TERMINAL COMPROMISE
Copyright © 1991 Winn Schwartau

Printed in the United States of America
First Printing, July 1991

Jacket by Schatz and Schatz

Published by Inter.Pact Press

ISBN 0-962-87000-5

A Note:

July, 1991

In writing a book like this, it is often difficult to distinguish fact from fiction.

That is because the fiction is all too probable, and the facts are unbelievable. Maybe it doesn't matter and they're the same after all. Other than a few well known names and incidents, the events in this book are fictional - to the best of my knowledge.

As I wrote this tale, I was endlessly coming upon new methods, new tactics, new ways to wage computer warfare. I found that if this story was to be told, I had to accept the fact that it would always be unfinished. The battle of the computers is one without an end in sight.

This story is an attempt to merge the facts as they are with the possibilities. The delineation between fact and fiction is clouded because the fiction of yesterday is the fact, the news, of today. I expect that distinction to become hazier over the next few years.

It is that incongruity that spawns a conjectural extrapolation indistinguishable from reality.

The construction of the model that gave birth to this tale was the culmination of many years of work, with a fictional narrative being the last thing in my mind. That was an accident necessitated by a need to reach the largest possible audience.

The reader will soon know why.

There were many people who have been invaluable in the preparation of this document, but I'll only mention a few. If the reader doesn't want to hear about my friends, please move on to the next chapter.

Mary C. Bell. Hi, Mom. Thanks for the flashlight.

Lazarus Cuttman. The greatest editor a writer has ever had. He kept me honest.

Miles Roban. That's an alias. He's the one who told me about the real NSA. I hope he doesn't get in trouble for what he said. I owe him Giradelli chocolates. 2 lbs. of them.

Dad. God rest.

Winn Schwartau
July, 1991

S herra

There is no adequate way to say thank you. You are the super-glue of the family. Let's continue to break the rules.

I Love You

A shley

She wrote three books before I finished the first chapter and then became a South-Paw.

A dam

Welcome, pilgrim.

TERMINAL COMPROMISE

Prologue

Friday, January 12, The Year After
The White House, Washington D.C.

The President was furious. In over 30 years of professional politics, not even his closest aides had ever seen him so totally out of character. The placid Texan confidence he normally exuded, part well designed media image, part real, was completely shattered.

"Are you telling me that we spent almost $4 trillion dollars, four goddamn trillion dollars on defense, and we're not prepared to defend our computers? You don't have a game plan? What the hell have we been doing for the last 12 years?" The President bellowed as loudly as anyone could remember. No one in the room answered. The President glared right through each of his senior aides.

"Damage Assessment Potential?" The President said abruptly as he forced a fork full of scrambled eggs into his mouth.

"The Federal Reserve and most Banking transactions come to a virtual standstill. Airlines grounded save for emergency operations. Telephone communications running at 30% or less of capacity. No Federal payments for weeks. Do you want me to continue?"

"No, I get the picture."

The President wished to God he wouldn't be remembered as the President who allowed the United States of America to slip backward 50 years. He waited for the steam in his collar to subside before saying anything he might regret.

* * * * *

Monday, August 6, 1945.
Japan

The classroom was coming to order. Shinzo Ito, the 12th graders' instructor was running a few minutes late and the students were in a fervent discussion about the impending end to the war. And of course it was to be a Japanese victory over the American Mongrels.

Ito-san was only 19 years old, and most of the senior class was only a year or two younger than he. The war had deeply affected all of them. The children of Japan were well acquainted with suffering and pain as families were wrenched apart - literally at the seams, and expected to hold themselves together by the honor that their sacrifices represented. They hardened, out of necessity, in order to survive and make it through the next day, the next week; and so they knew much

1

about the war. Since so many of the men had gone to war, women and children ran the country. 10 and 11 year old students from the schools worked as phone operators. It was an honorable cause, and everyone contributed; it was only fitting. Their fathers and loved ones were fighting selflessly and winning the war.

Many of the children's fathers had gone to war, valiantly, and many had not come home. Many came home in pieces, many others, unrecognizable. And when some fathers had gone off to war, both they and their families knew that they would never return. They were making the Supreme Sacrifice for their country, and more importantly, a contribution to their honorable way of life.

The sons and daughters of kamikazes were treated with near reverence. It was widely believed that their father's honor was handed down to their offspring as soon as word had been received the mission had been successful. Albeit a suicide mission.

Taki Homosoto was one 17 year old boy so revered for his father's sacrifice. Taki spoke confidently about such matters, about the war, about American atrocities, and how Japan would soon defeat the round faced enemy. Taki had understood, on his 17th birthday that his father would leave . . .and assuredly die as was the goal of the kamikaze. He pretended to understand that it made sense to him.

In the last 6 months since his father had left, Taki assumed, at his father's request, the patriarchal role in the immediate family. The personal anguish had been excruciating. While friends and family and officials praised Taki's father and family, inside Taki did not accept that a man could willingly leave his family, his children, him . . .Taki, never to return. Didn't his father love him? Or his sister and brother? Or his mother?

Taki's mother got a good job at one of the defense plants that permeated Hiroshima, while Taki and his brother and sister continued their schooling. But the praise, the respect didn't make up for not having a father to talk to, to play with and to study with. He loved his mother, but she wasn't a father.

So Taki compensated and overcompensated and pretended that his father's sacrifice was just, and good, and for the better of society, and the war effort and his family. Taki spoke as a juvenile expert on the war and the good of Japan and the bad of the United States and the filthy Americans with their unholy practices and perverted ways of life, and how they tortured Japanese prisoners. Taki was an eloquent and convincing orator to his peers and instructors alike.

At 8:15 A.M., the Hiroshima radio station, NHK, rang its old school bell. The bell was part of a warning system that announced impending attacks from the air, but it had been so overused that it was mostly ignored. The tolls from the bell were barely noticed by the students or the teachers in the Honkawa School. Taki though, looked out the window toward the Aioi Bridge. His ears perked and his eyes scanned the clear skies over downtown Hiroshima. He was sure he heard something . . .but no . . .

The first sensation of motion in the steel reinforced building came long seconds after the blinding light. Since the rolling earth motions in 1923 devastated much of Tokyo, schoolchildren and households nationwide practiced earthquake preparedness and were reasonably expectant of another major tremor at any time.

But the combination of light from 10,000 suns and the deafening roar gave those who survived the blast reason to wish they hadn't. Blindness was instant for those who saw the sky ignite. The classroom was collapsing around them. In the air was the noise of a thousand trains at once...even louder. In seconds the schoolhouse was in rubble.

The United States of America had just dropped the Atomic Bomb on Hiroshima, Japan. This infamous event would soon be known as *ayamachi* - the Great Mistake.

* * * * *

Tuesday, August 7, 1945

Taki Homosoto opened his eyes. He knew he was lying on his back, but all else was a clutter of confusion. He saw a dark ceiling, to what he didn't know, and he hurt. He turned his head and saw he was on a cot, maybe a bed, in a long corridor with many others around him. The room reeked of human waste and death.

"Ah . . .you are awake. It has been much time." The voice came from behind him. He turned his head rapidly and realized he shouldn't have. The pain speared him from his neck to the base of his spine. Taki grimaced and made a feeble attempt at whimpering. He said nothing as he examined the figure in the white coat who spoke again. "You are a very lucky young man, not many made it."

What was he talking about . . .made it? Who? His brain wanted to speak but his mouth couldn't. A slight gurgling noise ushered from his throat but nothing else. And the pain . . .it was everywhere at once . . .all over . . .he wanted to cry for help . . .but was unable. The pain overtook Taki Homosoto and the vision of the doctor blackened until there was no more.

Much later, Taki reawoke. He assumed it was a long time later, he been awake earlier . . .or had that been a dream. The doctor...no he was in school and the earthquake . . .yes, the earthquake . . .why don't I remember? I was knocked out. Of course. As his eyes adjusted to the room, he saw and remembered that it wasn't a dream. He saw the other cots, so many of them, stretching in every direction amidst the cries of pain and sighs of death.

Taki tried to cry out to a figure walking nearby but only a low pitched moan ushered forth. Then he noticed something odd . . .an odd smell. One he didn't recognize. It was foul . . .the stench of burned . . .burned what? The odor made him sick and he tried to breathe through his mouth but the awful odor still penetrated his glands. Taki knew that he was very hurt and very sick and so were a lot of others. It took him some time, and a lot of energy just to clear his thoughts. Thinking hurt - it concentrated the aching in his head, but the effort took away some of his other pain, or at least it successfully distracted him from focussing on it.

There were cries from all around. Many were incomprehensible babblings, obviously in agony. Screams of "*Eraiyo!*", ("the pain is unbearable!") were constant. Others begged to be put out of their misery. Taki actually felt fortunate; he couldn't have screamed if he had wanted to, but out of guilt he no longer felt the need to.

Finally, the same doctor, was it the same doctor? appeared over his bed again. "I hope you'll stay with us for a few minutes?" The doctor smiled. Taki responded as best he could. With a grunt and the raising and lowering of his eyelids. "Let me just say that you are in very good condition . . .much better than the others," the doctor gestured across the room. "I don't mean to sound cruel, but, we do need your bed, for those seriously hurt." The doctor sounded truly distraught. What had happened?

A terrified look crossed Taki's face that receded into a facial plead. His look said, "I can't speak so answer my questions . . .you must know what they are. Where am I? What happened? Where is my class?"

"I understand your name is Taki Homosoto?" the doctor asked. "Your school identification papers . . ."

Taki blinked an affirmative as he tried to cough out a response.

"There is no easy way to tell this. We must all be brave. America has used a terrible weapon upon the people of Japan. A special new bomb so terrible that Hiroshima is no longer even a shadow of itself. A weapon where the sky turns to fire and buildings and our people melt . . .where the water sickens the living and those who seem well drop in their steps from an invisible enemy. Almost half of the people of Hiroshima are dead or dying. As I said, you are a lucky one."

Taki helped over the next days at the Communications Hospital in what was left of downtown Hiroshima. When he wasn't tending to the dying, he moved the dead to the exits so the bodies could be cremated, the one way to insure eternal salvation. The city got much of its light from pyres for weeks after the blasts.

He helped distribute the kanpan and cold rice balls to the very few doctors and to survivors who were able to eat. He walked the streets of Hiroshima looking for food, supplies, anything that could help. Walking through the rubble of what once was Hiroshima fueled his hate and his loathing for Americans. They had wrought this suffering by using their pikadon, or flash-boom weapon, on civilians, women and children. He saw death, terrible, ugly death, everywhere; from Hijiyama Hill to the bridges across the wide Motoyas River.

The Aioi bridge spontaneously became an impromptu symbol for vengeance against the Americans. Taki crossed the remnants of the old stone bridge, which was to be the hypocenter of the blast if the Enola Gay hadn't missed its target by 800 feet. A tall blond man in an American military uniform was tied to a stone post. He was an American POW, one of 23 in Hiroshima. A few dozen people, women in bloodstained kimonos and mompei and near naked children were hurling rocks and insults at the lifeless body. How appropriate thought Taki. He found himself mindlessly joining in. He threw rocks at the head, the body, the legs. He threw rocks and yelled. He threw rocks and yelled at the remains of the dead serviceman until his arms and lungs ached.

Another 50,000 Japanese died from the effects of radiation within days while Taki continued to heal physically. On August 17, 9 days after the atomic bombing of Nagasaki and 2 days after Emperor Hirohito's broadcast announcing Japan's surrender, a typhoon swamped Hiroshima and killed thousands more. Taki blamed the Americans for the typhoon, too.

Taki was alone for the first time in his life. His family dead, even his little sister. Taki Homosoto was now a hibakusha, a survivor of Hiroshima, an embarrassing and dishonorable fact he would desperately try to conceal for the rest of his life.

* * * * *

Forty Years Later . . .
January, 1985, Gaithersburg, Maryland.

A pristine layer of thick soft snow covered the sprawling office and laboratory filled campus where the National Bureau of Standards sets standards for the country. The NBS establishes exactly what the time is, to the nearest millionth of a millionth of a second. They make

5

sure that we weigh things to the accuracy of the weight of an individual atom. The NBS is a veritable technological benchmark to which everyone agrees, if for no other reason than convenience.

It was the NBS's turn to host the National Computer Security Conference where the Federal government was ostensibly supposed to interface with academia and the business world. At this exclusive symposium, only two years before, the Department of Defense introduced a set of guidelines which detailed security specifications to be used by the Federal agencies and recommended for the private sector.

A very dry group of techno-wizards and techno-managers and techno-bureaucrats assemble for several days, twice a year, to discuss the latest developments in biometric identifications techniques, neural based cryptographic analysis, exponential factoring in public key management, the subtleties of discretionary access control and formalization of verification models.

The National Computer Security Center is a Department of Defense working group substantially managed by the super secret National Security Agency. The NCSC's charter in life is to establish standards and procedures for securing the US Government's computers from compromise.

1985's high point was an award banquet with slightly ribald speeches. Otherwise the conference was essentially a maze of highly complex presentations, meaningless to anyone not well versed in computers, security and government-speak. An attendee's competence could be well gauged by his use of acronyms. "If the IRS had DAC across its X.25 gateways, it could integrate X9.17 management, DES, MAC and X9.9 could be used throughout. Save the government a bunch!" "Yeah, but the DoD had an RFI for an RFQ that became a RFP, specced by NSA and based upon TD-80-81. It was isolated, environmentally speaking." Boring, thought Miles Foster. Incredibly boring, but it was his job to sit, listen and learn.

Miles Foster was a security and communications analyst with the National Security Agency at Fort Meade, Maryland. It was part of the regimen to attend such functions to stay on top of the latest developments from elsewhere in the government and from university and private research programs.

Out of the 30 or so panels that Miles Foster had to attend, pro forma, only one held any real interest for him. It was a mathematical presentation entitled, "Propagation Tendencies in Self Replicating Software". It was the one subject title from the conference guide about which he knew nothing. He tried to figure out what the talk was going to be about, but the answer escaped him until he heard what the author, Dr. Les Sternman had to say.

Miles Foster wrote an encapsulated report of Dr. Brown's presentation with the 23 other synopses he was required to generate for the NSA. Proof of Attendance.

SUBJECT:

Dr. Les Sternman - Professor of Computer Science, Sheffield University presented an updated version of his doctoral thesis.

CONTENTS:

Dr. Sternman spoke about unique characteristics of certain software that can be written to be self-replicating. He examined the properties of software code in terms of set theory and adequately demonstrated that software can be written with the sole purpose of disguising its true intents, and then replicate or clone itself throughout a computer system without the knowledge of the computer's operators.

He further described classes of software that, if designed for specific purposes, would have undetectable characteristics. In the self replicating class, some would have crystalline behaviors, others mutating behaviors, and others random behaviors. The set theory presentations closely paralleled biological transmission characteristics and similar problems with disease detection and immunization.

It became quite clear from the Dr. Sternman's talk, that surreptitiously placed software with self-replicating properties could have deleterious effects on the target computing system.

CONCLUSIONS

It appears prudent to further examine this class of software and the ramifications of its use. Dr. Sternman presented convincing evidence that such propagative effects can bypass existing protective mechanisms in sensitive data processing environments. There is indeed reason to believe that software of this nature might have certain offensive military applications.

Dr. Sternman used the term 'Virus' to describe such classes of software.

> **Miles Foster**
> **Senior Analyst**
> **Y-Group/SF6-143G-1**

After he completed his observations of the conference as a whole, and the seminars in particular, Miles Foster decided to eliminate Dr. Brown's findings from the final submission to his superiors. He wasn't sure why he left it out, it just seemed like the right thing to do.

* * * * *

Chapter 1

August, 4 Years Ago.
National Security Agency
Fort George S. Meade, Maryland.

Thousands of disk drives spun rapidly, at over 3600 rpm. The massive computer room, Computer Room C-12, gently whirred and droned with a life of its own. The sublime, light blue walls and specially fitted blue tint light bulbs added a calming influence to the constant urgency that drove the computer operators who pushed buttons, changed tapes and stared at the dozens of amber screens on the computers.

Racks upon racks of foreboding electronic equipment ringed the walls of Room C-12 with arrays of tape drives interspersed. Rats nests of wire and cable crept along the floor and in and out of the control centers for the hundreds of millions of dollars of the most sophisticated computers in the world. Only five years ago, computing power of this magnitude, now fit in a room the size of an average house would have filled the Pentagon. All of this, all of this power, for one man.

Miles Foster was locked in a room without windows. It contained a table, 4 chairs, and he was sure a couple of cameras and microphones. He had been held for a least six hours, maybe more; they had taken his watch to distort his time perception.

Within 2 minutes of the time Miles Foster announced his resignations as a communications expert with the National Security Agency, S Group, his office was sealed and guarded by an armed marine. His computer was disconnected, and he was escorted to a debriefing room where he had sporadically answered questions asked by several different Internal Affairs Security Officers.

While Miles Foster was under virtual house arrest, not the preferred term, but an accurate one, the Agency went to work. From C-12, a group of IAS officers began to accumulate information about Miles Foster from a vast array of computer memory banks. They could dial up any major computer system within the United States, and most around the world. The purpose, ostensibly, of having such power was to centralize and make more efficient security checks on government employees, defense contractors and others who might have an impact on the country's national security. But, it had other purposes, too.

Computer Room C-12 is classified above Top Secret, it's very existence denied by the NSA, the National Security Agency, and unknown to all but a very few of the nation's top policy makers.

Congress knows nothing of it and the President was only told after it had been completed, black funded by a non-line item accountable budget. Computer Room C-12 is one of only two electronic doors into the National Data Base - a digital repository containing the sum total knowledge and working profiles of every man, woman and child in the United States. The other secret door that guards America's privacy is deep within the bowels of the Pentagon.

From C-12, IAS accessed every bank record in the country in Miles' name, social security number or in that of his immediate family. Savings, checking, CD's. They had printouts, within seconds, of all of their last year's credit card activity. They pulled 3 years tax records from the IRS, medical records from the National Medical Data Base which connects hospitals nationwide, travel records from American carriers, customs checks, video rental history, telephone records, stock purchases. Anything that any computer ever knew about Miles Foster was printed and put into eleven 6" thick files within 2 hours of the request from the DIRNSA, Director, National Security Agency.

Internal Affairs was looking for some clue as to why a successful and highly talented analyst like Miles Foster would so abruptly resign a senior analyst position. While Miles was more than willing to tell them his feelings, and the real reasons behind his resignation, they wanted to make sure that there weren't a few little details he wasn't telling them. Like, perhaps gambling debts, women on the side, (he was single) or women on the wrong side, overextended financial obligations, anything unusual. Had he suddenly come into money and if he did, where did he get it? Blackmail was considered a very real possibility when unexpected personnel changes occur.

The files vindicated Miles Foster of any obvious financial anomalies. Not that he knew he needed vindication. He owned a Potomac condominium in D.C., a 20 minutes against traffic commute to Fort Meade where he had worked for years, almost his entire professional life. He traveled some, Caribbean cruises, nothing ostentatious but in style, had a reasonable savings account, only used 2 credit cards and he owed no one anything significant. There was nothing unusual about his file at all, unless you think that living within ones means is odd. Miles Foster knew how to make the most out of a dollar. Miles Foster was clean.

The walls of his drab 12 foot square prison room were a dirty shade of government gray. There was an old map on the wall and Miles noticed that the gray paint behind it was 7 shades lighter than the surrounding paint. Two of the four fluorescent bulbs were out, hiding some of the peeling paint on the ceiling. Against one wall was a row of file cabinets with large iron bars behind the drawer handles, insuring that no one, no one, was getting into those files without permission. Also prominent on each file cabinet was a tissue box sized padlock.

Miles was alone, again. When the IAS people questioned him, they were hard on him. Very hard. But most of the time he was alone.

Miles paced the room during the prolonged waits. He poked here and there, under this, over that; he found the clean paint behind the map and smirked.

When the IAS men returned, they found Miles stretching and exercising his tight 5' 9" physique to help relieve the boredom.

He was 165 lbs. and in excellent shape for almost 40. Miles wasn't a fitness nut, but he enjoyed the results of staying in shape - women, lots of women. He had a lightly tanned Mediterranean skin, dark, almost black wavy hair on the longish side but immaculately styled. His demeanor dripped elegance, even when he wore torn jeans, and he knew it. It was merely another personal asset that Miles had learned how to use to his best advantage. Miles was regularly proofed. He had a face that would permit him to assume any age from 20 to 40, but given his borderline arrogance, (he called it aloofness,) most considered him the younger. Nonetheless, women, of all ages went for it.

One peculiar trait made women and girls find Miles irresistible. He had an eerie but conscious muscular control over his dimples. If he were angry, a frown could mean any number of things depending upon how he twitched his dimples. A frown could mean, "I'm real angry, seriously", or "I'm just giving you shit", or "You bore me, go away", or more to Miles' purpose, "You're gorgeous, I wanna fuck your brains out". His dimples could pout with a smile, grin with a sneer, emphasize a question; they could accent and augment his mood at will.

But now, he was severely bored. Getting even more disgusted with the entire process. The IAS wasn't going to find anything. He had made sure of that. After all, he was the computer expert.

Miles heard the sole door to the room unlock. It was a heavy, 'I doubt an ax could even get through this' door. The fourth IAS man to question Miles entered the room as the door was relocked from the other side.

"So, tell us again, why did you quit?" The IAS man abruptly blurted out even before sitting in one of the old, World War II vintage chairs by the wooden table.

"I've told you a hundred times and you have it on tape a hundred times." The disgust in his voice was obvious and intended. "I really don't want to go through it again."

"Tough shit. I want to hear it. You haven't told me yet." This guy was tougher, Miles thought.

"What are you looking for? For God's sake, what do you want me to say? You want a lie that you like better? Tell me what it is and I'll give it back to you, word for word. Is that what you want?" Miles gave away something. He showed, for the first time, real anger. The intellect in Miles saw what the emotion was doing, so his brain quickly secreted a complex string of amino acids to calm him down. Miles decided that he should go back to the naive, 'what did I do?' image and stick to the plan.

He put his head in his hands and leaned forward for a second. He gently shook and looked up sideways. He was very convincing. The IAS man thought that Miles might be weakening.

"I want the fucking truth," the IAS man bellowed. "And I want it now!"

Miles sighed. He was tired and wanted a cigarette so bad he could shit, and that pleasure, too, he was being denied. But he had prepared himself for this eventuality; serious interrogation.

"O.K., O.K." Miles feigned resignation. He paused for another heavy sigh. "I quit 'cause I got sick of the shit. Pure and simple. I like my work, I don't like the bureaucracy that goes with it. That's it. After over 10 years here, I expected some sort of recognition other than a cost of living increase like every other G12. I want to go private where I'll be appreciated. Maybe even make some money."

The IAS man didn't look convinced. "What single event made you quit? Why this morning, and not yesterday or tomorrow, or the next day, or next week. Why today?" The IAS man blew smoke at Miles to annoy him and exaggerate the withdrawal symptoms. Miles was exhausted and edgy.

"Like I said, I got back another 'don't call us, we'll call you' response on my Public-Private key scheme. They said, 'Not yet practical' and set it up for another review in 18 months. That was it. Finis! The end, the proverbial straw that you've been looking for. Is that what you want?" Miles tried desperately to minimize any display of arrogance as he looked at the IAS man.

"What do you hope to do in the private sector? Most of your work is classified." The IAS man remained cool and unflustered.

"Plenty of defense bandits who do crypto need a good comm guy. I think the military call it the revolving door." Miles' dimpled smugness did not sit well with IAS.

"Yeah, you'll probably go to work for your wop friends in Sicily." The IAS man sarcastically accused.

"Hey - you already know about that!" That royally pissed off Miles. He didn't appreciate any dispersion on his heritage. "They're relatives, that's it. Holidays, food, turkey, ham, and a bunch of booze. And besides," Miles paused and smiled, "there's no such thing as the Mafia."

By early evening they let him relieve himself and then finally leave the Fort. He was given 15 minutes to collect his personal items, under guard, and then escorted to the front gate. All identification was removed and his files were transferred into the 'Monitor' section, where they would sit for at least one year. The IAS people had finally satisfied themselves that Miles Foster was a dissatisfied, underpaid government employee who had had enough of the immobility and rigidity of a giant bureaucratic machine that moves at a snail's pace. Miles smiled at the end of the interrogation. 'Just like I said,' he thought, 'just like I said.'

There was no record in his psychological profiles, those from the Agency shrinks, that suggested Miles meant anything other than what he claimed. Let him go, they said. Let him go. Nowhere in the records did it show how much he hated his stupid, stupid bosses, the bungling bureaucratic behemoths who didn't have the first idea of what he and his type did. Nowhere did Miles' frustration and resultant build up of resentment and anger show up in any file or on any chart or graph. His strong, almost overbearing ego and over developed sense of worth and importance were relegated to a personality quirk common to superbright ambitious engineering types. It fit the profile.

Nowhere, either, was it mentioned that in years at NSA, Miles Foster had submitted over 30 unsolicited proposals for changes in cryptographic and communications techniques to improve the security of the United States. Nowhere did it say, they were all turned down, tabled, ignored.

At one point or another, Miles had to snap. The rejection of proposal number thirty-four gave him the perfect reason to quit.

* * * * *

Miles Foster looked 100% Italian despite the fact his father was a pure Irishman. "Stupido, stupido" his grandmother would say while slamming the palm of her hand into forehead. She was not exactly fond of her daughter marrying outside the family. But, it was a good marriage, 3 great kids, or as good as kids get and Grandmama tolerated the relationship. Miles the oldest, was only 7 when his father got killed as a bystander at a supermarket robbery.

Mario Dante, his homosexual uncle who worked in some undefined, never mentioned capacity for a Vegas casino, assumed the paternal role in raising Miles. With 2 sisters, a mother, an aunt and a grandmother all living under the same roof with Miles, any male companionship, role model if you will, was acceptable. Mario kept the Family Honor, keeping his sexual proclivities secret until Miles turned 18. Upon hearing, Miles commented, "Yeah, so? Everyone knows Uncle Mario's a fag. Big deal."

Mario was a big important guy, and he did business, grownup business. That was all Miles was supposed to know. When Miles was 13, Mario thought it would be a good idea for him to become a man. Only 60 miles from Las Vegas lived the country's only legal brothels. Very convenient. Miles wasn't going to fool around with any of that street garbage. Convention girls. Miles should go first class the first time.

Pahrump, Nevada is home to the only legalized prostitution in the United States. Mario drove fast, Miles figured about 130mph, in his Red Ferrari on Highway 10, heading West from Vegas. Mario was drinking Glen Fetitch, neat, and he steered with only one hand, hardly looking at the road.

The inevitable occurred. Gaining on them, was a Nevada State Trooper. The flashing lights and siren reminded Mario to slow down and pull over. He grinned, sipped his drink and Miles worried. Speeding was against the law. So was drinking and driving. The police officer walked over to the driver side of the Ferrari. Uncle Mario lowered the window to let the officer lean into the car. As the trooper bent over to look inside the flashy low slung import, Mario pulled out a handgun from under the seat and stuck it into the cop's face.

Mario started yelling. "Listen asshole, I wasn't speeding. Was I? I don't want nothing to go on my insurance. I gotta good driving record, y'know?" Mario was crazy! Miles had several strong urges to severely contract his sphincter muscles.

"No sir, I wanted to give you a good citizenship citation, for your contributions to the public good." The cop laughed in Uncle Mario's face.

"Good to see you still gotta sensa'humor." Uncle Mario laughed and put the gun back in his shoulder holster. Miles stared, dumbfounded, still squeezing his butt cheeks tight.

"Eh, Paysan! Where you going so fired up? You know the limit's 110?" They both guffawed.

"Here!" Mario pointed at Miles. "'Bout time the kid took a ride around the world, y'know what I mean?" Miles wasn't sure what it meant, but he was sure it had to do with where he was going to lose his virginity.

"Sheeeee-it! Uptown! Hey kid, ask for Michelle and take 2 from Column B, then do it once for me!" To a 13 year male Italian virgin, Mario and the cop were making fun of him. "I remember my first time. It was in a pick up truck, out in the desert. Went for fucking ever! Know what I mean? "The cop winked at Miles who was humiliated. To Miles' relief, Mario finally gave the cop an envelop, while being teasingly reprimanded. "Hey, Mario, take it a little easy out here, will yah? At least on my watch, huh?"

"Yeah, sure. No problem. Ciao."

"Ciao."

They were off again, doing over 100 in seconds. The rest of the evening went as planned. Miles thanked his uncle in a way that brought tears to Mario's eyes. Miles said, "You know, Uncle Mario. When I grow up, I want to be just like you."

"He's just a boy, Mario! How could you!" Miles' mother did not react favorably to the news of her son's manhood. She was trying to protect him from the influence of her relatives. Miles was gauged near genius with a pronounced aptitude for mathematics and she didn't want his life to go to waste.

His mother had married outside of the family, the organized crime culture, the life one inherits so easily. She loved her family, knew that they dealt in gambling, some drugs, an occasional rough-up of an opponent, but preferred to ignore it. She married a man she loved, not one picked for her, but had lost him 6 years before. They could not have her son.

Her wishes were respected, in the memory of Miles father, and also because it wasn't worth having a crazed Sicilian woman ranting and raving about. But Miles was delectable bait to the Family. His mathematical wizardry could assist greatly in gaming operations, figure the odds, new angles, keep the dollars in the house's favor despite all advertising claims to the contrary.

But, there was respect and honor in their promise to his mother. Hands off was the rule that came all the way from the top. He was protected. Miles was titillated with the attention, but he still listened to his mother. She came before all others. With no father, she became a little of both, and despite anyone's attempts, Miles knew about Mario.

Miles was such a subject of adoration by his mother, aunt and grandmother, siblings aside, that Miles came to expect the same treatment from everyone, especially women. They praised him so, he always got top honors, the best grades, that he came to require the attention and approval.

Living with 5 women and a gay uncle for 11 years had its effect. Miles was incredibly heterosexual. Not anti-gay at all, but he had absolutely no interest in men. He adored women, largely because of his mother. He put women on pedestals, and treated them like queens. Even on a beer budget Miles could convince his lady that they were sailing the Caribbean while baking in the desert suburbs of Las Vegas. Women succumbed, willingly, to Miles' slightest advance. He craved the approval, and worked long and hard to perfect his technique. Miles Foster was soon an expert. His mother never openly disapproved which Miles took as approval.

By the time Miles went off to college to study advanced mathematics and get a degree, he had shattered half of the teen-age hearts within 50 miles of Vegas. Plus, the admiration from his female family had allowed him to convince himself that he was going to change the world. He was the single most important person that could have an effect on civilization. Invincible. Can do no wrong. Miles was the end-all to be-all. If Miles said it, it must be so, and he bought into the program. What his mother or girl friends called self confidence others called conceit and arrogance. Even obnoxious.

His third love, after his mother and himself, was mathematics. He believed mathematics to be the answer to every problem. All questions can be reduced to formulas and symbols. Then, once you have them on a piece of paper, or in a computer . . .the answer will appear.

His master thesis was on that very subject. It was a brilliant soliloquy on the reducibility of any multi-dimensional condition to a defined set of measured properties. He postulated that all phenomenon was discrete in nature and none were continuous. Given that arguable position, he was able to develop a set of mathematical tools that would permit dissection of a problem into much smaller pieces. Once in manageable sizes, the problem would be worked out piece by piece until the pieces were reassembled as the answer. It was a tool that had very definite uses in the government.

He was recruited by the Government in 1976. They wanted him to put his ingenious techniques to good use. The National Security Agency painted an idyllic picture of the ultimate job for a mathematician - the biggest, fastest and best computers in the world at your fingertips. Always the newest and the best. Whatever you need, it'll be there. And that's a promise. Super secret important work - oh how his mother would be proud. Miles accepted, but they never told him the complete truth. Not that they lied, of course. However, they never bothered to tell him, that because of his family background, guilt by association if you wish, his career would be severely limited.

Miles made it to senior analyst, and his family was proud, but he never told them that over 40% of the staff in his area were senior analysts. It was a high tech desk job that required his particular skills as a mathematician. The NSA got from him what they wanted; his mathematical tools modified to work for government security projects. For a couple of years, Miles happily complied - then he got itchy to work on other projects. After all, he had come up with the idea in the first place, it was time he came up with another.

In typical bureaucratic manner, the only way to get something new done is to write a proposal; enlist support and try to push it through committee. Everyone made proposals. You not only needed a good idea for a good project, good enough to justify the use of 8 billion dollars worth of computers, but you needed the connections and assistance of others. You scratch mine, I'll scratch yours.

During his tenure at NSA, Miles attempted to institute various programs, procedures, new mathematical modes that might be useful. While technically his concepts were superior, his arrogance, his better-than-everyone, my shit doesn't stink attitude proved to be an insurmountable political obstacle. He was unable to ever garner much support for his proposals. Thus, not one of them was ever taken seriously. Which compounded the problem and reinforced Miles' increasingly sour attitude towards his employer. However, with dimples in command, he successfully masked his disdain. To all appearance he acceded to the demands of the job, but off the job, Miles Foster was a completely different person.

* * * * *

The telephone warbled on the desk of the IAS Department Chief. The digital readout on the phone told him that it was an internal call, not from outside the building, but he didn't recognize the number.

"Investigations," The chief answered.

"This is Jacobs. We're checking up on Foster."

"Yessir?" DIRNSA? Calling here?

"Is he gone?"

"Yessir."

"Anything?"

"No sir."

"Good. Close the file."

"Sir?"

"Close it. Forever."

* * * * *

September, 4 Years Ago
Georgetown, Washington, D.C.

Miles Foster set up shop in Washington D.C. as a communications security consultant. He and half of those who lived within driving distance of the Capitol were known as Beltway Bandits, a simultaneously endearing and self-deprecating title given to those who make their living selling products or services to the Federal Government. Miles was ex-NSA and that was always impressive to potential clients. He let it be known that his services would now be available to the private sector, at the going rates.

As part of the revolving door, from Government to industry, Miles' value would decrease with time, so he needed to get a few clients quickly. The day you leave public service all of your knowledge is current, and therefore valuable, especially to companies who want to sell widgets to the government. As the days and months wear on, new policies, new people, new arrangements and confederacies are in place. Washington's transient nature is probably no more evident than through the political circle where everyone is aware of whom is talking to whom and about what. This Miles knew, so he stuck out his tentacles to maximize his salability.

He restructured his dating habits. Normally Miles would date women whom he knew he could fuck. He kept track of their menstrual cycles to make sure they wouldn't waste his time. If he thought a particular female had extraordinary oral sex skills, he would make sure to seduce her when she had her period. Increased the odds of good blow job.

Now though, Miles restricted his dating, temporarily, to those who could help start his career in the private sector. "Fuck the secretary to get to the boss!" he bragged unabashedly.

Miles dragged himself to many of the social functions that grease the wheels of motion in Washington. The elaborate affairs, often at the expense of government contractors and lobbyists, were a highly visible, yet totally legal way to shmooze and booze with the influentia in the nation's capital. The better parties, the ones for generals, for movers and for shakers, for dignitaries and others of immediate importance, are graced with a generous sprinkling of strikingly beautiful women. They are paid for by the hosts, for the pleasure of their guests. The Washington culture requires that such services are discreetly handled. Expense reports and billings of that nature therefore cite French Caterers, C.T. Temps, Formal Rentals and countless other harmless, inoffensive and misleading sounding company names.

Missile Defense Systems, Inc. held one of the better parties in an elegant old 2 story brick Georgetown home. The building was a former embassy, which had been discarded long ago by its owners in favor of a neo-modern structure on Reservoir Road. The house was appointed with a strikingly southern ante-bellum flair, but tastefully done, not overly decorated. The furniture was modern, comfortable, meant to be and used enjoyed, yet well suited to classic Americana formality.

The hot September night was punctuated with an occasional breeze. The breaths of relief from Washington's muggy, swamp-like summer air were welcomed by those braving the heat in the manicured gardens outside, rather than the refreshing luxury of the air conditioned indoors.

It was a straight cocktail party, a stand-up affair, with a hundred or so Pentagon types attending. It began at seven, and unless tradition was broken, it would be over by 10 as the last of the girls finds her way into a waiting black limousine with her partner for the night. Straight politics, Miles thought.

9:30 neared, and Miles felt he had accomplished most of what he had set out to do - meet people, sell himself, play the game, talk the line, do the schtick. He hadn't, though, yet figured out how he was going to get laid tonight.

As he sipped his third Glenfiddich on the rocks, he spotted a woman whom he hadn't seen that evening. Maybe she had just arrived, maybe she was leftovers. Well, it was getting late, and he shouldn't let a woman go to waste, so let's see what she looks like from the front. She looked aimlessly through the French doors at the backyard flora.

Miles sauntered over to her and introduced himself. "Hi, I'm Miles Foster." He grinned wide, dimples in force, as she turned toward him. She was gorgeous. Stunning even. About an inch taller than Miles, she wore her shimmering auburn hair shoulder length. Angelic, he thought. Perfectly formed full lips and statuesque cheek bones underscored her sweetly intense brown eyes. Miles went to work, and by 10P.M., he and Stephanie Perkins were on their way to Deja Vu on 22nd. and M Street for drinks and dance. By 10:30 he had nicknamed her Perky because her breasts stood at constant attention. By 11:30 they were on their way to Miles' apartment.

At 2:00 AM Miles was quite satisfied with himself. So was Perky. His technique was perfect. Never a complaint. Growing up in a house without men taught Miles what women wanted. He learned how to give it to them, just the way they liked it. The weekend together centered around the bed; playing, making love, giggling, ordering in Chinese and pizza. Playing more, watching *I Love Lucy* reruns, drinking champagne, and making love. Miles bounced quarters on her taut stomach and cracked eggs on her exquisitely tight derriere. By Sunday morning, Miles found that he actually liked Stephanie. It wasn't that he didn't like his other women, he did. It was just, well, this one was different. He 'really' liked her. A very strange feeling for Miles Foster.

"Miles?" Stephanie asked during another period of blissful afterglow. She snuggled up against him closer.

"Yeah?" He responded by squeezing her buttocks. His eyes were still closed.

"In a minute stud, yes." She looked up reassuringly at him. "Miles, would you work for anyone?" She kissed his chest.

"What do you mean?" he asked in return. He wasn't in the mood for shop talk.

"Like, say, a foreigner, not an American company. Would you work for them?"

"Huh?" Miles looked down inquisitively. "Foreigner? I guess so. Why do you ask?" He sounded a tad concerned.

"Oh, no reason." She rubbed him between his legs. "Just curious. I thought you were a consultant, and consultants work for anyone who can pay. That's all."

"I am, and I will, but so what?" He relaxed as Stephanie's hands got the desired result.

"Well," she stroked him rhythmically. "I know some people that could use you. They're not American, that's all. I didn't know if you cared."

"No, I don't care," he sighed. "It's all the same to me. Unless they're commies. My former employer would definitely frown on that."

"Would you mind if I called them, and maybe you two can get together?" She didn't miss a beat.

"No go ahead, call them, anything you want, but can we talk about this later?" Miles begged.

* * * * *

Miles felt very much uninformed on his way to the Baltimore Washington Airport. He knew that he was being flown to Tokyo Japan, first class, by a mystery man who had prepaid him $10,000 for a 1 hour meeting. Not a bad start, he thought. His reputation obviously preceded him. Stephanie was hired to recruit him, that was obvious. And that bothered Miles. He was being used. Wasn't he? Or had he seduced her and the trip was a bonus? He still liked Stephanie, just not as much as before. It never occurred to Miles, not for a second, that Stephanie might not have liked him.

At JFK in New York, Miles connected to the 20 hour flight to Tokyo through Anchorage, Alaska. He had a brief concern that this was the same route that KAL Flight 007 had taken in 1983 before it was shot down by the Soviets, but he was flying an American carrier with a four digit flight number. He allowed that thought to remove any traces of worry.

The flight was a couple of hours out of New York when one of the flight attendants came up to him. "Mr. Foster?"

"Yes?" He looked up from the New York City Times he was reading.

"I believe you dropped this?" She handed Miles a large sealed envelope. His name had been written across the front with a large black marker.

"Thank you," said Miles. He took it gratefully.

When she left, he opened the strange envelope. It wasn't his. Inside there was a single sheet of paper. Miles read it.

MR. FOSTER

WELCOME TO JAPAN.

YOU WILL BE MET AT THE NARITA AIRPORT BY MY DRIVER AND CAR. THEY ARE AT YOUR DISPOSAL.

WE WILL MEET IN MY OFFICE AT 8:00 AM, WEDNES-DAY, SEPTEMBER 23. ALL ARRANGEMENTS HAVE BEEN MADE FOR YOUR PLEASURES.

RESPECTFULLY

TAKI HOMOSOTO

The name meant nothing to him so he forgot about it. He had more important things to do. His membership in the Mile High Club was in jeopardy. He had not yet made it with a female flight attendant.

They landed, 18 hours and 1 day later in Tokyo. Miles was now a member in good standing.

* * * * *

Thursday, September 3
Dallas-Fort Worth International Airport

"DFW, this is American 1137, heading 125 at 3500."

"Roger American 1137, got you loud and green. Maintain 125, full circle 40 miles then 215 for 40."

"Traffic Dallas?"

"Heavy. Weather's been strong. On again off again. Piled up pretty good."

"Sheers?"

"None so far. Ah, you're a 37, you carry a sheer monitor. You got it made. Have to baby sit some 0's and 27's. May be a while."

"Roger Dallas. 125 40, 215 40. Maintaining 12 point 5."

"Roger 1137."

The control tower at DFW airport was busier than normal. The dozen or so large green radar screens glowed eerily and made the air traffic controllers appear pallid under the haunting light emitting from around the consoles. Severe weather patterns, afternoon Texas thunderstorms had intermittently closed the airport forcing planes to hold in a 120 miles circle over Dallas and Fort Worth.

Many of the tower crew had been at their stations for 2 hours past their normal quitting time due to street traffic delays and highway pileups that had kept shift replacements from arriving on time. Planes were late coming in, late departing, connections were being missed. Tensions were high on the ground and in the air by both the airline personnel and travelers alike. It was a chaotic day at Dallas-Fort Worth International Airport.

"Chad? Cm'ere," said Paul Gatwick, the newest and youngest, and least burnt out of the day shift flight controller.

Chad Phillips came right over. "What you got?" He asked looking at the radar screen.

"See these three bogies?" Paul pointed at three spots with his finger.

"Bogies? What are those symbols?"

"They just appeared, out of nowhere. I don't think they're there. And over here," he pointed, "that was Delta 210. It's gone." Paul spoke calmly, in the professional manner he was trained. He looked up at Chad, awaiting instructions.

"Mike," Chad said to the controller seated next to Paul. "Switch and copy 14, please. Fast." Chad looked over to Mike's screen and saw the same pattern. "Paul, run a level 2 diagnostic. What was the Delta pattern?"

"Same as the others, circle. He's at 45 doing a 90 round."

"Tell him to hold, and verify on board transponder." Chad spoke rapidly and his authority wasn't questioned.

"Mike, see if we can get any visuals on the bogies. They might be a bounce."

Chad took charge and, especially in this weather, was concerned with safety first and schedules last. In less than a minute he had verified that Delta 210 was not on any screen, three other ghost planes meandered through the airspace, and that their equipment was functioning properly.

"Dallas," the calm pilot voice said, "American 1137, requesting update. It's getting a little tight up here."

"Roger, 1137," Gatwick said nervously. "Give me a second here . . ."

"Dallas, what's the problem?"

"Just a check . . ."

Chad immediately told the operator of the ETMS computer to notify the FAA and Department of Transportation that a potential situation was developing. The Enhanced Traffic Management System was designed to create a complete picture of every airplane flying within domestic air space.

All status information, on every known flight in progress and every commercial plane on the ground, is transmitted from the 22 ARTCC's, (Air Route Traffic Control Centers) to an FAA Technical Center in Atlantic City and then sent by land and satellite to a DoT Systems Center. There, an array of DEC VAX super mini computers process the constant influx of raw data and send back an updated map across the ETMS every five minutes.

Chad zoomed in on the picture of the country into the DFW approach area and confirmed that the airplanes in question were not appearing on the National Airspace System data fields or displays. Something was drastically wrong.

"Chad, take a look here!" Another controller urgently called out.

His radar monitor had more bogies than Paul's. "I lost a Delta, too, 1258."

"What is it?"

"37."

"Shit," said Chad. "We gotta get these guys wide, they have to know what's happening. He called over to another controller. "Get on the wire, divert all traffic. Call the boss. We're closing it down." The controllers had the power to close the airport, and direct all flight operations from the tower. Airport management wasn't always fond of their autonomy, but the tower's concern was safety at all costs.

"Another one's gone," said Paul. "That's three 37's gone. Have they had a recall lately?"

The ETMS operator asked the computer for a status on 737's elsewhere. "Chad, we're not the only ones," she said. "O'Hare and LAX have problems, too."

"OK, everybody, listen up," Chad said. "Stack 'em. pack 'em and rack 'em. Use those outer markers, people. Tell them to believe their eyes. Find the 37's. Let 'em know their transponders are going . . . Then, bring 'em down one by one."

The emergency speaker suddenly rang out. "Shit! Dive!" The captain of American 1137 ordered his plane to accelerate groundward for 10 seconds, descending 500 feet, to avoid hitting an oncoming, and lost, DC-9.

"Dallas, Mayday, Mayday. What the fuck's going on down there? This is worse than the freeway . . ."

The emergency procedure was one they had practiced over and over, but rarely was it necessary for a full scale test. The FAA was going to be all over DFW and a dozen other airports within hours, and Chad wanted to be prepared. He ordered a formal notification to Boeing that had identified a potentially serious malfunction. Please make your emergency technical support crews available immediately.

Of the 100 plus flights under DFW control all 17 of the Boeing 737's disappeared from the radar screen, and replaced by dozens of bogies with meaningless signatures.

"Dallas, American 1137 requests emergency landing . . .we have several injured passengers who require immediate medical assistance."

"Roger, 1137," Gatwick blurted back. "Copy, EP. Radar status?"

"Nominal," said the shaken American pilot.

"Good. Runway 21B. We'll be waiting."

* * * * *

By 5:00 PM, Pacific time, Boeing was notified by airports across the country that their 737's were having catastrophic transponder failure. Takeoffs were ordered stopped at major airports and the FAA directed that every 737 be immediately grounded. Chaos reigned in the airline terminals as delays of several hours to a day were announced for most flights. Police were needed to quell angry crowds who were stuck thousands of miles from home and were going to miss critical business liaisons. There is nothing we can do, every airline explained to no avail.

Slowly, the planes were brought down, pilots relying on VFR since they couldn't count on any help from the ground. At airports where weather prohibited VFR landings, and the planes had enough fuel, they were redirected to nearby airports. Nearly a dozen emergency landings in a 2 hour period set new records that the FAA preferred didn't exist. A field day for the media, and a certain decrease in future passenger activity until the shock wore off.

The National Transportation Safety Board had representatives monitoring the situation within an hour of the first reports from Dallas, San Francisco, Atlanta, and Tampa. When all 737's were accounted for, the individual airports and the FAA lifted flight restrictions and left it to the airlines to straighten out the scheduling mess. One hundred thousand stranded passengers and almost 30% of the domestic civilian air fleet was grounded.

It was a good thing their reservation computers hadn't gone down. Damn good thing.

* * * * *

DISASTER IN AIR CREATES PANIC ON GROUND

by Scott Mason

"A national tragedy was avoided today by the quick and brave actions of hundreds of air traffic controllers and pilots working in harmony," a spokesperson for The Department of Transportation said, commenting on yesterday's failure of the computerized transponder systems in Boeing 737 airplanes.

"In the interest of safety for all concerned, 737's will not be permitted to fly commercially until a full investigation has taken place." the spokesperson continued. "That process should be complete within 30 days."

In all, 114 people were sent to hospitals, 29 in serious condition, as a result of injuries sustained while pilots performed dangerous gut wrenching maneuvers to avoid mid-air collisions.

Neither Boeing nor the Transportation Safety Board would comment on how computer errors could suddenly affect so many airplanes at once, but some computer experts have pointed out the possibility of sabotage. According to Harold Greenwood, an aeronautic electronics specialist with Air Systems Design in Alpharetta, Georgia, "there is a real and definite possibility that there has been a specific attack on the airline computers. Probab-

24

ly by hackers. Either that or the most devastating computer programming error in history."

Government officials discounted Greenwood's theories and said there is no place for wild speculation that could create panic in the minds of the public. None the less, flight cancellations busied the phones at most airlines and travel agencies, while the gargantuan task of rescheduling thousands of flights with 30% less planes began. Airline officials who didn't want to be quoted estimated that it would take at least a week to bring the system back together.

Airline fares will increase next Monday by at least 10% and as much as 40% on some routes that will not be restored fully.

The tone of the press conference held at the DoT was one of both bitterness and shock as was that of sampled public opinion.

"I think I'll take the train."

"Computers? They always blame the computers. Who's really at fault?"

"They're just as bad as the oil companies. Something goes a little wrong and they jack up the prices."

The National Transportation Safety Board said it would also institute a series of preventative maintenance steps on other airplanes' computer systems to insure that such a global failure is never repeated.

Major domestic airlines announced they would try to lease additional planes from other countries, but could not guarantee prior service performance for 3 to 6 months. Preliminary estimates place the cost of this debacle at between $800 Million and $2 Billion if the entire 737 fleet is grounded for only 2 weeks.

The Stock Market reacted poorly to the news, and transportation stocks dove an average of 27% in heavy trading.

The White House issued a brief statement congratulating the airline industry for its handling of the situation and wished its best to all inconvenienced and injured travelers.

Class action suits will be filed next week against the airlines and Boeing as a result of the computer malfunction. This is Scott Mason, riding the train.

* * * * *

"Doug," pleaded 39 year old veteran reporter Scott Mason. "Not another computer virus story . . ." Scott childishly shrugged his shoulders in mock defeat.

"Stop your whining," Doug ordered in fun. "You are the specialist," he chided.

When the story first came across the wire, Scott was the logical choice. In only seven years as a reporter Scott Mason had developed quite a reputation for himself, and for the New York City Times. Doug had had to eat his words more times than he cared to remember, but Scott's head had not swelled to the size of the fan club, which was the bane of so many successful writers. He knew he was good, just like he had told Doug

"There is nothing sexy about viruses anymore," said Scott trying to politely ignore his boss so he would just leave.

"Christ Almighty," the chubby balding sixtyish editor exploded. Doug's periodic exclamatory outbursts at Scott's nonchalance on critical issues were legendary. "The man who puts Cold Fusion on the front page of every paper in the country doesn't think a virus is sexy enough for the public. Good night!"

"That's not what I'm saying." Scott had to defend this one. "I finally got someone to go on the record about the solar payoff scandals between Oil and Congress . . ."

"Then the virus story will give you a little break," kidded Doug. "You've been working too hard."

"Damn it, Doug," Scott defied. "Viruses are a dime a dozen and worse, there's no one behind it, there's nobody there. There's no story . . ."

"Then find one. That's what we pay you for." Doug loudly muttered a few choice words that his paper wouldn't be caught dead printing. "Besides, you're the only one left." As he left he patted Scott on the back saying, "thanks. Really."

"God, I hate this job."

Scott Mason loved his job, after all it was his invention seven years ago when he first pitched it to Doug. Scott's original idea had worked. Scott Mason alone, under the banner of the New York City Times, virtually pioneered Scientific Journalism as a media form in its own right.

Scott Mason was still its most vocal proponent, just as he was when he connived his way into a job with the Times, and without any journalistic experience. It was a childhood fantasy.

Doug remembered the day clearly. "That's a new one on me," Doug had said with amusement when the mildly arrogant but very likable Mason had cornered him, somehow bypassing personnel. Points for aggressiveness, points for creativity and points for brass balls. "What is Scientific Journalism?"

"Scientific Journalism is stripping away all of the long technical terms that science hides behind, and bringing the facts to the people at home."

"We have a quite adequate Science Section, a computer column, and we pick up the big stories." Doug had tried to be polite.

"That's not what I mean," Scott explained. "Everybody and his dead brother can write about the machines and the computers and the software. I'm talking about finding the people, the meaning, the impact behind the technology."

"No one would be interested," objected Doug.

Doug was wrong.

Scott Mason immediately acclimated to the modus operandi of the news business. He locked onto the collapse of Kaypro Computers and the odd founding family who rode serendipity until competence was required for survival. As his first major story, the antics of the Kay family earned Mason a respectable following in his articles and contributions as well as several libel ånd slander suits from the Kays. Trouble was, it's not against the law to print the truth or third party speculations, as long as they're not malicious. Scott instinctively knew how to ride the fine edge between false accusations and impersonal objectivity.

Cold Fusion, the brief prayer for immediate, cheap energy independence made headlines, but Scott Mason dug deep and found that some of the advocates of Cold Fusion had vested interests in palladium and iridium mining concerns. He also discovered how the experiments had been staged well enough to fool most experts. Scott had located one expert who wasn't fooled and could prove it. Scott Mason rode the crest of the Cold Fusion story for months before it became old news and the Hubble Telescope disaster took its place.

The fiasco of the Hubble Telescope was nothing new to Scott Mason's readers. He had published months before its launch that the mirrors were defective, but the government didn't heed the whistle blower's advice. The optical measurement computers which grind the mirrors of the telescope had a software program that was never tested before being used on the Hubble. The GSA had been tricked by the contractor's test results and Scott found the discrepencies.

When Gene-Tech covered up the accidental release of mutated spores into the atmosphere from their genetic engineering labs, Scott Mason was the one reporter who had established enough of a reputation as both a fair reporter, but also one that understood the technology. Thanks to Mason's early diagnosis and the Times responsible publishing, a potentially cataclysmic genetic disaster was averted.

The software problems with Star Wars and Brilliant Pebbles, the payoffs that allowed defective X-Ray lasers to be shipped to the testing ground outside of Las Vegas - Scott Mason was there. He traced the Libyan chemical weapons plant back to West Germany which triggered the subsequent destruction of the plant.

Scott's outlook was simple. "It's a matter of recognizing the possibilities and then the probabilities. Therefore, if something is possible, someone, somewhere will do it. Guaranteed. Since someone's doing it, then it's only a matter of catching him in the act."

"Besides," he would tell anyone who would listen, "computers and technology and electronics represent trillions of dollars annually. To believe that there isn't interesting, human interest and profound news to be found, is pure blindness. The fear of the unknown, the ignorance of what happens on the other side of the buttons we push, is an enemy wrapped in the shrouds of time, well disguised and easily avoided.

Scott successfully opened the wounds of ignorance and technical apathy and he made Times the de facto standard in Scientific Journalism.

His reputation as an expert in anything technical endeared him to fellow Times' reporters. Scott often became the technical backbone of articles that did not carry his name. But that was good. The journalists' barter system. Scott Mason was not considered a competitor to the other reporters because of his areas of interest and the skills he brought with him to the paper. And, he didn't flaunt his knowledge. To Scott's way of thinking, technical fluency should be as required as the ABC's, so it was with the dedication of a teacher and the experience of simplification that Scott undertook it to gladly help anyone who wanted to learn. His efforts were deeply appreciated.

* * * * *

Chapter 2

Friday, September 4
San Francisco, California

Mr. Henson?"

"Yes, Maggie?" Henson responded over the hands free phone on his highly polished black marble desk. He never looked up from the papers he was perusing.

"There's a John Fullmaster for you."

"Who?" he asked absent mindedly.

"Ah . . .John Fullmaster."

"I don't know a Fullman do I? Who is he?"

"That's Fullmaster, sir, and he says its personal."

Robert Henson, chairman and CEO of Perris, Miller and Stevenson leaned back in the plush leather chair. A brief perplexed look covered his face and then a sigh of resignation. "Very well, tell him I'll take it in a minute."

As the young highly visible leader of one of the most successful Wall Street investment banking firms during the merger mania of the 1980's, he had grown accustomed to cold calls from aggressive young brokers who wanted a chance to pitch him on sure bets. Usually he simply ignored the calls, or referred them to his capable and copious staff. Upon occasion, though, he would amuse himself with such calls by putting the caller through salesmen's hell; he would permit them to give their pitch, actually sound interested, permit the naive to believe that their call to Robert Henson would lead them to a pot of gold, then only to bring them down as harshly as he could. It was the only seeming diversion he had from the daily grueling regimen of earning fat fees in the most somber of Wall Street activities. He needed a break anyway.

"Robert Henson. May I help you?" he said into the phone. It was as much a command as a question. From the 46th. floor South West corner office, Henson stared out over Lower New York Bay where the Statue of Liberty reigned.

"Thank you for taking my call Mr. Henson." The caller's proper Central London accent was engaging and conveyed assurance and propriety. "I am calling in reference to the proposed merger you are arranging between Second Boston Financial and Winston Ellis Services. I don't believe that the SEC will be impressed with the falsified figures you have generated to drive up your fees. Don't you agree."

Henson bolted upright in his chair and glared into the phone. "Who the hell is this?" he demanded.

"Merely a concerned citizen, sir." The cheeky caller paused. "I asked, sir, don't you agree?"

"Listen," Henson shouted into the phone. "I don't know who the hell you are, nor what you want, but all filings made with the SEC are public and available to anyone. Even the press whom I assume you represent . . ."

"I am not with the press Mr. Henson," the voice calmly interrupted. "All the same, I am sure that they would be quite interested in what I have to say. Or, more precisely, what I have to show them."

"What the hell are you talking about?" Henson screamed.

"Specifically, you inflated the earnings of Winston Ellis over 40% by burying certain write downs and deferred losses. I believe you are familiar with the numbers. Didn't you have them altered yourself?"

Henson paled as the caller spoke to him matter of factly. His eyes darted around his spacious and opulent office as though someone might be listening. He shifted uneasily in his chair, leaned into the phone and spoke quietly.

"I don't know what you're taking about."

"I think you do, Mr. Henson."

"What do you want?" Henson asked cautiously.

"Merely your acknowledgment, to me, right now, that the figures were falsified, at your suggestion, and . . ."

"I admit nothing. Nothing." Henson hung up the phone.

Shaken, he dialed the phone, twice. In his haste he misdialed the first time. "Get me Brocker. Now. This is Henson."

"Brocker," the other end of the phone responded nonchalantly.

"Bill, Bob here. We got troubles."

* * * * *

"Senator Rickfield? I think you better take this call." Ken Boyers was earnest in his suggestion. The aged Senator looked up and recognized a certain urgency. The youthful 50 year old Ken Boyers had been with Senator Merrill Rickfield since the mid 1960's as an aide de campe, a permanent fixture in Rickfield's national success. Ken preferred the number two spot, to be the man in the background rather the one in the public light. He felt he could more effectively wield power without the constant surveillance of the press. Only when events and deals were completely orchestrated were they made public, and then Merrill could take the credit. The arrangement suited them both.

Rickfield indicated that his secretary and the two junior aids should leave the room. "What is it Ken?"

"Just take the call, listen carefully, and then we'll talk."

"Who is it, Ken. I don't talk to every. . ."

"Merrill . . .pick up the phone." It was an order. They had worked together long enough to afford Ken the luxury of ordering a U.S. Senator around.

"This is Senator Rickfield, may I help you?" The solicitous campaign voice, smiling and inviting, disguised the puzzled look he gave his senior aid. Within a few seconds the puzzlement gave way to open mouthed silent shock and then, only moments later to overt fear. He stared with disbelief at Ken Boyers. Aghast, he gently put the phone back in its cradle.

"Ken," Rickfield haltingly spoke. "Who the hell was that and how in blazes did he know about the deal with Credite Suisse? Only you, me and General Young knew." He rose slowly rose and looked accusingly at Ken.

"C'mon Merrill, I have as much to lose as you..."

"The hell you do." He was growling. "I'm a respected goddamned United States Senator. They can string me up from the highest yardarm just like they did Nixon and I'm not playing to lose. Besides, I'm the one the public knows while you're invisible. It's my ass and you know it. Now, and I mean now, tell me what the hell is going on? There were only three of us . . ."

"And the bank," Ken quickly interjected to deflect the verbal onslaught.

"Fuck the bank. They use numbers. Numbers, Ken. That was the plan. But this son of a bitch knew the numbers. Damn it, he knew the numbers Ken!"

"Merrill, calm down."

"Calm down? You have some fucking nerve telling me to calm down. Do you know what would happen if anyone, and I mean anyone finds out about . . ." Rickfield looked around and thought better of finishing the sentence.

"Yes I know. As well as you do. Jesus Christ, I helped set the whole thing up. Remember?" He approached Merrill Rickfield and touched the Senator's shoulder. "Maybe it's a hoax? Just some lucky guess by some scum bag who . . ."

"Bullshit." The senator turned abruptly. "I want a tee off time as soon as possible. Even sooner. And make damn sure that bastard Young is there. Alone. It's a threesome."

* * * * *

John Faulkner was lazing at his estate in the eminently exclusive, obscenely expensive Bell Canyon, 20 miles north of Los Angeles. Even though it was Monday, he just wasn't up to going into the office. As Executive Vice President of California National Bank, with over 20 billion in assets, he could pick and choose his hours. This Tuesday he chose to read by the pool and enjoy the warm and clear September California morning. The view of the San Gabriel mountains was so distracting that his normal 30 minute scan of the Wall Street Journal took nearly 2 hours.

His estate was the one place where Faulkner was guaranteed privacy and anonymity. High profile Los Angeles banking required a social presence and his face, along with his wife's, graced the social pages every time an event of any gossip-magnitude occurred. He craved his private time.

Faulkner's standing instruction with his secretary was never to call him at home unless "the bank is nuked, or I died" which when translated meant, "Don't call me, I'll call you." His wife was the only other person with the private phone number he changed every month to insure his solitude.

The phone rang. It never rang. At least not in recent memory. He used it to dial out; but it was never used to receive calls. The warble surprised him so, that he let it ring three times before suspiciously picking it up. Damn it, he thought. I just got a new number last week. I'll have to have it changed again.

"Hello?" he asked suspiciously.

"Good morning Mr. Faulkner. I just called to let you know that your secret is safe with me." Faulkner itched to identify the voice behind the well educated British accent, but that fleeting thought dissipated at the import of the words being spoken.

"Who is this? What secret?"

"Oh, dear me. I am sorry, where are my manners. I am referring to the millions you have embezzled from your own bank to cover your gambling losses last year. Don't worry. I won't tell a soul." The line went dead.

Sir George dialed the next number on his list after scanning the profile. The phone was answered by a timid sounding gentleman. Sir George began his fourth pitch of the day. "Mr. Hugh Sidneys? I would like to talk to you about a small banking problem I think you have . . ."

Sir George Sterling made another 34 calls that day. Each one alarmingly similar to the first three. Not that they alarmed him. They merely alarmed, often severely, the recipients of his calls. In most cases he had never heard of the persons he was calling, and the contents of his messages were often cryptic to him. But it didn't take him long to realize that every call was some form of veiled, or not so veiled threat. His instructions had been clear. Do not threaten. Just pass on the contents of the messages on his list to their designees. He was not to leave any message unless he had confirmed, to the best of his ability that he was actually speaking to the party in question. If he received any trouble in reaching his intended targets, by secretaries or aides, he was only to pass on a preliminary message. These were especially cryptic, but in all cases, perhaps with a little prod, his call was put through.

At the end of the first day of his assignment, Sir George Sterling walked onto his balcony overlooking San Francisco Bay and reflected on his good fortune. *If he hadn't been stuck in Athens last year, wondering where his next score would come from. How strange the world works,* he thought. Damn lucky he became a Sir, and at the tender age of 29, at that.

His title, actually purchased from The Royal Title Assurance Company, Ltd. in London in 1987 for a mere 5000 pounds had permitted George Toft to leave the perennial industrial smog of the eternally drizzly commonness of Manchester, England and assume a new identity. It was one of the few ways out of the dismal existence that generations before him had tolerated with a stiff upper lip. As a petty thief he had done 'awright', but one score had left him with more money than he had ever seen. That is when he became a Sir, albeit one purchased.

He spent several months impressing mostly himself as he traveled Europe. With the help of Eliza Doolittle, Sir George perfected his adapted upper crust London accent. His natural speech was that of a Liverpuddlian with a bag of marbles in his mouth - totally unintelligible when drunk to the non-local. But his royal speech was now that of a Gentleman from the House of Lords. Slow and precise when appropriate or a practiced articulateness when speaking rapidly. It initially took some effort, but he could now correct his slips instantly. No one noticed anymore. Second nature it became for George Sterling, né Toft.

Athens was the end of his tour and where he had spent the last of his money. George, Sir George, sat sipping Metaxa in Sintigma Square next to the Royal Gardens and the imposing Grand Britannia Hotel styled in 19th century rococo elegance. As he enjoyed the balmy spring Athens evening pondering his next move, as either George Toft of Sir George Sterling, a well dressed gentleman sat down at his tiny wrought iron table.

"Sir George?" The visitor offered his hand.

George extended his hand, not yet aware that his guest had no reason whatsoever to know who he was.

"Sir George? Do I have the Sir George Sterling of Briarshire, Essex?" The accent was trans European. Internationally cosmopolitan. German? Dutch? It didn't matter, Sir George had been recognized.

George rose slightly. "Yes, yes. Of course. Excuse me, I was lost in thought, you know. Sir George Sterling. Of course. Please do be seated."

The stranger said, "Sir George, would you be offended if I offered you another drink, and perhaps took a few minutes of your valuable time?" The man smiled genuinely and sat himself across from George before any reply. He knew what the answer would be.

"Please be seated. Metaxa would it be for you, sir?" The man nodded yes. "*Garcon*?" George waved two fingers at one of the white-jacketed waiters who worked in the outdoor cafe. "*Metaxa, parakalo!*" Greek waiters are not known for their graciousness, so a brief grunt and nod was an acceptable response. George returned his attention to his nocturnal visitor. "I don't believe I've had the pleasure . . ." he said in his most formal voice.

"Sir George, please just call me Alex. Last names, are so, well, so unnecessary among men like us. Don't you agree?"

George nodded assent. "Yes, quite. Alex then, it is. How may I assist you?"

"Oh no, Sir George, it is I who may be able to assist you. I understand that you would like to continue your, shall we say, extended sabbatical. Would that be a fair appraisal?" The Metaxas arrived and Alex excused the waiter with two 1000 Drachma notes. The overtipping guaranteed privacy.

George looked closely at Alex. Very well dressed. A Saville suit? Perhaps. Maybe Lubenstrasse. He didn't care. This stranger had either keen insight into George's current plight or had heard of his escapades across the Southern Mediterranean. Royalty on Sabbatical was an unaccostable lie that regularly passed critical scrutiny.

"Fair. Yes sir, quite fair. What exactly can you do for me, or can we do for each other?"

"An even more accurate portrayal my friend, yes, do for each other." Alex paused for effect and to sip his Metaxa. "Simply put Sir George, I have the need for a well spoken gentleman to represent me for a period of perhaps, 3 months, perhaps more if all goes well Would that fit into your schedule?"

"I see no reason that I mightn't be able to, take a sabbatical from my sabbatical if . . .well now, how should I put this . . ."

" . . .that you are adequately compensated to take time away from your valuable projects?"

"Yes, yes quite so. Not that I am ordinarily for hire, you understand, it's just that . . .". Alex detected a slight stutter as Sir George spoke.

Alex held up both hands in a gesture of understanding. "No need to continue my dear Sir George. I do thoroughly recognize the exorbitant costs associated with your studies and would not expect your efforts, on my behalf of course, to go unrewarded."

George Toft was negotiating with a man he had never met, for a task as yet unstated. The only reason he didn't feel the discomfort that one should in such a situation is that he was in desperate need of money. And, this stranger did seem to know who he was, and did need his particular type of expertise, whatever that was.

"What exactly do you require of me . . .Alex. That is, what form of representation have you in mind?" He might as well find out what he was supposed to do before naming a price.

Alex laughed. "Merely to be my voice. It is so simple, really. In exchange for that, and some travel, first class and all expenses to which you are accustomed, you will be handsomely paid." Alex looked for Sir George's reaction to the proposed fees. He was pleased with what he saw in George's face.

A year's pay for a month's work? Bloody hell, this bloke's gonna pay me to play? Crikey, this is too good to be true. What's the catch. As George ruminated his good fortune and the Metaxa, Alex continued.

"The job is quite simple, really, but requires a particular delicacy with which you are well acquainted. Each day you will receive a list of names. There will be instructions with each name. Call them at the numbers provided. Say only what is written. Keep notes of each call you make and I will provide you with the means to transmit them to me in the strictest of confidence. You and I will have no further personal contact, either if you accept or do not accept my proposition. If we are able to reach mutually agreeable terms, monies will be wired to a bank account in your name." Alex opened his jacket and handed George an envelop. "This is an advance if you accept. It is $25,000 American. There is a phone number to call when you arrive in San Francisco. Follow the instructions explicitly. If you do not, there will be no lists for you, no additional monies and I will want this money back. Any questions Sir George?" Alex was smiling warmly but as serious as a heart attack.

Alex scanned the contents of the envelope. America. He had always wanted to see the States.

"Yes, Alex, I do have one question. Is this legal?" George peered at Alex for a clue.

"Do you really care?"

"No."

"Off you go then. And good luck."

* * * * *

Sir George Sterling arrived in San Francisco airport the following evening. He flew first class and impressed returning American tourists with his invented pedigree and his construed importance. What fun. After the virtually nonexistent customs check, he called the number inside the envelop. It rang three times before answering. Damn, it was a machine, he thought.

"Welcome to the United States Sir George. I hope you had a good flight." The voice was American, female, and flight attendant friendly. "Please check into the San Francisco Airport Hilton. You will receive a call at 11 AM tomorrow. Good night." A dial tone replaced the lovely voice. He dialed the number again.

A mechanical voice responded instead. "The number you have called is no longer in service. Please check the number or call the operator for assistance. The number you have called is no longer in service..."

George dialed the number twice more before he gave up in frustration. He had over $20,000 in cash, knew no one in America and for the first time in years, he felt abandoned. What kind of joke was this? Fly half way around the world and be greeted with an out of service number. But the first voice had known his name . . .the Hilton. Why not?

At precisely 11AM, the phone in Sir George Sterling's suite rang. He was still somewhat jet lagged from his 18 hours of flying and the span of 10 time zones. The Eggs Benedict was exquisite, but Americans could learn something about tea. The phone rang again. He casually picked it up.

"Good morning, Sir George. Please get a pencil and paper. You have fifteen seconds and then I will continue." It was the same alluring voice from yesterday. The paper and pen were right there at the phone so he waited through 14 seconds of silence. "Very good. Please check out of the hotel and pay cash. Proceed to the San Francisco airport and from a pay phone, call 5-5-5-3-4-5-6 at 1 P.M. Have a note book and two pens with you. Good Bye. "

The annoying dial tone returned. Shit, what a waste of time.

At 1P.M. he called the number as he was instructed. He figured that since he was to have a notebook and pens he might need to be writing for a while, so he used one of the phone booths that provides a seat and large writing surface.

"Good afternoon Sir George. In 10 seconds, your instructions will begin." Again, that same voice, but it almost appeared condescending to him now. Isn't that the way when you can't respond. The voice continued. "Catch the next flight to New York City. Stay at the Grand Hyatt Hotel at Grand Central Station on 42nd. Street and Park Avenue. Not a suite this time, Sir George, just a regular room." Sir George was startled at Alex's attention to detail.

"You will stay there for 14 days. On 56th street and Madison avenue is a school called CTI, Computer Training Institute. You are to go to CTI and enroll in the following classes: DOS, that's D-O-S for beginners, Intermediate DOS and Advanced DOS. You will also take WordPerfect I and II. Lastly, and most importantly you will take all three classes on Tele-Communications. They call it TC-I, TC-II and TC-III. These 8 classes will take you 10 days to complete. Do not forget to pay in cash. I will now pause for 10 seconds." Alex was writing furiously. Computers? He was scared silly of them. Not that he had ever had the opportunity or the need or the desire to use them, just from lack of exposure and the corresponding ignorance. But if this meant he could keep the $25,000 he would do it. What the hell.

"After you enroll, go to 45 West 47th street to a store called Discount Computer Shoppe. Buy the following equipment with cash. One Pro-Start 486-80 computer with 8 Meg RAM. That's 8 M-E-G R-A-M and ask for a high resolution color Monitor. Also purchase, and have them install a high speed Modem, M-O-D-E-M. Do not, I repeat, do not purchase a printer of any type. No printers Sir George. You are never to use a printer. Ever. Lastly, you will purchase a copy of Word Perfect and Crosstalk. If you wish any games for your amusement, that is up to you. When you have completed your studies you will call 212-555-6091. Do not call that number before you have completed your studies. This is imperative."

Sir George was just writing, not comprehending a thing. It was all gibberish to him. Pure gibberish.

"Sir George." The female voice got serious, very serious for the first time in their relationship. "You are to speak to no one, I repeat, no one, of the nature of your business, the manner in which you receive instructions, or why computers have a sudden interest for you. Otherwise our deal is off and your advance will be expected to be returned. Am I clear?"

George responded quickly, "Yes!" before seeing the lunacy of answering a machine.

"Good," the voice was friendly again. "Learn your lessons well for you will need the knowledge to perform your tasks. Until we speak again, I thank you, Sir George Sterling." The line went dead.

George Toft took his computer classes very seriously. He had in fact bought a few games to amuse himself and he found himself really enjoying the work. It was new, and exciting. His only social distractions were the sex shops on Times Square. Red Light Amsterdam or the Hamburg they weren't, so midnight antics with the Mario Brothers prevailed most evenings. Besides, there was a massive amount of homework. Bloody hell, back to school. He excelled in his studies which pleased George a great deal. In fact most of the students in Sir George's computer classes excelled. The teachers were very pleased to have a group of students that actually progressed more rapidly than the curriculum called for. Pleasant change from the E Train Bimbos from Queens.

The computer teachers didn't know that a vast majority of the class members had good reason to study hard. Most of them had received their own $25,000 scholarships.

* * * * *

Sunday, September 6
SDSU Campus, San Diego, California.

WTFO

the computer screen displayed. That was hackerese, borrowed from the military for What The Fuck? Over! It was a friendly greeting that offended no one.

Back on. Summer finals are over. Everyone still there?

BOOM'S STILL AT UCLA, I JUST TALKED TO CRACKER, MAD MAX, ALPHA, SCROLLER, MR. MAGIC . . .YEAH . . .WE MISSED YOU. LOOKING FORWARD TO A GOOD VA-CATE?

Yeah, 4 days before next term starts . . .Has anyone got the key to the NPPS NASA node?

THEY CLOSED IT AGAIN.. WE'RE STILL LOOKING. WE WERE BACK INTO AMEX, THOUGH. CLEANED UP A FEW DEBTS FOR UNSUSPECTING CARD MEMBERS. HAPPY LABOR DAY TO THEM. GOOD FUN.

And CHAOS? Anyone?

BEST I'VE EVER HEARD. 4 NEW VIRUSES SET TO GO OFF. HIGHLY POTENT VARIATIONS OF JERUSALEM-B.

THEN SOME RUMORS ABOUT COLUMBUS DAY, BUT NOTH-ING HARD.

When you get the code send me copy, OK?

SURE. HEY, REMEMBER SPOOK? STILL ASKING TO JOIN NEMO. SEEMS HE'S BEEN UP TO A LOT OF SUCCESSFUL NO GOOD. WE'RE ABOUT READY TO LET HIM IN. HE BROUGHT A LOT TO THE PARTY.

Careful! Remember 401

YEAH, I KNOW. HE'S CLEAN. GOOD GOVT STUFF . . .HE BROUGHT US THE NEWEST IRS X.25 SIGN-ONS, 2 MILNET SUPERUSER PASSWORDS AND, DIG THIS, VETERAN'S BENEFIT AND ADMINISTRATION, OFFICE OF POLICY AT THE VA.

What you gonna do, boy? In them thar computers?

I FIGURE I'D GIVE A FEW EXTRA BENEFITS TO SOME NEEDY GI'S WHO'VE BEEN ON THE SHORT END.

Excellent! Hey, Lori's on the line. gotta go

TA

<<< CONNECTION TERMINATED >>>

The screen of his communications program returned to a list of names and phone numbers. Lori said she'd be over in an hour and Steven Billings was tempted to dial another couple of numbers before his date with Lori. But if he found something interesting it might force him to be late, and Lori could not tolerate playing second fiddle to a computer.

Steven Billings, known as "KIRK, where no man has gone before", by fellow hackers, had finished his midterms at San Diego State University. The ritual labors were over and he looked forward to some relax time. Serious relax time.

The one recreation he craved, but downplayed to Lori, was spending time with his computer. She was jealous in some respects, in that it received as much attention from Steve as she did. Yet, she also understood that computers were his first love, and they were part of his life long before she was. So, they came with the territory. Steve attended, upon occasion, classes at SDSU, La Jolla. For a 21 year old transplant from Darien, Connecticut, he lived in paradise.

Steve's single largest expense in life was his phone bill, and instead of working a regular job to earn spending money, Steve tutored other students in their computer courses. Rather than flaunt his skills to his teachers and risk extra assignments, he was more technically qualified than they were, he kept his mouth shut, sailed through classes, rarely studied and became a full time computer hacker. He translated his every wish into a command that the computer obeyed.

Steve Billings did not fill the picture of a computer nerd. He was almost dashing with a firm golden tanned 175 pound body, and dark blond hair that caused the girls to turn their heads. He loved the outdoors, the hot warmth of the summer to the cooler warmth of the winter, surfing at the Cardiff Reef and betting on fixed jai-alai games in Tijuana. He played soccer, and OTL, a San Diego specific version of gloveless and topless co-ed beach softball. In short, he was a guy. A regular guy.

The spotlessly groomed image of Steve Billings in white tennis shorts and a "Save the Whales" tank-top eclectically co-existed with the sterile surroundings of the mammoth super computer center. The Cray Y-MP is about as big and bad a computer as money can buy, and despite Steve's well known skills, the Super Computing Department Head couldn't help but cringe when Steve leaned his surf board against the helium cooled memory banks of the twelve million dollar computer.

He ran his shift at the computer lab so efficiently and effortlessly that over time he spent more and more of his hours there perusing through other people's computers. Now there was a feeling. Hacking through somebody else's computer without their knowledge. The ultimate challenge, an infinity of possibilities, an infinity of answers.

The San Diego Union was an awful paper, Steve thought, and the evening paper was even worse. So he got copies of the New York City Times when possible, either at a newsstand, borrowed from yesterday's Times reader or from the library. Nice to get a real perspective on the world. This Sunday he spent the $4.00 to get his own new, uncrumpled and unread copy of his revered paper, all 34 pounds of it. Alone. Peace.

Reading by the condo pool an article caught his eye. Steve remembered a story he had heard about a hacker who had invaded and single handedly stopped INTERNET, a computer network that connected tens of thousands of computers around the country.

* * * * *

Government Defense Network Halted by Hacker

by Scott Mason, New York City Times

Vaughn Chase, a 17 year old high school student from Galbraith High School in Ann Arbor, Michigan was indicted today on charges that he infected the nationwide INTERNET network with a computer virus. This latest attack upon INTERNET is reminiscent of a similar incident launched by Robert Morris of Cornell University in November, 1988.

According to the Computer Emergency Response Team, a DARPA sponsored group, if Mr. Chase had not left his name in the source code of his virus, there would have been no way to track down the culprit.

A computer virus is a small software program that is secretly put into a computer, generally designed to cause damage. A virus attaches itself to other computer programs secretively. At some time after the parasite virus program is 'glued' into the computer, it is reawakened on a specific date or by a particular sequence of events.

Chase, though, actually infected INTERNET with a Worm. A Worm is a program that copies itself, over and over and over, either filling the computer's memory to capacity or slowing down its operation to a snail's pace. In either case, the results are devastating - effectively, the computer stops working.

Chase, a math wizard according to his high school officials, released the Worm into Internet in early August with a detonation date of September 1, which brought thousands of computers to a grinding halt.

INTERNET ties together tens of thousands of computers from the Government, private industry, universities and defense contractors all over the country. Chase said he learned how to access the unclassified computer network from passwords and keys distributed on computer Bulletin Boards.

Computer security experts worked for 3 days to first determine the cause of the network slowdown and then to restore the network to normal operation. It has been estimated that almost $100 Million in damage was caused by Mr. Chase's Worm. Mr. Chase said the Worm was experimental, and was accidentally released into INTERNET when a piece of software he had written malfunctioned. He apologized for any inconvenience he caused.

The Attorney General of the State of Michigan is examining the legal aspects of the case and it is expected that Mr. Chase will be tried within a year. Mr. Chase was released on bond on his own recognizance.

This is Scott Mason wondering why the Pentagon doesn't shoot worms instead of bombs at enemy computers.

* * * * *

Steve Billings signed on to the SDSU/BBS from his small Mission Beach apartment. It was a local university Bulletin Board Service or BBS. A BBS is like a library. There are libraries of software which is free, and as a user you are reciprocally expected to donate software into the Public Domain. Conference Halls or Conversation Pits on the BBS are free-for-all discussions where people at their keyboards anywhere in the world can all have a 'live' conversation. Anyone, using any computer, anywhere in the world can call up any BBS using regular phone lines. No one cared or knew if you were skinny, fat, pimpled, blind, a double for Christy Brinkley or too chicken shit to talk to girls in person. Here, everyone was equal.

LOGON: Billings 234

PASSWORD: XXXXXXXXXXXXXXXX

There was a brief pause.

WELCOME TO THE SD/BBS. STEVE BILLINGS, YOU ARE USER #109

Steve chose option #12, SERVICES, from the menu.

The menu changed to a list of further options. Each option would permit the user to gain access to other networks around the country. From one single entry point with a small computer, anyone could 'dial up' as it's called, almost any of over 20,000,000 computers in the country tied into any of ten thousand different networks.

SD/BBS WINDOW ON THE WORLD

NETWORK SERVICES MENU

Steve selected CALNET, a network at Cal Tech in Los Angeles. Many universities have permanently connect their computers.

LOGON: Billings014

PASSWORD: XXXXKIRKXXXX

Again, there was a pause, this time a little longer. Now, from his room, he was talking to a computer in Los Angeles. There was another menu of options, and a list of other widely dispersed computer networks. He requested the SUNYNET computer, the State

University of New York Network. From there, he asked the computer for a local phone line so he could dial into a very private, very secret computer called NEMO.

It took Steve a grand total of 45 seconds to access NEMO in New York, all at the price of a local phone call.

NEMO was a private BBS that was restricted to an elite few. Those whose qualifications and reputations allowed them entry into the exclusive domain of hacking. NEMO was born into this world by Steve and a few of his friends while they were in high school in Darien. NEMO was a private club, for a few close friends who enjoyed their new hobby, computers.

NEMO's Menu was designed for the professional hacker.

1. PASSWORDS

2. NEW NETS

3. DANGER ZONES

4. CRACKING TOOLS

5. WHO'S NEW?

6. PHREAKING

7. CRYPTO

8. WHO ELSE?

9. U.S. NETWORKS

10. INTERNATIONAL NETWORKS

11. FOR TRADE

12. FORTUNE 500 DOORKEYS

He selected (8), WHO ELSE? Steve wanted to see who else was 'on-line' now. He wanted to talk about this Chase guy who was giving hackers a bad name. The computer responded:

CONVERSATION PIT: LA CREME, RAMBO. DO YOU WANT TO JOIN IN?

That was great! Two of the half dozen of NEMO's founders were there. La Creme de la Creme was KIRK's college roommate, but he had not yet returned to San Diego for the fall term. RAMBO, 'I'll get through any door' was the same age as Kirk and Creme, but chose to study at Columbia in New York's Harlem. Hackers picked alter- ego monikers as CB'ers on the highways did; to project the desired image. Steve and his cohorts picked their aliases when they were only 15, and kept them ever since.

Steve typed in a 'Y' and the ENTER key.

WHO ARE YOU?

NEMO was asking for an additional password.

Kirk

Steve typed. A brief pause, and the computer screen came to life.
WELCOME TO THE CONVERSATION PIT, KIRK. HOW HAVE YOU BEEN?

That was his invitation to interrupt any conversation in progress. Steve typed in,

Dudes!

HOW'D EXAMS GO? <LA CREME>

Greased'em. Ready to come back?

FAST AS THE PLANE WILL GO. PICK ME UP? 7:20 ON AMERICAN?

Sure. Hey, what's with the Morris copy cat? Some phreak blowing it for the rest of us.

SO YOU HEARD. CHASE IS REALLY GONNA FUCK THINGS UP. <RAMBO>

What the hell really happened? I read the Times. Said that he claimed it was accident.

ACCIDENTAL ON PURPOSE MAYBE <LA CREME>

HOW MANY WAYS ARE THERE TO INFECT A NATIONAL DEFENSE NETWORK? ONE THAT I KNOW OF. YOU PUT THE VIRUS IN THERE. THAT'S NO ACCIDENT. <RAMBO>

Ten-Four. Seems like he don't wanna live by the code. Must be some spoiled little brat getting too big for his britches . . .

BEST GUESS IS THAT HE DID IT TO IMPRESS HIS OLD MAN. HE SUPPOSEDLY CREATED AN ANTIDOTE, TOO. HE WANTED TO SET OFF A BIG VIRUS SCARE AND THEN LOOK LIKE A HERO WITH A FAST FIX. THE VIRUS WORKED ALL TOO WELL. THE ANTIDOTE, IF THERE WAS ONE SUCKED. SO INTERNET HAS GAS SO BAD, COMPUTING CAME TO A HALT FOR A COUPLE OF DAYS TILL THEY CLEANED OUT THE PROVERBIAL SEWERS. <LA CREME>

SURE SOUNDS LIKE A PUBLICITY GAG TO ME <RAMBO>

Jeez. Anyone else been hit yet?

NO, BUT WE'VE BEEN EXTRA CAREFUL SINCE. A LOT OF DOORS HAVE BEEN CLOSED SO IT'S BACK TO SQUARE ONE ON A BUNCH, BUT WE DIDN'T LOSE EVERYTHING. THE DOORKEY DOWNLOAD WILL UPDATE YOU. <RAMBO>

OK, I'll be supersleuth. Any word on CHAOS? Legion of Doom, The Crusaders?

IT'S ONE BIG DEAL IN THE E-MAIL: NEW CHAOS VIRUSES, EVERY DICK AND JANE IS WRITING THEIR OWN VIRUSES. COMPUTING WITH AIDS.

Funny. Why don't you put a rubber on your big 640K RAM? Or your mouse?

GOT SOMETHING AGAINST SAFE COMPUTING? IF HALF OF WHAT THEY SAY IS TRUE, WE'RE ALL IN TROUBLE. TAKE A LOOK AT THE PUBLIC BBS's. QUITE A CHAT. <LA CREME>

Will do. any word on the new Central Census Data Base? Everything about every American stored in one computer. All of their personal data, ripe for the picking. Sounds like the kind of library that would do the bad guys a lot of good.

CAN'T FIND A DOOR FROM THE INTERNET GATE. THE JUSTICE LINK WAS STILL GOOD YESTERDAY AND THE FBI STILL HASN'T CHANGED A PASSWORD, SO THAT SHOULD BE AN EASY OPEN ONCE WE FIND THE FRONT DOOR. GIMME A COUPLE OF DAYS AND WE SHOULD KNOW DAN QUAYLES' JOCK SIZE. <RAMBO>

Zero! Ha! Keep me in mind.

* * * * *

Steve copied several pages of names, phone numbers and passwords from NEMO's data base into his computer 3000 miles across the country. These were the most valuable and revered types of files in the underground world of hackerdom. They include all of the information needed to enter and play havoc inside of hundreds of secret and private computers.

National Institute of Health   **301-555-6761**
USER: Fillstein   **PASSWORD: Daddy1**
USER: Miller9   **PASSWORD: Secret**
VMS 1.01
SUPERUSER: **PASSWORD: SUPERUSER**

VTEK NAS, Pensacola, Fla   **904-555-2113**
USER: Major101   **PASSWORD: Secret**
USER: General22   **PASSWORD: Secret1**
USER: Forestall   **PASSWORD: PDQS**

45

IBM, Armonk, Advanced Research   **914-555-0965**
USER: Port1   PASSWORD: Scientist
USER: Port2   PASSWORD: Scientist
USER: Port3   PASSWORD: Scientist

There were 17 pages of updated and illegal access codes to computer systems across the country. Another reason NEMO was so secret. Didn't want just anybody climbing the walls of their private playground. Can't trust everyone to live by the Code.

Steve finished downloading the files from NEMO's distant data base and proceeded to print them out for a hardcopy reference. He laughed to himself. Big business and government never wizened up. Predictable passwords, like 'secret' were about as kindergarten as you could get. And everyone wonders why folks like us parade around their computers. Here in Steve's hand was a list of over 250 updated and verified private, government and educational institutions who had left the keys to the front door of their computers wide open. And those were just the ones that NEMO knew about today.

There is no accurate way to determine how many groups of hackers like NEMO existed. But, even if only 1/10 of 1% of computer users classified themselves as hackers, that's well over 100,000 people breaking into computers. Enough reason to give Big Business cause for concern. Yet, no one did anything serious to lock the doors.

Steve spent the next several hours walking right into computer systems all over the country. Through the Bank of California in San Francisco, (Steve's first long distance call) he could reach the computers of several corresponding banks. He read through the new loan files, saw that various developers had defaulted on their loans and were in serious trouble. Rates were going to start rising. Good enough for a warm up.

Steve still wanted back into the NASA launch computers. On line launch information, results of analysis going back 20 years, and he had had a taste of it, once. Then, one day, someone inside of NASA got smart and properly locked the front door. He and NEMO were ever on the search for a key back into NASA's computers.

He figured that Livermore was still a good bet to get into NASA. That only meant a local call, through the SD/BBS to Cal Tech then into Livermore. From San Diego, to LA, to San Francisco for a mere 25 cents.

Livermore researchers kept the front doors of their computers almost completely open. Most of the workers, the graduate students, preferred a free exchange of information between all scientists, so their computer security was extraordinarily lax. For a weapons research laboratory, funded by the Department of Energy, it was a most incongruous situation.

Much of the information in the Livermore computers was considered sensitive but unclassified, whatever that meant in government- speak, but for an undergraduate engineering major cum hacker, it was great reading. The leading thinkers from the most technically demanding areas in science today put down their thoughts for everyone to read. The Livermore scientists believed in freedom of information, so nearly everyone who wanted in, got in - to the obvious consternation and dismay of Livermore management. And its funding agency.

Steve poked around the Livermore computers for a while and learned that SDI funding was in more serious jeopardy than publicly acknowledged. He discovered that the last 3 underground nuclear test explosions outside of Las Vegas were underyield, and no one knew why. Then he found some super-technical proposals that sounded like pure science fiction:

Moving small asteroids from between Mars and Jupiter into orbit around the Earth would make lovely weapons to drop on your enemies. War mongers.

All of this fascinating information, available to anyone with a computer and a little chutzbah.

Steve finally shut down his computer and his hacking when Lori called and insisted they go to the movies. She felt a minor sense of victory. Lori 1, Computer 0. She liked to keep score.

* * * * *

Alexander Spiradon had picked Sir George and his other subjects carefully, as he was trained to do.

He had spent the better part of 20 years working for West German Intelligence at the Bundeposte making less money than he required to live in the style he desired. The German Post Office runs not only the mail system, but also most communications as well as the phone company. To supplement his income, he occasionally performed extracurricular activities for special interest groups throughout Europe. A little information to the IRA in Northern Ireland, a warning to the Red Brigade about an impending raid. Even the Hizballah, the Party of God for Lebanese terrorists had occasion to use Alex's Services. Nothing that would compromise his country, he rationalized, just a little help to the various political factions that have become an annoyance to their respective governments.

Alex suddenly resigned in 1984 when he had collected enough freelance fees to support his habits, but he was unaware that his own agency had had him under surveillance for years, waiting for him to slip up. He hadn't, and with predictable German Government efficiency, upon his departure from the RDD, his file was promptly retired and his subsequent activities ignored.

Alex began his full time free-lance career as a 'Provider of Information'. With fees of no less than 250,000 DM, Alex didn't need to work much. He could pick and choose his clients as he weighed the risks and benefits of each potential assignment. With his network of intelligence contacts from Scotland Yard, Le Surite, and the Mossad, he had access to the kind of information that terrorists pay dearly for.

It was a good living. No guns, no danger, just information.

His latest client guaranteed Alex three years of work for a flat fee in the millions of Deutch Marks. It was the intelligence assignment of a lifetime, one that insured a peaceful and prosperous retirement for Alex. He wasn't the perennial spy, politically or dogmatically motivated. Alex wanted the money.

After he had completed his computer classes and purchased the equipment from the list, Sir George dialed the number he had been given. He half expected a live person to congratulate him, but also realized that that was a foolish wish. There was no reason to expect anything other than the same sexy voice dictating orders to him.

"Ah, Sir George. How good of you to call. How were your classes?" George nearly answered the alluring telephone personality again, but he caught himself.

"Very good," the voice came back in anticipated response. "Please get a pencil and paper. I have a message for you in 15 seconds." That damned infernal patronization. Of course I have a bleeding pen. Not a pencil. Idiot.

"Are you ready?" she asked. George made an obscene gesture at the phone.

"Catch a flight to San Francisco tonight. Bring all of the computer equipment you have purchased. Take a taxi to 14 Sutherland Place on Knob Hill. Under the mat to Apartment 12G you will find two keys. They will let you into your new living quarters. Make yourself at home. It is yours, and the rent is taken care of as is the phone bill. Your new phone number is 4-1-5-5-5-5-6-3-6-1. When you get settled, dial the following number from your computer. You should be well acquainted with how to do that by now. The number is 4-1-5-5-5-5-0-0-1-5. Your password is A-G-O-R-A. Under the mattress in the bedroom is a PRG, Password Response Generator. It looks like a credit card, but has an eight digit display. Whenever you call Alex, he will ask you for a response to your password. Quickly enter whatever the PRG says. If you lose the PRG, you will be terminated." The voice paused for a few seconds to George's relief.

"You will receive full instruction at that point. Good Bye." A dial tone replaced the voice he had come to both love and hate. Bloody hell, he thought. I'm down to less than $5000 and now I'm going back to San Francisco? What kind of bleedin' game is this?

Apartment 12G was a lavish 2 bedroom condominium with a drop dead view of San Francisco and water in 3 directions. Furnished in high tech modern, it offered every possible amenity; bar, jacuzzi, telephone in the bathroom and full channel cable. Some job. But, he kept wondering to himself, when does the free ride end? Maybe he's been strung along so far that he can't let go. One more call, just to see how the next chapter begins.

George installed his computer in the second bedroom on a table that fit his equipment exactly.

C:\cd XTALK
C:\XTALK\xtalk

His hard disk whirred for a few seconds. He chose the Dial option and entered the phone number from the keyboard and then asked the computer to remember it for future use. He omitted the area code. Why had he been given an area code if he was dialing from the same one? George didn't pursue the question; if he had he would have realized he wasn't alone.

The modem dialed the number for him. His screen went momentarily blank and then suddenly came to life again.

<<<CONNECT 2400 BAUD>>>
DO YOU WANT TO SPEAK TO ALEX? (Y/N?)

George entered a "Y"

PASSWORD:

George entered AGORA. The letters did not echo to the screen. He hoped he had typed then correctly. Apparently he did, for the screen then prompted him for his RESPONSE.

He copied the 8 characters from the PRG into the computer. There was a pause and then the screen filled.

SIR GEORGE,

WELCOME TO ALEX. IT IS SO GOOD TO SPEAK TO YOU AGAIN.

OVER THE NEXT SEVERAL MONTHS YOU WILL BE GIVEN NAMES AND NUMBERS TO CALL. THERE ARE VERY SPECIFIC QUESTIONS AND STATEMENTS TO BE MADE TO EACH PERSON YOU CALL. THERE IS TO BE NO DEVIA-

TION WHATSOEVER. I REPEAT, NO DEVIATION WHAT-
SOEVER. IF THERE IS, YOUR SERVICES WILL BE IMMEDI-
ATELY TERMINATED. WE HOPE THAT WILL NOT BE
NECESSARY.

EACH MORNING YOU ARE TO DIAL ALEX AND REQUEST
THE FILE CALLED SG.DAT. DO NOT, I REPEAT, DO NOT AT-
TEMPT TO ACCESS OR DOWNLOAD ANY OTHER FILES,
OR YOU WILL BE TERMINATED AT ONCE.

FOLLOW THE INSTRUCTIONS IN EACH FILE, EXACTLY.
KEEP AN EXACT LOG OF THE EVENTS AS THEY
TRANSPIRE ON EACH CALL.

\<PUSH SPACE BAR FOR MORE\>

George pushed the space bar. The screen was again filled.

ALEX REQUIRES PRECISE INFORMATION. WHATEVER
YOU ARE TOLD BY THE PEOPLE YOU CALL MUST BE
RELAYED AS IT IS OCCURS, TO THE LETTER.

AT THE END OF EACH DAY, YOU ARE TO UPLOAD YOUR
FILE, CALLED SG.TOD. YOUR COMPUTER WILL AUTOMAT-
ICALLY PUT A DATE AND TIME STAMP ON IT.

THEN ERASE THE SG.DAT FILE FROM THAT DAY. IF YOU
ARE UNABLE TO REACH ANYONE ON THE LISTS, JUST IN-
DICATE THAT IN YOUR DAILY REPORTS. DO NOT, REPEAT,
DO NOT TRY TO CALL THE SAME PERSON THE NEXT
DAY. IS THAT CLEAR?

The screen was awaiting a response. George typed in "Y".

GOOD. THIS IS QUITE SIMPLE, IS IT NOT?

Y

DO YOU THINK YOU CAN HANDLE THE JOB?

Y

WHAT KIND OF PRINTER DO YOU HAVE?

None

ARE YOU SURE?

Y

WILL YOU BUY ONE?

N

GOOD. ARE YOU INTERESTED IN MONEY?

Finally, thought Sir George, the reason for my existence.

Y

AN ACCOUNT HAS BEEN OPENED IN YOUR NAME AT THE
BANK OF AMERICA, REDMOND BRANCH 3 BLOCKS FROM
YOU. THERE IS $25,000 IN IT. EACH MONTH OF SUC-
CESSFUL WORK FOR ALEX WILL BE REWARDED WITH
ANOTHER PAYMENT. U.S. TAXES ARE YOUR RESPON-
SIBILITY. IS THAT A PROBLEM?

N

WILL YOU DISCUSS YOUR JOB OR ITS NATURE WITH
ANYONE? ANYONE AT ALL?

N

EVEN UNDER FORCE?

Force, what the hell does that mean? I guess the answer is No,
thought George.

N

I HOPE NOT, FOR YOUR SAKE. GOOD LUCK SIR GEORGE.
YOU START MONDAY.
<<<CONNECTION TERMINATED>>>

Sir George was a little confused, maybe a lot confused. He was
the proud owner of a remote control job, a cushy one as far as he could
tell, but the tone of the conversation he just had with the computer
was worrisome. Was he being threatened? What was the difference
between 'Services Terminated' and 'Terminated' anyway. Maybe he
shouldn't ask. Keep his mouth shut and do a good job.

Hey, he thought, dismissing the possible unpleasant consequences
of failure. This is San Francisco, and I have three days off in a new
city. Might as well find my way around the town tonight. According
to the guide books I should start at Pier 39.

* * * * *

Chapter 3

Tuesday, September 8,
New York City

But they told me they wouldn't tell! They promised." Hugh Sidneys pleaded into his side of the phone. "How did you find out?" At first Scott thought the cartoon voice was a joke perpetrated by one of his friends, or more probably, his ex-wife. Even she, though, coudn't possibly think a crank phone call was a twisted form of art. No, it had to be real.

"I'm sorry Mr. Sidneys. We can't give out our sources. That's confidential. But are you saying that you confirm the story? That it is true?"

"Yes, no. Well . . ." the pleading slid into near sobbing. "If this gets out, I'm ruined. Ruined. Everything, my family . . .how could you have found out? They promised!" The noise from the busy metro room at the New York City Times made it difficult to hear Sidneys.

"Can I quote you, sir? Are you confirming the story?" Scott pressed on for that last requisite piece of every journalistic puzzle . . .confirmation of a story that stood to wreck havoc in portions of the financial community. And Washington. It was a story with meat, but Scott Mason needed the confirmation to complete it.

"I don't know. . .If I tell what I know now, that maybe . . .that would mean I was being helpful . . .maybe I should get a lawyer . . ." The call from Scott Mason to First State Savings and Loan on Madison Avenue had been devastating. Hugh Sidneys was just doing what he was told to do. Following orders.

"Maybe, Hugh. Maybe." Scott softened toward Sidneys, thinking the first name approach might work. "But, is it true, Hugh? Is the story true?"

"It doesn't matter anymore. Do what you want." Hugh Sidneys hung up on Mason. It was as close to a confirmation as he needed. He wrote the story.

* * * * *

At 39, Scott Byron Mason was already into his second career. Despite the objections of his overbearing father, he had avoided the family destiny of becoming a longshoreman. "If it's good enough for me, it's good enough for my kids." Scott was an only child, but his father had wanted more despite his mother's inability to carry another baby to full term.

Scott caught the resentment of his father and the doting protection of his mother. Marie Elizabeth Mason wanted her son to have more of a future than live another generation in the lower middle class doldrums of Sheepshead Bay, Brooklyn. Not that Scott was aware of his predicament; he was a dreamer.

Her son showed aptitude. By the age of six Scott knew two words his father never learned - how and why. His childhood curiosity led to more than a few mishaps and spankings by the hot tempered Horace Mason. Scott took apart everything in the house in an attempt to see what made it tick. Sometimes, not often enough, Scott could reassemble what he had broken down to its smallest components. Despite his failings and bruised bottom Scott wasn't satisfied with, "that's just the way it is," as an answer to anything.

Behind his father's back, Marie had Scott take tests and be accepted to the elite Bronx High School of Science, an hour and a half train ride from Brooklyn. To Scott it wasn't yet an escape from Brooklyn, it was a chance to learn why and how machines worked.

Horace gave Marie and Scott a three day silent treatment until his mother finally put an end to it. "Horace Stipton Mason," Evelyn Mason said with maternal command. "Our son has a gift, and you will not, I repeat, you will not interfere with his happiness."

"Yes dear."

"The boy is thirteen and he has plenty of time to decide what he's going to do with himself. Is that clear?"

"Yes dear."

"Good." She would say as she finished setting the table. "Dinner is ready. Wash your hands boys." And the subject was closed.

But throughout his four years at the best damn high school in the country, Horace found ample opportunity to pressure Scott about how it was the right thing to follow in the family tradition, and work at the docks, like the three generations before him.

The issue was never settled during Scott's rebellious teen age years. The War, demonstrating on the White House lawn, getting gassed at George Washington, writing for the New York Free Press, Scott was even arrested once or twice or three times for peaceful civil disobedience. Scott Mason was seeing the world in a new way. He was rapidly growing up, as did much of the class of 1970.

Scott's grades weren't good enough for scholarships, but adequate to be accepted at several good universities.

"I already paid for his education," screamed Horace upon hearing that Scott chose NYU to keep costs down. He would live at home. "He broke every damn thing I ever bought, radios, TV's, washers. He can go to work like a man."

With his mother's blessing and understanding, Scott moved out of the house and in with three roommates who also attended City College, where all New Yorkers can get a free education. Scott played very hard, studied very little and let his left of center politics guide his social life. His engineering professors remarked that he was underutilizing his god-given talents and that he spent more time protesting and objecting that paying attention. It was an unpredictable piece of luck that Scott Mason would never have to make a living as an engineer. He would be ablt to remain the itinerate tinkerer; designing and building the most inane creations that regularly had little purpose beyond satisfying technical creativity.

"Can we go with it?" Scott asked City Editor Douglas McQuire and John Higgins, the City Times' staff attorney whose job it was to answer just such questions. McQuire and Mason had been asked to join Higgins and publisher Anne Manchester to review the paper's position on running Mason's story. Scott was being lawyered, the relatively impersonal cross examination by a so-called friendly in-house attorney. It was the single biggest pain in the ass of Scott's job, and since he had a knack for finding sensitive subjects, he was lawyered fairly frequently. Not that it made him feel any less like being called to the principal's office every time.

Scott's boyish enthusiasm for his work, and his youthful appearance allowed some to underestimate Scott's ability. He looked much younger than his years, measuring a slender 6 feet and just shy of 160 pounds. His longish thin sandy hair and a timeless all about Beach Boy face made him a good catch on his better days. Now that he was back in circulation again at almost 40. The round wire rimmed glasses he donned for an extreme case of myopia were visible stylized memories of his early rebel days, conveying a sophisticated air of radicalism. Basically clean cut, he preferred shaving every two or three, or occasionally four days. He blamed his poor shaving habits on his transparent and sensitive skin 'just like Dick Nixon's'.

The four sat in Higgins' comfortable dark paneled office furnished with black leather and brass sconce lamps. With 2 walls full of books and generous seating, the ample office resembled an elegant and subdued law library. Higgins chaired the meeting from behind his leather trimmed desk. Scott brought a tall stack of files and put them on the glass topped coffee table.

"We need to go over every bit, from the beginning. OK?" Higgins made it sound more like an order than responsible journalistic double checking. Higgins didn't interfere in the news end of the business; he kept his opinions to himself. But it was his responsibility to insure that the City Times' was kept out of the receiving end of any litigation. That meant that as long as a story was properly researched, sourced, and confirmed, the contents were immaterial to him. That was the Publisher's choice, not his.

Mason had come to trust Higgins in his role as aggravating mediator between news and business. Scott might not like what he had to say, but he respected his opinion and didn't argue too much. Higgins was never purposefully adversarial. He merely wanted to know that both the writers and the newspaper had all their ducks in a row. Just in case. Libel suits can be such a pain, and expensive.

"Why don't you tell me, again, about how you found out about the McMillan scams." Higgins turned on a small micro-cassette recorder. "I hope you don't mind," he said as he tested it. "Keeps better notes than I do," he offhandedly said. Nobody objected. There would have been no point in objecting even if anyone cared. It was an unspoken truism that Higgins and other good attorneys taped many of their unofficial depositions to protect themselves in case anything went terribly wrong. With a newspaper as your sole client, the First Amendment was always at stake.

"OK," Scott began. His reporter's notebook sat atop files full of computer printouts. "A few days ago, on September 4, that's a Friday, I got an anonymous call. The guy said, 'You want some dirt on McMillan and First State S&L?' I said sure, what do you have and who is this?

"So then you knew who Francis McMillan was?" Higgins looked up surprised.

"Of course," Mason said. "He's the squeaky clean bank President from White Plains. Says he knows how to clean up the S&L mess, gets lots of air time. Probably making a play for Washington. Big time political ambitions. Pretty well connected at Treasury. I guess they listen to him."

"In a nutshell." Higgins agreed. "And . . .then?"

Mason sped through a couple of pages of scribbled notes from his pad. "My notes start here. 'Who I am don't matter but what I gotta say does. You interested'. Heavy Brooklyn accent, docks, Italian, who knows. I said something like, 'I'm listening' and he says that McMillan is the dirtiest of them all. He's been socking more money away than the rest and he's been doing it real smart. So I go, 'so?' and he says he can prove it and I say 'how' and he says 'read your morning mail'." Mason stopped abruptly.

"That's it?" Higgins asked.

"He hung up. So I forgot about it till the next morning."

"And that's when you got these?" Higgins said pointing at the stack of computer printouts in front of Mason. "How were they delivered?"

"By messenger. No receipt, nothing. Just my name and the paper's." Mason showed Higgins the envelope in which the files came.

"Then you read them?"

"Well not all of them, but enough." Scott glanced at his editor. "That's when I let Doug know what I had."

"And what did he say?" Higgins was keeping furious notes to back up the tape recording.

"'Holy shit', as I remember." Everyone laughed. Ice breakers, good for the soul, thought Mason. People are too uptight. Higgins indicated that Scott should continue.

"Then he said 'we gotta go slow on this one,' then he whistled and Holy Shat some more." Once the giggles died down, Mason got serious. "I borrowed a bean counter from the basement, told him I'd put his name in the paper if anything came of it, and I picked his brain. Ran through the numbers on the printouts, and ran through them again. I really worked that poor guy, but that's the price of fame. By the next morning we knew that there were two sets of books on First State." Mason turned a couple pages in his files.

"It appears," Scott said remembering that he was selling the importance of the story to legal and the publisher, "that a substantial portion of the bank's assets are located in numbered bank accounts all over the world." Scott said with finality.

Higgins interrupted here. "So what's wrong with that?" he challenged.

"They've effectively stolen a sandbagged and inflated reserve account with over $750 Million it. Almost 10% of stated assets. It appears from these papers," Scott waved his hand over them, "that the total of the reserve accounts will be taken, as a loss, in their next SEC reporting." Mason stopped and looked at Higgins as though Higgins would understand everything.

Higgins snorted as he made more notes.

"That next morning," Mason politely ignored Higgins. "I got a call again, from what sounded like the same guy."

"Why do you say that? How did you know?" Higgins inquired to Mason's dismay.

Mason sighed. "Cause he said, 'it's me remember?' and spoke like Archie Bunker. Good enough for you?" Mason grinned wide. Mason had the accent down to a tee. Higgins gave in to another round of snickers.

"He said, 'you like, eh?'" Mason spoke with an exaggerated New York accent and used the appropriate Italian hand gesture for 'eh!'. "I said, 'I like, but so what?'. I still wasn't sure what he wanted. He said, 'they never took a loss, yet. Look for Friday. This Friday.

They're gonna lose a bunch.' I said, 'how much' and he said, 'youse already know'." Mason's imitation of a Brooklyn accent was good enough for a laugh.

"He then said, 'enjoy the next installment', and that was the last time I spoke to him. At any rate, the next package contained a history of financial transactions, primarily overseas; Luxembourg, Lietchenstein, Switzerland, Austria, Hong Kong, Sidney, Macao, Caymans and such. They show a history of bad loans and write downs on First State revenues.

"Well, I grabbed the Beanie from the Basement and said, help me with these now, and I got research to come up with the 10K's on First State since 1980 when McMillan took over. And the results were incredible." Mason held out a couple of charts and some graphs.

"We compared both sets of books. The bottom lines on both are the same. First State has been doing very well. McMillan has grown the company from $1 Billion to $12 Billion in 8 years. Quite a job, and the envy of hundreds of every other S&L knee deep in their own shit." Higgins cringed. He thought Ms. Manchester should be shielded from such language. "The problem is that, according to one set of books, First State is losing money on some investments merely by wishing them away. They disappear altogether from one report to the next. Not a lot of money, but a few million here and there."

"What have you got then?" Higgins pressed.

"Nobody notices 'cause the losses are all within the limits of the loss projections and reserve accounts. Sweet and neat! Million dollar embezzlement scam with the SEC's approval."

"How much follow up did you do?" Higgins asked as his pen flew across the legal pad.

"Due to superior reporting ability," Scott puffed up his chest in jest, "I found that a good many account numbers listed in the package I received are non-existent. But, with a little prodding, I did get someone to admit that one of them was recently closed and the funds moved elsewhere.

"Then, this is the clincher, as the caller promised, today, I looked for the First State SEC reports, and damned if the numbers didn't jive. The books with the overseas accounts are the ones with the real losses and where they occur. The 'real' books don't."

"The bottom line, please."

"Someone has been embezzling from First State, and when they're through it'll be $3 Billion worth." Scott was proud of himself. In only a few days he had penetrated a huge scam in the works.

"You can't prove it!" Higgins declared. "Where's the proof? All you have is some unsolicited papers where someone has been playing a very unusual and admittedly questionable game of 'what if'. You have a voice on the end of a phone with no name, no nothing, and a so-called confirmation from some mid level accountant at the bank who dribbles on about 'having to do it' but never saying what 'it' is. So what does that prove?"

"It proves that McMillan is a fraud, a rip-off," Scott retorted confidently.

"It does not!"

"But I have the papers to prove it," Scott shuffled through the folders.

"Let me explain something, Scott." Higgins put down his pen and adapted a friendlier tone. "There's a little legal issue called right to privacy. Let me ask you this. If I came to you and said that Doug here was a crook, what would you do?"

"Ask you to prove it," Scott said.

"Exactly. It's the same here."

"But I have the papers to prove it, it's in black and white."

"No Scott, you don't. What you have is some papers with accusations. They're unsubstantiated. They could have easily been phonied. You know what computers can do better than I do. Now here's the key point. Everybody in this country is due privacy. You don't know where these came from, or how they were obtained, do you?"

"No," Scott hesitantly admitted.

"So, someone's privacy has been compromised, in this case McMillan's. If, and I'm saying, if, these reports are accurate, I would take the position that they are stolen, obtained illegally. If we print what we have now, the paper could be on the receiving end of a slander and libel suit that could put us out of business. We even could be named as a co-conspirator in a criminal suit. I can't let that happen. It's our obligation to guarantee responsible journalism."

"I see." Scott didn't agree.

"Scott, you're good, real good, but you have to see it from the paper's perspective." Higgins' tone was now conciliatory. "This is hard stuff, and there's just not enough here, not to go with it yet. Maybe in a few days when you can get a little more to tie it up. Not now. I'm sorry."

Case closed.

Shit, shit shit, thought Scott. Back to square one.

Hugh Sidneys was nondescript, not quite a nebbish, but close. At five foot five with wisps of brown scattered over his balding pate, he only lacked horn rimmed glasses to complete the image. His bargain basement suits almost fit him, and he scurried rather than walked down the hallways at First State Savings and Loan where he had been employed since graduating from SUNY with a degree in accounting 24 years ago.

His large ears accentuated the oddish look, not entirely out of place on the subways at New York rush hour. His loyalty to First State was known throughout the financial departments; he was almost a fixture. His accounting skills were extremely strong, even remarkable if you will, but his personality and appearance, and that preposterous cartoon voice, held him back from advancing up the official corporate ladder.

Now, however, Hugh Sidneys was scared.

He needed to do something . . .and having never been in this kind of predicament before . . .he thought about the lawyer . . .hiring one like he told that reporter . . .but could he afford that . . .and he wasn't sure what to do . . .was he in trouble? Yes, he was . . .he knew that. That reporter . . .he sounded like he understood . . .maybe he could help . . .he was just asking questions . . .what was his name . . .?

"Ah, Mr. Mason?" Scott heard the timid man's Road Runner voice speak gently over the phone. Scott had just returned to his desk from Higgins' office. It was after 6PM and time to catch a train back home to Westchester.

"This is Scott Mason."

"Do you remember me?"

Scott recognized the voice immediately but said nothing.

"We spoke earlier about First State, and I just . . .ah . . .wanted to . . .ah . . .apologize . . .for the way I acted."

Scott's confirmation. Hugh Sidneys, the Pee Wee Herman sounding beancounter from First State. What did he want?

"Yes, of course, Mr. Sidneys. How can I help you?" He opened his notebook. He had just had his story nixed and he was ready to go home. But Sidneys . . .maybe . . .

"It's just that, well, I'm nervous about this . . ."

"No need to apologize, Hugh." Scott smiled into the phone to convey sincerity. "I understand, it happens all the time. What can I do for you tonight?"

"Well, I, ah, thought that we might, maybe you could, well I don't know about help, help, it's so much and I didn't really know, no I shouldn't have called . . .I'm sorry . . ." The pitch of Sidneys' voice rose as rambled on.

"Wait! Don't hang up. Mr. Sidneys. Mr. Sidneys?"

"Yes," the whisper came over the earpiece.

"Is there something wrong . . .are you all right?" The fear, the sound of fear that every good reporter is attuned to came over loud and clear. This man was terrified.

"Yes, I'm OK, so far."

"Good. Now, tell me, what's wrong. Slowly and calmly." He eased Sidneys off his panic perch.

Scott heard Sidneys compose himself and gather up the nerve to speak.

"Isn't there some sorta rule," he stuttered, "a law, that says if I talk to you, you're a reporter, and if I say that I don't want you to tell anybody, then you can't?" Sidneys was scared, but wanted to talk to someone. Maybe this was the time for Scott to back off a little.

"That's called off the record, Hugh. And it's not a law." Scott was amused at the naivete that Hugh Sidneys showed. "It's a gentleman's agreement, a code of ethics in journalism. You can be off the record, on the record, or for background, not for attribution, for confirmation, there's a whole bunch of 'em." Scott realized that Hugh knew nothing about the press so he explained the options slowly. "Which one would you like?" Scott wanted it to seem that Sidneys was in control and making the rules.

"How about we just talk, and you tell me what I should do . . .what you think . . .and . . .I don't want anything in the paper. You have one for that?" Hugh was feeling easier on the phone with Scott.

"Sure do. We'll just call it off the record for now. Everything you tell me, I promise not to use it without your permission. Will that do?" Scott smiled broadly. If you speak loudly with a big smile on your face, people on the other end of the phone think you're honest and that you mean what you say. That's how game show hosts do it.

"OK." Scott heard Sidneys inhale deeply. "Those papers you say you have? Remember?"

"Sure do. Got them right here." Scott patted them on his cluttered desk.

"Well, you can't have them. Or you shouldn't have them. I mean it's impossible." Hugh was getting nervous again. His voice cracked.

"Hugh, I do have them, and you all but confirmed that for me yesterday. A weak confirmation, but I think you know more than you let on . . ."

"Mr. Mason . . ."

"Please, call me Scott!"

"OK . . .Scott. What I'm trying to say is that what you say you have, you can't have cause it never existed."

"What do you mean never existed?" Scott was confused, terribly confused all of sudden. He raised his voice. "Listen, I have reams of paper here that say someone at First State is a big crook. Then you say, 'sure it's real' and now you don't. What's your game, Mister?" Playing good-cop bad-cop alone was difficult, but a little pressure may bring this guy down to reality.

"Obviously you have them, that's not the point." Sidneys reacted submissively to Scott's ersatz domineering personality. "The only place that those figures ever existed was in my mind and in my computer. I never made a printout. They were never put on paper." Hugh said resolutely.

Scott's mind whirred. Something is wrong with this picture. He has papers that were never printed, or so says a guy whose stability is currently in question. The contents would have far reaching effects on the S&L issue. A highly visible tip of the iceberg. McMillan, involved in that kind of thing? Never, not Mr. Clean. What was Sidneys getting at?

"Mr. Sidneys . . .Hugh . . .do you have time to have a cup of coffee somewhere. It might be easier if we sat face to face. Get to know each other."

Rosie's Diner was one of the better Greasy Spoons near the Hudson River docks on Manhattan's West Side. The silver interior and exterior was not a cliche when this diner was built. Rosie, all 280 pounds of her, kept the UPS truckers coming back for over 30 years. A lot of the staff at the paper ate here, too. For the best tasting cholesterol in New York, saturated fats, bacon and sausage grease flavored starches, Rosie's was the place. Once a month at Rosie's would guarantee a reading of over 300.

Scott recognized Hugh from a distance. No one dressed like that comes in here. Had to be an accountant. Hugh hugged his briefcase while nervously looking around the diner. Scott called the short pale man over to the faded white formica and dull chrome booth. Hugh ordered a glass of water, while Scott orderd enough to make a light dinner of their meeting.

"So, Hugh, please continue with what you were telling me on the phone." Scott tried to sound empathetic.

"It's like I said, I don't know how you got them or they found out. It's impossible." The Pee Wee Herman voice was uncannily accurate in person.

"Who found out? Does someone else know . . .?"

"OK," Hugh sighed. "I work for First State, right? I work right with McMillan although nobody except a few people know it. They think I do market analysis and research. What I'm really doing is helping shelter money in offshore investment accounts. There are some tax benefits, I'm not a tax accountant so I don't know the reasons, but I manage the offshore investments."

"Did you think that was illegal?"

"Only a little. Until recently that is."

"Sorry, continue." Scott nibbled from the sandwich on his plate.

"Well there was only 1 set of books to track the offshore invest-ments. They wanted them to be kept secret for various reasons. McMillan and the others made the deals, not me. I just moved the money for them." Again Hugh was feeling paranoid.

"Hugh, you moved some money around illegally, maybe. So what? What's the big deal?" Scott gulped some hot black coffee to chase the pastrami that almost went down the wrong pipe.

Sidneys continued after sipping his water and wetting his lips. "Four days ago I got this call, from some Englishman who I'd never spoken to before. He said he has all the same figures and facts you said you have. He starts reading enough to me and I know he's got what he says he got. Then he says he wants me to cooperate or he'll go public with everything and blow it right out of the water." Hugh was perspiring with tension. His fists were clenched and knuckles white.

"And then, I called you and you came unglued. Right?" Scott was trying to emotionally console Hugh, at least enough to get something more. "Do you think you were being blackmailed? Did he, the English guy, demand anything? Money? Bribes? Sex?" Scott grinned. Hugh obviously did not appreciate the attempt at levity.

"No, nothing. He just said that I would hear from him shortly. That was it. Then, nothing, until you called. Then I figured I missed his call." Hugh was working himself into another nervous frenzy.

"Did he threaten you?"

"No. Not directly. Just said that it would be in my best interest to cooperate."

"What did you say?"

"What could I say? I mumbled something about doing nothing wrong but he said that didn't matter and I would be blamed for everything and that he could prove it."

"Could he prove it?" Hugh was scribbling furiously in his notebook.

"If he had the files in my computer I guess I would look pretty guilty, of something, but there's no way anyone could get in there. I'm the only one, other than McMillan who can get at that stuff. It's always been a big secret. We don't even make any printouts of it. It's never on paper, just in the computer." Hugh fell back in the thinly stuffed torn red Naugahyde bench seat and gulped from his water glass.

Scott shook his head as he scanned the notes he had been making. This didn't make any sense at all. Here was this little nerdy man, with a convoluted tale of embezzlement and blackmail, off shore money . . .and he was scared. "Hugh," Scott began slowly. "Let me see if I've got this right. You were part of a scheme to shift investments overseas, falsify reports, yet the investments always made a reasonable return in investment." Hugh nodded in agreement silently.

"Then, after how many, 8 years of this, creating a secret little world that only you and McMillan know about . . ."

"A few others knew, I have the names, but only McMillan could get the information from the computer. No one else could. I set it up that way on purpose." Hugh interrupted.

"OK, then you receive a call from some Englishman who says he's got the numbers you say are so safe and then I get a copy. And the numbers agree with the results that First State reported. Is that about it?" Scott asked, almost mocking the apparent absurdity.

"Yeah, that's it. That's what happened." Hugh Sidneys was such a meek man.

"That leaves me with a couple of possible conclusions. One, you got yourself in over your head, finally decided to cut your losses and make up this incredible story. Maybe make a deal with the cops or the Feds and try to be hero. Maybe you're the embezzler and want out before it's too late. Born again beancounter. It's a real possibility." Hugh's face grimaced; no, that's not what happened, it's just as I told you.

"Or, two, McMillan is behind the disclosures and effectively sabotaging his own plans. For what reasons I could hardly venture a guess now. But, if what you are saying is true, it's either you or McMillan." Scott liked the analysis. It was sound and took into account all available information, omitting any speculation.

"Then why would someone want to threaten me?"

"Either you never got the call," the implication was obvious, "or McMillan is trying, quite effectively to spook you." Scott put a few dollars on the table next to the check.

"That's it? You won't say anything, will you? You promised!" Hugh leaned into Scott, very close.

Scott consoled Hugh with a pat on his wrinkled suit sleeve. "Not without speaking to you first. No, that wouldn't be cricket. Don't worry, I'll call you in a couple of days."

His editor, Doug McGuire agreed that Scott should keep on it. There might be a story there, somewhere. Go find it. But don't forget about the viruses.

* * * * *

The headline of the National Exposé, a weekly tabloid caught Scott's attention on his way home that evening in Grand Central Station.

EXCLUSIVE!
S&L RIP OFF EXPOSED!

Scott's entire story, the one he wasn't permitted to print was being read by millions of mid-American supermarket shopping housewives. In its typically sensationalistic manner, the article claimed that the Expose was in exclusive possession of documents that proved Mc-Millan was stealing 10's of millions from First State S&L. It even printed a fuzzy picture of the same papers that Scott had received.

How the hell?

* * * * *

Chapter 4

Thursday, September 10
Houston, Texas.

Angela Steinem dialed extension 4343, Network Administration for MIS at the Treadline Oil Company in Houston, Texas. It rang three times before Joan Appleby answered. Joan was the daytime network administrator for Building 4. Hundreds of IBM personal computers were connected together so they could share information over a Novell local area network.

"Joan, I don't bug you much, right?" Angela said hesitantly.

"Angela, how about a good morning, girl?" They were good friends outside of work but had very little business contact.

"Sorry, mornin'. Joan, I gotta problem."

"What's troubling ya hon." Joan spoke with a distinct Texas twang.

"A little bird just ate my computer."

"Well, then I guess I'd be lookin' out for Big Bird's data dump." Joan laughed in appreciation of the comedy.

"No really. A little bird flew all over my computer and ate up all the letters and words on the screen. Seriously."

"Y'all are putting me on, right?" Angela's voice lilted.

"No. No, I'm serious. It was like a simple video game, Pac-Man or something, ate up the screen. I couldn't get it to come back so I turned my computer off and now it won't do anything. All it says is COMMAND.COM cannot be found. Now, what the hell does that mean?"

Joan Appleby now took Angela seriously. "It may mean that we have some mighty sick computers. I'll be right there."

By the end of the workday, the Treadline Oil Company was essentially at a standstill. Over 4,000 of their internal microcomputers, mainly IBM and Compaq's were out of commission. The virus had successfully struck.

Angela Steinem and her technicians shut down the more than 50 local area networks and gateways that connected the various business units. They contacted the National Computer Virus Association in San Mateo, California, NIST's National Computer Center Laboratories and a dozen or so other watchdog groups who monitor computer viruses.

This was a new virus. No one had seen it before. Sorry, they said. If you can send us your hard disk, we may be able find out what's going on . . .otherwise, your best bet is to dismantle the entire computer system, all 4,000 plus of them, and start from scratch.

Angela informed the Vice President of Information Systems that it would be at least a week, maybe ten days before Treadline would be fully operational again.

Mary Barnsider, secretary to Larry Gompers, Junior democratic representative from South Carolina was stymied.

Every morning between 7:30 and 8:00 AM she opened her boss's office and made coffee. Most mornings she brought in Dunkin' Donuts. It was the only way she knew to insure that her weight would never ebb below 200 pounds. Her pleasant silken skin did not match the plumpness below. At 28 she should have known that meeting Washington's best and brightest required a more slender physique.

This morning she jovially sat down at her Apple Macintosh computer with 3 creme filled donuts and a mug of black coffee with 4 sugars. She turned on the power switch and waited as the hourglass icon indicated that the computer was booting. It was going through its self diagnostics as it did every time power was applied.

Normally, after a few seconds, the Mac would come alive and the screen would display a wide range of options from which she could select. Mary would watch the procedure carefully each time - she was an efficient secretary.

This time, however, the screen displayed a new message, one she had not seen in the 9 months she had worked as Congressman Gompers' front line.

RAM OPTIMIZER TEST PROCEDURE....

INITIALIZING...

THIS PROGRAM IS DESIGNED TO TAKE MAXIMUM ADVANTAGE OF SYSTEM STORAGE CAPABILITIES. THE TEST WILL ONLY TAKE A FEW SECONDS...

WAITING....

WARNING: DO NOT TURN OFF COMPUTER DURING SELF TEST!

As she was trained, she heeded her computer's instructions. She watched and waited as the computer's hard disk whirred and buzzed. She wasn't familiar with the message, but it sounded quite official, and after all, the computer is always right.

And she waited. Some few seconds, she thought, as she dove into her second donut. And she waited through the third donut and another mug of too sweet coffee.

She waited nearly a half an hour, trying to oblige the instructions from the technocratic box on her desk. The Mac continued to work, so she thought, but the screen didn't budge from it's warning message.

What the hell, this has taken long enough. What harm can it cause if . . .

She turned the power switch off and then back on. Nothing.

The computer did absolutely nothing. The power light was on, the disk light was on, but the screen was as blank as a dead television set.

Mary Coldtree called Violet Beecham, a co worker in another office down the hall.

"'Morning Vi. Mary."

Violet sounded agitated. "Yeah, Mare, what is it?"

"I'm being a dumb bunny and need a hand with my computer. Got a sec?" Mary's sweetness oozed over the phone.

"You, too? You're having trouble? My computer's as dead as a doornail. Won't do nothing. I mean nothing." Violet was clearly frustrated and her concern was evident to Mary.

"Dead? Vi, mine is dead too. What happened to yours?"

"Damned if I know. It was doing some self check or something, seemed to take forever and then . . .nothing. What about yours?"

"Same thing. Have you called MIS yet?"

"Not yet, but I'm getting ready to. I never did trust these things. Give me a typewriter any day."

"Sure Vi. I'll call you right back."

Mary looked up the number for MIS Services, the technical magicians in the basement who keep the 3100 Congressional computers alive.

"Dave here, can I help you?" The voice spoke quickly and indifferently.

"Mary Barnsider, in Gompers office. My computer seems to be having a little problem . . ." Mary tried to treat the problem lightly.

"You and half of Congress. Listen . . .is it Mary? This morning is going to be a slow one. My best guess is that over 2500 computers died a quick death. And you know what that means."

"No, I don't . . ." Mary said hesitantly.

"It means a Big Mac Attack."

"A what?"

"Big Mac, it's a computer virus. We thought that Virus-Stop software would stop it, but I guess there's a new strain out there. Congress is going to be ordering a lot of typewriters and legal pads for a while."

"You mean you can't fix it? This virus?"

"Listen, it's like getting the flu. Once you got it, you got it. You can't pretend you aren't sick. Somebody took a good shot at Congress and well . . .they won. We're gonna be down for a while. Couple of weeks at least. Look, good luck, but I gotta go." Dave hung up.

Mary ate the other three donuts intended for her boss as she sat idle at her desk wondering if she would have a job now that there were no more computers on Capitol Hill.

* * * * *

CONGRESS CATCHES FLU - LOSES FAT IN PROCESS

Scott Mason, New York City Times

The Congressional Budget Office announced late yesterday that it was requesting over $1 Million in emergency funding to counter a devastating failure of Congress's computers.

Most of the computers used by both Senators and Representatives are Apple Macintosh, but Apple Computer issued a quick statement denying any connection between the massive failures and any production problems in their machines.

The CBO said that until the problems were corrected, estimates to take up to four weeks, that certain normal Congressional activities would be halted or severely curtailed. Electronic mail, E- Mail that has saved taxpayers millions, will be unavailable for communications until October at a minimum. Inter-office communications, those that address legislative issues, proposed bills, and amendments have been destroyed and will require ". . .weeks and weeks and weeks of data entry just to get back where we started. This is a disaster."

The culprit is, of course, a computer virus. The question on everyone's mind is, was this virus directed at Congress, or were they merely an anonymous and unfortunate victim?

I have an IBM PC clone at home. Technically it's an AT with a hard disk, so I'm not sure if that's an XT, and AXT, an XAT, an ATX or . . .well whatever. I use it to write a lot of my stories and then I can send the story to the computer at work for an overdiligent editor to make it fit within my allotted space.

It never occurred to me that a computer could get sick.

I am, as we all are, used to our 'TV going on the Fritz', or 'Blowing a Fuse'. It seems like a lot of things blow: a gasket blows, a light bulb blows, a tire blows or blows out, the wind blows. I am sure that the Thomas W. Crapper, the 19th century inventor of the flush toilet would not be pleased that in 1988 man has toasters and other cooking devices that 'crap out'. The Phone Company 'screws up', the stock market 'goes to hell in a handbasket' and VCR's 'work for s__t'.

It never occurred to me that a computer could get sick.

Computers are supposed to 'crash'. That means that either Aunt Tillie can't find the ON switch or her cat knocked it on the floor. Computers have 'fatal errors' which obviously means that they died and deserve a proper burial.

It never occurred to me that a computer could get sick.

In the last few weeks there have been a lot of stories about computers across the country getting ill. Sick, having the flu, breathing difficulty, getting rashes, itching, scratching themselves . . .otherwise having a miserable time.

Let's look at the medical analogy to the dreaded computer virus that indiscriminately attacks and destroys any computer with which it comes in contact.

Somewhere in the depths of the countryside of the People's Republic of China, a naturally mutated submicroscopic microbe has the nerve to be aerodynamically transferred to the smoggy air of Taiwan. Upon landing in Taipei, the microbe attaches itself to an impoverished octogenarian who lives in an overpopulated 1 room apartment above a fish store.

The microbe works its way into this guy's blood stream, unbeknownst to him, and in a few days, he's sicker than a dog. But this microbe is smart, real smart. It has heard of antibiotics, and in the spirit of true Darwinism, it replicates itself before being killed off with a strengthened immunity. So, the microbe copies itself and when Kimmy Chen shakes hands with his customers, some of them are lucky enough to receive an exact duplicate, clone if you will, of his microbe.

Then they too, get ill.

The microbe thus propagates its species until the entire East Coast of the U.S. has billions and trillions of identical microbes costing our fragile economy untold millions of dollars in sick pay.

However, the microbe is only so smart. After a while, the microbe mutates itself into a benign chemical compound that no longer can copy itself and the influenza epidemic is over. Until next year when Asian Flu B shows up and the process begins all over again. (The same group of extremists who believe that the Tri-Lateral commission runs the world and Queen Elizabeth and Henry Kissinger are partners in the heroin trade think the AMA is behind all modern flu epidemics. No comment.)

The point of all of this diatribe is that computers can get sick too. With a virus.

Don't worry, mom. Your computer can't give you the flu anymore than a your pet wharthog can get feline leukemia.

It all started years ago, before Wozniak and Apple and the PC.

Before personal computers there were mainframes; huge room sized computers to crunch on numbers. One day, years ago, Joe, (that's not a real name, it's changed to protect him) decided it would be great fun to play a prank on Bill, another programmer who worked at a big university. Joe wrote a little program that he put into Bill's big computer. Every time Bill typed the word 'ME' on his keyboard, the computer would take over. His video screen would fill up with the word 'YOU', repeating itself hundreds and thousands of times. Bill's computer would become useless.

That was called a practical joke to computer programmers. Joe and Bill both got a laugh out of it, and no harm was done. Then Bill decided to get back at Joe. He put a small program into Joe's big computer. Every day at precisely 3:00 P.M., a message appeared: 'Do Not Pass GO!'.

It was all good fun and became a personal challenge to Joe and Bill to see how they could annoy each other.

Word spread about the new game. Other graduate students at the university got involved and soon computer folks at Cal Tech, MIT, Carnegie Mellon, Stanford and elsewhere got onto the bandwagon. Thus was born the world's first computer disease, the virus.

This is Scott Mason. Using a typewriter.

✻ ✻ ✻ ✻ ✻

November, 3 Years Ago
Sunnyvale, California.

When Data Graphics Inc. went public in 1987, President and founder Pierre Troubleaux, a nationalized American born in Paris momentarily forgot that he had sold his soul to achieve his success. The company, to the financial community known as DGI, was on the road to being in as much favor as Lotus or Microsoft. Annual sales of $300 Million with a pre-tax bottom line of over $55 Million were cause celebre on Wall Street. The first public issues raised over $200 Million for less than 20% of the common stock. With a book value in excess of $1 Billion, preparation for a second offering began immediately after the first sold out in 2 hours.

The offering made Pierre Troubleaux, at 29, a rich man; a very rich man. He netted almost $20 Million in cash and another $100 Million in options over 5 years. No one objected. He had earned it. DGI was the pearl of the computer industry in a time of shake ups and shake outs. Raging profits, unbridled growth, phenomenal market penetration and superb management.

Perhaps the most unique feature of DGI, other than its President's deal with the devil, was that it was a one product company. DGI was somewhat like Microsoft in that they both got rich and famous on one product. While Microsoft branched out from DOS into other product areas, DGI elected to remain a one product company and merely make flavors of its products available for other companies which marketed them under their own names.

Their software product was dubbed dGraph, a marketing abbreviated term for data-Graphics. Simply put, dGraph let users, especially novices, run their computers with pictures and icons instead of complex commands that must be remembered and typed. dGraph theoretically made IBM computers as easy to use as a Macintosh. Or, the computer could be trained to follow instructions in plain English. It was a significant breakthrough for the industry.

DGraph was so easy to use, and so powerful in its abilities that it was virtually an instant success. Almost every computer manufacturer offered dGraph as part of its standard fare. Just as a computer needed DOS to function, it was viewed that you needed dGraph before you even loaded the first program. Operating without dGraph was considered archaic. "You don't have dGraph?" "How can you use your computer without dGraph?" "I couldn't live without d-Graph." "I'd be lost without dGraph."

The ubiquitous non-technical secretaries especially loved dGraph. DGraph was taught at schools such as Katherine Gibbs and Secre-Temps who insisted that all its girls were fluent in its advanced uses. You just can't run an office without it!

As much as anything in the computer industry is, dGraph was a standard. Pierre Troubleaux was unfortunately under the misimpression that the success for DGI was his and his alone and that he too was a standard . . .a fixture. The image the press and media experts portrayed to the public that he was the company's singular genius, with remarkable technical aptitude to see "beyond the problem to the solution . . .".

The official DGI biography of Pierre Troubleaux, upon close examination, reads like that of an inflated resume by a person applying for a position totally outside his field of expertise. Completely unsuited for the job. But the media hype had relegated that minor inconsistency to old news.

In reality Troubleaux was a musician. He was an accomplished pianist who also played another 20 instruments, very, very well. By the age of 10 he was considered something of a prodigy and his parents decided that they would move from Paris to New York, the United States, for proper schooling. Pierre's scholarships at Julliard made the decision even easier.

Over the years Pierre excelled in performances and was critically acclaimed as having a magnificent future where he could call the shots. Either as a performer and composer. But Pierre had other ideas. He was rapt in the study of the theory of music. How notes related to each other. How scales related to each other. What made certain atonalities subjectively pleasing yet others completely offensive. He explored the relationships between Eastern polyphonic scales and the Western 12 note scale. Discord, harmony, melody, emotional responses; these were the true loves of Pierre Troubleaux.

Upon graduation from Julliard he announced, that contrary to his family's belief and desire, he would not seek advanced training. Rather, he would continue his study of musical relationships which by now had become an obsession. There was little expertise in this specific area, so he pursued it alone. He wrote and arranged music only to provide himself with enough funds to exist in his pallid Soho loft in downtown Manhattan.

He believed that there was an inherent underlying Natural Law that guided music and musical appreciation. If he could find that Law, he would have the formula for making perfect music every time. With the Law at the crux of all music, and with control of the Law, he ruminated, one could write a musical piece to suit the specific goals of the writer and create the desired effect on the listener. By formula.

In 1980 Pierre struggled to organize the unwieldy amount of data he had accumulated. His collections of interpretive musical analysis filled file cabinets and countless shelves. He relied on his memory to find anything in the reams of paper, and the situation was getting out of control. He needed a solution.

Max Jones was a casual acquaintance that Pierre had met at the Lone Star Cafe on the corner of 13th and 5th Avenue. The Lone Star was a New York fixture, capped with a 60 foot iguana on the roof. They both enjoyed the live country acts that played there. Max played the roll of an Urban Cowboy who had temporarily given up Acid Rock in favor of shit kickin' Southern Rock. Pierre found the musical phenomenon of Country Crossover Music intriguing, so he rationalized that drinking and partying at the Lone Star was a worthwhile endeavor which contributed to his work. That may have been partially true.

puter junkie, rock'n'roll aficionado and recreational drug user, Max maintained the integrity of large and small computer systems to pay the bills.

"That means they pretend to pay me and I pretend to work. I don't really do anything productive."

Max was an "ex-hippie who put on shoes to make a living" and a social anarchist at heart. At 27, Max had the rugged look that John Travolta popularized in the 70's but on a rock solid trim six foot five 240 pound frame. He dwarfed Pierre's mere five feet ten inches.

Pierre's classic European good looks and tailored appearance, even in jeans and a T-shirt were a strong contrast to Max's ruddiness. Pierre's jet black hair was side parted and covered most of his ears as it gracefully tickled his shoulders.

Piercing black eyes stared over a prominent Roman nose and thin cheeks which tapered in an almost feminine chin. There was never any confusion, though; no one in their right mind would ever view Pierre as anything but a confirmed and practiced heterosexual. His years of romantic achievements proved it. The remnants of his French rearing created an unidentifiable formal and educated accent; one which held incredible sex appeal to American women.

Max and Pierre sipped at their beers while Max rambled on about how wonderful computers were. They were going to change the world.

"In a few years every one on the planet will have his own computer and it will be connected to everyone else's computer. All information will be free and the planet will be a better place to live and . . .so on . . ." Max's technical sermons bordered on religious preaching. He had bought into the beliefs of Steven Jobs, the young charismatic founder and spiritual guiding force behind Apple Computer.

Pierre had heard it before, especially after Max had had a few. His view of a future world with everyone sitting in front of a picture tube playing with numbers and more numbers . . .and then a thought hit him.

"Max . . .Max . . ." Pierre was trying to break into another one of Max's Apple pitches.

"Yeah . . .oh yeah, sorry Amigo. What's that you say?" Max sipped deeply on a long neck Long Star beer.

"These computers you play with . . ."

"Not play, work with. Work with!" He pointed emphatically at nothing in particular.

"O.K., work with. Can these computers play, er, work with music?"

Max looked quizzically at Pierre. "Music, sure. You just program it in and out it comes. In fact, the Apple II is the ideal computer to play music. You can add a synthesizer chip and . . ."

"What if I don't know anything about computers?"

"Well, that makes it a little harder, but why doncha let me show you what I mean." Max smiled wide. This was what he loved, playing with computers and talking to people about them. The subject was still a large mystery to the majority of people in 1980.

Pierre winced. He realized that if he took up Max on his offer he would be subjected to endless hours of computer war stories and technical esoterica he couldn't care less about. That may be the price though, he thought. I can always stop.

Over the following months they became fast friends as Pierre tutored under Max's guiding hand. Pierre found that the Apple had the ability to handle large amounts of data. With the new program called Visi-Calc, he made large charts of his music and their numbers and examined their relationships.

As Pierre learned more about applying computers to his studies in musical theory, his questions of Max and demands of the Apple became increasingly complex. One night after several beers and a couple of joints Pierre asked Max what he thought was a simple question.

"How can we program the Apple so that it knows what each piece of data means?" he inquired innocently.

"You can't do that, man." Max snorted. "Computers, yes even Apples are stupid. They're just a tool. A shovel doesn't know what kind of dirt it's digging, just that it's digging." He laughed out loud at the thought of a smart shovel.

Pierre found the analogy worth a prolonged fit of giggles through which he managed to ask, "But what if you told the computer what it meant and it learned from there. On its own. Can't a computer learn?"

Max was seriously stoned. "Sure I guess so. Sure. In theory it could learn to do your job or mine. I remember a story I read by John Garth. It was called Giles Goat Boy. Yeah, Giles Goat Boy, what a title. Essentially it's about this Goat, musta been a real smart goat cause he talked and thunk and acted like a kid." They both roared at the double entendre of kid. That was worth another joint.

"At any rate," Max tried to control his spasmodic chuckles. "At any rate, there were these two computers who competed for control of the world and this kid, I mean," laughing too hard to breath, "I mean this goat named Giles went on search of these computers to tell them they weren't doing a very good job."

"So, what has that got to do with an Apple learning," Pierre said wiping the tears from his eyes.

"Not a damn thing!" They entered another spasm of laughter. "No really. Most people either think, or like to think that a computer can think. But they can't, at least not like you and me. " Max had calmed down.

"So?" Pierre thought there might still be a point to this conversation.

"So, in theory, yeah, but probably not for a while. 10 years or so."

"In theory, what?" Pierre asked. He was lost.

"In theory a machine could think."

"Oh." Pierre was disappointed.

"But, you might be able to emulate thinking. H'mmmm." Max retreated into mental oblivion as Abbey Road played in the background. Anything from Apple records was required listening by Max.

"Emulate. Emulate? What's that? Hey, Max. What's emulate.? Hey Max, c'mon back to Earth. Emulate what?"

Max jolted back to reality. "Oh, copy. You know, act like. Emulate. Don't they teach you emulation during sex education in France?" They both thought that that was the funniest thing ever said, in any language for all of written and pre-history.

The substance of the evening's conversation went downhill from there.

A few days later Max came by Pierre's loft. "I been thinking."

"Scary thought. About what?" Pierre didn't look up from his Apple.

"About emulating thought. You know what we were talking about the other night."

"I can't remember this morning much less getting shit faced with you the other night."

"You were going on and on about machines' thinking. Remember?"

"Yes," Pierre lied.

"Well, I've been thinking about it." Max had a remarkable ability to recover from an evening of illicit recreation. He could actually grasp the germ of a stoned idea and let a straight mind deal with it the following day. "And, I maybe got a way to do what you want."

"What do I want?" Pierre tried to remember.

"You want to be able to label all of your music so that to all appearances, each piece of music knows about every other piece of music. Right?"

"Kinda, yeah, but you said that was impossible . . ." Pierre trailed off.

"In the true sense, yes. Remember emulation, though? Naw, you were too stoned. Here's the basic idea." Max ran over to the fridge, grabbed a beer and leapt into a bean bag chair. "We assign a value to every piece of music. For example, in music we might assign a value to each note. Like, what note it is, the length of the note, the attack and decay are the raw data. That's just a number. But the groupings of the notes are what's important. The groupings. Get it?"

Pierre was intrigued. He nodded. Maybe Max did understand after all. Pierre leaned forward with anticipation and listened intently, unlike his usual in one ear out the other treatment he normally gave Max's sermons.

"So what we do is program the Apple to recognize patterns of notes; groupings, in any size. We do it in pictures instead of words. Maybe a bar, maybe a scale, maybe even an entire symphony orchestra. All 80 pieces at once!" Max's enthusiasm was contagious. "As the data is put in the computer, you decide what you want to call each grouping. You name it anything you want. Then we could have the computer look for similar groupings and label them. They could all be put on a curve, some graphic of some kind, and then show how they differ and by how much. Over time, the computer could learn to recognize rock'n'roll from Opera from radio jingles to Elevator Music. It's all in the patterns. Isn't that what you want?" Max beamed while speaking excitedly. He knew he had something here.

Max and Pierre worked together and decided to switch from the Apple II computer to the new IBM PC for technical reasons beyond Pierre's understanding. As they labored, Max realized that if he got his "engine" to run, then it would be useful for hundreds of other people who needed to relate data to each other but who didn't know much about computers.

In late 1982 Max's engine came to life on its own. Pierre was programming in pictures and in pure English. He was getting back some incredible results. He was finding that many of the popular rock guitarists were playing lead riffs that had a genealogy which sprang from Indian polyphonic sitar strains.

He found curious relationships between American Indian rhythms and Baltic sea farer's music. All the while, as Pierre searched the reaches of the musical unknown, Max convinced himself that everyone else in the world would want his graphical engine, too.

Through a series of contacts within his Big Eight company, Max was put in touch with Hambrecht Quist, the famed Venture Capital firm that assisted such high tech startups as Apple, Lotus and other shining stars in the early days of the computer industry. Max was looking for an investor to finance the marketing of his engine that would change the world. His didactic preaching and circumlocution didn't get him far. While everyone was polite at his presentations, afterwards they had little idea of what he was talking about.

"The Smart Engine permits anyone to cross-relate individual or matrices of data with an underlying attribute structure that is defined by the user. It's like creating a third dimension. Data is conventionally viewed in a two dimensional viewing field, yet is really a one dimension stream. In either source dimensional view, the addition of a 3 dimensional attribute structure yields interrelationships that are not inherently obvious. Thus we use graphical representations to simplify the entire process."

After several weeks of pounding the high risk financial community of the San Francisco Bay area, Max was despondent. Damn it, he thought. Why don't they understand. I outline the entire theory and they don't get it. Jeez, it's so easy to use. So easy to use. Then the light bulb lit in his mind. Call Pierre. I need Pierre. Call Pierre in New York.

"Pierre, it's Max." Max sounded quite excited.

"How's the Coast."

"Fine, Fine. You'll find out tomorrow. You're booked on American #435 tomorrow."

"Max, I can't go to California, I have so much work to do."

"Bullshit. You owe me. Or have I forgotten to bill you for the engine?" He was calling in a favor.

"Hey, it was my idea. You didn't even understand what I was talking about until . . ."

"That's the whole point, Pierre. I can't explain the engine to these Harvard MBA asswipes. It was your idea and you got me to understand. I just need you to get some of these investors to understand and then we can have a company and make some money selling engines." Max's persistence was annoying, but Pierre knew that he had to give in. He owed it Max.

The new presentations Max and Pierre put on went so well that they had three offers for start up financing within a week. And, it was all due to Pierre. His genial personality and ability to convey the subtleties of a complex piece of software using actual demonstrations from his music were the touchy-feely the investors wanted. It wasn't that he was technical; he really wasn't. But Pierre had an innate ability to recognize a problem, theoretically, and reduce it to its most basic components. And the Engine was so easy to use. All you had to do was . . .

It worked. The brainy unintelligible technical wizard and charismatic front man. And the device, whatever it was, it seemed to work.

The investors installed their own marketing person to get sales going and Pierre was asked to be President. At first he said he didn't want to. He didn't know how to run a company anyway. That doesn't matter, the investors said. You are a salable item. A person whom the press and future investors can relate to. We want you to be the image of the company. Elegance, suave, upper class. All that European crap packaged for the media. Steve Jobs all over again.

Pierre relented, as long as he could continue his music.

Max's engine was renamed dGraph by the marketing folks and the company was popularly known as DGI. Using Byte, Personal Computing, Popular Computing and the myriad computer magazines of the early 1980's, dGraph was made famous and used by all serious computer users.

DGraph could interface with the data from other programs, dBase II, 123, Wordstar and then relate it in ways never fathomed. Automatically. Users could assign their own language of, at that time, several hundred words, to describe the third dimension of data. Or, they could do it in pictures. While the data on the screen was being manipulated, the computer, unbeknownst to the operator, was constantly forming and updating relationships between the data. Ready to be called upon at any time.

As the ads said, "dGraph for dData."

As success reigned, the demand upon Pierre's time increased so that he had little time for his music. By 1986 he lived a virtual fantasy. He was on the road, speaking, meeting with writers, having press conferences every time a new use for dGraph was announced. He was loved by the media. He swam in the glory of the attention by the women who found his fame and image an irresistible adjunct to his now almost legendary French accent and captivating eyes.

Pierre and Max were the hottest young entrepreneurs in Silicon Valley; the darlings of the VC community. And the company sparkled too. It was being run by professionals and Max headed up the engineering group. As new computers appeared on the market, like the IBM AT, additional power could be effectively put into the Engine and Voila! a new version of dGraph would hit the market to the resounding ring of an Instant Hit on Softsel's Top 40.

Max, too, liked his position. He was making a great deal of money, ran his own show with the casualness of his former hippie days, yet could get on the road with Pierre any time he needed a break. Pierre got into the act hook, line and sinker and Max acted the role of genius behind 'The Man'. That gave Max the freedom to avoid the microscope of the press yet take a twirl in the fast lane whenever he felt the urge.

The third round of funding for DGI came from an unexpected place. Normally when a company is as successful as DGI, the original investors go along for the ride. That's how the VC's who worked with Lotus, Compaq, Apple and others were getting filthy stinking rich. The first two rounds went as they had planned, the third didn't.

"Mr. Troubleaux," Martin Fisk, Chairman of Underwood Investments said to Pierre in DGI's opulent offices. "Pierre, there is only one way to say this. Our organization will no longer be involved with DGI. We have sold our interest to a Japanese firm who has been trying to get into the American computer field."

"What will that change? Anything?" Pierre was nonplused by the announcement.

"Not as far as you're concerned. Oh, they will bring in a few of their own people, satisfy their egos and protect their investment, that's entirely normal. But, they especially want you to continue on as President of DGI. No, no real changes."

"What about Max?" Pierre had true concern for his friend.

"He'll remain, in his present capacity. Essentially the financial people will be reporting to new owners that's all."

"Are we still going to go public? That's the only way I'm gonna make any real money."

Martin was flabbergasted. Pierre wasn't in the least interested as to why the company changed hands. He only wanted to know about the money, how much money he would make and when. Pierre never bothered to ask, nor was it offered, that Underwood would profit over 400 percent in under 2 years on their original investment. The Japanese buyer was paying more than the company was worth now. They had come in offering an amount of money way beyond what an opening offer should have been. Underwood did a search on the Japanese company and its American subsidiary, Data Tech. They were real, like $30 Billion real, and they were expanding into the information processing field through acquisitions, primarily in the United States.

Underwood sold it's 17% stake in DGI for $350 Million, more than twice its true value. They sold quickly and quietly. Even though Pierre and Max should have had some say in the transfer, Underwood controlled the board of directors and technically didn't need the founder's consensus. Not that it overtly appeared to matter to Pierre. Max gave the paper transfer a cursory examination, at least asked the questions that were meaningless to the transformed Pierre, and gave the deal his irrelevant blessings.

After the meeting with the emissaries from DGI's new owner, OSO Industries, Pierre and Max were confident that nothing would change for them. They would each continue in their respective roles. The day to day interference was expected to be minimal, but the planned public offering would be accelerated. That suited Pierre just fine; he would make out like a bandit.

Several days before the date of issue, Pierre received a call from Tokyo.

"Mr. Troubleaux?" The thick Japanese accent mangled his name so badly Pierre cringed.

"Yes, this is Pierre Troubleaux," he said exaggerating his French accent. The Japanese spoke French as well as a hair-lipped stutterer could recite "Peter Piper picked a peck of pickled peppers."

"I wish to inform you, sir, that the Chairman of OSO is to visit your city tomorrow and participate in your new successes. Would this be convenient?"

Pierre had only one possible response to the command performance he was being 'invited' to. Since OSO had bought into DGI, Pierre was constantly mystified by the ritualism associated with Japanese business. They could say "Yes!" a hundred times in a meeting, yet everyone present understood that the speakers really meant "No Way, Jose!" There of course was the need for a quality gift for any visitor from Japan. Johnny Walker Black was the expected gift over which each recipient would feign total surprise. Pierre had received more pearl jewelry from the Japanese than he could use for 10 wives. But the ritual was preserved.

"Of course it will. I would be most honored. If you could provide me with details of his flight I will see to it that he receives appropriate treatment."

"Very good Mr. Troubleaux." Pierre stifled a smirk at the mispronunciation. "Your trouble will not go unrewarded."

"Mr. Homosoto, it is so good of you to visit at this time. Very auspicious, sir." Pierre was kissing some ass.

"Troubleaux-San," Homosoto's English had a touch of Boston snobbery in it, "you have performed admirably, and we all look to continued successes in the future. I expect, as I am sure you do, that the revenues raised from your public stock offering will provide your company with the resources to grow ten fold." It was a statement that demanded an answer. Another Japanese quirk.

"Yessir, of course. As you know, Mr. Homosoto, I am not involved in the day to day operations and the forecasting. My function is more to inspire the troops and carry the standard, so to speak. I will have to rely upon the expertise of others to give you the exact answers you seek."

"That is not necessary, I have all I need to know about your business and its needs. Your offer is most kind."

"Why do you call DGI my business? Aren't we in this together? Partners?" Pierre clarified the idiom for the rotund bespectacled Chairman of OSO Industries.

"Hai! Of course, my friend, we are partners, and you will be very wealthy in a few days." That statement had the air of an accusation more than good wishes. "There is one little thing, though. It is so small that I don't wish to mention it."

Well then don't, thought Pierre. "Nothing is so small it shouldn't be mentioned. Please, proceed Homosoto-San. How may I help?"

"That's it exactly!" Homosoto beamed. "I do need your help. Not today, but in the future, perhaps a small favor."

"Anytime at all, sir. Whatever I can I will." Pierre was relieved. Just some more Japanese business practices that escaped him.

Homosoto leaned in towards Pierre. His demeanor had shifted to one of a very serious man. "Mr. Troubleaux, how can I be sure that you won't disappoint me? How can I be sure?"

The question threw Pierre for a loop. How can he be sure? I don't know. Maybe this was only an Oriental game of mumbley peg or chicken. "Sir, what would I need to do to convince you of my willingness to comply?" When in doubt, ask.

Homosoto relaxed again, leaned back in the plush office chair and smiled. "In my country, Mr., Troubleaux, honor is everything. You have nothing, nothing without your honor. Every child man and woman in Japan knows that. We are raised with the focus of growth being honor. During the war between our countries, so many years ago, many found honor by making the supreme sacrifice. Kamikaze pilots are of whom I am speaking, Mr. Troubleaux."

Pierre's face must have given away the panic that instantly struck him. Suicide? This guy is truly nuts.

"Do not worry, Mr. Troubleaux, I can see what you are thinking. No. I only speak of kamikaze pilots to serve as example of honor. The kind that brought honor to Japan in the face of defeat. That is something Americans will never understand. But then again you're not American are you?"

"I was born a Frenchman, but I naturalized over 20 years ago, at the same time my parents did."

"Ah yes. I remember. Then honor does mean more to you than to most Americans. That will be quite good. Now, for the future favor. I require nothing of you today, other than the guarantee of your honor. Is that agreeable to you, Mr. Troubleaux?" Homosoto was pushing with the facade of friendliness. Pierre's concern was not alleviated. All the same, he reluctantly nodded his assent.

"Very good. Now for the favor." Homosoto stood up and reached inside his size 48, ill fitting suit. Pierre was amazed at how much money the Japanese had, yet were apparently unable to ever wear clothes that fit properly.

Homosoto handed a 5 1/4" floppy disk to Pierre. Pierre took it carefully from Homosoto and looked at the label. The diskette was marked only with:

FILE1.EXE to FILE93.EXE

He looked inquisitively at Homosoto, his eyes asking, Yeah, so? What's this got to do with anything?

"I see now you are confused. It is so simple, really. Sometime in the future, you will be instructed to add one of the files on this disk onto the dGraph programs you sell. That's it. So simple. So I have your word Mr. Troubleaux? Honor among men."

Pierre's mind was racing. Put a file onto a program? What does that do? What's on it? Does it help dGraph? No that can't be it. What is it? Why so secret. What's with the honor bit? From the Chairman of OSO, not a technician? One floppy disk? Pierre smelled a fox in the chicken coup.

"Mr. Homosoto, sir. I mean no disrespect. But, I hardly know what to think. I don't even know what this disk is. You are asking me to promise something I don't understand. What if I don't agree. At least until I know what I'm doing? I need to know what's going on here." he said holding the disk up prominently.

"I prefer to think, Mr. Troubleaux of what occurs as long as you do agree to maintain the honor between us. It is so much more pleasant." Homosoto edged towards the doors of Troubleaux's office as he spoke.

"When you agree to act honorably, perform for me this small, insignificant favor, Mr. Troubleaux, you will get to keep the $20 Million you make this Friday and you will be permitted to continue living. Good Afternoon." Homosoto closed the door behind him.

* * * * *

Alexander Spiradon was pleased. His students were doing well. Sir George was the last. The other students from the New York computer school had already checked in; they didn't have as far to travel. Everything was in place, not quite a year to the day since he and Taki Homosoto had set their plans in action. Alex hadn't spoken to Homosoto in a couple of months. It was now time to report to Homosoto in Tokyo. It was 17 hours earlier there - Homosoto would probably be at his desk. The modem dialed a local Brookline number. The phone in Brookline subsequently dialed a number in Dallas, Texas, which dialed another phone in Tacoma, Washington. The

Tacoma phone had the luxury of dialing the international number for Homosoto's private computer.

Call forwarding services offered the ultimate in protection. Any telephone tracing would take weeks, requiring the cooperation of courts from every state where a forwarded phone was located. Then, the State Department would have to coordinate with the Japanese Embassy. An almost impossible task, if anyone had the resources. It took about 45 seconds for the call to be completed.

<<<CONNECTION>>>
PASSWORD:

Alex entered his password, GESUNDHEIT and his forced response from his own PRG card. His computer terminal paused. If he was on satellite to Japan, or to Dallas or anywhere else, his signal could travel a hundred thousand miles or more each time he sent a character from his keyboard.

CRYPT KEY:

Alex Spiradon chose 43. Each communication he had with Homosoto was also protected with full encryption. If someone was able to isolate their conversations, all they would get would be sheer garbage, a screen full of unintelligible symbols and random characters. By choosing 43, Alex told his computer and Homosoto's computer to use Crypt Key 43, one of over 100 secret keys that both computers held in their memory. This cryptographic scheme, using the U.S.'s Data Encryption Standard, DES, and ANSI standard X9.17 was the same one that the Treasury Department and Federal Reserve used to protect the transmission of over $1 trillion of funds transfers daily.

<<<TRANSMISSION ENCODED>>>

That was the signal for Alex to send the first words to Homosoto.

Good Morning, Homosoto-San.

AND TO YOU MY ESTEEMED PARTNER. YOU HAVE SOMETHING TO REPORT.

Yes. All is in place.

PLEASE CLARIFY . . .MY MEMORY IS NOT WHAT IT WAS.

Of course. The last of the Operators are in place. We call him Sir George. That makes 8 altogether. San Francisco, (SF), New York, (NY), Los Angeles, (LA), Boston, (BM), Atlanta, (AG) Chicago, (CI), Washington, (DC) and Dallas, (DT).

AND THEY CAN BE TRUSTED?

They are aware of the penalty. If not, we have others that will replace them. Besides, you are rewarding them most handsomely for their efforts.

SO I AM. I EXPECT RESULTS. AND THE OTHERS?

The Mail Men are waiting as well. Four of them in NY, DC, LA and DT.

YOU SAY MAIL MEN. WHAT IS THAT TERM?

They will deliver our messages in writing to those who need additional proof of our sincerity. They know nothing other than they get paid, very well, to make sure that the addressees are in receipt of their packages.

VERY GOOD. AND THEY TOO ARE RESPONSIBLE?

Yes. Elimination is a strong motivation. Besides, they know nothing.

WHAT IF THEY READ THE CONTENTS?

That can only help. They do not know where the money comes from. Most need the money more than their lives. My contacts make my choices ideal. Death is . . .so permanent.

I AGREE. IT MAKES MEN HONORABLE, DOES IT NOT?

Most of the time, yes. There are always exceptions, and we are prepared for that, too.

THE SEKIGUN-HA ARE AT YOUR DISPOSAL.

Thank you. The Ground Hogs, the first are in place.

HOW MANY AND WHERE.

Over 50 so far. I will keep recruiting. We have 11 in the long distance phone companies and at AT&T, 3 at IBM, 14 in government positions, 12 in major banks, a couple of insurance companies, 3 Hospitals are compromised . . .and a list of others. We will keep the channels full, I promise.

HOW WILL THEY FUNCTION?

They will gain access to the information we need, and when we call, they will perform. I will add more as we proceed. It amazes me, these Americans. Anything for a buck.

DO NOT DISAPPOINT ME.

I will not. That is my promise. When will the information be ready?

SOON. TOMORROW THE FIRST READER INFORMATION WILL BE SENT TO YOU. CALLS MAY BEGIN IN DAYS. YOU ORGANIZE IT. THE GROUND HOGS ARE NOT TO BE AC-

TIVATED FOR SEVERAL WEEKS. THEY ARE TO PERFORM THEIR JOBS AS IF NOTHING IS WRONG. DO THEY UN-DERSTAND?

Ground Hogs receive 2 paychecks. They understand their obliga-tions. We pay 10 times their salary for their allegiance. The Operators and Mail Men will start soon.

THERE IS NO SUCH THING AS ALLEGIANCE. DON'T YOU KNOW THAT YET?

Americans pay homage to the almighty dollar, and nothing else. They will be loyal.

AS YOU ARE MOTIVATED MY FRIEND, I DO NOT FORGET THAT. BUT OTHERS CAN OFFER MORE DOLLARS AND WE CAN BE FOUND. I CANNOT RISK THAT, UNDER ANY CIR-CUMSTANCES. DO YOU UNDERSTAND THE RISK?

Completely. I am responsible for my people.

AND THEY ARE PREPARED FOR THEIR JOBS?

Yes. That is my responsibility, to insure the security of our task. No one must know. I know my job.

DO IT WELL. I WILL LEAVE YOU.

<<<CONNECTION TERMINATED>>>

* * * * *

Chapter 5

Monday, September 14
New York City

Doug! Doug!" Scott shouted across the city room. As in most newspaper offices, the constant scurry of people bumping into each other while reading and walking gave the impression of more activity than there really was. Desks were not in any particular pattern, but it wasn't totally chaotic either. Every desk had at least one computer on it. Some two or three. Scott pushed back into place those that he dislodged while running to McGuire's desk.

Doug McGuire noticed the early hour, 8:39 AM on the one wall clock that gave Daylight Savings Time for the East Coast. The other dozen or so clocks spanned the time zones of the globe. It wasn't like Scott to be his energetic youthful self before noon, EST.

"Doug, I need you." Scott shouted from 3 desks away. "It'll just take a minute."

Scott nearly dragged the balding, overweight, sometimes harsh 60 year old Doug McGuire across the newsroom. They abruptly halted in front of Scott's desk. Boxes full of files everywhere; on the floor, piled 3 or 4 high, on his desk. "Will you look at this. Just look at this!" He stuck a single sheet of paper too close into Doug's face. Doug pushed it away to read it out loud.

McGuire read from the page. "A Message from a Fan. Thanks." Doug looked perplexed. He motioned at the paper hurricane on Scott's desk. "So, what is this mess? Where did it come from?"

Scott spoke excitedly. "I got another delivery, about an hour ago. I think it's from the same guy who sent the McMillan stuff." He perused the boxes.

"Why do you say that?" Doug asked curiously.

"Because of what's in here. I haven't been able to go through much of it, obviously, but I scanned through a few of the boxes. There's dirt on almost every company in the Fortune 1000. Copies of memoranda, false figures, confidential position statements, the truth behind a lot of PR scandals, it goes on and on. There's even a copy of some of the shredded Ollie North papers. Or so they say they are. Who knows. But, God! There are notes about behind the scene plays on mergers, who's screwing who to get deals done . . .it's all here. A hundred years of stories right here . . .".

"Let's see what we've got here." Doug was immediately hooked by the treasure trove of potential in from of them coupled with Scott's enthusiasm. The best stories come from the least likely places. No

86

reporter ever forgets the 3rd rate burglary at the Watergate that brought down a President.

By late afternoon, Scott and several of the paper's researchers had set up a preliminary filing system. They categorized the hundreds of files and documents and computer printouts by company, alphabetically. The contents were amazing. Over 150 of the top American corporations were represented directly, and thousands of other by reference. In every case, there was a revelation of one or more particularly embarrassing or illegal activities. Some were documented accounts and histories of past events and others that were in progress. Many of the papers were prognostications of future events of questionable ethics or legality. It reminded Scott of Jeanne Dixon style predictions. Fat chance, he thought.

From Wall Street's ivory tower deals where payoffs are called consulting fees; and in banking circles where delaying transfers of funds can yield millions of dollars in interest daily; from industrial secrets stolen or purchased from such and such a source, the laundry list was long. Plans to effect such a business plan and how to disguise its true purposes from the ITC and SEC. Internal, very upper level policies which never reach the company's Employee Handbook; policies of discrimination, attitude, and protective corporate culture which not only transcend the law but in many cases, morality. The false books, the jimmied numbers . . .they were in the boxes too, but that was almost accepted accounting practice as long as you didn't get caught. But the depth of some of the figures was amazing. Like how one computer company brought in Toshiba parts and sold them to the government despite the ban on Toshiba components because of their sale of precision lathes to the Soviets.

"Jesus," said Scott after a lengthy silence of intent reading. "This shit nails everyone, even the Government."

There were well documented dossiers on how the EPA made unique exclusions hundred of times over based upon the financial lobbying clout of the particular offender. Or how certain elected officials in Washington had pocketed funds from their PAC monies or how defense contractors were advised in advance of the contents of an upcoming billion dollar RFP.

The cartons of files were absolute political dynamite. And, if released, could have massive repercussions in the world financial community.

There was a fundamental problem, though. Scott Mason was in possession of unsupported accusations; not unreasonable accusations. They were certainly believable. All he really had was leads, a thousand leads in ten thousand different directions, with no apparent coherency or theme, received from an anonymous and dubious donor.

And there was no way of immediately gauging the veracity of their contents. He clearly remembered what is was like to be lawyered. That held no appeal at the moment.

The next obvious question was, who would have the ability to gather this amount of information, most of which was obviously meant to be kept very, very private. Papers meant not for anyone but instead only a select group of insiders.

Finally, and just as important to the reporter; why? What would someone gain from telling all the nasty goings on inside of Corporate America. There have been so many stories over the years about this company or that screwing over the little guy. How the IRS and the government operated substantially outside of legal channels. The kinds of things that the Secretary of the Treasury would prefer were kept under wraps. Sometimes stories of this type made the news, maybe a trial or two, but not exactly noteworthy in the big picture. White collar crime wasn't as good as the Simpsons or Roseanne, so it went largely ignored.

Scott Mason needed to figure out what to do with his powder keg. So, as any good investigative reporter would do, he decided to pick a few key pieces and see if the old axiom was true. Where there's smoke, there's fire.

* * * * *

Fire. That's exactly what Franklin Dobbs didn't want that Monday morning. He and 50 other Corporate CEO's across the country received their own unsolicited packages by courier. Each CEO received a dossier on his own company. A very private dossier containing information that technically didn't, or wasn't officially supposed to exist. Each one read their personalized file cover to cover in absolute privacy. And shock set in.

Only a few of the CEO's in the New York area had ever heard of Scott Mason before, and little did they know that he had the complete collection of dossiers in his possession at the New York City Times. Regardless, boardrooms shook to their very core. Wall Street trading was untypically low for a Monday, less than 50,000,000 shares. But CNN and other financial observers attributed the anomaly to random factors unconnected to the secret panic that was spreading through Corporate America.

By 6 P.M., CEO's and key aides from 7 major corporations headquartered in the metropolitan New York area had agreed to meet. Throughout the day, CEO's routinely talk to other corporate leaders as friends, acquaintances, for brain picking and G2, market probing or otherwise in the course of business. Today, though, the scurry of inter-Ivory-Tower calls was beyond routine.

Through a complicated ritual dance of non-committal consent, questions never asked and answers never given, with a good dose of Zieglerisms, a few of the CEO's communicated to each other during the day that they were not happy with the morning mail. A few agreed to talk together. Unofficially of course, just for a couple of drinks with friends, and there's nothing wrong, we admit nothing, of course not.

These are the rules strictly obeyed for a non-encounter that isn't happening. So they didn't meet in a very private room, upstairs at the Executive Club, where sensitive meetings often never took place. One's presence in that room is as good as being in a black hole. You just weren't there, no matter what. Perfect.

The room that wasn't there was heavily furnished and dark. The mustiness lent to the feeling of intrigue and incredulity. Massive brown leather couches and matching oversized chairs surrounded by stout mahogany tables were dimly lit by the assortment of low wattage lamp fixtures. There was a huge round dining table large enough for all of Camelot, surrounded by mammoth chairs in a large anteroom. The brocade curtains covered long windows that stretched from the floor to ornate corner moldings of the 16 foot ceilings.

One tired old black waiter with short cropped white hair appeared and disappeared skillfully and invisibly. He was so accustomed to working with such distinguished gentlemen, and knew how important their conversations were, that he took great pride in refilling a drink without being noticed. With his little game, he made sure that drinks for everyone were always full. They spoke openly around Lambert. Lambert had worked the room since he was 16 during World War II. Lambert saw no reason to trade occupations; he was treated decently, and he doubled as a bookie for some members which added to his income. There was mutual trust.

"I don't know about you gentlemen," said Porter Henry, the energetic and feisty leader of Morse Technologies, defense subcontractor. "I personally call this blackmail." A few nods.

"I'm not about to admit to anything, but have you been threatened?" demanded Ogden Roberts, Chairman of National First Interstate.

"No, I don't believe any of us have, in so many words. And no, none of us have done anything wrong. We are merely trying to keep sensitive corporate strategies private. That's all. But, I do take the position that we are being intimidated. I think Porter's right. This is tantamount to blackmail. Or the precursor at a minimum."

They discussed, in the most circumlocutous manner, possibilities. The why, how, and who's. Who would know so much, about so many, supposedly sacrosanct secrets. Therefore there must have been a lot of whos, mustn't there? They figured about 50 of their kindred CEO's had received similar packages, so that meant a lot of whos were behind the current crisis in privacy. Or maybe just one big who. O.K., that's narrowed down real far; either a lot of whos, one big who, or somewhere in between.

Why? They all agreed that demands would be coming, so they looked for synergy between their firms, any sort of connections that spanned at first the seven of those present, to predict what kinds of demands. But it is difficult to find hard business connections between an insurance company, a bank, 2 defense contractors, a conglomerate of every drug store product known to man and a fast food company. The thread wasn't there.

How? That was the hardest. They certainly hadn't come up with any answers on the other two questions, so this was asking the impossible. CEO's are notorious for not knowing how their companies work on a day to day basis. Thus, after 4 or 5 drinks, spurious and arcane ideas were seriously considered. UFO's were responsible, I once saw one . . .my secretary, I never really trusted her at all . . .the Feds! Must be the IRS . . .(my/his/your) competitor is doing it to all of us . . .the Moonies, maybe the Moonies . . .

"Why don't we just go to the Feds?" asked Franklin Dobbs who did not participate in the conjecturing stream of consciousness free for all. Silence cut through the room instantly. Lambert looked up from his corner to make sure they were all still alive.

"I'm serious. The FBI is perfect. We all operate interstate, and internationally. Would you prefer the NYPD?" He said derogatorally waiting any voices of dissent.

"C'mon Frank. What are we going to tell them?" Ogden Roberts the banker asked belligerently. The liquor was having an effect. "Certainly not the truth . . ." he cut himself short, realizing that he came dangerously close to admitting some indefinable wrong he had committed. "You know what I mean," he quickly added.

"We don't go into all of the detail. An abbreviated form of the truth, all true, but maybe not everything. I am sure we all agree that we want to keep this, ah, situation, as quiet as possible." Rapid assent came from all around.

"All we need to say is that we have been contacted, by phone, in a threatening manner. That no demands have been made yet, but we are willing to cooperate with the authorities. That would give us all a little time, to re-organize our priorities, if you see what I mean?" Dobbs added. The seven CEO's were thoughtful.

"Now this doesn't mean that we all have to agree on this," Franklin Dobbs said. "But as for me, I have gone over this, in limited detail, with my attorney, and he agrees with it on a strategic level. If someone's after you, and you can't see 'em, get the guys with the White Hats on your side. Then do some housekeeping. I am going to the FBI. Anybody care to join me?"

It was going to be a lonesome trip.

* * * * *

September, 4 Years Ago
Tokyo, Japan.

Oso Industries maintained its world headquarters in the OSO World Bank Building which towered 71 stories over downtown Tokyo. From the executive offices on the 66th floor, on a clear day, the view reached as far as the Pacific. It was from these lofty reaches that Taki Homosoto commanded his $30 Billion empire which spread across 5 continents, 112 countries, and employed almost a quarter million people.

OSO Industries had diversified since it humble beginnings as a used tire junkstore.

The Korean conflict had been a windfall for OSO. Taki Homosoto started a tire retreading business in 1946, during the occupation. The Americans were so smart, he thought. Bring over all of your men, tanks, jeeps and doctors not telling us the truth about radiation, and you forget spare tires. Good move, Yankee.

Taki gouged the Military on pricing so badly, and the Americans didn't seem to care, that the Pentagon didn't think twice about paying $700 for toilet seats decades later. Taki did give great service - after all his profits were so staggeringly high he could afford it. Keep the American's happy, feed their ego, and they'll come back for more. No sense of pride. Fools.

When the Americans moved in for Korea, Tokyo was both a command post for the war effort and the first choice of R&R by servicemen. OSO Industries was in a perfect position to take advantage of the US Government's tire needs throughout the conflict. OSO was already in place, doing a good job; Taki had bought some friends in the US military, and a few arrangements were made to keep business coming his way.

Taki accumulated millions quickly. Now he needed to diversify.

Realizing that the war would come to an end some day, Homosoto began making plans. OSO Radio sets appeared on the market before the end of the Korean Police Action. Then, with the application of the transistor, the portable radio market exploded. OSO Industries made more transistor radios than all other Japanese electronics firms combined. Then came black and white televisions. The invention of the single beam color TV tube again brought OSO billions in revenues every year.

Now, OSO was the model of a true global corporation. OSO owned banks and investment companies. Their semiconductor and electronics products were household words. They controlled a vast network of companies; electronic game manufacturers, microwave and appliance manufacturers, and notably, acres and acres of Manhattan Island, California and Hawaii. They owned and operated communications companies, including their own geosynchronous satellite. OSO positioned itself as a holding company with hundreds of subsidiaries, each with their own specialty, operating under thousands of names. Homosoto wove an incredibly complex web of corporate influence and intrigue.

OSO was one of the 10 largest corporations in the world. Reaganomics had already assisted in making OSO and Homosoto himself politically important to both Japan and the US. Exactly how Homosoto wanted it. The leaders of the US, Senators, Congressmen, appointees, lobbyists, in fact much of Washington coddled up to Homosoto. His empire planned years in advance. The US Government, unofficially craved his insights, and in characteristic Washington style, wanted to be near someone important. Homosoto relished it. Ate it up. He was a most cordial, unassuming humble guest. He played the game magnificently.

Almost the entire 66th floor of the OSO Bank Building was dedicated to Homosoto and his immediate staff. Only a handful of the more than 200,000 people that OSO Industries employed had access to the pinnacle of the OSO tower which graced the Tokyo skyline.

The building was Designed by Pie, and received international acclaim as an architectural statement. The atrium in the lobby vaulted almost 700 feet skyward precursoring American hotel design in the next decade. Plants, trees over 100 feet tall and waterfalls graced the atria and the overhanging skylobbies. The first floor lobby was designed around a miniature replica of the Ging Sha forest, fashioned with thousands of Bonzai trees. The mini forest was built to be viewed from various heights within the atrium to simulate a flight above the earth at distances from 2 to 150 miles.

The lobby of OSO Industries was a veritable museum. The Van Gogh collection was not only the largest private or public assemblage in the world, but also represented over $100 Million spent in Sothby and Christies auctions worldwide since 1975.

To get to the elevator to the 66th floor, a security check was performed, including a complete but unobtrusive electronic scan of the entire person and his belongings. To all appearances, the procedure was no more than airport security. However to the initiate or the suspect, it was evident from the accuracy with which the guards targeted specific contraband on a person or in his belongings that they knew more than they were telling. The OSO guards had the girth of Sumo wrestlers, and considering their sheer mass, they received little hassle. Very few deemed it prudent to cross them.

The lobby for all of its grandeur, ceilings of nearly 700 feet, was a fairly austere experience. But, the elevator to the 66th floor altered that image at once. It was this glass walled elevator, the size of a small office, with appropriately comfortable furnishings, that Miles Foster rode. From the comfort of the living room setting in the elevator, he enjoyed a panorama of the atrium as it disappeared beneath him. He looked at the forest and imagined what astronauts saw when they catapulted into orbit. The executive elevator was much slower than the others. Either the residents in the penthouse relished the solitude and view or they had motion sickness. Nonetheless, it was most impressive.

"Ah, Mister Foster! Welcome to OSO. Please to step this way." Miles Foster was expected at the terminus of the lift which opened into an obscenely large waiting room that contained a variety of severe and obviously uncomfortable furniture. Aha! Miles, thought. That's exactly what this is. Another art gallery, albeit a private one for the eyes of his host and no one else. White walls, white ceilings, polished parquet floors, track lighting, recessed lights, indirect lights. Miles noticed that the room as pure as the driven snow didn't have any windows. He didn't recognize much of the art, but given his host, it must have represented a sizable investment.

Miles was ushered across the vast floor to a set of handsomely carved, too tall wooden doors with almost garish gold hardware. His slight Japanese host barely tapped on the door, almost inaudibly. He paused and stood at attention as he blurted an obedient "Hai!"

The aide opened both doors from the middle, and in deference to Mr. Foster, moved to one side to let the visitor be suitably impressed. Homosoto's office was a total contrast to his gallery. Miles first reaction was astonishment. It was slightly dizzying. The ceiling slanted to a height of over 25 feet at the outer walls, which were floor to ceiling glass. The immense room provided not only a spectacular view of Tokyo and 50 miles beyond, but lent one the feeling of being outside.

Coming from the U.S. Government, such private opulence was not common. It was to be expected in his family's places of business, the gaming parlors of Las Vegas, but not in normal commerce. He had been to Trump Tower in New York, but that was a public building, a place for tourists. This office, he used the word liberally, was palatial.

It was decorated in spartan fashion with cherry wood walls. Artwork, statues, figurines, all Japanese in style, sat wherever there was an open surface. A few gilt shelves and marble display tables were randomly scattered around the room. Not chaoticly; just the opposite. The scattering was exquisitely planned. There was a dining alcove, privatized by lavish rice paper panels for eating in *suhutahksi*. Eating on the floor was an honored ritual. There was a small pit under the table for curling one's legs on the floor.

A conference table with 12 elegant wooden chairs sat at the opposite end of the cavernous office. In the center of the room, at the corner of the building, was Homosoto's desk, or work surface if you prefer. It was large enough for four, yet Homosoto, as he stood to greet Foster, appeared to dwarf his environment and desk. Not in size, but in confidence. His personage was in total command. The desk and its equipment were on a platform some 6" above the rest of the room. The intended effect was not lost on Foster.

The sides of the glossy cherrywood desk were slightly elevated to make room for a range of video monitors, communications facilities, and computers which accessed Homosoto's empire. A vast telephone console provided tele-conferencing to OSO offices worldwide. Dow Jones, CNN, Nippon TV were constantly displayed, visible only to Homosoto. This was Homosoto's Command Central as he liked to call it.

Foster gawked at the magnificent surroundings as he stood in front of his assigned seat. A comfortable, plush, black leather chair. It was one of several arranged in a sunken conversation pit.

Homosoto acknowledged Foster's presence with the briefest of nods as he stepped down off of his aerie. Homosoto wore expensive clothes. A dark brown suit, matching solid tie and the omnipresent solid white starched shirt. It didn't fit, like most Japanese business uniforms.

He was short, no more than five foot six, Miles noticed, after Homosoto got down to the same level as the rest of the room. On the heavy side, he walked slowly and deliberately. Eyes forward after the obligatory nod. His large head was sparsely covered with little wisps of hair in nature's futile attempt to drape the top of his freckled skull. Even at 59 Homosoto's hair was still pitch black. Miles wasn't sure if Grecian Formula was available in Japan. The short crop accentuated the ears.

A rounded face was peppered with spots, dark freckles perhaps, or maybe carcinoma. His deep set black eyes stared through the object of his attention. Homosoto was not the friendly type, thought Miles.

Homosoto stood in front of Miles, extended his hand and bowed the most perfunctory of bows. Miles took his hand, expecting a strong grip. Instead he was greeted with a wet fish handshake which wriggled quickly from his grasp. Homosoto didn't give the slightest indication of a smile. The crow's feet around his eyes were caused by pudginess, not happiness. When he sat opposite Foster in a matching chair, he began without any pleasantries.

"I hear you are the best." Homosoto stared at Foster. It was a statement that required a response.

Foster shifted his weight a little in the chair. What a way to start. This guy must think he's hot shit. Well, maybe he is. First class, all expense paid trip to Tokyo, plus consultation fees. In advance. Just for one conversation, he was told, we just want some advice. Then, last night, and the night before, he was honored with a sampling of the finest Oriental women. His hot button. All expenses paid, of course. Miles knew he was being buttered up, for what he didn't know, but he took advantage of it all.

"That's what's your people tell you."

Foster took the challenge and glared, albeit with a smirk dimpled smile, politely, right back at Homosoto. Homosoto continued his stare. He didn't relax his intensity.

"Mr. Foster," Homosoto continued, his face still emotionless. "Are you as good as they say?" he demanded.

Miles Foster defiantly spat out the one word response. "Better."

Homosoto's eyes squinted. "Mr. Foster, if that is true, we can do business. But first, I must be convinced. I can assure you we know quite a bit about you already, otherwise you wouldn't be here." Miles noticed that Homosoto spoke excellent English, clipped in style, but Americanized. He occasionally stretched his vowels, to the brink of a drawl.

"Yeah, so what do you know. Pulled up a few data bases? Big Deal." Miles cocked his head at Homosoto's desk. "I would assume that with that equipment, you can probably get whatever you want."

Homosoto let a shimmer of a smile appear at the corners off his mouth. "You are most perceptive, Mr. Foster." Homosoto paused and leaned back in the well stuffed chair. "Mr. Foster, tell me about your family."

Miles neck reddened. "Listen! You called me, I didn't call you. All I ever knew about OSO was that you made ghetto blasters, TV's and vibrators. So therefore, you wanted me, not my family. If you had wanted them you would have called them." Miles said loudly. "So, keep my family the fuck out of it."

"I do not mean to offend," Homosoto said offensively. "I just am most curious why you didn't go to work for your family. They have money, power. You would have been a very important man, and a very rich one." Homosoto said matter of factly. "So, tone must wonder why you went to work for your Government? Aren't your family and your government, how shall I say, on opposite sides?"

"My family's got nothing to do with this or you. Clear?" Miles was adamant. "But, out of courtesy for getting me laid last night, I might as well tell you. I went to the feds cause they have the best computers, the biggest equipment and the most interesting work. Not much money, but I have a backup when I need it. If I went to work for my family, as you put it, I would have been a glorified bean-counter. And that's not what I do. It would have been no challenge. Boring, boring, boring!" Miles smiled sarcastically at Homosoto. "Happy now?"

Homosoto didn't flinch. "Does that mean you do not disapprove of your family's activities? How they make money?"

"I don't give a fuck!" Miles yelled. "How does that grab you? I don't give a flying fuck. They were real good to me. Paid a lot of my way. I love my mother and she's not a hit man. And I really don't know what my uncle does to whom. Nor do I care. They're family, that's it. How much clearer do you want it?"

Homosoto grinned and held up his hands. "My apologies Mr. Foster. I mean no disrespect. I just like to know who works for me."

"Hey, I don't work for you yet."

"Of course, a simple slip of the tongue."

"Right." Miles snapped sarcastically.

Homosoto ignored this last comment. The insincere smile left his face, replaced with a more serious countenance. "Why did you leave your post with the National Security Agency, Mr. Foster?"

Another inquisition, thought Miles. What a crock. Make it good for the gook.

"'Cause I was working for a bunch of bungling idiots who insured their longevity by creating an invincible bureaucracy." Miles decided that a calm beginning might be more appropriate. "They had no real idea of what was going on. Their heads were so far up their ass they had a tan line across their chests. Whenever we had a good idea, it was either too novel, too expensive or needed additional study. Or, it was relegated to a committee that might react in 2 years. What a pile of bullshit, a waste of time. We could have achieved a lot more without all the interference."

"Mr. Foster, you say, 'we'. Who is 'we'?" Homosoto pointedly asked Miles.

"The analysts, the people who did the real work. There were hundreds of us on the front lines. The guys who sweated weekends and nights to make our country safe from the Communists. The managers just never got with the program."

"Mr. Foster, how many of the other analysts, in your opinion, are good?"

Miles stepped back in his mind to think about this. "Oh, I guess I knew a half dozen guys, and one girl, who were pretty good. She was probably the best, other than me," he bragged. "Some chicken."

"Excuse me? Chicken?"

"Oh, sorry." Miles looked up in thought. "Ah, chicks, fox, looker, sweet meat, gash, you know?"

"Do you mean she's very pretty?"

Miles suppressed an audible chuckle. "Yeah, that's right. Real pretty, but real smart, too. Odd combination, isn't it?" he smiled a wicked smile.

Homosoto ignored the crudeness. "What are your politics, Mr. Foster?"

"Huh? My politics? What the hell has that got to do with anything?" Miles demanded.

"Just answer the question, please, Mr. Foster?" Homosoto quietly ordered.

Miles was getting incensed. "Republican, Democrat? What do you mean? I vote who the fuck I want to vote for. Other than that, I don't play."

"Don't play?" Homosoto briefly pondered the idiom. "Ah, so. Don't play. Don't get involved. Is that so?"

"Right. They're all fucked. I vote for the stupidest assholes running for office. Any office. With any luck he'll win and really screw things up." Homosoto hit one of Miles hot buttons. Politics. He listened attentively to Miles as he carried on.

"That's about the only way to fix anything. First fuck it up. Real bad. Create a crisis. Since the Government ignores whoever or whatever isn't squeaking that's the only way to get any attention. Make noise. Once you create a crisis, Jeez, just look at Granada and Panama and Iraq to justify Star Wars, you get a lot of people on for the ride. Just look at the national energy debate. Great idea, 30 years and $5 trillion late. Then, 'ooooh!', they say. 'We got a big problem. We better fix it.' Then they all want to be heroes and every podunk politico shoots off his mouth about the latest threat to humanity. "

"That's your politics?"

97

"Sure. If you want to get something fixed, first fuck it up so bad that everyone notices and then they'll be crawling up your ass trying to help you fix it."

"Very novel, Mr. Foster. Very novel and very cynical." Homosoto looked mildly amused.

"Not meant to be. Just true."

"It seems to me that you hold no particular allegiance. Would that be a fair observation?" Homosoto pressed the point.

"To me. That's my allegiance. And not much of anything else." Miles sounded defensive.

"Then, Mr. Foster, what does it take to make you a job offer. I am sure money isn't everything to a man like you." Homosoto leaned back. All 10 of his fingers met in mirror image fashion and performed push ups on each other.

Foster returned Homosoto's dare with a devastating stare-down that looked beyond Homosoto's face. It looked right into his mind. Foster used the knuckles from both hands for supports as he leaned on the table between them. He began speaking deliberately.

"My greatest pleasure? A challenge. A great challenge. Yes, the money is nice, don't get me wrong, but the thrill is the challenge. I spent years with people ignoring my advice, refusing to listen to me. And I was right so many times when they were wrong. Then they would start blaming everyone else and another committee is set up to find out what went wrong. Ecch! I would love to teach them a lesson."

"How unfortunate for them that they failed to recognize your abilities and let your skills serve them. Yes, indeed, how unfortunate." Homosoto said somberly.

"So," Miles said arrogantly as he retreated back to his seat. "You seem to be asking a lot of questions, and getting a lot of answers. It is your dime, so I owe you something. But, Mr. Homosoto, I would like to know what you're looking for."

Homosoto stood up erect. "You, Mr. Foster, You. You are what I have been looking for. And, if you do your job right, I am making the assumption you will accept, you will become wealthier than you ever hoped. Ever dreamed. Mr. Foster, your reputation precedes you." He sincerely extended his hand to Foster. "I do believe we can do business." Homosoto was beaming at Miles Foster.

"O.K., O.K., so if I accept, what do I do?" said Miles as he again shook Homosoto's weak hand.

"You, Mr. Foster, are going to lead an invasion of the United States of America."

* * * * *

Chapter 6

3 Years Ago
Sunnyvale, California.

Pierre Troubleaux was staggered beyond reason. His life was just threatened and he didn't know what to do about it. What the hell was this disk anyway? Military secrets? Industrial espionage? Then why put it on the dGraph disks and programs? Did I just agree? What did I say? I don't remember what I said? Maybe I said maybe.

Panic yielded to confusion. What is so wrong? This was just some old Japanese guy who was making some veiled Oriental threat. No, it was another one of those cultural differences. Like calisthenics before work at those Japanese companies that saturate the West Coast. Sure it sounded like a threat, but this is OSO Industries we are talking about. That would be like the head of Sony using extortion to sell Walkmen. Impossible. All the same, it was scary and he had no idea what was on the disk. He called Max.

"Max! What are you doing?" What he meant, and Max understood, was 'I need you. Get your ass up here now.'

"On my way Amigo."

The next few minutes waiting for Max proved to be mentally exhausting. He thought of hundreds of balancing arguments for both sides of the coin. Be concerned, this guy is nuts and meant it, or I misunderstood something, or it got lost in the translation. He prayed for the latter.

"Yo, what gives?" Max walked into Pierre's office without knocking.

"Tell me what's on this!" Pierre thrust the disk up at Max's large physique.

Max held the disk to his forehead and gazed skyward. "A good start. Yes, a good start." Max grinned.

Pierre groaned, knowing full well that the Kreskin routine had to be completed before anything serious was discussed. Max brought the disk to his mouth and blew on it so the disk holder bulged in the middle. Max pulled out the disk and pretended to read it. "What do you call 1000 lawyers at the bottom of the ocean." Pierre chuckled a half a chuck. He wasn't in the mood, but then he had no love for lawyers.

"Max! Please."

"Hey, just trying new material . . . "

" . . . that's 5 years old." Pierre interrupted.

"All right already. Gimme a break. OK, let's have a look." They went behind Pierre's desk and inserted the disk in his IBM AT. Max asked the computer for a listing of the diskette's contents. The screen scrolled and stopped.

C:\a:
A:\dir

FILE84.EXE	01/01/80	704
FILE85.EXE	01/01/80	2013
FILE86.EXE	01/01/80	1900
FILE87.EXE	01/01/80	567
FILE88.EXE	01/01/80	2981
FILE89.EXE	01/01/80	4324
FILE90.EXE	01/01/80	1280
FILE91.EXE	01/01/80	1395
FILE92.EXE	01/01/80	2374
FILE93.EXE	01/01/80	3912
	93 Files	1457 Bytes Remaining

A:\

"Just a bunch of small programs. What are they?" Max's lack of concern was understandable, but it annoyed Pierre all the same.

"I don't know, that's what I'm asking you. What are they? What kind of programs?"

"Shit, Pierre, I don't know. Games maybe? Small utilities? Have you used them yet?"

"No, not yet, someone just gave them to me. That's all." Pierre's nervousness betrayed him.

"Well let's try one, see what it does." Max typed in FILE93. That would run the program.

A few seconds later the disk stopped and the computer returned to its natural state, that of the C:\. "That one didn't work. Let's try 92. H'mmmm. That's curious, it don't do nothing neither. Looks like a bunch of crap to me. What are they supposed to do?" Max shrugged his shoulders.

Max kept trying a few more of the numbered programs. "I don't know, really. Maybe it's just a joke."

"Some joke, I don't get it. Where's the punch line? Damn, nothing." Max punched a few more keys. "Let me have this. I wanna take me a look a closer look," Max said as he pulled the diskette from the machine.

"Where are you going with that?"

"To my lab. I'll disassemble it and see what's what. Probably some garbage shareware. I'll call you later."

At 4PM Max came flying through Pierre's office door again. Pierre was doing his magic . . .talking to the press on the phone.

"Where did you get this?" bellowed Max as he strutted across the plush carpet holding a diskette in his hand?

Pierre waved him silent and onto the couch. He put up one finger to indicate just a minute. Pierre cut the reporter short on an obviously contrived weak excuse. He promised to call back real soon. He meant that part. He would call back.

"Pierre, where did you get this?" Max asked again.

"Nowhere. What's on it," he demanded.

"Viruses. Lots of 'em."

"You mean it's sick? Like contagious?" Pierre was being genuine.

"No you Frog idiot. Computer viruses."

"What is a computer virus? A machine can't get sick."

"How wrong you are ol' buddy. You're in for a lesson now. Sit down." Pierre obliged. This was Max's turf.

"Here goes. If I lose you, just holler, O.K., Amigo?" Pierre had grown to hate being called Amigo, but he had never asked Max to stop. Besides, now wasn't the appropriate time to enlighten Max as to the ins and outs of nick name niceties. Pierre nodded silent agreement.

"Computers basically use two type of information. One type of information is called data. That's numbers, words, names on a list, a letter, accounting records whatever. The second type are called programs, we tweaks call them executables. Executables are almost alive. The instructions contained in the executables operate on the data. Everything else is a variation on a theme."

"Yeah, so the computer needs a program to make it work. Everyone knows that. What about these?"

"I'm getting there. Hold on. There are several types of executables, some are COM files, SYS and BAT files act like executables and so do some OVR and OVL files. In IBM type computers that's about it. Apples and MACs and others have similar situations, but these programs are for IBM's. Now imagine a program, an executable which is designed to copy itself onto another program."

"Yeah, so. That's how dGraph works. We essentially seam ourselves into the application."

"Exactly, but dGraph is benign. These," he holds up the diskette, "these are contaminated. They are viruses. I only looked at a couple of them, disassembly takes a while. Pierre, if only one of these programs were on your computer, 3 years from now, the entire contents of your hard disk would be destroyed in seconds!" Pierre was stunned. It had never occurred to him that a program could be harmful.

"That's 3 years from now? So what? I probably won't have the same programs on my computer then anyway. There's always something new."

"It doesn't matter. The viruses I looked at here copy themselves onto other programs and hide themselves. They do nothing, nothing at all except copy themselves onto other programs. In a few days every program on your computer, I mean every one would be infected, would be sick. Every one would have the same flu if you wish. And then, 3 years from now, any computer that was infected would destroy itself. And, the virus itself would be destroyed as well. Kind of like Jap kamikazes from World War II. They know exactly when they will die and hope to take a lot of others with them. In this case the virus commits suicide in 3 years. Any data or program within spitting distance, so to speak, goes too."

"So why doesn't someone go looking for viruses and come up with antidotes?"

"It's not that simple. A well written virus will disguise itself. The ones you gave me, at least the ones I disassembled not only hide themselves, but they are dormant until activation; in this case on a specific date." Max continued the never ending education of Pierre. "Besides, it's been proven that there is no way to have a universal piece of software to detect viruses. Can't be done."

"Whew . . .who comes up with this stuff?" Pierre was trying to grasp the importance of what he was hearing.

"Used to be a UNIX type of practical joking; try writing a program that would annoy fellow programmers. Pretty harmless fooling around. No real damage, just embarrassment that called for a similar revenge. It was a game of one upmanship within university computer science labs. I saw a little of it while I worked at the school computer labs, but again it was harmless shenanigans. These though. Wow. Deadly. Where the hell did you get them?"

Pierre was in a quandary. Tell or don't tell. Do I or don't I? He trusted Max implicitly, but what about the threat. Naw, I can tell Max. Anything.

"Homosoto."

"What?" asked Max incredulously.

"Homosoto. He gave it to me." Pierre was solemn.

"Why? What for?"

"He said that I was to put it on the dGraph disks that we sell."

"He's crazy. That's absolutely nuts. Do you know what would happen?" Max paced the floor as he spoke angrily. "We sell thousands of dGraph's every month. Tens of thousands. And half of the computer companies ship dGraph with their machines. In 3 years time we may have over a couple of million copies of dGraph in the field. And who knows how many millions more programs would be infected, too. Tens of millions of infected programs . . .my God! Do you know how many machines would be destroyed . . . well maybe not all destroyed but it's about the same thing. The effects would be devastating." Max stopped to absorb what he was saying.

"How bad could it be? Once they're discovered, can't your viruses be destroyed?" Pierre was curious about the newly discovered power.

"Well, yes and no. A virus that is dormant for that long years is also called a Time Bomb and a Trojan Horse. There would be no reason to suspect that a legitimate software company would be shipping a product that would damage computers. The thought is absurd . . .it's madness. But brilliant madness. Even if a few of the viruses accidentally go off prematurely, the virus destroys itself in the process. Poof! No smoking gun. No evidence. Nobody would have clue until V-Day."

"V-Day?"

"Virus Day."

"Max, what's in this for Homosoto? What's the angle?"

"Shit, I can't think of one. If it ever got out that our programs were infected it would be the end of DGI. All over. On the other hand, if no one finds out before V-Day, all the PC's in the country, or Jesus, even the world, self destruct at once. It's then only a matter of time before DGI is caught in the act. And then, amigo, it's really over. For you, me and DGI. What exactly did Homosoto say?"

Pierre was teetering between terror and disbelief. How had he gotten into this position. His mind wandered back over the last few years since he and Max had come up with the Engine. Life had been real good. Sure, I don't get much music in anymore, and I have kinda got seduced by the fast lane, but so what? So, I take a little more credit than credit's due, but Max doesn't mind. He really doesn't.

The threat. Was it real? Maybe. He tried to convince himself that his mind was playing tricks on itself. But the intellectual exercises he performed at lightening speed, cranial neuro-synapses switching for all they were worth, did not permit Pierre the luxury of a respite of calm.

"He said he wanted me to put this on dGraph programs. Sometime in the future. That's about it." There was no reason to speak of the threats. No, no reason at all. His vision became suddenly clear. He was being boxed into a corner.

"Well . . .?" Max's eyes widened as he expected a response from Pierre.

"Well what?"

"Well, what are you going to tell him? Or, more like where are you going to tell him to go? This is crazy. Fucking crazy, man."

"Max, let me handle it. " Some quietude returned to Pierre. A determination and resolve came from the confusion. "Yeah, I'll take care of it."

"Mr. Homosoto, we need to speak." Pierre showed none of the international politic that usually was second nature. He called Homosoto at the San Jose Marriott later that afternoon.

"Of course, Mr. Troubleaux. I will see you shortly." Homosoto hung up.

Was that a Japanese yes for a yes, or a yes for a no? Pierre wasn't sure, but he was sure that he knew how to handle Homosoto. Homosoto didn't have the common courtesy to say he would not be coming until the following morning.

In the plushness of Pierre's executive suite, Homosoto sat with the same shit eating grin he had left with the day before. Pierre hated that worse than being called amigo.

"Mr. Troubleaux, you asked to speak to me. I assume this concerns a matter of honor between two men." Homosoto spoke in a monotone as he sat stiffly.

"You're damned right it does." Pierre picked up the diskette from his desk. "This disk, this disk . . .it's absolutely incredible. You know what's here, you know what kind of damage it can cause and you have the gall, the nerve to come in here and ask me, no, worse yet, tell me to distribute these along with dGraph? You're out of your mind, Mister." Pierre was in a rage. "If you think we're a bunch of pawns, to do your dirty little deeds, you have another thing coming."

Unfazed, Homosoto rose slowly and started for the door.

"Where do you think you're going? Hey, I asked you where you're going? I'm not finished with you yet. Hey, fuck the deal. I don't want the goddamned money. We'll stay private and wait for someone honest to come along." Pierre was speaking just as loudly with hand, arm and finger gestures. While not all of the gestures were obscene, there was no doubt about their meaning.

Homosoto spoke gently amidst Pierre's ranting. "I will give you some time to think about it." With that, he left and shut the door in Pierre's bright red face.

Three days later DGI stock would be officially unleashed upon the public. Actually institutional buyers had already committed to vast amounts of it, leaving precious little for the small investor before driving the price up. That morning Pierre was looking for Max. They had a few last minute details to iron out for the upcoming press conferences. They had to prepare two types of statements. One if the stock purchase went as expected, sold out almost instantly at or above the offering price, and another to explain the financial bloodbath if the stock didn't sell. Unlikely, but their media advisors forced them to learn both positions, just in case.

His phone rang. "Pierre, Mike Fields here." Fields was DGI's financial media consultant. He worked for the underwriters and had a strong vested interest in the outcome. He didn't sound like a happy camper.

"Yes, Mike. All ready for tomorrow? I'm so excited I could burst." Pierre pretended.

"Yes, so am I, but we have a problem."

Pierre immediately thought of Homosoto. "What kind of problem, Mike?" Pierre asked suspiciously.

"Uh, Max, Pierre, it's Max."

"What about Max?"

"Pierre, Max is dead. He died in a car crash last night. I just found out a few minutes ago. I gather you didn't know?"

Of all the possible pieces of bad news that Mike Fields could have brought him, this was the farthest from his mind. Max dead? Not possible. Why, he was with him till after 10 last night.

"Max, dead? No way. What happened? I don't believe it. This is some kind of joke, right?"

"Pierre, I'm afraid I'm all too serious, unless CHiPs is in on it. They found a car, pretty well burned up, at the bottom of a ravine on the 280. Looks like he went through the barrier and down the, well, you know what . . .I . . ."

"I get the idea. Mike. Who . . ." Pierre stuttered.

"It was an accident, Pierre. One of those dumb stupid accidents. He may have had a blow out, fell asleep at the wheel, oh . . .it could be a million things. Pierre, I am sorry. So sorry. I know what you guys meant to each other. What you've been through . . ."

"Mike, I have to go," Pierre whispered. The tears were welling up in his eyes.

"Wait, Pierre," Mike said gingerly. "Of course we're gonna put off the offering until . . ."

"No. Don't." Pierre said emphatically.

"Pierre, your best friend and partner just died and you want to go through with this . . .at least wait a week . . .Wall Street will be kind on this . . ."

"I'll call you later. No changes. None." Pierre hung up. He hung his head on his desk, shattered with conflicting emotions. He was nothing without Max. Sure, he gave great image. Knew how to do the schtick. Suck up to the press, tell a few stories, stretch a few truths, all in the name of marketing, of course. But without Max, Max understood him. Damn you Max Jones. You can't do this to me.

His grief vacillated from anger to despair until the phone rang. He ignored the first 7 rings. Maybe they would go away. The caller persisted.

"Yes," he breathed into the phone.

"Mr. Troubleaux," it was Homosoto. Just what he fucking needed now.

"What?"

"I am most sorry about your esteemed friend, Max Jones. Our sympathies are with you. Is there anything I can do to help you in this time of personal grief." Classic Japanese manners oozed over the phone wire.

"Yeah. Moral bankruptcy is a crime against nature, and you have been demonstrating an extreme talent for vivid androgynous self gratification." Pierre was rarely rude, but when he was, he aped Royal British snobbery at their best.

"A physical impossibility, Mr. Troubleaux," Homosoto said dryly. "I understand your feelings, and since it appears that I cannot help you, perhaps we should conclude our business. Don't you agree Mr. Troubleaux?" The condescension dripped from Homosoto's words. The previous empathy was gone as quickly as if a light had been extinguished.

"Mr. Homosoto, the offering will still go through, tomorrow as scheduled. I assume that meets with your approval?" The French can be so caustic. It makes them excellent taxi cab drivers.

"That is not the business to which I refer. I mean business about honor. I am sure you remember our last conversation."

"Yes, I remember, and the answer is still no. No, no, no. I won't do it."

"That is such a shame. I hope you will not regret your decision." There it was again, Pierre thought. Another veiled threat.

"Why should I?"

"Simply, and to the point as you Americans like it, because it would be a terrible waste if the police obtained evidence you murdered your partner for profit."

"Murdered? What in hell's name are you talking about?" Crystal clear visions scorched across Pierre's mind; white hot fire spread through his cranium. Was Homosoto right? Was Max murdered? Searing heat etched patterns of pain in his brain.

"What I mean, Mr. Troubleaux is that there is ample evidence, enough to convince any jury beyond a reasonable doubt, that you murdered your partner as part of a grander scheme to make yourself even richer than you will become tomorrow. Do I make myself clear?"

"You bastard. Bastard," Pierre hissed into the phone. Not only does Homosoto kill Max, but he arranges to have Pierre look like the guilty party. What choice did he have. At least now. There's no proof, is there? The police reports are apparently not ready. No autopsy. Body burned? What could Homosoto do?

"Fuck you all the way to Hell!" Pierre screamed at the phone in abject frustration and then slammed the receiver down so hard the impact resistant plastic cracked.

At that same instant, Sheila Brandt, his secretary, carefully opened the door his door. "Pierre, I just heard. I am so sorry. What can I do?" She genuinely felt for him. The two had been a great team, even if Pierre had become obsessed with himself. Her drawn face with 40 years of intense sun worshiping was wracked with emotional distress.

"Nothing Sheil. Thanks though . . .what about the arrangements . . .?" The helpless look on his face brought out the mother in her even though she was only a few years older.

"Being taken care of . . .do you want to . . .?"

"No, yes, whatever . . .that's all right, just keep me advised . . ."

"Yessir. Oh, I hate to do this, but your 9AM appointment is waiting. Should I get rid of him?"

"Who is it? Something I really give a shit about right now?"

"I don't know. He's from personnel."

"Personnel? Since when do I get involved in that?"

"That's all I know. Don't worry I'll have him come back next week . . ." she said thinking she had just relieved her boss of an unnecessary burden that could wait.

"Sheil? Send him in. Maybe it'll get my mind off of this."

"If you're sure . . ." Scott nodded at her affirmatively. "Sure, Pierre, I'll send him in."

An elegantly dressed man, perhaps a dash over six feet, of about 30 entered. He walked with absolute confidence. If this guy was applying for a job he was too well dressed for most of DGI. He looked more like a tanned and rested Wall Street broker than a . . .well whatever he was. The door closed behind him and he grasped Pierre's hand.

"Good morning Mr. Troubleaux. My name is Thomas Hastings. Why don't we sit for moment." Their hands released as they sat opposite each other in matching chairs. Pierre sensed that Mr. Hastings was going to run the conversation. So be it. "I am a software engineer with 4 advanced degrees as well 2 PhD's from Caltech and Polytechnique in Paris. There are 34 US patents either in my name alone or jointly along with over 200 copyrights. I have an MBA from Harvard and speak 6 languages fluently . . ."

Pierre interrupted, "I am impressed with your credentials, and your clothes. What may I do for you."

"Oh dear, I guess you don't know. I am Max Jones' replacement. Mr. Homosoto sent me. May I have the diskette please?"

* * * * *

The financial section of the New York City Times included two pieces on the DGI offering. One concerned the dollars and cents, and the other was a related human interest story, with financial repercussions. Max Jones, the co-founder of DGI, died in a car accident 2 days before the company was to go public. It would have earned him over $20 Million cash, with more to come.

The article espoused the "such a shame for the company" tone on the loss of their technical wizard and co-founder. It was a true loss to the industry, as much as if Bill Gates had died. Max, though, was more the Buddy Holly of software, while Gates was the Art Garfunkle. The AP story, though, neglected to mention that the San Jose police had not yet ruled out foul play.

* * * * *

Wednesday, September 16
New York City

Scott arrived in the City Room early to the surprise of Doug. He was a good reporter; he had the smarts, his writing was exemplary and he had developed a solid readership, but early hours were not his strong point.

"I don't do mornings," Scott made clear to anyone who thought he should function socially before noon. If they didn't take the hint, he behaved obnoxiously enough to convince anyone that his aversion to mornings should be taken seriously.

Doug assumed that Scott had a purpose in arriving so early. It must be those damned files. The pile of documents that alleged America was as crooked as the Mafia. Good leads, admittedly, but proving them was going to be a bitch. Christ, Scott had been going at them with a vengeance. Let him have some rope.

Scott got down to business. He first called Robert Henson, CEO of Perris, Miller and Stevenson. Scott's credentials as a reporter for the New York City Times got him past the secretary easily. Henson took the call; it was part of the job.

"Mr. Henson? This is Scott Mason from the Times. I would like to get a comment on the proposed Boston-Ellis merger." Scott sounded officious.

"Of course, Mr. Mason. How can I help?" Robert Henson sounded accommodating.

"We have the press releases and stock quotes. They are most useful and I am sure that they will be used. But I have other questions." Scott hoped to mislead Henson into thinking he would ask the pat questions he was expected to ask.

"Yes, thank you. My staff is very well prepared, and we try to give the press adequate information. What do you need?" Scott could hear the smiling Henson ready to play the press game.

"Basically, Mr. Henson. I have some documents that suggest that you inflated the net earnings of Second Boston to such a degree that, if, and I say, if, the deal goes through, your firm will earn almost one million dollars in extra fees. However, the figures I have do not agree at all with those filed with the SEC. Would you care to comment?" Scott tried not to sound accusatory, but it was difficult not to play the adversary.

Henson didn't try to conceal the cough he suddenly developed at the revelation. "Where," he choked, "Where do you get that information?"

"From a reliable source. We are looking for a confirmation and a comment. We know the data is correct." Scott was playing his King, but he still held an Ace if he needed it.

"I have no comment. We have filed all required affidavits with the appropriate regulatory agencies. If you need anything else, then I suggest you call them." Henson was nervous and the phone wires conveyed his agitation.

"I assume, Mr. Henson, that you won't mind if I ask them why files from your computer dispute figures you gave to the SEC?" Scott posed the question to give Henson an option.

"That's not what I said," Henson said abruptly. "What computer figures?"

"I have a set of printouts that show that the earnings figures for Second Boston are substantially below those stated in your filings. Simple and dry. Do you have a comment?" Scott stuck with the game plan.

"I . . .uh . . .am not familiar . . .with . . .the . . .ah . . ." Henson hesitated and then decided to go on the offensive. "You have nothing. Nothing. It's a trap," Henson affirmed.

"Sir, thank you for your time." Scott hung up after Henson repeatedly denied any improprieties.

"This is Scott Mason for Senator Rickfield. I am with the New York City Times." Scott almost demanded a conversation with Washington's leading debunker of the Defense Department's over spending.

"May I tell the Senator what this is in reference to?" The male secretary matter of factly asked.

"Yes of course." Scott was overly polite. "General Young and Credit Suisse."

"Excuse me?" the young aide asked innocently.

"That will do. I need a comment before I go to print." Scott commanded an assurance that the aid was not used to hearing from the press.

"Wait one moment please," the aide said. A few seconds of Muzak on hold bored Scott before Senator Merrill Rickfield picked up the call. He was belligerent.

"What the hell is this about?" The senator demanded.

"Is that for the record?" Scott calmly asked.

"Is what for the record? Who the hell is this? You can't intimidate me. I am a United States Senator." The self assurance gave away nervousness.

"I mean no disrespect, Senator. I am working on an article about political compromise. Very simple. I have information that you and General Young, shall we say, have . . .an understanding. As a member of the Senate Intelligence Committee, you have helped pass legislation that gave you both what you wanted. General Young got his weapons and you have a substantial bank account in Geneva. Comments, Senator?"

Rickfield was beside himself but was forced to maintain a formal composure. "Sir. You have made some serious accusations, slanderous at best, criminal I suspect. I hope you are prepared to back up these preposterous claims." Scott heard desperation in the Senator's voice.

"Yessir, I am. I go to print, with or without your comments," Scott lied. A prolonged pause followed. The first person who spoke lost, so Scott busied himself with a crossword puzzle until Rickfield spoke.

"If you publish these absurdities, I will sue you and your paper right into bankruptcy. Do you copy?"

"I copy , Senator. Is that for attribution?" Scott knew that would piss off Rickfield. The line went dead.

Scott made similar calls for a good part of the day, and he continued to be amazed.

From call to call, the answers were the same. "How did you get that?" "Where did you find out?" "There's no way you could know that." "I was the only one who had access that . . ." "That was in my private files . . ."

Blue Tower Nuclear Plant denied that Scott held internal memos instructing safety engineers to withhold critical flaws from the Nuclear Regulatory Committee. General Autos denied using known faulty parts in Cruise Control mechanisms despite the fact that Scott held a copy of a SECRET internal memorandum. He especially upset the Department of Defense when he asked them how Senors Mendez and Rodriguez, CIA operatives, had set up Noriega.

The Center for Disease Control reacted with abject terror at the thought of seeing the name of thousands of AIDS victims in the newspaper. Never the less, the CDC refused to comfirm that their files had been penetrated or any of the names on the list. Useless.

Everyone he called gave him virtually the same story. Above and beyond the official denial to any press; far from the accusatory claims which were universally denied for a wide variety of reasons, all of his contacts were, in his opinion, honestly shocked that he even had a hint of their alleged infractions.

Scott Mason began to feel he was part of a conspiracy, one in which everyone he called was a victim. One in which he received the same formatted answer; more surprise than denial.

Scott knew he was onto a story, but he had no idea what it was. He had in his possession damning data, from an anonymous source, with, thus far, no way to get a confirmation. Damn. He needed that for the next time he got lawyered.

When he presented his case to his editor, Scott's worst fears were confirmed. Doug McGuire decided that a bigger story was in the making. Therefore, we don't go. Not yet. That's an order. Keep digging.

"And while you're at it," Doug said with the pleasure of a father teasing his son, "follow this up, will you? I need it by deadline."

Scott took the AP printout from Doug and read the item.

"No," Scott gasped, "not another virus!" He threw the paper on his desk. "I'm up to my ass in . . ."

"Viruses," Doug said firmly, but grinning.

"Have a heart, these things are such bullshit."

"Then say so. But say something."

* * * * *

Chapter 7

Thursday, September 17
New York City Times

Christopher Columbus Brings Disease to America

By Scott Mason

Here's a story I can't resist, regardless of the absurdity of the headline. In this case the words are borrowed from a story title in last week's National Exposé, that most revered of journalistic publications which distributes half truths and tortured conclusions from publicity seeking nobodies.

The headline should more appropriately be something like,
"Terror Feared in New Computer Virus Outbreak", or
"Experts See Potential Damage to Computer Systems", or
"Columbus Day Virus: Imaginary Panic?"

According to computer experts, this Columbus Day, October 12, will mark a repeat appearance of the now infamous Columbus Day Virus. As for the last several years, that is the anticipated date for a highly viral computer virus to 'explode'. The history behind the headline reads from an Ian Fleming novel.

In late 1988, a group of West German hackers and computer programmers thought it would be great fun to build their own computer virus. As my regular readers recall, a computer virus is an unsolicited and unwanted computer program whose sole purpose is to wreak havoc in computers. Either by destroying important files or otherwise damaging the system.

We now know that that these Germans are part of an underground group known as CHAOS, an acronym for Computer Hackers Against Open Systems, whatever the heck that means. They work together to promote computer systems disruption worldwide.

In March of 1989, Amsterdam, Holland, hosted an international conference of computer programmers. Are you ready for the name? Intergalactic Hackers Conference. Some members were aware of the planned virus. As a result of the negative publicity hackers have gotten over the last few years, the Conference issued a statement disavowing the propagation and creation of computer viruses. All very honorable by a group of people whose sole purpose in life is to invade the privacy of others.

Somewhere, somehow, something went wrong, and the CHAOS virus got released at the Intergalactic Hackers meetings. In other words, files and programs, supposedly legitimate ones, got corrupted by this disreputable band, and the infections began spreading.

The first outbreak of the Columbus Day Virus occurred in 1989, and caused millions of dollars of down computer time, reconstruction of data banks and system protection.

Again we are warned, that the infection has continued to spread and that some strains of the virus are programmed to detonate over a period of years. The Columbus Day Virus is called by its creators, the "Data Crime Virus", a name befitting its purpose. When it strikes, it announces itself to the computer user, and by that time, it's too late. Your computer is kaput!

What makes this particular computer virus any more tantalizing than the hundred or so that have preceded it? The publicity the media has given it, period, each and every year since 1989.

The Data Crime, aka Columbus Day Virus has, for some inescapable reason attracted the attention of CNN, ABC, CBS, NBC and hundreds of newspapers including this one. The Associated Press and other reputable media have, perhaps due to slow news weeks, focused a great deal of attention on this anticipated technological Armageddon.

Of course there are other experts who pooh-pooh the entire Virus issue and see it as an over-exploited media event propelled by Virus Busters. Sam Moscovitz of Computer Nook in Dallas Texas commented, "I have never seen a virus in 20 years. I've heard about them but really think they are a figment of the media's imagination."

Virus Busters are people or firms who specialize in fighting alleged computer viruses by creating and selling so-called antidotes. Virus Busting Sean McCullough, President of The Virus Institute in San Jose, California thinks that most viruses are harmless and users and companies overreact. "There have been no more that a few dozen viral outbreaks in the last few years. They spread more by rumor than by infection." When asked how he made his living, he responded, "I sell antidotes to computer viruses." Does he make a good living? "I can't keep up with the demand," he insists.

The Federal Government, though, seems concerned, and maybe for good reason. On October 13, a Friday by chance, another NASA space shuttle launch is planned. Friday the 13th is another date that computer virus makers use as the intended

113

date of destruction. According to an official spokesman, NASA has called in computer security experts to make sure that their systems are " . . .clean and free from infection. It's a purely precautionary move, we are not worried. The launch will continue as planned."

Viruses. Are they real? Most people believe they are real, and dangerous, but that chances of infection are low. As one highly respected computer specialist put it, "The Columbus Day Virus is a low risk high consequence possibility. I don't recommend any panic." Does he protect his own computer agaist viruses? "Absolutely. I can't risk losing my computers."

Can anybody? Until October 12, this is Scott Mason, hoping my computer never needs Tylenol.

* * * * *

Scarsdale, New York.

The Conrail trains were never on time.

Scott Mason regularly tried to make it to the station to ride the 7:23 from the wealthy Westchester town of Scarsdale, New York into Grand Central Station. If he made it. It was a 32 minute ride into the City on good days and over 2 hours when the federally subsidized rail service was under Congressional scrutiny.

The ritual was simple. He fell into his old Porsche 911, an upscale version of a station car, and drove the 2 miles to the Scarsdale train station. He bought a large styrofoam cup full of decent black coffee and 3 morning papers from the blind newsman before boarding the express train. Non-stop to Harlem, and then on to 42nd St. and Park Avenue and wake up time.

Tyrone Duncan followed a similar routine. Except he drove his silver BMW 850i to the station. The FBI provided him with a perfectly good Ford Fairlane with 78,000 miles on it when he needed a car in New York. He was one of the few black commuters from the affluent bedroom community and his size made him more conspicuous than his color.

Scott and Tyrone were train buddies. Train buddies are perhaps unique in the commuterdom of the New York suburbs. Every morning you see the same group of drowsy, hung over executives on their way to the Big Apple. The morning commute is a personal solace for many. Your train buddy knows if you got laid and by whom. If you tripped over your kids toys in the driveway, your train buddy knew. If work was a bitch, he knew before the wife. Train buddies are buddies to the death or the bar, whichever comes first.

114

While Scott and Tyrone had been traveling the same morning route since Scott had joined the paper, they had been friends since their wives introduced them at the Scarsdale Country Club 10 years ago. Maggie Mason and Arlene Duncan were opposites; Maggie, a giggly, spacey and spontaneous girl of 24 and Arlene, the dedicated wife of a civil servant and mother of three daughters who were going to toe the line, by God. The attachment between the two was not immediately explainable, but it gave both Scott and Ty a buddy with their wives' blessing.

The physical contrast between the two was comical at times. Duncan was a 240 pound six foot four college linebacker who had let his considerable bulk accumulate around the middle. Scott, small and wiry was 10 years Ty's junior. On weekends they played in a very amateur local basketball league where minimum age was thirty five, but there, Scott consistently out maneuvered Tyrone's bulk.

During the week, Tyrone dressed in impeccable Saville Row suits he had made in London while Scott's uniform was jeans, sneakers and T-Shirt of choice. His glowing skull, more dark brown than ebony, with fringes of graying short hair emphasized the usually jovial face that was described as a cross between rolly-polly and bulbous. Scott on the other hand always seemed to need a haircut.

Coffee in hand, Tyrone plopped down opposite Scott as the train pulled out of the open air station.

"You must be in some mood," Tyrone said laughing.

Scott laid down his newspaper and vacantly asked why.

"That shirt," Ty smirked. "A lesson in how tomake friends and influence people."

"Oh, this?" Scott looked down at the words on his chest:

I'm O.K.
You're A Shithead.

"It only offends them that oughta be offended."

"Shitheads?"

"Shitheads."

"Gotcha," Ty said sarcastically. "Right."

"My mother," groused Scott. "VCR lessons." Ty didn't understand.

"I gave my mom a VCR last Christmas," Scott continued. "She ooh'd and ah'd and I thought great, I got her a decent present. Well, a couple of weeks later I went over to her place and I asked how she liked the VCR. She didn't answer, so I asked again and she mumbled that she hadn't used it yet. I fell down," Scott laughed out loud.

"'Why?' I asked her and she said she wanted to get used to it sitting next to her TV for a couple of months before she used it." Tyrone caught a case of Scott's roaring laughter.

"Wheeee!" exclaimed Tyrone. "And you're an engineer?"

"Hey," Scott settled down, "my mom calls 911 to change a lightbulb." They laughed until Scott could speak. "So last night I went over for her weekly VCR lesson."

"If it's anything like Arlene's mother," Tyrone giggled, "trusting a machine to do something right, when you're not around to make sure it is right, is an absolutely terrifying thought. They don't believe it works."

"It's a lot of fun actually," Scott said fondly. "It tests my ability to reduce things to the basics. The real basics. Trying to teach a seventy year old about digital is like trying to get a square ball bearing to roll."

Even so, Scott looked forward to those evenings with his mom. He couldn't imagine it, the inability to understand the simplicity of either 'on' or 'off'. But he welcomed the tangent conversations that invariably resulted when he tried to explain how the VCR could record one channel and yes mom, you can watch another channel at the same time.

Scott never found out that his mother deprogrammed the VCR, cleared its memory and 'Twelved' the clock an hour before he arrived to show her how to use it. And after he left, she reprogrammed it for her tastes only to erase it again before his next visit. If he had ever discovered her ruse it would have ruined her little game and the ritual starting point for their private talks.

"By the way," Scott said to Tyrone. "What are you and Arlene doing Sunday night?"

"Sunday? Nothing, why?" Tyrone asked innocently.

"My mom is having a little get together and she'd love the two of you . . ."

"Is this another one of her seances?" Tyrone asked pointedly.

"Well, not in so many words, but it's always possible . . ."

"Forget it." Tyrone said stubbornly. "Not after what happened last time. I don't think I could get Arlene within 20 miles of your mother. She scared the living shit out of her . . .and I have my doubts."

"Relax," Scott said calmly. "It's just her way of keeping busy. Some people play bingo, others play bridge . . ."

"And your mother shakes the rafters trying to raise her husband from the dead," said Scott with exaperation. "I don't care what you say, that's not normal. I like your mother, but, well, Arlene has put her foot down." Tyrone shuddered at the thoughts of that evening.

No one could explain how the wooden shutters blew open or the table wobbled. Tyrone preferred, just as his wife did, to pretend it never happened.

"Hey," Tyrone said with his head back behind the newspaper. "I see you're making a name for yourself elsewhere, too."

"What do you mean?" Scott asked.

"Don't give me that innocent shit. I'm a trained professional," Tyrone joked. He held up the New York City Times turned to Scott's Christopher Columbus article. "Your computer crime pieces have been raising a few eyebrows down at the office. Seems you have better sources than we do. Our Computer Fraud division has been going nuts recently."

"Glad you can read." Scott enjoyed the compliment. "Just a job, but I gotta story much more interesting. I can't publish it yet, though."

"Why?"

"Damn lawyers want us to have our facts straight. Can you believe it?" Scott teased Tyrone. "Besides, blackmail is so, so personal."

Tyrone stopped in mid-sip of his hot coffee. "What blackmail?" The frozen visage caught Scott off guard. They rarely spoke of their respective jobs in any detail, preferring to remain at a measured professional distance. Thus far their professional interests had not sufficiently overlapped to affect their personal relationship.

"It's a story, that, well, doesn't have enough to go into print, but, it's there, I know it. Off the record, O.K.?" Scott wanted to talk.

"Mums the word."

"A few days ago I received some revealing documents papers on a certain company. I can't say which one." He looked at Tyrone for approval.

"Whatever," Tyrone urged anxiously.

Scott told Tyrone about his nameless faceless donor and what Higgins had said about the McMillan situation and the legality of the apparently purloined information. Tyrone listened in fascination as Scott outlined a few inner sanctum secrets to which he was privy.

Tyrone got a shiver up his spine. He tried to disguise it.

"Can I ask you a question?" Tyrone quietly asked.

"Sure. Go for it."

"Was one of the companies Amalgamated General?"

Scott shot Tyrone a look they belied the answer.

"How did you know?" Scott asked suspiciously.

"And would another be First Federated and State National Bank?" Tyrone tried to subdue his concern. All he needed was the press on this.

117

Scott could not hide his surprise. "Yeah! And a bunch of others. How'd you know?"

Tyrone retreated back into his professional FBI persona. "Lucky guess."

"Bullshit. What's up?" Scott's reporter mindset replaced that of the lazy commuter.

"Nothing, just a coincidence." Tyrone picked up a newspaper and buried his face behind it.

"Hey, Ty. Talk ol' buddy."

"I can't and you know it." Tyrone sounded adamant.

"As a friend? I'll buy you a lollipop?" Scott joked.

Ty snickered. "You know the rules, I can't talk about a case in progress."

"So there is a case? What is it?" Scott probed.

"I didn't say that there was a case," Ty countered.

"Yes you did. Case in progress were your words, not mine. C'mon what's up?"

"Shit, you media types." Tyrone gave himself a few seconds to think. "I'll never know why you became a reporter. You used to be a much nicer pain in the ass before you became so nosy." Scott sat silently, enjoying Ty's awkwardness.

Tyrone hated to compromise the sanctity of his position, but he realized that he, too, needed some help. Since he hadn't read any of this in the papers, there had to be journalistic responsibility from both Scott and the paper. "Off, off, off the record. Clear?" He was serious.

"Done."

The train rumbled into the tunnel at the Northern tip of Manhattan. They had to raise their voices to hear each other, but that meant they couldn't be heard either.

"As near as I can tell," Tyrone hesitantly began. "There's a well coordinated nationwide blackmail operation in progress. As of yesterday, we have received almost a hundred cases of alleged blackmail. From Oshkosh, Baton Rouge, New York, Miami, Atlanta, Chicago, LA, the works. Small towns to the metros. It's an epidemic and the local and state cops are absolutely buried. They can't handle it, and besides it's way out of their league. So who do they all call? Us. Shit. I need this, right? There's no way we can handle this many cases at once. No way. Washington's going berserk."

"Who's behind it?" Scott asked knowing he wouldn't get a real answer.

"That's the rub. Don't have a clue. Not a clue. There's no pattern, none at all. We assumed it was organized crime, but our informants say they're baffled. Not the mob, they swear. They knew about it before we did. Figures." Tyrone's voice echoed a professional frustration.

"Motives?"

"None. We're stuck."

"Sounds like we're both on the same hunt."

The train slowed to a crawl and then a hesitant stop at Grand Central. Thousands of commuters lunged at the doors to make their escape to the streets of New York above them. Scott wondered if any of them were part of Duncan's problems.

"Scott?" Tyrone queried on the escalator.

"Yeah?"

"Not a word. O.K.?"

Scott held up his right hand with three fingers. "Scott's honor!" That was good enough for Tyrone.

They walked up the stairs and past a newsstand that caught both of their eyes instantly. The National Expose had another sensationalistic headline:

FBI POWERLESS IN NATIONAL BLACKMAIL SCHEME

They fought for who would pay the 75 cents for the scandal filled tabloid, bought two, and started reading right where they stood.

"Jesus," Tyrone said more breathing than saying the word. "They're going to make a weekly event of printing every innuendo."

"They have the papers, too," muttered Scott. "The whole blasted lot. And they're printing them." Scott put down the paper. "This makes it a brand new ball game . . ."

"Just what I need," Tyrone said with disgust.

"That's the answer," exclaimed Scott. "The motive. Who's been affected so far?"

"That's the mystery. No one seems to have been affected. What's the answer?" Tyrone demanded loud enough to attract attention. "What's the answer?" he whispered up close.

"It's you." Scott noted.

Tyrone expressed surprise. "What do you mean, me."

"I mean, it seems that the FBI has been affected more than anyone else. You said you're overloaded, and that you can't pay attention to other crimes."

"You're jumping to conclusions." Tyrone didn't follow Scott's reasoning and cocked his head quizzically.

"What if the entire aim of the blackmail was to overwork the FBI, overload it with useless cases? What if the perpetrators really have other crimes in mind? Maybe they have already hit their real targets. Isn't it possible that the FBI is an unwilling dupe, a decoy in a much larger scheme that isn't obvious yet?" Scott liked the sound of his thinking and he saw that Tyrone wasn't buying his argument.

"It's possible, I guess . . .but . . ." Tyrone didn't have the words to finish his foggy thoughts. It was too far left field for his linear thinking. "No, this is as crazy as the time you thought that UFO's were invading Westchester in '85. Then there was the time you said that Colombian drug dealers put cocaine in the water supply . . ."

"That wasn't my fault . . ."

" . . .and the Trump Noriega connection and the other 500 wild ass conspiracies you come up with."

Scott dismissed Tyrone's friendly criticism by ignoring the derisions. "As I see it," Scott continued, "the only victim is the FBI. None of the alleged victims have been harmed, other than ego and their paranoia levels. Maybe the FBI was the target all along. Given the lack of hard data they had," Scott suggested, "it's as good a theory as any other."

"With what goal?" Duncan accepted the logic for the moment.

"So when the real thing hits, you guys are too fucked up to react."

* * * * *

The Federal Bureau of Investigation
Federal Square, Manhattan.

The flat white and glass square building, designed in the '60's, built shoddily by the lowest bidder in 1981, in no way echoed the level of technical sophistication hidden behind the drab exterior. The building had no personality, no character, nothing memorable about it, and that was exactly the way the tenants wanted it.

The 23 story building extended 6 full floors below the congested streets of Lower Manhattan. Throughout the entire structure well guarded mazes held the clues to the locations of an incredible array of computing power, some of the world's best analytical tools, test equipment, forensic labs, communications facilities and a staff of experts in hundreds of technical specialties required to investigate crimes that landed in their jurisdiction.

The most sensitive work was performed underground, protected by the solid bedrock of Manhattan island. Eavesdropping was impossible, almost, and operational privacy was guaranteed. Personal privacy was another matter, though. Most of the office staff worked out in an open office floorplan. The walls between the guard stations and banks of elevators consisted solely of bulletproof floor to ceiling triple pane glass. Unnerving at first, no privacy.

There was a self-imposed class structure between the "bugs", those who worked in the subterranean chambers and the "air-heads" who worked where the daylight shone. There was near total separation between the two groups out of necessity; maintain isolation between those with differing need-to-know criteria. The most visible form of self-imposed isolation, and unintended competitiveness was that each camp spent Happy Hour at different bars. A line that was rarely crossed.

Unlike the mechanism of the Corporate Ladder, where the higher floors are reserved for upper, top, elite management, the power brokers, at the FBI the farther down into the ground you worked, the more important you were. To the "airheads", "bugs" tried to see how low they could sink in their acquisition of power while rising up on the Government pay scale.

On level 5, descending from street level 1, Tyrone sat on the edge of his large Government issue executive desk to answer his ringing phone. It was Washington, Bob Burnsen, his Washington based superior and family friend for years.

"No, really. Thanks," Ty smiled. "Bob, we've been through this before. It's all very flattering, but no. I'm afraid not. And you know why. We've been through this all . . ." He was being cut off by his boss, so he shut up and listened.

"Bob . . .Bob . . .Bob," Tyrone was laughing as he tried to interrupt the other end of the conversation. "OK, I'll give it some more thought, but don't get your hopes up. It's just not in my cards." He listened again.

"Bob, I'll speak to Arlene again, but she feels the same way I do. We're both quite content and frankly, I don't need the headaches." He looked around the room as he cocked the earpiece away from his head. He was hearing the same argument again.

"Bob, I said I would. I'll call you next week." He paused. "Right. If you don't hear from me, you'll call me. I understand. Right. O.K., Bob. All right, you too. Goodbye."

He hung up the phone in disbelief. They just won't leave me alone. Let me be! He clasped his hands in mock prayer at the ceiling.

* * * * *

Tyrone Duncan joined the FBI in 1968, immediately after graduating cum laude from Harvard Law. Statistically the odds were against him ever being accepted into the elite National Police Force. The virtually autonomous empire that J. Edgar Hoover had created over 60 years and 12 presidents ago was very selective about whom it admitted. Tyrone Duncan was black.

His distinguished pre-law training had him prepared to follow into his father's footsteps, as a partner with one of Boston's most prestigious law firms. Tyrone was a member of one of the very few rich and influential black families in the North East. His family was labeled "Liberal" when one wasn't ashamed of the moniker.

Then came Selma. At 19, he participated in several of the marches in the South and it was then that he first hand saw prejudice. But it was more than prejudice. It was hate, it was ignorance and fear. It was so much more than prejudice. It was one of the last vestiges left over from a society conquered over a century ago; one that wouldn't let go of its misguided myopic traditions.

Fear and hate are contagious. Fueled by the oppressive heat and humidity, decades of racial conflict, several 'Jew Boy Nigger Lovers' were killed that summer in Alabama. The murder of the civil rights workers made front page news. The country was outraged, at the murders most assuredly, but national outrage turned quickly to divisional disgust when local residents dismissed the crime as a prank, or even congratulated the perpetrators for their actions.

The FBI was not called in to Alabama to solve murders, per se; murder is not a federal crime. They were to solve the crime because the murderers had violated the victim's civil rights. Tyrone thought that that approach was real slick, a nice legal side step to get what you want. Put the lawyers on the case. When he asked the FBI if they could use a hand, the local overworked, understaffed agents graciously accepted his offer and Tyrone spent the remainder of the summer filing papers and performing other mundane tasks while learning a great deal.

On the plane back to Boston, Tyrone Duncan decided that his despite his father's urging, after law school he would join the FBI.

Tyrone Duncan, graduate cum laude, GPA 3.87, Harvard Law School, passed the Massachussettes Bar on the first try and sailed through the written and physical tests for FBI admission. He was over 100 pounds lighter than his current weight. His background check was unassailable except for his family's prominent liberal bent. He had every basic qualification needed to become an FBI Agent. He was turned down.

Thurman Duncan, his prominent lawyer father was beside himself, blaming it on Hoover personally. But Tyrone decided to 'investigate' and determine who or what was pulling the strings. He called FBI personnel and asked why he had been rejected. They mumbled something about 'experience base' and 'fitting the mold'. That was when he realized that he was turned down solely because he was black. Tyrone was not about to let a racial issue stand in his way.

He located a couple of the agents with whom he had worked during the last summer. After the pleasantries, Tyrone told them that he was applying for a position as an assistant DA in Boston. Would they mind writing a letter . . .

Tyrone Duncan was right on time at the office of the FBI Personnel Director. Amazing, Tyrone thought, the resemblance to Hoover. The four letters of recommendation, which read more like votes for sainthood were a little overdone, but, they were on FBI stationary. Tyrone asked the Personnel Director if they would reconsider his application, and that if necessary, he would whitewash his skin.

The following day Tyrone received a call. Oh, it was a big mix-up. We misfiled someone else's charts in your files and, well, you understand, I'm sure. It happens all the time. We're sorry for any inconvenience. Would you be available to come in on Monday? Welcome to the FBI.

Tyrone paid his dues early. Got shot at some, chased long haired left wing hippie radicals who blew up gas stations in 17 states for some unfathomable reason, and then of course, he collected dirt on imaginary enemies to feed the Hoover-Nixon paranoia. He tried, fairly successfully to stay away from that last kind of work. In Tyrone's not so humble opinion, there were a whole lot more better things for FBI agents to be doing than worry about George McGovern's toilet habits or if some left wing high school kids and their radical newspaper were imaginarily linked to the Kremlin. Ah, but that was politics.

Three weeks after J. Edgar Hoover died, Tyrone Duncan was promoted to Section Chief in the New York City office. A prestigious position. This was his first promotion in 8 years at the bureau. It was one that leaped over 4 intermediate levels. The Hoover era was gone.

After hanging up the phone with Bob Bernsen, Tyrone sat behind his desk going over his morning reports. No planes hijacked, no new counterfeiting rings and nary a kidnapping. What dogged him. though, was the flurry of blackmail and extortion claims. He re- read the digested version put out by the Washington headquarters that was faxed to him in the early hours, ready for his AM perusal.

The apparent facts confounded his years of experience. Over 100 people, many of them highly placed leaders of American industry had called their respective regional FBI offices for help. A call into the FBI is handled in a procedural manner. The agent who takes the call can identify the source of the call with a readout on his special phone. A service that the FBI had for years but was only recently becoming available to the public. Thus, if the caller had significant information, but refused to identify himself, the agent had a reliable method to track him down. Very few people who called the FBI realized that a phone inquiry to an FBI office triggered a sequence of automatic events that was complete before the call was over.

The phone call was of course monitored and taped. And the phone number of the caller was logged in the computer and displayed to the agent. Then the number was crosschecked against files from the phone company. What was the exact location of the caller? To whom was the phone registered? A calling and billing history was made instantly available if required.

If the call originated from a phone registered to an individual, his social security number was retrieved and within seconds of the receipt of the call, the agent knew a plethora of information about the caller. Criminal activities, bad credit records; the type of data that would permit the agent to scale the validity of the call. For business phones, a cross check determined any and all dubious dealings that might be valuable in a determination.

Thus, the profile that emerged from the vast number of callers who intimated blackmail activities created a ponderous situation. They all, to a call, originated from the office or home of major corporate movers and shakers. Top American businessmen who, while not beyond the reach of the law, were from the FBI's view, upstanding citizens. Not pristine, but certainly not mad men with a record of making outlandish capricious claims. It was not in their interest to bring attention to themselves.

What puzzled Tyrone, and Washington, was the sudden influx of such calls. Normally the Bureau handles a handful of diversified cases of blackmail, and a very small percentage of those pan out into legitimate and solvable cases. Generally, veiled vague threats do not materialize into prosecutable cases. Tyrone Duncan sat back thoughtfully.

What is the common element here? Why today, and not a year ago or on April Fools Day? Do these guys all play golf together? Is it a joke? Not likely, but a remote possibility. What enemies have they made? Undoubtedly they haven't befriended everyone with whom they have had contact, but what's the connection? Tyrone's mind reeled through a maze of unlikelihoods. Until, the only common element he could think of stared at him right in the face. There was a single dimension of commonality between all of the callers. They had, to a company, to a man, all dealt with the same organization for years. The U.S. Government.

The thought alone caused a spasm to his system. His body literally leapt from his chair for a split second as he caught his breath. The government. Shit. No way. Is it possible? I must be missing something, surely. This is crazy. Or is it? Doesn't the IRS have records on everyone? Then the ultimate paranoid thought hit him square in the cerebellum. He playfully pounded his forehead for missing the connection.

Somewhere, deep in the demented mind of some middle management G-9 bureaucrat, Duncan thought, an idea germinated that he could sell to another overworked, underpaid civil servant; his boss. The G-9 says, 'I got a way to make sure the tax evaders pay their share, and it won't cost Uncle Sam a dime!'. His boss says, 'I got a congressional hearing today, I'm too busy. Do some research and let me see a report.'

So this overzealous tax collector prowls around other government computers and determines that the companies on his hit list aren't necessarily functioning on the up and up. What better way to get them to pay their taxes than to let them know that we, the big We, Big Brother know, and they'd better shape up.

He calls a few of them, after all he knows where the skeletons and the phone numbers are buried, and says something like, 'Big Brother is listening and he doesn't like what he hears.' And he says, 'we'll call you back soon, real soon, so get your ducks in a row' and that scares the shit out of the corporate muckity-mucks.

Tyrone smiled to himself. What an outlandish theory. Absurd, he admitted, but it was the only one he could say fit the facts. Still, is it possible? The government was certainly capable of some pretty bizarre things. He recalled the Phoenix program in Viet Nam where suspected Viet Cong or innocent civilians were tossed out of helicopters at 2000 feet to their deaths in the distorted hope of making another one talk.

Wasn't Daniel Ellsburg a government target? And the Democrats were in 1972 targets of CREEP, the Committee to Re-Elect the President. And the Aquarius project used psychics to locate Soviet Boomers and UFO's. Didn't we give LSD to unsuspecting soldiers to see if they could function adequately under the influence? The horror stories swirled through his mind. And they became more and more unbelievable, yet they were all true. Maybe it was possible. The United States government had actually instituted a program of anonymous blackmail in order to increase tax revenues. Christ, I hope I'm wrong. But, I'm probably not.

The buzzer on the intercom of his phone jarred Tyrone from his daydream speculations.

"Yes?" He answered into space.

"Mr. Duncan, a Franklin Dobbs is here for his 10 o'clock appointment. Saunderson is out and so you're elected." Duncan's secretary was too damned efficient, he thought. Why not give it to someone else. He pushed his intercom button.

"Gimme a second, I gotta primp." That was Tyrone's code that he needed a few minutes to graduate from speculative forensics and return to Earth to deal with real life problems. As usual, Gloria obliged him. In exactly 3 minutes, his door opened.

"Mr. Duncan, this is Franklin Dobbs, Chairman and CEO of National Pulp. Mr. Dobbs, Mr. Duncan, regional director." She waited for the two men to acknowledge each other before she shut the door behind her.

"Mr. Duncan?" Dobbs held his hand out to the huge FBI agent. Duncan accepted and pointed at a vacant chair. Dobbs sat obediently.

"How can I help you, Mr. Dobbs?"

"I am being blackmailed, and I need help." Dobbs looked straight into Duncan's coal black eyes.

The IRS, thought Duncan. "By whom?" he asked casually.

"I don't know." Dobbs was firm.

"Then how do you know you are being blackmailed?" Duncan wanted to conceal his interest. Keep it low profile.

"Let me tell you what happened."

Good start, thought Duncan. If only half of us would start in such a logical place.

"Two days ago I received a package by messenger. It contained the most sensitive information my company has. Strategic positions, contingency plans, competitive information and so on. There are only a half dozen people in my company that have access to that kind of information. And they all own enough stock to make sure that they aren't the culprits."

"So who is?" interjected Tyrone as he made notes.

"I don't know. That's the problem."

"What did they ask for?" Duncan looked directly into Dobbs' eyes. To both force an answer and look for signs of deceit. All he saw was honesty and real fear.

"Nothing. Nothing at all. All I got was the package and a brief message."

"What was the message?" Tyrone asked.

"We'll be in touch. That's it."

"So where's the threat? This hardly seems like a case for the FBI." Tyrone was baiting the hook. See if the fish is real.

"None, not yet. But that's not the point. What they sent me were copies, yet they looked more like the originals, of information that would negatively affect my company. It's the sort of information that we would not want made public. If you know what I mean."

"I know what you mean," he agreed.

"I need to stop it. Before it's too late?"

"Too late?" asked Duncan.

"Too late. Before it gets out."

"What gets out, Mr. Dobbs?" Duncan stared right into and beyond Dobbs' eyes.

"Secrets. Just secrets." Dobbs paused to recompose himself. "Isn't there a law . . .?"

"Yes, there is Mr. Dobbs. And if what you say is true, you are entitled to protection." Duncan decided to bait Dobbs a bit more. "Even if the information is illegal in nature."

"I grant you I'm no Mother Teresa. I'm a businessman, and I have to make money for my investors. But in the files that I received were exact copies of my personal files that no one, and I mean no one has access to. They were my own notes, ideas in progress. Nothing concrete, just work in progress. But someone, somehow has gotten a hold of it all. And, by my thinking, there's no way to have gotten it without first killing me, and I'm here. So how did they get it? That's what I need to know." Dobbs paused. "And then, I need to stop them." His soliloquy was over.

"Who else is affected?" Duncan asked. Dobbs' pause made the answer perfectly clear. Dobbs wasn't alone.

"I only speak for myself. No one else." Dobbs rose from the chair. "It's eminently clear. There's not a damned thing you can do,. Good day." Dobbs left the room abruptly giving Tyrone plenty of time to think.

* * * * *

Chapter 8

Monday, September 21
New York

14 Dead As Hospital Computer Fails

by Scott Mason

Fourteen patients died as a result of massive computer failure this weekend at the Golda Meier Medical Center on 5th. Avenue.

According to hospital officials, the Meditrix Life Support Monitors attached to many of the hospital's patients were accidentally disconnected from the nurses stations and the hospital's main computer. Doctors and nurses were unaware of any malfunction because all systems appeared to be operating correctly.

The LSM's are connected to a hospital wide computer network that connects all hospital functions in a central computer. Medical records, insurance filings and treatments as well as personnel and operations are coordinated through the Information Systems department.

Golda Meier Medical Center leads the medical field in the used of technologically advanced techniques, and has been applying an artificial intelligence based Expert System to assist in diagnosis and treatment. Much of the day to day treatment of patients is done with the LSM continually measuring the condition of the patient, and automatically updating his records. The Expert System then determines what type of treatment to recommend. Unless there is a change in the patient's condition that warrants the intervention of a doctor, drugs and medicines are prescribed by the computer.

According to computer experts who were called in to investigate, the Expert System began misprescribing medications and treatments early Saturday morning. Doctors estimate that over 50%, about 300, of the hospital's patients received incorrect treatment. Of those, 14 died and another 28 are in critical condition.

Until this weekend, the systems were considered foolproof. The entire computer system of Golda Meier Medical Center has been disconnected until a more intensive investigation is completed.

In response to the news, the Jewish Defense League is calling the incident, "an unconscionable attack against civilized behavior and the Jewish community in particular." They have called for a full investigation into the episode and have asked the Mossad, Israel's crack intelligence agency for assistance.

No group or individuals have yet taken credit for the crime. The AMA has petitioned the Drug and Food Administration to look into the matter.

Gerald Steinmetz, chief counsel for the Center, said in interviews that he had already been contacted by attorney's representing the families of some of the victims of this tragedy. He anticipates extended legal entanglements until such time that the true cause can be determined and blame can accurately be assigned. The hospital denies any wrong doing on its or its staff's part.

This is Scott Mason, determined to stay healthy.

* * * * *

December, 4 Years Ago
Tokyo, Japan

Miles Foster arrived at Narita Airport as another typhoon shattered the coast of Japan. It was the roughest plane ride he had ever taken; and after 2 weeks of pure bliss. Boy, that Homosoto sure knows how to show a guy a good time.

After their first meeting at the OSO World Bank Building, Miles had flown to Tahiti and spent 18 delightful days on the outer resort of Moorea, courtesy of OSO Industries, with all of the trimmings. He was provided with a private beach house containing every modern amenity one could want. Including two housekeepers and a cook. Only one of the housekeepers knew how to keep house. The other knew how to keep Miles satisfied.

Marasee was a Pacific Islander who was well schooled in advanced sexual techniques. At barely 5 feet tall and 96 pounds, her long silken black hair was as much a sexual tool as her hands and mouth. Her pristine dark complexion and round face caused Miles to think that he was potentially guilty of crimes against a minor, but after their first night together, he relented that Marasee knew her business very well.

"Mr. Homosoto-San," she purred in delicately accented English, "wants you to concentrate on your work." She caressed his shoulders and upper body as she spoke. "He knows that a man works best when he has no worries. It is my job to make sure that you are relaxed. Completely relaxed. Do you understand?"

Her eyes longed for an affirmative answer from Miles. At first he was somewhat baffled. Homosoto had indeed sent him on this trip, vacation, to work, undisturbed. But Miles thought that he would have to fend for himself for his physical pleasures. He was used to finding ways to satisfy his needs.

"Homosoto-San says that you must be relaxed to do very serious business. Whenever you need relaxation, I am here."

The food was as exquisite as was Marasee. He luxuriated in the eternally perfect weather, the beach, the waves and he even ventured under water on a novice scuba dive. But, as he knew, he was here to concentrate on his assigned task, so he tried to limit this personal activities to sharing pleasure with Marasee.

In just a few days, a relaxed Miles felt a peace, a solace that he had never known before. He found that his mind was at a creative high. His mind propelled through the problems of the war plans, and the solutions appeared. His brain seemed to function independent of effort. As he established goals, the roads to meet them appeared magically before him, in absolute clarity. He was free to explore each one in its entirety, from beginning to end, undisturbed.

If a problem confounded him, he found that merely forgetting about it during an interlude with Marasee provided him with the answer. The barriers were broken, the so-called 'walls of defense' crumbled before as he created new methods of penetration no one had ever thought of before.

As his plan coalesced into a singular whole, he began to experience a euphoria, a high that was neither drug nor sexually induced. He could envision, all at once, the entire grand strategy; how the myriad pieces effortlessly fit together and evolved into a picture perfect puzzle. Miles became able to manipulate the attack scenarios in his mind and make slight changes in one that would have far reaching implications in another portion of the puzzle. He might change only one slight aspect, yet see synergistic ramifications down a side road. This new ability, gained from total freedom to concentrate and his newfound worry free life, gave Miles new sources of pleasure and inspiration.

As his plans came together, Miles yearned for something outside of his idyllic environment. His strategies grew into a concrete reality, one which he knew he could execute, if Homosoto wasn't feeding him a line of shit. And, for the $100,000 Homosoto gave him to make plans. he was generally inclined to believe that this super rich, slightly eccentric but obviously dangerous man was deadly serious.

As the days wore on, Miles realized that, more than anything in his life, even more than getting laid, he wanted to put his plan to the test. If he was right, of which he was sure, in a few short years he would be recognized as the most brilliant computer scientist in the world. In the whole damn world.

His inner peace, the one which fed his creativity, soon was overtaken by the unbridled ego which was Miles Foster's inner self. The prospect of success fostered new energies and Miles worked even harder to complete the first phase of his task. To the occasional disappointment of Marasee, Miles would embroil himself in the computer Homosoto provided for the purpose. Marasee had been with many men, she was an expert, but Miles gave her as much pleasure as she to him. As his work further absorbed him, she rued the day her assignment would be over.

Miles left Tahiti for Tokyo without even saying goodbye to Marasee.

The ritualistic scanning and security checks before Miles got onto the living room elevator at the OSO Building in Tokyo evidenced that Homosoto had not told anyone else how important Miles was. Even though he recognized the need for secrecy in their endeavors, Miles was irked by the patronizing, almost rude treatment he received when he was forced to pass the Sumo scrutiny.

The elevator again opened into the grand white gallery on the 66th floor.

"Ah . . .so good to see you again Mr. Foster. Homosoto-San is anxious to see you." A short Japanese manservant escorted Miles to the doors of Homosoto's office. The briefest of taps invited the bellow of "Hai!" from its inner sanctum.

Homosoto was quick to rise from his pedestaled throne and greeted Miles as if they were long lost friends.

"Mr. Foster . . .it is so good to see you. I assume everything was satisfactory? You found the working conditions to your liking?" Homosoto awkwardly searched for the vain compliment. He pointed at the leather seating area in which they had first discussed their plans. They sat in the same chairs they had last time they met.

Miles was taken aback by the warm reception, but since he was so important to Homosoto, it was only fitting to be treated with respect.

Miles returned the courtesy with the minimum required bow of the head. It was a profitable game worth playing. "Very much so, Mr. Homosoto. It was most relaxing . . .and I think you will be very pleased with the results." Miles smiled warmly, expecting to be heavily complimented on his promise. Instead, Homosoto ignored the business issue.

"I understand that Miss Marasee was most pleased . . .was she not?" The implication was clear. For the first time, Miles saw a glimmer of a dirty old man looking for the sordid details.

"I guess so. I was too busy working to pay attention." Miles tried to sluff off the comment.

"That is what she says. That you were too busy for her . . .or to say goodbye and thank her for her attentions. Not an auspicious beginning Mr. Foster." Miles caught the derision in Homosoto's voice and didn't appreciate it one little bit.

"Listen. My affairs are my affairs. I am grateful for the services . . .but I do like to keep my personal life just that. Personal." Miles was polite, but firm. Homosoto nodded in understanding.

"Of course, Mr. Foster, I understand completely. It is merely for the sake of the young woman that I mention it. There is no offense intended. It is shall we say . . .a cultural difference?"

Miles didn't believe in the cultural difference to which he referred, but he didn't press the point. He merely nodded that the subject was closed. A pregnant pause followed before Homosoto interrupted the silence.

"So, Mr. Foster. I really did not expect to see you for another few weeks. I must assume that you have made some progress in planning our future endeavors." Homosoto wore a smile that belied little of his true thoughts.

"You bet your ass, I did." Homosoto winced at the colorful language. It was Miles' way of maintaining some control over the situation. His dimples recessed even further as he enjoyed watching Homosoto's reaction. "It turned out to be simpler than even I had thought."

"Would you be so kind as to elaborate?"

"Gotcha." Miles opened his briefcase and brought out a sheath of papers with charts and scribbles all over them. "Basically the technology is pretty simple. Here are the fundamental systems to use in the attack, there are only four of them. After all, there are no defenses, so that's not a problem."

"Problem?" Homosoto raised his eyes.

"Perhaps not problem. As you can see here, putting the technical pieces together is not the issue. The real issue is creating an effective deployment of the tools we create." Miles was matter of fact and for the first time Homosoto saw Miles as the itinerant professional he was capable of being. The challenge. Just as Miles promised earlier, 'give me a challenge, the new, the undone and I will be the best.' Miles was shining in his own excellence, and his ego was gone, totally gone. His expertise took over.

"I have labeled various groups that we will need to pull this off."

"Pull off? Excuse me . . ."

"Oh, sorry. Make it work? Have it happen?"

"Ah yes, So sorry."

"Not at all." Miles looked at Homosoto carefully. Was there a mutual respect actually developing?

"As I said, we will have to have several groups who don't even know about each other's existence. At NSA we call it containment, or need to know."

Homosoto cursorily examined the printouts on the table in front of him, but preferred to address Miles' comments. "Could you explain, please? I don't see how one can build a car if you don't know what it's going to look like when you're done. You suggest that each person or group functions without the knowledge of the others? How can this be efficient?"

Miles smiled. For the first time he felt a bit of compassion for Homosoto, as one would feel for the naive child asking why 1 plus 1 equals 2. Homosoto was used to the Japanese work ethic: Here's a beautiful picture of a car, and all 50,000 of us are going to build it; you 5,000 build the engines, you 5,000 build the body and so on. After a couple of years we'll have built a fabulous automobile that we have all shared as a common vision.

Homosoto had no idea of how to wage a war, although he apparently could afford it. Miles realize he could be in control after all, if he only sold Homosoto on his abilities, and he was well on the way.

"You see, Mr. Homosoto, what we are trying to do requires that no one, except a few key people like you and I, understand what is going on. As we said in World War II, loose lips sink ships." Homosoto immediately bristled at the mention of the war. Miles hardly noticed as he continued. "The point is, as I have it laid out here, only a handful of people need to know what we are trying to achieve. All of the rest have clearly defined duties that they are expected to perform as we ask. Each effectively works in a vacuum. Efficient not exactly. Secure, yes. I imagine you would like to keep this operation as secret as possible."

Homosoto took immediate notice and bolted his response. "Hai! Of course, secrecy is important, but how can we be sure of compliance by our . . .associates?"

"Let me continue." Miles referred back to the papers in front of him. "The first group is called the readers, the second will be dedicated to research and development." Homosoto smiled at the R&D reference. He could understand that. "Then there will be a public relations group and a communications group. A software company will be needed, there's another group I call the Mosquitoes and a little manufacturing which I assume you can handle." Miles looked for Homosoto's reaction.

"Manufacturing, very easy. I don't fully understand the others, but I am most impressed with your outline. You mentioned problem. Can you explain?" Homosoto had become a different person. One who showed adolescent enthusiasm. He moved to the edge of his seat.

"As with any well designed plan," Miles boasted, "there are certain situations that need to be addressed. In this case, I see several." Miles was trying to hook Homosoto onto the proverbial deck.

"I asked for problem." Homosoto insisted.

"To properly effect this plan we will need two things that may make it impossible."

Homosoto met the challenge. "What do you need?"

Miles liked the sound of it. You. What do *you* need. "This operation could cost as much as $50 million. Is that a problem?"

Homosoto looked squarely at Miles. "No problem. What is the second thing you need?"

"We will need an army. Not an army with guns, but a lot of people who will follow orders. That may be more important than the money."

Homosoto took a momentary repose while he thought. "How big an army will you need?"

"My guess? Today? I would say that for all groups we will need a minimum of 500 people. Maybe as many as a thousand."

Homosoto suddenly laughed out loud. "You call that an army? 1000 men? An army? That is a picnic my friend." Homosoto was enjoying his own personal joke. "When you said army, Mr. Foster I imagined tens of thousands of people running all around the United States shooting their guns. A thousand people? I can give you a thousand dedicated people with a single phone call. Is that all you need?" He continued his laughter.

Miles was taken aback and had difficulty hiding his surprise. He had already padded his needs by a factor of three. "With a few minor specialties and exceptions, yes. That's it. If we follow this blue print." He pointed at the papers spread before them.

Homosoto sat back and closed his eyes is apparent meditation. Miles watched and waited for several minutes. He looked out the expanse of windows over Tokyo patiently as Homosoto seemed to sleep in the chair across from him. Homosoto spoke quietly with his eyes still closed.

"Mr. Foster?"

"Yes?" Miles was ready.

"Do you love your country?" Homosoto's eyelids were still.

Miles had not expected such a question.

"Mr. Foster? Did you hear the question?"

"Yes, I did." He paused. "I'm thinking."

"If you need to think, sir, then the answer is clear. As you have told me, you hold no allegiance. Your country means nothing to you."

"I wouldn't quite put it that way . . ." Miles said defensively. He couldn't let this opportunity escape.

"You hold your personal comfort as your primary concern, do you not? You want the luxuries that the United States offers, but you don't care where or how you get them? Is that not so? You want your women, your wine, your freedom, but you will take it at any expense. I do not think I exaggerate. Tell me Mr. Foster, if I am wrong."

Miles realized he was being asked to state his personal allegiances in mere seconds. Not since he was in the lower floors of the NSA being interrogated had he been asked to state his convictions. He knew the right answer there, but here, he wasn't quite sure. The wrong answer could blow it. But, then again, he was $110,000 ahead of the game for a few weeks work.

"I need to ask you a question to answer yours." Miles did not want to be backed into a corner. "Mr. Homosoto. Do you want me to have allegiance to my country or to you?"

Homosoto was pleased. "You debate well, young man. It is not so much that I care if you love America. I want, I need to know what you do love. You see, for me, I love Japan and my family. But much of my family was taken from me in one terrible instant, a long time ago. They are gone, but now I have my wife, my children and their children. I learned, that if there is nothing else, you must have family. That must come first, Mr. Foster. Under all conditions, family is first. All else is last. So my allegiance shifted, away from country, to my family and my beliefs. I don't always agree with my government, and there are times I will defy their will. I can assure you, that if we embark upon this route, neither I nor you will endear ourselves to our respective governments. Does that matter to you?"

Miles snickered. "Matter? After what they did to me? Let me tell you something. I gave my country most of my adult life. I could have gone to work with my family . . .my associates . . ."

"I am aware of your background Mr. Foster," Homosoto interrupted.

"I'm sure you are. But that's neither here nor there. I could have been on easy street. Plug a few numbers and make some bucks for the clan." The colloquialism escaped Homosoto, but he got the gist of it. "But I said to myself, 'hey, you're good. Fixing roulette wheels is beneath you.' I needed, I still need the diversion, the challenge, so I figured that the Feds would give me the edge I needed to make something of myself." Miles was turning red around his neck.

"The NSA had the gear, the toys for me to play with, and they promised me the world. Create, they said, lead America's technology into the 21st. century. What a pile of shit. Working at the NSA is like running for President. You're always trying to sell yourself, your ideas. They don't give a shit about how good your ideas are. All they care is that you're asshole buddies with the powers that be. To get something done there, you need a half dozen committees with their asses greased from here to eternity for them to say maybe. Do you know the difference between ass kissing and having your head up your ass?"

"If I understand your crudities, I assume this is an American joke, then, no Mr. Foster, I do not know the difference."

"Depth perception." Miles looked for a reaction to his anatomical doublette. There was none other than Homosoto's benign smile indicating no comprehension. "O.K., never mind, I'll save it. At any rate, enough was enough. I gotta do something with my life." Miles had said his piece.

"In other words, money is your motivation?"

"Money doesn't hurt, sure. But, I need to do what I believe. Not that that means hurting my country, but if they don't listen to what makes sense, maybe it's best that they meet their worst enemy to get them off of their keesters." Miles was on a roll.

"Keesters?" Homosoto's naivete was amusing.

"Oops!" Miles exclaimed comically. "Butts, asses, fannies?" He patted his own which finally communicated the intention.

"Ah yes." Homosoto agreed. "So you feel you could best serve your country by attacking it?"

Miles only thought for a few seconds. "I guess you could put it that way. Sure."

"Mr. Foster, or should I say General Foster?" Miles beamed at the reference. "We shall march to success."

"Mr. Homosoto," Miles broke the pagential silence. "I would like to ask you the same question. Why?"

"I was wondering when you were going to ask me that Mr. Foster," Homosoto said with his grin intact. "Because, Mr. Foster, I am returning the favor."

* * * * *

Chapter 9

September, 1982
South East Iraq

Ahmed Shah lay in a pool of his own blood along with pieces of what was once another human being.

The pain was intolerable. His mind exploded as the nerve endings from the remains of his arms and legs shot liquid fire into his cerebral cortex. His mind screamed in sheer agony while he struggled to stay conscious. He wasn't sure why, but he had to stay awake . . .*can't pass out . . .sleep, blessed sleep . . .release me from the pain . . .Allah! Oh take me Allah . . .I shall be a martyr fighting for your holy cause . . .in your name . . . for the love of Islam . . .for the Ayatollah . . .take me into your arms and let me live for eternity in your shadow . . .*

The battle for Abadan, a disputed piece of territory that was a hub for Persian Gulf oil distribution had lasted days. Both Iran and Iraq threw waves of human fodder at each other in what was referred to in the world press as " . . .auto-genocide . . ." Neither side reacted to the monumental casualties that they sustained. The lines of reinforcements were steady. The dead bodies were thick on the battlefield; there was no time to collect them and provide a proper burial. New troops had as much difficulty wading through the obstacle courses made up of human corpses as staying alive.

Public estimates were that the war had already cost over 1,000,000 lives for the adversaries. Both governments disputed the figures. The two agreed only 250,000 had died. The extremist leaders of both countries believed that the lower casualty numbers would mollify world opinion. It accomplished the exact opposite. Criticism was rampant, in the world courts and the press. Children were going to battle. Or more appropriately, children were marching in the front lines, often without weapons or shoes, and used as cover for the advancing armed infantrymen behind them. The children were disposable receptacles for enemy bullets. The supreme sacrifice would permit the dead pre-adolescents the honor of martyrdom and an eternal place with Allah.

Mothers wailed and beat their breasts in the streets of Teheran as word arrived of loved ones and friends who died in Allah's war against the Iraqi infidels. Many were professional mourners who were hired by others to represent families to make them look bigger and more Holy. Expert wailing and flagellation came at a price. The bulk of the civilized world, even Brezhnev's evil Soviet empire denounced the use of unarmed children for cannon fodder.

The war between Iran and Iraq was to continue, despite pleas from humanity, for another 6 years.

Ahmed Shah was a 19 year old engineering student at the exclusive Teheran University when the War started. He was reared as a dedicated Muslim by wealthy parents. Somehow his parents had escaped the Ayatollah's scourge after the fall of the Shah. Ahmed was never told the real reason, but a distribution of holy *rials* certainly helped. They were able to keep a beautiful home in the suburbs of Teheran and Ahmed's father kept his professorship at Teheran University. Ahmed was taught by his family that the Shah's downfall was the only acceptable response to the loss of faith under his regime.

"The Shah is a puppet of the Americans. Ptooh!" His father would spit. "The Yanqis come over here, tell us to change our culture and our beliefs so we can make them money from our oil!" For a professor he was outspoken, but viewed as mainstream by the extremist camps. Ahmed learned well. For the most part of his life all Ahmed knew was the Ayatollah Khomeini as his country's spiritual leader. News and opinion from the West was virtually non-existent so Ahmed developed as a devout Muslim, dedicated to his country and his religion.

When the War began he thought about enlisting immediately, but the University counselors convinced him otherwise.

"Ahmed Shah, you are bright and can offer Iran great gifts after you complete your studies. Why not wait, the War will not be forever, and then you can serve Allah with your mind, not your body."

Ahmed took the advice for his first year as a university student, but guilt overwhelmed him when he learned about how many other young people were dying in the cause. From his parents he would hear of childhood friends who had been killed. Teheran University students and graduates were honored daily in the Mosque on campus. The names were copied and distributed throughout the schools. True martyrs. Ahmed's guilt compounded as the months passed and so many died. He had been too young to participate in the occupation of the American Embassy. How jealous he was.

Why should I wait to serve Allah? He mused. Today I can be of service, where he needs me, but if I stay and study, I will not be able to bid his Will for years. And what if Iraq wins? There would be no more studies anyway. Ahmed anguished for weeks over how he could best serve Iran, his Ayatollah and Allah.

After his freshman finals, on which he excelled, he joined the Irani Army. Within 60 days he was sent to the front lines as a communications officer.

They had been in the field 3 days, and Ahmed had only gotten to know a few of the 60 men in his company when the mortars came in right on top of them. The open desert offers little camouflage so the soldiers built fox holes behind the larger sand dunes. They innaccurately thought they were hidden from view. More than half the company died instantly. Pieces of bodies were strewn across the sandy tented bivouac.

Another 20 were dying within 50 yards of where Ahmed writhed in agony. Ahmed regained consciousness. Was it 5 minutes or 5 hours later. He had no way of knowing. The left lower arm where he wore his wristwatch was gone. A pulpy stump. As were his legs. Mutilated . . .the highest form of insult and degradation. *Oh, Allah, I have served you, let me die and come to you now. Let me suffer no more.*

Suddenly his attention was grabbed by the sound of a jeep coughing its way to a stop. He heard voices.

"This one's still alive." Then a shot rang out. "So's this one." Another shot. A few muted voices from the dying protested and asked for mercy. "Ha! I give Mercy to a dog before you." A scream and 2 shots. They were Iraqi! Killing off the wounded. *Pigs! Infidels! Mother Whores!*

"You, foreskin of a camel! Your mother lies with dogs!" Ahmed screamed at the soldiers, which had two results. One, it kept him a little more alert and less aware of his pain, and two, it attracted the attention of the two soldiers from the jeep.

"Ola! Who insults the memory of my mother who sits with Allah? Who?" One soldier spun around and tried to imagine which one of the pieces of bodies that surrounded him still had enough life to speak. He scanned the sand nearby. Open eyes were not a sure sign of life nor was the presence of four limbs. There needed to be a head.

"Over here camel dung. Hussein fucks animals who give birth to the likes of you." Ahmed's viciousness was the only facial feature that gave away he was alive. The soldiers saw their tormentor.

"Prepare to meet with your Allah, now," as one soldier took aim at Ahmed's head.

"Go ahead! Shoot, pig shit. I welcome death so I won't have to see your filth . . ." Ahmed defied the soldier and the automatic rifle aimed at him.

The other soldier intervened. "No, don't kill him. That's too easy and we would be honoring his last earthly request. No, this one doesn't beg for mercy. At least he's a man. Let's just make him suffer." The second soldier raised his gun and pointed at the junction of Ahmed's two stumps for legs. Two point blank range shots shattered the three components of his genitals. Ahmed let out a scream so primal, so anguished, so penetrating that the soldiers bolted to escape the sounds of death. The scream continued, briefly interrupted by a pair of shots that caught the two soldiers square in the middle of the back as they ran. They dropped onto the hot desert sand with matched thuds.

Ahmed didn't hear the shots over the sounds coming from his larynx. He didn't hear anything after that for a very long time.

Unfortunately for Ahmed Shah, he survived.

He woke up, or more accurately, regained semi-consciousness more than a week after he was picked up at the site of the mortar attack. He was wired up to tubes and machines in an obviously well equipped hospital. He thought, *I must be back in Teheran . . .then fog . . .a blur . . .a needle . . .feel nothing . . .stay awake . . .move lips . . .talk . . .*

"Doctor, the patient was awake." The nurse spoke to the physician who was writing on Ahmed's medical chart.

"He'll wish he wasn't. Let him go. Let him sleep. Hell hasn't begun for him yet." The Doctor moved onto the chart on the next bed in the busy ward.

Over the next few days while grasping at consciousness, and with the caring attention of the nurses, Ahmed pieced together the strands of a story . . .what happened to him.

The Iraqis were killing the wounded, desperate in their attempts to survive the onslaught of Irani children. All must die, take no prisoners were their marching orders. In the Iraqi Army you either did exactly as you were told, with absolute obedience, or you were shot on sight as a traitor. Some choice. We lost at Abadan, the Iraqi's thought, but there will be more battles to win.

Ahmed was the only survivor from his company, and there was no earthly reason that could explain why he lived. He was more dead than alive. His blood coagulated well in the hot desert sun, otherwise the blood loss alone would have killed him. The medics found many of his missing pieces and packed them up for their trip to the hospital, but the doctors were unable to re-attach anything of significance.

He was a eunuch. With no legs and only one good arm.

Weeks of wishing himself dead proved to be the source of rest that contributed to his recovery. Was he man? Was he woman? Was he, God forbid, neither? Why had he not just died along with the others, why was he spared! Spared, ha! *If I had truly been spared I would be living with Allah! This is not being spared. This is living hell and someone will pay.* He cried to his parents about his torment and his mother wailed and beat her breast. His father listened to the anger, the hate and the growing strength within his son's being. Hate could be the answer that would make his son, his only son, whole again. Whole in spirit at least.

The debates within Ahmed's mind developed into long philosophical arguments about right, wrong, revenge, avenge, purpose, cause and reason. He would take both sides of the issue, and see if he could beat himself with his alter rationales. The frustration at knowing one's opponents' thoughts when developing your own counter argument made him angry, too. He finally started arguing with other patients. He would take any position, on any issue and debate all night. Argumentative, contrary, but recovering completely described the patient.

Over the months his strength returned and he appeared to come to grips with his infirmaries. As much as anyone can come to terms with such physical mutilations. He covered his facial wounds with a full black beard that melded into his full short cropped kinky hair.

Ahmed graduated from Teheran University in 1984 with a cruel hatred for anything Anti-Islam. One major target of his hatred was President Reagan, the cowboy president, the Teflon president, the evil Anti-Muslim Zionist loving American president. Of course there was plenty of room to hate others, but Reagan was so easy to hate, so easy to blame, and rarely was there any disagreement.

He thought of grand strategies to strike back at the U.S.. After all, didn't they support the Iraqis? And the Iraqis did this to him. It wasn't the soldiers' fault. They were just following orders: Do or Die. Any rational person would have done the same thing. He understood that. So he blamed Reagan, not Hussein. And he blamed the American people for their stupidity, their isolationism, their indifference to the rest of the world. They are all so smug and caught up in their own little petty lives, and there are causes, people are dying for causes, and the American fools don't even care. And Reagan personified them all.

How does a lousy movie actor from the 1950's get to be President of the United States? Ahmed laughed to himself at the obvious answer. He was the most qualified for the job.

His commentaries and orations about the Imperialists, the United States, England, even the Soviet Union and their overwhelming influence in the Arab world made Ahmed Shah a popular man on the campus of Teheran University. His highly visible infirmities assisted with his credibility.

In his sixth semester of study, Ahmed's counselor called him for a conference. Besides his counselor there was another man, Beni Farjani, from the government. Beni was garbed in Arab robes and turbans that always look filthy. Still, he was the officious type, formal and somber. His long white hair snuck through the turban, and his face showed ample wrinkles of wisdom.

He and the Counselor sat alone, on one side of a large wooden conference table that could easily have seated 20. Ahmed stopped his motorized wheel chair at the table, Farjani spoke, and curiously, the Counselor rose from his chair and slipped out of the room. Ahmed and the Government official were alone.

"My name is Beni Farjani, Associate Director to the Undersecretary of Communications and Propaganda. I trust you are well."

Ahmed long since gave up commenting on his well being or lack thereof. "It is good to meet you, sir." He waited for more.

"Ahmed Shah, you are important to the state and the people of Iran." Farjani said it as though his comment was already common knowledge. "What I am here to ask you, Ahmed Shah, is, are you willing again to serve Allah?"

"Yes, of course . . .?" He bowed his head in reverence.

"Good, because we, that is the members of my department think that you might be able to assist on a small project we have been contemplating. My son, you have the gift of oration, speaking, moving crowds to purpose. I only wish I had it!" Beni Farjani smiled solemnly at Ahmed.

"I thank Allah for His gift. I am only the humble conduit for his Will."

"I understand, but you have now, and will have much to be proud of. I believe you graduate in 6 months. Is that correct?"

"Yes, and then I go to Graduate School . . ."

"I am afraid that won't be possible Ahmed Shah." Farjani shook a kindly wrinkled finger at him. "As soon as you graduate, your Government, at Allah's bidding, would like you to move to the United States."

"America?" Ahmed gaped in surprise.

"We fear that America may invade Iran, that we may go to war with the United States." The words stunned Ahmed. Could he be serious? Sure, relations were in pretty bad shape, but was Farjani saying that Iran was truly preparing for War? Jihad? Holy War against the United States?

"We need to protect ourselves," Farjani spoke calmly, with authority. "America has weapons of mass destruction that can reach our land in minutes, while we have nothing to offer in retaliation. Nothing, and that is a very frightening reality that the people of Iran must live with every day. A truly helpless feeling." Ahmed was listening carefully, and so far what he heard was making a great deal of sense.

"Both the Soviets and the Americans can destroy each other and the rest of the world with a button. Their armies will never meet. A few missiles and it's all over. A 30 minute grand finale to civilization. They don't have to, nor would we expect either the Soviets or the Americans to ask the rest of the world if they mind. They just go ahead and pull the trigger and everyone else be damned.

"And yes, there have been better times when our nation has had more friends, when all Arabs thought and acted as one; especially against the Americans. They have the most to gain and the most to lose from invading and crossing our borders. They would love nothing more than to steal our land, our oil and even take over OPEC. All in the name of world stability. They'll throw around National Security smoke screens and do what they want." Farjani was speaking quite excitedly.

Ahmed was fascinated. A man from the Government who was nearly as vitriolic as he was about America. The only difference was Ahmed wanted to attack, and Farjani wanted to defend. He didn't think it opportune to interrupt. Farjani continued.

"The Russians want us as a warm water port. They have enough oil, gas and resources, but they crave a port that isn't controlled by the Americans such as in the Black Sea and through the Hellespont. So they too, are a potential enemy. You see don't you, Ahmed, that Allah has so graced our country everyone else wants to take it away from us?" Ahmed nodded automatically.

"So we need to create a defense against outside aggressors. We do not have weapons that can reach American shores, that is so. But we have something that the Americans will never have, because they will never understand. Do you know what that is?"

Before Ahmed could answer Farjani continued.

"Honor and Faith to protect our heritage, our systems, our way of life." Ahmed agreed.

"We want you, Ahmed Shah to build a network of supporters, just like you, all across the United States that will come to our service when we need them. To the death. Your skills will capture the attention of those with kindred sentiments. You will draw them out, from the schools, from the universities.

"Ahmed Shah, there are over 100,000 Irani and Arab students in the United States today. Many, many of them are sympathetic to our causes. Many of them are attending American Universities, side by side with their future enemies, learning the American way so we may better fight it. You will become one of them and you will find others that can be trusted, counted on, depended upon when we call.

"Your obvious dedication and personal tragedies," Farjani pointed at the obvious affliction, "will be the glue to provide others with strength. You will have no problems in recruiting. That will be the easy part."

"If recruiting is so easy, then what will be the hard task?"

"Holding them back. You will find it most difficult to restrain your private army from striking. Right under the American's noses, you will have to keep them from bursting at the seams until the day comes when they are needed. If could be weeks, it could be years. We don't know. Maybe the day will never come. But it is your job to build this Army. Grow it, feed it and keep our national spirit alive until such time that it becomes necessary to defend our nation, Allah and loyal Muslims everywhere. This time, though, we will fight America from within, inside her borders.

"There hasn't been a foreign war on American soil since 1812. Americans don't know what is like to have their country ruined, ravaged, blown up before their eyes. We need a defense against America, and when it is deeded by Allah, our army will strike back at America where is hurts most. In the streets of their cities. In their homes, parks and schools. But first we must have that army. In place, and willing to act.

"You will find out all the details in good time, I assure you. You will require some training, though, and that will begin shortly. Everything you need to serve will be given you. Go with Allah.

Ahmed trained for several months with the infamous terrorist group Abu Nidal. He learned the basics that every modern terrorist needs to know to insure success against the Infidels.

Shah moved to New York City on December 25, 1986. Christmas was a non issue. He registered at Columbia as a graduate researcher in the engineering department to legitimize his student visa and would commence classes on January 2.

Recruitment was easy, just as Farjani had said.

Ahmed built a team of 12 recruiters whom he could trust with his life. Seven professional terrorists, unknown to the American authorities, thoroughly sanitized, came with him to the United States under assumed visas and the other 5, already in the U.S. were personally recommended by Farjani.

His disciples settled in strategic locations; New York was host to Ahmed and another Arab fanatic trained in Libya. They both used Columbia University as their cover. Washington D.C. was honored with a Syrian terrorist who had organized mass anti-US demonstrations in Damascus as the request of President Assad. Los Angeles and San Francisco were homes to 4 more engineering type desert terrorist school graduates who were allowed to move freely and interact with the shakers and movers in high technology disciplines. Miami, Atlanta, Chicago, Boston, and Dallas were also used as recruitment centers for developing Ahmed's personal army.

If the media had been aware of the group's activities they would have made note that Ahmed's inner circle was very highly skilled not only in the use of C4 and Cemex, the Czechoslovakian plastic explosive that was responsible for countless deaths of innocent bystanders, but that were all very well educated. Each spoke English like a native, fluent in colloquialisms and idioms unique to America.

Much of his army had skills which enabled them to acquire positions of importance within engineering departments of companies such as IBM, Apple, Hughes Defense Systems, Chase Manhattan, Prudential Life, Martin Marietta, Westinghouse, Compuserve, MCI and hundreds of similar organizations. Every one of their employers would have attested to their skills, honor and loyalty to their adopted country. Ahmed's group was well versed in deception. After all, they answered to a greater cause.

What even a seasoned reporter might not find out though, was that all 12 of Ahmed's elite recruiters had to pass a supreme test often required by international political terrorist organizations. To guarantee their loyalty to the cause, whatever that cause might be, and to weed out potential external infiltrators, each member had to have killed at least one member of their immediate family.

It requires extraordinary hardening, to say the least, to kill your mother or father. Or to blow up the school bus that carried your pre teen sister to school. Or engage your brother in a mock fight and then sever his head from his body. The savagery that permitted one access into this elite circle is beyond the comprehension of most Western minds. Yet such acts were expected to demonstrate one's loyalty to a supreme purpose or belief.

The events surrounding Solman Rushdie and the Satanic Verses were a case in point. Each of those who volunteered to assassinate him at the bequest of the Ayatollah Khomeini had in fact already killed not only innocent women and children in order to reach their assigned terrorist targets, but had brought the head of their family victims to the tables of their superiors. A deed for which they were honored and revered.

These were the men, all of them men, who pledged allegiance to Ahmed Shah and the unknown, undefined assignments they would in the future be asked to complete. To the death if necessary, and without fear. These men were reminiscent of the infamous moles that Stalin's Soviet Empire had placed throughout the United Kingdom and the United States in the 1930's to be awakened at some future date to carry out strikes against the enemy from within. The only difference with Ahmed's men was that they were trained to die, not to survive. And unlike their Mole counterparts, they were awake the entire time, focused on their mission. Clearly it was only a matter of time before they would be asked to follow orders with blind obedience. Their only reward was a place in the Muslim heaven.

145

Meanwhile, while awaiting sainthood, their task was to find others with similar inclinations, or those who could be corralled into their system of beliefs. It was unrealistic, they knew, to expect to find an entire army of sympathizers who would fight to the death or perform suicide missions in the name of Allah. But they found it was very easy to find many men, never women, who would follow orders and perform the tasks of an underground infantryman.

The mass influx of Arabs into the United States was another great mistake of the Reagan '80's as it opened its doors to a future enemy. The immigration policy of the U.S. was the most open in the entire world. So, the Government allowed the entry of some of the world's most dangerous people into the country, and then gave them total freedom, with its associated anonymity. Such things could never happen at home, Ahmed thought. We love our land too much to permit our enemies on our soil. It is so much easier to dispose of them before they can cause damage.

So the thinking went, and Ahmed and his cadre platooned themselves often, in any of the thousands of American resort complexes, unnoticed, to gauge the progress of their assignments.

By early 1988, Ahmed's army consisted of nearly 1000 fanatic Muslims who would swallow a live grenade if the deed guaranteed their place in martyrdom. And another several thousand who could be led into battle under the right conditions. And more came and joined as the ridiculous immigration policies continued unchecked.

They were students, businessmen, flight attendants who were now in the United States for prolonged periods of time. All walks of life were included in his Army. Some were technicians or bookkeepers, delivery men, engineers, doctors; most disciplines were represented. Since Ahmed had no idea when, if ever, he and his army would be needed, nor for what purpose, recruiting a wide range of talents would provide Allah with the best odds if they were ever needed. They were all men. Not one woman in this man's army, Ahmed thought.

The biggest problem, just as Farjani had predicted, was the growing sense of unrest among the troops. The inner 12 had been professionally trained to be patient. Wait for the right moment to strike. Wait for orders. Do nothing. Do not disclose your alliances or your allegiances to anyone. No one can be trusted. Except your recruiter. Lead a normal life. Act like any American immigrant who flourishes in his new home. Do not, at all costs, give yourself away. That much was crucial.

Periodically, the inner 12 would assign mundane, meaningless tasks to various of their respective recruits. Americans called it busy work. But, it kept interest alive, the belief in the eventual victory of the Arab Nation against the American mongrels. It kept the life in their organization flowing, not dulled by the prolonged waiting for the ultimate call: Jihad, a holy war against America, waged from inside its own unprotected borders. It was their raison d'étre. The underlying gestalt for their very existence.

* * * * *

February 6, 1988
New York City

"It is time." Ahmed could not believe the words - music to his ears. It was not a long distance call; too clear. Must be local, or at least within the U.S.. The caller spoke in Ahmed's native tongue and conveyed an excitement that immediately consumed him. He sat in his wheelchair at a computer terminal in an engineering lab at Columbia University's Broadway campus. While he had hoped this day would come, he also knew that politicians, even Iran's, promised a glory that often was buried in diplomacy rather than action. Praise be Allah.

"We are ready. Always for Allah." Ahmed was nearly breathless with anticipation. His mind wandered. Were we at war? No, of course not. The spineless United States would never have the strength nor will to wage war against a United Arab State.

"That is good. For Allah." The caller agreed with Ahmed. "But it is not the war you expect."

Ahmed was taken aback. He had not known what to expect, exactly, but, over the months he had conjured many scenarios of how his troops would be used to perform Allah's Will. His mind reeled. "For whom do you speak?" Ahmed asked pointedly. There was a hint of distrust in Ahmed's question.

"Farjani said you would question. He said, 'there hasn't been a war on U.S. soil since 1812'. He said you would understand."

Ahmed understood. Only someone that was privy to their conversations would have known that. His heart quickened with anticipation. "Yes, I understand. With whom do I speak?" Ahmed asked reverently.

"My name is of no consequence. I am only a humble servant of Allah with a message. You are to follow instructions exactly, without reservation."

"Of course. I, too, am but a servant of God. What are my instructions?" Ahmed felt like standing at parade attention if only he had legs.

"This will not be our war. It will be another's. But our purposes are the same. You will act as his army, and are to follow his every request. As if Allah came to you himself and so ordered himself."

Ahmed beamed. He glowed with perspiration. Finally. The chance to act. And he would, his army would perform admirably. He listened carefully as the anonymous caller gave him his instructions. He noted the details as disbelief sank in. This is jihad? Yes, this is jihad. You are expected to comply. I am clear, but are you sure? Yes, I am sure. Then I will follow orders. As ordered. Will we speak again? No, this is your task, your destiny. The Arab Nation calls upon you now. Do you answer? Yes, I answer. I will perform. We, our army will perform.

"*Insha'allah.*"

"Yes, God Willing."

Ahmed Shah put his teaching schedule on hold by asking for and receiving an immediate sabbatical. He then booked and took a flight to Tokyo three days later.

"I need an army, and I am told you can provide such services for me. Is that so?" Homosoto asked Ahmed Shah though he already knew the answer.

Ahmed Shah and Taki Homosoto were meeting in a private palace in the outskirts of Tokyo. Ahmed wasn't quite sure to whom it belonged, but he was following orders and in no way felt in danger. The grounds were impeccable, a Japanese Versailles. The weather was cool, but not uncomfortably so. Both men sat under an arbor that would be graced with cherry blossoms in a few months. Each carried an air of confidence, an assurity not meant as arrogance, but rather as an assertion of control, power over their respective empires.

"How large is your army?" Homosoto knew the answer, but asked anyway.

"One thousand to the death. Three thousand to extreme pain, another ten thousand functionaries." Ahmed Shah said with pride.

Homosoto laughed a convivial Japanese laugh, and lightly slapped his knees. "Ah, comrade. To the death, so familiar, that is why you are here, but, I hope that will not be necessary. You see, this war will be one without bullets." Homosoto said waiting for the volatile Arab's reaction.

This was exactly what Ahmed feared. A spineless war. How could one afford to wage a war against America and not expect, indeed, plan for, the death of some troops. There was no Arab translation for pussy-wimp, but the thought was there.

"How may I be of service?"

"The task is simple. I have need of information, much information that will be of extreme embarrassment to the United States. Their

Government operates illegally, their companies control the country with virtual impunity from law, in many cases the law's sanction. It is time that they are tried for their crimes." Homosoto tailored his words so that his guest would acquire an enthusiasm similar to his.

"Yes," Ahmed agreed. "They need to learn a lesson. But, Mr. Homosoto, how can that be done without weapons? I assume you want to attack their planes, their businesses, Washington perhaps?" Ahmed was hopeful for the opportunity to give his loyal troops the action they desired.

"In a manner of speaking, yes, my friend. We shall strike where they least expect it, and in a way in which they are totally unprepared." Homosoto softened his speech to further his pitch to gain Ahmed Shah's trust and unity. "I am well aware of the types of training that you and your people have gone through. However, you must be aware, that Japan is the most technically advanced country in the world, and that we can accomplish things is a less violent manner, yet still achieve the same goals. We shall be much more subtle. I assume you have been informed of that by your superiors." Homosoto waited for Ahmed's response.

"As you say, we have been trained to expect, even welcome death in the struggle against our adversaries. Yet I recognize that a joint effort may be more fruitful for all of us. It may be a disappointment to some of my people that they will not be permitted the honor of martyrdom, but they are expected to follow orders. If they do not comply, they will die without the honor they crave. They will perform as ordered."

"Excellent. That is as I hoped." Homosoto beamed at the developing understanding. "Let me explain. My people will provide you with the weapons of this new war, a type of war never before fought. These are technological weapons that do not kill the enemy. Better, they expose him for what he is. It will be up to your army to use these weapons and allow us to launch later attacks against the Americans.

"There are to be no independent actions or activities. None without my and your direction and approval. Can you abide by these conditions?"

"At the request of my Government and Allah, I will be happy to serve you in your war. Both our goals will be met." Ahmed glowed at the opportunity to finally let his people do something after so much waiting.

Homosoto arose and stood over Ahmed. "We will make a valuable alliance. To the destruction of America." He held his water glass to Ahmed.

Ahmed responded by raising his glass. "To Allah, and the cause!"

They both drank deeply from the Perrier. Homosoto had one more question.

"If one or more of your men get caught, will they talk?"

"They will not talk."

"How can you be so sure?" Homosoto inquired naively.

"Because, if they are caught, they will be dead."

"An excellent solution."

* * * * *

Chapter 10

Tuesday, October 13
New York

COMPUTER ASSAULT
CLAIMS VICTIMS

by Scott Mason

For the last few weeks the general press and computer media have been foretelling the destruction to be caused by this year's version of the dreaded Columbus Day Virus. AKA Data Crime, the virus began exploding yesterday and will continue today, depending upon which version strikes your computer.

With all of the folderall by the TV networks and news channels, and the reports of anticipated doom for many computers, I expected to wake up this morning and learn that this paper didn't get printed, my train from the suburbs was rerouted to Calcutta and Manhattan's traffic lights were out of order. No such luck. America is up and running.

That doesn't mean that no one got struck by computer influenza, though. There are hundreds of reports of widespread damage to microcomputers everywhere.

The Bala Cynwyd, PA medical center lost several weeks of records. Credit Card International was struck in Madrid, Spain and can't figure out which customers bought what from whom. A few schools in England don't know who their students are, and a University in upstate New York won't be holding computer classes for a while.

William Murray of the Institute for Public Computing Confidence in Washington, D.C., downplayed the incident. "We have had reports of several small outbreaks, but we have not heard of any particularly devastating incidents. It seems that only a few isolated sites were affected."

On the other hand, Bethan Fenster from Virus Stoppers in McLean, Virginia, maintains that the virus damage was much more widespread. She says the outbreaks are worse than reported in the press. "I personally know of several Fortune 100 companies that will be spending the next several weeks putting their systems back in order. Some financial institutions have been nearly shut down because their computers are inoperable. It's the worst (computer) virus outbreak I've ever seen."

Very few companies would confirm that they had been affected by the Columbus Day Virus. "They won't talk to you," Ms. Fenster said. "If a major company announced publicly that their computers were down due to criminal activity, there would be a certain loss of confidence in that company. I understand that they feel a fiduciary responsibility to their stockholders to minimize the effects of this."

Despite Ms. Fenser's position, Forsythe Insurance, North-East Airlines, Brocker Financial and the Internal Revenue Service all admitted that they have had a 'major' disruption in their computer services and expect to take two to six weeks to repair the damage. Nonetheless, several of those companies hit, feel lucky.

"We only lost about a thousand machines," said Ashley Marie, senior network manager at Edison Power. "Considering that we have no means of protecting our computers at all, we could have been totally put out of business." She said that despite the cost to repair the systems, her management feels no need to add security or protective measures in the future. "They believe that this was a quirk, a one time deal. They're wrong," Ms. Marie said.

Many small companies that said they have almost been put out of business because they were struck by the Columbus Day Virus. "Simply not true," commented Christopher Angel of the Anti-Virus Brigade, a vigilante group who professes to have access to private information on computer viruses. "Of all of the reports of downed computers yesterday, less than 10% are from the Data Crime. Anyone who had any sort of trouble is blaming it on the virus rather than more common causes like hardware malfunction and operator error. It is a lot more glamorous to admit being hit by the virus that has created near hysteria over the last month."

Whatever the truth, it seems to be well hidden under the guise of politics. There is mounting evidence and concern that computer viruses and computer hackers are endangering the contents of our computers. While the effects of the Columbus Day Virus may have been mitigated by advance warnings and precautionary measures, and the actual number of infection sites very limited, computer professionals are paying increasing attention to the problem.

This is Scott Mason, safe, sound and uninfected.

* * * * *

Wednesday, October 14
J. Edgar Hoover Building, FBI Headquarters
Washington, D.C.

The sweltering October heat wave of the late Indian summer penetrated the World War II government buildings that surrounded the Mall and the tourist attractions. Window air conditioners didn't provide the kind of relief that modern workers were used to. So, shirtsleeves were rolled up, the nylons came off, and ties were loose if present at all.

The streets were worse. The climatic changes that graced much of North America were exaggerated in Washington. The heat was hotter, the humidity wetter. Sweat was no longer a five letter word, it was a way of life.

Union Station, the grand old train station near the Capitol Building provided little relief. The immense volume of air to be cooled was too much for the central air conditioners. They were no match for mother nature's revenge on the planet for unforgiving hydrocarbon emissions. As soon as Tyrone Duncan detrained from the elegant Metroliner he had ridden this morning from New York's Penn Station, he was drenched in perspiration. He discovered, to his chagrin, that the cab he had hailed for his ride to headquarters had no air conditioning. The stench of the city, and the garbage and the traffic fumes reminded him of home. New York.

Tyrone showed his identification at the J. Edgar Hoover Building wishing he had the constitution to wear a seersucker suit. There is no way on God's earth a seersucker could show a few hours wear as desperately as his $1200 Louis Boston did, he thought. Then, there was the accompanying exhaustion from his exposure to the dense Washington air. Duncan had not been pleased with the panic call that forced him to Washington anyway. His reactions to the effects of the temperature humidity index did not portend a good meeting with Bob Bernsen.

Bob had called Tyrone night before, at home. He said, we have a situation here, and it requires some immediate attention. Would you mind being here in the morning? Instead of a question, it was an unissued order. Rather than fool around with hours of delays at La Guardia and National Airport, Tyrone elected to take the train and arrive in the nation's capitol just after noon. It took, altogether just about the same amount of time, yet he could travel in relative luxury and peace. Burnson was waiting for him.

Bob Burnson held the title of National Coordinator for Tactical Response for the FBI. He was a little younger that Duncan, just over 40, and appeared cool in his dark blue suit and tightly collared shirt. Burnson had an unlikely pair of qualities. He was both an extraordinarily well polished politician and a astute investigator. Several years prior, though, he decided that the bureaucratic life would suit him just fine, and at the expense of his investigative skills, he attacked the political ladder with a vengeance.

Despite the differences between them, Burnson a willing compatriot of the Washington machine and Duncan preferring the rigors of investigation, they had developed a long distance friendship that survived over the years. Tyrone was most pleased that he had a boss who would at least give his arguments a fair listen before being told that for this or that political reason, the Bureau had chosen a different line of reasoning. So be it, thought Duncan. I'm not a policy maker, just a cop. Tyrone sank into one of the government issue chairs in Burnson's modern, yet modest office ringed with large windows that can't open.

"How 'bout that Arctic Chill?" Burnson's short lithe 150 pound frame showed no wear from the heat. "Glad you could make it."

"Shee . . .it man," Tyrone exhaled as he wiped his shiny wet black face and neck. He was wringing wet. "Like I had a choice. If it weren't for the company, I'd be at the beach getting a tan." He continued to wipe his neck and head with a monogrammed handkerchief.

"Lose a few pounds, and it won't hurt so bad. You know, I could make an issue of it." Bob poked fun.

"And I'm outta here so fast, Hoover'll cheer from his grave," he sweated. The reference to the FBI founder's legendary bigotry was a common source of jokes in the modern bureau.

"No doubt. No doubt." Burnson passed by the innuendo. "Maybe we'd balance the scales, too." He dug the knife deeper in reference to Tyrone's weight..

"That's two," said Duncan.

"O.K., O.K.," said Burnson feigning surrender. "How's Arlene and the rest of the sorority?" He referred to the house full of women with whom Tyrone had spent a good deal of his life.

"Twenty degrees cooler." He was half serious.

"Listen, since you're hear, up for a bite?" Bob tried.

"Listen, how 'bout we do business then grab a couple of cold ones. Iced beer. At Camelot? That's my idea of a quality afternoon." Camelot was the famous downtown strip joint on 18th and "M" street from which former Mayor Marion Berry had been 86'd for unpublished reasons. It was dark and frequented by government employees for lunch, noticeably the ones from Treasury.

"Deal. If you accept." Bob's demeanor shifted to the officious.

"Accept what?" Tyrone asked suspiciously.

"My proposition."

"Is this another one of your lame attempts to promote me to an office job in Capitol City?"

"Well, yes and no. You're being re-assigned." No easy way to say it.

"To what?" exclaimed Tyrone angrily.

"To ECCO."

"What the hell is ECCO?"

"All in good time. First, to the point," Bob said calmly. "How much do you know about this blackmail thing?"

"Plenty. I read the reports, and I have my own local problems. Not to mention that the papers have picked it up. If it weren't for the National Exposé printing irresponsibly, the mainstream press would have kept it quiet until there was some confirmation."

"Agreed," said Burnson. "They are being spoken to right now, about that very subject, and as I hear it, they will have more lawsuits on their doorstep than they can afford to defend. They really blew it this time."

"What else?" Bob was listening intently.

"Not much. Loose, unfounded innuendo, with nothing to follow up. Reminds me of high school antics or mass hysteria. Just like UFO flaps." Tyrone Duncan dismissed the coincidences and the though tof Scott' conspiracy theory. "But it does make for a busy day at the office."

"Agree, however, you only saw the reports that went on the wire. Not the ones that didn't go through channels."

"What do you mean by that?" Duncan voiced concern at being out of the loop.

"What's on the wire is only the tip of the iceberg. There's a lot more."

"What else?"

"Senators calling the Director personally, asking for favors. Trying to their secrets secret. A junior Midwest senator has some quirky sexual habits. A Southern anti-pornography ballbreaker happens to like little boys. It goes on and one. They've all received calls saying that their secrets will be in the newspapers' hands within days."

"Unless?" Duncan awaited the resolved threat.

"No unless, which scares them all senseless. It's the same story everywhere. Highly influential people who manage many of our countries' strategic assets have called their senators, and asked them to insure that their cases are solved in a quiet and expedient political manner. Sound familiar?" Burnson asked Duncan.

"More than vaguely," Tyrone had to admit. "How many?"

"As of this morning we have 17 Senators asking the FBI to make discreet investigations into a number of situations. 17! Not to mention a couple hundred executive types with connections. Within days of each other. They each, so far, believe that theirs is an isolated incident and that they are the sole target of such . . .threats is as good a word as any. Getting the picture?"

Tyrone whistled to himself. "They're all the same?"

"Yes, and there's something else. To a man, each claimed that there was no way the blackmailer could know what he knew. Impossible." Burnson scratched his head. "Strange. Same story everywhere. That's what got the Director and his cronies in on this. And, then me . . .and that's why you're here," Burnson said with finality.

"Why?" Tyrone was getting frustrated with the roundabout diatribe.

"We're pulling the blackmail thing to the national office and a special task force will take over. A lot of folks upstairs want to pull you in and stick you in charge of the whole operation, but I told them that you weren't interested, that you like it the way it is. So, I struck a deal." Burnson sounded proud.

Duncan wasn't convinced. "Deal? What deal? Since when do you talk for me?" Tyrone didn't think to thank Bob for the front line pass interference. Keep the politicos out of his hair.

"Have you been following any of the computer madness recently?" Burnson spoke as though he expected Tyrone to know nothing of it.

"Can't miss it. From what I hear, a lot of people are getting pretty spooked that they may be next."

"It gets more interesting than what the papers say," Bob said while opening a desk drawer. He pulled out a large folder and lay it across his desk. "We have experienced a few more computer incidents than is generally known, and in the last several weeks there has been a sudden increase in the number of attacks against Government computers."

"You mean the INTERNET stuff and Congress losing it's mind?" Tyrone laughed at the thought that Congress would now use their downed computers as an excuse for not doing anything.

"Those are only the ones that have made it to the press. It's lot worse." Bob scanned a few pages of the folder and paraphrased while reading. "Ah, yes, the NPRP, National Pretrial Reporting Program over at Justice . . .was hit with a series of computer viruses . .

.apparently intentionally placed . . .in VMS computers, whatever the hell those are." Bob Burnson was not computer fluent, but he knew what the Bureau's computer could do.

"The Army Supply Center at Fort Stewart, Georgia had all of its requisitions for the last year erased from the computer." Bob chuckled as he continued. "Says here that they have had to pool the guys' money to go to Winn Dixie to buy toilet paper and McDonald's has offered a special GI discount until the system gets back up."

"Ty," Bob said. "Of course, some people on the hill have raised a stink since their machines went down. Damn crybabies. So ECCO is being activated."

"What the hell is ECCO?" Tyrone asked again.

"ECCO stands for Emergency Computer Crisis Organization. It's a computer crisis team that responds to . . .well I guess, computer crises." Bob opened the folder again. "It was formed during the, and I quote, ' . . .the panic that followed the first INTERNET Worm in November of 1988.'"

Tyrone's mouth hung open. "What panic?"

"The one that was kept under absolute wraps," Bob said, slightly lowering his voice. "At first no one knew what the INTERNET event was about. Who was behind it. Why and how it was happening. Imagine 10's of thousands of computers stopping all at once. It scared the shit out of the National Security Council, remember we and the Russians weren't quite friends then, and we thought that military secrets were being funneled straight to the Kremlin. You can't believe some of the contingency plans I heard about."

"I had no idea . . ."

"You weren't supposed to," Bob added. "Very few did. At any rate, right afterward DARPA established CERT, the Computer Emergency Response Team at Carnegie Mellon, and DCA set up a Security Coordination Center at SRI International to investigate problems in the Defense Data Network. Livermore and the DOE got into the act with Computer Incident Advisory Capability. Then someone decided that the bureaucracy was still too light and it deserved at least a fourth redundant, overlapping and rival group to investigate on behalf of Law Enforcement Agencies. So, there we have ECCO."

"So what's the deal?" asked Tyrone. "What do I have to do?"

"The Director has asked ECCO to investigate the latest round of viruses and the infiltration of a dozen or so sensitive and classified computers." Bob watched for Ty's reaction, but saw none yet. He wondered how he would take the news. "This time, we would like to be involved in the entire operation from start to finish. Make sure the investigation is done right. We'd like to start nailing some of the bastards on the Federal level. Besides you have the legal background and we are treading on some very new and untested waters."

"I can imagine. So what's our role?"

"Your role," Bob emphasized 'Your', "will be to liaison with the other interested agencies."

"Who else is playing?" asked Tyrone with trepidation.

"Uh, that is the one negative," stammered Bob. "You've got NSA, CIA, NIST, the NSC, the JCS and a bunch of others that don't matter. The only rough spot is the NSA/NIST connection. Everyone else is there just to make sure they don't miss anything."

"What's their problem?"

"Haven't heard, huh?" laughed Bob. "The press hasn't been kind. They've been in such a pissing match for so long that computer security work came to a virtual halt . . .I don't want to spoil the surprise . . .you'll see," he added chuckling.

Tyrone sat back in the chair, he was cool enough now not to stick to it, closed his eyes and rotated his head to work out the kinks. Bob never had gotten used to Tyrone's peculiar method of deep thought; he found it most unnerving.

Bob's intents were crystal clear, not that Tyrone minded. He had no desire to move to D.C.; indeed he would have quit instead. He wanted to stay with the Bureau and the action, but in his comfortable New York existence. Otherwise, no. But, if he could get Bob off his back by this one favor. Sure it might not be real action, watching computer jockies play with themselves . . .but it might be an interesting change in pace.

"Yes, under a couple of condition." Tyrone was suddenly a little too agreeable and smug after his earlier hesitancy.

"Conditions? What conditions?" Bob's suspicion was clear.

"One. I do it my way, with no, and I mean, absolutely no interference." Duncan awaited a reply to his first demand.

"What else?"

"I get to use who I want to use, inside or outside the Bureau."

"Outside? Outside? We can't let this outside. The last thing in the world we want is publicity."

"You're gonna get it anyway. Let's do it right this time."

"What do you mean by that?" Bob asked somewhat defensively.

"What I mean is," Tyrone spoke up, sounding confident, "that the press are already on this computer virus thing and hackers and all. So, let's not advertise it, but when it comes up, let's deal with it honest."

"No way," blurted out Bob. "They'll make it worse than it is."

"I have that covered. A friend of my works for a paper, and he is a potential asset."

"What's the trade?"

"Not much. Half day leads, as long as he keeps it fair."

"Anything else?" Bob asked, not responding to Ty.

"One last thing," Tyrone said sitting up straighter. "After this one, you promise to let me alone and work my golden years, the way I want, where I want until my overdue retirement."

"I don't know if I can . . ."

"Then forget it," interrupted Tyrone. "I'll just quit." It was the penultimate threat and bluff and caught Bob off balance.

"Wait a minute. You can't hold me hostage . . ."

"Isn't that what you're doing to me?" Touché!

Bob sat back in though. To an event, Duncan had been right on. He had uncannily been able to solve, or direct the solution of a crime where all others had failed. And, he always put the Bureau in the best possible light. If he didn't go with him now, he'd lose him for sure.

"And, I may need some discretionary funds." Duncan was making a mental list of those things he thought he needed. But his sources of information were the most valuable. Without them, it would be a bad case of babysitting sissy assed bureaucrats staking out their ground.

"Yes to the money. Ouch, but yes to hands off your promotion. Maybe, to the reporter. It's my ass, too, you know."

"You called me," Tyrone said calmly. "Remember?"

I can't win this one, thought Bob. He's never screwed up yet. Not big time. As they say, with enough rope you either bring in the gang or hang yourself. "I want results." That's all Bob had to say. "Other than that, I don't give a good goddamn what you do." Bob resigned.

"One more thing," Tyrone slipped in.

"What is it?" Bob was getting exasperated.

"It happens out of New York, not here."

"But . . ."

"No buts. Period."

"O.K., New York, but you report here when I need you. Agreed?"

"Agreed," said Tyrone agreeably. "Deal?"

"Yes, except no to the press. Even this reporter of yours. Agreed?"

"Whatever," Tyrone told Bob.

* * * * *

From his hotel room, Tyrone Duncan called Scott Mason at his home. It was after 11PM EST, and Ty was feeling no pain after several hours of drinking and slipping $10 bills into garter belts at Camelot.

"RCA, Russian Division," Scott Mason answered his phone.

"Don't do that," Tyrone slurred. "That'll trigger the monitors."

"Oh, sorry, I thought you wanted the plans for the Stealth Bomber . . ."

"C'mon, man," Tyrone pleaded. "It's not worth the paperwork."

Scott choked through his laughter. "I'm watching a Honeymooner rerun. This better be good."

"We need to talk."

* * * * *

Thursday, October 15
Washington, D.C.

The stunning view of the Potomac was complete with a cold front that brought a wave of crisp and clear air, a much needed change from the brutal Indian Summer. His condo commanded a vista of lights that reflected the power to manipulate the world. Miles reveled in it. He and Perky lounged on his 8th. floor balcony after a wonderfully satisfying romp in his waterbed. For every action there is an equal an opposite reaction. Sex in a waterbed meant the expenditure of the least energy for the maximum pleasure. Ah, the beauty of applied mathematics.

Perky and Miles had continued to see each other on a periodically irregular basis since they met. She was a little more than one of Miles' sexual release valves. She was a semi-sorta-kinda girl friend, but wouldn't have been if Miles had known that she reported their liaisons back to her boss. Alex was not interested in how she got her information. He only wanted to know if there were any digressions in Miles mission.

They sipped Grande Fine from oversized brandy glasses. The afterglow was magnificent and they saw no reason to detract from it with meaningless conversation. Her robe barely covered her firm breasts and afforded no umbrage for the triangle between her legs. She wasn't ashamed of her nakedness, job or no job. She enjoyed her time with Miles. He asked for nothing from her but the obvious. Unlike the others whom she entertained who often asked her for solicitous introductions to others who wielded power that might further their own particular lobby. Miles was honest, at least. He even let her spend the night upon occasion.

At 2 AM, as they gazed over the reflections in the Potomac, Miles' phone warbled. He ignored the first 5 rings to Perky's annoyance.

"Aren't you going to answer?" Her unspoken thoughts said, *do whatever you have to do to make that infernal noise stop.*

"Expecting a call?" Miles said. His eyes were closed, conveying his internal peace. The phone rang again.

"Miles, at least get a machine." The phone rang a seventh time.

"Fuck." He stood and his thick terrycloth robe swept behind him as he walked into the elegantly simple modern living room through the open glass doors. He put down his glass and answered on the 8th ring.

"It's late," he answered. His 'I don't give a shit' attitude was evident.

"Mr. Foster, I am most displeased." It was Homosoto. Miles curled his lips in disgust as Perky looked in from her balcony vantage.

Miles breathed heavily into the phone. "What's wrong now?" Miles was trying to verbally show his distaste for such a late call.

"Our plans were explicit. Why have you deviated?" Homosoto was controlled but forthright.

"What the hell are you talking about?" Miles sipped loudly from the brandy glass.

"I have read about the virus, the computer virus. The whole world in talking about it. Mr. Foster, you are early. I thought we had an understanding."

"Hey!" Foster yelled into the phone. "I don't know where you get off calling me this way at 2 in the morning, but you've got your head up your ass."

"Excuse me Mr. Foster, I do not and could not execute such a motion. However, do not forget we did have an agreement." Homosoto was insistent.

"What the fuck are you talking about?" Miles was adamant.

"Since you insist on these games, Mr. Foster. I have read with great interest about the so called Columbus Day Virus. I believe you have made a great error in judgment."

Miles had just had about enough of this. "If you've got something to say, say it." he snorted into the phone.

"Mr. Foster. Did we not agree that the first major strike was not to occur until next year?"

"Yeah," Miles said offhandedly. He saw Perky open her eyes and look at him quizzically. He made a fist with his right hand and made an obscene motion near his crotch.

"Then, what is this premature event?" Homosoto persisted.

"Not mine." Miles looked out to the balcony. Perky was invitingly licking her lips. Miles turned away to avoid distraction.

"Mr. Foster, I find it hard to believe that you are not responsible."

"Tough shit.

"Excuse me?" Homosoto was taken aback.

"Simple. Neither you nor I are the only persons who have chosen to build viruses or destructive computer programs. We are merely taking a good idea and taking it to its logical conclusion as pure form of offensive weaponsry. This one's not mine nor yours. It's someone elses."

The phone was silent for a few seconds. "You are saying there are others?" The childlike naivete was coming through over 12,000 miles of phone wire.

"Of course there are. This will probably help us."

"How do you mean?"

"There are a thousands of viruses, but none as effective as the ones which we use. A lot of amateurs use them to build their egos. Jerusalem-B, Lehigh, Pakistani, Brain, Marijuana, they all have names. They have no purpose other than self aggrandizement. So, we will be seeing more and more viruses appear that have nothing to do with our efforts. I do not hope you will call every time you hear of one. You know our dates. "

"Is there no chance for error?"

"Oh yes! There is, but it will be very isolated if it occurs. Most viruses do not receive as much attention as this one, and probably won't until we are ready. And, as I recall we are not ready." Miles was tired of the timing for this hand holding session. Ms. Perkins was beckoning.

"I hope you are right. My plans must not be interfered with."

"Our plans," Miles corrected. "My ass is on the line, too. I don't need you freaking every time the press reports a computer going on the fritz. It's gonna happen, a lot."

"What will happen, Mr. Foster?" Homosoto was able to convey disgust with a Japanese accent like no other he had ever met.

"We've been through this before."

"Then go through it again," Homosoto ordered.

Miles turned his back to Perky and sat on the couch inside where he was sure he could speak in privacy. "Listen here Homo," Miles scowled. "In the last couple of years viruses have been become techno-yuppie amusements. The game has intensified as the stakes have increased. Are you aware . . .no I'm sure you're not, that the experts here say that, besides our work, almost every local area network in the country is infected with a virus of one type or another. Did you know that?"

"No, Mr. Foster, I didn't. How do you know that?" Homosoto sounded unconvinced.

"It's my fucking job to know that. And you run an empire?"

"Yes, I remember, and I hope you do, Mr. Foster, that you work for me." Acute condescending was an executive Oriental trait that Miles found unsettling.

"For now, I do."

"You do, and will until our job is over. Is that clear Mr. Foster? You have much to lose."

Miles sank deep into the couch, smirking and puckering his dimples. He wanted to convey boredom. "I a job. You an empire."

"Do not be concerned about me. Good night Mr. Foster."

Homosoto had quickly cut the line. Just as well, thought Miles. He had enough of that slant-eyed slope-browed rice-propelled mother-fucker for one night. He had bigger and better and harder things to concern him.

* * * * *

October 31, 1989
Falls Church, Virginia.

"What do you mean gone?"

"Gone. Gone. It's just gone." Fred Porter sounded panicked.

Larry Ferguson, the Senior Vice President of First National Bank did not appreciate the news he was getting from the Transfer Department in New York. "Would you be kind enough to explain?" he said with disdain.

"Yessir, of course." Porter took a deep breath. "We were running a balance, the same one we run every day. And every day, they balance. The transfers, the receipts, the charges . . .everything. When we ran them last night, they didn't add up. We're missing a quarter billion dollars."

"A quarter billion dollars? You better have one good explanation, son."

"I wish I did," Porter sighed.

"All right, let's go through it top to bottom." Ferguson knew that it was ultimately his ass if $250 Million was really missing.

"It's just as I told you."

"Then tell me again!" Ferguson bellowed.

"Yessir, sorry. We maintain transfer accounts as you know."

"Of course I know."

"During the day we move our transfer funds into a single account and wait till the end of the day to move the money to where it belongs. We do that because . . ."

"I know why we do it. Cause for every hundred million we hold for half a day we make $16,000 in interest we don't have to pay out."

"Yessir, but that's not official . . ."

"Of course it's not you idiot . . ."

"I'm sorry sir."

"As you were saying . . ." Ferguson was glad he had moved the psychological stress to his underling.

"When we got to the account, about 9:00 AM, it was empty. That's it. Empty. All the money was gone."

"And, pray tell, where did it go?" Templeton said sarcastically.

"We don't know. It was supposed to have been transferred to hundreds of accounts. Here and abroad. There's no audit of what happened."

"Do you know how long it will take you to pay for this screw up Porter?" Templeton demanded.

"Yessir."

"How long?"

"A hundred lifetimes," Porter said dejectedly.

"Longer. A lot longer." Ferguson really knew that Porter wouldn't pay any price. As long as the computer records showed he wasn't at fault, he would continue to be a valued employee. Ferguson himself was bound to be the scape goat.

"What do you want me to do, sir?" Porter asked.

"You've done enough. Just wire me the records. I need them yesterday. I have to talk to Weinhauser." Ferguson hung up in disgust. It was not going to be a good day.

* * * * *

Chapter 11

Wednesday, November 4
The Stock Exchange, New York

Wall Street becomes a ghost town by early evening with the nighttime population largely consisting of guards, cleaning and maintenance people. Tightly packed skyscrapers with their lighted windows create random geometric patterns in the moonless cityscape and hover ominously over dimly lit streets.

Joe Patchok and Tony Romano worked as private guards on the four to midnight shift at the Stock Exchange on Cortland Street in lower Manhattan. For a couple of young college guys, this was the ideal job. They could study in peace and quiet, nothing ever happened, no one bothered them, and the pay was decent.

They were responsible for the 17th. and 18th. floors which had a sole entrance and exit; controlled access. This was where the central computers for the Stock Exchange tried to maintain sanity in the market. The abuses of computer trading resulting in the minicrash of 1987 forced a re-examination of the practice and the subsequent installation of computer brakes in an effort to dampen severe market fluctuations.

Hundreds of millions of shares exchanged every day are recorded in the computers as are the international, futures and commodities trades. The dossiers on thousands upon thousands of companies stored in the memory banks and extensive libraries were used to track investors, ownership, offerings, filings and provide required information to the government.

Tony sat at the front guard desk while Joe made the next hourly check through the offices and computer rooms. Joe strolled down the halls, brilliantly lit from recessed ceiling fixtures. The corridor walls were all solid glass, giving the impression of more openness than was really provided by the windowless, climate controlled, 40% sterile environment. There was no privacy working in the computer rooms.

The temperature and humidity were optimized; the electricity content of air was neutralized both electrostatically and by nuclear ionization, and the air cycled and purified once an hour. In the event of a catastrophic power failure, which is not unknown in New York, almost 10,000 square feet was dedicated to power redundancy and battery backup. In case of fire, heat sensors trigger the release of halon gas and suck all of the oxygen from the room in seconds. The Stock Exchange computers received the best care.

Joe tested the handle on the door of each darkened room through the myriad glass hallways. Without the computers behind the glass walls, it might as well have been a House of Mirrors. He noticed that the computer operators who work through the night were crowded together at the end of a hall next to the only computer rooms with activity. He heard them muttering about the cleaning staff.

"Hey guys, problem?" Joe asked.

"Nah, we escaped," a young bearded man in a white lab coat said pointing into the room. "His vacuum cleaner made one God awful noise, so we came out here till he was done."

"New cleaning service," Joe said offhandedly.

The dark complexioned cleaning man wore a starchy white uniform with Mohammed's Cleaning Service emblazoned across the back in bold red letters. They watched him, rather than clean the room, fiddle with the large barrel sized vacuum cleaner.

"What's he doing?"

"Fixing that noise, I hope."

"What's he doing now?"

"He's looking at us and, saying something . . ."

"It looks like he's praying . . ."

"Why the hell would he . . ."

The entire 46 story building instantly went dark and the force of the explosion rocked Tony from his seat fifty yards away. He reached for the flashlight on his belt and pressed a series of alarms on the control panel even though the video monitors were black and the emergency power had not come on. Nothing. He ran towards the sound of the blast and yelled.

"Hello? Hey?" he yelled nervously into the darkness.

"Over here, hurry," a distant pained voice begged.

Tony slid into a wall and stopped. He pointed his flashlight down one hall. Nothing.

"Over here."

He jumped sideways and pointed the beam onto a twisted maze of bodies, some with blood geysering into the air from their necks and arms and legs. Tony saw that the explosion had shattered the glass walls into thousands of high velocity razor sharp projectiles. The corpses had been pierced, stabbed, severed and mutilated by the deadly shards. Tony felt nauseous; he was going to be sick right then.

"Tony." A shrapnelled Joe squeaked from the mass of torn flesh ahead of him.

"Holy shit . . ." Tony's legs turned to jelly as he bent over and gagged.

"Help me!"

The force of the blast had destroyed the glass partitions as far as his light beam would travel. He pointed the light into the room that exploded. The computer equipment was in shambles, and then he saw what was left of the cleaning man. His severed head had no recognizable features and pieces of his body were strewn about. Tony suddenly vomited onto the river of blood that was flowing his way down the hallway.

"I gotta go get help," Tony said choking. He pushed against the wall to give him the momentum to overcome the paralysis his body felt and ran.

"No, help me . . ."

He ran down the halls with his flashlight waving madly towards guard his station and the elevators. They were out, too. Maybe the phone on the console. Dead. He picked up the walkie-talkie and pushed the button. Nothing. He banged the two way radio several times on the counter in the futile hope that violence was an electronic cure-all. Dead. Tony panicked and threw it violently into the blackness.

Neither the small TV, nor his portable radio worked either.

* * * * *

"I know it's almost midnight," Ben Shellhorne said into the cellular phone. He cupped his other ear to hear over the commotion at the Stock Exchange building.

"Quit your bitching. Look at it this way; you might see dawn for the first time in your life." Ben joked. All time was equal to Ben but he knew that Scott said he didn't do mornings. "Sure, I'll wait," Ben said in disgus and waited with agitation until Scott came back to the phone. "Good. But don't forget that beer isn't just for breakfast."

He craned his neck to see that the NYPD Bomb Squad had just left and gave the forensics team the go ahead. No danger.

"Listen," Ben said hurriedly. "I gotta make it quick, I'm going in for some pictures." He paused and then said, "Yes, of course after the bodies are gone. God, you can be gross." He paused again. "I'll meet you in the lobby. One hour."

Ben Shellhorn, a denizen of the streets, reported stories that sometimes didn't fit within the all-the-news-that's-fit-to-print maxim. Many barely bordered on the decent, but they were all well done. For some reason, unknown even to Ben, he attracted news whose repulsiveness made them that much more magnetic to readers. Gruesome lot we are, he thought.

That's why one of his police contacts called him to say that a bunch of computer nerds were sliced to death. The Cheers rerun was bringing him no pleasure, so, sure, what the hell; it's a nice night for a mutilation.

"It's getting mighty interesting, buddy boy," Ben said meeting Scott as he stepped out of his filthy Red 911 in front of the Stock Exchange an hour later. His press credentials performed wonders at times. Like getting behind police lines and not having to park ten blocks away.

The police had brought in generators to power huge banks of lights to eerily light up the Stock Exchange building, all 500 feet of it. Emergency vehicles filled the wide street, everything from ambulances, fire engines, riot vehicles and New York Power. Then the DA's office, lawyers for the Exchange, insurance representatives and a ton of computer people.

"What the hell happened here?" Scott asked looking at the pandemonium on the cordoned off Cortland Street. "Where are all the lights?" He turned and gazed at the darkened streets and tall buildings. "Did you know a bunch of the street lights are out, too?" Scott meandered in seeming awe of the chaos.

"This is one strange one," Ben said as they approached the building entrance. "Let me ask you a question, you're the techno- freak."

Scott scowled at him for the reference but didn't comment.

"What kind of bomb stops electricity?"

"Electricity? You mean power?" Scott pointed at the blackened buildings and streets and Ben nodded. "Did they blow the block transformers?"

"No, just a small Cemex, plastic, bomb in one computer room. Did some damage, but left an awful lot standing. But the death toll was high. Eleven dead and two probably not going to make it. Plus the perp."

Scott gazed around the scene. The dark sky was pierced by the top floors of the World Trade Center, and there were lights in the next blocks. So it's not a blackout. And it wasn't the power grid that was hit. A growing grin preceded Scott shaking his head side to side.

"What is it?" Ben asked.

"A nuke."

"A nuke?"

"Yeah, that's it, a nuke," Scott said excitedly. "A nuke knocks out power. Of course."

"Right," Ben said mockingly. "I can hear it now: Portion of 17th. Floor of Exchange Devastated by Nuclear Bomb. News at Eleven."

"Never mind," Scott brushed it off. "Can we get up there?" He pointed at the ceiling. "See the place?"

Ben pulled a few strings and spent a couple of hundred of Scott's dollars but succeeded in getting to the corpse-less site of the explosion. Scott visually poked around the debris and noticed a curved porcelain remnant near his feet. He wasn't supposed to touch, but, what was it? And the ruby colored chunks of glass? In the few seconds they were left alone, they snapped a quick roll of film and made a polite but hasty departure. At $200 a minute Scott hoped he would find what he was looking for.

"Ben, I need these photos blown up, to say, 11 X 17? ASAP."

The press conference at 4:15 in the morning was necessary. The Stock Exchange was not going to open Thursday. The lobby of the Stock Exchange was aflood with TV camera lights, police and the media hoards. Voices echoed loudly, unbounded among the marble walls and floor and made hearing difficult.

"We don't want to predict what will happen over the next 24 hours," the exhausted stocky spokesman for the Stock Exchange said loudly, to make himself heard over the din. "We have every reason to expect that we can make a quick transition to another system."

"How is that done?"

"We have extensive tape vaults where we store everything from the Exchange computers daily. We will either use one of our backup computers, or move the center to a temporary location. We don't anticipate any delays."

"What about the power problem?" A female reporter from a local TV news station asked.

"Con Ed is on the job," the spokesman said   pleased they were picking on someone else. "I have every confidence they will have things up and flying soon."

"What caused the power outage?"

"We don't have the answer to that now."

Scott edged to the front of the crowd to ask a question. "What if," Scott asked the spokesman. "If the tapes were destroyed?"

"Thank God they weren't . . ." he said haltingly.

"Isn't is true," Scott ventured accusingly, "that in fact you already know that every computer in this building is dead, all of the emergency power backup systems and batteries failed and that every computer tape or disk has been completely erased?" The other reporters stood open mouthed at the unexpected question.

Scott spoke confidently, knowing that he was being filmed by the networks. The spokesman nervously fumbled with some papers in his hand. The press pool waited for the answer that had silenced the spokesman. He stammered, "We have no . . .until power is restored a full determination of the damage cannot be made . . ."

Scott pressed the point. "What would happen if the tapes were all erased?"

"Uh, I, well . . ." he glanced from side to side. On his left were two men dressed in matching dark blue suits, white shirts and sunglasses. "It is best not to speculate until we have more information."

"Computer experts have said that if the tapes are erased it would take at least thirty days to recreate them and get the Exchange open again. Is that correct?"   Scott exaggerated. He was the computer expert to whom he referred. Journalistic license.

"Under the conditions," the spokesman said trying to maintain a credible visage to front for his lies, "I also have heard some wildly exaggerated estimates. Let me assure you," the politician in him came out here. "That the Exchange will in no way renege on its fiduciary responsibilities to the world financial community."   He glanced at his watch. "I'm afraid that's all the time I have now. We will meet here again at 9:00 A.M. for a further briefing. Thank you." He quickly exited under the protection of one of New York's finest as the reporters all shouted at once their last questions. Scott didn't bother. It never works.

One of the men in the blue suits leaned over to the other and spoke quietly in his ear. "Who is that guy asking all those questions?"

"Isn't that the reporter the Director was talking about?"

"Yeah. He said we should keep an eye on him."

* * * * *

Thursday,   November 5

<<<AUTOCRYPT MODE>>>
MR. SHAH

Ahmed heard his computer announce that Homosoto had signed on. He pushed the joystick on the arm of his electric wheelchair and proceeded over to the portable computer that was outfitted with an untraceable cellular modem. Even if the number was traced after four interstate call forwards after the original overseas link, finding him was an entirely different matter. Ahmed entered the time base PRG code from the ID card he kept strapped to his wheelchair.

yes.

CONGRATULATIONS ON THE STOCK EXCHANGE.

yes. we were well served by martyrs. they are to be honored.

CAN YOU HAVE MORE READY?

8 more.

WHEN

1 month.

GOOD. PUT THEM HERE. SOCIAL SECURITY ADMINISTRA-
TION, IMMIGRATION AND NATURALIZATION, AMERICAN EX-
PRESS, NEW YORK FEDERAL RESERVE, STATE FARM
INSURANCE, FANNY MAE, CITIBANK AND FEDERAL EX-
PRESS.

done.

DO IT AS SOON AS POSSIBLE. THEN MAKE MORE.
<<<CONNECTION TERMINATED>>>

* * * * *

Friday, November 6
New York City

The Stock Exchange didn't open Friday either.

Scott Mason had made enough of a stink about the erased tapes
that they could no longer hide under the cover of computer malfunctions. It was finally admitted that yes, the tapes were needed to verify
all transactions, especially the computer transactions, and they had
been destroyed along with the entire contents of the computer's
memory and hard disks. Wiped out. Totally.

The Exchange didn't tell the press that the National Security
Agency had been quietly called in to assist. The NSA specializes in
information gathering, and over the years with tens of billions of
dollars in secret appropriations, they have developed extraordinary
methods to extract usable information from where there is apparently
none.

The Exchange couriered a carton of computer tapes to NSA's Fort
Meade where the most sophisticated listening and analysis tools in the
world live in acres upon acres of underground laboratories and data
processing centers. What they found did not make the NSA happy.
The tapes had in fact been totally erased. A total unidirectional
magnetic pattern.

Many 'erased' tapes and disks can be recovered. One of the
preferred recovery methods is to use MNR, Magnetic Nuclear Resonance, to detect the faintest of organized magnetic orientations. Even
tapes or disks with secret information that have been erased many
times can be 'read' after an MNR scan.

The electromagnetic signature left remnant on the tapes, the
molecular alignment of the ferrous and chromium oxide particles in

this case were peculiarly characteristic. There was little doubt. The NSA immediately called the Exchange and asked them, almost ordered them, to leave the remaining tapes where they were.

In less than two hours an army of NSA technicians showed up with crates and vehicles full of equipment. The Department of Energy was right behind with equipment suitable for radiation measurements and emergency responses.

DOE quickly reached no conclusion. Not enough information. Initially they had expected to find that someone had stumbled upon a way to make highly miniaturized nuclear weapons. The men from the NSA knew they were wrong.

* * * * *

It took almost six weeks for the Stock Exchange to function at its previous levels. Trading was reduced to paper and less than 10,000,000 shares daily for almost two weeks until the temporary system was expanded with staff and runners. Daily trading never exceeded 27,000,000 shares until the computers came back on line.

The SEC and the Government Accounting Office released preliminary figures indicating the shut down of the Exchange will cost the American economy almost $50 Billion this year. Congress is preparing legislation to provide emergency funding to those firms that were adversely affected by the massive computer failure.

The Stock Exchange has said that they will institute additional physical and computer security to insure that there is no repeat of the unfortunate suicide assault.

* * * * *

Sunday, November 8
Scarsdale, New York

"You never cease to amaze me," Tyrone said as entered Scott's ultra modern house. "You and this freaking palace. Just from looking at you, I'd expect black lights, Woodstock posters and sleeping bags." He couldn't recall if he had ever seen Scott wear anything but jeans, t-shirts or sweat shirts and spotlessly clean Reboks.

Scott's sprawling 8000 square foot, free-form, geometric white-on-white home sat on 2 acres at the end of a long driveway heavily treed with evergreens so that seclusion was maintained all year long. Featured in Architectural Digest, the designers made generous use of glass brick inside and out. The indoor pool boasted sliding glass walls

172

and a retractable skylight ceiling which gave the impression of out-door living, even in the midst of a harsh winter.

"They're in the music room." Scott proceeded to open a set of open heavy oaken double doors. "Soundproof, almost," he said cheerily. A 72 inch video screen dominated one wall and next to it sat a large control center with VCR's, switchers and satellite tuner. Scott's audio equipment was as complex as Ty had ever seen and an array of speaker systems flanked the huge television.

"Toys, you got the toys, don't you?" joked Tyrone.

"The only difference is that they cost more," agreed Scott. "You wanna see a toy and a half? I invented it myself."

"Not another one?" groaned Tyrone. "That idiot golf machine of yours was ..."

"Capable of driving 350 yards, straight as an arrow."

"And as I remember, carving up the greens pretty good." Scott and his rolling Golf Gopher had been thrown off of several courses already.

"A few modifications, that's all," laughed Scott.

Scott led Tyrone through the immense family-entertainment room into a deep navy blue, white accented Euro-streamlined automated kitchen. It was like no other kitchen he had ever seen. In fact, other than the sinks and the extensive counters, there was no indication that this room was intended for preparing food. Scott flipped a switch and suddenly the deep blue cabinet doors faded into a transparent tint baring the contents of the shelves. The fronts of the stoves, refrigerator and freezer and other appliances exposed their function and controls.

"Holy Jeez ..." Ty said in amazement. Last month this had been a regular high tech kitchen of the 80's. Now it was the Jetsons. "That's incredible ...you invented that?"

"No," dismissed Scott. "That's just a neat trick of LCD panels built into the cabinets. This was my idea." He pressed an invisible switch and 4 ten inch openings appeared on the counter top near the sink. "Combination trash compacter re-cycler. Glass, plastic, aluminum, metal and paper. Comes out by the garbage, ready to go to the center."

"Lazy son of a bitch aren't you?" Tyrone laughed loudly.

"Sure, I admit my idea of gardening is watching someone mow the lawn." Scott feigned offense. "But this is in the name of Green. I bet if you had one, you'd use it and Arlene would get off your ass."

"No way," Tyrone objected. "My marriage is too good to screw up. It's the only thing left we still fight about, and we both like it just the way it is. Thanks, but no thanks. I'm old fashioned."

Scott showed Tyrone how to use the kitchen and he found that no matter what he wanted, there was button for it, a hidden drawer or a disguised appliance. "I still buy dishwashers at Sears. How the hell do you know how to use this stuff," Ty said fumbling with the automatic bottle opener as it dropped the removed caps into the hole for the metal compactor.

Tyrone had come over to Scott's house for a quiet afternoon o Sunday football. An ideal time because Arlene had gone to Boston for the weekend with his daughters. Freedom!

They made it to the Music Room with their beers as the kickoff was midfield. "So how's the promotion going?" Scott asked Tyrone in half jest. Over the last few weeks, Ty had spent most of his time in Washington and what little time was left with his family.

"Promotion my ass. It's the only way I can NOT get a promotion." Tyrone added somberly, "and it may be my last case."

"What do you mean?" Scott asked.

"It has gotten outta hand, totally our of hand. We have to spend more time protecting the rights of the goddamned criminals than solving crimes. That's not what it should be about. At least not for me."

"You're serious about this," Scott said rhetorically.

"Hey, sooner or later I gotta call it quits," Ty replied soberly. "But this computer thing's gonna make my decision easier."

"That's what I asked. How's the promotion?"

"Let's just say, more of the same but different. Except the inter-agency crap is amazing. No one commits to anything, and everything needs study and nothing gets done." Tyrone sighed.

He had been in Washington working with NIST, NSA, DoD and every other agency that thought it had a vested interest in computers and their protection. Their coordination with CERT and ECCO was a joke, even by government standards.

At the end of the first quarter, the 49'ers were holding a solid 10 point leads. Scott grabbed a couple more beers and began telling Tyrone about the incident a the Exchange. The New York Police had taken over the case, declaring sovereignty over Wall Street and its enclaves.

"They don't know what they have, though," Scott said immodestly.

"The talk was a small scale nuke . . ."

"But the DOE smashed that but fast," Scott interrupted. "What if I told you that the it was only the computers that were attacked? That the deaths were merely coincidental?"

Tyrone groaned as the 49'ers fumble the ball. "I'd listen," he said noncommittally.

"It was a classified magnetic bomb. NSA calls them EMP-T."

"Empty? The empty bomb?" Tyrone said skeptically. "Since when does NSA design bombs?"

"Listen," said Scott trying to get Ty's attention away from the TV. "Have you ever heard of C-Cubed, or C3?"

"No." He stared at the San Francisco defense being crushed.

"Command, Control and Communications It's a special government program to deal with nuclear warfare."

"Pleasant thought," said Tyrone.

"Yeah, well, one result of a nuclear blast is a terrific release of electromagnetic energy. Enough to blow out communications and power lines for miles. That's one reason that silos are hardened - to keep the communications lines open to permit the President or whoever's still alive to shoot back."

"Like I said," Tyrone shuddered, "pleasant thought." He stopped suddenly at turned to Scott. "So it was a baby nuke?"

"No, it was EMP-T," Scott said in such a way to annoy Ty. "Electro Magnetic Pulse Transformer." The confusion on Tyrone's face was clear. "O.K., it's actually pretty simple. You know what interference sounds like on the radio or looks like on a TV?"

"Sure. My cell phone snaps crackles and pops all of the time."

"Exactly. Noise is simply electromagnetic energy that interferes with the signal. Right?" Scott waited for Tyrone to respond that he understood so far.

"Good. Imagine a magnetic pulse so strong that it not only interferes with the signal, but overloads the electronics themselves. Remember that electricity and magnetism are the same force taking different forms."

Tyrone shook his head and curled his mouth. "Right. I knew that all the time." Scott ignored him.

"The EMP-T bomb is an electromagnetic explosion, very very short, only a few microseconds, but incredibly intense." Scott gestured to indicate the magnitude of the invisible explosion. "That was the bomb that went off at the Stock Exchange."

"How can you possibly know that?" Tyrone asked with a hint of professional derision. "That requires a big leap of faith . . ."

Scott leaned over to the side of the couch and picked up the two items he had retrieved from the Exchange.

"This," Scott said handing a piece of ceramic material to Ty, "is superconducting material. Real new. It can superconduct at room temperature. And this," he handed Tyrone a piece of red glass, "is a piece of a high energy ruby laser."

Tyrone turned the curios over and over in his hands. "So?" he asked.

"By driving the output of the laser into a High Energy Static Capacitive Tank, the energy can be discharged into the super coil. The instantaneous release of energy creates a magnetic field of hundreds of thousands of gauss." Scott snapped his fingers. "And that's more than enough to blow out computer and phone circuits as well as erase anything magnetic within a thousand yards."

Tyrone was now ignoring the football action. He stared alternately at Scott and the curious glass and ceramic remnants. "You're bullshitting me, right? Sounds like science fiction."

"But the fact is that the Stock Exchange still isn't open. Their entire tape library is gone. Poof! Empty, thus the name EMP-T. It empties computers. Whoever did this has a real bad temper. Pure revenge. They wanted to destroy the information, and not the hardware itself. Otherwise the conventional blast would have been stronger. The Cemex was used to destroy the evidence of the EMP-T device."

"Where the hell do these bombs come from."

"EMP-T technology was originally developed as part of a Top Secret DARPA project for the DoD with NSA guidance a few years back."

"Then how do you know about it?"

"I did the documentation for the first manuals on EMP-T. Nothing we got from the manufacturer was marked classified and we didn't know or care."

"What was the Army going to do with them?" asked Tyrone, now with great interest.

"You know, I had forgotten all about this stuff until the other night, and then it all came back to me," Scott said mentally reminiscing. "At the time we thought it was a paranoid joke. Another government folly. The EMP-T was supposed to be shot at the enemy to screw up his battlefield computers and radar and electronics before the ground troops or choppers went it. As I understand it, EMP-T bombs are made for planes, and can also be launched from Howitzers and tanks. According to the manufacturer, they can't be detected and leave a similar signature to that of a conventional nuclear blast. If there is such a thing as a conventional nuke."

"Who else knows about this," Tyrone asked. "The police?"

"You think the NYPD would know what to look for?" Scott said snidely. "Their bomb squad went home after the plastic explosive was found."

"Right. Forget where I was."

"Think about it," Scott mused out loud. "A bomb that destroys all of the computers and memory but leaves the walls standing."

"Didn't that asshole Carter want to build a nuke that would only kill people but leave the city intact for the marauding invaders? Neutron bombs, weren't they?"

"There's obviously nothing immoral about nuking computers," Scott pontificated. "It was all part of Star Wars. Reagan's Strategic Defense included attacking enemy satellites with EMP-T bombs. Get all of the benefits and none of the fallout from a nuke. There's no accompanying radiation."

"How easy is it to put one of the empty-things together?" Tyrone missed another 49'er touchdown.

"Today?" Scott whistled. "The ones I saw were big, clumsy affairs from the 70's. With new ceramics, and such, I would assume they're a lot smaller as the Stock Exchange proves. A wild guess? I bet that EMP-T is a garage project for a couple of whiz kids, or if the government orders them, a couple hundred thou each." Scott laughed at the absurdity of competitive bidding for government projects. Everyone knew the government paid more for everything. They would do a lot better with a VISA card at K-Mart.

"I think I better take a look." Tyrone hinted.

"I thought you would, buddy. Thought you would." Scott replied.

They returned to the game 12 seconds before half time. The gun went off. Perfect timing. Scott hated football. The only reason in his mind for the existence of the Super Ball was to drink beer with friends and watch the commercials.

"Shit," declared Tyrone. "I missed the whole damned second quarter." He grabbed another beer to comfort his disappointment.

"Hey," Scott called to Tyrone. "During the next half, I want to ask you something."

Tyrone came back into the Music Room snickering. "What the hell is that in your bathroom?" Tyrone laughed at Scott.

"Isn't that great?" asked the enthused Scott. "It's an automatic toilet seat."

"Now just what the devil is an automatic toilet seat? It pulls it out and dries it off for you?" He believed that Scott was kidding with some of his half baked inventions. That Scott subjected any of his guests to their intermittent functioning was cruel and inhuman punishment according to Tyrone.

"You're married with three girls. Aren't they always on your case about the toilet seat?"

"I've been married 26 years," Tyrone said with pride. "I conquered toilet seats on our honeymoon. She let me know right then that she was boss and what the price of noncompliance was."

"Ouch, that's not fair," Scott said in sympathy. "I sleep-piss." He held his hands out in front. "That's the only side effect from too much acid. Sleep pissing."

Tyrone scrunched his face in disgust.

Scott spoke rapidly and loudly. "So for those of us who forget to lower the seat after use, for those who forget to raise the seat; for those who forget to raise the lid, Auto-Shit." Ty had tried to ignore him, but Scott's imitation of a hyperactive cable shopping network host demanded that one at least hear him out. Ty's eyes teared.

"Make that woman in your life happy today. No more mess, fuss or morning arguments. No more complaints from the neighbors or the health department. Auto-Shit. The toilet that knows your needs. The seat for the rest of us. Available in 6 designer colors. Only $49.95, Mastercard, Visa, No COD. Operators are standing by."

Tyrone fell over on his side laughing. "You are crazy, man. Sleep pissing. And, if you don't know it, no one, I mean no one in his right mind has five trash compactors." Tyrone waved his hand at Scott. "Ask me what you were gonna ask me."

"Off the record, Ty," Scott started, "how're the feds viewing this mess?"

Tyrone hated the position he was in, but Scott had given him a lead recently. It was time to reciprocate.

"Off?"

"So far off, so far off that if you turned the light On it would still be off."

"It's a fucking mess," Tyrone said quickly. He was relieved to be able to talk about it. "You can't believe it. I'm down there to watch a crisis management team in action, but what do I find?" He shook his head. "They're still trying to decide on the size of the conference table." The reference caught Scott's ear. "No, it's not that bad, but it might as well be."

"How is this ECCO thing put together? Who's responsible?"

"Responsible? Ha! No one," Tyrone chuckled as he recounted the constant battles among the represented agencies. "This is the perfect bureaucratic solution. No one is responsible for anything, no one is accountable, but they all want to run the show. And, no one agency clearly has authority. It's a disaster."

"No one runs security? In the whole government, no one runs security?" Scott sounded aghast.

"That's pushing it a little, but not too far off base."

"Oh, I gotta hear this," Scott said reclining in the deep plush cloth covered couch.

"Once upon a time, a super secret agency, no one ever spoke the initials, but it begins with the National Security Agency, got elected by the Department of Defense to work out communications security during the Cold War. They took their job very seriously.

"Then along came NIST and IBM who developed DES. The DOD formed the Computer Security Initiative and then the Computer Security Evaluation Center. The DOD CSEC became the DOD Computer Security and then after NSA realized that everybody knew who they were, it became the NCSC. Following this?"

Scott nodded only not to disrupt the flow.

"O.K.. In 1977, Carter signed a bill that said to NSA, you take over the classified national security stuff, but gave the dregs, the unclassified stuff to the NTIA, a piece of Commerce. But that bill made a lot of people unhappy. So, along comes Reagan who says, no that's wrong, before we get anything constructive done, let me issue a Directive, number 145, and give everything back to NSA.

"That pissed off even more people and Congress then passed the Computer Security Act of 1987, stripped NSA of what it had and gave NIST the unclassified stuff. As a result, NSA closed the NCSC, NIST is underbudgeted by a factor of 100 and in short, they all want a piece of a very small pie. That took over 4 years. And that's whose fault it is.

"Whose?"

"Congress of course. Congress passes the damn laws and then won't fund them. Result? I get stuck in the middle of third tier rival agency technocrats fighting over their turf or shirking responsibility, and . . .you get the idea. So I've got ECCO to talk to CERT to talk to NIST to talk to . . .and it goes on ad nauseum."

"Sorry I asked," joked Scott.

"In other words," Ty admitted, "I don't have the first foggy idea what we'll do. They all seem hell bent on power instead of fixing the problem. And the scary part?"

"What's that?"

"It looks like it can only get worse."

* * * * *

Tuesday, November 11
White House Press Room

"Mr. President," asked the White House correspondent for Time magazine. "A recent article in the City Times said that the military has been hiding a super weapon for years that is capable of disabling enemy computers and electronics from a great distance without any physical destruction. Is that true, sir, and has the use of those weapons contributed to the military's successes over the last few years?"

"Ah, well," the President hesitated briefly. "The Stealth program was certainly a boon to our air superiority. There is no question about that, and it was kept secret for a decade." He stared to his left, and the press pool saw him take a visual cue from his National Security Director. "Isn't that right Henry?" Henry Kennedy nodded aggressively. "We have the best armed forces in the world, with all the advantages we can bring to bear, and I will not compromise them in any way. But, if there is such a classified program that I was aware of, I couldn't speak of it even if I didn't know it existed." The President picked another newsman. "Next, yes, Jim?"

During the next question Henry Kennedy slipped off to the anteroom and called the Director of the National Security Agency. "Marv, how far have you gotten on this EMP-T thing?" He waited for a response. "The President is feeling embarrassed." Another pause. "So the Exchange is cooperating?" Pause. Wait. "How many pieces are missing?" Pause. "That's not what Mason's article said." Longer pause. "Deal with it."

Immediately after the press conference, the President, Phil Musgrave, his Chief of Staff, Henry Kennedy and Qunton Chambers his old time ally and Secretary of State had an impromptu meeting in the Oval Office.

They sat in the formal Queen Anne furniture as an elegant silver coffee and tea service was brought in for the four men. Minus Treasury Secreatry Martin Royce, this was the President' inner circle, his personal advisory clique who assisted in making grand national policy. Anything goes in one of these sessions, the President had made clear in the first days of his Administration. Anything.

We do not take things personally here, he would say. We have to explore all options. All options. Even if they are distasteful. And in these meeting, treat me like one of the guys. "Yes, sir, Mr. President." The only formality of their caucuses was the President's fundamental need to mediate the sometimes heated dialogues between his most trusted aids. They were real free-for-alls.

"Henry," the President said. "Before we start, who was that reporter? Where the hell did that question come from; the one about the weapon stuff?"

"Forget him. The story started at the City Times. Scott Mason, sir." Musgrave replied quickly. His huge football center sized body overwhelmed the couch on which he sat. "He's been giving extensive coverage to computer crime."

"Well, do we have such a bomb?" he asked with real curiosity.

"Ah, yessir," Henry Kennedy responded. "It's highly classified. But the object is simple. Lob in a few of the EMP-T bombs as they're called, shut down their communications and control, and move in during the confusion. Very effective, sir."

"Well, let's see what we can do about keeping secrets a little better. O.K., boys?" The President's charismatic hold over even his dear friends and long time associates made him one of the most effective leaders in years. If he was given the right information.

The President scanned a few notes he had made on a legal pad. "O

"Can I forget about it?" the President closely scrutinized Henry for any body language.

"Yessir."

The President gave Henry one more glance and made an obvious point of highlighting the item. The subject would come up again.

* * * * *

Chapter 12

Thursday, November 14
NASA Control Center, Johnson Space Center

The voice of Mission Control spoke over the loudspeakers and into hundreds of headsets.

THE GROUND LAUNCH SEQUENCER HAS BEEN IN-ITIATED. WE'RE AT T-MINUS 120 SECONDS AND COUNT-ING.

The Space Shuttle Columbia was on Launch Pad 3, in its final preparation for another secret mission. As was expected, the Department of Defense issued a terse non-statement on its purpose: "The Columbia is carrying a classified payload will be used for a series of experiments. The flight is scheduled to last three days."

In reality, and most everyone knew it, the Columbia was going to release another KH-5 spy satellite. The KH-5 series was able, from an altitude of 110 miles, to discern and transmit to Earth photos so crisp, it could resolve the numbers on an automobile license plate. The photographic resolution of KH-5's was the envy of every government on the planet, and was one of the most closely guarded secrets that everyone knew about.

T-MINUS 110 SECONDS AND COUNTING.

Mission control specialists at the Cape and in Houston monitored every conceivable instrument on the Shuttle itself and the ground equipment that made space flight possible.

A cavernous room full of technicians checked and double checked and triple checked fuel, temperature, guidance, computers systems, backup systems, relays, switches, communications links, telemetry, gyros, the astronauts' physiology, life support systems, power supplies . . .everything had a remote control monitor.

"The liquid hydrogen replenish has been terminated, LSU pressurization to flight level now under way. Vehicle is now isolated from ground loading equipment."

T-MINUS 100 SECONDS AND COUNTING

"SRB and external tank safety devices have been armed. In-hibit remains in place until T-Minus 10 seconds when the range safety destruct system is activated."

The Mission Control Room had an immense map of the world spread across its 140 feet breadth. It showed the actual and projected trajectories of the Shuttle. Along both sides of the map were several large rear projection video screens. They displayed the various camera angles of the launch pad, the interior of the Shuttle's cargo hold, the cockpit itself and an assortment of other shots that the scientists deemed important to the success of each flight.

T-MINUS 90 SECONDS AND COUNTING

"At the T-Minus one minute mark, the ground launch sequencer will verify that the main shuttle engines are ready to start."

T-MINUS 80 SECONDS AND COUNTING

"Liquid hydrogen tanks now reported at flight pressure."
The data monitors scrolled charts and numbers. The computers spewed out their data, updating it every few seconds as the screens flickered with the changing information.

T-MINUS 70 SECONDS AND COUNTING

The Voice of Mission Control continued its monotone countdown. Every airline passenger is familiar with the neo-Texas twang that conveys sublime confidence, even in the tensest of situations.

The Count-down monitor above the global map decremented its numbers by the hundredths of seconds, impossible for a human to read but terribly inaccurate by computer standards.

"Coming up on T-Minus one minute and counting."

T-MINUS 60 SECONDS

"Pressure systems now armed, lift off order will be released at T-Minus 16 seconds."
The voice traffic became chaotic. Hundreds of voices give their consent that their particular areas of responsibility are ship-shape. The word *nominal* sounds to laymen watching the world over as a classic understatement. If things are great, then say 'Fuel is Great!'. NASA prefers the word *nominal* to indicate that systems are performing as the design engineers predicted in their simulation models.

T-MINUS 50 SECONDS AND COUNTING.

The hoses that connect the Shuttle to the Launch Pad began to fall away. Whirls of steam and smoke appeared around portions of the boosters. The tension was high. 45 seconds to go.
"SRB flight instrumentation recorders now going to record."
Eyes riveted to computer screens. It takes hundreds of computers to make a successful launch. Only the mission generalists watch over the big picture; the screens across the front of the behemoth 80 foot high room.

183

T-MINUS 40 SECONDS AND COUNTING

"**External tank heaters now turned off in preparation for launch.**"

Screens danced while minds focused on their jobs. It wasn't until there were only 34 seconds left on the count down clock that anyone noticed.

The main systems display monitor, the one that contained the sum of all other systems information displayed a message never seen before by anyone at NASA.

"CHRISTA MCAULIFFE AND THE CHALLENGER WELCOME THE CREW OF THE SPACE SHUTTLE COLUMBIA."

"**We have a go for auto sequence start. Columbia's forward computers now taking over primary control of critical vehicle functions through lift-off.**"

T-MINUS 30 SECONDS AND COUNTING

"What the hell is that?" Mission Specialist Hawkins said to the technician who was monitoring the auto-correlation noise reduction systems needed to communicate with the astronauts once in space.

TWENTY NINE

"What?" Sam Broadbent took off his earpiece.

TWENTY EIGHT

"Look at that." Hawkins pointed at the central monitor.

TWENTY SEVEN

"What does that mean? It's not in the book."

TWENTY SIX

"I dunno. No chances though." Hawkins switched his intercom selector to 'ALL', meaning that everyone on line, including the Mission Control Director would hear.

TWENTY FIVE

"We have an anomaly here . . ." Hawkins said into his mouthpiece.

TWENTY FOUR

"Specify anomaly, comm." The dry voice returned. Hawkins wasn't quite sure how to respond. The practice runs had not covered this eventuality.

TWENTY THREE

"Look up at Video 6. Switching over." Hawkins tried to remain unflustered.

TWENTY TWO

"Copy comm. Do you contain?"

TWENTY ONE

"Negative Mission Control. It's an override." Hawkins answered.

TWENTY - FIRING SEQUENCE NOMINAL

The voice of Mission Control annoyed Hawkins for the first time in his 8 years at NASA.
"Confirm and update."

NINETEEN

Hawkins blew his cool. "Look at the goddamned monitor for Chrissakes. Just look!" He yelled into the intercom.

EIGHTEEN

"Holy . . .who's . . .please confirm, local analysis," the sober voice sounded concerned for the first time.

SEVENTEEN

"Confirmed anomaly." "Confirmed." "Confirmed." "Confirmed." The votes streamed in.

SIXTEEN

"We have a confirm . . ."

T-MINUS 15 SECONDS AND COUNTING.

TEN

"We have a go for main engine start."

SEVEN

SIX

FIVE

"We have a main engine start . . .We have a cut off."
"Columbia, we have a monitor anomaly, holding at T-minus 5."
"That's a Roger, Houston," the commander of Space Shuttle Columbia responded calmly.

"We have a manual abort override, Columbia's on board computers confirm the cut-off. Can you verify, Columbia?"

"That's a Roger."

The huge block letter message continued to blaze across the monitors. Craig Volker spoke rapidly into his master intercom system. "Cut network feed. Cut direct feed. Cut now! Now!" All TV networks suddenly lost their signal that was routed through NASA's huge video switches. NASA's own satellite feed was simultaneously cut as well. If NASA didn't want it going to the public it didn't get sent.

CNN got the first interview with NASA officials.

"What caused today's flight to be aborted?"

"We detected a slight leak in the fuel tanks. We believe that the sensors were faulty, that there was no leak, but we felt in the interest of safety it would be best to abort the mission. Orbital alignment is not critical and we can attempt a relaunch within 2 weeks. When we know more we will make further information available." The NASA spokesman left abruptly.

The CNN newsman continued. "According to NASA, a malfunctioning fuel monitor was the cause of today's aborted shuttle launch. However, several seconds before the announced abort, our video signal was cut by NASA. Here is a replay of that countdown again."

CNN technicians replayed one of their video tapes. The video monitors within Mission Control were not clear on the replay. But the audio was. "Look at the goddamned monitor for Chrissakes. Just look." Then the video went dead.

* * * * *

San Diego, California

Steve Billings received an urgent message on his computer's E-Mail when he got home from classes. All it said was:

PHONE HOME

He dialed NEMO directly this time.

<<<CONNECTION>>>

He chose CONVERSATION PIT from the menu. La Creme was there, alone and probably waiting.

What's the panic?

YOU DON'T KNOW? <CREME>

Just finished exams . . .been locked up in student hell . . .

NASA ABORT . . .SHUTTLE WENT TO SHIT. <CREME>

So? More Beckel fuel problems I s'pose.

UH . . .UH. NOT THIS TIME. NASA GOT AN INVITATION. <CREME>

From aliens? SETI finally came through?

NOPE. FROM CHRISTA MCAULIFFE. <CREME>

Right.

SERIOUS. SHE WELCOMED THE CREW OF COLUMBIA. <CREME>

Get real . . .

I AM. CHECK OUT CNN. THEY RECONSTRUCTED THE VIDEO SIGNAL BEFORE NASA SHUT THE FEED DOWN. THE MONITORS HAD A GREETING FROM CHRISTA. ABORTED THE DAMN MISSION. <CREME>

I don't get it.

NEITHER DO I. BUT, DON'T YOU PLAY AROUND IN NASA COMPUTERS? <CREME>

Sure I do. Poke and Play. I'm not alone.

AND REPROGRAM THE LAUNCH COMPUTERS? <CREME>

Never. It's against the Code.

I KNOW THAT, BUT DO YOU? <CREME>

What are getting at?

OK GOOD BUDDY . . .STRAIGHT SHOOTING. DID YOU GO IN AND PUT SOME MESSAGES ON MISSION CONTROL COMPUTERS? <CREME>

Fuck, no. You know better than that.

I HOPED YOU'D SAY THAT. <CREME>

Hey . . .thanks for the vote of confidence.

NO OFFENSE DUDE. HADDA ASK. THEN IF YOU DIDN'T WHO DID? <CREME>

I don't know. That's sick.

NO SHIT SHERLOCK. NASA'S ONE PISSED OFF PUPPY. THEY HAVEN'T GONE PUBLIC YET, BUT THE MEDIA'S GOT IT PEGGED THAT HACKERS ARE RESPONSIBLE. WE MAY HAVE TO LOCK IT UP.

Damn. Better get clean.

YOU LEAVE TRACKS?

Nah. They're security is for shit. No nothing. Besides, I get in as SYSOP. I can erase my own tracks.

BETTER BE SURE.

I ain't going back, not for a while.

THERE'S GONNA BE SOME SERIOUS HEAT ON THIS.

Can't blame 'em. What d'you suggest? I'm clean, really.

BELIEVE YOU GUY. I DO. BUT WILL THEY?

I hope so . . .

* * * * *

Friday, November 15
New York City Times

NASA SCRUBS MISSION: HACKERS AT PLAY?

by Scott Mason

NASA canceled the liftoff of the space shuttle Columbia yesterday, only five seconds prior to liftoff. Delays in the troubled shuttle program are nothing new. It seems that just about everything that can go wrong has gone wrong in the last few years. We watch fuel tanks leak, backup computers go bad, life support systems malfunction and suffer through a complete range of incomprehensible defects in the multi-billion dollar space program.

We got to the moon in one piece, but the politics of the Shuttle Program is overwhelming.

Remember what Senator John Glenn said during his historic 3 orbit mission in the early days of the Mercury Program. "It worries me some. To think that I'm flying around up here in a machine built by the lowest bidder."

At the time, when the space program had the support of the country from the guidance of the young Kennedy and from the fear of the Soviet lead, Glenn's comment was meant to alleviate the tension. Successfully, at that. But since the Apollo fire and the Challenger disaster, and an all too wide array of constant technical problems, political will is waning. The entire space program suffers as a result.

Yesterday's aborted launch echoes of further bungling. While the management of NASA is undergoing critical review, and executive replacements seem imminent, the new breed will have to live with past mistakes for some time. Unfortunately, most Americans no longer watch space launches, and those that do tune out once the astronauts are out of camera range. The Space Program suffers from external malaise as well as internal confusion.

That is, until yesterday.

In an unprecedented move, seconds after the countdown was halted, NASA cut its feeds to the networks and all 4 channels were left with the omnipresent long lens view of the space shuttle sitting idle on its launch pad. In a prepared statement, NASA blamed the aborted flight on yet another leak from the massive and explosive 355,000 gallon fuel tanks. In what will clearly become another public relations fiasco, NASA lied to us again. It appears that NASA's computers were invaded.

CNN scooped the other networks by applying advanced digital reconstruction to a few frames of video. Before NASA cut the feed, CNN was receiving pictures of the monitor walls from Mission Control in Houston, Texas. Normally those banks of video monitors contain critical flight information, telemetry, orbital paths and other data to insure the safety of the crew and machinery.

Yesterday, though, the video monitors carried a message to the nation:

CHRISTA MCAULIFFE AND THE CHALLENGER WELCOME THE CREW OF THE SPACE SHUTTLE COLUMBIA.

This was the message that NASA tried to hide from America. Despite the hallucinations of fringe groups who are prophesizing imminent contact with an alien civilization, this message was not from a large black monolith on the Moon or from the Red Spot on Jupiter. A Star Baby will not be born.

The threatening words came from a deranged group of computer hackers who thought it would be great sport to endanger the lives of our astronauts, waste millions of taxpayer dollars, retard military space missions and make a mockery of NASA. CNN confronted NASA officials with undisputable evidence within minutes after the attempted launch, and the following statement was issued:

"The Space Shuttle Columbia flight performing a military mission, was aborted 5 seconds prior to lift-off. First reports indicated that the reason was a minor leak in a fuel line. Subsequent analysis showed, though, that the Side Band Com-

munications Monitoring System displayed remote entry anomalies inconsistent with program launch sequence. Automatic system response mechanisms put the count-down on hold until it was determined that intermittent malfunctions could not be repaired without a launch delay. The launch date has been put back until November 29."

Permit me to translate this dribble of NASA-speak with the straight skinny.

The anomaly they speak of euphemistically was simple: A computer hacker, or hackers, got into the NASA computers and caused those nauseating words to appear on the screen. The implication was obvious. Their sickening message was a distinct threat to the safety of the mission and its crew. So, rather than an automatic systems shut-down, as the CNN tape so aptly demonstrates, a vigilant technician shouted, "Look at the g____ed monitor for Chrissakes! Just look!"

While the NASA computers failed to notice that they had been invaded from an outside source, their able staff prevented what could have been another national tragedy. Congratulations!

If computer hackers, those insidious little moles who secretively poke through computer systems uninvited and unchecked, are the real culprits as well placed NASA sources suggest, they need to be identified quickly, and be prosecuted to the fullest extent possible. There are laws that have been broken. Not only the laws regarding computer privacy, but legal experts say that cases can be made for Conspiracy, Sedition, Blackmail, Terrorism and Extortion.

But, according to computer experts, the likelihood of ever finding the interlopers is " . . .somewhere between never and none. Unless they left a trail, which good hackers don't, they'll get away with this Scott free."

Hackers have caused constant trouble to computer systems over the years, and it they have been increasing in both number and severity. This computer assault needs to be addressed immediately. America insists on it. Not only must the hacker responsible for this travesty be caught, but NASA must also explain how their computers can be compromised so easily. If a bunch of kids can enter one NASA communications computer, then what stops them from altering flight computers, life support systems and other computer controlled activities that demand perfect operation?

NASA, we expect an answer.

This is Scott Mason, waiting for NASA to lift-off from its duff and get down to business.

* * * * *

Friday, November 15
New York City.

Scott Mason picked up the phone on the first ring.

"Scott Mason," he said without thinking.

"Mr. Mason? This is Captain Kirk." The voice was serious, but did not resonate as did the distinctive voice that belonged to William Shatner. Scott laughed into the phone.

"Live long and prosper." Mason replied in an emotionless voice.

"I need to talk to you." The voice came right back.

"So talk." Scott was used to anonymous callers so he kept the rhythm of the conversation going.

"You have it all wrong. Hackers aren't the bad lot." The voice was earnest.

"What are you talking about?" Scott asked innocuously.

"Your articles keep saying that hackers cause all the trouble on computers. You're wrong."

"Says who?" Scott decided to play along.

"Says me. You obviously don't know about the Code."

"What code?" This was getting nowhere fast.

"Listen, I know your phone is tapped, so I only have another few seconds. Do you want to talk?"

"Tapped? What is this all about?" The annoyance was clear in Scott's voice.

"You keep blaming everything on hackers. You're wrong."

"Prove it." Scott gave this phone call another 10 seconds.

"I've been inside the NASA computers."

That got Scott to wake up from the droll papers on his desk. "Are you telling me you wrote the message . . .?" Scott could not contain his incredulity.

"God, no." Captain Kirk was firm. "Do you have a modem? At home?"

"Yeah, so what." Scott gave the caller only another 5 seconds.

"What's the number?"

"Is this love or hate?" Time's up thought Scott.

"News."

"What?"

"News. Do I talk to you or the National Exposé? I figured you might be a safer bet." The voice who called himself Captain Kirk gave away nothing but the competitive threat was effective.

"No contest. If it's real. What have you got?" Scott paid attention.

"What's the number?" The voice demanded. "Your modem."

"O.K. 914-555-2190." Scott gave his home modem number.

"Be on at midnight." The line went dead.

Scott briefly mentioned the matter to his editor, Doug, who in turn gave him a very hard time about it. "I thought you said virus hacker connection was a big ho-hum. As I recall, you said they weren't sexy enough? What happened"

"Eating crow can be considered a delicacy if the main course is phenomonal."

"I see," laughed Doug. Creative way out, he thought.

"He said he'd been plowing around NASA computers," Scott argued.

"Listen, ask your buddy Ben how many crackpots admit to crimes just for the attention. It's crap." Doug was too jaded, thought Scott.

"No, no, it's legit," Scott said defensively. "Sounds like a hacker conspiracy to me."

"Legit? Legit?" Doug laughed out loud. "Your last column just about called for all computer junkies to be castrated and drawn and quartered before they are hung at the stake. And now you think an anonymous caller who worse yet claims to be a hacker, is for real? C'mon, Scott. You can't have it both ways. Sometimes your conspiracies are bit far fetched . . ."

"And when we hit, it sells papers." Scott reminded his boss that it was still a business.

Nonetheless, Doug made a point that hit home with Scott. Could he both malign computer nerds as sub-human and then expect to derive a decent story from one of them? There was an inconsistency there. Even so, some pretty despicable characters have turned state's evidence and made decent witnesses against their former cohorts. Had Captain Kirk really been where no man had been before?

"You don't care if I dig a little?" Scott backed off and played the humble reporter.

"It's your life." That was Doug's way of saying, "I told you there was a story here. Run!"

"No problem, chief." Scott snapped to mock attention and left his editor's desk before Doug changed his mind.

* * * * *

Midnight
Scarsdale, New York

Scott went into his study to watch Nightline after grabbing a cold beer and turned on the light over his computer. His study could by all standards be declared a disaster area, which his ex-wife Maggie often had. In addition to the formal desk, 3 folding tables were piled high with newspapers, loose clippings, books, scattered notes, folders, magazines, and crumpled up paper balls on the floor. The maid had refused to clean the room for 6 months since he blamed her for disposing of important notes that he had filed on the floor. They were back on good terms, he had apologized, but his study was a no-man's, or no maid's land.

Scott battled to clear a place for his beer as his computer booted up. Since he primarily used his computer for writing, it wasn't terribly powerful by today's standards. A mere 386SX running at 20 megahertz and comparatively low resolution VGA color graphics. It was all he needed. He had a modem in it to connect to the paper's computer. This way he could leave the office early, write his articles or columns at home and still have them in by deadline. He also owned a GRiD 396 laptop computer for when he traveled, but it was buried beneath a mound of discarded magazines on one of the built-in floor to ceiling shelves that ringed the room.

Scott wondered if Kirk would really call. He had seemed paranoid when he called this afternoon. Phones tapped? Where did he ever get that idea? Preposterous. Why wouldn't his phone at home be tapped if the ones at work were? We'll see.

Scott turned the old 9" color television on the corner of the desk to Nightline. Enough to occupy him even if Kirk didn't call.

He set the ComPro communications program to Auto-Answer. If Kirk, or anyone else did call him, the program would automatically answer the phone and his computer would alert him that someone else's computer had called his computer.

He noticed the clock chime midnight as Nightline went overtime to further discuss the economic unification of Europe. Including much of Eastern Europe. Fascinating, he thought. I grow up in the 60's and 70's when we give serious concern to blowing up the world and today our allies of a half century ago, turned Cold War enemy, are talking about joining NATO.

At 12:02, Scott Mason's computer beeped at him. The beeping startled him.

He looked at the computer screen as a first message appeared.

WTFO

Scott didn't know what to make of it, so he entered a simple response.

Hello.

The computer screen paused briefly then came alive again.

ARE YOU SCOTT MASON?

Scott entered 'Yes'.

THIS IS KIRK

Scott wondered what the proper answer was to a non-question by a computer. So he retyped in his earlier greeting.

Hello. Again.

IS THIS YOUR FIRST TIME?

What a question! Scott answered quickly.

Please be gentle.

NO . . .AT CHATTING ON COMPUTER . . .

I call the computer at work. First time with a stranger. Is it safe?

Scott had a gestalt realization. This was fun. He didn't talk to the paper's computer. He treated it as an electronic mailbox. But this, there was an attractiveness to the anonymity behind the game. Even if this Kirk was a flaming asshole, he might have discovered a new form of entertainment.

VERY GOOD. YOU'RE QUICK.

Not too quick, sweetheart.

IS THIS REALLY SCOTT MASON?

Yes.

PROVE IT.

Kirk, or whoever this was, was comfortable with anonymity, obviously. And paranoid. Sure, play the game.

You screwed up the NASA launch.

I DID NOT!!!!!!!!!! OK, IT'S YOU.

Glad to know it.

YOU GOT IT ALL WRONG.

What do I have wrong?

ABOUT HACKERS. WE'RE NOT BAD. ONLY A FEW BAD AP-PLES, JUST LIKE COPS AND REPORTERS. I HOPE YOU'RE A GOOD GUY.

You called me, remember?

STILL, IT'S NOT LIKE YOU THINK.

Sure, I think.

NO NO NO . . .HACKERS. WE'RE BASICALLY A GOOD LOT WHO ENJOY COMPUTERS FOR COMPUTERS SAKE.

That's what I've been saying

REALLY. HEY, DO YOU KNOW WHAT A HACKER REALLY IS?

A guy who pokes his nose around where it's not wanted. Like in NASA computers.

YEAH, THAT'S WHAT THE PRESS SAYS AND SO THAT'S WHAT THE COUNTRY THINKS. BUT IT AIN'T NECESSARI- LY SO.

So, change my mind.

LET ME GIVE YOU THE NAMES OF A FEW HACKERS. BILL GATES. HE FOUNDED MICROSOFT. WORTH A COUPLE OF BILLION. MITCH KAPOR. FOUNDED LOTUS. STEVE WOZNIAK FOUNDED APPLE. GET THE POINT?

You still haven't told me what you think a hacker is.

A HACKER IS SOMEONE WHO HACKS WITH COMPUTERS. SOMEONE WHO ENJOYS USING THEM, PROGRAMMING THEM, FIGURING OUT HOW THEY WORK, WHAT MAKES THEM TICK. PUSHING THEM TO THE LIMIT. EXTRACTING EVERY LAST INCH OF POWER FROM THEM. LET ME ASK YOU A QUESTION. WHAT DO YOU CALL SOMEONE WHO PLAYS WITH AMATEUR RADIOS?

A Ham.

AND WHAT DO YOU CALL SOMEONE WHO HAS A CAL- CULATOR IN HIS SHORT POCKET WITH A DOZEN BALLPOINT PENS?

In my day it was a sliderule, and we called them propeller heads.

THAT TRANSLATES. GOOD. AND WHAT DO YOU CALL SOMEONE WHO FLIES AIRPLANES FOR FUN?

A fly boy, space jockey . . .

A CAR TINKERER?

A grease monkey

AND SOMEONE WHO JUMPS OUT OF PLANES?

Fucking crazy!!!!

FAIR ENOUGH. BUT HERE'S THE POINT. DIFFERENT STROKES FOR DIFFERENT FOLKS. AND IT JUST SO HAP- PENS THAT PEOPLE WHO LIKE TO PLAY WITH COM- PUTERS ARE CALLED HACKERS. IT'S AN OLD TERM FROM THE 60'S FROM THE COLLEGES, AND AT THAT TIME IT WASN'T DEROGATORY. IT DIDN'T HAVE THE SAME NEGATIVE CONNOTATIONS THAT IT DOES TODAY THANKS TO YOU. HACKERS ARE JUST A BUNCH OF PEOPLE WHO PLAY WITH COMPUTERS INSTEAD OF CARS, BOATS, AIRPLANES, SPORTS OR WHATEVER. THAT'S IT, PURE AND SIMPLE.

Ok, let's accept that for now. What about those stories of hackers running around inside of everybody else's computers and making computer viruses and all. Morris and Chase were hackers who caused a bunch of damage.

WHOA! TWO SEPARATE ISSUES. THERE ARE A NUMBER OF HACKERS WHO DO GO PROBING AND LOOKING AROUND OTHER PEOPLE'S COMPUTERS. AND I AM PROUD TO ADMIT THAT I AM ONE OF THEM.

Wait a minute. You first say that hackers are the guys in the white hats and then you admit that you are one of those criminal types who invades the privacy of others.

THERE IS A BIG DIFFERENCE BETWEEN LOOKING AROUND A COMPUTER READING ITS FILES AND DESTROY-ING THEM. I REMEMBER READING ABOUT THIS GUY WHO BROKE INTO PEOPLE'S HOUSES WHEN THEY WERE OUT OF TOWN. HE LIVED IN THEIR HOUSE UNTIL THEY CAME BACK AND THEN LEFT. HE USED THEIR FOOD, THEIR TV, THEIR SHOWER AND ALL, BUT NEVER STOLE ANYTHING OR DID ANY DAMAGE. THAT'S KINDA WHAT HACKERS DO.

Why? For the thrill?

OH, I GUESS THAT MAY BE PART OF IT, BUT IT'S REALLY MORE THAN THAT. IT'S A THIRST, AT LEAST FOR ME, FOR KNOWLEDGE.

That's a line of crap.

REALLY. LET'S COMPARE. LET'S SAY I WAS WORKING IN A GARAGE AND I WAS A CAR ENTHUSIAST BUT I DIDN'T OWN AND COULDN'T AFFORD A FERRARI. SO, DURING THE DAY WHEN MY CUSTOMERS ARE AT WORK, I TAKE THEIR CARS OUT FOR A RIDE . . .AND I EVEN REPLACE THE GAS. I DO IT FOR THE THRILL OF THE RIDE, NOT FOR THE THRILL OF THE CRIME.

So you admit hacking is a crime?

NO NO NO NO. AGREED, ENTERING SOME COMPUTERS IS CONSIDERED A CRIME IN SOME STATES, BUT IN THE STATE OF TEXAS, IF YOU LEAVE YOUR COMPUTER PASSWORD TAPED TO THE BOTTOM OF YOUR DESK DRAWER YOU CAN GO TO JAIL. I BET YOU DIDN'T KNOW THAT.

You made that up.

CHECK IT OUT. I DON'T KNOW THE LEGAL JARGON, BUT IT'S TRUE. THE ISSUE IS, FOR THE GUY WHO DRIVES PEOPLE'S CARS WITHOUT THEIR PERMISSION, THAT IS REALLY A CRIME. I GUESS A GRAND FELONY. RIGHT?

EVEN IF HE DOES NOTHING BUT DRIVE IT AROUND THE BLOCK. BUT WITH COMPUTERS IT'S DIFFERENT.

How is it different?

FIRST THERE'S NO THEFT.

What about theft of service?

ARGUABLE.

Breaking and entering.

NOT ACCORDING TO MY FRIEND. HIS FATHER IS A LAWYER.

But, you have to admit, you are doing it without permission.

NO, NOT REALLY.

Aw, come on.

LISTEN. LET'S SAY THAT YOU LIVE IN A HOUSE.

Nice place to make a home.

AND LET'S SAY THAT YOU AND YOUR NEIGHBORS DECIDE TO LEAVE THE KEYS TO YOUR HOUSES ON THE CURB OF YOUR STREET EVERY DAY. EVEN WHEN YOU'RE HOME. SO THAT ANYONE WHO COMES ALONG CAN PICK UP THE KEYS AND WALK INTO YOUR HOUSE ANYTIME THEY WANT TO.

That's crazy.

OF COURSE IT IS. BUT WHAT WOULD HAPPEN IF YOU DID THAT AND THEN YOUR HOUSE GOT BROKEN INTO AND YOU WERE ROBBED?

I guess the police would figure me for a blithering idiot, a candidate for the funny farm, and my insurance company might have reason not to pay me after they cancelled me. So what?

THAT'S WHAT I DO. AND THAT'S WHAT MY FRIENDS DO. WE LOOK AROUND FOR PEOPLE WHO LEAVE THE KEYS TO THEIR COMPUTERS LYING AROUND FOR ANYONE TO PICK UP. WHEN WE FIND A SET OF KEYS, WE USE THEM.

It can't be that simple. No one would leave keys lying around for hackers.

WRONGO MEDIA BREATH. IT'S ABSURDLY SIMPLE. I DON'T KNOW OF VERY MANY COMPUTERS THAT I CAN'T GET INTO. SOME PEOPLE CALL IT BREAKING AND ENTERING. I CALL IT A WELCOME MAT. IF YOU DON'T WANT ME IN YOUR COMPUTER, THEN DON'T LEAVE THE FRONT DOOR OPEN.

If what you're saying is true . . .

IT IS. COMPLETELY. I HAVE THE KEYS TO HUNDREDS OF COMPUTERS AROUND THE COUNTRY AND THE WORLD. AND ONE WAY OR ANOTHER THE KEYS WERE ALL LEFT LYING IN THE STREET. SO I USED THEM TO HAVE A LOOK AROUND.

I don't know if I buy this. But, for now, I'll put that aside. So, where do these hacker horrors come from?

AGAIN LET'S COMPARE. IF YOU LEFT YOUR KEYS IN FRONT OF YOUR HOUSE AND HALF OF YOUR TOWN KNEW IT AND 100 PEOPLE WENT INTO YOUR HOUSE TO LOOK AROUND, HOW MANY WOULD STAY HONEST AND JUST LOOK?

Not many I guess.

BUT WITH HACKERS. THERE'S A CODE OF ETHICS THAT MOST OF US LIVE BY. BUT AS IN ANY GROUP OR SOCIETY THERE ARE A FEW BAD APPLES AND THEY GIVE THE REST OF US A BAD NAME. THEY GET A KICK OUT OF HURTING OTHER PEOPLE, OR STEALING, OR WHATEVER. HERE'S ANOTHER SOMETHING FOR YOUR FILE. EVERY COMPUTER SYSTEM IN THE COUNTRY HAS BEEN ENTERED BY HACKERS. EVERY SINGLE ONE.

That's impossible.

TRY ME. I'VE BEEN INTO OVER A THOUSAND MYSELF AND THERE ARE THOUSANDS OF GUYS LIKE ME. AT LEAST I'M HONEST.

Why should I believe that?

WE'RE TALKING AREN'T WE.

Throw me off the track.

I COULD HAVE IGNORED YOU. I'M UNTRACEABLE.

By the way, what's your name.

CAPTAIN KIRK.

No, really.

REALLY. ON BBS THAT'S MY ONLY NAME.

How can I call you?

YOU CAN'T. WHAT'S YOUR HANDLE?

Handle? Like CB? Never had one.

YOU NEED ONE DUDE. WITHOUT IT YOU'RE A JUST A REPORTER NERD.

Been called worse. How about Spook? That's what I'm doing.

CAN'T. WE ALREADY GOT A SPOOK. CAN'T HAVE TWO. TRY AGAIN.

What do you mean we?

WE. MY GROUP. YOU'VE ALREADY HEARD OF 401 AND
CHAOS AND THE LEGION OF DOOM. WELL, I AM PART OF
ANOTHER GROUP. BUT I CAN'T TELL YOU WHAT IT'S
CALLED. YOU'RE NOT PART OF THE INNER CIRCLE. I
KNOW WHAT I'LL CALL YOU. REPO MAN.

repo man

REPORTER MAN. SUSPICIOUS TOO.

I suspect that hackers are up to no good.

OK, SOME AREN'T, BUT THEY'RE THE EXCEPTION. HOW
MANY MASS GOOD SAMARITANS OTHER THAN MOTHER
TERESA DO YOU WRITE ABOUT? NONE. ONLY IF
THEY'RE KILLED IN ACTION. BUT, MASS MURDERERS
ARE NEWS. SO ALL YOU NEWS FIENDS MAKE HEAD-
LINES ON DEATH AND DESTRUCTION. THE MEDIA SELLS
THE HYPE AND YOU CAN'T DENY IT.

*Got me. You're right, that's what the public buys. But not all
news is bad.*

EXACTLY. SEE THE POINT.

*At least we don't do the crime, just report it. What about these
viruses. I suppose hackers are innocent of that too.*

BY AND LARGE YES. PEOPLE THAT WRITE VIRUSES AND
INFECT COMPUTERS ARE THE COMPUTER EQUIVALENT
TO SERIAL KILLERS. OR HOW ABOUT THE GUY WITH
AIDS, WHO KNOWS HE'S GOT IT AND SCREWS AS MANY
PEOPLE AS HE CAN TO SPREAD IT AROUND. VIRUSES
ARE DANGEROUS AND DEMENTED. NO HACKER OF THE
CODE WOULD DO THAT.

You keep mentioning this code. What is the code?

IT'S A CODE OF ETHICS THAT MOST OF US LIVE BY. AND
IT'S CRUCIAL TO A STABLE UNDERGROUND CULTURE
THAT SURVIVES BY ITS WITS. IT GOES LIKE THIS:
NEVER INTENTIONALLY DAMAGE ANOTHER COMPUTER.

That's it?

PRETTY SIMPLE HUH?

*So, you said earlier that you poke around NASA computers. And
NASA just had a pretty good glitch that rings of hackers. Someone broke the code.*

EXACTLY. BUT NO ONE'S TAKING CREDIT.

*Why would they? Isn't that a sure giveaway and a trip up the
river?*

YES AND NO. MORRIS FOR EXAMPLE ADMITTED HIS MIS-TAKE. HE SAID HE WAS WRITING A VIRUS FOR THE EXER-CISE AND IT GOT OUT OF CONTROL. OOPS, HE SAID, AND I'M INCLINED TO BELIEVE HIM BECAUSE HE DIDN'T COVER HIS TRACKS. IF HE WAS SERIOUS ABOUT SHUT-TING DOWN INTERNET HE WOULDN'T HAVE BEEN FOUND AND HE WOULDN'T HAVE ADMITTED IT IF THEY EVER CAUGHT HIM. PROVING HE DID IT IS NEXT TO IMPOS-SIBLE.

So?

SO, HACKERS HAVE STRONG EGOS. THEY LIKE TO GET CREDIT FOR FINDING THE KEYS TO COMPUTERS. IT BUILDS THEM A REPUTATION THAT THEY FEED ON. VIRUS BUILDERS ARE THE SAME. IF SOMEONE BUILDS A VIRUS AND THEN FEEDS IT INTO THE SYSTEM, HE WANTS TO GET CREDIT FOR IT. SO HE TAKES CREDIT.

And then gets caught, right?

WRONGO AGAIN, LET'S SAY I TOLD YOU THAT IT WAS ME THAT DID THAT STUFF AT NASA.

So it was you?

NO NO. I SAID, IF IT WAS ME, WHAT WOULD YOU DO ABOUT IT?

Uh . . .

WHAT?

I'm thinking.

WHO WOULD YOU TELL?

The police, NASA,

WHAT WOULD YOU TELL THEM?

That you did it.

WHO AM I?

Good point. Who are you?

I DIDN'T DO IT AND I'M NOT GOING TO TELL YOU WHO I AM. YOU SEE, MOST OF US DON'T KNOW EACH OTHER. WE'VE ONLY MET OVER THE COMPUTER. IT JUST DON'T MATTER WHO I AM.

I don't know if I buy everything you say, but it is something to think about. So what about the NASA thing.

I DON'T KNOW. NOBODY DOES.

You mean, I gather, nobody has owned up to it.

EXACTLY

How can I describe you? If I wanted to use you in an article.

STUDENT AT A MAJOR UNIVERSITY.

Sounds like a Letter to Penthouse Forum.

TRY THE SEX BBS.

If you've done nothing wrong, why not come forward?

NOT EVERYONE BELIEVES WHAT WE DO IS HARMLESS.
NEITHER DO YOU. YET. MIGHT BE BAD FOR MY HEALTH.

What time is it?

WON'T WORK GUY. TIME ZONES I UNDERSTAND. ONE
THING. IF YOU'RE INTERESTED, I CAN ARRANGE A TRIP
THROUGH THE FIRST TRUST BANK COMPUTERS,

Arrange a trip? Travel agent on the side.

IN A WAY WE ARE ALL TRAVEL AGENTS. JUST THOUGHT
YOU MIGHT BE INTERESTED.

Let's say I am.

JUST CALL 212-555-9796. USE THE PASSWORD
MONEYMAN AND THE ID IS 9796. LOOK AROUND ALL YOU
WANT. USE F1 FOR HELP. I'LL CALL YOU IN A COUPLE
OF DAYS. LEAVE YOUR COMPUTER ON.

<<<CONNECTION TERMINATED>>>

* * * * *

Chapter 13

Wednesday, November 25

HACKERS HAMPER HOLIDAY HELLO'S

By Scott Mason

As most of my readers know by now, I have an inherent suspicion of lame excuses for bureaucratic bungling. If any of you were unable to make a long distance phone call yesterday, you weren't alone.

AT&T, the long distance carrier that provides the best telephone service in the world, handles in excess of 100,000,000 calls daily. Yesterday, less than 25% got through. Why? There are two possible answers: AT&T's official response and another, equally plausible and certainly more sinister reason that many experts claim to be the real culprit.

According to an AT&T spokesperson from its Basking Ridge, New Jersey office, "In my 20 years with AT&T, I have not seen a crisis so dramatic that it nearly shut down operations nationwide." According to insiders, AT&T came close to declaring a national emergency and asking for Federal assistance.

Airlines and hotel reservation services reported that phone traffic was down between 65-90%! Telemarketing organizations said that sales were off by over 80%.

Perhaps an understanding of what goes on behind the scenes of a phone call is in order.

When you pick up your phone, you hear a dial tone that is provided by the Local Exchange Company, or as it is more commonly called, a Baby Bell. The LEC handles all local calls within certain dialing ranges. A long distance call is switched by the LEC to the 4ESS, a miracle of modern communications. There are 114 Number 4 Electronic Switching Systems used in all major AT&T switching offices across the country. (A few rural areas still use relays and mechanical switches over 40 years old. When it rains, the relays get sticky and so does the call.)

Now here's the invisible beauty. There are 14 direct connects between each of the 114 4ESS's and every other 4ESS, each capable of handling thousands of call at once. So, rarely do we ever get a long distance busy signal. The systems automatically reroute themselves.

The 4ESS then calls its own STP, Signal Transfer Point within an SS7 network. The SS7 network determines from which phone number the call originated and its destination. (More about that later!) It sends out an IAM, Initial Address Message, to the destination 4ESS switch and determines if a line is available to complete the call. The SS7 is so powerful it can actually create up to 7 additional virtual paths for the heaviest traffic. 800 numbers, Dial a Porn 900 numbers and other specially coded phone numbers are translated through the NCP Network Control Point and routed separately. Whew! Had enough? So have I.

The point is, massive computer switches all across our nation automatically select the routing for each call. A call from Miami to New York could be sent through 4ESS's in Dallas, Los Angeles and Chicago before reaching its ultimate destination. But what happened yesterday?

It seems that the switches got real stupid and slowed down. For those readers who recall the Internet Worm in November of 1988 and the phone system slowdown in early 1990, computers can be infected with errors, either accidentally or otherwise, and forced to misbehave.

AT&T's explanation is not satisfying for those who remember that AT&T had said, "it can never happen again."

Today's official explanation is; "A minor hardware problem in one of our New York City 4ESS switches caused a cascading of similar hardware failures throughout the network. From all appearances, a faulty piece of software in the SS7 networks was the culprit. Our engineers are studying the problem and expect a solution shortly. We are sorry for any inconvenience to our valued customers."

I agree with AT&T on one aspect: it was a software problem.

According to well placed sources who asked to remain anonymous, the software problems were intentionally introduced into AT&T's long distance computers, by person or persons yet to be identified. They went on to say that internal investigation teams have been assigned to find out who and how the "bug" was introduced. Regardless of the outcome of the investigation, AT&T is expected, they say, to maintain the cover of a hardware failure at the request of the public relations Vice President.

AT&T did, to their credit, get long distance services up and running at 11:30 P.M. last night, only 9 hours after the problem first showed up. They re-installed an older SS7 software version that is widely known to contain some "operational anomalies" according to the company; but they still feel that it is more reliable than what is currently in use.

If in fact, the biggest busy signal in history was caused by intruders into the world's largest communications systems, then we need to ask ourselves a few questions. Was yesterday a symbolic choice of dates for disaster or mere coincidence? Would the damage have been greater on a busier business day? Could it affect our defense systems and the government's ability to communicate in case of emergency? How did someone, or some group, get into AT&T's computers and effect an entire nation's ability to do business. And then, was there a political motivation sufficient to justify an attack on AT&T and not on Sprint or MCI?

Perhaps the most salient question we all are asking ourselves, is, When will it happen again?

This is Scott Mason, busy, busy, busy. Tomorrow; Is big brother listening?

* * * * *

Friday, November 27
Times Square, New York

The pre-winter overnight snowstorm in New York City turned to sleet and ice as the temperature dropped. That didn't stop the traffic though, as hundreds of thousands of cars still crawled into Manhattan to insure downtown gridlock. If the streets were drivable, the city wouldn't stop. Not for a mere ice storm.

Steam poured from subway grates and manhole covers as rush hour pedestrians huddled from the cold winds, tromping through the grimy snow on the streets and sidewalks.

The traffic on 42nd street was at a near standstill and the intersection at Broadway and 7th Avenues where the Dow Chemical Building stood was unusually bad. Taxis and busses and trucks and cars all fought for space to move.

As the southbound light on 7th turned green, a dark blue Ford Econoline van screeched forward and cut off two taxis to make a highly illegal left turn. It curved too quickly and too sharply for the dangerously icy conditions and began to slide sideways. The driver turned the wheel hard to the left, against the slide, compensating in the wrong direction and then he slammed on the brakes. The van continued to slide to the right as it careened toward the sidewalk. The van rotated and headed backwards toward the throngs of pedestrians. They didn't notice until it was too late.

The van spun around again and crashed through a McDonald's window into the crowded breakfast crowds. As it crushed several patrons into the counter, the van stopped, suddenly propelling the driver through the windshield into the side of the yogurt machine. His neck was broken instantly.

Getting emergency vehicles to Times Square during the AM rush hour is in itself a lesson in futility. Given that 17 were pronounced dead on the scene and another 50 or more were injured, the task this Monday morning was damned near impossible.

City-ites come together in a crisis, and until enough paramedics arrived, people from all walks of life tended to the wounded and respectfully covered those beyond help. Executives in 3 piece suits worked with 7th avenue delivery boys in harmony. Secretaries lay their expensive furs on the slushy street as pallets for the victims.

It was over two hours before all the wounded were transferred to local hospitals and the morgue was close to finishing its clean up efforts. Lt. Mel Kavitz, 53rd. Precinct, Midtown South NYPD made it to the scene as the more grisly pieces were put away. He spoke to a couple of officers who had interviewed witnesses and survivors. The media were already there adding to the frigid chaos. Two of the local New York TV stations were broadcasting live, searching out sound-bytes for the evening news and all 3 dailies had reporters looking for quotable quotes. Out of the necessity created by such disasters, the police had developed immunity to the media circus.

"That's it lieutenant. Seems the van made a screwball turn and lost control." The young clean-shaven patrolman shrugged his shoulders. Only 27, he had still been on the streets long enough not to let much bother him.

"Who's the driver?" Lt. Kavitz scanned the scene.

"It's a foreign national, one . . .ah . . .Jesef Mumballa. Second year engineering student at Columbia." The young cop looked down and spoke quietly. "He didn't make it."

"I'm not surprised. Look at this mess." The Lieutenant took it in stride. "Just what McDonalds needs. Another massacre. Anything on him?" Kavitz asked half suspecting, half hoping.

"Clean. As clean as a rag head can be."

"O.K., that's enough. What about the van?"

"The van?"

"The van!" Kavitz said pointedly at the patrolman. "The van! What's in it? Has anybody looked?"

"Uh . . .no sir. We've been working with the injured . . .I'm sure you . . ."

"Of course, I'm sorry." Kavitz waved off the explanation. "Must have pretty rough." He looked around and shook his head. "Anything else officer?"

"No sir, that's about it. We still don't have an exact count though."

"It'll come soon enough. Soon enough." Kavitz left the young patrolman and walked into the bloodbath, pausing only briefly before opening the driver's side door. "Let's see what's in this thing."

* * * * *

"D'y'hear about the mess over at Times Square?" Ben Shellhorne walked up to Scott Mason's desk at the City Times.

"Yeah, pretty gruesome. The Exchange . . .McDonald's. You really scrape the bottom, don't you?" Scott grinned devilishly at Ben.

"Maybe some guys do, not me." Ben sat down next to Scott's desk. "But that's not the point. There's something else."

"What's that?" Scott turned to Ben.

"The van."

"The van?" Scott asked.

"Yeah, the van. The van that busted up the McBreakfast crowd."

"What about it?"

Ben hurried. "Well, it was some sort of high tech lab on wheels. Computers and radios and stuff. Pretty wild."

"Why's that so unusual? Phone company, computer repair place, EPA monitors, could be anything." Scott seemed disinterested.

"If that were true, you're right. But this was a private van, and there's no indication of what company it worked for. And the driver's dead. Personal ID only. No company, no numbers, no nothing, except this."

He handed several tattered computer printouts to Scott. "Look familiar?"

Scott took the papers and perused them. They were the same kind that Scott had received from Vito, his unknown donor. These were new documents as far as Scott could tell - he didn't recognize them as part of his library. They only contained some stock tips and insider trading information from a leading Wall Street brokerage house. Pretty tame stuff.

"These," Scott pointed at the papers, "these were in the van?"

"That's what I said." Ben said triumphantly.

"How did you get them?" Scott pushed.

"I have a few friends on the force and, well, this is my beat you know. Crime, disaster, murder, violence, crisis, death and destruction on the streets. Good promo stuff for the Big Apple."

"Are there any more?" Scott ignored Ben's self pity.

"My guy said there were so many that a few wouldn't make any difference."

"Holy Christ!" Scott said aloud as he sat back in thought.

"What is it? Scott? Does this mean something?"

"Can I have these, Ben? Do you need them?"

"Nah! There's no blood on 'em? Not my kinda story. I just remembered that secret papers and computers are your thing, so they're yours." Ben stood up. "Just remember, next time you hear about a serial killer, it's mine."

"Deal. And, hey, thanks a lot. Drinks on me." Scott caught Ben before he left. "Ben, one more thing."

"Yeah?" Ben stopped.

"Can you get me into that van. Just to look around? Not to touch, just to look?" Scott would have given himself a vasectomy with a weed eater to have a look. This was his first solid lead on the source of the mysterious and valuable documents that he had been stymied on for so long. He had been unable to publish anything significant due to lack of confirming evidence. Any lead was good lead, he thought.

"It may cost another favor, but sure, what the hell. I'll set it up. Call you." Ben waved as he walked off leaving Scott to ponder the latest developments.

* * * * *

The interior of the dark blue Ford Econoline van was not in bad shape as the equipment was bolted into place. The exterior though was thoroughly trashed, with too many blood stains for Scott to stomach. It was a bad wreak, even for the Police Impound.

While Ben kept his cooperative keeper of the peace occupied, he signaled to Scott that he would only have a minute, so please, make it quick.

Scott entered the van with all his senses peaked. He wanted to take mental pictures and get as much detail as he could. Both sides of the van contained riveted steel shelving, with an array of equipment bolted firmly in place. It was an odd assortment of electronics, noticed Scott. There were 2 IBM personal computers with large WYSIWYG monitors. What You See Is What You Get monitors were generally used for intensive word processing or desktop publishing. In a van? Odd.

A digital oscilloscope and waveform monitor were stacked over one of the computers. Test equipment and no hand tools? No answer. Over the other computer sat a small black and white television and a larger color television monitor. Two cellular phones were mounted behind the drivers seat. Strange combination. Then he noticed what appeared to be a miniature satellite dish, only 8 or so inches across. He recognized it as a parabolic microphone. Aha! That's it. Some sort of spy type surveillance vehicle. Tracking drug dealers and assorted low lifes. But, a privately registered vehicle, no sign of any official affiliations to known enforcement agencies?

Scott felt his minute was gone in only a few seconds.

"Well, you find what you're looking for?" Ben asked Scott after they had left the police garage grounds over looking the Hudson River.

Scott looked puzzled. "It's more like by not finding anything, I eliminated what it's not."

Ben scowled. "Hey riddle man, back to earth. Was it a waste or what?"

"Far from it." Scott's far away glaze disappeared as his personal Eureka! set in. "I think I may have stumbled, sorry, you, stumbled onto to something that will begin to put several pieces in place for me. And if I'm right, even a little bit right, holy shit. I mean, hoooolly shit."

"Clue me in, man. What's the skinny. You got Pulitzer eyes." Ben tried to keep up with Scott as their pace quickened.

"I gotta make one phone call, for a confirmation. And, if it's a yes, then I got, I mean we got one fuckuva story."

"No, it's yours, yours. Just let me keep the blood and guts. Besides, I don't even know what you're talking about, you ain't said shit. Keep it. Just keep your promise on the drinks. O.K.?"

Scott arrived at Grand Central as the huge clock oppose the giant Kodak photograph struck four o'clock. He proceeded to track twenty two where the four thirteen to Scarsdale and White Plains was waiting. He walked down to the third car and took a seat that would only hold two. He was saving it for Ty.

Tyrone Duncan hopped on the crowded train seconds before it left the station. He dashed down the aisle of the crowded car. There was only one empty seat. Next to Scott Mason. Scott's rushed call gave Ty an excuse to leave work early. It had been one of those days. Ty collapsed in a sweat on the seat opposite Scott.

"Didn't your mother tell you it's not polite to keep people waiting?" Scott made fun of Tyrone.

"Didn't your mama tell you not to irritate crazy overworked black dudes who carry a gun?"

Scott took the hint. It was safest to ignore Ty's diatribe completely. "I think I got it figured out. Thought you might be interested." Scott teased Duncan.

Tyrone turned his head away from Scott. "If you do, I'll kiss your bare ass on Broadway. We don't have shit." He sounded disgusted with the performance of his bureau.

Scott puffed up a bit before answering. The pride did not go unnoticed by Duncan. "I figured out how these guys, these blackmailers, whoever they are, get their information." Scott paused for effect which was not lost on Duncan.

"I don't care anymore. I've been pulled from the case." Tyrone said sounding exhausted.

"Well," Scott smirked. "I think you just might care, anyway."

Tyrone felt himself being pulled into Scott's trap. "What have you got?"

Scott relished the moment. The answer was so simple. He saw the anticipation in Tyrone's face, but they had become friends and didn't feel right about prolonging the tension. "Van Eck."

Duncan was expecting more than a two word answer that was absolutely meaningless to him. "What? What is Van Eck? The expressway?" He said referring to the New York Expressway that had been a 14 mile line traffic jam since it opened some 40 years ago.

"Not Van Wyck, Van Eck. Van Eck Radiation. That's how they get the information."

Duncan was no engineer, and he knew that Scott was proficient in the discipline. He was sure he had an education coming. "For us feeble minded simpletons, would you mind explaining? I know about Van Allen radiation belts, nuclear radiation . . .but OK, I give. What's this Van Eck?"

Scott had not meant to humble Tyrone that much. "Sorry. It's a pretty arcane branch of engineering, even for techy types. How much do you know about computers? Electronics?"

"Enough to get into trouble. I can wire a stereo and I know how to use the computers at the Bureau, but that's about it. Never bothered to get inside those monsters. Consider me an idiot."

"Never, just a novice. It's lecture time. Computers, I mean PC's, the kind on your desk and at home are electronic devices, that's no great revelation. As you may know, radio waves are caused by the motion of electrons, current, down a wire. Ever heard or seen interference on your TV?"

"Sure. We've been down this road before, with your EMP-T bombs." Tyrone cringed at the lecture he had received on secret defense projects.

"Exactly. Interference is caused by other electrical devices that are running near the radio or TV. Essentially, everything that runs on electricity emanates a field of energy, an electromagnetic field. Well, in TV and radio, an antenna is stuck up in the air to pick up or 'hear' the radio waves. You simply tune it in to the frequency you want to listen to."

"I know, like on my car radio. Those are preset, though."

"Doesn't matter. They still pick the frequency you want to listen to. Can you just hold that thought and accept it at face value?" Scott followed his old teaching techniques. He wanted to make sure that each and every step of his explanation was clearly understood before going on to the next. Tyrone acknowledged that while he wasn't an electronic engineer, he wasn't stupid either.

"Good. Well computers are the same. They radiate an electromagnetic field when they're in use. If the power is off then there's no radiation. Inside the computer there are so many radiated fields that it looks like garbage, pure noise to an antenna. Filtering out the information is a bitch. But, you can easily tune into a monitor."

"Monitors. You mean computer screens?" Tyrone wanted to clarify his understanding.

"Monitors, CRT's, screens, cathode ray tubes, whatever you want to call them. The inside of most monitors is just like television sets. There is an electron beam that writes to the surface of the screen, the phosphor coated one. That's what makes the picture."

"That's how a TV works? I always wondered." Duncan was only half kidding.

"So, the phosphor coating gets hit with a strong electron beam, full of high voltage energy, and the phosphor glows, just for a few milliseconds. Then, the beam comes around again and either turns it on or leaves it off, depending upon what the picture is supposed to show. Make sense?"

"That's why you can go frame to frame on a VCR, isn't it? Every second there are actually lots of still pictures that change so quickly that the eye is fooled into thinking it's watching motion. Really, it's a whole set of photographs being flipped through quickly." Duncan picked up the essentials on the first pass. Scott was visibly impressed.

"Bingo! So this beam is directed around the surface of the screen about 60 times every second."

"What moves the beam?" Duncan was following closely.

"You are one perceptive fuck aren't you? You nailed it right on the head." Scott enjoyed working with bright students. Duncan's smile made his pudgy face appear larger than it was. "Inside the monitor are what is called deflection coils. Deflection coils are magnets that tell the beam where to strike the screen's surface. One magnet moves the beam horizontally across the screen from left to right, and the other magnet, the vertical one, moves the beam from the top to the bottom. Same way as in a TV." Scott paused for a moment. He had given similar descriptions before, and he found it useful to let is audience have time to create a mental image.

"Sure, that makes sense. So what about this radiation?" Duncan impatiently asked. He wanted to understand the full picture.

"Well, magnets concentrate lots of electrical energy in a small place, so they have more intensive, or stronger magnetic fields . . .electromagnetic radiation if you will. In this case, the radiation from a computer monitor is called Van Eck radiation, named after the Dutch electrical engineer who described the phenomena." Scott sounded pleased with his Radiation 101 course brief.

Tyrone wasn't satisfied though. "So how does that explain the blackmail and the infamous papers you have? And why do I care? I don't get it." The confused look on Tyrone's face told Scott he hadn't successfully tutored his FBI friend.

"It's just like a radio station. A computer monitor puts out a distinctive pattern of surface radio waves, from the coils and pixel radiations from the screen itself, at a comparatively high power. So, with a little radio tuner, you can pick up the signals on the computer screen and read them for yourself. It's the equivalent of eavesdropping on a computer."

The stunned grimace on Duncan's face was all Scott needed to see to realize that he now had communicated the gist of the technology to him.

"Are you telling me," Tyrone searched for the words and spoke slowly, "that a computer broadcasts what's going on inside it? That anyone can read anyone else's computer?"

"In a sense yes, but not what's stored on the computer, only what's appearing on the screen at that moment." Tyrone looked out the window as they passed through Yonkers, New York. He whistled quietly to himself.

"Isn't that bad enough?" The wheels turned inside Tyrone Duncan's head as he sought the ramifications to what he had just been told.

"How did you find out? Where did you . . .?" The questions spewed forth.

"There was a wreck, midtown, and there was a bunch of equipment in it. Then I checked it out with a couple of . . .engineer friends who are more up on this than I am. They confirmed it."

"This stuff was in a van? How far away does this stuff work?" Duncan gave away his concern.

"According to my sources, with the proper gear, two or three miles is not unreasonable. In New York, maybe only a half a mile. Interference and steel buildings and all. Manhattan is a magnetic sewer, as they say."

"Shit, this could explain a lot." The confident persona of the FBI professional returned. "The marks all claim that there was no way for the information to get out, yet it did. Scott, is it possible that . . .how could one person get all this stuff? From so many companies?" The pointed question was one of devil's advocacy.

"That's the scary part, I think. If I'm right. But this is where I need your help." Scott had given his part, now to complete the tale he needed the cooperation of his friend. The story was improving.

"Jesus," Duncan said quietly contemplating the implications.

"Most people believe that their computers are private. If they knew that their inner most secrets were really being broadcast for anyone to hear, it might change their behavior a little." Scott had had the time to think about the impact if this was made

"No shit Sherlock. It makes me wonder who's been listening in on our computers all these years. Maybe that's why our jobs seem to get tougher every day." Duncan snapped himself back from the mental digression. "Where do you go from here?"

Scott was prepared. He had a final bombshell to lay on Duncan before specifying his request. "There are a couple of things that make me think. First, there is no way that only one guy could put together the amount of information that I have. I've told you how much there is. From all over the country. That suggests a lot more than one person involved. I don't know how many, that's your job.

"Two, these blackmail threats. Obviously whoever is reading the computers, Van Ecking them is what I call it, has been sending the information to someone else. Then they, in turn, call up their targets and let them know that their secrets are no longer so secret. Then three, they have been probably sending the information to other people, on paper. Like me and the National Expose. I have no idea if any others are receiving similar packages. What I see here, is a coordinated effort to . . .well, I don't what, but to do something." Scott held Tyrone's complete attention.

"You still haven't told me what you need. Lay it on me, buddy. There can't be much more."

"Doesn't it make sense that if we had one van, and the equipment inside, we could trace it down, and maybe see if there really are other Van Eck vans out there? For an operation that's this large, there would have to be a back up, a contingency . . ." The excitement oozed from Scott as his voice got louder.

"Shhhh . . ." Tyrone cautioned. "The trains have ears. I don't go for conspiracy theories, I never have. Right now all we have is raw, uncorrelated data. No proof. Just circumstantial events that may have nothing to do with each other . . ."

"Bullshit. Look at this." Scott opened up his briefcase and handed a file folder to Tyrone.

"What is it? Looks like a news story, that . . . uh . . . you wrote and, it's about some mergers. Big deal." Duncan closed the folder. "What does this have to do with anything?"

"This. Yes, I wrote the story. Two days ago. It hasn't been printed yet." Scott took the folder back. "I found this copy in the van that was wrecked two days ago. It was Van Eck'ed from my computer the day I wrote it. They've been watching me and my computer."

"Now wait a second. There are a hundred possible answers. You could have lost a copy . . . or someone got it from your wastebasket." Duncan wasn't convincing either to himself or to Scott. Scott smirked as Tyrone tried to justify the unbelievable.

"You want to play?" Scott asked.

"I think I'd better. If this is for real, no one has any privacy anymore."

"I know I don't."

* * * * *

213

Chapter 14

Sunday, November 29
Columbia University, New York

T he New York City Times put the story on page eleven. In contrats, the New York Post, in Murdoch's infinite wisdom, had put pictures of the dead and dying on the front page. With the McDonalds' window prominent.

Ahmed Shah reacted with pure intellectual detachment to the debacle on Seventh Avenue and 42nd. St.   Jesef was a martyr, as much of one as those who had sacrificed their lives in the Great War against Iraq. He had to make a report. From his home, in the Spanish Harlem district of the upper West Side of Manhattan, 3 blocks from his Columbia University office, he wheeled over to his computer that he always kept turned on.

C:\cd protalk

C:\PROTALK\protalk

He dialed a local New York number that was stored in the Protalk communications program. He had it set for 7 bits, no parity, no stop bits.

<<<DIALING>>>

The local phone number he dialed answered automatically and redialed another number, and then that one dialed yet another number before a message was relayed back to Ahmed Shah. He was accustomed to the delay. While waiting he lit up a Marlboro. It was the only American cigarette that came close to the vile taste of Turkish camel shit cigarettes that he had smoked before coming to the United States. A few seconds later, the screen came to life and displayed

PASSWORD:

Ahmed entered his password and his PRG response.

CRYPT KEY:

He chose a random crypt key that would be used to guarantee the privacy of his conversations.

<<<TRANSMISSION ENCODED>>>

That told Ahmed to begin his message, and that someone would be there to answer.

Good Morning. I have some news.

NEWS?

We have a slight problem, but nothing serious.

PROBLEM? PLEASE EXPLAIN.

One of the readers is gone.

HOW? CAPTURED?

No, the Americans aren't that smart. He died in a car crash.

WILL THIS HURT US?

No. In New York we have another 11 readers. But we have lost one vehicle. The police must have it.

THAT IS NOT GOOD. WHO WAS IT?

A martyr.

CAN THE POLICE FIND ANYTHING?

He had false identification. They will learn nothing.

BE SURE THEY DON'T. DESTROY THE CAR.

They can learn nothing. Why?

IT IS TOO EARLY FOR THEM TO FIND OUT ABOUT US. HOW LONG HAS IT BEEN?

I read about it today. The crash was yesterday.

DO ANY OF THE OTHERS KNOW?

It would not matter if they did. They are loyal. The papers said nothing of the van. They cared only about the Americans who died eating their breakfasts.

GOOD. REMOVE ALL EVIDENCE. REPLACE HIM.

It will be done.

<<<CONNECTION TERMINATED>

* * * * *

Monday, November 30
New York City

The fire at the New York City Police Impound on 22nd St., and the Hudson River was not newsworthy. It caused, however, a deluge of paperwork for the Sergeant whose job it was to guard the confiscated vehicles. Most of those cars damaged in the firestorm had been towed for parking infractions. It would cost the city tens of thousands of dollars, but not at least for three or four months. The city would take as long as possible to process the claims. Jesef Mumballa's vehicle was completely destroyed as per Homosoto's order. The explosion that had caused the fire was identified as coming from his van, but little importance was placed with that obscure fact.

Ben Shellhorne noticed, though. Wasn't that the van that Scott Mason had shown such interest in yesterday? A car bombing, even if on police property was not a particularly interesting story, at least in New York. But Ben wanted that drink. Maybe he could parlay it into two.

"Scott, remember that van?" Ben called Scott on the internal office phones.

"Yeah, what about it?"

"It's gone."

"What do you mean gone?"

"Somebody blew it up. Took half the cars in the impound with it. Sounds like Cemex. Just thought you might care. You were pretty hot about seeing it yesterday." Scott enjoyed Ben's nonchalance. He decided to play it cool.

"Yeah, thanks for the call. Looks like another lead down the tubes."

"Know whatcha mean."

Scott called Tyrone at his office. He was surprised that he was successful in getting a response two times in a row.

"4543." Duncan answered obliquely.

"Just an anonymous call." Scott didn't disguise his voice. The message would be obvious.

"So?"

"A certain van in a certain police impound was just blown up. Seemed le Plastique was involved. Thought you might want to know."

"Thanks." The phone went dead.

Within 30 minutes, 6 FBI agents arrived at the police impound station. It looked like a war zone. Vehicles were strewn about, many the victim of fire, many with substantial pieces missing.

With the signature of the New York District Chief on appropriate forms, the FBI took possession of one Ford Econoline van, or what was left of it. The New York police were just as glad to be rid of it. It was one less mess they had to worry about. Fine, take it. It's yours. Just make sure that the paperwork covers our asses. Good, that seems to do it. Now get out. Fucking Feds.

* * * * *

Tyrone Duncan took the Trump Shuttle down to Washington's National Airport. The 7:30 flight was dubbed the Federal Express by the stewardesses because it was primarily congressmen, diplomats and other Washington denizens who took this flight. They wanted to get to D.C. before the cocktail parties began and found the 2-drink flight an excellent means to tune up. Duncan was met out in front by a driver who held up a sign that read 'Burnson'.

He got into the car in silence and was driven to a residence on P Street off Wisconsin in Georgetown. The brick townhouse looked like every other million dollar home in the affluent Washington bedroom community. But this one was special. It not only served as a home away from home for Bob Burnson when he worked late, but it was also a common neutral meeting place far from prying eyes and ears. This night was one such case.

An older, matronly lady answered the door.

"May I help you?" She went through the formality for the few accidental tourists who rang the bell.

"I'm here to see Mr. Merriweather. He's expecting me." Merriweather was the nom-de-guerre of Bob Burnson, at least at this location. Duncan was ushered into the elegant old sitting room, where the butleress closed the door behind him. He double-checked that she was gone and walked over to the fireplace. The marble facade was worn in places, from overuse he assumed, but nonetheless, traces of its 19th century elegance remained. He looked up at the large full length standing portrait of a somber, formal man dressed in a three piece suit. Undoubtedly this vain portrait was his only remaining legacy, whoever he was. Tyrone pressed a small button built into the side of the picture frame.

An adjoining bookcase slipped back into the wall, exposing a dark entry. Duncan squeezed his bulk through the narrow wedge provided by the opened bookcase.

The blank wall behind him closed and the lights in the room he entered slowly brightened. Three people were seated at an oversized table with black modern executive chairs around it. The room was large. Too large to fit behind the 18 foot width of a Georgetown brownstone. The adjacent building must be an ersatz cover for the privacy that this domicile required. The room was simple, but formal. Stark white walls and their nondescript modern paintings were illuminated by recessed lights. The black trim work was the only accent that the frugal decorator permitted.

217

His old friend and superior Bob Burnson was seated in the middle. The other two men were civil servants in their mid 40's as near as Duncan could determine. Both wore Government issue blue suits, white shirts and diagonally striped maroon ties. Their hair was regulation above the ears, immaculately kept. Reminded Duncan of the junior clerks on Wall Street. They could only afford suits from the discount racks, but still tried to make a decent impression. The attempt usually failed, but G-Men stuck to the tradition of poor dress. He had never seen either of the men that flanked Burnson, which wasn't unusual. He was a New Yorker who carefully avoided the cacophony of Washington politics. He played the political game once nearly 30 years ago to secure his position, but he had studiously avoided it since.

"Thanks for making it on such short notice," Burnson solicitously greeted Duncan. He did it for the benefit of the others present.

"Yes sir. Glad to help." Duncan groaned through the lie. He had been ordered to this command performance.

"This is," Burnson gestured to his right, "Martin Templer, our CIA liaison, And," pointing to his left, "Charlie Sorenson, assistant DIRNSA, from the Fort." They all shook hands perfunctorily. "Care for a drink?" Burnson asked. "We're not on Government time."

Duncan looked and saw they were all drinking something other than Coke. The bar behind them showed recent use. "Absolut on the rocks. If you have it." It was Duncan's first time to 'P Street' as this well disguised location was called. Burnson rose and poured the vodka over perfectly formed ice cubes. He handed the drink to Duncan and indicated he should take a seat.

They exchanged pleasantries, and Duncan spoke of the improvement in the Northeast corridor Shuttle service; the flight was almost on time. Enough of the niceties.

"We don't want to hold you up more than necessary, but since you were here in town we thought we could discuss a couple of matters." Burnson was the only one to speak. The others watched Duncan too closely for his taste. What a white wash. He was called down here, pronto. Since I'm here, my ass.

"No problem sir," he carried the charade forward.

"We need to know more about your report. This morning's report." Sorenson, the NSA man spoke. "It was most intriguing. Can you fill us in?" He sipped his drink while maintaining eye contact with Duncan.

"Well, there's not much to say beyond what I put in." Suspicion was evident in Duncan's voice. "I think that it's a real possibility that there is a group whom may be using highly advanced computer equipment as weapons. Or at least surveillance tools. A massive operation is suspected. I think I explained that in my report."

"You did Tyrone," Bob agreed. "It's just that there may be additional considerations that you're not aware of. Things I wasn't even aware of. Charlie, can you elaborate?" Bob looked at the NSA man in deference.

"Thanks, Bob, be glad to." Charlie Sorenson was a seasoned spook. His casual manner was definitely practiced. "Basically, we're following up on the matter of the van you reported, and the alleged equipment it held." He scanned the folder in front of him. "It says here," he perused, "that you discovered that individuals have learned how to read computer signals, unbeknownst to the computer users." He looked up at Duncan for a confirmation. Tyrone felt slightly uncomfortable. "Is that right?"

"Yes Sir," Duncan replied. "From the information we've received, it appears that a group has the ability to detect computer radiation from great distances. This technique allows someone to compromise computer privacy . . ."

"We know what it is Mr. Duncan." The NSA man cut him off abruptly. Duncan looked at Burnson who avoided his stare. "What we want to know is, how do you know? How do you know what CMR radiation is?" There was no smile or sense of warmth from the inquisitor. Not that there had been since the unpropitious beginning of this evening.

"CMR?" Tyrone wasn't familiar with the term.

"Coherent Monitor Radiation. What do you know?"

"There was a van that crashed in New York a couple of days ago." Duncan was not sure what direction this conversation was going to take. "I have reason to believe it contained computer equipment that was capable of reading computer screens from a distance."

"What cases are you working on that relate to this?" Again the NSA man sounded like he was prosecuting a case in court.

"I have been working on a blackmail case," Duncan said. "Now I'm the agency liaison with ECCO and CERT. Looking into the INTERNET problems."

The two G-men looked at each other. Templer from the CIA shrugged at Sorenson. Burnson was ignored.

"Are you aware that you are working in an area of extreme national security?" Sorenson pointedly asked Duncan.

Tyrone Duncan thought for a few seconds before responding. "I would imagine that if computers can be read from a distance then there is a potential national security issue. But I can assure you, it was brought to my attention through other means." Duncan tried to sound confident of his position.

"Mr. Duncan," Sorenson began, "I will tell you something, and I will only tell you because you have been pre-cleared." He waited for a reaction, but Duncan did not give him the satisfaction of a sublimation. Cleared my ass. Fucking spooks. Duncan had the common sense to censor himself effectively.

"CMR radiation, as it is called, is a major threat facing our computers today. Do you know what that means?" Sorenson was being solicitous. Tyrone had to play along.

"From what I gather, it means that our computers are not safe from eavesdropping. Anyone can listen in." Tyrone spoke coldly. Other than Bob, he was not with friends.

"Let me put it succinctly," Sorenson said. "CMR radiation has been classified for several years. We don't even admit that it exists. If we did, there could be panic. As far as we are concerned with the public, CMR radiation is a figment of an inventive imagination. Do you follow?"

"Yes," Duncan agreed, "But why? It doesn't seem to be much of a secret to too many people?"

"That poses two questions. Have you ever heard of the Tempest Program?"

"Tempest? No. What is it?" Duncan searched his mind.

"Tempest is a classified program managed by the Department of Defense and administered by the National Security Agency. It has been in place for years. The premise is that computers radiate information that our enemies can pick up with sophisticated equipment. Computers broadcast signals that tell what they're doing. And they do it in two ways. First they radiate like a radio station. Anyone can pick it up." This statement confirmed what Scott had been saying. "And, computers broadcast their signals down the power lines. If someone tried, they could listen to our AC lines and essentially know what the computer was doing. Read classified information. I'm sure you see the problem." Sorenson was trying to be friendly, but he failed the geniality test.

Duncan nodded in understanding.

"We are concerned because the Tempest program is classified and more importantly, the Agency has been using CMR for years."

"What for?"

"The NSA is chartered as the ears and eyes of the intelligence community. We listen to other people for a living."

"You mean you spy on computers, too? Spying on civilians? Isn't that illegal?" Tyrone remembered back when FBI and CIA abuses had totally gotten out of hand.

"The courts have determined that eavesdropping in on cellular phone calls is not an invasion of privacy. The Agency takes the same position on CMR." Sorenson wanted to close the issue quickly.

Duncan carefully prepared his answer amidst the outrage he was feeling. He sensed an arrogant Big Brother attitude at work. He hated the 'my shit doesn't stink' attitude of the NSA. All in the name of National Security. "Until a couple of days ago I would have though this was pure science fiction."

"It isn't Mr. Duncan. Tempest is a front line of defense to protect American secrets. We need to know what else there is; what you haven't put in your reports." The NSA man pressed.

Duncan looked at Bob who had long ago ceased to control the conversation. He got no signs of support. In fact, it was almost the opposite. He felt alone. He had had little contact with the Agency in his 30 years of service. And when there was contact it was relegated to briefings, policy shifts. . .pretty bureaucratic stuff.

"As I said, it's all in the report. When there's more, I'll submit it." Duncan maintained his composure.

"Mr. Duncan, I don't think that will do." Martin Templer spoke up again. "We have been asked to assist the NSA in the matter."

"Whoah! Wait a second." Duncan's legal training had not been for naught. He knew a thing or two about Federal charters and task designations. "The NSA is just a listening post. Your guys do the international spook stuff, and we do the domestic leg work. Since when is the Fort into investigations?"

"Ty? They're right." The uneasiness in Bob's voice was prominent. "The protection of classified information is their responsibility. A group was created to report on computer security problems that might have an effect on national security. On that committee is the Director of the NSA. In essence, they have control. Straight from 1600. It's out of our hands."

Tyrone was never the technical type, and definitely not the politician. Besides, there was no way any one human being could keep up with the plethora of regulations and rule changes that poured out of the three branches of government. "Are you telling me that the NSA can swoop down on our turf and take the cases they want, when they want?" Duncan hoped he had heard wrong.

"Mr. Duncan, I think you may be under a mistaken impression here." Sorenson sipped his drink and turned in the swivel chair. "We don't want anything to do with your current cases, especially the alleged blackmail operation in place. That is certainly within the domain of the FBI. No. All we want is the van." The NSA man realized he may have come on a little strong and Duncan had misunderstood. This should clear everything up nicely.

Tyrone decided to extricate himself from any further involvement with these guys. He would offer what he knew, selectively.

"Take the van, it's yours. Or what's left of it."

"Who else knows about CMR? How is works?" Sorenson wanted more than the van.

Duncan didn't answer. An arrogance, a defiance came over him that Bob Burnson saw immediately. "Tell them where you found out, Ty." He saw Duncan's negative facial reaction. "That's an order."

How could he minimize the importance of Scott's contribution to his understanding of CMR radiation. How could he rationalize their relationship. He thought, and then realized it might not matter. Scott had said he already had his story, and no one had done anything wrong. Actually they had only had a casual conversation on a train, as commuter buddies, what was the harm? It really exposed him more than Scott if anything came of it.

"From an engineer friend of mine. He told me about how it worked."

The reaction from the CIA and NSA G-Men was poorly concealed astonishment. Both made rapid notes. "Where does he work? For a defense contractor?"

"No, he's also a reporter."

"A reporter?" Sorenson gasped. "For what paper?" He breathlessly prayed that it was a local high school journal, but his gut told him otherwise.

"The New York City Times." Duncan said, confident that Scott could handle himself and that the First Amendment would if all else failed.

"Thank you very much Mr. Duncan." Sorenson rapidly rose from his chair. "You've been most helpful. Have a good flight back."

* * * * *

Tuesday, December 1
New York City

The morning commute into the City was agonizingly long for Scott Mason. He nearly ran the 5 blocks from Grand Central Station to the paper's offices off Times Square. The elevator wait was interminable. He dashed into the City Room, bypassing his desk, and ran directly toward editor Doug McQuire's desk. Doug saw him coming and was ready.

"Don't stop here. We're headed up to Higgins." Doug tried to deflect the verbal onslaught from Scott.

"What the fuck? I work on a great story, you said you loved it, and then I finally get the missing piece and then . . .this?" He pushed the morning paper in Doug's face. "Where the hell is my story? And don't give me any of this 'we didn't have the room' shit. You yourself thought we were onto something bigger . . ."

Doug ignored Scott as best he could, but on the elevator to the 9th floor, Scott was still in his face.

"Doug, I am not a pimple faced cub reporter. I never was, that's why you hired me. You've always been straight with me . . ."

Scott trailed behind Doug as they walked down the hallway to Higgins' office. He was still calling Doug every name in the book as they entered the room. Higgins sat behind his desk, no tie, totally un-Higgins-like. Scott shot out another nasty remark.

"Hey, you look like shit."

"Thanks to you," the bedraggled Higgins replied.

"What? You too? I need this today." Scott's anger displayed concern as well.

"Sit down. We got troubles." Higgins could be forceful when necessary. Apparently he felt this was an appropriate time to use his drill sergeant voice. It startled Scott so he sat on the edge of his seat. He wasn't through dishing out what he thought about having a story pulled this way.

Higgins waited for nearly half a minute. Let some calm, normalcy return before he started.

"Scott, I pulled the story, Doug didn't. And, if it makes you feel any better, we've both been here all night. And we've had outside counsel lose sleep, too. Congratulations."

Scott was confused. Congratulations? "What are you . . .?"

"Hear me out. In my 14 years at this paper, this is the first time I've ever had a call from the Attorney General's office telling me, ordering me, that I, we had better not run a story. I am as confused as you." Higgins' sincerity was real; tired, but real.

Scott suddenly felt a twinge of guilt, but not enough to remove the anger he still felt. "What ever happened to the first amendment?" Irate confusion was written all over his face.

"Here me out before you blow a fuse." Higgins sounded very tired. "About 10:30 last night I got a call from the Print Chief. He said that the NYPD was at the plant with a restraining order that we not print a story you had written. What should they do, he asked. Needless to say I had to come down, so I told him, hold the presses, for a half hour. I called Ms. Manchester and she met me here just after eleven. The officer had court orders, from Washington, signed by the Attorney General personally, informing us that if we published certain information, allegedly written by you, the paper could be found in violation of some bullshit national security laws they made up on the spot.

"I called Doug, who was pleased to hear from me at midnight, I can assure you, and he agreed. Pull it. Whatever was going on, the story was so strong, that we can always print it in a few days once we sort it out. We had no choice. But now, we need to know, what is going on?" Higgins was clearly exhausted.

Scott was at a loss for words. "I . . .uh . . . dunno. What did the court order say?"

"That the paper will, will is their word, refrain from printing anything with regards to CMR. And CMR was all over your article. Nobody here knew much about it, other than what was in the article, and we couldn't reach you, so we figured that we might save ourselves a bushel of trouble by waiting. Just a day or two," he quickly added.

"How the hell did they find out . . ." Scott's mind immediately blamed Tyrone. He had been betrayed. Used. Goddamn it. He knew better than to trust a Fed. Fuck. Tyrone must have gone upstairs and told his cronies that I was onto a story and . . .well one thing led to another. But Jeez . . .the Attorney General's office.

"Scott, what is going on here?" Higgins asked but Doug wanted to know as well. "It looks like you've got a tiger by the tail. And the tiger is in Washington. Seems like you've pissed off some important people. We need to know the whole bit. What are you onto?"

"It's all in the story," Scott said, emotionally drained before 9:00 AM. "Whatever I know is there. It's all been confirmed, Doug saw the notes." Doug nodded, yes, the reporting was as accurate as is expected in such cases.

"Well," Higgins continued, "it seems that our friends in Washington don't want any of this printed, for their own reasons. Is any of this classified, Scott?"

"If it is, I don't know it," Scott lamely explained. He felt up against an invisible wall. "I got my confirmations from a couple of engineers and a hacker type who is up on computer security stuff. This stuff is chicken feed compared to SDI and the Stealth Bomber."

"So why do they care?"

"I have an idea, but I can't prove it yet," offered Scott.

"Lay it on us, kid," said Doug approvingly. He loved controversial reporting, and this had the makings of . . .

"What if between this and the Exchange we fell into a secret weapons program . . ." Scott began.

"Too simple. Been done before without this kind of backlash," Higgins said dismissing the idea.

"Except, these weapons can be built by any high school kid with an electronics lab and a PC," Scott retorted undaunted. "Maybe not as good, or as powerful, but nonetheless, effective. If you were the government, would you want every Tom, Dick and Shithead to build home versions of cruise missiles?"

"I think you're exaggerating a little, Scott." Higgins pinched his nose by the corners of his eyes. Doug? What do you think?"

Doug was amazingly collected. "I think," he said slowly, "that Scott is onto a once in a lifetime story. My gut tells me this is real. And still, we only have a small piece of the puzzle."

"Scott? Get right back on it,"Doug ordered. "I want to know what the big stink is. Higgins will use outside counsel to see if they dig anything up, but I believe you'll have better luck. It seems that you've stumbled on something that the Government wants kept secret. Keep up the good work."

Scott was being congratulated on having a story pulled, which aroused mixed emotions within him. His boss thought it wonderful that it was pulled. It all depends what side of the fence you're on, I guess.

"I have a couple of calls to make." Scott excused himself from Higgins' domain to get back to his desk. He dialed Duncan's private number.

"4543," Duncan answered gruffly.

"Fuck you very much." Scott enjoyed slamming down the phone as hard as he could.

Scott's second call wouldn't be for hours. He wished it to be sooner, so the day passed excruciatingly slowly. But, it had to wait. Safety was a concern, not getting caught was paramount. He was going to break into a bank.

* * * * *

Washington, D.C.

"I will call you in 5 minutes."

Miles Foster heard the click of the phone in his ear. It was Homosoto. At midnight no less. He had no choice. It was better to speak to Homosoto over the computer than live. He didn't have to hear the condescension. He turned his Compaq 286 Deskpro back on and initiated the auto-answer mode on the modem through the Pro-Talk software package.

Miles was alone. He had sent Perky home a few minutes before.

He heard his modem ring, and saw the computer answer. The computer automatically set the communications parameters and matched the crypt key as chosen by the caller, undoubtedly Homosoto. Miles set his PRG code to prove to the computer that it was really him and he waited for the first message.

WE NEED TO TALK.

That was obvious, why state the obvious, thought Miles. He typed,

I am listening.

ONE OF THE READERS IS DEAD. HIS EQUIPMENT HAS BEEN CAPTURED.

By whom?

THE NEW YORK POLICE. THERE WAS A CAR ACCIDENT. THEN THE FBI GOT THE READER. THEN THE NSA, YOUR NSA, STEPPED IN AND TOOK OVER. THEY EVEN HAVE IN-TERFERED WITH THE PRESS. SCOTT MASON WROTE A STORY ON THE READERS AND THE GOVERNMENT STOPPED HIM.

How? We don't do that sort of stuff.

OBVIOUSLY YOU DO, MR. FOSTER. I HAVE MY SOURCES AS YOU DO.

They don't screw with the press, though. That's frowned on.

MAYBE SO, BUT TRUE. WE NEED TO GET THIS MASON BACK ON THE TRACK. HE IS WHAT WE NEED.

Why him?

SIMPLE. WE HAVE SENT READER INFORMATION TO SEVERAL NEWSPAPERS. THE ONLY ONE TO PRINT HAS BEEN YOUR NATIONAL EXPOSE. THAT PAPER, I BELIEVE IS SOLD AT SUPERMARKETS AND READ BY WOMEN WHO WATCH SOAP OPERAS. MR. MASON IS AN ENGINEER WHO UNDERSTANDS. WE NEED HIM BACK. HE IS VALU-ABLE TO OUR PLAN. IN YOUR COUNTRY PEOPLE LISTEN TO THE PRESS. BUT YOUR GOVERNMENT STOPPED HIM. WE CANNOT LET HIM FAIL.

How much does he know?

AS MUCH AS WE WANT HIM TO. NO MORE. WE WANT TO FEED HIM A LITTLE AT A TIME, AS WE PLANNED. I AM AFRAID HE WILL BE DISCOURAGED AND ABANDON THE HUNT. YOU KNOW HOW CRITICAL THE PRESS IS. THEY ARE OUR MOUTHPIECE.

Yes, I agree. I wish I knew how you find out these things.

MANY PEOPLE OWE ME MANY FAVORS. WE MAY HAVE LOST AFTER PEARL HARBOR, BUT WE WON WITH THE

TRANSISTOR RADIO AND THE VCR. THE WAR IS NOT OVER.

What do you want me to do?

MAKE SURE THAN MR. MASON IS KEPT INFORMED. HE IS BRIGHT. HE UNDERSTANDS. HIS VOICE WILL BE HEARD. HE MUST NOT BE STOPPED. I WILL DO WHAT I CAN AS WELL. PUT HIM BACK ON THE TRACK.

I know how to do that. That will not be a problem. Do we still have readers?

YES, WE LOST ONLY ONE. WE HAVE MANY MORE.

How many?

MR. FOSTER, YOU WROTE THE PLAN. DID YOU FORGET?

No, I know. Curiosity.

KILLED THE CAT AS YOU SAY.

It is my plan.

WHICH I BOUGHT. I WANT THE PUBLICITY, AS PLANNED. SEE THAT WE GET IT.

Sure.

MR. FOSTER? ONE MORE THING

Yes.

I DO NOT HAVE A SLOPED BROW NOR IS RICE MY PRIMARY MEANS OF PROPULSION.

Just an expression.

KEEP IT TO YOURSELF.

<<<CONNECTION TERMINATED>>>

* * * * *

Midnight, Wednesday, December 2
Scarsdale, New York

Since he had met Kirk, Scott had developed a mild affection for the long distance modem-pal, and pretended informer. Now, it was time to take advantage of his new asset. Maybe the Government carries weight with their spook shit, but a bank can't push hard enough to pull a story, if it's true. And Kirk, whoever that was, offered Scott the ideal way to prove it. Do it yourself.

So he prepared himself for a long night, and he would definitely sleep in tomorrow; no matter what! Scott so cherished his sleep time. He wormed his way through the mess of the downstairs "study in disaster," and made space by redistributing the mess into other corners.

He felt a commitment, an excitement that was beyond that of developing a great story. Scott was gripped with an intensity that was a result of the apprehension of invading a computer, and the irony of it all. He was an engineer, turned writer, using computers as an active journalistic instrument other than for word processing. To Scott, the computer, being the news itself, was being used as a tool to perform self examination as a sentient being, as a separate entity. Techno-psychoanalysis?

Is it narcissistic for man's tools to use themselves as both images of the mirror of reflective analysis? They say man's brain can never fully understand itself. Is the same true with computers? And since they grow in power so quickly compared to man's snail-like millennia by millennia evolution, can they catch up with themselves?

Back to reality, Scott. The Great American Techno-Philosophy and Pulitzer could wait. He had a bank to rob. Scott left his computer on all the time since Kirk had first called. If the Intergalactic Traveler called back, the computer would answer, and Kirk could leave a message. Scott checked the Mail Box in the ProCom communications program. No calls. Not that his modem was a popular number. Only he, his office computer and Kirk knew it. And the phone company, but everyone knows about them . . .

Just as the clock struck midnight, Kirk jumped in his seat. Not only was the bell chiming an annoying 12 mini-gongs, but his computer was beeping. It took a couple of beeps from the small speaker in his computer to realize he was receiving a call. The 14" color screen came alive and it entered terminal mode from the auto-answer screen that Scott had left yesterday.

WTFO

The screen rang out. Scott knew the answer.

naft

VERY GOOD! COULDN'T HAVE SAID IT BETTER MYSELF.

Welcome pilgrim, what has brought thee to these shores?

I GUESS WRITERS HAVE AN ADVANTAGE ON COMM. MAKE YOURSELF VERY COLORFUL. CREATE ANY PICTURE YOU WANT.

Seems a bit more sporting that hiding behind techy-talk.

YEAH, WELL, I'LL WORK ON IT.

So, as Maynard G. Crebbs asked, "You Rang?"

AH! DOBIE GILLIS. NICK AT NIGHT!

No, the originals.

WHEN WAS THAT?

You've just dated yourself. Thanks.

TO-FUCKING-SHAY! NOT AS OLD AS YOU. READY FOR A
TRIP TO THE BANK?

Your read my mind . . .

I FIGURED YOU'D WIMP OUT ON A SOLO TRIP, FIRST TIME
AND ALL. THOUGHT I MIGHT BE ABLE TO HELP. I MAKE A
HELL OF A CHAUFFEUR.

What do you mean?

I MEAN I'M GOING TO TAKE YOU FOR A RIDE.

You're kidding. Just like Superman carries Lois Lane?

JUST ABOUT. FIRST I'M GOING TO SEND YOU A COPY OF
'MIRAGE' SOFTWARE.

When?

RIGHT NOW. THEN, YOU'LL USE MIRAGE. ALL YOU HAVE
TO DO IS EXECUTE FROM THE COMMAND LINE AFTER I
DOWN LOAD.

English kimosabe.

OK, ITS SIMPLE. WHEN I SAY SO, YOU ENTER ALT-F9.
THAT SETS YOU UP TO RECEIVE. NAME THE FILE
MIRAGE.EXE. THERE'S ONLY ONE. THEN WHEN IT SAYS
ITS DONE, PRESS CTRL-ALT-R. YOU WILL HAVE A DOS
LINE APPEAR. ENTER MIRAGE.EXE AND RETURN.

Stop! I'm writing . . .

USE PRTSCR

What's that

IS YOUR PRINTER ON LINE?

Yes

WHENEVER YOU WANT TO PRINT WHAT'S ON THE
SCREEN ENTER 'SHIFT- PrtScr'. LOOK FOR IT. HIT IT
NOW.

Thanks! Got it.

OR SAVE THE WHOLE THING TO A FILE. USE CTRL-ALT-S.
THEN PICK A NEW FILE NAME. MEANS MONGO EDITING
THOUGH.

Done! I like Ctrl-Alt-S. Suits me fine. No memory needed.

HIT ALT-F9. MIRAGE IS COMING.

Scott did as instructed. The entire procedure made sense intellectually, but inside, there was an inherent disbelief that any of these simple procedures would produce anything meaningful. It is inherently difficult to feel progress, a sense of achievement without instantaneous feedback that all was well.

Less than a minute later, the screen told Scott it was finished. Did he want to Save the file? Yes. Please name it. Mirage.Exe. Would you like to receive another? No. Do you want to exit to Command line? Yes. He entered Mirage.Exe as Kirk had instructed, hoping that he was still waiting at the other end. The screen displayed various copyrights and Federal warnings about illegal copying of software, the very crime Scott had just committed.

The video suddenly split into two windows. The bottom window looked just like the screen he used to talk to Kirk, except much smaller. Only 10 out of a possible 25 lines. The upper half of the screen was new: MIRAGE-Remote View (C) 1988.

Kirk announced himself.

WTFO

Yup! I got something. Two screens.

GOOD. THAT MEANS EVERYTHING PROBABLY WORKED. LET'S TEST IT. YOU AND I TALK JUST AS USUAL, ON THE SMALL WINDOW, LIKE WE'RE DOING NOW. ON THE TOP WINDOW, YOU WILL SEE WHAT I'M DOING. EXCEPT IN MINIATURE. BECAUSE YOU ONLY HAVE 15 LINES TO SEE, AND A NORMAL SCREEN IS 25 LINES, THE PROGRAM COMPRESSES THE SIGNAL TO DISPLAY IT IN FULL. DO YOU HAVE A DECENT MONITOR?

vga 14 inch

GOOD. YOU WON'T HAVE ANY PROBLEMS. REMEMBER, WHENEVER YOU WANT A COPY OF THE SCREEN, HIT SHIFT-PRTSCR.

Can't I save everything?

CTRL-ALT-S, YEAH.

Done. Anything else?

YOU CAN'T INTERFERE. JUST ALONG FOR THE RIDE.

A Sunday drive in the country . . .

WITH ME DRIVING. HA! FASTEN YOUR SEAT BELTS.

Scott watched with his fingers sitting on the keyboard with anticipation. A phone number was displayed on top line in the Upper Window: 18005555500.

<DIALING>

In a few seconds the screen announced,

WELCOME TO USA-NET, THE COMPLETE DATA BASE.

The graphics got fancy but in black and white.

ARE YOU A FIRST TIME USER? NO

ID? XXXXXXXXXXXXXXX

PASSWORD? XXXXXXXX

The video monitor did not let Scott see the access codes.

Welcome to USA-NET, Kirk.

Time synchronizing: 0:04:57 December 18,

DO YOU WANT THE MAIN MENU? Y

Scott's large window began to scroll and fill with lines after line of options:

(A) Instructions

(B) Charges

(C) Updating

(D) OAG

(E) Shopping Menus

(F) Trading Menus

(G) Conversation Pits

In all there were 54 choices displayed. The lower window came alive.

SEE HOW IT WORKS?

Fascinating.

THAT WAS JUST A TEST. NOW FOR THE REAL THING.
SURE YOU WANNA GO?

Scott had gone this far. He would worry about the legalities in the morning. Higgins would have his work cut out for him.

Aye, aye, Captain.

ENGAGE WARP ENGINES.

The upper window changed again.

QUIT? Y

ARE YOU SURE? Y

<<<CONNECTION TERMINATED>>>

Another number flashed in the upper window. 12125559796.

<DIALING>

After less than 2 rings the screen announced that they had arrived at the front doors to the computer system at First State Bank, in New York. Another clue. Kirk was not from New York. He used an area code.

Scott felt like looking back over his shoulders to see who was watching him. His automatic flight-or-fight response made the experience more exhilarating. He tried to force his intellect to convince himself that he was far from view, unobservable, undetectable. Only partially successful, he remained tense realizing that he was borderline legal.

<<<CONNECTION>>>

PORT CONTROL SECURITY, CENTRAL DATA PROCESSING CENTER, FIRST STATE BANK. O/S VMS R31

SECURITY: SE-PROTECT, 4.0 REV. 3.12.1 10, OCT, 1989

TIME: 00:12:43.1

DATE: 04 December

PORT: 214

ARE YOU SYSTEMS ADMINISTRATOR? YES

ENTER SYS-ADMIN ID CODE SEQUENCE: 8854

<WAITING . . .>

PRIMARY SYS-ADMIN AUTHENTICATION ACCEPTED. PLEASE BEGIN SECONDARY IDENTIFICATION.

PASSWORD: 4Q-BAN/HKR

<WAITING . . .>

SECONDARY SYS-ADMIN AUTHENTICATION ACCEPTED. PLEASE BEGIN FINAL IDENTIFICATION.

ID: 374552100/1

<WAITING . . .>

WELCOME TO CENTRAL DATA PROCESSING, FIRST STATE BANK, NEW YORK CITY. YOU ARE THE SYSTEMS ADMINISTRATOR.

****

WARNING!!!
PLEASE ONLY INITIATE CHANGES WHICH HAVE BEEN TESTED ON BACKUP PROCESSORS. SEVERE DAMAGE MAY RESULT FROM IMPROPER ADMINISTRATION.
****

Scott watched in fascination. Here he was, riding shotgun on a trip through one of New York's largest bank computers, and there was no resistance. He could not believe that he had more security in his house than a bank with assets of over $10 Billion. The bottom window showed Kirk's next message.

WHAD'YA THINK?

Pretty stupid

WHAT?

That the bank doesn't have better control

VIVE LE HACKER!!!

* * * * *

Wednesday, December 2
New York City

"Doug," Scott came into the office breathlessly, "we have to see Higgins. I gotta great . . ."

"Hey, I thought you were gonna come in late today? Wire in the copy?" He looked at the New York clock on the wall. It was 9:15. Scott broke the promise he made to himself to come in late.

"Yeah, well, I underslept." He brandished a thick file of computer printouts. "Before I write this one, I want Higgins and every other lawyer God put on this green Earth to go over it."

"Since when did you get so concerned with pre-scrutiny. As I remember, it was only yesterday that you threatened to nuke Higgins' house and everyone he ever met." Doug pretended to be condescending. Actually, the request was a great leap forward for Scott and every other reporter. Get pre- lawyered, on the approach, learn the guidelines, and maybe new rules before plowing ahead totally blind.

"Since I broke into a bank last night!" Scott threw the folder down on Doug's desk. "Here. I'm going to Rosie's for a cholesterol fix. Need a picker upper."

When Scott came back from a breakfast of deep fried fat and pan grilled grease he grabbed his messages at the front desk. Only one mattered:

Higgins. 11:00. Be there. Doug.

Still the boss, thought Scott.

Higgins' job was to approve controversial material, but it generally didn't surround only one reporter, on so many different stories within such a short time span.

"Good to see you, Mason," snorted Higgins.

"Right. Me too," he came back just as sarcastically. "Doug." He acknowledged his editor with only slightly more civility.

"John, the boy's been up all night," Doug conciliated to Higgins. He called all his reporters boys. "And Scott, lighten up." He was serious.

"Sure, Doug," he nodded.

Higgins began. "O.K., Scott, what is it this time? Doug said you broke into a bank, and I haven't had time to go over these." He held up the thick file of printouts. "In 25 words or less." The legal succinctness annoyed Scott.

"Simple. I tied in with a hacker last night, 'round midnight. He had the passwords to get into the First State computers, and well, he showed me around. Showed me how much damage can actually be done by someone at a keyboard. The tour lasted almost 2 hours."

"That's it?" Asked Higgins.

"That's it? Are you kidding? Let me tell you a few things in 25 words or more!" Scott was tired and the lack of sleep made him irritable.

"I did a little checking before I went on this excursion. You bank at First, don't you, John?"

It was a setup question. "Yes," Higgins said carefully.

"I thought so. Here let me have that file. Gimme a minute," he said flipping pages. "Here it is, and yes, correct me if I say anything that you don't agree with." His curtness and accusatory sound put both Higgins and Doug off. Where was he going?

"John W. Higgins, social security number, 134-66-9241. Born Rockville, Maryland, June 1, 1947. You currently have $12,435.16 in your checking account, $23,908.03 in savings . . ."

Higgins' jaw and pen dropped simultaneously. Doug saw the shock on his face while Scott continued.

"Your mortgage at 115 Central Park West is $2,754.21. Your portfolio is split between, let's see, CD's, T-Bills, the bank acts as your broker, and you have three safety deposit boxes, only one of which your wife, Helen Beverly Simons, has access to. You make a deposit every two weeks . . ."

"Stop! How the hell do you know . . ."

"Jeez, you make that much? Can I be a lawyer too, huh? Please Mr. Higgins?"

Higgins threw his chair back and stormed around his desk to grab the papers from Scott. Scott held them away.

"Let me see those!" Higgins demanded.

"Say please. Say Pretty please."

"Scott!" Doug decided enough was enough. Scott had made his point. "Cool it. Let him have them."

"Sure, boss!" He grinned widely at Doug who could not, for reasons of professional conduct, openly condone Scott's performance, no matter how effective it was.

Higgins looked at the top pages from where Scott was reading. He read them intently, looking from one to the other. Slowly, he walked back to his desk, and sat down, nearly missing the chair because he was so engrossed.

Without looking up he spoke softly. "This is unbelievable. Unbelievable. I can't believe that you have this." Suddenly he spoke right to Scott. "You know this is privileged information, you can't go telling anyone about my personal finances. You do know that, right?" The concern was acute.

"Hey, I don't really give a damn what you make, but I needed to shake the tree. This is serious."

"Scott, you've got my total, undivided attention now. The floor's yours. You have up to 100 words." Humor wasn't Higgins' strong point, or his weak point, or any point, but Scott appreciated the gesture. Doug could relax, too. A peace treaty, for now.

"Thanks, John." Scott was sincere. "As you know I've been running a few stories on hackers, computer crimes, what have you." Higgins rolled his eyes. He remembered. "A few weeks ago I got a call from Captain Kirk. He's a hacker."

"What do you know about him?" Higgins was again taking notes. The tape recorder was nowhere to be seen.

"Not much, yet, but I have a few ideas. I would hazard to guess that he is younger. Maybe in his late '20's, not from New York, maybe the Coast, and has a sense of responsibility."

"How do you know this?"

"Well, I don't know, I guessed from our conversations."

"Why didn't you just ask?"

"I did. But, he wants his anonymity. It's the things he says, the way he says them. The only reason I know he's a he is because he called me on the phone first."

"When did you speak to him?" Higgins inquired.

"Only once. After that it's been over computer."

"So it could be anyone really?"

"Sure, but that doesn't matter. It's what he did. First, we entered the computer . . ."

"What do you mean we?" Higgins shot Scott a disapproving stare.

"We. Like him and me. He tied my computer to his so I could watch what he was doing. So, he gets into the computer . . ."

"How?"

"With the passwords. There were three."

"How did he get them?"

"From another hacker I assume. That's another story." The constant interruptions exasperated Scott. "Let me finish, then grill me. O.K.?"

Higgins nodded.

"So, once we were in, he could do anything he wanted. The computer thought he was the Systems Administrator, the head honcho for all the bank's computer operations. So we had free reign. The first place we went was to Account Operations. That's where the general account information on the bank's customers is kept. I asked him for information on you. Within seconds I knew a lot about you." Higgins frowned deeply. "From there, he asked for detailed information on your files; credit cards, payment history, delinquencies, loans on cars, IRA's, the whole shooting match."

"I have to interrupt here, Scott." Higgins said edgily. "Could he, or you, have made changes, to, ah . . .my account?"

"We did!"

"You made changes? What changes?" Higgins was aghast.

"We took all your savings and invested them in a new startup fast food franchise called Press Rat and Wharthog Sandwiches, Inc."

"You have got be kidding." Scott saw the sweat drops at Higgins' hairline.

"Yeah, I am. But he did show me how easy it is to make adjustments in account files. Like pay off loans and have them disappear, invoke foreclosures, increase or decrease balances, whatever we wanted to do."

"Jesus Christ!"

"That's not the half of it. Not even a millionth of it. See, we went through lots of accounts. The bank computer must hold hundreds of thousands of account records, and we had access to them all. If we had wanted to, we could have erased them all, or zeroed them out, or made everyone rich overnight."

"Are you telling me," Higgins spoke carefully, "that you and this . . .hacker, illegally entered a bank computer and changed records and . . ."

"Whoah!" Scott held up his hands to slow Higgins down. "We left everything the way it was, no changes as far as I could tell."

"Are you sure?"

"No, I'm not. I wasn't in the driver's seat. I went along for the ride."

"What else did you do last night, Scott?" Higgins sounded re-signed to more bad news. The legal implications must have been too much for him to handle.

"We poked around transfer accounts, where they wire money from one bank to another and through the Fed Reserve. Transaction ac-counts, reserves, statements, credit cards. Use your imagination. If a bank does it, we saw it. The point is, John, I need to know two things."

John Higgins sat back, apparently exhausted. He knew what was coming, at least half of it. His expression told Scott to ask away. He could take it.

"First, did I do anything illegal, prosecutable? You know what I mean. And, can I run with it? That's it."

Higgins' head leaned back on the leather head rest as he began to speak deliberately. This was going to be a lawyer's non-answer. Scott was prepared for it.

"Did you commit a crime?" Higgins speculated. "My gut reaction says no, but I'm not up on the latest computer legislation. Did you, at any time, do anything to the bank's computers?"

"No. He had control. I only had a window."

"Good, that helps." The air thickened with anticipation as Doug and Scott both waited for words of wisdom. "I could make a good argument that you were a reporter, with appropriate credentials, inter-viewing an individual, who was, coincidentally, at the same time, committing a crime. That is, if what he did was a crime. I don't know the answer to that yet.

"There have been countless cases where a reporter has witnessed crimes and reported on them with total immunity. Yes, the more I think about it, consider this." Higgins seemed to have renewed ener-gy. The law was his bible and Scott was listening in the congregation. "Reporters have often gone into hostage situations where there is no doubt that a crime is in progress, to report on the condition of the hostages. That's O.K.. They have followed drug dealers into crack houses and filmed their activities."

Higgins thought a little more. "Sure, that's it. The arena doesn't change the rules. You said you couldn't affect the computers, right?" He wanted a confirmation.

"Right. I just watched. And . . .asked him to do certain things."

"No you didn't! Got that? You watched, nothing else!" Higgins cracked sharply at Scott. "If anyone asks, you only watched."

"Gotcha." Scott recognized the subtle difference. He did not want to be an aider or abettor of a crime.

"So, that makes it easy. If you were in the hackers home, watching him over his shoulder, that would be no different from watching him over a computer screen." He sounded confident. "I guess." He sounded less confident. "There is very little case history on this stuff, so, if it came to it, we'd be in an interesting position to say the least. But, to answer your question, no, I don't think that you did anything illegal."

"Great. So I can write the story and . . ." Scott made a forgone conclusion without his lawyers advice. There was no way Higgins would let him get away with that.

"Hold your horses. You say write a story, and based upon what I know so far, I think you can, but with some rules."

"What kind of rules?" Skepticism permeated Scott's slow responses.

"Simple ones. Are you planning on printing the passwords to their computers?"

"No, not at all. Why?"

"Because, that is illegal. No doubt about it. So, good, rule one is easy. Two, I want to read over this entire file and have a review of everything before it goes to bed. Agreed?" Higgins looked at Doug who had not contributed much. He merely nodded, of course that would be fine.

"Three, no specifics. No names of people you saw, nothing exact. We do not want to be accused of violation of privacy in any way, shape or form."

"That's it?" Scott was pleasantly surprised. What seemed like common sense to him was a legal spider web that Higgins was required to think through.

"Almost. Lastly, was this interview on the record?"

Damn good question, Scott thought. "I dunno. I never asked, it didn't seem like a regular interview, and since I don't know Kirk's real name, he's not the story. It was what he did that is the story. Does it matter?"

"If the shit hits the fan it might, but I think we can get around it. Just be careful what you say, so I don't have to redline 90% of it. Fair enough?"

Scott was pleased beyond control. He stood to thank Higgins. "Deal. Thanks." Scott began to turn.

"Scott?" Higgins called out. "One more thing."

Oh no, he thought, the hammer was dropping. He turned back to Higgins. "Yeah?"

"Good work. You're onto something. Keep it up and keep it clean."

"No problem." Scott floated on air. "No, problem at all."

Back at his desk, Scott called Hugh Sidneys. He still worked at First State, as far as he knew, and it was time to bring him out of the closet, if possible.

"Hugh?" Scott said affably. "This is Scott Mason, over at the Times?"

"Yeah? Oh, hello," Sidneys said suspiciously. "What do you want?"

"Hugh, we need to talk." Scott went to the meat of the matter.

"About what?"

"I think you know. Would you like to talk here on the phone, or privately?" Sometimes leaving the mark only two options, neither particularly attractive, would keep him within those bounds. Sidneys was an ideal person for this tact.

The pregnant pause conveyed Sidney's consternation. The first person to speak would lose, thought Scott. Hugh spoke.

"Ah, I think it would be . . .ah . . .better . . .if we spoke . . .at . . ."

"How about the same place?" Scott offered.

"OK," Hugh was hesitant. "I guess so . . .when?"

"Whenever you want. No pressure." Scott released the tension.

"I get off at 5, how about . . .?"

"I'll be there."

"Yes ma'am. This is Scott Mason. I'm a reporter for the Times. I will only take a few seconds of his time. Is he in?" Scott used his kiss-the-secretary's-ass voice. Better then being aggressive unless it was warranted.

"I'll check, Mr. Mason," she said. The phone went on hold. After a very few seconds, the Montevani on hold was replaced with a gruff male voice.

"Mr. Mason? I'm Francis MacMillan. How may I help you?" He conveyed self assuredness, vitality and defensiveness.

"I won't take a moment, sir." Scott actually took several seconds to make sure his question would be formed accurately. He probably only had one chance. "We have been researching an article on fraudulent investment practices on the part of various banks; some fall out from the S&L mess." He paused for effect. "At any rate, we have received information that indicts First State of defrauding it's investors. In particular, we have records that show a complicated set of financial maneuvers that are designed to drain hundreds of millions of dollars from the assets of First State. Do you have any comment?"

Total silence. The quality of fiber phone lines made the silence all the more deafening.

"If you would like some specifics, sir, I can provide them to you," Scott said adding salt to the wound. "In many cases, sir, you are named as the person responsible for these activities. We have the documents and witnesses. Again, we would like a comment before we go to print."

Again Scott was met with silence. Last try.

"Lastly, Mr. MacMillan, we have evidence that your bank's computers have been invaded by hackers who can alter the financial posture of First State. If I may say so, the evidence is quite damning." Scott decided not to ask for a comment directly. The question was no longer rhetorical, it was implicit.

If feelings could be transmitted over phone wires, Scott heard MacMillan's nerve endings commence a primal scream. The phone explosively hung up on Scott.

* * * * *

Thursday, December 3
First State Bank, New York

Francis MacMillan, President of First State Savings and Loan, bellowed at the top of his lungs. Three Vice Presidents were in his office before 7:00 AM.

"Who the fuck's in charge of making sure the damned computers are safe?"

The V.P. of Data processing replied. "It's Jeanne Fineman, sir."

"Fire him."

"Jeanne is a woman . . ."

"Fire them both. I want them out of here in 10 minutes." McMillan's virulent intensity gave his aids no room for dissent.

"Sir, why, it's almost Christmas, and it wasn't her fault . . ."

"And no bonus. Make sure they never work near banks, or computers ever again! Got that?" Everyone nodded in shock.

"Al?" McMillan shouted. "Buy back our stock, quietly. When the market hears this we're in for a dump. No one will believe us when we respond, and it will take us a day to get out an answer."

"How much?" Al Shapiro asked.

"You figure it out. Just keep it calm." Shapiro noted it agreeably.

"Where the hell are the lawyers? I want that pinko-faggot news-paper stopped by tonight." McMillan's rage presaged a very, very bad day at First State.

"And someone, someone, find me that shit hole worm Sidneys. I want him in my office in 30 seconds. Now," he violently thrust his arms in the air, "get the hell out of here until you have some good news."

* * * * *

Friday, December 4

RUN ON FIRST STATE AS IT STALLS ON OWN BAILOUT

by Scott Mason

Since yesterday afternoon, First State Savings and Loan has been in asset-salvation mode. Upon reports that computer hack-ers have had access to First State's computers and records for some time, and can change their contents at will, the stock market reacted negatively by a sell-off. In the first 15 minutes of trading, First State's stock plummeted from 48 1/2 to 26 1/4, a reduction of one half its value. Subsequently, the stock moved up with block buying. At the noon bell, the stock had risen modestly to 31. It is assumed that First State itself is repurchasing their own stock in an attempt to bolster market confidence.

However, at 2:00PM, First State contacted banking officials in New York and Washington, as well as the SEC, to announce that a rush of worried depositors had drained the bank of it's available hard currency reserves, and would close until the fol-lowing morning when cash transfers would permit the bank to continue payments.

Last quarter cash holding were reported at in excess of $3 Billion, and First State has acknowledged that any and all monies would be available to those who desired it. In a press release issued by First State at 1:00 PM they said, "A minor compromise of our computers has caused no discernible damage to the computers, our customers or the bank. A thorough inves-tigation has determined that the hacker was either a figment of the imagination of a local paper or was based upon unfounded hearsay. The bank's attorneys are reviewing their options."

The combination of the two announcements only further depressed First State stock. It stood at 18 7/8 when the SEC blocked further trading.

This is Scott Mason, who reported the news as he saw it. Accurately.

* * * * *

Chapter 15

Sunday, December 6
Washington, D.C.

Miles Foster was busy at one of the several computers in his Washington D.C. condo. It was necessary, on a daily basis, to stay in contact with a vast group of people who were executing portions of his master plan. He thought it was going quite well, exceedingly so in fact. Spread over 3 continents he remote controlled engineers and programmers who designed methods to compromise computers. With his guidance, though. He broke them into several groups, and none of them knew they were part of a much larger organization, nor did they have any idea of their ultimate objective.

Each of his computer criminals was recruited by Alex; that's the only name that Miles knew. Alex. Miles had drawn up a list of minimum qualifications for his 'staff'. He forwarded them to Homosoto, who, Miles guessed, passed them on to the ubiquitous yet invisible Alex. That obviously wasn't his real name, but suitable for conversation.

Miles had developed a profile of the various talents he required. One group needed to have excellent programming skills, with a broad range of expertise in operating systems. An operating system is much like English or any other language. It is the O/S that allows the computer to execute its commands. Unless the computer understands the O/S, the computer is deaf, dumb and blind. As a child learns to communicate, a computer is imbued with the basic knowledge to permit it to function. It is still essentially stupid. That is, it can't do anything on its own without instructions, but it can understand them when they are given.

In order to violate a computer, a thorough understanding of the O/S, or language of the computer is a must. Good programmers, learn the most efficient way to get a computer to perform the desired task. There are, as in any field, tricks of the trade. Through experience, a programmer will learn how to fool the computer into doing things it might not be designed to do. By taking advantage of the features of the Operating System, many of them unknown and therefore undocumented by the original designers of the O/S, a computer programmer is able to extract additional performance from the equipment.

Similarly, though, such knowledge allows the motivated programmer to bypass critical portions of the Operating System to perform specific jobs and to circumvent any security measures that may be present. For example, in most of the 65,000,000 or so DOS computers in the world, it is common knowledge that when you ERASE a file, you really don't erase it. You merely erase the NAME of the file. If a secretary was told to dispose of document from a file cabinet, and she only removed the name of each file, but left the contents remaining in the file drawers, she would certainly have reason to worry for her job. Such is an example of one of the countless security holes that permeate computer land.

To take advantage of such glaring omissions, several software companies built programs that allowed users to retrieve 'erased' files.

These were among the skills that Miles wanted his people to have. He needed them to be fluent in not only DOS, but Unix, Xenix, VMS, Mac and a host of other Operating Systems. He needed a group that knew the strengths and weaknesses of every major O/S to fulfill his mission. They needed to be able to identify and exploit the trap doors and holes in all operating and security systems. From an engineering standpoint, Miles found it terrifically exciting. Over the three years he had been working for Homosoto, Miles and his crew designed software techniques and hardware tools that he didn't believe were even contemplated by his former employer.

The qualifications he sent to Homosoto were extensive, detailed and demanding. Miles wasn't convinced that anyone but he could find the proper people. The interview process alone was crucial to determining an applicant's true abilities, and a mediocre programmer could easily fool a non-technical person. While Miles and Homosoto agreed that all programmers should be isolated from each other, Miles felt he should know them more than by a coded name over modem lines. Miles lost that battle with one swift word from Homosoto.

No.

To Miles' surprise, within a few days of providing Homosoto with his recruitment lists, his 'staff' began calling him on his computer. To call Miles, a computer needed his number, and the proper security codes. To a man, or woman, they all did. And, as he spoke to them over the public phone lines, in encrypted form of course, he was amazed at their quality and level of technical sophistication. Whoever Alex was, he knew how to do his job.

Over a period of a few months, Miles commanded the resources of over 100 programmers. But, Miles thought, there was something strange about most of those with whom he spoke. They seemed ready to blindly follow instructions without questioning the assigned tasks. When a programmer takes a job or an assignment, he usually knows that he will be designing a data base, or word processor or other application program. However, Miles' staff was to design programs intended to damage computers.

He was assembling the single largest virus software team in the world, and none of them questioned the nature or ethics of the work.

Miles would have thought that while there is considerable technical talent around the world, finding people who would be willing to work on projects to facilitate the interruption of communications and proper computer operations would have been the most difficult part of recruitment. He realized he was wrong, although he did not know why. Technical mercenaries perhaps? He had never seen an ad with that as a job title, but, what the hell. Money can buy anything. Weapons designers since Oppenheimer have had to face similar moral dilemmas, and with widespread hatred of things American, recruitment couldn't have been all that difficult.

As he sat in his apartment, he was receiving the latest virus designs from one of his programmers who lived in the suburbs of Paris, France. While there was somewhat of a language barrier when they spoke, the computer language was a common denominator, and they all spoke that fluently. It broke down communications errors. Either it was in the code, or it wasn't.

Miles knew this designer only as Claude. Claude's virus was small, less than 2K, or 2000 characters, but quite deadly. Miles went over it and saw what it was designed to do. Ooh, clever, thought Miles. As many viruses do, this one attached itself to the Command.Com file of the DOS Operating System. Rather than wait for a specific future date, the next time the computer was booted, or turned on, Claude's virus in the O/S would play havoc with the chips that permit a printer to be connected to the computer. In a matter of seconds, with no pre-warning, the user would hear a small fizzle, and smell the recognizable odor of electronic burn. During the time the user poked his nose around the computer, to see if the smell was real or imaginary, the virus would destroy the contents of the hard disk.

According to Claude, whose English was better than most Frenchmen, there was a psychological advantage to this type of double- duty virus. The victim would realize that his computer needed repair and take it be fixed at his local computer shop. But, alas! Upon its return, the owner would find his hard disk trashed and attempt to blame the repairman. Deviously clever. Of course this type of virus would be discovered before too long. After a few thousand computers had their printer port blown up, word would get around and the virus would be identified. But, meanwhile, oh what fun.

As Miles prepared to send Claude's latest and greatest to another of his staff for analysis and debugging, the computer dedicated to speaking to Homosoto beeped at him. He glanced over at NipCom. He labeled all his computers with abbreviations. In this case, Nippon Communications seemed appropriate.

   <<<CONNECTION>>>

  MR. FOSTER

Miles scooted his chair over to NipCom and entered his PRG response..

Here Boss-san. What's up

YOU TELL ME.

Huh?

I READ THE PAPERS. AGAIN YOU MOVE PRECIPITOUSLY.

What are you talking about?

FIRST STATE BANK. YOUR INFECTORS ARE WITHOUT DISCIPLINE

I still don't know what you mean

THE PAPERS HAVE SAID THAT FIRST STATE BANK WAS INVADED BY HACKERS AND THEIR STOCK DROPPED VERY MUCH. IT IS STILL NOT TIME.

Oh, that. Good bit of work.

NO SO MR FOSTER. I AM NOT PLEASED WITH YOU

Me, why? I didn't have anything to do with it

EXPLAIN

Nothing to explain. My group doesn't do that, and even if they did, so what.

WHAT ABOUT THE VIRUSES? I READ EVERY DAY OF NEW COMPUTER VIRUS. THEY MUST BE STOPPED.

Why? It's all in good fun. Let 'em release them all they want.

THEY WILL HURT OUR PLANS

Bull. If anything, they help us.

HOW IS THAT?

Getting folks good and nervous. They're beginning to wonder who they can trust. It sure as hell won't be the government.

BUT IT IS IN THE PAPERS.

So?

THE BANKS WILL PROTECT THEMSELVES. THEY WILL SEE WHAT THE HACKERS DO AND MAKE OUR JOB MORE DIFFICULT.

Not a chance. Listen, there are hundreds, maybe thousands or more of small time hackers who poke around computers all the time. Sometimes they do some damage, but most of the time they are in it for thrill. The challenge. They are loosely organized at best. Maybe a few students at a university, or high school who fancy themselves computer criminals. Most of them wouldn't know what to do with the information if they took it.

The only reason this one hit the papers is because First is under investigation anyway, some fraud stuff. Literally thousands of computers are attacked every day, yet those don't appear in the paper or TV. It's kind of like rape. Companies don't want to admit they've been violated. And since damage has been limited, at least as far as the scale upon which we function, it's a non-issue.

I DO NOT SEE IT THAT WAY.

Well, that's the way it is. There are maybe a half dozen well coordinated hacking groups who care to cause damage. The rest of them, ignore them. They're harmless.

I WISH I BELIEVED THAT

There's not much we can do about it.

WHY NOT STOP THEM

We can't. Look at our plans. We have hundreds of people who have a single purpose. We operate as a single entity. The hackers are only a small thorn. Industry can't do much about them, so they ignore them. It is better that we ignore them, too.

FIND THEM

Who?

THE FIRST BANK ATTACKERS

Why?

I WANT THEM STOPPED

I told you, you can't do that. It's impossible. Call the Arab.

LOOK AT US, MR FOSTER. NOTHING IS IMPOSSIBLE.

What do you want me to do with them?

TELL ME WHO THEY ARE. I WILL TAKE CARE OF IT.

I'll see what I can do.

DO IT.

<<<CONNECTION TERMINATED>>>

Fuck, thought Miles. Sometimes Homosoto can be such an asshole. He doesn't really understand this business. I wonder how he got into it in the first place.

He remembered that he had to get Claude's virus properly analyzed and tested, so he sent it off to an American programmer who would perform a sanity-check on it. If all went well he would then send it out for distribution into America's computers through his BBS system set up just for that purpose.

With Diet Coke and Benson and Hedges Ultra Lights in hand he figured he might as well have someone look into Homosoto's paranoia. With some luck they could get a lead on this anonymous hacker and maybe Homosoto would leave him alone for a few hours. The constant interruptions and micro-management was a perpetual pain in the ass.

Miles moved over to his BBS computer and told ProCom to dial 1-602-555-3490. That was the phone number of the Freedom BBS, established by Miles and several recruits that Alex had so ably located. It was mid morning Arizona time. Revere should be there.

<<<CONNECTION>>>

Welcome to the Freedom BBS
Owned and Operated by the
Information Freedom League
(Non-profit)

Are You a Member of the IFL? Y
ID: XXXXXXXXX
PASSWORD: XXXXXXXX
Pause . . .
WELCOME TO THE FREEDOM BBS, MF. HOW ARE YOU TODAY?

✳ ✳ ✳ ✳ ✳ ✳ ✳ ✳ ✳ ✳ ✳ ✳ ✳ ✳

FREEDOM FLASH!!!!!!!!!!
Another hacker has been convicted of a computer crime and has been sentenced to 1 Year in jail, a fine of $25,000 and 2000 hours of community service!

His crime? Larry Johnson, a respected hacker from Milwaukee, WI, was a founding member of the 401 Group over 10 years ago. Since then he has been hacking systems successfully and was caught after he added $10,000 to his bank account.

GOOD FOR THE SECRET SERVICE! Congratulations Guys!
The IFL believes in a free exchange of information for all those who wish to be willing participants. We whole-heartedly condemn all computer activities that violate the law and code of computer ethics. All members of IFL are expected to heed all

current computer legislation and use computers exclusively for the betterment of mankind.

Any IFL member found to be using computers in any illegal fashion or for any illegal purpose will be reported to the Computer Crime Division of the Secret Service in Washington, D.C.

Remember, hacking is a crime!

* * * * * * * * * * * * * * * * * *

A little thick, thought Miles, but effective.   And a stroke of genius. He patted himself on the back every time he saw how effective Freedom, his computer warfare distribution system was.

DO YOU WANT THE MAIN MENU? No

DO YOU WANT TO SPEAK TO REVERE? Y

LET ME SEE IF HE IS HERE, OR IF YOU NEED TO LEAVE A MESSAGE.

ONE MOMENT PLEASE. . .

THE SYSOP IS WAITING.   PLEASE ENTER YOUR PIN: XXXX-XXXX

Pause . . .

MF? IS THAT YOU?

Betch'ure ass. Revere? How's trix?

SAME OL' SAME OL'. YOU?

Trying to make a profit. Hey, we gotta talk.

OUT LOUD?

No whisper.

OK. LET ME SET IT.

<CRYPT KEY SELECTION>

Pause . . .

<CRYPT KEY EXCHANGE>

Pause . . .

<TRANSMISSION ENCODED>

MF?

Still here.

GOOD. SURPRISES THE SHIT OUT OF ME EVERY TIME THIS WORKS.

Me too.

WHAT CAN I DO? GOT ANOTHER PRESENT?

Couple of days, sure. Some doosies.

WHAT'YA GOT?

A graphics program that kicks the living shit out of VGA Master and Paint Man. Deadly too.

HOW?

Copies portions of itself into Video RAM and treats it as a TSR. Next program you load gets infected from Video RAM and spreads from there. Undetectable unless you're running debug at the same time and looking for it. Then it stealths itself into all V-RAM applications and spreads outside the O/S.

TRIGGERS?

I forget the exact trigger mechanism, but it gives constant parity errors. Nothing'll run.

OK! LOOKIN' GOOD.

Also have a few Lotus utilities, a couple of games.

THE GAMES ARE GOING GREAT GUNS. WE SHOULD BE SELLING THEM IN THE STORES.

How many?

AS OF A WEEK AGO, MORE THAN 240,000 PACK-LADIES HAVE BEEN DOWN LOADED. THAT'S OUR BEST SELLER.

Anyone sending money?

SURPRISINGLY, YES. WE'RE TURNING A PROFIT.

Shit. That's not what we wanted.

CAN'T KEEP A GOOD PROGRAM DOWN.

Yeah Yeah Yeah. need some info.

THAT'S OUR MIDDLE NAME. WHAT DO YOU NEED.

You hear about the First Bank hacker?

SURE! I GOT A DOZEN PEOPLE TAKING CREDIT FOR IT.

You're kidding

NO! IT'S A GOOD ONE. BRING A BANK TO IT'S KNEES. STOP STOCK TRADING. SEC INVESTIGATION. A LOT OF OUR FOLKS WOULD HAVE BEEN PROUD.

Was it us?

NO WAY.

Then who, really?

DAMNED IF I KNOW OR CARE.

Care

WHAT? SINCE WHEN DO WE CARE ABOUT THE AMATEURS?

Since now. Things are heating up too soon. I need to know who pulled the job.

I CAN GET A LOT OF PEOPLE TO ADMIT IT, BUT I CAN'T VERIFY IT.

Whoever did it is not likely to advertise it openly. We may need to pull him into the open.

GOTCHA

Here's my thinking. Assume the hack is just a kid. He's getting no credit and receives a shitty allowance. So, we offer a reward. Whoever can prove that they are the one's who broke into First Bank, we'll send them a new 386. Whatever, use your imagination.

THINK HE'LL BITE?

If it's a pro, no. But this doesn't ring of a pro. The newspapers know too much.

AND IF WE FIND HIM?

Just get me his number and shipping address. Make sure he gets the computer too.

OK BOSS. ANYTHING ELSE?

Keep up the good work. Oh, yeah. I need the estimates.

NO PROBLEM. THEY LOOK GREAT. IN JUST OVER 2 YEARS, WE HAVE GIVEN AWAY OVER 1,300,000 INFECTED PROGRAMS AND NONE HAVE GONE OFF YET. ACCORDING TO PLAN.

Love it. Peace.

BYE, YOU MF.

<<<CONNECTION TERMINATED>>>

* * * * *

Monday, December 7
New York City

The phone on Scott Mason's desk had been unusually, but gratefully quiet. Higgins had been able to keep the First State lawyers at bay with the mounds of information the paper had accumulated on MacMillan's doings. The bank's stock was trading again, but at a dilution of over 75%. Most individual customers had cashed out their accounts, including Higgins, and only those long term portfolios remained. Scott's stories on First Bank had won him recognition by his peers. No awards, but an accolade at the New York Journalists Club dinner. Not bad, he thought.

Now the hard work continued for him. The full background analyses, additional proof, more witnesses now that Sidneys was under Federal indictment and out of work. MacMillan was in trouble, but it was clear to Scott, that if the heat got turned up too much, there was a cache of millions offshore for the person with the right access codes.

His phone rang.

"Scott Mason."

"Hey, Scott this is Kirk. We gotta talk, I'm in trouble." Kirk sounded panicked.

"Damn Klingons," Scott cracked.

"Seriously, I'm in trouble. You gotta help me out."

Scott realized this was no prank. "Sure, sure, calm down. What happened?"

"They found me, and they got into my computer and now it's gone . . .shit, I'm in trouble. You gotta help me."

"Kirk!" Scott shouted. "Kirk, relax, ground yourself. You're not making sense. Take it from the beginning."

Kirk exhaled heavily in Scott's ear, taking several deep breaths. "O.K., I'm O.K., but should we be talking on the phone?"

"Hey, you called me . . ." Scott said with irritation.

"Yeah, I know, but I'm not thinking so good. You're right, I'll call you tonight."

Click.

* * * * *

Nightline was running its closing credits when Scott's home computer beeped at him. Though Kirk had not told him when to expect a call, all other communications had begun precisely at midnight, so Scott made a reasonable deduction.

The dormant video screen came to life as the first message appeared.

MASON

That was unlike Kirk to start a conversation that way.

wtfo

ITS ME. KIRK.

Now it was Scott's turn to be suspicious.

Prove it.

AW CMON

Prove it.

I CALLED YOU TODAY

So did half of the crack pots in New York

I'M IN TROUBLE

So were the others.

OK. WE WENT THROUGH THE BANK AND HAD SOME FUN WITH PRESSED RAT AND WHARTHOG, INC.

Good enough. You sound as scared here as you did on the phone. I thought computers didn't have emotion.

I DO.

OK, what's up.

THEY FOUND ME

Who?

THE PEOPLE FROM FIRST STATE BANK.

How? What?

I RECEIVED A MESSAGE ON MY COMPUTER, E-MAIL. IT SAID, STAY AWAY FROM FIRST STATE BANK. YOUR HACK-ING CAREER IS OVER. OR ELSE.

What did you do?

CALLED A FEW FRIENDS WHO THINK THEY'RE FUNNY.

And?

HONOR AMONG THIEVES. IT WASN'T THEM. SO I FIGURED IT WAS FOR REAL.

You sure?

AS SURE AS I CAN BE. MY ACTIVITIES ARE SUPPOSED TO BE SECRET. NO ONE KNOWS. EXCEPT YOU.

And you think I did something.

THE THOUGHT CROSSED MY MIND MORE THAN ONCE, I'LL TELL YOU. BUT, I THINK I HAVE ELIMINATED YOU

Thanks, Why?

NO MOTIVATION. I'M MORE USE TO YOU ALIVE THAN DEAD.

Excuse me?

AS LONG AS MY IDENTITY AND ACTIVITIES REMAIN
SECRET, I'M ALIVE AS A HACKER AND CAN CONTINUE TO
DO WHAT I DO. AS SOON AS I'M FOUND OUT, IT'S OVER.
BUT THAT'S NOT THE PROBLEM.

What is?

I CAME HOME THIS MORNING AND FOUND THAT SOME-
ONE BROKE IN AND TRASHED EVERYTHING. COM-
PUTERS, PRINTERS, MONITORS, THE WHOLE BALL OF
WAX. AND THERE WAS A NOTE.

What did it say?

WE KNOW WHAT YOU'VE DONE. STAY OUT OF OUR COM-
PUTERS OR YOU WILL BE SORRY. IT WAS SIGNED FIRST
STATE BANK.

That doesn't make sense.

WHAT DOESN'T

*Nobody except terrorists leave their calling card, and then only
when they're sure they can't be caught. I would bet dollars to
donuts that First State had nothing to do with it.*

ARE YOU SURE?

*No, I'm not sure, not 100%, but it doesn't add up. You've
stepped on somebody's toes, and it may or may not have anything
to do with First State. They're just trying to scare you.*

AND DOING A DAMNED GOOD JOB OF IT

Have you called the police.

NO. NOT YET. I'M NOT IN THE LINE OF WORK THEY
PROBABLY APPROVE OF.

*So I see. Who else knew about your trips through the bank, other
than me. I will assume I'm not the guilty party.*

A COUPLE OF HACKER FRIENDS, MY GIRLFRIEND, THAT'S
ABOUT IT.

No one else?

NOT THAT I CAN THINK OF.

*Let me ask you. If you wanted to find out who was hacking
where, how would you find out? Let's say you wanted to know
what your friends were doing. Is there a way?*

NOT WITHOUT A LOT OF EXPENSIVE EQUIPMENT. NO.
YOU WOULD HAVE TO TELL SOMEONE.

And you told no one? No one?

WELL, THERE WAS FREEDOM.

What's Freedom?

FREEDOM IS A NATIONAL BBS SYSTEM. IT'S FAIRLY NEW.

What do they do?

LIKE MOST BBS'S, IT'S AN OPEN FORUM FOR EXCHANGE
OF INFORMATION, PROGRAMS, ETC. IT IS ONE OF THE
LARGEST IN THE COUNTRY. THEY HAVE BBS AFFILIATES
IN 50 OR 60 CITIES. THEY ALSO RUN A SHAREWARE SER-
VICE.

Is that significant?

MOST SHAREWARE COMPANIES SELL THEIR SOFTWARE
ON OTHER PEOPLE'S BBS'S. THE CONCEPT IS SIMPLE.
THEY GIVE AWAY THEIR SOFTWARE FOR FREE. IF YOU
LIKE IT, YOU ARE SUPPOSED TO SEND IN A FEW DOL-
LARS AS A REGISTRATION, AND THAT'S HOW THEY MAKE
MONEY. IT'S PART OF THE CULTURE, DON'T BECOME
RICH ON SOFTWARE. FREEDOM WRITES A TREMENDOUS
AMOUNT OF SOFTWARE AND THEY PUT IT ON THEIR OWN
AS WELL AS OTHER BBS'S. IT'S REAL SMART. THEY BASI-
CALLY HAVE THEIR OWN METHOD TO DISTRIBUTE THEIR
SOFTWARE.

Do they make money?

WHO KNOWS. IT LOOKS LIKE A BIG OPERATION. VERY
FEW SHAREWARE PEOPLE MAKE MONEY, AND FREEDOM
SAYS ITS NON-PROFIT.

Non-Profit did you say? Are you sure?

THAT'S WHAT THEY SAY.

What's their number?

I ONLY HAVE THE LA NUMBER.

So you are from the Coast.

SHIT. YEAH. I'M FROM THE COAST.

That was an accident. I really don't care.

I KNOW. IT MAY NOT MATTER. I MAY GIVE IT UP. I DON'T
NEED MY COMPUTERS BEING BLOWN TO SMITHERINES
TO TELL ME I'M BARKING UP THE WRONG TREE.

Maybe it is the right tree.

WHAT?

Never mind. So, you said you told them?

WELL, KIND OF. YOU SEE, THEY ARE VERY MUCH
AGAINST HACKING. THEY ALWAYS TALK ABOUT
PROSECUTING HACKERS, HOW BAD WE ARE. AFTER THE

FIRST STATE ARTICLES YOU WROTE, A LOT OF PEOPLE ON THE CHAT LINE CLAIMED TO HAVE DONE THE JOB. NOT THAT WE REALLY DID ANYTHING. WE JUST LOOKED AROUND. ALL THESE GUYS ADMITTED TO HAVE DONE IT, SO I ADDED MY TWO CENTS AND SAID I DID IT. I THOUGHT IT MIGHT ADD TO THE CONFUSION.

Apparently it did.

WHAT DOES THAT MEAN?

Let's say I had something to hide, and let's even say I was First State.

SO

So, a bunch of people claim to have wrecked havoc on a computer. What easier way to cover all the possible bases than to threaten them all.

YOU MEAN EVERYONE WHO ADMITTED IT? OR CLAIMED IT?

Right. Get to them all.

BUT HOW WOULD FIRST STATE KNOW ABOUT IT?

I'm not saying they did. Do you know any of the others who claimed responsibility?

NOT PERSONALLY. ONLY ONE GUY NAMED DA VINCI I'VE TALKED TO.

Can you call him?

SURE, HE'S ON FREEDOM ALL THE TIME.

Don't use Freedom. Is there any other way to contact him? On another BBS?

IT WOULDN'T BE HARD TO FIND OUT, BUT WHY NOT FREEDOM?

Look. This BBS may be the only link between the First State hack you and I were in on, by the way, did you use my name?

DIDN'T NEED TO. YOU WROTE THE ARTICLE. YOU'RE GETTING VERY WELL KNOWN.

Thanks for the warning. HA! At any rate, you check it out with this Da Vinci character and once you know, just call me at the office, and say something like, the Mona Lisa frowned. That means he got a message similar to yours. If the Mona Lisa smiles, then we can figure out something else. OK?

SURE. HEY, QUESTION.

Answer.

SERIOUSLY.

I'm serious.

WHAT DO YOU THINK'S GOING ON? YOU BELIEVE IT'S HACKERS, DON'T YOU?

Let me ask you a question. How many surrealistic painters does it take to screw in a lightbulb?

I GIVE. HOW MANY

A fish.

I DON'T UNDERSTAND

That's the point. Neither do I. Yet. But you can help. According to what you're saying, there may be some weirdness with Freedom. What do you recommend so I can dig a little deeper. Into the whole cult of hacking. And don't worry. I don't hang sources. Besides, I think we may need each other.

HOW DO YOU MEAN.

I think you should talk to the authorities.

NO WAY

Wait. I have a friend, ex-friend, who knows about this kind of thing, at least a little, and he might be of some help to you. I just don't think it should go unreported. Would you talk to him?

LIVE OR MEMOREX?

He probably would want a face to face, but I can't say for sure.

FORGET IT. BUT I CAN HELP YOU WITH MORE SOURCES. AT LEAST I CAN TELL YOU WHERE TO GO.

So can a lot of people.

REALLY. NEXT WEEK, THERE'S A CONVENTION OF SORTS FOR HACKERS.

A convention?

WELL, IT'S MORE LIKE AN UNDERGROUND MEETING, A LARGE ONE. WHERE HACKERS FROM ALL OVER GET TOGETHER AND COMPARE NOTES. IT'S A GREAT DEAL OF FUN, AND FOR YOU, MIGHT BE A SOURCE OF LEADS. GENERALLY SPEAKING OF COURSE. YOU CAN'T BE A BULL IN A CHINA SHOP.

In other words, reporters are taboo.

KIND OF. YOU'LL NEED AN INVITATION, I CAN PROBABLY SWING THAT. BEYOND THAT, YOU'RE ON YOUR OWN. IT'S A VERY PRIVATE CLUB.

Where is this meeting?

IN AMSTERDAM.

Holland?

YUP.

Why there?

SIN CITY IS AS GOOD FOR HACKERS AS IT IS FOR DRUGS AND SEX. SO I'M TOLD. HA HA. THE POLICE DON'T REALLY CARE WHAT YOU DO.

What goes on?

BESIDES THE USUAL AMSTERDAM ANTICS? A COUPLE OF HUNDRED OF THE BEST HACKERS IN THE WORLD SHOW UP TO SET CODES OF ETHICS FOR THEMSELVES, JUST LIKE FREEDOM DOES. IN REALITY, THOUGH, WE STROKE OUR EGOS AND PARADE AROUND WITH OUR LATEST CLAIMS TO FAME AND INVASIONS OF COM-PUTERS. WAR STORIES. CRACKING AND HACKING TECH-NIQUES ARE SHARED, PEOPLE LIE TO EACH OTHER ABOUT THEIR ACHIEVEMENTS AND TALK ABOUT WHAT THEY'LL DO THE NEXT YEAR. PROGRAMASTERBATION.

Some name. Is that really what they call it?

NAH, JUST A TERM WE USE. I WENT LAST YEAR AND HAD A BALL, LITERALLY. IN FACT, THAT'S WHERE I LEARNED HOW TO GET INTO FIRST STATE. IT WAS SECOND RATE INFORMATION, FIRST STATE IS NOT EXACTLY YOUR HIGH PROFILE BANK TO CRACK.

Understood. How do I get in, what's it called?

IT'S CALLED THE INTERGALACTIC HACKERS CON-FERENCE, I-HACK FOR SHORT. ONLY THE BEST GET TO GO.

You're kidding. Interplanetary. So what do you do to get me in?

I CALL YOU AGAIN. I'LL GET YOU AN INVITE.

That's great, I really appreciate that. Will you be there?

NOT THIS YEAR. CAN'T SPARE THE TIME. DON'T ACT LIKE A REPORTER. PARANOIA RUNS RAMPANT.

Will anyone talk to me, as a reporter?

THAT'S UP TO YOU. ASK THE RIGHT QUESTIONS AND SHOW SYMPATHY FOR THEIR ACTIVITIES. IF YOU'RE LUCKY YOU'LL MEET THE RIGHT PERSON WHO CAN GIVE YOU A HANDS ON CRACKING LESSON. FAIR ENOUGH?

Again, thanks. I'll expect your call. And, I'll let you know what my Fed-Friend says about your problem.

TA.

<<<CONNECTION TERMINATED>>>

* * * * *

Tuesday, December 8
Vienna, Austria

Vienna is not only the geographic center of Europe - for 45 years it has been the geopolitical center as well. A neutral country, as is Switzerland, it contains the highest concentration of KGB and CIA operatives in the world. Perhaps that is why Martin Templer chose to meet Alex Spiradon there a week after his meeting with Tyrone Duncan at P Street.

Situated by the Danube of Strauss fame, Vienna, Austria is an odd mixture of the old, the very old and nouveau European high tech. Downtown Vienna is small, a semi-circle of cobblestone streets and brash illuminated billboards at every juncture.

Templer contacted Alex through intermediaries stationed in Zurich. The agreed upon location was the third bench from St. Stephen's Cathedral on the Stephansplatz, where Vienna's main street, Karntnerstrasse-Rotenturmstrasse changes names. No traffic is allowed on the square, on Kartnerstrasse or on Grabenstrasse, so it always packed with shoppers, tourists and street musicians. Ideal for a discreet meeting.

"Have you ever seen Vienna from Old Steffel?" A deep voice came from behind where Martin was seated. He looked around and saw it was Alex.

"Many years ago. But I prefer the Prater." He spoke of the fairgrounds 2 kilometers from town where the world's oldest Ferris Wheel offered an unparalleled view of the Viennese surrounds. Templer smiled at his old ally from German intelligence. Today though, Alex was an asset to the Agency, as he had been since he had gone freelance some years ago. An expensive asset, but always with quality information.

"Did you know that St. Stephen's," Alex gestured at the pollution stained church, "is one of the finest examples of Gothic architecture in Europe? And Vienna's paradox?"

Templer had never been a history buff. He shook his head.

"Most of Vienna is Baroque, in fine fashion, but there are isolated examples of Gothic. Yet, they seem to coexist. In peace." Alex's poetic words rolled off of his well educated tongue. The allegory was not lost on Templer. Western and Eastern intelligence services used Vienna as a no-man's land, where information and people were regularly exchanged.

"It is a new world," commented Templer. "The threats are different."

Alex took the hint. "Let us walk," he urged.

They slowly strolled up the Kartnerstrasse as the Austrian nightlife took on its own distinct flavor.

"How long has it been, my friend?" Alex casually asked. He disliked rushing into business, the way the Americans favored.

"Damned if I know. 4, 5, 6 years? Too long. We've had some good times."

"'85, '86 was it? So much travel blurs the senses." Alex wrinkled his forehead in thought. "Wasn't it the Pelton affair? Yes, that would be summer of '85." He referred to Ron Pelton, the ex-NSA analyst who sold American cryptographic secrets to the Soviets.

"Yeah," Templer laughed. "That poor jerk. I'd forgotten all about that. Never would have caught on to the scam if it weren't for Slovnov. The KGB should tell their own to stay out of the Moulin Rouge. Not good for business. Ivan had to trade Slovnov for Pelton. We didn't find out for a year that they wanted Pelton out anyway. He was too fucked up for them."

"And now? Who do you spy on since Sam and Ivan are brothers again?" Alex openly enjoyed speaking obliquely.

"Spy? Ha!" Templer shook his head. "I got pushed upstairs. Interagency cooperation, political bullshit. I do miss the streets though, and the friends . . .on both sides."

"Don't you mean on all sides?" Cocktail semantics made Alex occasionally annoying.

"No, I mean both. At least we had class; we knew the rules and how to play. Now every third rate country tries to stick their nose in and they screw it up. One big mess." Templer was a staunch anti-Communist when there were Communists, but he respected their agents' highly professional attitude, and yes, ethics.

"Touché! I have missed our talks and our disagreements. I never could talk you into something you did not believe in, could I?" Alex slapped Templer lightly on his back. Templer didn't answer. "Ah, you look so serious. You came for business, not old memories?"

"No, Alex, I'd love to chat, and we will, but I do need to get a couple of questions answered, and then, I can relax. Perhaps a trip to Club 24?" Templer pointed at the bright yellow kiosk with the silhouettes of naked women emblazoned on it. For a mere $300, you can buy a bottle of Chevas Regal and share it with one or two or more of the lovely skimpily clad ladies who adorned the bar seats. All else was negotiable in private.

"Done. Let us speak, now. What can I do for you?" Alex approved of the plan.

"I need some information," Templer said seriously.

"That is my business, of course."

"We have a problem in the States . . ."

"As usual," Alex interrupted.

"Yes," Templer grinned, "as usual. But this one is not usual. Someone, someone with connections, is apparently using computers as a blackmail tool. The FBI is investigating domestically, and, well, it's our job, to look outside. So, I figure, call Alex. That's why I'm here."

Alex disguised his surprise. How had they found him? He now needed to find out what, if anything, they knew.

"Blackmail? Computers? That's not a lot to go on." Alex maintained absolute composure.

"Here's what we know. And it's not much. There appears to be a wholesale blackmail operation in place. With the number of complaints we have gotten over the last few months, we could guess that maybe 10, or 20 people, maybe more are involved. They're after the big boys; the banks, some senators, folks with real money and power. And it's one professional job. They seem to get their information from computers, from the radiation they emanate. It's something we really want to keep quiet."

Alex listened quietly. If Templer was being straight, they didn't know much, certainly not the scope of the operation nor Alex's own involvement. It was possible, though, that Templer was playing dumb, and trying to elicit clues from Alex. If he was a suspect.

"What sort of demands are being made?" Alex was going to play the game to the hilt.

"None. Yet."

"After 2 months? You say? And no demands? What kind of blackmail is that?" Alex ineffectively stifled a laugh. "This sounds like some Washington paranoia. "You really don't know what to do without an adversary, so you create one," Alex chuckled.

"Alex, c'mon. No shit, we got some muckity mucks with their heads in a tail spin and our asses in a sling. I don't know what's happening, but, whatever it is, it's causing a pile of shit bigger than Congress and smellier."

"And you thought I might know something about it?" Alex ventured.

"Well, no, or yes, or maybe," Templer said coyly. "Who's got a grudge? Against so many people? And then, who's also got the technology to do it? There must be a lot of smart people and money in on it. You have the best ears in Europe." The compliment might help.

"Thank you for the over-statement, but I have only a small group on whom I can rely. Certainly your own agency can find out before I can." Deniability and humility could raise the ante.

"We have our good days, but too many bad days." Templer was being sincere concluded Alex. "Listen, I need the streets. If there's nothing, then there's nothing. It could be domestic, but it smells of outside influence. Can you help?"

Alex stopped to light up a non-filter Gaulloise. He inhaled deeply as his eyes scanned the clear sky. He wanted to have Templer think there might be something.

"How much is this information worth?" Alex was the perfect mercenary, absolutely no allegiance to anyone other than himself.

"We have about fifty grand for good info. But for that price, it had better be good."

Alex had to laugh to himself at the American's naivete. Homosoto was paying him a hundred times that for one job. Being a freelancer means treating all customers as equals, and there was no way he would jeopardize his planned retirement for a cause or for a friend. This would be easy.

"Phew!" Alex whistled. "Hot off the griddle, huh? I'll see who knows what. It may take a while, a week, ten days, but I'll get back to you with anything I find. No promises, though."

"I know it's a long shot, but we have to look at all angles. I really appreciate it." Templer sounded relieved. He had just recruited, for no money down, the best source of information in Europe. "Let's go have a bottle of Chevas. On me." The American taxpayer was about to pay for the sexual relief of a mercenary enemy.

Alex made it home at 4:00 AM after the romp in Club 24. Or was it Club 1? He no longer knew, nor cared. Despite his intense intoxication, he had to talk to his employer. Somehow he managed to get his computer alive. He dialed the number in Tokyo, not knowing whether Homosoto would be in the office.

ENTER PASSWORD

ENTER CRYPT KEY

He responded to both, nearly blinded from the Chevas, yet his professionalism demanded that he make immediate contact if possible.

<<<CONNECTION>>>

Alex missed the message for several seconds before forcing himself alert. He quickly entered his opening words before the connection would shut down.

I have been contacted.

262

Homosoto apparently never went home. He got an immediate response.

BY WHOM

The CIA

The screen paused for several seconds. Alex was too drunk to notice.

HOW?

An old frrrriend. He called for a meeeeeeting.

WHAT DID HE WANT?

He asked about the US operations.

HOW MUCH DOES HE KNOW?

They kkknnow about the blackmail. But, they're fishing

FISH

Fishing. Looking for answers. They know nothing.

TELL ME MORE. I AM NOT HAPPY.

The FBI is looking for an answer, who is behind the propaganda. They think it is very important, take it seriously. They brought in the CIA and, probably, the NSA. The effect is beginning. We should be pleased.

AND THE PRESS? IS IT IN THE PAPERS?

No, it was suppressed. The Government still controls the press.

AND YOU. WHY CONTACT YOU?

The same reason you did. It is pure coincidence.

I AM NOT CONVINCED.

An old friend, colleague, called, for a meeting. He asked for my help. He tried to hire me to find out if it was foreign.

WHAT DID YOU SAY?

I told him the streets, the rumors, know nothing. That is true. He never suspected me. I was surprised. He offered me money to give him information.

HOW MUCH MONEY?

$50,000 US

I PAY YOU A THOUSAND TIMES THAT

No, only 100 times.

DOES IT MATTER?

Only if they equal your money.

MAKE SURE THEY DO NOT. IT IS NOT WORTH YOUR LIFE.

The CIA does not have that kind of money. That is why the Russians learned so much for so little. The US does not think they should pay to keep their secrets.

THEY ARE WRONG. WE CALL IT INSURANCE.

They call it blackmail. They do not have the funds.

WHAT WILL YOU TELL THEM?

I will tell them that it is not from here. No, it must be from the US. They will believe me. I will charge them for that information.

AND THEY WILL BELIEVE YOU?

If I make them pay, yes. If I give it for free, no. That's the American way. They will believe what is easiest to believe. They do not know that this is my last job. They cannot know. If they think that, they will suspect me. And then, you.

WHY ME?

They will use drugs I cannot resist. So, I must make sure I convince them.

AND IF THEY OFFER MONEY. AS MUCH AS I DO?

Then we negotiate.

THEN YOU WILL DIE.

<<<CONNECTION TERMINATED>>>

* * * * *

Chapter 16

Wednesday, December 9
New York

The late afternoon pace of the City Room at the Times tended to be chaotic. As deadlines approached and the paper was laid out for the printers, the flurry of activity was associated with an increase in the loudness of the room. Scott Mason listened with one hand over his right ear and the phone so awkwardly pressed between his left ear and shoulder that his glasses sat askew on his face. Suddenly hanging up the phone, Scott sprung up shouting, "I got it." Several people stopped and stared in his direction, but seeing nothing of concern or interest to them, they returned to their own world.

Scott ripped a page from a notebook and ran into and around his co-workers. "Doug, I got it. Confirmed by the President."

"You're kidding me?" Doug stopped his red pencil mid-stroke. "Give it to me from the top." He turned in his swivel chair to face Scott more directly.

"It goes like this. A few weeks ago Sovereign Bank in Atlanta found that someone had entered their central computers without permission." Scott perused his notes. "It didn't take long for them to find the intruder. He left a calling card. It said that the hackers had found a hole to crawl through undetected into their computers. Was the bank interested in knowing how it was done? They left a Compuserve Mail Box."

"As you can imagine the bank freaked out and told their computer people to fix whatever it was. They called in the FBI, that's from my contact, and went on an internal rampage. Those good ol' boys don't trust nobody," Scott added sounding like a poor imitation of Andy from Mayberry

"Anybody that could spell computer was suspect and they turned the place upside down. Found grass, cocaine, ludes, a couple of weapons and a lot of people got fired. But no state secrets. You talk about a dictatorship," commented Scott on the side. "There's no privacy at all. They scanned everyone's electronic mail boxes looking for clues and instead found them staring at invasion of privacy suits from employees and ex-employees who were fired because of the contents of their private mail.

"The computer jocks unplugged the computers, turned them inside out and screwed them back together. Nothing. They found nada. So they tighten the reins and give away less passwords, to less people. That's all they figured they could do."

"This is where the fun starts." Scott actively gestured with his hands as he shifted weight to his other foot. "A few days later they discover another message in their computer. Says something like, 'sorry Charlie' or something to that effect. The hackers were back. And this time they wanted to sell their services to the bank. For a nominal fee, say, a million bucks, we'll show you how to sew up the holes."

"Well, what does that sound like to you?" Scott asked Doug.

"Extortion."

"Exactly, and ape-shit doesn't begin to describe what the bank did. Bottom line? They made a deal. We'll pay you a million bucks as consultants for 10 years. You agree to stay out of the machines unless we need you. Immunity unless you break the deal."

"What happened?" Doug said with rapt attention.

"Sovereign bank now has three fourteen year old consultants at a hundred grand a year," Scott said choking with laughter on his words.

"You're kidding," exclaimed Doug slapping his knees.

"No shit. And everyone is pretty happy about it. The kids have a way to pay for a good college, they're bright little snots, and they get off. The bank figures it's making an investment in the future and actually may have gotten off cheap. It woke them up to the problems they could face if their computers did go down for a month. Or if they lost all their records. Or if someone really wanted to do damage. Thoughts like that trigger a panic attack in any bank exec. They'd rather deal with the kids.

"In fact, they're turning it into a public relations coup. Dig this," Scott knew the story like the back of his hand. "The bank realized that they could fix their security problems for a couple of million bucks. Not much of an investment when you're guarding billions. So they design a new ad campaign: Sovereign. The Safest Your Money Can Be."

"Now that's a story," said Doug approvingly. "Important, fun, human, and everyone comes out a winner. A story with a moral. Confirmed?"

"Every bit. From the president. They announce it all tomorrow and we print tonight with their blessing. Exclusive."

"Why? What did you have to do . . ?"

"Nothing. He likes the work we've been doing on the computer capers and crime and all and thought that we would give it fair coverage. I think they're handling it like absolute gentlemen."

"How fast do you type?"

"Forty mistakes a minute. Why?"

"You got 40 minutes to deadline."

* * * * *

Friday, December 11
Washington, D.C.

Throughout his years of Government service at the National Security Agency, Miles Foster had become a nine to fiver. Rarely did he work in the evening or on weekends. So the oddball hours he had to work during his association with Homosoto were irritating and made him cranky. He could function well enough, and crankiness was difficult to convey over a computer terminal, but working nights wasn't much to his liking. It interfered with his social responsibilities to the women.

The master plan Miles had designed years ago for Homosoto was now calling for phase two to go into effect. The beauty of it all, thought Miles, was that it was unstoppable. The pieces had been put into play by scores of people who worked for him; the programmers, the Freedom League BBS's and the infectors. Too much had already gone into play to abort the mission. There was no pulling back.

Only a few weeks were left before the first strike force landed. The militaristic thinking kept Miles focussed on the task at hand, far away from any of the personalization that might surface if he got down to thinking about the kinds of damage he was going to be inflicting on millions of innocent targets. Inside, perhaps deep inside, Miles cared, but he seemed to only be aware of the technical results of his efforts in distinction to the human element. The human elements of frustration, depression, helplessness - a social retreat of maybe fifty years, that was going to be the real devastation above and beyond the machinery. Just the way Homosoto wanted it. To hurt deep down.

Miles had come to learn of the intense hatred that Homosoto felt toward the United States. In his more callous moments, especially when he and Homosoto were at odds over any particular subject, Miles would resort to the basest of verbal tactics.

"You're just pissed off 'cause we nuked your family." It was meant to sting and Homosoto's reactions were unpredictable. Often violent, he had once thrown priceless heirlooms across his office shattering in a thousand shards. A three hour lecture ensued on one occasion, tutoring Miles about honorable warfare. Miles listened and fell asleep during more than one sermon.

But at the bottom of it, Homosoto kept a level head and showed he knew what he was doing. The plans they formulated were coming together though Miles had no direct control over many pieces. The Readers were run by another group altogether; Miles only knew they

267

were fundamentalist fanatics. He didn't really care as long as the job was getting done. And the groundhogs; he designed them, but they were managed by others. Propaganda, yet another, just as the plan called for. Extreme compartmentalization, even at the highest level.

Only Homosoto knew all the players and therefore had the unique luxury of viewing the grand game being played. Though Miles designed every nuance, down to the nth degree of how to effect the invasion properly, he was not privileged to push the chessmen around the board. His rationalization was that he was being paid a great deal of money for the job, and, he was working for a more important cause, one that would make it all worthwhile. Perhaps in another year or two when the final phases were complete, and the United States was even more exposed and defenseless than it was right now, the job would be done.

Miles' ruminating provided a calming influence during the interminable months and years that distanced the cause and effect. In the intelligence game, on the level that he had operated while with the NSA, he would receive information, process it, make recommendation and determinations, and that was that. Over. Next.

Now though, Miles had designed the big picture, and that meant long range planning. No more instant gratification. He was in control, only partially, as he was meant to be. He was impressed with the operation. That nothing had gone awry so far consoled Miles despite the fact that Homosoto called him almost every day to ask about another computer crime he had heard about.

This time is was Sovereign Bank. Homosoto had heard rumors that they were being held hostage by hackers and was concerned that some of Miles' techy's had gone out on their own.

Homosoto reacted to the Sovereign issue as he had many others that he seemed so concerned about. Once Miles gave him an explanation, he let the matter drop. Not without an appropriate warning to Miles, though, that he had better be right.

The number of computer crimes was increasing more rapidly than Miles or anyone in the security field had predicted only a few years ago and the legal issues were mounting faster than the state or federal legislatures could deal with them. But, as Miles continually reassured Homosoto, they were small timers with no heinous motivation. They were mostly kids who played chicken with computers instead of chasing cars or smoking crack. A far better alternative, Miles offered.

Just kids having a little fun with the country's most important computer systems. No big deal. Right. How anyone can leave the front door to their computer open, or with the keys lying around, was beyond him. Fucking stupid.

His stream of consciousness was broken when his NipCom computer announced that Homosoto was calling. Again. Shit. I bet some high school kids changed their school grades and Homosoto thinks the Rosenburgs are behind it. Paranoid gook.

<<<TRANSMISSION ENCRYPTED>>>

MR FOSTER

That's me. What's wrong.

NOTHING. ALL IS WELL.

That's a change. Nobody fucking with your Nintendo, huh?

YOUR HUMOR ESCAPES ME, AT TIMES

S'pozed 2

WHAT?

Never Mind. What do you need?

WE ARE CLOSE

I know.

OF COURSE YOU DO. A BRIEF REPORT PLEASE.

Sure. Freedom is doing better than expected. Over a million now, maybe a million and a half. The majors are sick, real sick. Alex has kept my staff full, and we're putting out dozens of viruses a week. On schedule.

GOOD

I'm gonna be out for a few days. I'll call when I get back.

SHOULDN'T YOU STAY WHERE YOU CAN BE REACHED?

I carry a portable. I will check my computer, as I always do. You have never had trouble reaching me.

THAT IS TRUE. WHERE DO YOU GO?

Amsterdam.

HOLLAND? WHY?

A hackers conference. I need a break anyway, so I thought I might as well make it a working vacation. The top hackers get together and stroke themselves, but I could pick something up. Useful to us.

DO BE CAREFUL, YOU ARE VALUABLE. NO ONE CAN KNOW WHO YOU ARE.

No one does. No one. I use my BBS alias. Spook.

* * * * *

San Francisco, California

Sir George Sterling checked his E-Mail for messages. There were only 2, both from Alex. The one week holiday had been good for Sir George. Well earned, he thought. In less than 3 months, he had called over 1,700 people on the phone and let them in on his little secrets, as he came to call them.

Every month Alex had forwarded money, regular like clockwork, and Sir George had diligently followed instructions. To the letter. Not so much in deference to the implicit threats issued him by Alex, over computer and untraceable of course, but by the prospect of continued income. He came to enjoy the work. Since he was in America and his calls were to Americans, he had the opportunity to dazzle them with his proper and refined accent before he let the hammer down with whatever tidbit of private information he was told to share with them.

In the beginning Sir George had little idea of what the motivation behind his job was, and still, he wasn't completely sure. He realized each call he made contained the undercurrent of a threat. But he never threatened anyone, his instructions were explicit; never threaten. So therefore, he reasoned, he must actually be making threats, no matter how veiled.

He rather enjoyed it all. Not hurting people, that wasn't his nature, but he savored impressing people with his knowledge and noting their reactions for his daily reports back to Alex. In the evenings Sir George searched out small American recreational centers inaccurately referred to as pubs. In fact they were disguised bars with darts and warm beer, but it gave Sir George the chance to mingle and flash his assumed pedigree. When asked what he did for a living, he truthfully said, "I talk to people." About what? "Whatever interests them."

He became somewhat of a celebrated fixture at several 'pubs' in Marin County where he found the atmosphere more to his liking, a perfectly civilized provincial suburb of San Francisco where his purchased affectations wore well on the locals who endlessly commuted to their high tech jobs in Silicon Valley 40 miles to the south.

Hawaii had been, as he said, "Quite the experience." Alex had informed him one day that he was to take a holiday and return ready for a new assignment, one to which now he was ideally suited. Sir George smiled to himself. A job well done, and additional rewards. That was a first for George Toft of dreary Manchester, England.

Since he did not have a printer, there was no way he would jeopardize his livelihood for a comfort so small, he read his E-Mail by copying the messages into Word Perfect, and then reading them at his leisure. All E-Mail was encrypted with the Public Private RSA algorithm, so he had to manually decrypt the messages with his private key and save them unencrypted. When he was done, he erased the file completely, to keep anyone else from discovering the nature of his work. Alex's first message was dated two days before he returned from Hawaii. It was actually cordial, as far as Alex could be considered cordial. After their first meeting in Athens, Alex had taken on a succinct if not terse tone in all communications.

Sir George:

Welcome back. I hope you had a most enjoyable holiday. It was well deserved.

We now enter phase two of our operations. We place much faith in your ability and loyalty. Please do not disrupt that confidence.

As in the past, you will be given daily lists of people to call. They are some of the people whom you have called before. As before, identify yourself and the nature of your call. I am sure your last call was so disturbing to them, they will take your call this time as well.

Then, once you have confirmed their identity, give them the new information provided, and ask them to follow the instructions given, to the letter. Please be your usual polite self.

Alex

The second message was more Alex-like:

Sir George:

If you have any problems with your new assignment, please call me to arrange your termination.

Alex.

* * * * *

"Hello? Are you there?" Sir George Sterling spoke with as much elegance he could muster. "This is John Fullmaster calling again for Robert Henson." Sir George remembered the name but not the specifics.

"One moment please," Maggie said. "Mr. Henson?" She said after dialing his intercom extension. "It's John Fullmaster for you. Line three"

"Who?"

"Mr. Fullmaster. He called once several months ago. Don't you remember?" He thought. Fullmaster. Fullmaster. Oh, shit. I thought he was a bad dream. Goddamn blackmailer. Never did figure how he knew about the Winston Ellis scam. Good thing that's been put to bed and over.

"All right, I'll take it." He punched up the third line. "Yeah?" He said defiantly.

"Mr. Henson? This is John Fullmaster. I believe we spoke a while back about some of your dealings? Do you recall?"

"Yes, I recall you bastard, but you're too late. The deal closed last month. So you can forget your threats. Fuck off and die." Henson used his best boardroom belligerence.

"Oh, I am sorry that you thought I was threatening you, I can assure you I wasn't." Sir George oozed politeness.

"Bullshit. I don't know how the blazes you learned anything about my business, and I don't really care . . ."

"I think you might care, sir, if you will allow me to speak for a moment." Sir George interjected. The sudden interruption caught Henson off guard. He stood his ground in silence.

"Thank you." Sir George waited for an acknowledgement which never arrived, so he continued. "Winston Ellis is old news, Mr. Henson, very old news. I read today, though, that Miller Pharmaceuticals is about to have its Anti-AIDS drug turned down by the FDA. Apparently it still has too many side effects and may be too dangerous for humans. I'm sure you've read the reports yourself. Don't you think it would be wise to tell your investors before they sink another $300 Million into a black hole from which there is no escape?" The aristocratic British accent softened the harshness of the words, but not the auger of the meaning.

Henson seethed. "I don't know who you are," he hissed, "but I will not listen to this kind of crap. I won't take it from . . ."

"Sorry," Sir George again interrupted, "but I'm afraid you will listen. The instructions are as follows. I want $5 Million in small bills in a silver Samsonite case to be placed into locker number 235 at Grand Central Station, first level. You have 48 hours to comply. If you do not have the money there, we will release these findings to the media and the SEC which will no doubt prompt an investigation into this and other of your dealings. Don't you think?"

Blackmail was an anathema to Robert Henson, although he should have felt quite comfortable in its milieu. It was effectively the same stunt he performed on many of his investors. Nobody treats Robert Henson this way, nobody. He needed time to think. The last time Fullmaster called it was a bluff, obviously, but then there were no demands. This time, he wanted something. But, how did he know? The FDA reports were still confidential, and he hoped to have completed raising the funds before the reports became public, another few weeks at most. He counted on inefficient government bureaucracy and indifference to delay any announcement. Meanwhile though, he would pocket several millions in banking fees.

"You got me. I'll do it. 235. Right?"

"Very good, Mr. Henson. I'm glad you see it my way. It has been a pleasure doing business with you." Sir George sounded like a used car salesman. "Oh, yes, I almost forgot. Please, Mr. Henson, no police. In that case, our deal is off."

"Of course, no police. No problem. Thanks for the call." Henson hung up. Fuck him. No money, no way.

* * * * *

"Mr. Faulkner, this is John Fullmaster." Sir George was sickeningly sweet. "Do you recall our last conversation?"

How couldn't he? This was the only call he had received on his private line since that maniac had last called. Faulkner had had the number changed at least a half a dozen times since, as a matter of course, but still, Fullmaster, if that was his real name, reached him with apparent ease.

"Yes, I remember," he said tersely. "What do you want now?"

"Just a piece of the action, Mr. Faulkner."

"What the hell does that mean?"

"Well, according to my records, you have lost quite a sum of money since our last conversation, and it would be such a shame, don't you agree, if California National Bank found out they lost another $2 million to your bad habits?" Sir George instinctively thought Faulkner was a California slime ball, never mind his own actions, and he briefly thought that he might actually be working for the side of good after all.

"You have a real doctor's bedside manner. What do you want?" Faulkner conveyed extreme nervousness.

"I think, under the circumstances that, shall we say, oh, one million would do it. Yes, that sounds fair."

"One million? One million dollars?" Faulkner shrieked from his pool side lounge chair.

"Yessir, that sounds just about right." Sir George paused for effect. "Now here is what I want you to do. Go to Las Vegas, and have your credit extended, and acquire small bills. Then, place the money in a silver Samsonite case at Union Station. Locker number 12. Is that simple enough?" British humor at its best.

"Simple, yes. Possible, no," Faulkner whispered in terror.

"Oh, yes, it is possible, as you well know. You cleared up the $2.4 Million you owed Caesar's only last week. Your credit is excellent."

"There's no way you can know that . . ." Then it occurred to him. The mob. He wasn't losing enough at the tables, they wanted more. Losing money was one thing, his way, but a sore winner is the worst possible enemy. He had no choice. There was only one way out.

"All right, all right. What locker number?"

"Twelve. Within 48 hours. And, I probably needn't mention it, but no police."

"Of course," Faulkner smiled to himself. At last the nightmare would be over.

"Thank you so very much. Have a nice day."

* * * * *

"Merrill! It's the blackmailer again. Merrill, do you hear me?" Ken Boyers tried to get Senator Rickfield out from the centerfold of the newest Playboy. "Merrill!"

"Oh sorry, Ken. Just reading the articles. Now what is it?" Rickfield put the magazine down, slowly, for one last lustful gaze.

"Merrill, that Fullmaster fellow, the one who called about the Credite Suisse arrangements . . ."

"Shut up! We don't talk about that in this office, you know that!" Rickfield admonished Ken.

"I know, but he doesn't," he said, pointing at the blinking light on the Senator's desk phone.

"I thought he went away. Nothing ever came of it, did it?"

"No, nothing, after we got General Young onto it," Boyers explained. "I thought he took care of it, in his own way. The problem just disappeared like it was supposed to."

"Well," Rickfield said scornfully, "obviously it didn't. Give me the goddamned phone." He picked it up and pressed the lighted button. His senatorial dignity was absent as he spoke.

"This is Rickfield. Who is this?"

"Ah, thank you for taking my call. Yes, thank you." Sir George spoke slowly, more slowly than necessary. This call was marked critical. That meant, don't screw it up. "My name is John Fullmaster and I believe we spoke about some arrangements you made with General Young and Credite Suisse."

"I remember. So what? That has nothing to do with me," Rickfield retorted. He grabbed a pen and wrote down the name, John Fullmaster. Ken looked at the scribbled writing and shrugged his shoulders.

"Ah, but I'm afraid it does. I see here that Allied Dynamics recently made a significant contribution to a certain account in

274

Credite Suisse. There are only two signators on the passbook. It also says here that they will be building two new factories in your state. Quite an accomplishment. I am sure your constituents would be proud."

The color drained from Rickfield's face. He put his hand over the mouthpiece to speak privately to Ken. "Who else knows? Don't bullshit me, boy. Who else have you told?"

"No one!" Boyers said in genuine shock. "I want to enjoy the money, not pay attorney's fees."

Rickfield waved Boyers away. He appeared satisfied with the response. "This is speculation. You can't prove a thing." Rickfield took a shot to gauge his opponent.

"Believe that if you wish, Senator, but I don't think it is in either of our best interests to play the other for the fool." Sir George saw that Rickfield did not attain his position as Chairman of the Senate Committee on Space, Transportation and Technology by caving in to idle demands or threats. In fact, in 34 years of Senate service, Senator Merrill Rickfield had survived 8 presidents, counseling most of them to varying degrees depending upon the partisan attitude of the White House.

At 65, much of the private sector would have forced him into retirement, but elected Government service permitted him the tenure to continue as long as his constituents allowed. Claude Pepper held the record and Merrill Rickfield's ego wanted to establish new definitions of tenure.

His involvement with General Chester Oliver Young was recent, in political terms; less than a decade. During the Reagan military buildup, nearly 3 trillion dollars worth, defense contractors expanded with the economy, to unprecedented levels and profits. Congress was convinced that $300 Billion per year was about right to defend against a Cold War enemy that couldn't feed its own people. The overestimates of the CIA, with selective and often speculative information provided by the country's intelligence gatherer, the NSA, helped define a decade of political and technological achievements: Star Wars, Stealth, MX, B1, B2 and other assorted toys that had no practical use save all out war.

With that kind of spending occurring freely, and the Senate Oversight Committee in a perpetual state of the doldrums, there was money to be made for anyone part of Washington's good ol' boy network. General Young was one such an opportunistic militarist. Promoted to one star general in 1978, after two lackluster but politically well connected tours in Vietnam, it was deemed prudent by the power brokers of that war to bring Young into the inner rings of the

Pentagon with the corresponding perks such a position brought. But Young had bigger and better ideas.

He saw countless ways to spend taxpayers money protecting them from the Communist threat of the Evil Empire, but had difficulty getting support from his two and three star superiors. It didn't take him long to realize that he had been token promoted to keep his mouth shut about certain prominent people's roles in the Vietnam era. Events that were better left to a few trusted memories than to the history books.

So Young decided to go out on his own and find support from the legislative branch; find an influential proponent for a few specific defense programs by which he could profit. Over the course of a few years, he and Senator Rickfield became fast friends, holding many of the same global views and fears, if not paranoias. When Allied Dynamics began losing Congressional support for an advanced jet helicopter project, Young went to Rickfield for help. After all, Allied was headquartered in Rickfield's home state, and wouldn't it be a great boon to the economy? The recession was coming to an end and that meant jobs.

Rickfield was unaware, initially, that Allied had an arrangement with General Young to donate certain moneys to certain charities, in certain Swiss bank accounts if certain spending programs were approved. Only when Rickfield offered some later resistance to the Allied projects did Young feel the need to share the wealth. After 25 years in Congress, and very little money put away to show for it, Rickfield was an easy target.

Rickfield's recruitment by Young, on Allied's behalf, had yielded the Senator more than enough to retire comfortably on the island paradise of his choice. Yet, Rickfield found an uncontrolled desire for more; considerations was his word for it, just as he had grown used to wielding power and influence in the nation's capital. Rickfield was hooked, and Credite Suisse was the certain Swiss bank in question. Ken Boyers was involved as well, almost from the start. They both had a lot to lose.

"No, I must assume that you are not a fool, and I know for a fact I am not one, so on that one point we do agree." Political pausing often allowed your opponent to hang himself with additional oration. Rickfield found the technique useful, especially on novices. "Please continue."

"Thank you." Sir George said with a hint of patronization. "To be brief, Senator, I want you to keep your money, I think that dedicated civil servants like yourself are grossly underpaid and underappreciated. No sir, I do not wish to deny you the chance to make your golden years pleasant after such a distinguished career."

"Then what is it. What do you want from me?" The Senator was doodling nervously while Ken paced the room trying to figure out what was being said at the other end of the phone.

"I'm glad you asked," said Sir George. "Beginning next month you are chairing a sub-committee that will be investigating the weaknesses and potential threats to government computer systems. As I remember it is called the Senate Select Sub-Committee on Privacy and Technology Containment. Is that right?"

"Yes, the dates aren't firm yet, and I haven't decided if I will chair the hearings or assign it to another committee member. So what?"

"Well, we want you to drag down the hearings. Nothing more." Sire George stated his intention as a matter of fact rather than a request.

Rickfield's face contorted in confusion. "Drag down? Exactly what does that mean, to you, that is?"

"We want you to downplay the importance of security for government computers. That there really is no threat to them, and that government has already met all of its obligations in balance with the new world order, if you will. The threats are mere scare tactics by various special interest groups and government agencies who are striving for long term self preservation." Sir George had practiced his soliloquy before calling Senator Rickfield.

"What the hell for?" Rickfield raised his voice. "Security? Big deal! What's it to you?"

"I am not at liberty to discuss our reasons. Suffice it to say, that we would be most pleased if you see to it that the hearings have minimal substance and that no direct action items are delivered. I believe that term you Americans so eloquently use is stonewall, or perhaps filibuster?"

"They're not the same things."

"Fine, but you do understand nonetheless. We want these hearings to epitomize the rest of American politics with procrastination, obfuscation and procedural gerrymandering." Sir George had learned quite a bit about the political system since he had moved to the States.

"And to what aim?" Rickfield's political sense was waving red flags.

"That's it. Nothing more."

"And in return?" The Senator had learned to be direct in matters of additional compensation since he had hooked up with the earthy General.

"I will assure you that the details of your arrangements with Allied Dynamics will remain safe with me."

"Until the next time, right? This is blackmail?"

"No. Yes." Sir George answered. "Yes, it is blackmail, but without the usual messiness. And no, there will be no next time. For, as soon as the hearings are over, it would be most advisable for you to take leave of your position and enjoy the money you have earned outside of your paycheck."

"And, if I don't agree to this?" Rickfield was looking at his options which seemed to be somewhere between few and none. Maybe he only had one.

"That would be so unfortunate." Sir George smiled as he spoke. "The media will receive a two page letter, it is already prepared I can assure you, detailing your illegal involvements with Allied, General Young and Mr. Boyers."

"What's in it for you? You don't want any money?" The confusion in Rickfield's mind was terribly obvious, and he was sliding on a logical Mobius loop.

"No Senator, no money. Merely a favor."

"I will let you know what I decide. May I have your number?"

"I do not need to contact you again. Your answer will be evident when the hearings begin. Whatever course you pursue, we will make an appropriate response."

* * * * *

"Scott!" A woman called across the noisy floor. "Is your phone off the hook?"

"Yeah, why?" He looked up and couldn't match the voice with a person.

"You gotta call."

"Who is it? I'm busy."

"Some guy from Brooklyn sounds like. Says he got a package for you?"

Holy shit. It's Vito! That was the name Scott had given to his anonymous caller. The one who had caused him so much work, so much research without being able to print one damn thing.

Not yet.

"Yeah, OK. It's back on." The phone rang instantly and Scott rushed to pick it up on the first ring.

"Yeah, Scott Mason here." He sounded hurried.

"Yo! Scott. It's me, your friend, rememba?" No one could forget the accent that sounded more fake than real. He had been nicknamed Vito for reference purposes by Scott.

"Sure do, fella," Scott said cheerily. "That bunch of shit you sent me was worthless. Garbage."

"Yeah, well, we may have fucked up a little on that. Didn't count on youse guys having much in the ethics department if youse know what I mean." Vito laughed at what he thought was a pretty good joke. "So, we all screw up, right? Now and again? Never mind that, I got something real good, something youse really gonna like."

"Sure you do."

"No, really, dig this. I gotta list of names that ..... "

"Great another list. Just what I need. Another list."

"Whad'ar'ya, a wise guy? Youse wanna talk or listen?" Scott didn't answer. "That's better, cause youse gonna like this. Some guy named Faulkner, big shit banker from La La Land is borrowing money from the mob to pay off a blackmailer. Another guy, right here in New York Shitty, a Wall Street big shot called Henson, him too. Another one named Dobbs, same thing. All being blackballed by the same guys. Youse want more?"

"I'm writing, quiet. Faulkner, Henson and Dobbs, right?"

"That's whad'I said, yeah."

"So how come you know so much?"

"That's my job. I deal in information. Pretty good, huh?"

"Maybe. I gotta check it out. That last stuff was . . ."

"Hey!" Vito interrupted, "I told youse 'bout that. Eh, paysan, what's a slip up among friends, right?"

"I'll ignore that. Gimme a couple of days, I'll call you."

"Like hell you will. I'll call you. You'll see, this is good stuff. No shit. All right? Two days."

Click.

* * * * *

Monday, December 14
Washington, D.C.

The FBI runs a little known counter intelligence operation from the middle of a run down Washington D.C. neighborhood on Half Street. Getting in and out is an exercise in evasive not to mention defensive driving. The South East quadrant of Wshington, D.C. is vying for the drug capital of the nation, and perhaps has the dubious distinction of having the highest murder rate per capita in the United States. Since the CI division of the FBI is a well kept secret, its location was strategically chosen to keep the casual passerby from stopping in for a chat. Besides, there was no identification on the front of the building.

Most Americans think that the CIA takes care of foreign spies, but their agents are limited to functioning on foreign land. On the domestic front the FBI Counter Intelligence Group is assigned to locate and monitor alien intelligence activities. For example, CI-3 is assigned to focus on Soviet and East Bloc activities, and other groups focus on their specific target countries. Thus, there is a certain amount of competition, not all of it healthy, between the two agencies chartered to protect our national interests. The CIA is under the impression that it controls all foreign investigations, even if they tread upon United States territory. This line of thinking has been a constant source of irritation and inefficiency since the OSS became the CIA during the Truman administration. Only during the Hoover reign at the FBI days was there any sense of peaceful coexistence. Hoover did what he damn well pleased, and if anyone stood in his way, he simply called up the White House and had the roadblock removed. Kennedy era notwithstanding, Hoover held his own for a 50 year reign.

Tyrone Duncan received an additional lesson on inter-agency rivalry when he was called down to Half Street. His orders were similar to those he had received from the safe house in Georgetown months before. *Stick to your hackers and viruses, period,* he was told. *If it smells of foreign influence, let the CI fight it out with Langley. Keep your butt clean.*

In 25 years of service, Tyrone had never been so severely admonished for investigating a case that he perceived as being domestic in nature. The thought of foreign influences at work had not occurred to him, until CI brought it up.

As far as he was concerned the quick trip from New York to Half Street was a bureaucratic waste of time and money. However, during the fifteen minute discussion he was told by his CI compatriots that both the blackmail and the ECCO investigations situations had international repercussions and he should keep his nose out of it. CI was doing just fine without Tyrone's help. The meeting, or warning as Tyrone Duncan took it, served to raise an internal flag.

There was a bigger picture, something beyond a classical blackmail operation and some hackers screwing with government computers, and he was being excluded. That only meant one thing. He was pushing someone's button and he didn't know how, where or why. The Trump Shuttle flight back to La Guardia gave Tyrone time to think about it, and that only incensed him further. Aren't we all on the same team? If I stumbled onto something, and you want me to back off, O.K., but at least let me know what I'm missing.

Twenty five years and a return to Hoover paranoia. He understood, and advocated, the need for secrecy, privacy and the trappings of confidentiality. But, compartmentalization of information this extreme was beyond the normal course to which he was accustomed. The whole thing stunk.

He arrived back at New York's Federal Square during lunch hour. Normally there was a minimal staff at that hour, or hour and half or two hours depending upon your rank. When the elevator doors opened on Level 5, 70 feet under lower Manhattan, he walked into a bustle of activity normally present only when visiting heads of state need extraordinary security. He was immediately accosted by eager subordinates. The onslaught of questions overwhelmed him, so he ignored them and walked through the maze directly to his office.

His head ringing, he plopped himself down behind his desk. He stared at the two agents who followed him all the way, plus his secretary stood in the open door, watching with amusement. Duncan was not appreciative of panic situations. His silence was contagious.

"Who's first?" He asked quietly.

The two agents looked at each other and one spoke. "Uh, sir, I think we have a lead in the blackmail operation." Duncan looked at the other, offering him a chance to speak.

"Yessir, it seems to have broken all over at once." Duncan opened his eyes wide in anticipation. Well, he, thought, go on.

The first agent picked up the ball. "Demands. The blackmailers are making demands. So far we have six individuals who said they were recontacted by the same person who had first called them a year ago."

Duncan sat upright. "I want a complete report, here, in 1 hour. We'll talk then. Thank you gentlemen." They took their cue to exit and brushed by Gloria White, Tyrone's secretary on their way out the door.

"Yes, Gloria?" Duncan treated her kindly, not with the administrative brusqueness he often found necessary to motivate some of his agents.

"Good morning, or afternoon, sir. Pleasant trip?" She knew he hated sudden trips to D.C. It was her way of teasing her boss.

"Wonderful!" Tyrone beamed with artificial enthusiasm. "Book me on the same flights every day for a month. Definite E-ticket ride."

"Do you remember a Franklin Dobbs? He was here some time ago, about, I believe the same matter you were just discussing?" Her demureness pampered Duncan.

"Dobbs? Yes, why?"

"He's been waiting all morning. Had to see you, no on else. Shall I show him in?"

"Yes, by all means, thank you."

"Mr. Dobbs, how good to see you again. Please," Duncan pointed at a chair in front of his desk. "Sit down. How may I help you?"

Dobbs shuffled over to the chair and practically fell into it. He sighed heavily and looked down at his feet. "I guess it's all over. All over."

"What do you mean? My secretary, said you were being blackmailed again. I think you should know I'm not working on that case anymore."

"This time it's different," Dobbs said, his eyes darting about. "They want money, a lot of money, more than we have. Last time I received a call, and I was told some very private and specific knowledge about our company, that we preferred to remain private. That information contained all our pricing, quotation methods, profit figures, overhead . . .everything our competitors could use."

"So you think your competition is blackmailing you," Duncan offered.

"I don't know. If they wanted the information, why call me and tell me? We haven't been able to figure it out."

"What about the others," Duncan thought out loud. "The others with access to the information?"

"Everyone is suspecting everyone else. It's not healthy. Now, after this, I'm thinking of packing it in."

"Why now? What's different?"

"The demands. I can't believe it's my competitors. Sure, it's a cut throat business, but, no, it's hard to believe."

"Stranger things have happened, Mr. Dobbs," Duncan tried to be soothing. "The demands, what were they?"

"They want three million dollars, cash. If we don't pay they said they'd give away our company secrets to our competitors. We don't have the cash."

Duncan felt for the man. Dobbs had been right. There was nothing the FBI could have done to help. No demands, no recontacts, and no leads, just a lot of suspicion. But, now, the Bureau was in a position to help.

"Mr. Dobbs, rest assured, we will pursue this case aggressively. We will assign you two of our top agents, and, in cases like this, we are quite successful." Duncan's upbeat tone was meant to lift Dobbs' spirits. "Was there anything else demanded?"

"No, nothing, they just told me not to go to the police."

"You haven't told anyone, have you?" Duncan asked.

"No, not even my wife."

"Mr. Dobbs, let me ask you a couple more things, then I will introduce you to some fine men who will help you. Do you know anyone else who is in your position? Other people who are being blackmailed in similar ways?"

Dobbs shuffled his feet under the chair, and picked at the edge of the chair. Duncan hit a raw nerve.

"Mr. Dobbs, I don't want names, no specifics. It's a general question. Do you know others?"

"Yes," Dobbs said almost silently.

"Do you know how many?" Duncan needed details if his current line of thinking would pan out into a viable theory.

"No, not exactly."

"Is it 5? 10? More than 10? 25? More than 25?" Dobbs nodded suddenly.

"Do you mean that you know of 25 other companies that are going through what you're going through? Twenty five?" Tyrone was incredulous at the prospects. The manpower alone to investigate that many cases would totally overwhelm his staff. There was no way. The ramifications staggered him. Twenty five, all at once.

"Yeah. At least."

"I know you can't tell me who they are . . ." Duncan hoped that Dobbs might offer a few.

"No. But, look at their stocks. They're not doing well. Our competitors seem to be getting the best of the deal."

Twenty five cases in New York alone, and he knows of at least 6 others, so far. The rekindled blackmail operation, after months of dead ends. Duncan wondered how big the monster behind the head could get. And how could the FBI handle it all. Poor bastard. Poor us.

* * * * *

Tuesday, December 15
New York

It was before 8:00 AM, and Scott cursed himself for arriving at his office at this ungodly hour. He had found the last piece of the puzzle, didn't sleep very much, and was in high gear before 6:00. Scott couldn't remember the last time he had been awake this early, unless it was coming round the long way. He scurried past security, shaking his ID card as he flew through the closing doors on the express elevator. The office hadn't yet come to life so Doug McGuire was available without a wait or interruption.

"I need some expense money," Scott blurted out at Doug.

"Yeah, so?" Doug sounded exasperated with Scott's constant requests for money. He didn't even look up from his impossibly disorganized desk.

"I'm serious . . ." Scott came back.

"So, am I." Doug firmly laid down his pen on his desk and looked at Scott. "What the hell kind of expenses do you need now?" Scott spent more money than several reporters combined, and he never felt bad about it. While a great deal of his work was performed at the office or at home, his phone bills were extraordinary as were his expenses.

Scott had developed a reputation as willing to go to almost any lengths to get a story. Like the time he hired and the paper paid for a call girl to entertain Congressman Daley from Wisconsin. She was supposed to confirm, in any way necessary, that LeMal Chemical was buying votes to help bypass certain approval cycles for their new line of drugs. She accidentally confirmed that he was a homosexual, but not before he slipped and the lady of the evening became the much needed confirmation.

As Scott put it, Daley's embarrassed resignation was unavoidable collateral damage in stopping the approval of a drug as potentially dangerous as thalidomide.

Or then there was the time that Scott received an anonymous tip that the Oil Companies had suppressed critical temperature-emission ratio calculations, and therefore the extent of the greenhouse effect was being sorely underestimated. As a result of his research and detective work, and the ability to verify and understand the physics involved, Scott's articles forced a re-examination of the dangers. He received a New York Writer's Award for that series.

When Doug had hired Scott, as a thirty-something cub reporter, they both thought that Scott would fit in, nice and neat, and write cute, introspective technical pieces. Neither expected Scott to quickly evolve into a innovative journalist on the offensive who had the embryo of a cult following.

But Scott Mason also performed a lot of the more mundane work that most writer's suffer with until the better stories can justify their full time efforts. New products, whiz bang electronic toys for the kitchen, whiz bangs for the bathroom. New computer this, new software that.

Now, though, he was on the track, due in part he admitted, to Doug coercing him into writing the computer virus bits. Yes, he was wrong and Doug was right. The pieces were falling in place. So, no matter what happened, it was Doug's fault.

"I'm going to Europe,"

"No you're not!" Thundered Doug.

"Yes I am, I gotta go . . ." Scott tried to plead his case.

"You aren't going anywhere, and that's final." Doug retorted without a pause. He stared challengingly through Scott.

"Doug," Scott visibly calmed himself, "will you at least hear me out, before telling me no? At least listen to me, and if I'm wrong, tell me why. O.K.?" Same routine, different day, thought Scott. The calmer, sincere request elicited empathy from Doug. Maybe he'd been too harsh.

"Sorry, it's automatic to say, 'no'. You know that they," he pointed down with his thumb, "have us counting paper clips. Sure, explain to me why I'm going to say 'no'," he joked. Doug's overtly stern yet fatherlike geniality returned.

"O.K.," Scott mentally organized his thoughts. He touched his fingers to his forehead and turned to sit on the edge of Doug's desk. A traditional no-no. "Without my notes . . ."

"Screw the notes, what have you got? If you don't know the material, the notes won't help. They're the details, not the story." Scott had heard this before.

"Sure, sorry." He gained confidence and went straight from the hip. "Fact One. The FBI is investigating a massive blackmail campaign that nobody wants us to talk about, and probably for good reason from what I can see. As of now, there is no clue at all to whom is behind the operation.

"Fact Two. My story got pulled by CIA, NSA or someone that pushed the AG's buttons. And this Tempest thing gets heads turning too fast for my taste." Doug nodded briefly. Scott made sense so far, both things were true.

"Three," Scott continued, "First State has been the target of hackers, plus, we have Sidneys . . ."

"Sort of. McMillan hasn't caved in on that yet."

"Agreed, but it's still good. You and I both know it." Doug grudgingly nodded in agreement.

"Then we have all those papers that came from a van, or more than one van I would guess, and not a damned thing we can do with them according to Higgins." Again, Doug nodded, but he wondered where all of this was going. "Then the EMP-T bombs, NASA, the Phone Company, and all of these viruses. What we have is a number of apparently dissimilar events that have one common denominator: computers."

Scott waited for a reaction from Doug that didn't come so he continued. "Don't you see, the van with the computer data, the endless files, the Sidneys problems, pulling my stories, the hackers? Even the viruses. They're starting to get a little out of hand. It's all the same thing!"

Doug rolled his head from side to side on his shoulder. Rather than boredom, Scott knew that Doug was carefully thinking through the logic of it. "Aren't you acting the engineer instead of the reporter here? Miss the old line of work 'eh?"

"Give me a break! You and your viruses are the ones who got me into this mess in the first place." Scott knew it would come up, so he had been ready and grabbed the opportunity Doug had just given him. "That's exactly the point!" Scott leaped off the desk to his feet. "All we have are technical threads, pieces of a puzzle. It's a classic engineering problem." Although Scott had never been a brilliant engineer, he could argue the issues fluently.

"Let me give you an example. When I was in defense electronics, whenever someone built something we had to document, without failure, it didn't work. Radar, navigation, communications, it didn't matter. The engineers forever were releasing products that failed on the first pass." Doug stopped rolling his head and looked at Scott with a blank stare.

"We had these terrifically advanced products meant to defend our country and they didn't work. So, we had to tell the engineers what was wrong so they could figure it out. Our own engineers and I got involved more times than we liked because the response time from the contractors was for shit. They didn't care any more. Since we hadn't designed it, we only saw the pieces that were on the fritz, we had symptoms and had to figure out what they meant in order to diagnose the failure so we could get the designers to come up with a fix. The point is, we only had shreds of evidence, little bits of technical information from which to try to understand the complete system. That's exactly what's going on here."

"So?" Doug said dead panned.

"So," Scott avoided getting incensed. "You're damn lucky you have me around. I see a pattern, a trail, that leads I don't know where, but I have to follow the trail. That's my job."

"What has Europe got to do with it?" Doug was softening.

"Oops, thanks! I almost forgot." Scott felt stupid for a second, but he was without notes, he rationalized. "Kirk is my hacker contact who I've been talking to over my computer. Gives me real good stuff. He says there's a conference of hackers in Amsterdam next week. It's a real private affair, and he got me an invite. I think, no I know, there's something bigger going down; somehow all of these pieces tie together and I need to find out how."

"That's it?" Scott looked disappointed at Doug's reaction.

"No, that's not it! You know that the Exposé has been publishing bits and pieces of the same stuff we haven't been publishing?"

Scott didn't know which of his arguments made the case, but Doug certainly reacted to the competitive threat. "How much?"

"How much what?" Scott wasn't ready for the question.

"For Europe? How much play money will you need. You know I have to sell this upstairs and they . . ."

"Airfare and a couple of nights plus food. That's it. If you want," Scott readied the trump card he had never used at the Times. "I'll pay for it myself, and submit it all when I come back. Then, you make the call. I'll trust you."

"You really think it's that important?" Doug said.

"Absolutely. No question. Something's going on that smells rotten, bad, and it includes the Government, but I have no idea how." Scott spoke as if he was on a soapbox. He had shot his wad. That was it. Anything more was a rehash of the same stuff and it would have been worthless to say more. He shut up and waited for Doug, who enjoyed making his better reporters anxious with anticipation.

"Have a good trip." Doug said nonchalantly. He leaned forward to hunch over his desk, and ignoring Scott, he went back to red-lining another writer's story.

* * * * *

Tuesday, December 15
Scarsdale, New York

Kirk delivered on his word. In his E-Mail repository at the Times, Scott found a message from Kirk. It was short, but all Scott needed to hear. Never mind how Kirk broke into the computers.

Tues. 12/15 00:02:14.1

< FREEDOM BBS >

Repo Man,

When you arrive, call 602-356. It's an Amsterdam number. Jon Gruptmann is your contact. I told him you were a reporter, but a good one. I said you're working to preserve freedom of electronic information and you were sick and tired of the police and media beating up on hackers. He thinks you want to give the other side of the story to the public.

Jon is one of the best in Holland and anywhere. He agreed to meet and talk with you himself. He will show you around. Have a good trip. Call me, oops, no can do.

Oh, Yes. Mona Lisa frowned. I will call you.

Kirk

< TRANSMITTED BY THE FREEDOM BBS SERVICE >

When Scott got home from work he checked his E-mail and found the same message from Kirk, telling him to be on the line tonight. The Mona Lisa frowned.   That meant to Scott that someone was interested enough in Kirk's activities, or alleged activities at First State to break in and ruin his computers. And Da Vinci's. Who was so scared of hackers, or of what they knew to go to these lengths? How many have had their computers ravaged?

As anticipated, midnight brought Kirk calling.

WE'RE GOING AFTER THEM

After who?

FREEDOM. NEMO AND SOME PHREAKS PHRIENDS ARE GOING TO FIND OUT WHAT'S GOING ON.

What's wrong?

DID YOU EVER TALK TO ANYONE AND FEEL THAT THINGS WEREN'T QUITE RIGHT?

Sure.

WELL SO DO I. DA VINCI IS A STRAIGHT WHITE HAT HACKER. I HAD HIM CHECKED OUT BY PHRIENDS. THEN I CALLED FREEDOM AND JOINED UP. I GAVE THEM A BUNCH OF SOFTWARE AND I TOOK SOME. I ASKED TO CHAT WITH THE SYSOP AND WE'VE BEEN TALKING DAILY. STRANGE GUY.

Strange? Over a computer?

YOU CAN TELL. HE SPOKE WITH AN ACCENT.

You're putting me on.

REALLY. EVER READ A VCR MANUAL TRANSLATED FROM THE JAPANESE? THEY LEAVE OUT THE the's FROM EVERYTHING. IT HAS AN ACCENT. AND THE WORD DUDE ESPECIALLY UPSET HIM.

Dude? Good reason to be suspicious.

THEN I HACKED HIS SYSTEM WHEN I KNEW HE WASN'T ON LINE. JUST TO LOOK AROUND MIND YOU.

How can you do that?

BBS'S ONLY COME IN SO MANY FLAVORS. THEY'RE PRETTY EASY TO CRACK, ESPECIALLY IF YOU HAVE A COPY TO WORK ON.

Ah hah!

I FOUND HUGE AREAS OF HIS COMPUTER NOT ASSIGNED TO THE BBS.

So?

A BBS COMPUTER IS DEDICATED TO ONE FUNCTION, BBS'ING. SO I POKED AROUND AND FOUND ANOTHER COMPLETE BBS SYSTEM, NOT PART OF FREEDOM. TOO MUCH WAS ENCRYPTED, THOUGH, TO LEARN MUCH. BUT WE WILL.

Don't get yourself into hot water again . . .

NOT TO WORRY. I'LL BECOME ONE OF THEM. PLAY THEIR GAMES. IT'S EASY TO BE ANYONE YOU WANT. I WANT TO SEE WHAT'S GOING ON BEHIND THE SCENES. SHOULDN'T TAKE LONG.

* * * * *

Friday, December 18
New York

U.S. Army on Virus Vigil!

by Scott Mason

In July of 1990, the United States Army joined the inner sanctum of the Computer Hacker.

The Pentagon had finally realized that the computer is as essential to battlefield operations and communications as is the gun and the radio.

Therefore, as the logic goes, why shouldn't the computers be directly attacked as are other military targets. In keeping with that line of thinking, the Army said, use computer viruses. Viruses are those little gremlins which roam throughout a computer system, hiding themselves in silicon gulches, waiting to ambush mountains of megabytes and erase deserts of data. Perfect for modern warfare.

The Army issued an RFP, (Request For Proposal) asking the private sector to study and design computer viruses and other methods to be used offensively against enemy computers. The half million dollar contract was awarded to a Beltway Bandit, a small government sub-contractor so named for their proximity to Interstate 495, which loops around Washington, D.C.

So, the Army is going into the hacking business, but this brings up quite a few questions.

Question I. How long has the Government known that computer viruses and other maladies could be used in a strategic militarily offensive fashion? RFP's are always preceded by much internal research and consultation with private industry. The Government typically will have issued RFI's, (Requests For Information) and RFQ's (Request For Quotes) and already have a darn good idea of what's available and from whom.

Question II. Has the Government already sponsored such research? The existence of the EMP-T Bomb has created quite a furor.

Question III. What if the Army created experimental computer viruses and they get loose? Who is responsible for silicon based biological warfare on desktop computers?

Question IV. Have any computer viral outbreaks actually been Government projects gone out of control?

Question V. If the Government knew that civilian and military computers could be systematically attacked and destroyed, why haven't we done anything to defend ourselves against a similar assault?

Last month's attack on the Stock Exchange by secret EMP-T bombs prompted an investigation into such military capabilities, and some surprising answers were uncovered.

In an attempt to get specific answers from various Government agencies, I located a secretive group called OCTAG/0N. (Offensive Computer Technology Applications Group/Zero-November). OCTAG/0N is a highly classified interagency project whose sole function is to develop methods to destroy or disable computers from great distances.

According to a highly placed source at the Pentagon, OCTAG/0N allegedly developed computer viruses that will destroy the enemy's hard disks. Successful deployment, to use Pentagon-ese, is the hard part. "If we can get at their computers," an engineer with OCTAG/0N said requesting anonymity, "we can stop them instantly. Getting them there has been the problem. But now we know how to get at their computers from great distances."

In the battlefield, for example, advanced tactical communications groups explode small Magnetic Bombs (EMP-T) which emit very strong electromagnetic pulses at certain frequencies. The EM pulses destroy nearby computers, (RAM, ROM, EPROM, Magnetic storage). Some computer systems are 'hardened' with extra shielding as in the Tempest program. Other computers, such as those in Air Force One, inside missile silos, or in the Pentagon War Room are additionally protected by the secret C^3I programs which 'super-hardens' the computers against the intense magnetic pulses associated with above ground nuclear explosions.

Intensely focussed energy beams of low power can totally disrupt an unshielded computer as far away as three miles. Synchronized Interference Techniques provide double duty to both listen in on and jam air borne computer traffic. One of OCTAG/0N's pet tricks is to broadcast a computer virus from a small antenna so that it is caught by a computers communicating on the same frequency. So simple, yet so devious.

In conversations with computer experts and the underground hacker community, the existence of such high tech weaponry has been confirmed, although the Department of Defense is still issuing a predictable 'no comment'.

So, I have to ask again. Why hasn't our Government been helping us protect ourselves against an apparently formidable computer weapons complement? I hope "The Other Guys" aren't so well armed.

This is Scott Mason, adding a chastity belt to my modem.

Chapter 17

Monday, December 28

AKA Software

by Scott Mason

The Christmas Virus is upon is. So is the anticipated New Years Eve and New Year's Day Virus.

Seems like wherever I look, someone is making a virus to attack my computer or celebrate a holiday.

Rather than another rash of warnings about the impending doom and gloom faced by your computers, my editor asked me to find the lighter side of computer viruses. I strongly objected, stating that I found nothing amusing about them. They were a deadly and cowardly form of terrorism that should be rewarded with beheading.

However, there is one thing . . .

The geniuses who come up with the names for viral infections; about as believable and laughable as a Batman comic.

I wonder what most of us would think if our doctor told us we have the Ping Pong virus instead of strep throat. Or in spring time we contracted the April Fool's Virus.

It is entirely within the realm of reason that America's computers go unprotected because of the sheer absurdity of the names we attach to each one. Comical names create a comical situation, so no one takes the issue seriously.

The Marijuana virus conjures up images of a stoned orgy, and why would a computer care about that. The Fu Manchu virus conjures up the Red Chinese Army crossing the Mississippi, which is clearly not the case, so it is ignored.

Viruses know no national boundary. The Pakistani virus, the Icelandic, the Israeli, Jerusalem A, Jerusalem B, Jerusalem C, Lehigh, Alameda, Vienna, Czech, Rumanian - I found over 900 current and active viruses that are identified by their reputed place of origin.

The Brain virus sounds more sinister than the Stoned Virus, and Friday the 13th viruses are as popular as the movie sequels. The Columbus Day Virus was actually dubbed by its authors as Data Crime, and might have generated more concern if not for the nick-nom-de-plume it inherited.

So to fulfill my editor's dream, I will list a few of the more creative virus names. Some were chosen by the programmers, others by the Virus Busters and others yet by the media. See what you think each virus would do to your computer, or when it will strike, merely from the name.

The Vatican Virus	*The Popeye Virus*
The Garlic Virus	*The Scrooge Virus*
Teenage Mutant Ninja Virus	*The Ides Virus*
The Quaalude Virus	*The Amphetamine Virus*
Super Virus	*The Tick Tock Virus*
The String Virus	*The Black Hole Virus*
The Stupid Virus	*Stealth*

I have a few of my own suggestions for future virus builders.
The Jewish Sex Virus (Dials your mother-in-law during a romantic interlude.)
The Ronald Reagan Virus (Puts your computer to sleep only in important meetings.)
The Pee Wee Herman Virus (Garbage In Garbage Out)
The Donald Trump Virus (Makes all of your spread sheets go into the red.)

Tomorrow, Viruses from Hell on Geraldo.
Namely, this is Scott Mason.

* * * * *

Tuesday, December 29
Washington, D.C.

"Why the hell do I have to find out what's going on in world from the goddamned papers and CNN instead of from the finest intelligence services in the world?" The President snapped sarcastically while sipping black coffee over his daily collection of major U.S. and foreign papers. International perspective, he said.

The early morning ritual of coffee, newspapers and a briefing by Chief of Staff Phil Musgrave provided the day with a smooth start. Usually.

"I've been asking for weeks about this computer craziness. All I get is don't worry, Mr. President," he said mimicking the classic excuses he was sick and tired of hearing. "We have it taken care of, Mr. President. No concern of yours, Mr. President, we have everything under control. We temporarily have our thumbs up our asses, Mr. President." Phil stifled a giggle behind his napkin.

"I'm sorry, Phil," the President continued, "but it irritates the shit out of me. The damn media knowing more about what's happening than we do. Where the hell is that report I asked for? The one on the bank hostage I've been requesting for a week?" The President's mood portended a rough day for the inner circle.

"Sir, as I understand it, it wasn't ready for your desk yet."

"Do the goddamned missiles have to land on the White House lawn before we verify it's not one of our own?"

Phil knew better than to attempt any dissuasion when the President got into these moods. He took notes, and with luck it would blow over in a couple of days. Today was not Phil's lucky day.

"I want a briefing. 2 Hours."

"Gentlemen," the President said from behind his desk in the oval office. "I'd like to read you something I had Brian put together." The efficiency of the White House Press Office under the leadership of Brian Packard was well known. The President had the best rapport with the press that any President had in a generation.

He slipped on his aviator style glasses and pulled the lobe of his left ear while reading from his desk. "Let's start here. Phone Company Invaded by Hackers; Stock Exchange Halted by Government Bomb; Computer Crime Costs Nation $12 Billion Annually; Viruses Stop Network; Banks Lose Millions to Computer Embezzlers; Trojan Horse Defeats Government Computers; NASA Spending Millions On Free Calls for Hackers." He looked for a reaction from his four key associates: Phil, Quinton Chambers, Martin Royce and Henry Kennedy. "If you don't know, these are headlines from newspapers and magazines across the country."

The President read further from his notes. "Viruses Infect Trans-Insurance Payments; Secret Service Computers Invaded; NSA and NIST in Security Rift; FBI Wasting Millions on Computer Blackmail Scheme; First National Bank Held Hostage; Sperm Bank Computer Records Erased; IRS Returns of the Super Rich." The President removed his glasses wanting answers.

"What is going on here, gentlemen?" the President asked directly. "I am baffled that everyone else but me seems to know there's a problem, and that pisses me off. Answers?"

He wondered who would be the first to speak up. Surprisingly, it was Henry, who normally waited to speak last. "Sir, we have active programs in place to protect classified computer systems."

"Then what are these about?" He waved a couple of sheets of paper in the air.

"Of course we haven't fully implemented security everywhere yet, but it is an ongoing concern. According to NSA, the rash of recent computer events are a combination of anomalies and the press blowing it all out of proportion."

"Do you believe Henry," the President asked, "that if there's smoke, a reasonable man will assume that there is a fire nearby?" Henry nodded obligingly. "And what would you think if there were a hundred plumes of smoke rising?"

Henry felt stumped. "Jacobs assured me that he had everything under control and . . ."

"As I recall Henry," the President interrupted, "you told me that a couple of months ago when the papers found out about the EMP-T bombs. Do you recall, Henry?"

"Yessir," he answered meekly.

"Then what happened?"

"We have to rely on available information, and as far as we know, as far as we're being told, these are very minor events that have been sensationalized by the media."

"It says here," the President again donned his glasses, "Defense Contractors Live with Hackers; Stealth Program Uncovered in Defense Department Computers; Social Security Computers At Risk. Are those minor events?" He pointed the question at not only Henry.

"There was no significant loss of information," Coletree rapidly said. "We sewed up the holes before we were severely compromised."

"Wonderful," the President said sarcastically. "And what ever happened to that bank in Atlanta? Hiring Those kids?"

"If I may, sir?" Phil Musgrave filled the silence. "That was a private concern, and we had no place to interfere. As is true in most of these cases. We can only react if government property is affected."

"What is being done about it? Now I mean."

"We have activated CERT and ECCO, independent computer crime units to study the problem further." As usual, Phil was impeccably informed. "Last years the Secret Service and FBI arrested over 70 people accused of computer crimes. The state of Pennsylvania over 500, California 300. Remember, sir, computer crimes are generally the states' problems."

"I'm wondering if it shouldn't be our problem, too," the President pondered.

"There are steps in that direction, as well. Next week the Senate hearings on Privacy and Technology Containment begin, and as I understand it, they will be focusing on exactly this issue."

"Who's running the show?" the President asked with interest.

"Ah," Phil said ripping through his notes. "Rickfield, sir."

"That bigot? Christ. I guess it could be worse. We could have ended up with Homer Simpson." The easing of tension worked to the President's advantage, for a brief moment. "I want the whole picture, the good and the bad, laid out for me." He scanned his private appointment book. "Two weeks. Is that long enough to find out why I'm always the last to know?"

* * * * *

Wednesday, December 30
New York

"Scott Mason," Scott said answering the phone with his mouth full of hot pastrami on rye with pickles and mayonnaise.

"Scott? It's Tyrone." Tyrone's voice was quiet, just about a whisper.

"Oh, hi." Scott continued to chew. Scott was unsuccessfully trying not to sound angry.

Other than following Scott's articles in the paper, they had had no contact since that eventful phone call a month ago. Since then, Scott had made sure that they rode on different cars during their daily commute into the city. It was painful for both of them since they had been close friends, but Scott was morally obligated, so he thought, to cut off their association after Tyrone broke the cardinal rule of all journalists; keep your sources protected. And, Tyrone had broken that maxim. Scott had not yet learned that the Bureau made their own rules, and that the gentleman's agreement of off-the-record didn't carry weight in their venue.

"How have you been?" Tyrone said cordially. "Good bit of work you been doing."

"Yeah, thanks, thanks," Scott said stiffly.

Tyrone had already determined that he needed Scott if his own agency wouldn't help him. At least Scott wasn't bound by idiotic governmental regulations that stifled rather than helped the cause. Maybe there was hope for cooperation yet, if his little *faux pas* could be forgiven.

"We need to talk. I've been meaning to call you." Though Tyrone meant it, Scott thought it was a pile of warmed up FBI shit.

"Sure, let's talk." Scott's apparent indifference bothered Tyrone.

"Scott, I mean it," he said sincerely. "I have an apology to make, and I want to do it in person. Also, I think that we both need each other . . .you'll understand when I tell you what's been going on." Tyrone's deep baritone voice conveyed honesty and a little bit of urgency. If nothing else, he had never known or had any reason to suspect Tyrone of purposely misleading or lying to him. And their friendship had been a good one. Plus, the tease of a secret further enticed Scott into agreeing.

"Yeah, what the hell. It's Christmas." Scott's aloofness came across as phony, but Tyrone understood the awkwardness and let it pass.

"How 'bout we meet at The Oyster Bar, Grand Central, and get shit faced. Merry Christmas from the Bureau."

The Oyster Bar resides on the second lower level of Grand Central Station, located eighty feet beneath Park Avenue and 42nd. Street. It had become a fairly chic restaurant bar in the '80's; the seafood was fresh, and occasionally excellent. The patronage of the bar ranged from the commuter who desperately quaffed down two or three martinis to those who enjoyed the seafaring ambience. The weathered hard wood walls were decorated with huge stuffed crabs, swordfish, lifesavers and a pot pourri of fishing accouterments. The ceilings were bathed in worn fishing nets that occasionally dragged too low for anyone taller than 6 feet.

Away from the bar, patrons could dine or drink in privacy, with dim ten watt lamps on each table to cut through the darkness. Tyrone was sitting at such a table, drink in hand when Scott craned his neck from the door to find his friend through the crowd. He ambled over, and Tyrone stood to greet him. Scott was cool, but willing to give it a try. As usual Tyrone was elegantly attired, in a custom tailored dark gray pin stripe suit, and a fitted designer shirt and a stylish silk tie of the proper width.

Scott was dressed just fine as far as he was concerned. His sneakers were clean, his jeans didn't have holes and the sweater would have gained him admission to the most private ski parties in Vermont. Maybe they were too different and their friendship had been an unexplainable anomaly; an accident.

Scott's stomach tightened. His body memory recalled the time the principal had suspended him from high school for spreading liquid banana peel on the hall floors and then ringing the fire drill alarm. The picture of 3000 kids and 200 teachers slipping and sliding and crawling out of the school still made Scott smile.

"What'll you have?" Tyrone gestured at a waiter while asking Scott for his preference.

"Corona, please."

Tyrone took charge. "Waiter, another double and a Corona." He waved the waiter away. "That's better." Tyrone was already slightly inebriated. "I guess you think I'm a real shit hole, huh?"

"Sort of," Scott agreed. "I guess you could put it that way." Scott was impressed with Ty's forthright manner. "I can think of a bunch more words that fit the bill." At least Tyrone admitted it. That was a step in the right direction.

Ty laughed, "Yeah, I bet you could, and you might be right." Scott's drink came. He took a thirsty gulp from the long neck bottle."

"Ease on down the road!" Ty held his half empty drink in the air. It was peace offering. Scott slowly lifted his and their drinks met briefly. They both sipped again, and an awkward silence followed.

"Well, I guess it's up to me to explain, isn't it?" Tyrone ventured.

"You don't have to explain anything, I understand," Scott said caustically.

"I don't think you do, my friend. May I at least have my last words before you shoot?" Tyrone's joviality was not as effective when nervous.

Scott remembered that he used the same argument with Doug only days before. He eased up. "Sure, ready and aimed, though."

"I'm quitting." Tyrone's face showed disappointment, resignation.

The beer bottle at Scott's lips was abruptly laid on the table. "Quitting? The FBI?" Tyrone nodded. "Why? What happened?" For one moment Scott completely forgot how angry he was.

The din of the Oyster Bar made for excellent cover. They could speak freely with minimal worry of being overheard.

"It's a long story, but it began when they pulled your article. God, I'm sorry, man," Tyrone said with empathy. The furrows on his forehead deepened as he searched for a reaction from Scott. Nothing.

Ty finished off his drink and started on the refill. "Unlike what you probably believe, or want to believe, when you called me that morning, I had no idea what you were talking about. It was several hours before I realized what had happened. If I had any idea . . ."

Scott stared blankly at Tyrone. *You haven't convinced me of anything*, Scott thought.

"As far as I knew, you were writing an article that had no particular consequence . . ."

"Thanks a shitload," Scott quipped.

"No, I mean, I had no idea of the national security implications, and besides, it was going to be in the paper the next day anyway." Tyrone shrugged with his hands in the air for added emphasis. "Tempest meant nothing to me. All I said was that you and I had been talking. I promise you, that's it. As a friend, that was the extent of it. They took it from there." Tyrone extended his hands in an open gesture of conciliation. "All I knew was that what you'd said about CMR shook some people up in D.C.. ECCO has been quite educational. Now I know why, and that's why I have to leave."

The genuineness from Tyrone softened Scott's attitude some. "I thought you spooks stuck together. Spy and die together."

Tyrone contorted his face to show disgust with that thought. "That'll be the day. In fact it's the opposite. A third of our budgets are meant to keep other agencies in the dark about what we're doing."

"You're kidding!"

"I wish I was." Tyrone looked disheartened, betrayed.

"At any rate," Tyrone continued, "I got spooked by the stunt with your paper and the Attorney General. I just couldn't call you, you'll see why. The Agency is supposed to enforce the law, not make it and they have absolutely no business screwing with the press. Uh-uh." Tyrone took a healthy sip of his drink. "Reminds me of times that are supposed to be gone. Dead in the past. Did you know that I am a constitutional lawyer?"

Scott ordered another beer and shook his head, no. Just a regular lawyer. Will wonders never cease?

"Back in the early 60's the South was not a good place for blacks. Or Negroes as we were called back then." Tyrone said the word Negro with disdain. He pulled his tie from the stiff collar and opened a button. "I went on some marches in Alabama, God, that was a hot summer. A couple of civil rights workers were killed."

Scott remembered. More from the movie Mississippi Burning than from memory.

Civil rights wasn't a black-white issue, Tyrone insisted. It was about man's peaceful co-existence with government. A legal issue. "I thought that was an important distinction and most people were missing the point. I thought I could make a difference working from inside the system. I was wrong, and I've been blinded by it until now . . .you know."

"When I was in college the politicians screamed integration while the poor blacks no more wanted to be bussed to the rich white neighborhood that the rich whites wanted the poor blacks in their schools." Tyrone spoke from his heart, his soul, with a touch of resentment that Scott had not seen before. But then, they had never spoken of it before. This was one story that he had successfully neglected to share. "Forced integration was government's answer to a problem it has never understood.

"It's about dignity. Dignity and respect, not government intervention. It's about a man's right to privacy and the right to lead his life the way he sees fit. Civil rights is about how to keep government from interfering with its citizens. Regardless of color." Tyrone was adamant.

"And that's why you're gonna quit?" Scott didn't see the connection.

"No, goddamnit, no," Tyrone shouted. "Don't you get it?" Scott shook his head. "They want to take them away." He spoke with finality and assumed Scott knew what he meant. The liquor fogged his brain to mouth speech connection.

"Who's gonna take what away?" Scott asked, frustrated by Ty's ramblings.

"I know it's hokey, but the Founding fathers had a plan, and so far it's survived two hundred years of scrutiny and division. I would like to think it can survive the computer age." Tyrone quieted down some. "My father used to tell me, from the time I was old enough to understand, that law was merely a measure of how much freedom a man was willing to sacrifice to maintain an orderly society."

"My father was a radical liberal among liberals," Tyrone remembered. "Even today he'll pick a fight at the family barbecue for his own entertainment. And he'll hold his own."

Scott enjoyed the image of a crotchety octogenarian stirring up the shit while his children isolated their kids from their grand father's intellectual lunacy. What was this about?

Tyrone caught himself and realized that he wasn't getting his point across. He took a deep breath and slouched back in the chair that barely held him.

"From the beginning," he said. "I told you about ECCO, and what a disaster it is. No authority, no control, no responsibility. And the chaos is unbelievable.

"I don't pretend to understand all of the computer jargon, but I do recognize when the NSA wants to control everything. There's a phenomenal amount of arrogance there. The NSA reps in ECCO believe that they are the only ones who know anything about computers and how to protect them. I feel sorry for the guys from NIST. They're totally underfunded, so they end up with both the grunt work and the brunt of the jokes from the NSA.

"NSA won't cooperate on anything. If NIST says it's white, NSA says it's black. If NIST says there's room to compromise, NSA gets more stubborn. And the academic types. At long last I now know what happened to the hippies: they're all government consultants through universities. And all they want to do is study, study, study. But they never come up with answers, just more questions to study.

"The vendors try to sell their products and don't contribute a damn thing," sighed Tyrone. "A bunch of industry guys from computer companies and the banks, and they're as baffled as I am."

"So why quit? Can't you make a difference?"

"Listen. The FBI views computer crimes as inter-state in nature and therefore under their domain."

Scott nodded in understanding.

"We are enforcement, only," Tyrone asserted. "We do not, nor should we make the laws. Separation of power; Civics 101. To accomplish anything, I have to be a private citizen."

"What do you want to accomplish?" asked Scott with great interest.

"I want to stop the NSA." Tyrone spoke bluntly and Scott sat too stunned to speak for long seconds.

"From what?" A sudden pit formed in Scott's stomach.

"I found out why they dumped on you about the CMR," Tyrone said. "I haven't been able to tell you before, but it doesn't matter any more." Tyrone quickly shook off the veiling sadness. "NSA has a built-in contradiction. On one hand they listen into the world and spy for America. This is supposed to be very secret, especially how they do it. It turns out that CMR is one of their 'secret' methods for spying on friends and foes alike.

"So, to keep our friends and foes from spying on us, they create the secret Tempest program. Except, they think it needs to be kept a military secret, and the public sector be damned. They actually believe that opening the issue to the public will hamper their intelligence gathering capabilities because the enemy will protect against it, too."

Scott listened in fascination. What he was learning now more than made up for the loss of one article. He felt bad now that he had overreacted and taken it out on Tyrone.

"Same goes for the EMP-T bomb," Tyrone added. "Only they didn't know that you were going to publish ahead of time like they did when I opened up my fat trap."

Scott's eyes suddenly lit up. "How much did you tell them?"

"That I knew you and you were writing an article. That's it."

"Then how did they know what I had written? It was pretty damned close. I assumed that you had . . ."

"No way, man," Tyrone held his hands up.

"Then how did . . .Ty? What if they're using CMR on my computers? Could they . . ."

Tyrone's predicament was to decide whether or not to tell Scott that he knew the NSA and others spied on Americans and gathered intelligence through remote control means. "I assume they're capable of anything."

"Shit!" Scott exclaimed. "Privacy goes right out the window. Damn." Scott rapidly spun in his chair and vacantly stared off in space. "Is that legal?"

"What? CMR? I looked into that briefly, and there's nothing on the books yet, but I did find out that tapping cellular phone conversations is legal."

"Phone tapping, legal?" Scott couldn't believe his ears.

"Cellular phones, yeah. The FCC treats them like TV sets, radios, satellites. Anyone can listen to any station."

"That's incredible," Scott said, mouth gaping. "I wonder how they'll handle RF LAN's."

"RF LAN's," asked Ty. "What are those?"

"A bunch of computers tied together with radios. They replace the wires that connect computers now. Can you imagine?" Scott saw the irony in it. "Broadcasting your private secrets like that? Hah! Or if you have your own RF network, all you have to do is dial up another one and all the information ends up right in your computer! Legal robbery. Is this a great country or what?"

"Now you know why I'm leaving. The NSA cannot be permitted to keep the public uninformed about vulnerabilities to their personal freedom. And hiding under the umbrella of national security gets old. A handful of paranoid un-elected, un-budgeted, non-accountable, mid-level bureaucrats are deciding the future of privacy and freedom in this country. They are the ones who are saying, 'no, no problem,' when they know damn well it is a problem. What they say privately is in diametric opposition to their public statements and positions."

Scott stifled a nervous laugh. Who wound Tyrone up? A conspiracy theory. Tyrone was drunk. "Don't you think that maybe you're taking this a little far," he suggested. For the first time in years the shoe was on the other foot. Scott was tempering somebody elses extremes.

"Why the hell do you think there's so much confusion at ECCO and CERT and the other computer SWAT teams? NSA interferes at every step." Tyrone responded. "And no, I am not taking this too far. I haven't taken it far enough. I sit with these guys and they talk as though I'm not there. I attend meetings where the policies and goals of ECCO are established. Shit, I trust the dope- smoking hippies from Berkeley more than anyone from the Fort." The bitterness came through clearly, but Scott could see it wasn't focussed on any one person or thing.

But Scott began to understand. For over 20 years Tyrone had insulated himself from the politics of the job and had seen only what he wanted to see; a national Police Force enforcing the laws. Tyrone loved the chase of the crime. The bits and pieces, the endless sifting of evidence, searching for clues and then building a case from shreds. The forensics of modern criminology had been so compelling for Tyrone Duncan that he had missed the impact that the mass proliferation of technology would have on his first love - The Constitution.

The sudden revelations and realizations of the last several weeks set his neurons and synapses into high gear. Tyrone introspectively examined his beliefs; he tried to review them from the perspective of an idealistic young man in his twenties. What would he have done then? He realized the answer was easier found now that he was a man of experience: Do Something About It.

Far from a rebel looking for a cause, the cause jumped all over Tyrone with a vengeance and the tenacity of a barnacle.

All at once Scott knew that Tyrone was serious and that he would be a better friend if he congratulated instead of castigated.

"You know, I kind of understand a little. Same thing with my ex-wife."

"Hey, that's not fair, man," Tyrone vigorously objected. "Maggie was a dingbat . . ."

"I know that and she knew that," Scott agreed, "but that was what made her Maggie." Tyrone nodded, remembering her antics. "And in some ways we still love each other. After ten years of fun, great fun, she wanted to get off of the planet more than I did, so she went to California." The softness in Scott's voice said he still cared about Maggie, that she was a cherished part of his life, that was and would remain in the past.

Scott shook off the melancholy and continued. "It's the same for you. You're married to the FBI, and while you still love it, you need to let it go to move on with your life."

"Y'know, I don't know why everyone says you're so stupid," Tyrone said with respect. "UFO's aside, you can actually make sense."

"Maybe, maybe not. Doesn't really matter. But I'm doing exactly what I want to do. And the day it stops being fun, I'm outta here."

"Isn't that the arrogance of wealth speaking?" Tyrone asked.

"And you're any different? The 22 room Tudor shack you live in is not exactly my vision of poverty. As I see it, it's one of the benefits," Scott said unembarrassed by his financial security. "Before I made my money, I swore that when I got rich, I would give something back. You know, to the planet or society or something. Do something useful and not for the money." Scott spoke with honest enthusiasm. "But I don't believe there's a rule that says I have to be miserable. I love what I do, and well, I don't know. The concept of career is different for me. I like the idea of doing a little bit of everything for the experience. You know, I drove a cab for one night. Glad I did, but never again."

"So?" asked Tyrone.

"So, do what you want to do and enjoy it. Period. As a friend of a friend says, live long and prosper."

Scott let Tyrone sit in contemplative silence as the waiter brought them two more. They were doing a good job of sticking to the plan of getting 'shiffaced'.

"You know," Tyrone opined. "INTERNET is only the tip of the iceberg. NASA is having ECCO and CERT look into over $12 Million in unaccounted-for telephone calls. The Justice Department sold old computers containing the names and other details of the Witness Protection Program to a junk dealer in Kentucky and they're suing him to get them back. The Secret Service is redesigning its protection techniques for the President since someone got into their computers and copied the plans. The computers at Mitre have been used by hackers for years to get at classified information. The public hears less than 1% of the computer problems in the government. And still, no one will do anything. There's even talk that the missing Plutonium that the Israelis theoretically stole in 1981 was actually a computer error."

"What do you want to do about it?" Scott was asking as a friend, not a reporter.

"First," said a newly determined Tyrone. "I'm gonna nail me some of these mothers, and I'll do it with your help. Then, after that?" Tyrone's old smile was suddenly back. "I think I'm gonna kick myself some government ass." Tyrone roared with laughter and Scott joined the contagious behavior. "In the meantime, I want to take a look at some blackmail. I think you may be right."

"About what? I don't listen to what I tell you."

"Remember you said that the blackmail scheme wasn't really blackmail." Tyrone shifted his weight in the chair and he reached for the words through is fogged mind. "You said it might be a way to make us too busy to see our own shadow. That it was a cover up for another dissociated crime."

"Yeah? It might be," Scott said.

Tyrone's body heaved while he snickered. "We finally have a lead. Demands have been made."

"What kind? Who? What do they want?" Scott's journalist mind clicked into gear. "What about the computer virus crap?"

"I'm kind of looking into both, but this morning my interest was renewed. A corporate type I met with this morning says not only he, but another 25 or more of his corporate brethren are getting the same treatment. If he's right, someone is demanding over $30 Million in ransoms."

"Jesus Christ! Is that confirmed?" Scott probed.

"Yes. That's why I said you were right."

The implications were tremendous, even to Scott's clouded mind. While the legal system might not be convinced that computer radiation was responsible for an obviously well coordinated criminal venture, he, as an engineer, realized how vulnerable anyone - everyone was. The questions raced through his mind all at once.

Over a few dozen oysters and not as many drinks, Scott and Ty proceeded to share their findings. Scott had documents up the ying-yang, documents he couldn't use in a journalistic sense, but might be valuable to the recent developments in Ty's case. He had moved the files to his home; they were simply taking too much space around his desk at the office. They were an added attraction to the disaster he called his study. Scott agreed to show Ty some of them. After the meeting with Franklin Dobbs this afternoon, and knowing there might be others in a similar situation, Ty wanted an informal look at Scott's cache.

"I've been holding back, Ty." Scott said during a lull in their conversation.

"How do you mean?"

"This morning, I got a call from a guy I had spoken to a few months ago; I assume he sent me those files, and he said that key executives throughout the country were being blackmailed. Some were borrowing money from the mob to pay them off."

"Do you have names? Who?" Tyrone's took an immediate interest.

"Let me see if I have'm here," he said as he reached for his small notebook in the sports jacket draped over the back of his chair. "Yeah, he only gave me three, not much to go on. A Faulkner, some banker from L.A., a Wall Street tycoon named Henson and another guy Dobbs, Franklin Dobbs."

"Dobbs! How the hell do you know about Dobbs?" Tyrone yelled so loud several remaining bar patrons looked over to see what the ruckus was.

"I told you, the call this morning." Scott was taken aback by the outburst. "What're you hollering about?"

"Shit, goddamned shit, I don't need this." Tyrone finished one and ordered another drink. He was keeping his promise; well on the way to getting severely intoxicated. "Dobbs. Dobbs is the poor fucker that came into my office today."

"You saw Dobbs? He admitted it?" Scott's heart raced at the prospect of a connection. Finally.

"Scott," Tyrone asked quietly. "I have no right to ask you this, but I will anyway. If you find anything, from Dobbs, can you hold back? Just for a while?" A slight pleading on Tyrone's part.

"Why?" Was this part of the unofficial trade with Ty for earlier information?

The waiter returned with the credit card. Tyrone signed the slip, giving the waiter entirely too much of a tip. "I'll tell you on the train. Let's go."

"Where?"

"To your house. You have a computer, don't you?"

"Yeah . . ."

"Well, let's see if we can find out who the other 25 are."

They took a cab from the Scarsdale station to Scott's house. No point in ending up in the clink for a DUI, even with a Federal Agent in tow. Scott's study was in such disarray that he literally scraped off books and papers from the couch onto the floor to find Ty a place to sit and he piled up bigger piles of files to make room for their beers on one of his desks.

Scott and Tyrone hadn't by any means sobered up on the train, but their thinking was still eminently clear. During the hour ride, they reviewed what they knew.

Several prominent businessmen were being actively blackmailed. In addition the blackmailer, or a confederate, was feeding information to the media. At a minimum the Times, and probably the Exposé. Perhaps other media as well were in receipt of similar information, but legitimate news organizations couldn't have much to do with it in its current form.

Presumably then, like Scott, other reporters were calling names in the files. Tyrone reasoned that such an exercise might be a well planned maneuver on the part of the perpetrators.

"Think about it this way," he said. "Let's say you get a call from someone who says they know something about you that you don't want them to. That'll shake you up pretty good, won't it?" Scott rapidly agreed. "Good. And the nature of the contact is threatening, not directly, perhaps, but the undercurrent leaves no doubt that the caller is not your best friend. Follow?"

"And then," Scott picked up, "a guy like me calls with the same information. The last person in the world he wants to know about his activities is a reporter, or to see it show up in the news, so he really freaks."

"Exactly!" Tyrone slapped his thigh. "And, if he gets more than one call, cardiac arrest is nearby. Imagine it. Makes for a good case of justifiable paranoia."

Tyrone nodded vigorously. "I've been in this game long enough to see the side effects of blackmail and extortion. The psychological effects can be devastating. An inherent distrust of strangers is common. Exaggerated delusions occur in many cases. But think about this. If we're right, you begin to distrust everyone, your closest friends, business associate, even your family. Suddenly, everyone is a suspect. Distrust runs rampant and you begin to feel a sense of isolation, aloneness. It feels like you're fighting the entire world alone. Solitude can be the worst punishment."

The analysis was sound. The far ranging implications had never occurred to Scott. To him it had been a simple case of extortion or blackmail using some high tech wizardry. Now, suddenly there was a human element. The personal pain that made the crime even that much more sinister.

"Well, we, I mean the FBI, have seven stake outs. It's a fairly simple operation. Money drops in public places, wait and pick up the guy who picks up the money." Tyrone made it sound so easy. Scott wondered.

"I bet it isn't that simple," Scott challenged.

"No shit, it ain't," Tyrone came back.

"So whaddya do?"

"Pay and have another beer." Tyrone tempered the seriousness of their conversation.

As Scott got up to go the kitchen he called out, "Hey, I been thinking."

"Yeah?" Tyrone yelled.

He popped a Bud and handed it to Tyrone. "Listen, I know this may be left field, but let's think it through." Scott sat behind his desk and put his feet on top of some books on the desk. He leaned back and put his hands behind his head. "We've been talking about the front end of this thing, the front lines where the victims are actually being blackmailed. The kind of stuff that makes headlines." Scott smiled devilishly at Ty who made a significant hand gesture in return. "And now you're talking about how to catch them when they pick up the money. Have you thought of the other side?"

"What other side?" Tyrone was still confused by Scott's logic.

"Assume for a moment that all this information is really coming from computers. The CMR. O.K.?" Ty grudgingly shrugged his shoulders. "O.K., you said that there are 7 cases across the country. Dobbs said he knew of more here. Right? Well, who gets the information?"

Confusion showed on Tyrone's face. "Gets the information?"

"Yeah, who runs around the country listening in on computers?" The question had been obvious to Scott. All of sudden Tyrone's face lit up.

"You mean the van?"

"Right. How many vans would it take to generate all this?" Scott pointed at several boxes over next to the disorganized shelves.

"Damned if I know!"

"Neither do I, but I'll make a wild guess and say that there are quite a few running around. One blew up, or more specifically, was blown up. You guys have pieces."

"Not any more," Ty said. "They were taken away by the CI boys. Said it was national security stuff. I was told to stay away from it. Told you about us Feds."

"Whatever," Scott waved away the sidebar. "The point is that if a whole bunch of these vans were used, that's not cheap. They held a lot of very expensive equipment. Why not look for the vans? They can't be that hard to find. Maybe you'll find your . . . "

"Holy Christ, Mother Mary and Joseph, why didn't I think of that." Tyrone stood up and aimlessly meandered amongst Scott's junk heaps. "We've been looking in one direction only. The van ceased to exist in our minds since CI took it. The Government can be a royal pain in the ass. The van, of course."

Just as Scott was going to describe how to find villains without wasting hundreds of hours scouring data banks, his computer beeped three times. Scott was shaken from his comfort. "What the . . .?" He looked at the clock. It was just midnight. Kirk! Kirk was calling and he totally had forgotten to mention the ransacking to Ty.

"Great! It's Kirk. I wanted you to meet him." As Scott leaned over the keyboard to answer the page, Tyrone looked quizzically at him.

"Who's Kirk?"

"This hacker, some kid on the West Coast. He's taught me a lot. Good guy. Hope to meet him someday." Scott pushed a few keys. The screen came alive.

WTFO

"Hey," said Tyrone, "that's what we used to say in the Reserves."

Gotta Spook here.

SPOOK? YOU KNOW SPOOK?

Who's Spook?

YOU SAID HE'S WITH YOU

Not Spook, a spook. FBI guy.

FBI? YOU PROMISED . . .

Don't worry. Tell him yourself. Who is Spook, anyway?

SPOOK IS A HACKER, ONE OF THE BEST. BEEN ON THE SCENE FOR YEARS. A FEW PEOPLE CLAIM TO HAVE MET HIM, BUT IT'S ALWAYS A FRIEND OF A FRIEND OF A FRIEND. HE KEEPS A LOW PROFILE. THE WORD IS SPOOK IS PLAYING SOME GOOD GAMES RECENTLY. THE FBI?

He's a friend. He doesn't know.

Tyrone had come over to the crowded desk to watch the exchange. "Who is this guy? What don't I know?"

Kirk, can I tell him? No one knows who you are?

I GUESS SO.

Be back . . .

Scott proceeded to tell Tyrone about the warnings that Kirk received, and then how his computers were destroyed. That the calling card warned him to stay away from First State Bank. And how another hacker calling himself Da Vinci on a BBS called Freedom might be a link. Then he admitted that he had been in on a bank robbery, or at least breaking and entering a bank's computer.

Tyrone had enough. "I'm not sure I want to hear anymore. You have been busy. So what can I do?"

"Tell Kirk what he can do," Scott asked.

"He could probably go to jail. Bank computers, my God! Is that where you get your stories? You live them and then report them in the third person. Stories for the inquiring mind."

"Are you through! I mean, are you through?" Scott sounded perturbed.

"It's true. What does this guy want?"

"Advice. Talk to him. Here." Scott motioned for Tyrone to sit at the keyboard.

"What do I do?"

"Just type," Scott said with exasperation. "You're as bad as my mother. Type!" Scott ordered.

This is Ty . . .

Scott pulled Ty's hands from the keyboard. "A handle, use a handle, like on a CB!"

"Oh, yeah, I forgot," Tyrone lied.

This is the FBI

Scott looked in shock. Tyrone laughed out loud. "He already knows who I am. So what? I've always liked saying that anyway." To Tyrone it was great fun.

KIRK HERE, FBI, WHERE NO MAN HAS GONE BEFORE

So I hear. Been to any good banks lately.

REPO MAN, WHAT'S UP

Can't take a joke?

YEAH. NO PROBLEM

Listen, I don't know you from Adam, and you don't have to talk to me, but I am curious. Did your computers really get bashed?

TOTALLY, DUDE.

Tyrone pointed his thumb at the computer. "Wise guy, eh?"

"Give him a chance. Generation gap." Tyrone didn't take kindly to references to his age. Sensitive area.

Why?

CAUSE SOMEONE THINKS I KNOW SOMETHING THAT I DON'T

That's clear.

THANKS

Do you want to make a formal complaint?

WOULD IT DO ANY GOOD?

No.

THEN, NO

You think it was First State?

YES.

Don't you go around poking into other computers, too?

SURE

So why not someone else?

THEY DIDN'T GET INTO BIG TROUBLE FROM REPO MAN'S ARTICLE?

"He knows who you are?" Tyrone asked.

"Sure. He likes calling me Repo Man for some reason that escapes me.

Where else do you go?

THAT WOULD BE TELLING

Gotcha. Well, I guess that's about it.

PHEW!

<<<CONNECTION TERMINATED>>>

"I guess you scared him off." Scott was amused.

"Sorry," Tyrone said.

"He'll call back," Scott waved off the apology. "When the coast is clear."

"Fuck off." Their friendship was returning to the level it once had been.

"Hey, it's getting beyond late," Scott ignored him. "What say we get together in a few days and sort through some of this."

"I know, but one thing. Can you get into your computers, at the paper?"

"Yeah, why?"

"Dobbs said that the others had had their stock go down pretty dramatically. Can you look up stock prices and performances over the last few months?"

"Yeah, do it all the time."

"Could you? I want to see if there are any names I recognize."

"No problem." Scott dialed the Times computer and identified himself. After going into the bank computer with Kirk, every time he dialed up his office, he felt an increased sense of power, and an increased sense of responsibility. He had access to massive amounts of information that if it got into the wrong hands . . .

He shook the thought. The computer offered the 'Stocks and Bonds Menu' and Scott set up a query in a modified SQL that was simple enough for reporters to use:

ALL STOCKS LOSING 35% OR MORE OF VALUE IN LAST YEAR.

The computer flashed a message, "Working". Scott leaned back. "Takes a few seconds. Oh, as I was saying, when I get back, I'll call and we'll see what we can screw together."

"Back from where?" Tyrone sounded accusatory but jealous.

"Europe. Amsterdam." Scott checked the computer screen. It was still busy.

"Rough life."

"No, it's only for a couple of days. There's a hackers conference. I've been invited, by Kirk as a matter of fact."

"Hackers conference, sounds like tons of fun." Tyrone was not impressed.

"The best hackers in the world are going to be there. I hope to get some leads on the First State mess. The Freedom BBS is not all it seems."

"Please stay in touch," Tyrone implored.

"Sure. Here we go. It's ready. Ah, let's see, there are 267 companies who meet that criterion. I guess that narrows it down for you."

"Smart ass. Ah, can you get those in New York only?"

"The city? Sure."

SORT BY ZIP 100XX

"That'll give us . . ."

"I know what it means." Tyrone shut Scott off in mock defense. In reality he didn't know much about computers, but some things were obvious even to the technically naive.

"That was fast," said Scott. "Only 17. Help any?"

"Might. Can I get that on paper?"

Scott gave him the print out of the public finances on the several unfortunate companies who had lost more than a third of their net worth in the last year. Tyrone folded it into his jacket pocket. "Hey, call me a cab. I'm too drunk to walk."

* * * * *

Wednesday, December 30
Lenox, Georgia

A faded blue Ford Econoline van sat in the Lenox Square parking lot. The affluent Atlanta suburb had been targeted from the beginning. Demographically it fit the bill to a tee.

From the outside, the van looked like a thousand other parked cars; empty, with their owners shopping in the huge mall. On the inside though, two men were intently operating a vast array of electronic equipment.

"Here comes another one," said the first. "How many does that make today?"

"A hundred and forty seven. Let's do it." The second man watched the enhanced color video image on a small monitor. A well dressed lady walked up to the ATM machine, card in hand. The first man pressed a switch on another monitor and the snow filled picture was transformed into an electronic copy of the ATM's video display.

Please Insert Card

The screen in the van echoed the ATM screen.

"Can you tune it in a bit?" asked the first man. " It's a little fuzzy."

"Yeah, we must have settled. Let me adjust the antenna." His hand grabbed a joystick on one of the tightly packed racks of equipment and gingerly moved it from left to right. "Is that better?" A small disguised antenna on the roof of the van aligned itself as the joystick commanded.

"Yeah . . .no . . .yeah, back again . . ."

"I see it. There."

"Thanks."

Enter Personal Identification Number:

A third monitor over the second man's cramped desk came to life as the number 3435 appeared across his screen.

"Got it. You, too?"
"On disk and saved."
"I'll back it up."
"Better not. Here comes another one."
"Busy day."

* * * * *

It was a very busy day. Ahmed Shah saw to it that his followers were kept busy, six days a week. As they had been for months.

When his army of a hundred plus Econoline vans were not raiding the contents of unsuspecting computers during the day, they became electronic ears which listened in on the conversations between the ATM's and their bank customers.

Ahmed's vans were used most efficiently. On the road, doing his bidding twenty four hours a day, every day but the Sabbath. Ahmed created cells of eight loyal anti-American sympathizers, regardless of nationality, to operate with each van. Each group operated as an independent entity, with only one person from each able to communicate privately with Ahmed over cellular modem. No cell knew any other cell. If one group was apprehended, they couldn't tell what they didn't know. Therefore, the rest of the cells remain intact.

Absolute loyalty was an unquestioned assumption for all members of Ahmed's electronic army. It had to be that way, for the bigger cause.

All day and night one of Ahmed Shah's computers in his lab at Columbia received constant calls from his cell leaders. During the day it was the most interesting information that they had captured from computer screens. At night, it was the passcodes to automatic bank tellers machines.

Once the passcodes were in hand, making fake ATM cards was a trivial task.

* * * * *

Chapter 18

Wednesday, January 6
Amsterdam, Holland

Scott Mason had a theory. It didn't matter than no one else believed it, or that they thought him daffy. It worked for him.

He believed that jet lag was caused by the human body traveling across mystical magnetic force fields called Ley lines. The physics of his theory made common sense to anyone but a scientist. It went like this: the body is electric and therefore magnetic fields can influence it. Wherever we live we are subject to the local influence of magnetic, electrical and Ley lines. If we move too quickly, as by plane, through Ley lines, the balance of our system is disturbed. The more Ley lines you traverse, the more upsetting it is to the system. Thus, jet lag.

But, Scott had a solution. Or more accurately, his mother had one which she had convinced him of years earlier. Scott carried with him a small box, the size of a pack of cigarettes, that had a switch and a blinking light. It was called an Earth Resonance Generator, or ERG. The literature said the ERG established a negative gravity field through a magnetic Mobius loop. Inside the box was a battery, a loop of wire, a light emitting diode and the back side of the switch. In short, nothing of electronic consequence or obvious function. There was no way in hell that this collection of passive components could do anything other than wear out batteries. All for $79.95 plus $4 shipping.

Scott first heard his mother proselytize about the magic of the ERG when he was ten or twelve. His father, the role model for Archie Bunker ignored her completely and said her rantings increased with certain lunar phases. Since his father wouldn't listen to her any longer, she endlessly lectured Scott about the virtues of the ERG whenever she returned from a trip. His father refused to travel, and had never even been on a plane.

His mother so persisted in her belief that she even tried experiments. On one of her trips to Rome, an eleven hour flight, she somehow talked the stewardesses into handing out the 400 questionnaires she'd brought with her onto the plane. It asked the passengers how they felt after the flight, and if they do anything special to avoid jet lag. She claims more than 200 were returned and that they overwhelmingly indicated that no one felt jet lag on that trip.

She attributed this immense success to the ERG effects which purportedly spread over the equivalent of one acre. In other words, the ERG takes care of an entire 747 or L-1011 or DC-10.

For years Scott successfully used the ERG to avoid jet lag. Some people put brown paper bags in their shoes, others eat yogurt and bean sprouts before a long flight. Maybe his solution was psychosomatic, Scott admitted to anyone who asked, but, so what? It still works, doesn't it? Scott was forever impressed that airport security had never, once, asked him what this little blinking black box was. Scary thought.

He arrived completely refreshed via KLM at the Amsterdam International Airport at 10:15 AM. While he had been to Europe many times, he had thus far missed the Amsterdam experience. He had heard that pot was legal in Amsterdam. In fact it was more than legal. Every morning the marijuana prices were broadcast on the local radio stations and Scott had every intention of sampling the wares. After 20 years of casual pot use, he preferred it immensely to the effects of drinking, and he was not going to miss out on the opportunity.

In New York no one harassed pot smokers, but technically, it still wasn't legal. Amsterdam represented the ultimate counterculture. This was the first time since Maggie had left for the Coast three years ago that Scott felt an independence, a freedom reminiscent of his rebellious teen years.

He gave the taxi driver the address of the Eureka! hotel, on the Amstel. During the half hour fifty guilder ride into downtown, the driver continuously chattered. "Amsterdam has more canals than Venice. Many more. Holland is mostly land reclaimed from the sea. We have the biggest system of dikes in Europe. Don't forget to see our diamond centers." He spoke endlessly with deep pride about his native land.

The Eureka! is a small four story townhouse with only 16 rooms that overlooked the Amstel, the largest canal in Amsterdam, similar to the Grand Canal in Venice. The Times had booked it because it was cheap, but Scott felt instantly at home. After settling in, Scott called the number that Kirk had given him.

"Hallo?" A thick Dutch accent answered the phone.

"Hello? I'm looking for Jon Gruptmann? This is Scott Mason.

"Ya, this is Jon."

"A mutual friend, Kirk, said I should call you."

"Ah, ya, ya. Repo Man, is it not?" The voice got friendly.

"That's what Kirk calls me."

"Ya, ya. He said you want to attend our meetings. Ya? Is that so?" Jon sounded enthusiastic.

"That's why I swam the Atlantic, all three thousand miles. I would love to!" Jon didn't sound like Scott expected a computer hacker to sound, whatever that was.

"Huh?" Jon asked. "Ah, ya, a joke. Goot. Let me tell you where we meet. The place is small, so it may be very crowded. I hope you do not mind." Jon sounded concerned about Scott's comfort.

"Oh, no. I'm used to inconvenience. I'm sure it will be fine."

"Ya, ya. I expect so. The meetings don't really begin until tomorrow. 11 AM. Is that goot for you?"

"Yes, just fine, what's the address?" Scott asked as he readied paper and pen.

"Ya. Go to the warehouse on the corner of Oude Zidjs Voorburg Wal and Lange Niezel. It's around from the Oude Kerksplein. Number 44."

"Hold it, I'm writing." Scott scribbled the address phonetically. A necessary trick reporters use when someone is speaking unintelligibly. "And then what?"

"Just say you're Repo Man. There's a list. And please remember, we don't use our given names."

"No problem. Fine. Thank you."

"Ya. What do you plan for tonight?" Jon asked happily.

"I hadn't really thought about it," Scott lied.

"Ya, ya. Well, I think you should see our city. Enjoy the unique pleasures Amsterdam has to offer."

"I might take a walk . . . or something."

"Ya, ya, or something. I understand. I will see you tomorrow. Ya?" Jon said laughing.

"Wouldn't miss it for the world."

"Do one favor?" Jon asked. "Watch your wallet. We have many pickpockets."

"Thanks for the warning. See you tomorrow." Click. *I grew up in New York*, Scott thought. *Pickpockets, big deal.*

* * * * *

Scott took a shower to remove the vestiges of the eleven hour trip; an hour ride to Kennedy, an hour and a half at the airport, a half hour on the tarmac, seven hours on the plane, and an hour getting into town.

He dressed casually in the American's travel uniform: jeans, jean jacket and warm sweater. He laced his new Reeboks knowing that Amsterdam is a walking city. Driving would be pure insanity unless the goal is sitting in two hour traffic jams. The single lane streets straddle the miles of canals throughout the inner city which is arranged in a large semi-circular pattern. Downtown, or old Amsterdam, is a dense collection of charming clean, almost pristine 4 story buildings built over a period of several hundred years. That's the word for Amsterdam; charming. From late medieval religious structures to townhouses that are tightly packed on almost every street, to the various Pleins where the young crowds congregate in the evenings, Amsterdam has something for everyone. Anne Frank's house to the Rembrandt Museum to a glass roofed boat trip down the canals through the diamond district and out into the Zeider Zee. Not to mention those attractions for the more prurient.

He ran down the two flights to the hotel lobby and found the concierge behind the Heineken bar which doubled as a registration desk. He wanted to know where to buy some pot.

"Not to find us selling that here," the Pakistani concierge said in broken English.

"I know. But where . . ." It was an odd feeling to ask which store sold drugs.

"You want Coffee Shop," he helpfully said.

"Coffee Shop?" Scott asked, skeptical of the translation.

"Across bridge, make right, make left." The concierge liberally used his hands to describe the route. "Coffee shop. Very good."

Scott thanked him profusely and made a quick exit thinking that in parts of the U.S., Texas came to mind, such a conversation could be construed as conspiracy. He headed out into the cool damp late morning weather. The air was crisp, clean, a pleasure to breathe deeply. The Amstel canal, not a ripple present, echoed the tranquility that one feels when walking throughout the city. There are only a half dozen or so 'main' streets or boulevards in Amsterdam and they provide the familiar intense international commercialism found in any major European city. It is when one begins to explore the back streets, the countless alleys and small passageways; the darkened corridors that provide a short cut to the bridge to the next islet; it is then that one feels the essence of Amsterdam.

Scott crossed over the bridge that spans the wide Amstel conscious of the small high speed car and scooters that dart about the tiny streets. He turned right as instructed and looked at the street names on the left. While Scott spoke reasonable French, Dutch escaped him. Bakkerstraat. Was that the name? It was just an alley, but there a few feet down on the right, was the JPL Coffee Shop. JPL was the only retail establishment on Bakkerstraat, and it was unassuming, some might call it derelict, in appearance. From a distance greater than 10 meters, it appeared deserted.

Through the large dirty plate glass window Scott saw a handful of patrons lazing on white wrought iron cafe chairs at small round tables. The Coffee shop was no larger than a small bedroom. Here goes nothing, Scott thought as he opened the door to enter. No one paid scant attention to him as he crossed over and leaned on the edge of the bar which was reminiscent of a soda fountain. A man in his young twenties came over and amiably introduced himself as Chris, the proprietor of the establishment. How could be of service?

"Ah . . . I heard I can buy marijuana here," Scott said.

"Ya, of course. What do you want?" Chris asked.

"Well, just enough for a couple of days, I can't take it back with me you know," Scott laughed nervously.

"Ya. We also have cocaine, and if you need it, I can get you heroin." Chris gave the sales pitches verbally - there was no printed menu in this Coffee Shop.

"No!" Scott shot back immediately, until he realized that all drugs were legal here, not just pot. He didn't want to offend. "Thanks anyway. Just some grass will do."

"How many grams do you want?"

Grams? How many grams? Scott mused that the metric Europeans thought in grams and Americans still in ounces and pounds. O.K., 28 grams to an ounce . . .

"Two grams," Scott said. "By the way, how late are you open?" Scott pushed his rounded spectacles back up his nose.

"Ah, sometimes 8, sometimes 10, sometimes late," Chris said while bringing a tissue box sized lock box to the top of the bar. He opened it and inside were several bags of pot and a block of aluminum foil the size of a candy bar. "You want hashish?" Chris offered.

Scott shook his head, 'no' so Chris opened one of the bags instead of the candy bar.

"You American?" A voice came from one of the tables. Scott looked around. "Here," the voice said. "Me too." The man got up and approached Scott. "Listen, they got two types of ganja here. Debilitating and Coma. I've made the mistake."

"Ya, we have two kinds," Chris agreed laughing. "This will only get you a little high," he said holding up a bag. "This one," he held up another, "will get you stoned."

"Bullshit," the American said. "Their idea of a little high is catatonic for us. Take my word for it. The Mexican shit we smoke? They'd give it to the dogs."

"You sold me," Scott said holding his hands up in surrender. "Just a little high is fine by me. Two grams, please," he said to Chris pointing at the less potent bag. "Thanks for the warning," he said to the American. "Where you from?" Scott asked.

"Oh, around. I guess you could call Washington my home."

"D.C.?"

"Yeah," the American nodded. "And you?" He leaned over the back of his chair to face Scott.

"Big Apple. Suburbs."

"What brings you here?"

"To Europe?" Scott asked.

"Amsterdam. Sin City. Diamonds?"

"No, I wish," Scott laughed. "News. A story brought me here for a couple of days."

Chris finished weighing Scott's purchase on a sensitive digital scale that measured the goods down to the nearest hundredth of a gram. Scott handed Chris $10 in Guilders and pocketed the pot. "Um, where can I get some papers?" Scott asked. Chris pointed to a glass on the bar with a complete selection of assorted paraphernalia.

"Hey, why don't you join me," the American asked. "I've been to Amsterdam before."

"Is it all right to smoke in here?" Scott asked looking around.

"Sure, that's what coffee shops are. The only other thing you can buy in here is sodas. No booze." The American spoke confidently as he lit up a joint and passed it to Scott.

"Thanks," Scott coughed as he handed it back. "Oh, I don't think I caught your name."

"Oh, just call me the Spook."

The Spook? thought Scott. What incredible synchronicity.

Scott's body instantly tensed up and he felt the adrenaline rush with an associated rise in pulse rate. Was this really the legendary Spook?

It is possible that he fell into a chance meeting with the hacker that Kirk and his friends refer to as the king of hackers? Spook? Gotta stay cool. Could he be that lucky? Was there more than one spook? Scott momentarily daydreamed, remembering how fifteen years before, in Athens, Greece he had opened a taxi door right into the face a lady who turned out to be an ex-high-school girl friend. It is a small world, Scott thought tritely.

"Spook? Are you a spy?" Scott comically asked, careful to disguise his real interest.

"If I answer that I'll have to kill you," the Spook laughed out loud in the quiet establishment. "Spy? Hardly. It's just a handle." Spook said guardedly. "What's yours?"

"Mine? Oh, my handle. They call me Repo Man, but it's really Scott Mason. Glad to meet you. Spook," he added handing back the intoxicating cigarette.

BINGO! Scott Mason in hand without even a search. Landing right in his lap. Keep your cool. Dead pan poker face. What unbelievable luck. Don't blow it, let's play this for all that it's worth. Your life just got very simple. Give both Homosoto and Mason exactly what they want with no output of energy.

"You said you're a reporter," Spook said inhaling deeply again. "What's the story?" At least he gets high, Spook thought. Mason could have been a real dip-shit nerd. Thank God for small favors.

"There's a hacker conference that I was invited to," Scott said unabashedly. "I'm trying to show the hacker's side of the story. Why they do what they do. How they legitimize it to themselves." Scott's mouth was rapidly drying out so he ordered a Pepsi. "I assume you're a hacker, too," Scott broached the issue carefully.

Spook smiled widely. "Yup. And proud of it."

"You don't care who knows?" Scott asked looking around to see if anyone was paying attention to their conversation. Instead the other patrons were engrossed in chess or huddled conversation. Only Chris, the proprietor listened from behind the bar.

"The Spook is all anyone knows. I like to keep it that way," Spook said as he laid the roach end of the joint in the ashtray. "Not bad, huh?" He asked Scott.

"Christ, no. Kinda hits you between the eyes." Scott rubbed them to clear off the invading fog.

"After a couple of days it won't get you so bad," Spook said. "You said you wanted to do a fair story on hackers, right?"

"Fair? A fair story? I can only try. If hackers act and talk like assholes then they'll come across like assholes, no matter what I do. However, if they make a decent case, hold a rational albeit arguable position, then maybe someone may listen."

"You sound like you don't approve of our activities." The Spook grinned devilishly.

"Honestly, and I shouldn't say this cause this is your grass," Scott said lighting the joint again. "No, I don't approve, but I figure there's at least 10 sides to a story, and I'm here to find that story and present all sides. Hopefully I can even line up a debate or two. Convincing me is not the point; my readers make up their own minds."

The word 'readers' momentarily jolted the Spook until he realized Scott meant newspaper readers, not his team of Van-Ecking eavesdroppers. Spook took the joint from Scott. "You sound like you don't want to approve."

"Having a hard time with all the crap going down with computers these days," Scott agreed. "I guess my attitude comes through in my articles."

"I've never read your stuff," Spook lied.

"Mainly in New York."

"That explains it. Ever been to Amsterdam?"

"No, I was going to get a map and truck around . . ."

"How about I show you around, and try to convince you about the honor of our profession?" Spook asked.

"Great!" Scott agreed. "But what about . . ." He made a motion to his lips as if he was holding a cigarette.

"Legal on the streets."

"You sure?"

"C'mon," Spook said rising from his chair. "Chris, see you later," he promised. Chris reciprocated and invited his two new friends to return any time.

Scott followed Spook up the alley named Bakkerstraat and into the Rembrandt Plein, a huge open square with cafes and street people and hotels. "At night," Spook said, "Rembrandt and another 4 or 5 pleins are the social hub of activity for the younger generation. Wished I had had this when I was a kid. How are your legs?" The Spook amorously ogled the throngs of young women twenty years his junior.

"Fine, why?"

"I'm going to show you Amsterdam."

Scott and the Spook began walking. The Spook knew his way around and described much of the history and heritage of the city, the country and its culture. This kind of educated hacker was not what Scott had expected. He had thought that today's hackers were nerds, the propeller heads of his day, but he was discovering through the Spook, that he may have been wrong. Scott remembered Clifford Stoll's Hanover Hacker was a well positioned and seemingly upstanding individual who was selling stolen computer information to the KGB. How many nerds would have the gumption to play in that league?

They walked to the outer edge of Old Amsterdam, on the Singelgracht at the Leidseplein. Without a map or the Spook, Scott would have been totally lost. The streets and canals were all so similar that, as the old phrase goes, you can't tell the players without a scorecard. Scott followed the Spook onto an electric street car. It headed down the Leidsestraat, one of the few heavily commercial streets and across the Amstel again.

The street car proceeded up the Nieuwezuds Voorburgwal, a wide boulevard with masses of activities on both sides. This was tourist madness, thought Scott.

"This is freedom," said the Spook.

"Freedom?" The word instantly conjured his memory of the Freedom League, the BBS he suspected was up to no-good. The Spook and Freedom?

"At the end of this street is the Train Station. Thousands of people come through this plaza every day to experience Amsterdam. Get whatever it is out of their system. The drugs, the women, the anarchy of a country that relies upon the integrity of its population to work. Can't you feel it?" The Spook positively glowed as he basked in the aura of the city.

Scott had indeed felt it during their several hours together. An intense sense of independence that came from a generation of socialism. Government regulated drugs, a welfare system that permitted the idle to live nearly as well as the working. Class structures blurred by taxes so extraordinarily high that most everyone lived in similarly comfortable conditions. Poverty is almost non-existent.

Yet, as the Spook explained to Scott, "This is not the world for an entrepreneur. That distinction still belongs to the ol' Red White and Blue. It's almost impossible to make any real money here."

The sun was setting behind the western part of the city, over the church steeples and endless rows of townhouses.

"Hungry yet?" Spook grinned at Scott.

"Hungry? I got a case of the munchies that won't quit. Let's eat." Scott's taste buds were entering panic mode.

"Good," the Spook said as he lit up another joint on the street car. "Let's eat." He hastily leapt off the slow moving vehicle. Scott followed him across the boulevard dodging cars, busses and bicycles. They stopped in front of a small Indonesian restaurant, Sarang Mas, ably disguised with a red and white striped awning and darkened windows.

"Ever had Indonesian food?"

"No, well maybe, in New York I guess . . ."

Miles dragged Scott into the unassuming restaurant and the calming strains of Eastern music replaced the city noises on the street outside. The red and white plastic checkered tablecloths severely clashed with the gilt of the pagoda shaped decorations throughout. But only by American tastes. Sarang Mas was a much touted and reputable restaurant with very fine native Indonesian chefs doing the preparations.

"Let me tell you something," the Spook said. "This food is the absolute finest food available, anywhere in the world, bar no idyllic island location, better than a trip to Hershey, Pennsylvania, to cure a case of the munchies. It's delicate, it's sweet, it's taste bud heaven, it's a thousand points of flavor you've never tried before." The Spook sounded like a hawker on the Home Shopping Network.

"Shut up," Scott joked. "You're just making it worse."

"Think of the oral orgasm that's coming. Anticipation." The waiter had appeared and waited patiently. It was still early and the first seating crowd was two hours away. "Do you mind if I order?"

"No, be my guest. Just make it fast food. Super fast food," Scott begged.

"Ah, let's have a couple of Sate Kambings to start, ah, and we'll share some Daguig Goreng, and some Kodok Goreng and ah, the Guila Kambing. And," Spook looked at Scott, "a couple of Heinekens?" Scott nodded. "And, if there's any way you could put that order into warp drive, my friend here," he pointed at Scott, "would appreciate it muchly."

"Very good," the dark skinned Indonesian waiter replied as he scurried back to the kitchen.

It still took half an hour for the appetizers to arrive. Scott chewed up three straws and tore two napkins into shreds while waiting.

"What is this," asked Scott as he voraciously dove into the food.

"Does it matter?"

"No," Scott bit into it. "Mmmmmmm . . .Holy shit, that's good, what is it?"

"Goat parts," the Spook said with a straight face.

Scott stopped chewing. "Which goat parts?" he mumbled staring over the top of his round glasses.

"The good parts," said the Spook taking two big bites. "Only the good parts."

"It's nothing like, eyeballs, or lips or . . ." Scott was grossing himself out.

"No, no, paysan, eat up. It's safe." The Spook made the Italian gesture for eating in reassurance. "Most of the time." The Spook chuckled as he ravaged the unidentifiable goat parts on his plate.

Scott looked suspiciously at the Spook, who seemed to be surviving. How bad could it be? It tasted great, phenomenal, but what is it? Fuck it. Scott wolfed down his goat parts in total ecstasy. The Spook was right. This was the best tasting food he had had, ever.

The rest of the meal was as sensorally exquisite as the appetizer. Scott felt relieved once the waiter had promised that the goat parts were from a goat roast, just like a rib roast or a pork roast. Nothing disgusting like ear lobes. Ecch!

"So you want to know why we do it," said the Spook in between nibbles of frog's legs. Scott had to think hard to realize that the Spook had shifted the conversation to hacking.

"It had occurred to me," responded Scott. "Why do you do it?"

"I've always liked biology, so hacking became the obvious choice," Spook said laughing. Scott looked perplexed but that didn't interrupt his voracious attack on the indescribably delicious foods on his plate.

"How old are you?" Asked the Spook.

"The Big four-oh is in range."

"Good, me too. Remember Marshall McCluhan?"

"The medium is the message guru." Scott had admired him and made considerable effort to attend a few of his highly motivating lectures.

"Exactly. He predicted it 20 years early. The Networked Society." The Spook paused to toss more food into his mouth. "How much do you know about computers?"

"I'm learning," Scott said modestly. Whenever asked that question he assumed that he was truly ignorant on the subject despite his engineering degree. It was just that computers had never held the fascination for him that they did for others.

"O.K., let me give you the low down." The Spook sucked down the last of the Heineken and motioned to the waiter for two more. He wiped his lips and placed his napkin beside the well cleaned plate. "At what point does something become alive?"

"Alive?" Scott mused. "When some carbon based molecules get the right combination of gases in the proper proportions of temperature and pressure . . ."

"C'mon, guy. Use your imagination," the Spook scoffed with his eyes twinkling. "Biologically, you're right, but philosophically that's pretty fucking lame. Bart Simpson could come up with better than that." The Spook could be most insulting without even trying. "Let me ask you, is the traffic light system in New York alive?"

"No way!" Retorted Scott. "It's dead as a doornail, programmed for grid lock." They both laughed at the ironic choice for analogy.

"Seriously, in many ways it can be considered alive," the Spook said. "It uses electricity as its source of power or food. Therefore it eats, has a digestive system and has waste product; heat. Agreed?"

Scott nodded. That was a familiar personification for engineering students.

"And, if you turn off the power, it stops functioning. A temporary starvation if you will. It interacts with its environment; in this case with sensors and switches that react to the conditions at any particular moment. And lastly, and most importantly, it has purpose." Scott raised his eyebrows skeptically. "The program, the rules, those are its purpose. It is coincidentally the same purpose that its designers had, but nonetheless it has purpose."

"That doesn't make it alive. It can't think, as we do, and there is no ego or personality," Scott said smugly.

"So what? Since when does plankton or slime mold join Mensa? That's sentience." Spook walked right over Scott's comment.

"O.K.," Scott acquiesced. "I'm here to play Devil's Advocate, not make a continent of enemies."

"Listen, you better learn something early on," Spook leaned in over the table. His seriousness caught Scott's attention. "You can disagree with us all you want, that's not a problem, most everyone does. But, we do expect fairness, personal and professional."

"Meaning?"

"Meaning," the dimples in Spook's smiling cheeks radiated camaraderie. "Don't give up on an argument so early if you believe in it. That's a chicken shit way out of taking a position. Real kindergarten." The Spook finished off his Heineken in two gulps.

Scott's tension eased realizing the Spook wanted the debate, the confrontation. This week could be a lot more fun than he had thought.

"At any rate, can you buy into that, that the traffic systems are alive?" The Spook asked again.

"I'll hold my final judgment in abeyance, but for sake of discussion, let's continue," acquiesced Scott.

"Fair enough. In 1947, I think that was the year, some guy said that he doubted there would be world wide market for more than three computers."

Scott choked on his beer. "Three? Ha! What mental moron came up with that?"

"Watson. Thomas Watson, founder of IBM," the Spook said dead pan.

"You're kidding."

"And what about Phil Estridge?"

"Who's that?"

"Another IBM'er," said the Spook. "He was kind of a renegade, worked outside of the mainstream corporate IBM mold. His bosses told him, *'hey, we need a small cheap computer to tie to our bigger computers. This little company Apple is selling too many for us not to get involved. By the way, Corporate Headquarters thinks this project is a total waste of money; they've been against it from the outset. So, you have 8 months.'* They gave him 8 months to build a computer that would set standards for generations of machines. And, he pulled it off. Damned shame he died.

"So, here we have IBM mis-call two of the greatest events in their history yet they still found ways to earn tens of billions of dollars. Today we have, oh, around 90 million computers in the world. Ninety million, that's a shitload of computers. And we're cranking out twelve million more each year.

"Then we tied over fifty million of these computers together. We used local area networks, wide area networks, dedicated phone lines, gate ways, transmission backbones all in an effort to allow more and more computers to talk to each other. With the phone company as the fabric of the interconnection of our computers we have truly become a networked society. Satellites further tighten the weave on the fabric of the Network. With a modem and telephone you have the world at your fingertips." The Spook raised his voice during his passionate monologue.

"Now we can use computers in our cars or boats and use cellular phone links to create absolute networkability. In essence we have a new life form to deal with, the world wide information Network."

"Here's where we definitely diverge," objected Scott, hands in the air. "Arriving at the conclusion that a computer network is a life form, requires a giant leap of faith that I have trouble with."

"Not faith, just understanding," the Spook said with sustained vigor. "We can compare networks to the veins and blood vessels in our bodies. The heart pumps the blood, the lungs replenish it, the other organs feed off of it. The veins serve as the thoroughfares for blood just as networks serve as highways for information. However, the Network is not static, where a fixed road map describes its operation. The Network is in a constant state of flux, in all likelihood never to repeat the same pattern of connections again.

"So you admit," accused Scott, "that a network is just a conduit, one made of copper and silicon just as the vein in a conduit?"

"Yes, a smart conduit," the Spook insisted. "Some conduits are much smarter than others. The Network itself is a set of rules by which information is transmitted over a conductive material. You can't touch a network. Sure, you can touch the computer, the network wire, you can touch the bits and pieces that make up the Network, but you cannot touch the Network. The Network exists as a synergistic byproduct of many dissimilar and physically isolated devices."

"I must admit Spook . . ."

"That's Mister Spook to you earth man," joked the Spook as he paid the waiter. "Sorry, continue."

"I could probably nickel and dime you into death by boredom on several points, but I will concede that they are arguable and better relegated for a long evening of total disagreement. For the sake of world peace I will not press the issue now."

"How very kind," mocked the Spook. "Let's get out of here, take a walk, and I'll continue your education."

If anyone else spoke to Scott so derogatorily, there would be instant conflict. The Spook, though, didn't raise the defense mechanism in Scott. Spook was actually a likable fellow, if somewhat arrogant.

They walked back down Nieuwezuds Voorburgwal and Beursplein very slowly. The Spook lit up another joint.

"What's this," said Scott appreciatively, "an endless supply?"

"When in Rome!" replied Spook. The brightly lit grand boulevard was a sample of the energy that permeates the Amsterdam night life. The train station was still a hub of activity in the winter darkness of early evening.

"So look at the Network. You can cut off its tentacles, that's better than legs and feet in this case, and they will reappear, reconnect somewhere else. Alternate routing bypasses trouble spots, self diagnostics help the Network doctors, priority and preferences are handled according to a clear set of rules." Spook waved his hands to reinforce his case.

"That's, ah, quite, ah, a theory. What do the experts say about this?" Scott was teetering on the edge of partial acceptance.

"Experts? We're the experts. That's why we hack, don't you see?" The answer was so obvious it didn't deserve a question. "Now, I can only speak for myself, but I find that the Network organism itself is what's interesting. The network, the spontaneously grown information organism that covers most of the planet Earth. I believe that is why all hackers start hacking. Innate curiosity about the way things work. Then, before our eyes, and behind the back of the world, the planet gets connected, totally connected to each other, and we haven't examined the ramifications of that closeness, computer-wise that is. That's what we do." The Spook sounded satisfied with his explanation.

Scott thought about it as they crossed Kerksplein and over canals to the Oude Zijds Voorbugwal. Was the Spook spouting off a lot of rationalized bullshit or were he and the likes of him actually performing valuable services, acting as technological sociologists to five billion clients? If a network was alive, thought Scott, it was alive in the sense that a town or village is alive, as the sum of its parts. As a society is alive. If the computer terminal and its operator are members of a global village, as are thousands of other computer users, might that not be considered a society? Communications are indeed different, but Scott remembered that Flatland was considered a valid society with a unique perspective on the universe. Is it any different than the telephone, which connects everyone on the planet? Shit, Spook made some sense.

They paused on a bridge by the Voorsbugwal, and a few blocks down the canal Scott saw a concentration of bright lights. "What's that?" He asked.

"Poontang," the Spook said lasciviously.

"Say wha?" Scott asked

"This is Horny Heaven, Ode to Orgasm, Pick a Perversion." The Spook proudly held his arms out.

"Aha, the Red Light District," Scott added dryly.

"Don't take the romance out of it, this is sleaze at it's best. Believe me I know." Somehow Scott had no doubts. With the way Spook was passionately describing the specific acts and services available within the 10 square block hotbed of sex, Scott knew that the Spook was no novice. They grabbed a couple of Heinekens from a bar and slowly strolled down one side of the carnal canal.

"I was going to go to the Yab Yub tonight, but since you've never been here before, I figured I owed you a tour."

"Yab Yub? Am I supposed to know . . ."

"The biggest bestest baddest whorehouse in Amsterdam," said Spook exuberantly.

"O.K., fine, and this is . . ."

"The slums."

"Thanks a lot," Scott said sarcastically.

"No, this is for middle class tourist sex. Yab Yub is first class but this'll do me just fine. How about you? Ready for some serious debauching?" The Spook queried.

"Huh?" Scott laughed anxiously. "Oh, I don't know, I've never been terribly fond of hookers."

"First time when I was 13. My uncle took me to a whorehouse for my birthday. Shit," the Spook fondly grinned at the memory. "I'll never forget the look on my mom's face when he told her. She lectured him for a week. Christ," he paused. "It's so funny, you know. My uncle's gay."

Scott was enjoying the conversation and the company of the Spook. Americans meeting up with kindred Americans in a foreign land is a breath of fresh air and the Spook provided that.

Scott window shopped as they walked, sidestepping the very few venturesome cars which attempted to penetrate the horny humanity on the crowded cobblestone streets. The variety of sexual materials was beyond comprehension. Spook seemed to be avidly fluent in their description and application. In one window, a spiked dildo of emmense girth and length dominated the display. Scott grimaced at the weapon while the Spook commented on it's possible uses at an adult sit'n'spin party.

"Here's the live sex show," the Spook said invitingly. "Pretty wild. Look at the pictures." Scott leaned over to view a set of graphic photographs that would have caused the Meese Commission on Pornography to double dose on its Geritol.

"Shit, they show this stuff on the street, huh?" Asked the surprised Scott. He wasn't naive, it's just quite a shock to see such graphic sexuality in such a concentration and in such an open manner. On Sundays when the Red Light District is closed until 6 PM, many Dutch families use the window dressings as the textbook for their children's' sex education. "No, let's keep going," Scott said unconvinced he would partake of the pleasures.

"Isn't this great?" The Spook blurted out as Scott was looking in the window of one of the hundred plus sex shops. "I just love it. Remember I was telling you about freedom in Amsterdam? It's kind of like the hacker's ethic."

Spook was going to equate sex and hacking? "Is that 'cause all hacker's are hard up?" Scott laughed.

"No, dig it." The Spook suddenly stopped to face Scott. "Freedom, total freedom implies and requires responsibility. Without that, the system would collapse into anarchy. Hacking is a manifestation of freedom. Once we have cracked a system, and are in it, we have freedom to do anything we want. But that freedom brings responsibility too, and, just like with sex so freely available, legally, it must be handled with care." Spook was sermonizing again, but was making more sense. His parallels were concise and poignant.

They walked further into the heart of the District and the Spook was constantly distracted by the quantity of red lights over the basement and first floor windows. He wanted to closely examine the contents of every one. In each window was a girl, sometimes two, clad in either a dental floss bathing suit or a see through penoire. Scott enjoyed the views, but thought that the Spook was acting somewhat obsessively. The calm, professional, knowledgeable hacker had reverted into a base creature, driven by hormonal compulsion. Or then again, maybe they were just stoned.

"I gotta pick the right one, just the right one," the Spook said. "Let's see what else is available. Got to find you a good one, too."

Scott shook his head. "I don't know . . ."

"What, you don't wanna get laid? What's the matter with you?" The Spook couldn't believe his ears.

The sheer intensity of the omnipresent sexual stimulation gave Scott the urge to pause and ask himself why. The desire was physically manifest, but the psychology of hookers; it wasn't his style. In the three years since he and Maggie had split, Scott occassioned to spend time with many ladies. He had kept himself in reasonable shape without doing becoming fanatic about it, and his high metabolism helped keep the body from degenerating ahead of schedule. So he had had his share of companionship and opportunity, but right now, he was enjoying the freedom of his work and the pleasures that

that offered. If a woman was in the cards, so be it, but it was not essential at the moment.

"Nothing, it's just that, well, I prefer to know the lady, if you know what I mean."

"Oh, no problem!" The Spook had an answer. "That's an all nighter and will cost you 1000 guilders."

"No, no," Scott said quickly. "That's not it. I just don't get a charge from hookers. Now, if some friends set it up to like a real pick-up, at the beach, a bar, whatever, as long as I didn't know. That could prove interesting. Hmmmm." He smiled to himself. "But honestly? I been a couple of times, just for giggles. And boy was it giggles."

Scott laughed out loud at the memory. "The first time it was a friend's birthday and a bunch of us put up enough to get him laid at the Chicken Ranch." That was the evening where Scott had lost almost two hours of his life on the drive back to Vegas. He speculated to himself, in private, that he may been abducted by alien creatures from a UFO. Right.

"I know the place," added the Spook.

"I was designated drunk driver so I drove him over to the high desert in the company van, about an hour's drive. Before we went in I insisted on a couple of beers. He was getting laid and I was nervous. Go figure. At any rate, the security cameras let us in and two very attractive ladies in slinky gowns lead us over to the couch. They immediately assumed that we were both there for, well, the services. I was too embarrassed to say no, that I wasn't interested, but then out came a line of 20 of the most gorgeous girls you could imagine. The madam, I forget her name, stepped in and begged our indulgence for the interruption. It seems, she said, that the BBC was filming a documentary on brothels, and they had a camera crew in the next room, and would we mind too terribly much if they filmed us?" Scott feigned extreme shock.

"Filmed you? For TV? Even I won't go that far," the Spook said impressed with Scott's story. "My movies are all first run private. Alphabetical from Adelle to Zelda."

"Not film that, pervert!" He had pegged the Spook. "They only filmed the selection process, the initial meetings and then the walk down the hallways to the bedrooms."

"So what'd you do?" The Spook asked with interest.

"We did the camera bit, Jim got laid and I take the fifth."

"You chicken shit asshole," hollered the laughing Spook.

Scott took that as a compliment from the male slut to whom he was speaking. "Listen, that was a long time ago, before I was married, and I don't want it to screw up our divorce. Three years of bliss."

The Spook kept laughing. "You really are a home boy, huh?" He gasped for air. They continued down a side street and back up the Oude Zijds Achterburgwal, the other main canal in the District, so Spook could check out more windows. Those with the curtain drawn indicated that either services were being rendered or that it was lunch hour. Hard to tell.

As they passed the Guys and Gals Sex Shop, the Spook abruptly stopped and stepped back toward the canal. He whistled to himself in appreciation of the sex goddesses that had captured his attention. In the basement window was a stunning buxom brunette, wearing an invisible g-string and bra. She oozed sexuality with her beckoning lips and fingers when she spotted the Spook's interest. In the first floor window above the brunette were two perfectly voluptuous poster blondes, in matching transparent peignoirs. They too, saw the Spook, and attempted to seduce him to their doorway. Scott was impressed that the ladies were so attractive.

"Some sweet meat, huh?" Said the Spook ogling his choices. "Well are you or aren't you?" He asked with finality. "I'm all systems go. You get first choice: 2 from window A or 1 from window B. What'll it be?"

Scott responded immediately. "I got a safer way. There are five billion people on the planet, and at any given time at least a million have to be having sex. So all I have to do is tune into the Planetary Consciousness, the ultimate archetype, and have an orgasm anytime I want."

"You're a sick motherfucker," laughed the Spook. "Transcendental group sex. At least I can tell the difference between pussy and praying." He asked Scott again to pick a girl.

"I have to pass. It's just not my thing." Spook glared at him askance. "No really, go ahead. I'm a bit tired, I just arrived this morning." He had forgotten to take his 3 hour afternoon nap and it was close to 6 in the morning body time. "I'll see you at the conference tomorrow. All right?"

"Fuckin' A!" The Spook beamed. "I get 'em all." He motioned to the girls that he would like to hire all three of them, at once. They indicated with their lips and hands that that would be a fine idea. "Listen, I don't mean to be rude, but . . ." the Spook said to Scott as he proceeded up the stairs to meet the female triumvirate. He turned briefly in the open doorway with two of the girls tugging at his clothes. "Scott! What happens if the medium gets sick? Think about it." The door closed behind the Spook as the girls shed their clothes.

"Medium? Jeez you are really fucked," laughed Scott. "Pervert!" He called out as the window curtains closed.

Scott got directions to the *Eureka!* from a live sex show salesman. For all the walking he and the Spook had done, miles and miles, it was odd that they had ended up only a few blocks away from the hotel. Ah, but that would figure, thought Scott. The Sex Starved Spook was staying at the *Europa* around the corner from Sin Street. Scott rolled a joint of his own to enjoy for the pleasant evening promenade home along the canals. Spook, what a character. In one breath, perfectly rational, but then the Jekyll and Hyde hormone hurricane. Wow.

What Scott Mason could never have imagined, indeed quite the opposite, was that the Spook was unable to respond to the three very attentive ladies he had hired for that very purpose. Nothing. No matter what stimuli they effected, the Spook's brain could not command his body to respond. His confusion alternated with embarrassment which made the problem only worse. Never before had the Spook had such a problem. Never. One of the ladies spoke to him kindly. "Hey, it happens to everyone once in a while." At hearing that he jumped up, removed the loose condom and zipped his pants while screaming, "Not to me. It doesn't happen to me!"

Scott did not know that the Spook bolted into the street and started running, in panic, away from the scene of his most private of failures. He ran all the way, in fact beating Scott to his hotel. He was driven by the terror of the first sexual failure in his life. The Spook felt emasculated as he sought a rationalization that would allow him to retain a shred of dignity.

He was used to commanding women, not being humiliated by them. What was wrong? Women fell all over him, but why this? This of all things? The Spook fell asleep on the top of his bed with his clothes on.

Scott did not know that he would not be seeing the Spook tomorrow.

* * * * *

Wednesday, January 6
Washington, D.C.

"Eight more!" exclaimed Charlie Sorenson into Martin Templer's face. "What the hell is going on?" The private office on twentieth and "L" Street was well guarded by an efficient receptionist who believed she worked for an international import export firm. Consulting offices were often easier for senior intelligence officials to use for clandestine, unrecorded meetings than one's own office. In the interest of privacy, naturally.

The two NSA and CIA agents from "P" Street held their clandestine meeting in a plain, windowless office meagerly furnished with a desk, a couple of chairs and a file cabinet.

Charlie turned his back on Templer and sighed. "I'm sorry, Marty. It's not you." He paced to the other side of the small confining room. "I'm getting pressure from all sides. That damned FBI guy is making a nuisance of himself. Asking too many questions. The media smells a conspiracy and the Director is telling me to ignore it." Sorenson stood in front of Templer. "And, now, no, it's not bad enough, but 8 more of the mothers go off. Shit!" He slammed his fist onto the desk.

"We can explain one to the Pentagon, but nine?" Martin asked skeptically.

"See what I mean?" Sorenson pointed.

Sorenson and Templer attended the ECCO and CERT roundups twice a week since they began after the first EMP-T explosion.

"These are the SATS?" Templer leaned over to the desk. Corners of several high resolution satellite photographs sneaked out from a partially open folder. Sorenson opened the folder and spread the photos across the surface. They weren't optical photographs, but the familiar map shapes of the central United States were visible behind swirls and patterns of a spectrum of colors. The cameras and computer had been instructed to look at selected bandwidths, just as infrared vision lets one see at night. In this case, though, the filters excluded everything but frequencies of the electromagentic spectrum of interest.

"Yeah," Sorenson said, pointing at one of the photos. "This is where we found the first one." On one of the photos, where an outline of the United States was visible, a dot of fuzzy light was visible in the Memphis, Tennessee area.

"That's an EMP-T bomb?" asked Templer.

"The electromagnetic signature, in certain bandwidths is the same as from a nuclear detonation." Sorenson pulled another photo out. It was a computer enhanced blowup of the first satellite photo. The bridges across the Mississippi were clearly visible. The small fuzzy dot from the other photograph became a larger fuzzy cloud of white light.

"I didn't know we had geosyncs over us, too," Templer said lightly.

"Officially we don't," Sorenson said seriously. Then he showed his teeth and said, "unofficially we have them everywhere."

"So who was hit?"

"Here?" He pointed at Memphis. "Federal Express. A few hours ago. They're down. Can't say when they'll be back. Thank God no one was killed. They weren't so lucky in Texas."

Sorenson pulled a couple more photographs and a fuzzy dot and it's fuzzy cloud mate were clearly visible in the Houston area. "EDS Computers," said Sorenson. "Six dead, 15 injured. They do central processing for hundreds of companies. Every one, gone. And then here." He scattered more photos with the now recognizable fuzzy white dots.

"Mid-State Farm Insurance, Immigration and Naturalization, National Bank, General Inter-Dynamics, CitiBank, and the Sears mail order computers." Sorenson spoke excitedly as he listed the latest victims of the magnetic cardiac arrest that their computer systems, and indeed, their entire organization suffered.

"Press?"

"Like stink on shit."

"What do they know?"

"Too much."

"What can we do?"

"Get to the bottom of this before Mason does."

* * * * *

Chapter 19

Thursday, January 7
Amsterdam, Holland

The following morning Scott awoke without telephone intervention by the front desk. He felt a little on the slow side, an observation he attributed to either the time difference, not the jet lag, or the minor after effect of copius cannabis consumption. The concierge called a cab and Scott told the driver where he thought he was going. Ya, no problem, it's a short ride.

To Scott's surprise he found himself passing by the same sex emporium where he had left the Spook last evening. Scott reminded himself to ask Spook how it went. The taxi stopped in front of an old building that appeared to have had no signs of use for years. It was number 44, but just in case, Scott asked the driver to wait a moment. He walked up the door and finding no bell, rapped on the heavy wooden door.

"Ya?" A muffled voice asked through the door.

"Is Jon there? This is Scott Mason." Scott knowingly looked at the cab driver.

"Who?"

Scott looked at the number again and then remembered what Jon had told him. "Sorry. This is Repo Man. Kirk said you'd expect me."

"Ah, ya! Repo Man." The door opened and Scott happily waved off the cab. "Welcome, please, come in." Scott entered a dark chamber as the door closed behind him. "I am Clay, that's French for key."

Wonderful, thought Scott. "Thanks for the invite. Is Jon here?"

"Everyone is here."

"I thought it didn't begin until eleven," Scott said looking at his watch.

"Ah, ya, well," the Dutch accented Clay said. "It is difficult to stop sometimes. We have been here all night."

Scott followed Clay up a darkened flight of steps. At mid landing Clay opened a door and suddenly the dungeon-like atmosphere vanished. Inside the cavernous room were perhaps 200 people, mostly men, excitedly conversing and huddling over computers of every imaginable model. The high ceiling was liberally dressed with fluorescent tubing which accentuated the green hues from many of the computer monitors. The walls were raw brick and the sparse decorations were all computer related. Windows at the two ends of the building added enough daylight to take some of the edge off of the pallid green aura.

"What should I do?" Asked Scott looking around the huge room which was probably overcrowded by modern safety counts.

"The Flying Dutchman said he will see you a little later," Clay said. "Many of our members know Repo Man is a reporter, and you are free to look and ask anything. Please enjoy yourself." Clay quickly disappeared into the congregation.

Scott suddenly felt abandoned and wished he could disappear. Like those dreams where you find yourself stark naked in a public place. He felt that his computer naivete was written all over his face and he would be judged thus, so instead he tried to ignore it by perusing the walls. He became amused at the selection of art, poster art, Scotch taped to the brick.

The first poster had Daffy Duck, or reasonable facsimile thereof, prepared to bring a high speed sledgehammer in contact with a keyboard. "Hit any key to continue," was the simple poster's message. Another portrayed a cobweb covered skeleton sitting behind a computer terminal with a repairman standing over him asking a pertinent question. "System been down long?"

One of the ruder posters consisted of Ronald Reagan with a superimposed hand making a most obscene manual gesture. The poster was entitled, "Compute This!"

Scott viewed the walls as if in an art gallery, not a hackers convention. He openly laughed when he saw a poster from the National Computer Security Center, a working division of the National Security Agency. A red, white and blue Uncle Sam, finger pointing, beckoned, "We want YOU! to secure your computer." In an open white space on the poster someone wrote in, "Please list name and date if you have already cracked into an NSA computer." Beneath were a long list of Hacker Handles with the dates they had entered the super secret agency's computers. Were things really that bad, Scott asked himself.

"Repo Man?"

Scott turned quickly to see a large, barrel chested, red haired man with an untamed beard in his early forties approach him rapidly. The man was determined in his gait. Scott answered, "Yes . . .?"

"Ya, I'm the Flying Dutchman," he said hurriedly in a large booming voice. "Welcome." He vigorously shook Scott's hand with a wide smile hidden behind the bushy red face. "You enjoyed Amsterdam last night, ya?" He expected a positive answer. Sex was no crime here.

"Well," Scott blushed. "I must say it was a unique experience," he said carefully so as not to offend Holland's proud hosts. "But I think the Spook had more fun than I did."

The Flying Dutchman's hand went limp. "Spook? Did you say Spook?" His astonishment was clear.

"Yeah, why?" Scott asked.

"The Spook? Here? No one has seen him in years."

"Yeah, well he's alive and well and screwing his brains out with three of Amsterdam's finest," Scott said with amusement. "What's the big deal?"

"The Spook, ya this is goot," the Flying Dutchman said clapping his hands together with approval. "He was the greatest phreak of his day. He retired years ago, and only been seen once or two times maybe. He is a legend."

"A phreak?"

"Oh, ya, ya. A phreak," he said speaking rapidly. "Before computers, in the 1960's and 1970's, hacking meant fighting the phone company. In America you call it Ma Bell, I believe. Captain Crunch was the epitome of phone phreaks."

These names were a bit much, thought Scott, but might add a sense of levity to his columns. "Captain Crunch?" Scott asked with skepticism.

"Ya, Captain Crunch. He blew the plastic whistle from a Captain Crunch cereal box into the phone," the Flying Dutchman held an invisible whistle to his lips. "And it opened up an inside line to make long distance calls. Then he built and sold Blue Boxes which recreated the tones to make free calls."

"Phreaking and computer hacking, they're the same?"

"Ya, ya, especially for the older hackers." The Flying Dutchman patted himself on the stomach. "You see hacking, some call it cracking, is taking a system to its limit. Exploring it, mastering the machine. The phones, computers, viruses, it's all hacking. You understand."

"Spook called hacking a technique for investigating new spontaneously generated lifeforms. He said a network was a living being. We got into quite an argument about it." Scott sounded mildly derisive of the theory.

The Dutchman crossed his arms, grinned wide and rocked back and forth on his heels. "Ya, ya. That sounds like the Spook. Cutting to the heart of the issue. Ya, you see, we all have our reasons why we hack, but ya, Spook is right. We forget sometimes that the world is one giant computer, with thousands and millions of arms, just like the brain. The neurons," he pointed at his head, "are connected to each other with synapses. Just like a computer network."

The Flying Dutchman's explanation was a little less ethereal than the Spook's and Scott found himself anticipating further enlightenment.

"The neuron is a computer. It can function independently, but because it's capacity is tiny, a neuron is really quite limited in what it can achieve alone. The synapse is like the network wire, or phone company wiring. It connects the neurons or computers together." The Dutchman spoke almost religiously as he animatedly drew wires and computers in the air to reinforce the concept. "Have you heard of neural networks?"

"Absolutely," Scott said. "The smart chips that can learn."

"Ya, exactly. A neural network is modeled after the brain, too. It is a very large number of cells, just like the brain's cells, that are only connected to each other in the most rudimentary way."

"Like a baby's brain?" Scott offered.

"Ya, ya, just like a baby. Very good. So like the baby, the neural net grows connections as it learns. The more connections it makes, the smarter it gets."

"Both the baby and the network?"

"Ya," Dutchman laughed. "So as the millions of neural connections are made, some people learn skills that others don't and some computers are better suited to certain tasks than others. And now there's a global neural network growing, across the face of the planet. Millions more computers are added and we connect them together, until any computer can talk to any other computer. Ya, the Spook is very much right. The Network is alive, and it is still learning."

Scott was entering a world where the machines, the computers, were personified, indeed imbued with a life of their own by their creators and their programmers. A highly complex world where inter-relatedness is infinitely more important than the specific function. Connections are issue. Didn't Spook remind him that the medium is the message?

But where, questioned Scott, is the line between man and machine? If computers are stupid, and man must program them to give them the appearance of intelligence, then the same must be true of the Network, the global information network. Therefore, when a piece of the Network is programmed to learn how to plan for future Network expansion and that piece of the Network calls another computer on the Network to inquire as to how it is answering the same problem for different conditions, don't man and machine merge? Isn't the Network acting as an extension of man? But then, a hammer is a tool as well, and no one calls a hammer a living being.

Unto itself it is not alive, Scott reasoned. The Network merely emulates the growth patterns and behavior of the cranial highway system. He was ready to concede that a network was more alive than a hammer, but he could not bring himself to carry the analogy any further yet.

"That gives me a lot to think about," Scott assured the Dutchman.

"Ya, ya, it does. Do you understand quantum physics?"

What the hell would make him ask that question, thought Scott. "I barely passed Quantum 101, the math was too far out for me, but, yes," he laughed kindly, "I do remember the basics. Very basic."

"Goot. In the global Network there is no way to predict where the next information packet will be sent. Will it start here," the Dutchman motioned to his far left, "or here? There's no way to know. All we can say, just as in physics, is that there is a statistical probability of data being transferred between any two points. Chance. And we can also view the Network in operation as both a wave and a particle."

"Wait," stopped Scott. "You've just gone over my head, but I get the point, I think. You and your associates really believe that this global Network is an entity unto itself and that it is growing and evolving on its own as we speak?"

"Ya, exactly. You see, no one person is responsible for the Network, its growth or its care. Like the brain, many different regions control their own piece of the Network. And, the Network can still function normally even if pieces of it are disconnected. The split brain studies."

"And you're the caretakers for the Network?" doubted Scott.

"No. As I said we all have our reasons. The common denominator is that we treat the Network as an incredibly powerful organism about which we know very, very little. That is our function - to learn."

The argument that the Flying Dutchman made was strong, and Scott was here to report, not create an international incident. "What is it that you do? For a living?"

"Ah, ya. I am Professor of Technological Sociology at the University of Amsterdam. The original proposal for my research came from personal beliefs and concerns; about the way the human race has to learn to cope in the face of great technology leaps. NATO is funding the research."

"NATO," exclaimed Scott. "They fund hacking?"

"No," laughed the Dutchman. "They know that hacking is necessary to gather the raw data my research requires, so they pretend not to notice or care. What we are trying to do is predict what the Baby, the global Network will look and act like when it grows up."

"Isn't crystal ball gazing easier?"

"Ya, it may be," the Dutchman agreed. "But now, why don't you look around? I am sure you will find it most educational."

The Dutchman asked again about the Spook. "Is he really here in Amsterdam?" *Yup!* "And he said he'd be here today?" *Yup!* "The Spook, at the conference? He hasn't made an appearance in years." *Well, that's what he told me, he'd be here.*

Scott profusely thanked his host and assured him that yes, he would ask for anything he needed. Thank you. Kirk had been vindicated, thought Scott who had expected a group of pimply faced adolescents with nerd shirts to be bouncing around like Spring Break in Fort Lauderdale. Instead he found a dedicated group of mostly men, with a set of principles and doctrines to which they adhered strictly. This was not an unruly bunch of hooligans changing their grades in the school computer. Right or wrong, this group cared deeply about what they were doing, and by and large, each one could rationalize a defensible argument to justify their activities.

Scott slowly explored the tables loaded with various types of computer gear. IBM clones were the most common, but an assortment of older machines, a CP/M or two, even a Commodore PET proved that expensive new equipment was not needed to become a respected hacker. Scott reminded himself that this group was the elite of hackerdom. These were the Hacker's Hackers.

In his discussions with Kirk, Scott figured he would see some of the tools of the trade. But he had no idea of the level of sophistication that was openly, and perhaps, illegally, being demonstrated. Then again, maybe that's why they hold their Hacker Ho Downs in Amsterdam.

Scott learned something very critical early on.

"Once you let one of us inside your computer, it's all over. The system is ours." The universal claim by hackers.

Scott no longer had any trouble accepting that. "So the security guy's job," one short balding middle aged American hacker said. "Is to keep us out. I'm a cracker." What's that? "The cracker is kind of like a safecracker, or lock picker. It's my job to figure out how to get into the computers." Scott had to stifle a giggle when he found out that this slight man's handle was appropriately Waldo.

Waldo went on to explain that he was a henpecked CPA who needed a hobby that would bore his wife to tears. So he locked himself in the basement, far away from her, and got hooked on computers. He found that rummaging through other computers was an amusing alternative to watching Honeymooner reruns while his wife kvetched. After a while, he said he discovered that he had a talent for cracking through the front doors of computers. On the professional hacker circuit that made Waldo a valuable commodity. The way it works, he explained, was that he would trade access codes for outlines of the contents of the computers. If he wanted to look further, he maintained a complete indexing system on the contents of thousands of computers world wide. He admitted it was the only exciting part of his life. "The most fun a CPA has," he said calmly, "is cutting up client's credit cards. But me," he added proudly, "I've been in and out of the IRS computers more times than Debbie did Dallas."

"The IRS computers? You've been in there?"

"Where else does a CPA go, but to the scene of the crime." Waldo laughed at his joke. "At first it was a game, but once I got into the IRS backplane, which connects the various IRS districts together, the things I found scared me. No one is in control over there. No one. They abuse taxpayers, basically honest taxpayers who are genuinely in trouble and need some understanding by their government. Instead they are on the receiving end of a vicious attack by a low level government paper slave who gets his thrills by seizing property. The IRS is immune from due process." Scott immediately thought of Tyrone and his constitutional ravings the other night.

"The IRS's motto is, 'guilty until we cash the check'. And IRS management ignores it. Auditors are on a quota basis, and if they don't recover their allotted amounts of back taxes, they can kiss their jobs goodbye." The innocent looking Waldo, too, had found a cause, a raison d'être, for hacking away at government computers.

"You know that, for a fact?" Asked Scott. This alone was a major story. Such a policy was against everything the Constitution stood for. Waldo nodded and claimed to have seen the internal policy memoranda. Who was in charge? Essentially, said Waldo, no one. It was anarchy, and you have to fight anarchy with anarchy. Besides, he continued, of all the government systems he had cracked, the IRS computers were absolute child's play.

"They have the worst security of any agency that should by all rights have the best. It's a crime against American citizens. Our rights and our privacy have shriveled to nothing." Waldo, the small CPA, extolled the virtues of fighting the system from within. From within he could battle the computers that had become the system.

"Have you ever, shall I say, fixed files in the IRS computers?"

"Many times," Waldo said proudly. "For my clients who were being screwed, sometimes I am asked to help. It's all part of the job," he said of his beloved avocation.

"How many systems have you cracked?" Asked Scott, visibly impressed.

"I am," Waldo said modestly, "the best. I have cracked 1187 systems in 3 years. 1040 was my personal goal for a while, then 1099, but it's kind of open ended now."

"That's almost one a day?"

"You could look at it like that, but sometimes you can get into 10 or twenty in one day. You gotta remember," Waldo said with pride, "a lot of homework goes into this. You just don't decide one day to crack a system. You have to plan it."

"So how do you do it?"

"O.K., it's really pretty simple. D'you speak software?"

"Listen, you make it real simple, and I won't interrupt. OK?"

"Interrupt. Hah! That's a good one. Here, let me show you on the computer," Waldo said as he leaned over to peck at the keyboard. "The first step to getting into computers is to find where they are located, electronically speaking, O.K.?" Scott agreed that you needed the address of the bank before you could rob it.

"So what we do is search for computers by running a program, like an exchange autodialer. Here, look here," Waldo said pointing at the computer screen. "We select the area code here, let's say 203, that's Connecticut. Then we pick the prefix, the first three numbers, that's the local exchange. So let's choose 968," he entered the numbers carefully. "That's Stamford. By the way, I wrote this software myself." Waldo spoke of his software as a proud father would of his first born son. Scott patted him on the back, urging him to continue.

"So we ask the computer to call every number in the 203-968 area sequentially. When the number is answered, the computer records whether a voice, a live person answered, or a computer answered or if it was a fax machine." Scott never had imagined that hacking was so systematic.

"Then, the computer records its findings and we have a complete list of every computer in that area," Waldo concluded.

"That's 10,000 phone calls," Scott realized. "It must cost a fortune and take forever?"

"Nah, not a dime. The phone company has a hole. It takes 200 milliseconds before a connection charge is made. It takes my program less than a second to record the response and we're off to the next call. It's all free, courtesy of TPC," Waldo bragged.

"TPC?" Questioned Scott.

"The Phone Company," Waldo chuckled.

"I don't see how you can do the entire country that way, 10,000 calls at a shot. In New York there must be ten million phones."

"Yes," agreed Waldo. "It is a never ending job. Phone numbers change, computers come and go, security gets better. But you have to remember, there are a lot of other people out there doing the same thing, and we all pool our information. You could ask for the number to almost any computer in the world, and someone in our group, somewhere, will have the number and likely the passwords."

"Jesus . . ."

"I run my program at night, every night, when I sleep. On a good night, if the calls are connected quickly enough, I can go through about a thousand phone numbers. I figure roughly a month per prefix."

"I am amazed, simply amazed. Truly impressed," said Scott. "You know, you always kind of imagine these things are possible, but until it stares you in the face it's black magic."

"You wanna know the best part?" Waldo said teasingly. "I get paid for it, too." Waldo crouched over and spoke to Scott secretively. "Not everyone here approves, but, I sell lists to junk fax mail-order houses. They want the fax lists. On a good night I can clear a couple hundred while my modem does the dialing."

The underground culture of Scott's day, demonstrating against the war, getting gassed while marching by George Washington University, getting thrown out of a Nixon rally at Madison Square Garden seemed so innocent in comparison. He continued to be in awe of the possible applications for a technology not as benign as its creators had intended.

Scott met other hackers; they were proud of the term even with the current negative connotations it carried. He saw how systemic attacks against the front door to computers were the single biggest challenge to hackers; the proverbial chase before the catch, the romance to many.

At another tabletop laden with computers Scott learned that there are programs designed to try passwords according to certain rules. Some try every possible combination of letters and numbers, although that is considered an antique method of brute force. More sophisticated hackers use advanced algorithms which try to open the computer with 'likely' passwords. *It was all very scientific, the approach to the problem*, thought Scott.

He met communications gurus who knew more about the switching networks inside the phone company than AT&T engineers. They had complete diagrams and function calls and source code for even the latest software revisions on the 4ESS switches and the new 5ESS that was being installed. "Once you're into the phone computers," one phone phreak extolled, "you have an immense amount of power at your fingertips. Incredible. Let me give you an example."

The speaker was another American, one that Scott would have classified as an ex-Berkeley-hippie still living in the past. His dirty shoulder length hair capped a skinny frame which held his jeans up so poorly that there was no question where the sun didn't shine.

"You know that the phone company is part of the Tri-Lateral Commission, working with Kissinger and the Queen of England to control the world. Right?" His frazzled speech was matched by an annoying habit of sweeping his stringy hair off his face every few words. "It's up to us to stop them."

Scott listened politely as Janis, (who adopted the moniker from his favorite singer) rewrote history with tortured explanations of how the phone company is the hidden seat of the American government, and how they have been lying to the public for decades. And the Rockefellers are involved too, he assured Scott.

"They could declare martial law, today, and take over the country. Those who control the communications control the power," he oracled. "Did you know," he took Scott into his confidence, "that phones are always on and they have computers recording everything you say and do in your own home. That's illegal!" Janis bellowed. *Not to mention crazy,* thought Scott.

One of Janis' associates came over to rescue Scott. "Sorry, he's a little enthusiastic and has some trouble communicating on the Earthly plane." Alva, as he called himself, explained coherently that with some of the newer security systems in place, it is necessary to manipulate the phone company switches to learn system passwords.

"For example, when we broke into a Bell computer that used CICIMS, it was tough to crack. But now they've added new security that, in itself, is flawless, albeit crackable," Alva explained. "Once you get past the passwords, which is trivial, the system asks you three unique questions about yourself for final identification. Pretty smart, huh?" Scott agreed with Alva, a voice of apparent moderation. "However, we were already in the phone switch computer, so we programmed in forwarding instructions for all calls that dialed that particular computer. We then intercepted the call and connected it to our computer, where we emulate the security system, and watched the questions and answers go back and forth. After a few hours, you have a hundred different passwords to use. There are a dozen other ways to do it, of course."

"Of course," Scott said sarcastically. Is nothing sacred? Not in this world it's not. All's fair in love, war and hacking.

The time flew as Scott learned what a tightly knitted clique the hackers were. The ethos 'honor among thieves' held true here as it did in many adolescent societies, most recently the American Old West. As a group, perhaps even a subculture, they were arduously taming new territory, each with their own vision of a private digital homestead. Each one taking on the system in their own way, they still needed each other, thus they looked aside if another's techno-social behavior was personally distasteful. The Network was big enough for everyone. A working anarchy that heralded the standard of John Paul Jones as their sole commandment: *Don't Tread On Me.*

He saw tapping devices that allowed the interception of computer data which traveled over phone lines. Line Monitors and Sniffers were commercially available, and legal; equipment that was nominally designed to troubleshoot networks. In the hands of a hacker, though, it graduated from being a tool of repair to an offensive weapon.

Small hand held radios were capable of listening in to the increasingly popular remote RF networks which do not require wires. Cellular phone eavesdropping devices permitted the owner to scan and focus on the conversation of his choice. Scott examined the electronic gear to find a manufacturer's identification.

"Don't bother, my friend," said a long haired German youth of about twenty.

"Excuse me?"

"I see you are looking for marks, yes?"

"Well, yes. I wanted to see who made these . . ."

"I make them, he makes them, we all make them," he said almost giddily. "This is not available from Radio Shack," he giggled. "Who needs them from the establishment when they are so easy to build."

Scott knew that electronics was indeed a garage operation and that many high tech initiatives had begun in entrepreneur's basements. The thought of home hobbyists building equipment which the military defends against was something of an anathema to Scott. He merely shook his head and moved on, thanking the makers of the eavesdropping machines for their demonstrations.

Over in a dimly lit corner, dimmer than elsewhere, Scott saw a number of people fiddling with an array of computers and equipment that looked surprisingly familiar. As he approached he experienced an immediate rush of déja vu. This was the same type of equipment that he had seen on the van, before it was blown up a couple of months ago. Tempest busting, he thought.

The group was speaking in German, but they were more than glad to switch to English for Scott's benefit. They sensed his interest as he poked around the assorted monitors and antennas and test equipment.

"Ah, you are interested in Van Eck?" asked one of the German hackers. They maintained a clean cut appearance, and through discussion Scott learned that they were funded as part of a university research project in Frankfurt.

Scott watched and listened as they set up a compelling demonstration. First, one computer screen displayed a complex graphic picture. Several yards away another computer displayed a foggy image that cleared as one of the students adjusted the antenna attached to the computer.

"Aha! Lock!" one of them said, announcing that the second computer would now display everything that the first computer did. The group played with color and black and white graphics, word processing screens and spreadsheets. Each time, in a matter of seconds, they 'locked' into the other computer successfully.

Scott was duly impressed and asked them why they were putting effort into such research. "Very simple," the apparent leader of the Frankfurt group said. "This work is classified in both your country and mine, so we do not have access to the answers we need. So, we build our own and now it's no more classified. You see?"

"Why do you need it?"

"To protect against it," they said in near unison. "The next step is to build efficient methods to fight the Van Eck."

"Doesn't Tempest do that?"

"Tempest?" the senior student said. "Ha! It makes the computer weigh a thousand pounds and the monitor hard to read. There are better ways to defend. To defend we must first know how to attack. That's basic."

"Let me ask you something," Scott said to the group after their lengthy demonstration. "Do you know anything about electromagnetic pulses? Strong ones?"

"Ya. You mean like from a nuclear bomb?"

"Yes, but smaller and designed to only hurt computers."

"Oh, ya. We have wanted to build one, but it is beyond our means."

"Well," Scott said smugly, "someone is building them and setting them off."

"Your stock exchange. We thought that the American government did it to prove they could."

An hour of ensuing discussion taught Scott that the technology that the DoD and the NSA so desperately spent billions to keep secret and proprietary was in common use. To most engineers, and Scott could easily relate, every problem has an answer. The challenge is to accomplish the so-called impossible. The engineer's pride.

Jon, the Flying Dutchman finally rescued Scott's stomach from implosion. "How about lunch? A few of the guys want to meet you. Give you a heavy dose of propaganda," he threatened.

"Thank God! I'm famished and haven't touched the stuff all day. Love to, it's on me," Scott offered. He could see Doug having a cow. How could he explain a thousand dollar dinner for a hundred hungry hackers?

"Say that too loud," cautioned the bearded Dutchman, "and you'll have to buy the restaurant. Hacking isn't very high on the pay scale."

"Be easy on me, I gotta justify lunch for an army to my boss, or worse yet, the beancounters." Dutchman didn't catch the idiom. "Never mind, let's keep it to a small regiment, all right?"

He never figured out how it landed on his shoulders, but Scott ended up with the responsibility of picking a restaurant and successfully guiding the group there. And Dutchman had skipped out without notifying anyone. Damned awkward, thought Scott. He assumed control, limited though it was, and led them to the only restaurant he knew, the Sarang Mas. The group blindly and happily followed. They even let him order the food, so he did his very best to impress the shit out of them by ordering without looking at the menu. He succeeded, with his savant phonetic memory, to order exactly what he had the night prior, but this time he asked for vastly greater portions.

As they were sating their pallets, and commenting on what a wonderful choice this restaurant was, Scott popped the same question to which he had previously been unable to receive a concise answer. Now that he had met this bunch, he would ask again, and if lucky, someone might respond and actually be comprehensible.

"I've been asking the same question since I got into this whole hacking business," Scott said savoring goat parts and sounding quite nonchalant. "And I've never gotten a straight answer. Why do you hack?" He asked. "Other than the philosophical credo of Network is Life, why do you hack?" Scott looked into their eyes. "Or are you just plain nosy?"

"I bloody well am!" said the one called Pinball who spoke with a thick Liverpudlian accent. His jeans were in tatters, in no better shape than his sneakers. The short pudgy man was mid-twenty-ish and his tall crewcut was in immediate need of reshaping.

"Nosy? That's why you hack?" Asked Scott in disbelief.

"Yeah, that's it, mate. It's great fun. A game the size of life." Pinball looked at Scott as if to say, that's it. No hidden meaning, it's just fun. He swallowed more of the exquisite food.

"Sounds like whoever dies with the most hacks wins," Scott said facetiously.

"Right. You got it, mate." Pinball never looked up from his food while talking.

Scott scanned his luncheon companions for reaction. A couple of grunts, no objection. What an odd assortment, Scott thought. At least the Flying Dutchman had been kind enough to assemble an English speaking group for Scott's benefit.

"We each have our reasons to hack," said the one who called himself Che2. By all appearance Che2 seemed more suited to a BMW than a revolutionary cabal. He was a well bred American, dressed casually but expensively. "We may not agree with each other, or anyone, but we have an underlying understanding that permits us to cooperate."

"I can tell you why I hack," said the sole German representative at the table who spoke impeccable English with a thick accent "I am a professional ethicist. It is people like me who help governments formulate rules that decide who lives and who dies in emergency situations. The right or wrong of weapons of mass destruction. Ethics is a social moving target that must constantly be re-examined as we as a civilized people grow and strive to maintain our innate humanity."

"So you equate hacking and ethics, in the same breath?" Scott asked.

"I certainly do," said the middle aged German hacker known as Solon. "I am part of a group that promotes the Hacker Ethic. It is really quite simple, if you would be interested." Scott urged him to continue. "We have before us, as a world, a marvelous opportunity, to create a set of rules, behavior and attitudes towards this magnificent technology that blossoms before our eyes. That law is the Ethic, some call it the Code." Kirk had called it the Code, too.

"The Code is quite a crock," interrupted a tall slender man with disheveled white hair who spoke with an upper crust, ever so proper British accent. "Unless everybody follows it, from A to Zed, it simply won't work. There can be no exceptions. Otherwise my friends, we will find ourselves in a technological Lord of the Flies."

"Ah, but that is already happening," said a gentleman in his mid-fifties, who also sported a full beard, bushy mustache and long well kept salt and pepper hair to his shoulders. "We are already well on the road to a date with Silicon Armageddon. We didn't do it with the Bomb, but it looks like we're sure as hell gonna do it with technology for the masses. In this case computers." Going only by 'Dave', he was a Philosophy Professor at Stanford. In many ways he spoke like the early Timothy Leary, using technology instead of drugs as a mental catalyst. Scott though of Dave as the futurist in the group.

"He's right. It is happening, right now. Long Live the Revolution," shouted Che2. "Hacking keeps our personal freedoms alive. I know I'd much prefer everyone knowing my most intimate secrets than have the government and TRW and the FBI and the CIA control it and use only pieces of it for their greed-sucking reasons. No way. I want everyone to have the tools to get into the Government's Big Brother computer system and make the changes they see fit."

Scott listened as his one comment spawned a heated and animated discussion. He wouldn't break in unless they went too far afield, wherever that was, or he simply wanted to join in on the conversation.

"How can you support freedom without responsibility? You contradict yourself by ignoring the Code." Solon made his comment with Teutonic matter of factness in between mouthfuls.

"It is the most responsible thing we can do," retorted Che2. "It is our moral duty, or responsibility to the world to protect our privacy, or rights, before they are stripped away as they have been since the Republicans bounced in, but not out, over a decade ago." He turned in his chair and glared at Scott. Maybe thirty years old, Che2 was mostly bald with great bushes of curly dark brown hair encircling his head. The lack of hair emphasized his large forehead which stood over his deeply inset eyes. Che2 called the Boston area his home but his cosmopolitan accent belied his background.

The proper British man known as Doctor Doctor, DRDR on the BBS's, was over six foot five with a greasy unruly frock of thick black hair which framed his ruddy pale face. "I do beg your pardon, but this so violates the tenets of civilized behavior. What this gentleman proposes is the philosophical antithesis of common sense and rationality. I suggest we consider the position that each of us in actual fact is working for the establishment, if I may use such a politically passé descriptor." DRDR's comment hushed the table. He continued. "Is it not true that security is being installed as a result of many of our activities?"

Several nods of agreement preceded a small voice coming from the far end of the table. "If you want to call it security." A small pre-adolescent spoke in a high pitched whine.

"What do you mean . . .I'm sorry, I don't know what to call you," asked Scott.

"GWhiz. The security is a toy."

GWhiz spoke unpretentiously about how incredibly simple it is to crack any security system. He maintained that there are theoretical methods to crack into any, and he emphasized any, computer. "It's impossible to protect a computer 100%. Can't be done. So that means that every computer is crackable." He offered to explain the math to Scott who politely feigned ignorance of decimal points. "In short, I, or anyone, can get into any computer they want. There is always a way."

"Isn't that a scary thought?" Scott asked to no one in particular.

Scott learned from the others that GWhiz was a 16 year old high school junior from Phoenix, Arizona. He measured on the high-end of the genius scale, joined Mensa at 4 and already had in hand scholarships from Westinghouse, Mellon, CalTech, MIT, Stanford to name a few. At the tender age of 7 he started programming and was now fluent in eleven computer languages. GWhiz was regarded with an intellectual awe from hackers for his theoretical analyses that he had turned into hacking tools. He was a walking encyclopedia of methods and techniques to both protect and attack computers. To GWhiz, straddling the political fence by arming both sides with the same weapons was a logical choice. Scott viewed it as a high tech MAD - Mutual Assured Destruction, computer wise.

"Don't you see," said the British DRDR, continuing as if there had been no interruption. "The media portrays us as security breaking phreaks, and that's exactly what we are. And that works for the establishment as well. We keep the designers and security people honest by testing their systems for free. What a great deal, don't you think? We, the hackers of the world, are the Good Housekeeping Seal of security systems by virtue of the fact that either we can or we cannot penetrate them. If that's not working for the system, I don't know what is."

"DRDR's heading down the right path." Dave the futurist spoke up. "Even though he does work for GCHQ."

"GCHQ?" Scott asked quickly.

"The English version of your NSA," said Pinball, still engrossed in his food.

"I do not!" protested DRDR. "Besides, what difference would it make if I did?" He asked more defensively.

"None, none at all," agreed Dave. "The effect is the same. However, if you are an MI-5 or MI-6 or whatever, that would show a great deal of unanticipated foresight on the part of your government. I wish ours would think farther ahead than tomorrow's headlines. I have found that people everywhere in the world see the problem as one of hackers, rather than the fundamental issues that are at stake. We hackers are manifestations of the problems that technology has bequeathed us. If any of our governments were actually responsive enough to listen, they would have a great deal of concern for the emerging infrastructure that doesn't have a leader. Now, I'm not taking a side on this one, but I am saying that if I were the government, I would sure as all hell want to know what was going on in the trenches. The U.S. especially."

Everyone seemed to agree with that.

"But they're too caught up in their own meaningless self-sustaining parasitic lives to realize that a new world is shaping around them." When Che2 spoke, he spoke his mind, leaving no doubt as to how he felt. "They don't have the smarts to get involved and see it first hand. Which is fine by me, because, as you said," he said pointing at DRDR, "it doesn't matter. They wouldn't listen to him anyway. It gives us more time to build in defenses."

"Defenses against what?" asked Scott.

"Against them, of course," responded Che2. "The fascist military industrial establishment keeps us under a microscope. They're scared of us. They have spent tens of billions of dollars to construct huge computers, built into the insides of mountains, protected from nuclear attack. In them are data bases about you, and me, and him and hundreds of millions of others. There are a lot of these systems, IRS, the Census Department has one, the FBI, The DIA, the CIA, the NSA, the OBM, I can go on." Che2's voice crescendo'd and he got more demonstrative as the importance he attributed to each subject increased. "These computers contain the most private information about us all. I for one, want to prevent them from ever using that information against me or letting others get at it either. Unlike those who feel that the Bill of Rights should be re-interpreted and re-shaped and re-packaged to feed their power frenzy, I say it's worked for 200 years and I don't want to fix something if it ain't broke."

"One needs to weigh the consequences of breaking and entering a computer, assay the purpose, evaluate the goal against the possible negatives before wildly embarking through a foreign computer. That is what we mean by the Code." Solon spoke English with Teutonic precision and a mild lilt that gave his accented words additional credibility. He sounded like an expert. "I believe, quite strongly, that it is not so complicated to have a major portion of the hacker community live by the Code. Unless you are intent on damage, no one should have any trouble with the simple Credo, 'leave things as you found them'. You see, there is nothing wrong with breaking security as long as you're accomplishing something useful."

"Hold on," interrupted Scott. "Am I hearing this right? You're saying that it's all right to break into a computer as long as you don't do any damage, and put everything right before you leave?"

"That's about it. It is so simple, yet so blanketing in its ramifications. The beauty of the Code, if everyone lived by it, would be a maximization of computer resources. Now, that is good for everyone."

"Wait, I can't stand this, wait," said Scott holding his hands over his head in surrender. He elicited a laugh from everyone but Che2. "That's like saying, it's O.K. for you to come into my house when I'm not there, use the house, wash the dishes, do the laundry, sweep up and split. I have a real problem with that. That's an invasion of my privacy and I would personally resent the shit out of it." Scott tried this line of reasoning again as he had with Kirk.

"Just the point," said DRDR. "When someone breaks into a house it's a civil case. But this new bloody Computer Misuse Act makes it a felony to enter a computer. Parliament isn't 100% perfect," he added comically. DRDR referred to the recent British attempts at legislative guidelines to criminalize certain computer activities.

"As you should resent it." Dave jumped in speaking to Scott. "But there's a higher purpose here. You resent your house being used by an uninvited guest in your absence. Right?" Scott agreed. "Well, let's say that you are going to Hawaii for a couple of weeks, and someone discovers that your house is going to be robbed while you're gone. So instead of bothering you, he house sits. Your house doesn't get robbed, you return, find nothing amiss, totally unaware of your visitor. Would you rather get robbed instead?"

"Well, I certainly don't want to get robbed, but . . . I know what it is. I'm out of control and my privacy is still being violated. I don't know if I have a quick answer." Scott looked and sounded perplexed.

"Goot! You should not have a quick answer, for that answer is the core, the essence of the ultimate problem that we all investigate every day." Solon gestured to their table of seven. "That question is security versus freedom. Within the world of academia there is a strong tendency to share everything. Your ideas, your thoughts, your successes and failures, the germs of an idea thrown away and the migration of a brainstorm into the tangible. They therefore desire complete freedom of information exchange, they do not wish any restrictions on their freedom to interact. However, the Governments of the world want to isolate and restrict access to information; right or wrong, we acknowledge their concern. That is the other side, security with minimal freedom. The banks also prefer security to freedom, although they do it very poorly and give it a lot, how do you say, a lot of lip service?"

Everyone agreed that describing a bank's security as lip service was entirely too complimentary, but for the sake of brevity they let it go uncontested.

"Then again, business hasn't made up its mind as to whether they should bother protecting information assets or not. So, there are now four groups with different needs and desires which vary the ratio of freedom to security. In reality of course there will be hundreds of opinions," Solon added for accuracy's sake. "Mathematically, if there is no security, dividing by 0 results in infinite freedom. Any security at all and some freedom is curtailed. So, therein the problem to be solved. At what cost freedom? It is an age old question that every generation must ask, weigh and decide for itself. This generation, indeed this decade, will do the same for information and freedom. They are inseparable."

Scott soaked in the words and wanted to think about them later, at his leisure. The erudite positions taken by hackers was astonishing compared to what he had expected. Yes, some of the goals and convictions were radical to say the least, but the arguments were persuasive.

"Let me ask you," Scott said to the group. "What happens when computers are secure? What will you do then?"

"They won't get secure," GWhiz said. "As soon as they come up with a defense, we will find a way around it."

"Won't that cycle ever end?"

"Technology is in the hands of the people," commented Che2. "This is the first time in history when the power is not concentrated with a select few. The ancients kept the secrets of writing with their religious leaders; traveling by ship in the open sea was a hard learned and noble skill. Today, weapons of mass destruction are controlled by a few mad men who are no better than you or I. But now, computers, access to information, that power will never be taken away. Never!"

"It doesn't matter." Dave was viewing the future in his own mind. "I doubt that computers will ever be secure, but instead, the barrier, the wall, the time and energy it takes to crack into them will become prohibitive for all but the most determined. Anyway, there'll be new technology to explore."

"Like what?" Asked Scott.

"Satellites are pretty interesting. They are a natural extension of the computer network, and cracking them will be lots easier in a couple of years." DRDR saw understanding any new technology as a personal challenge.

"How do you crack a satellite? What's there to crack?"

"How about beaming your own broadcasts to millions of people using someone else's satellite?" DRDR speculated. "It's been done before, and as the equipment gets cheaper, I can assure you that we'll be seeing many more political statements illegally being made over the public airwaves. The BBC and NBC will have their hands full. In the near future, I see virtual realities as an ideal milieu for next generation hackers."

"I agree," said Solon. "And with virtual realities, the ethical issues are even more profound than with the Global Network."

Scott held up his hands. "I know what *I* think it is, but before you go on, I need to know how you define a virtual reality." The hackers looked at each until Dave took the ball.

"A virtual reality is fooling the mind and body into believing something is real that isn't real." Scott's face was blank. "Ever been to Disneyland?" Dave asked. Scott nodded. "And you've ridden Star Tours?" Scott nodded again. "Well, that's a simple virtual reality. Star Tours fools your body into thinking that you are in a space ship careening through an asteroid belt, but in reality, you are suspended on a few guy wires. The projected image reinforces the sensory hallucination."

"Now imagine a visual field, currently it's done with goggles, that creates real life pictures, in real time and interacts with your movements."

Scott's light bulb went off. "That's like the Holo-Deck on Star Trek!"

"That is the ultimate in virtual reality, yes. But before we can achieve that, imagine sitting in a virtual cockpit of a virtual car, and seeing exactly what you would see from a race car at the Indy 500. The crowds, the noises, and just as importantly, the feel of the car you are driving. As you drive, you shift and the car reacts, you feel the car react. You actually follow the track in the path that you steer. The combination of sight, sound and hearing, even smell, creates a total illusion. In short, there is no way to distinguish between reality and delusion."

"Flight simulators for the people," chimed in Che2.

"I see the day when every Mall in America will have Virtual Reality Parlors where you can live out your fantasies. No more than 5 years," Dave confidently prognosticated.

Scott imagined the Spook's interpretation of virtual realities. He immediately conjured up the memory of Woody Allen's Orgasmatron in Sleeper. The hackers claimed that computer generated sex was less than ten years away.

"And that will be an ideal terrain for hackers. That kind of power over the mind can be used for terrible things, and it will be up to us to make sure it's not abused." Che2 maintained his position of guardian of world freedom.

As they finished their lunch and Scott paid the check, they thanked him vigorously for the treat. They might be nuts, but they were polite, and genuine.

"I'm confused about one thing," Scott said as they left the restaurant and walked the wide boulevard. "You all advocate an independence, an anarchy where the individual is paramount, and the Government is worse than a necessary evil. Yet I detect disorganization, no plan; more like a leaf in a lake, not knowing where it will go next." There were no disagreements with his summary assessment.

"Don't any of you work together? As a group, a kind of a gang? It seems to me that if there was an agenda, a program, that you might achieve your aims more quickly." Scott was trying to avoid being critical by his inquisitiveness.

"Then we would be a government, too, and that's not what we want. This is about individual power, responsibility. At any rate, I don't think you could find two of us in enough agreement on anything to build a platform." As usual, Solon maintained a pragmatic approach.

"Well," Scott mused out loud. "What would happen if a group, like you, got together and followed a game plan. Built a hacker's guide book and stuck to it, all for a common cause, which I realize is impossible. But for argument's sake, what would happen?"

"That would be immense power," said Che2. "If there were enough, they could do pretty much what they wanted. Very political."

"I would see it as dangerous, potentially very dangerous," commented DRDR. He pondered the question. "The effects of synergy in any endeavor are unpredictable. If they worked as group, a unit, it is possible that they would be a force to be reckoned with."

"There would be only one word for it," Dave said with finality. "They could easily become a strong and deadly opponent if their aims are not benevolent. Personally, I would have to call such a group, terrorists."

"Sounds like the Freedom League," Pinball said off handedly.

Scott's head jerked toward Pinball. "What about the Freedom League?" He asked pointedly.

"All I said is that this political hacking sounds like the Freedom League." Pinball said innocently. "They bloody well go on for a fortnight and a day about how software should be free to anyone that needs it, and that only those that can afford it should pay. Like big corporations."

"I've heard of Freedom before," piped Scott.

"The Freedom League is a huge BBS, mate. They have hundreds of local BBS's around the States, and even a few across the pond in God's country. Quite an operation, if I say."

Pinball had Scott's full attention. "They run the BBS's, and have an incredible shareware library. Thousands of programs, and they give them all away."

"It's very impressive," Dave said giving credit where credit was due. "They prove that software can be socially responsible. We've been saying that for years."

"What does anybody know about this Freedom League?" Scott asked suspiciously.

"What's to know? They've been around for years, have a great service, fabulous BBS's, and reliable software."

"It just sounds too good to be true," Scott mused as they made it back to the warehouse for more hours of education.

* * * * *

355

Until late that night, Scott continued to elicit viewpoints and opinions and political positions from the radical underground elements of the 1990's he had traveled 3000 miles to meet. Each encounter, each discussion, each conversation yielded yet another perspective on the social rational for hacking and the invasion of privacy. Most everyone at the InterGalactic Hackers Conference had heard about Scott, the Repo Man, and knew why he was there. He was accepted as a fair and impartial observer, thus many of them made a concerted effort to preach their particular case to him. By midnight, overload had consumed Scott and he made a polite exit, promising to return the following day.

Still, no one had heard from or seen the Spook.

Scott walked back to his hotel through the Red Light District and stopped to purchase a souvenir or two. The sexually explicit T-Shirts would have both made Larry Flynt blush and be banned on Florida beaches, but the counterfeit $1 bills, with George Washington and the pyramid replaced by closeups of impossible oral sexual acts was a compelling gift. They were so well made, that without a close inspection, the pornographic money could easily find itself in the till at a church bake sale.

There was a message waiting for Scott when he arrived at the *Eureka!* It was from Tyrone and marked urgent. New York was 6 hours behind, so hopefully Ty was at home. Scott dialed USA Connect, the service that allows travelers to get to an AT&T operator rather than fighting the local phone system.

"Make it good." Tyrone answered his home phone.

"Hey, guy. You rang?" Scott said cheerily.

"Shit, it's about time. Where the hell have you been?" Tyrone whispered as loud as he could. It was obvious he didn't want anyone on his end hearing. "You can thank your secretary for telling me where you were staying." Tyrone spoke quickly.

"I'll give her a raise," lied Scott. He didn't have a secretary. The paper used a pool for all the reporters. "What's the panic?"

"Then you don't know." Tyrone caught himself. "Of course you didn't hear, how could you?"

"How could I hear what?"

"The shit has done hit the fan," Tyrone said drawling his words. "Two more EMP-T bombs. The Atlanta regional IRS office and a payroll service in New Jersey. A quarter million folks aren't getting paid tomorrow. And I'll tell you, these folks is mighty pissed off."

"Christ," Scott said mentally chastising himself for not having been where the action was.

What lousy timing.

"So dig this. Did you know that the Senate was having open subcommittee hearings on Privacy and Technology Protection?"

"No."

"Neither do a lot of people. It's been a completely underplayed and underpromoted effort. Until yesterday that is. Now the eyes of millions are watching. Starting tomorrow."

"Tomorrow?" Scott yelled across the Atlantic. "That's the eighth. Congress doesn't usually convene until late January . . ."

"Used to," Ty said. "The Constitution says that Congress shall meet on January third, after the holidays. Since the Gulf War Congress has returned in the first week. 'Bout time they did something for their paychecks."

"Damn," Scott thought out loud.

"I knew that would excite you," Tyrone said sarcastically. "and there's more. Congressman Rickfield, you know who he is?" Asked Tyrone.

"Yeah, sure. Long timer on the Hill. Got as many enemies as he does friends. Wields an immense amount of power," Scott recalled.

"Right, exactly. And that little weasel is the chair."

"I guess you're not on his Christmas list," Scott observed.

"I really doubt it," Tyrone said. "But that's off the record. He's been a Southern racist from day one, a real Hoover man. During the riots, in the early '60's, he was not exactly a proponent of civil rights. In fact that slime ball made Wallace look like Martin Luther King." Tyrone sounded bitter and derisive in his description of Rickfield. "He has no concept what civil rights are. He makes it a black white issue instead of one of constitutional law. Stupid bigots are the worst kind." The derision in Ty's voice was unmistakable.

"Sounds like you're a big fan."

"I'll be a fan when he hangs high. Besides my personal and racial beliefs about Rickfield, he really is a low life. He, and a few of his cronies are one on the biggest threats to personal freedom the country faces. He thinks that the Bill of Rights should be edited from time to time and now's the time. He scares me. Especially since there's more like him."

It was eminently clear that Tyrone Duncan had no place in this life for Merrill Rickfield.

"I know enough about him to dislike him, but on a crowded subway he'd just be another ugly face. Excuse my ignorance . . ." Then it hit him. Rickfield. His name had been in those papers he had received so long ago. What had he done, or what was he accused of doing? Damn, damn, what is it? There were so many. Yes, it was Rickfield, but what was the tie-in?

"I think you should be there, at the hearings," Tyrone suggested.

"Tomorrow? Are you out of your mind? No way," Scott loudly protested. "I'm 3000 miles and 8 hours away and it's the middle of the night here," Scott bitched and moaned. "Besides, I only have to work one more day and then I get the weekend to myself . . . aw, shit."

Tyrone ignored Scott's infantile objections. He attributed them to jet lag and an understandable urge to stay in Sin City for a couple more days. "Hollister and Adams will be there, and a whole bunch of white shirts in black hats, and Troubleaux . . ."

"Troubleaux did you say?"

"Yeah, that's what it says here . . ."

"If he's there, then it becomes my concern, too."

"Good, glad you thought of it," joked Tyrone. "If you catch an early flight, you could be in DC by noon." He was right, thought Scott. The time difference works in your favor in that direction.

"You know," said Scott, "with what I've found out here, today alone, maybe. "Jeeeeeesus," Scott said cringing in indecision.

"Hey! Get your ass back here, boy. Pronto." Tyrone's friendly authority was persuasive. "You know you don't have any choice." The guilt trip.

"Yeah, yeah, yeah."

Scott called his office and asked for Doug. He got the voice mail instead, and debated about calling him at home. *Nah*, he thought, *I'll just leave a message. This way I'll just get yelled at once.*

"Hi, Doug? Scott here. Change in plans. Heard about EMP-T. I'm headed to Washington tomorrow. The story here is better than I thought and dovetails right into why I'm coming back early. I expect to be in DC until Tuesday, maybe Wednesday. I'll call when I have a place. Oh, yeah, I learned a limerick here you might like. The Spook says the kids around here say it all the time. 'Mary had a little lamb, its fleece was white as snow. And everywhere that Mary went, the lamb was sure to go. It followed her to school one day and a big black dog fucked it.' That's Amsterdam. Bye."

* * * * *

Chapter 20

Friday, January 8
Washington, D.C.

T he New Senate Office Building is a moderately impressive structure on the edge of one of the worst sections of Washington. Visitors find it a perpetual paradox that the power seat of the Western World is located within a virtual shooting gallery of drugs and weapons. Scott arrived at the NSOB near the capitol, just before lunchtime. His press identification got him instant access to the hearing room and into the privileged locations where the media congregated. The hearings were in progress and as solemn as he remembered other hearings broadcast on late night C-SPAN.

He caught the last words of wisdom from a government employee who worked for NIST, the National Institute of Standards and Technology. The agency was formerly known as NBS, National Bureau of Standards, and no one could adequately explain the change.

The NIST employee droned on about how seriously the government, and more specifically, his agency cared about privacy and information security, and that ". . .the government was doing all it could to provide the requisite amount of security commensurate with the perceived risk of disclosure and sensitivity of the information in question." Scott ran into a couple of fellow reporters who told him he was lucky to show up late. All morning, the government paraded witnesses to read prepared statements about how they were protecting the interests of the Government.

It was an intensive lobbying effort, they told Scott, to shore up whatever attacks might be made on the government's inefficient bungling in distinction to its efficient bungling. To a man, the witnesses assured the Senate committee that they were committed to guaranteeing privacy of information and unconvincingly assuring them that only appropriate authorized people have access to sensitive and classified data.

Seven sequential propagandized statements went unchallenged by the three senior committee members throughout the morning, and Senator Rickfield went out of his way to thank the speakers for their time, adding that he was personally convinced the Government was indeed doing more than necessary to obviate such concerns.

The underadvertised Senate Select Sub Committee on Privacy and Technology Protection convened in Hearing Room 3 on the second floor of the NSOB. About 400 could be accommodated in the huge light wood paneled room on both the main floor and in the balcony that wrapped around half of the room. The starkness of the room was emphasized by the glare of arc and fluorescent lighting.

Scott found an empty seat on a wooden bench directly behind the tables from which the witnesses would speak to the raised wooden dais. He noticed that the attendance was extraordinarily low; by both the public and the press. Probably due to the total lack of exposure.

As the session broke for lunch, Scott asked why the TV cameras? He thought this hearing was a deep dark secret. A couple of fellow journalists agreed, and the only reason they had found out about the Rickfield hearings was because the CNN producer called them asking if they knew anything about them. Apparently, Scott was told, CNN received an anonymous call, urging them to be part of a blockbuster announcement. When CNN called Rickfield's office, his staffers told CNN that there was no big deal, and that they shouldn't waste their time. In the news business, that kind of statement from a Congressional power broker is a sure sign that it is worth being there. Just in case. So CNN assigned a novice producer and a small crew to the first day of the hearings. As promised, the morning session was an exercise in terminal boredom.

The afternoon session was to begin at 1:30, but Senator Rickfield was nowhere to be found, so the Assistant Chairperson of the committee, Junior Senator Nancy Deere assumed control. She was a 44 year old grandmother of two from New England who had never considered entering politics. Nancy Deere was the consummate wife, supporter and stalwart of her husband Morgan Deere, an up and coming national politician who had the unique mixture of honesty, appeal and potential. She had spent full time on the campaign trail with Morgan as he attempted to make the transition from state politics to Washington. Morgan Deere was heavily favored to win after the three term incumbent was named a co-conspirator in the rigging of a Defense contract. Despite the pending indictments, the race continued with constant pleadings by the incumbent that the trumped up charges would shortly be dismissed. In the first week after the Grand Jury was convened, the voter polls indicated that Deere led with a 70% support factor.

Then came the accident. On his way home from a fund raising dinner, Morgan Deere's limousine was run off an icy winter road by a drunk driver. Deere's resulting injuries made it impossible for him to continue the campaign or even be sure that he would ever be able to regain enough strength to withstand the brutality of Washington politics.

Within days of the accident, Deere's campaign manager announced that Nancy Deere would replace her husband. Due to Morgan's local popularity, and the fact that the state was so small that everyone knew everyone else's business, and that the incumbent was going to jail, and that the elections were less than two weeks away, there was barely a spike in the projections. No one seemed to care that Nancy Deere had no experience in politics; they just liked her.

What remained of the campaign was run on her part with impeccable style. Unlike her opponent who spent vast sums to besmirch her on television, Nancy's campaign was largely waged on news and national talk shows. Her husband was popular, as was she, and the general interest in her as a woman outweighed the interest in her politics. The state's constituency overwhelmingly endorsed her with their votes and Senator Nancy Deere, one of the few woman ever to reach that level as an elected official, was on her way to Washington.

Nancy Deere found that many of the professional politicians preferred to ignore her; they were convinced she was bound to be a one termer once the GOP got someone to run against her. Others found her to be a genuine pain in the butt. Not due to her naivete, far from that, she adeptly acclimated to the culture and the system. Rather, she was a woman and she broke the rules. She said what she felt; she echoed the sentiments of her constituency which were largely unpopular politically. Nancy Deere didn't care what official Washington thought; her state was behind her with an almost unanimous approval and it was her sworn duty to represent them honestly and without compromise. She had nothing to lose by being herself. After more than a year in Washington, she learned how the massive Washington machinery functioned and why it crawled with a hurry up and wait engine.

In Rickfield's absence, at 1:40 PM Senator Nancy Deere called the session to order. Her administrative demeanor gave no one pause to question her authority. Even the other sole Congressional representative on the sub-committee fell into step. While Senator Stanley Paglusi technically had seniority, he sat on the committee at Rickfield's request and held no specific interest in the subject matter they were investigating. He accepted the seat to mollify Rickfield and to add to his own political resume.

"Come to order, please," she announced over the ample sound system. The voluminous hearing room reacted promptly to the authoritative command that issued forth from the petite auburn haired Nancy Deere who would have been just as comfortable auctioning donated goods at her church. She noticed that unlike the morning session, the afternoon session was packed. The press pool was nearly full and several people were forced to stand. What had changed, she asked herself.

After the procedural formalities were completed, she again thanked those who had spoken to the committee in the morning, and then promised an equally informative afternoon. Nancy, as she liked to be called on all but the most formal of occasions introduced the committee's first afternoon witness.

"Our next speaker is Ted Hammacher, a recognized expert on the subject of computer and information security. During 17 years with the Government, Mr. Hammacher worked with the Defense Investigatory Agency and the National Security Agency as a DoD liaison. He is currently a security consultant to industry and the government and is the author of hundreds of articles on the subject." As was required, Nancy Deere outlined Hammacher's qualifications as an expert, and then invited him to give his opening statement.

The television in Rickfield's office was tuned to C-SPAN which was broadcasting the hearings as he spoke into the phone.

"Only a couple more and then I'm off to spend my days in the company of luscious maidens on the island of my choice," he bragged into the phone. The Senator listened intently to the response. "Yes, I am aware of that, but it doesn't change the fact that I'm calling it quits. I cannot, I will not, continue this charade." He listened quietly for several minutes before interjecting.

"Listen, General, we've both made enough money to keep us in style for the rest of our lives, and I will not jeopardize that for anything. Got it?" Again he listened. "I don't know about you, but I do not relish the idea of doing ten to twenty regardless of how much of a country club the prison is. It is still a prison." He listened further.

"That's it, I've had it! Don't make me use that file to implicate you, the guys over at State and our Import . . .hey!" Rickfield turned to Ken Boyers. "Who started the afternoon session?" He pointed at the TV.

"It looks like Senator Deere," Ken said.

"Deere? Where does that goddamned bitch get off . . ." He remembered the phone. "General? I have to go, I've got a suffragette usurping a little power, and I have to put her back in her place. You understand. But, on that other matter, I'm out. Done. Finito. Do what you want, but keep me the fuck out of it." Rickfield hung up abruptly and stared at the broadcast. "Some housebroken homemaker is not going to make me look bad. Goddamn it, Ken," Rickfield said as he stood up quickly. "Let's get back out there."

"Thank you Senator Deere, and committee members. I am honored to have a chance to speak to you here today. As a preface to my remarks, I think that a brief history of security and privacy from a government perspective may be in order. One of the reasons we are here today is due to a succession of events that since the introduction of the computer have shaped an ad hoc anarchism, a laissez-faire attitude toward privacy and security. Rather than a comprehensive national policy, despite the valiant efforts of a few able Congressmen, the United States of America has allowed itself to be lulled into technical complacency and indifference. Therefore, I will, if the committee agrees, provide a brief chronological record."

"I for one would be most interested," said Senator Deere. "It appeared that this morning our speakers assumed we were more knowledgeable that we are. Any clarifications will be most welcome." The crowd agreed silently. Much of the history was cloaked in secrecy.

The distinguished Ted Hammacher was an accomplished orator, utilizing the best that Washington diplomatic-speak could muster. At 50 years old, his short cropped white hair capped a proper military bearing even though he had maintained a civilian status throughout his Pentagon associations. "Thank you madam chairman." He glanced down at the well organized folder and turned a page.

"Concerns of privacy can be traced back thousands of years with perhaps the Egyptian pyramids as the first classic example of a brute force approach towards privacy. The first recorded attempts at disguising the contents of a written message were in Roman times when Julius Caesar encoded messages to his generals in the field. The Romans used a simple substitution cipher where one letter in the alphabet is used in place of another. The cryptograms found in the Sunday paper use the same techniques. Any method by which a the contents of a message is scrambled is known as encryption."

The CNN producer maintained the sole camera shot and his attention on Ted Hammacher. He missed Senator Rickfield and his aid reappear on the dais. Rickfield's eyes penetrated Nancy Deere who imperceptibly acknowledged his return. "You should not overstep your bounds," Rickfield leaned over and said to her. "You have five years to go. Stunts like this will not make your time any easier."

"Senator," she said to Rickfield as Hammacher spoke. "You are obviously not familiar with the procedures of Senate panel protocol. I was merely trying to assist the progress of the hearings in your absence, I assure you." Her coolness infuriated Rickfield.

"Well, then, thank you," he sneered. "But, now, I am back. I will appreciate no further procedural interference." He sat up brusquely indicating that his was the last word on the subject. Unaware of the political sidebar in progress, Hammacher continued.

"Ciphers were evolved over the centuries until they reached a temporary plateau during World War II. The Germans used the most sophisticated message encoding or encryption device ever devised. Suitably called the Enigma, their encryption scheme was nearly uncrackable until the Allies captured one of the devices, and then under the leadership of Alan Turing, a method was found to regularly decipher intercepted German High Command orders. Many historians consider this effort as being instrumental in bringing about an end to the war.

"In the years immediately following World War II, the only perceived need for secrecy was by the military and the emerging intelligence services, namely the OSS as it became the modern CIA, the British MI-5 and MI-6 and of course our opponents on the other side. In an effort to maintain a technological leadership position, the National Security Agency funded various projects to develop encryption schemes that would adequately protect government information and communications for the foreseeable future.

"The first such requests were issued in 1972 but it wasn't until 1974 that the National Bureau of Standards accepted an IBM proposal for an encryption process known as Lucifer. With the assistance of the NSA who is responsible for cryptography, the Data Encryption Standard was approved in November of 1976. There was an accompanying furor over the DES, some saying that the NSA intentionally weakened it to insure that they could still decrypt any messages using the approved algorithm.

"In 1982 a financial group, FIMAS endorsed a DES based method to authenticate Electronic Funds Transfer, or EFT. Banks move upwards of a trillion dollars daily, and in an effort to insure that all monies are moved accurately and to their intended destinations, the technique of Message Authentication Coding was introduced. For still unknown reasons it was decided that encrypting the contents of the messages, or transfers, was unnecessary. Thus, financial transactions are still carried out with no protection from eavesdropping."

"Excuse me, Mr. Hammacher, I want to understand this," interrupted Senator Deere. "Are you saying that, since 1976, we have had the ability to camouflage the nation's financial networks, yet as of today, they are still unprotected?" Rickfield looked over at Nancy in disgust but the single camera missed it.

"Yes, ma'am, that's exactly the case," replied Hammacher.

"What does that mean to us? The Government? Or the average citizen?"

"In my opinion it borders on insanity. It means that for the price of a bit of electronic equipment, anyone can tap into the details of the financial dealings of banks, the government and every citizen in this country."

Senator Deere visibly gulped. "Thank you, please continue."

"In 1984, President Reagan signed National Security Decision Directive 145. NSDD-145 established that defense contractors and other organizations that handle sensitive or classified information must adhere to certain security and privacy guidelines. A number of advisory groups were established, and to a minimal extent, the recommendations have been implemented, but I must emphasize, to a minimal extent."

"Can you be a little more specific, Mr. Hammacher?" Asked Senator Deere.

"No ma'am, I can't. A great deal of these efforts are classified and by divulging who is not currently in compliance would be a security violation in itself. It would be fair to say, though, that the majority of those organizations targeted for additional security measures fall far short of the government's intentions and desires. I am sorry I cannot be more specific."

"I understand completely. Once again," Nancy said to Hammacher, "I am sorry to interrupt."

"Not at all, Senator." Hammacher sipped from his water glass. "As you can see, the interest in security was primarily from the government, and more specifically the defense community. In 1981, the Department of Defense chartered the DoD Computer Security Center which has since become the National Computer Security Center operating under the auspices of the National Security Agency. In 1983 they published a series of guidelines to be used in the creation or evaluation of computer security. Officially titled the Trusted Computer Security Evaluation Criteria, it is popularly known as the Orange Book. It has had some minor updates since then, but by and large it is an outdated document designed for older computer architectures.

"The point to be made here is that while the government had an ostensible interest and concern about the security of computers, especially those under their control, there was virtually no overt significance placed upon the security of private industry's computers. Worse yet, it was not until 1987 that any proposed criteria were developed for networked computers. So, as the world tied itself together with millions of computers and networks, the Government was not concerned enough to address the issue. Even today, there are no secure network criteria that are universally accepted."

"Mr. Hammacher." Senator Rickfield spoke up for the first time. "You appear to have a most demeaning tone with respect to the United States Government's ability to manage itself. I for one remain unconvinced that we are as derelict as you suggest. Therefore, I would ask that you stick to the subject at hand, the facts, and leave your personal opinions at home."

Nancy Deere as well as much of the audience listened in awe as Rickfield slashed out at Hammacher who was in the process of building an argument. Common courtesy demanded that he be permitted to finish his statement, even if his conclusions were unpopular or erroneous.

Hammacher did not seem fazed. "Sir, I am recounting the facts, and only the facts. My personal opinions would only be further damning, so I agree, that I will refrain." He turned a page in his notebook and continued.

"Several laws were passed, most notably Public Law 100-235, the Computer Security Act of 1987. This weak law called for enhanced cooperation between the NSA and NIST in the administration of security for the sensitive but unclassified world of the Government and the private sector. Interestingly enough, in mid 1990 it was announced, that after a protracted battle between the two security agencies, the NCSC would shut down and merge its efforts with its giant super secret parent, the NSA. President Bush signed the Directive effectively replacing Reagan's NSDD-145. Because the budgeting and appropriations for both NSA and the former NCSC are classified, there is no way to accurately gauge the effectiveness of this move. It may still be some time before we understand the ramifications of the new Executive Order.

"To date every state has some kind of statute designed to punish computer crime, but prosecutions that involve the crossing of state lines in the commission of a crime are far and few between. Only 1% of all computer criminals are prosecuted and less than 5% of those result in convictions. In short, the United States has done little or nothing to forge an appropriate defense against computer crime, despite the political gerrymandering and agency shuffling over the last decade. That concludes my opening remarks." Hammacher sat back in his chair and finished the water. He turned to his lawyer and whispered something Scott couldn't hear.

"Ah, Mr. Hammacher, before you continue, I would like ask a few questions. Do you mind?" Senator Nancy Deere was being her usual gracious self.

"Not at all, Senator."

"You said earlier that the NSA endorsed a cryptographic system that they themselves could crack. Could you elaborate?" Senator Nancy Deere's ability to grasp an issue at the roots was uncanny.

"I'd be pleased to. First of all, it is only one opinion that the NSA can crack DES; it has never been proven or disproven. When DES was first introduced some theoreticians felt that NSA had compromised the original integrity of IBM's Lucifer encryption project. I am not qualified to comment either way, but the reduction of the key length, and the functional feedback mechanisms were less stringent than the original. If this is true, then we have to ask ourselves, why? Why would the NSA want a weaker system?"

A number of heads in the hearing room nodded in agreement with the question; others merely acknowledged that it was NSA bashing time again.

Hammacher continued. "There is one theory that suggests that the NSA, as the largest eavesdropping operation in the world wanted to make sure that they could still listen in on messages once they have been encrypted. The NSA has neither confirmed or denied these reports. If that is true, then we must ask ourselves, if DES is so weak, why does the NSA have the ultimate say on export control. The export of DES is restricted by the Munitions Control, Department of State, and they rely upon DoD and the NSA for approval.

"The export controls suggest that maybe NSA cannot decrypt DES, and there is some evidence to support that. For example, in 1985, the Department of Treasury wanted to extend the validation of DES for use throughout the Treasury, the Federal Reserve System and member banks. The NSA put a lot of political muscle behind an effort to have DES deaffirmed and replaced with newer encryption algorithms. Treasury argued that they had already adapted DES, their constituents had spent millions on DES equipment for EFT and it would be entirely too cumbersome and expensive to make a change now. Besides, they asked, what's wrong with DES? They never got an answer to that question, and thus they won the battle and DES is still the approved encryption methodology for banks. It was never established whether DES was too strong or too weak for NSA's taste.

"Later, in 1987, the NSA received an application for export of a DES based device that employed a technique called infinite encryption. In response to the frenzy over the strength or weakness of DES, one company took DES and folded it over and over on itself using multiple keys. The NSA had an internal hemorrhage. They forbade this product from being exported from the United States in any form whatsoever. Period. It was an extraordinary move on their part, and one that had built-in contradictions. If DES is weak, then why not export it? If it's too strong, why argue with Treasury? In any case, the multiple DES issue died down until recently, when NSA, beaten at their own game by too much secrecy, developed a secret internal program to create a Multiple-DES encryption standard with a minimum of three sequential iterations.

"Further embarrassment was caused when an Israeli mathematician found the 'trap door' built into DES by the NSA and how to decode messages in seconds. This quite clearly suggests that he government has been listening in on supposedly secret and private communications.

"Then we have to look at another event that strongly suggests that NSA has something to hide."

"Mr. Hammacher!" Shouted Senator Rickfield. "I warned you about that."

"I see nothing wrong with his comments, Senator," Deere said, careful to make sure that she was heard over the sound system.

"I am the chairman of this committee, Ms. Deere, and I find Mr. Hammacher's characterization of the NSA as unfitting this forum. I wish he would find other words or eliminate the thought altogether. Mr. Hammacher, do you think you are capable of that?"

Hammacher seethed. "Senator, I mean no disrespect to you or this committee. However, I was asked to testify, and at my own expense I am providing as accurate information as possible. If you happen to find anything I say not to your liking, I do apologize, but my only alternative is not to testify at all."

"We accept your withdrawal, Mr. Hammacher, thank you for your time." A hushed silence covered the hearing room. This was not the time to get into it with Rickfield, Nancy thought. He has sufficiently embarrassed himself and the media will take care of the rest. Why the hell is he acting this way? He is known as a hard ass, a real case, but his public image was unblemished. Had the job passed him by?

A stunned and incensed Hammacher gathered his belongings as his lawyer placated him. Scott overheard bits and pieces as they both agreed that Rickfield was a flaming asshole. A couple of reporters hurriedly followed them out of the hearing room for a one on one interview.

"Is Dr. Sternman ready?" Rickfield asked.

A bustle of activity and a man spoke to the dais without the assistance of a microphone. "Yessir, I am."

Sternman was definitely the academic type, Scott noted. A crumpled ill fitting brown suit covering a small hunched body that was no more than 45 years old. He held an old scratched briefcase and an armful of folders and envelopes. Scott was reminded of the studious high school student that jocks enjoy tripping with their feet. Dr. Sternman busied himself to straighten the papers that fell onto the desk and his performance received a brief titter from the crowd.

"Ah, yes, Mr. Chairman," Sternman said. "I'm ready now." Rickfield looked as bored as ever.

"Thank you, Dr. Sternman. You are, I understand, a computer virus expert? Is that correct?"

"Yessir. My doctoral thesis was on the subject and I have spent several years researching computer viruses, their proliferation and propagation." Rickfield groaned to himself. Unintelligible mumbo jumbo.

"I also understand that your comments will be brief as we have someone else yet to hear from today." It was as much a command as a question.

"Yessir, it will be brief."

"Then, please, enlighten us, what is a virus expert and what do you do?" Rickfield grinned menacingly at Dr. Arnold Sternman, Professor of Applied Theoretical Mathematics, Massachusetts Institute of Technology.

"I believe the committee has received an advance copy of some notes I made on the nature of computer viruses and the danger they represent?" Rickfield hadn't read anything, so he looked at Boyers who also shrugged his shoulders.

"Yes, Dr. Sternman," Nancy Deere said. "And we thank you for your consideration." Rickfield glared at her as she politely upstaged him yet again. "May I ask, though, that you provide a brief description of a computer virus for the benefit of those who have not read your presentation?" She stuck it to Rickfield again.

"I'd be happy to, madam Chairwoman," he said nonchalantly. Rickfield's neck turned red at the inadvertent sudden rise in Senator Deere's stature. For the next several minutes Sternman solemnly described what a virus was, how it worked and a history of their attacks. He told the committee about Worms, Trojan Horses, Time Bombs, Logic Bombs, Stealth Viruses, Crystal Viruses and an assorted family of similar surreptitious computer programs. Despite Sternman's sermonly manner, his audience found the subject matter fascinating.

"The reason you are here, Dr. Sternman, is to bring us up to speed on computer viruses, which you have done with alacrity, and we appreciate that." Rickfield held seniority, but Nancy Deere took charge due to her preparation. "Now that we have an understanding of the virus, can you give us an idea of the type of problems that they cause?"

"Ah, yes, but I need to say something here," Sternman said.

"Please, proceed," Rickfield said politely.

"When I first heard about replicating software, viruses, and this was over 15 years ago, I, as many of my graduate students did, thought of them as a curious anomaly. A benign subset of computer software that had no anticipated applications. We spent months working with viruses, self cloning software and built mathematical models of their behavior which fit quite neatly in the domain of conventional set theory. Then an amazing discovery befell us. We proved mathematically that there is absolutely no effective way to protect against computer viruses in software."

Enough of the spectators had heard about viruses over the past few years to comprehend the purport of that one compelling statement. Even Senator Rickfield joined Nancy and the others in their awe. No way to combat viruses? Dr. Sternman had dropped a bombshell on them.

"Dr. Sternman," said Senator Deere. "Could you repeat that?

"Yes, yes," Sternman replied, knowing the impact of his statement. "That is correct. A virus is a piece of software and software is designed to do specific tasks in a hardware environment. All software uses basically the same techniques to do its job. Without all of the technicalities, if one piece of software can do something, another piece of software can un-do it. It's kind of a computer arms race.

"I build a virus, and you build a program to protect against that one virus. It works. But then I make a small change in the virus to attack or bypass your software, and Poof! I blow you away. Then you build a new piece of software to defend against both my first virus and my mutated virus and that works until I build yet another. This process can go on forever, and frankly, it's just not worth the effort."

"What is not worth the effort, Doctor?" Asked Nancy Deere. "You paint a most bleak picture."

"I don't mean to at all, Senator." Dr. Sternman smiled soothingly up at the committee and took off his round horn rim glasses. "I wasn't attempting to be melodramatic, however these are not opinions or guesses. They are facts. It is not worth the effort to fight computer viruses with software. The virus builders will win because the Virus Busters are the ones playing catch-up."

"Virus Busters?" Senator Rickfield mockingly said conspicuously raising his eyebrows. His reaction elicited a wave of laughter from the hall.

"Yessir," said Dr. Sternman to Rickfield. "Virus Busters. That's a term to describe programmers who fight viruses. They mistakenly believe they can fight viruses with defensive software and some of them sell some incredibly poor programs. In many cases you're better off not using anything at all.

"You see, there is no way to write a program that can predict the potential behavior of other software in such a way that it will not interfere with normal computer operations. So, the only way to find a virus is to already know what it looks like, and go out looking for it. There are several major problems with this approach. First of all, the virus has already struck and done some damage. Two it has already infected other software and will continue to spread. Three, a program must be written to defeat the specific virus usually using a unique signature for each virus, and the vaccine for the virus must be distributed to the computer users.

"This process can take from three to twelve months, and by the time the virus vaccine has been deployed, the very same virus has been changed, mutated, and the vaccine is useless against it. So you see, the Virus Busters are really wasting their time, and worst of all they are deceiving the public." Dr. Sternman completed what he had to say with surprising force.

"Doctor Sternman," Senator Rickfield said disdain. "All of your theories are well and good, and perhaps they work in the laboratory, but isn't it true, sir, that computer viruses are an overblown issue that the media has sensationalized and that they are nothing more than a minor inconvenience?"

"Not really, Senator. The statistics don't support that conclusion," Dr. Sternman said with conviction. "That is one of the worst myths." Nancy Deere smiled to herself as the dorky college professor handed it right to a United States Senator. "The incidence of computer viruses has been on a logarithmic increase for the past several years. If a human disease infected at the same rate, we would declare a medical state of emergency."

"Doctor," implored Rickfield. "Aren't you exaggerating . . .?"

"No Senator, here are the facts. There are currently over 2500 known computer viruses and strains that have been positively identified. Almost three thousand, Senator." The good Doctor was a skilled debater, and Rickfield was being sucked in by his attack on the witness. The figure three thousand impressed everyone. A few low whistles echoed through the large chamber. Stupid move Merrill, though Nancy.

"It is estimated, sir," Dr. Sternman dryly spoke to Rickfield, "that every single network in the United States, Canada and the United Kingdom is infected with at least one computer virus. That is the equivalent of having one member of every family in the country being sick at all times. That is an epidemic, and one that will not go away. No sir, it will not." Sternman's voice rose. "It will not go away. It will only get worse."

"That is a most apoplectic prophesy, Doctor. I think that many of us would have trouble believing the doom and gloom you portend." Rickfield was sloughing off the Doctor, but Sternman was here to tell a story, and he would finish.

"There is more, Senator. Recent reports show that over 75% of the computers in the People's Republic of China are infected with deadly and destructive software. Why? The look on your face asks the question. Because, almost every piece of software in that country is bootleg, illegal copies of popular programs. That invites viruses.

Since vast quantities of computers come from the Pacific Rim, many with prepackaged software, new computer equipment is a source of computer viruses that was once considered safe. Modem manufacturers have accidentally had viruses on their communications software; several major domestic software manufacturers have had their shrink-wrapped software infected.

"If you recall in 1989, NASA brought Virus Busters to Cape Kennedy and Houston to thwart a particular virus that threatened a space launch. A year later as everyone remembers, NASA computers were invaded forcing officials to abort a flight. The attacks go on, and they inflict greater damage than is generally thought.

"Again, these are our best estimates, that over 90% of all viral infections go unreported."

"Doctor, 90%? Isn't that awfully high?" Nancy asked.

"Definitely, yes, but imagine the price of speaking out. I have talked to hundreds of companies, major corporations, that are absolutely terrified of anyone knowing that their computers have been infected. Or they have been the target of any computer crime for that matter. They feel that the public, their customers, maybe even their stockholders, might lose faith in the company's ability to protect itself. So? Most viral attacks go unreported.

"It's akin to computer rape." Dr. Sternman had a way with words to keep his audience attentive. Years of lecturing to sleeping freshman had taught him a few tricks. "A computer virus is uninvited, it invades the system, and then has its way with it. If that's not rape, I don't know what is."

"Your parallels are most vivid," said a grimacing Nancy Deere. "Let's leave that thought for now, and maybe you can explain the type of damage that a virus can do. It sounds to me like there are thousands of new diseases out there, and every one needs to be isolated, diagnosed and then cured. That appears to me to a formidable challenge."

"I could not have put it better, Senator. You grasp things quickly." Sternman was genuinely complimenting Nancy. "The similarities to the medical field cannot go unnoticed if we are to deal with the problem rationally and effectively. And like a disease, we need to predict the effects of the infection. What we have found in that area is as frightening.

"The first generation of viruses were simple in their approach. The designers correctly assumed that no one was looking for them, and they could enter systems without any deterrence. They erase files, scramble data, re-format hard drives . . .make the computer data useless.

"Then the second generation of viruses came along with the nom-de-guerre stealth. These viruses hid themselves more elaborately to avoid detection and had a built in self-preservation instinct. If the virus thinks it's being probed, it self destructs or hides itself even further.

"In addition, second generation viruses learned how to become targeted. Some viruses have been designed to only attack a competitor's product and nothing else."

"Is that possible?" Asked Nancy Deere.

"It's been done many times. Some software bugs in popular software are the result of viral infections, others may be genuine bugs. Imagine a virus who sole purpose is to attack Lotus 123 spreadsheets. The virus is designed to create computational errors in the program's spreadsheets. The user then thinks that Lotus is to blame and so he buys another product. Yes, ma'am, it is possible, and occurs every day of the week. Keeping up with it is the trick.

"Other viruses attack on Friday the 13th. only, some attack only at a specified time . . .the damage to be done is only limited by imagination of the programmers. Third generation viruses were even more sophisticated. They were designed to do damage not only to the data, but to the computer hardware itself. Some were designed to overload communications ports with tight logical loops. Others were designed to destroy the hard disk by directly overdriving the disk. There is no limit to the possibilities.

"You sound as though you hold their skills in high regard, Doctor." Rickfield continued to make snide remarks whenever possible.

"Yessir, I do. Many of them have extraordinary skills, that are unfortunately misguided. They are a new breed of bored criminal."

"You mentioned earlier Doctor, that there were over 2500 known viruses. How fast is the epidemic, as you put it, spreading?" Senator Nancy Deere asked while making prolific notes throughout.

"For all intents and purposes Senator, they spread unchecked. There is a certain amount of awareness of the problem, but it is only superficial. The current viral defenses include signature identification, cyclic redundancy checks and intercept verification, but the new viruses can combat those as a matter of rule. If the current rate of viral infection continues, it will be a safe bet that nearly every computer in the country will be infected ten times over within three years."

Dr. Arnold Sternman spent the next half hour answering insightful questions from Nancy Deere, and even Puglasi became concerned enough to ask a few. Rickfield continued with his visceral comments to the constant amazement of the gallery and spectators. Scott could only imagine the raking Rickfield would receive in the press, but being Friday, the effects will be lessened. Besides, it seemed as if Rickfield just didn't give a damn.

Rickfield dismissed and perfunctorily thanked Dr. Sternman. He prepared for the next speaker, but Senator Deere leaned over and asked him for a five minute conclave. He was openly reluctant, but as she raised her voice, he conceded. In a private office off to the side, Nancy Deere came unglued.

"What kind of stunt are you pulling out there, Senator?" She demanded as she paced the room. "I thought this was a hearing, not a lynching."

Rickfield slouched in a plush leather chair and appeared unconcerned. "I am indeed sorry," he said with the pronounced drawl of a Southern country gentleman, "that the young Senatoress finds cross examination unpleasant. Perhaps if we treated this like a neighborhood gossip session, it might be easier."

"Now one damned minute," she yelled while pointing a finger right at Rickfield. "That was not cross-examination; it was harassment and I for one am embarrassed for you. And two, do not, I repeat, do not, ever patronize me. I am not one of your cheap call girls." She could not have knocked Rickfield over any harder with a sledgehammer.

"You bitch!" Rickfield rose to confront her standing nine inches taller. "You stupid bitch. You have no idea what's at stake. None. It's bigger than you. At this rate I can assure you, you will never have an ear in Washington. Never. You will be deaf, dumb and blind in this town. I have been on this Hill for thirty years and paid my dues and I will not have a middle aged June Cleaver undermine a lifetime of work just because she smells her first cause."

Undaunted, Nancy stood her ground. "I don't know what you're up to Senator, but I do know that you're sand bagging these hearings. I've raised four kids and half a neighborhood, plus my husband talked in his sleep. I learned a lot about politicians, and I know sand bagging when I see it. Now, if you got stuck with these hearings and think they're a crock, that's fine. I hear it happens to everyone. But, I see them as important and I don't want you to interfere."

"You are in no position to ask for anything."

"I'm not asking. I'm telling." Where did she get the gumption, she asked herself. Then it occurred to her; *I'm not a politician, I want to see things get fixed.* "I will take issue with you, take you on publicly, if necessary. I was President of the PTA for 8 years. I am fluent in dealing with bitches of every size and shape. You're just a bastard."

* * * * *

Chapter 21

Friday, January 8
Washington, D.C.

As the hour is late, I am tempted to call a recess until tomorrow morning." Senator Merrill Rickfield said congenially from the center seat of the hearing room dais. His blow up with Nancy left him in a rage, but he ably disguised the anger by replacing it with overcompensated manners.

"However," he continued, "I understand that we scheduled someone to speak to us who has to catch a plane back to California?" Rickfield quickly glanced about the formal dais to espy someone who could help him fill in the details. Ken Boyers was engrossed in conversation and had to be prodded to respond. "Ken," Rickfield whispered while covering the microphone with his hand. He leaned over and behind his seat. "Is that right, this True Blue guy flew in for the day and he's out tonight?" Ken nodded, "yes, it was the only way we could get him."

"What makes him so bloody important?" Rickfield acted edgy.

"He's one of the software industry's leading spokesman. He owns dGraph," Ken said, making it sound like he was in on a private joke.

"So fucking what? What's he doing here?" Rickfield demanded. Keeping it to a whisper was hard.

"Industry perspective. We need to hear from all possible viewpoints in order to . . ." Ken explained.

"Oh, all right. Whatever. If this goes past five, have someone call my wife and tell her I'll see her tomorrow." Rickfield sat back and smiled a politician-hiding-something smile.

"Excuse me, ladies and gentlemen, a little scheduling confusion. I guess there's a first time for anything." Rickfield's chuckle told those-in-the-know that it was time to laugh now. If Rickfield saw someone not laughing at one of his arthritic jokes, he would remember. Might cost a future favor, so it was simpler to laugh. The mild titter throughout the hall that followed gave Rickfield the few seconds he needed to organize himself.

"Yes, yes. Page 239. Everyone there?" Rickfield scanned the other committee members and aides flipping pages frantically to find the proper place.

"We now have the pleasure of hearing from Pierre, now correct me if I say this wrong, Trewww-Blow?" Rickfield looked up over his glasses to see Pierre seated at the hearing table. "Is that right?" Scott had been able to keep his privileged location for the busier afternoon session by occupying several seats with his bags and coat. He figured correctly that he would be able to keep at least one as the room filled with more people than had been there for the morning session.

"Troubleaux, yes Senator. Very good." Pierre had turned on 110% charm. Cameras from the press pool in front of the hearing tables strobe-lit the room until every photographer had his first quota of shots. Troubleaux was still the computer industry's Golden Boy; he could do no wrong. Watching the reaction to Pierre's mere presence, Senator Rickfield instantly realized that True Blue here was a public relations pro, and could be hard to control. What was he gonna say anyway? Industry perspective my ass. This hearing was as good as over before it started until the television people showed up, Rickfield thought to himself with disgust.

"Mr. Trew-blow flew in extra special for this today," Rickfield orated. "And I'm sure we are all anxious to hear what he has to say." His Southern twang rang of boredom. Scott, who was sitting not 6 feet from where Pierre and the others testified, overheard Troubleaux's attorney whisper, "Sarcastic bastard."

Rickfield continued. "He is here to give us an overview of the problems that software manufacturers face. So, unless anyone has any comments before Mr. Trew-blow, I will ask him to read his opening statement."

"I do, Mr. Chairman," Senator Nancy Deere said. She said it with enough oomph to come across more dynamic on the sound system than did Rickfield. Political upstaging. Rickfield looked annoyed. He had had enough of her today. One thing after another, and all he wanted was to get through the hearings as fast as possible, make a "Take No Action" recommendation to the Committee and retire after election day. Mrs. Deere was making that goal increasingly difficult to reach.

"I recognize the Junior Senator. He said the word 'Junior' as if it was scrawled on a men's room wall. His point was lost on nobody, and privately, most would agree that it was a tasteless tactic.

"Thank you, Mr. Chairman," Senator Nancy Deere said poising herself. "I, too, feel indeed grateful, and honored, to have Mr. Troubleaux here today. His accomplishments over the last few years, legendary in some circles I understand, have been in no way inconsequential to the way that America does business. By no means do I wish to embarrass Mr. Troubleaux, and I do hope he will forgive me." Pierre gave Nancy a forgiving smile when she glanced at him. "However, I do feel it incumbent upon this committee to enter into the record the significant contributions he has made to the computer industry. If there are no objections, I have prepared a short biography." No one objected.

"Mr. Troubleaux, a native Frenchman, came to the United States at age 12 to attend Julliard School of Music on scholarship. Since founding dGraph, Inc. with the late Max Jones, dGraph and Mr. Troubleaux have received constant accolades from the business community, the software industry and Wall Street." It sounded more to Scott that she was reading past achievements before she handed out a Grammy.

"Entrepreneur of the Year, 1984, 1985, 1986, 1988, Cupertino Chamber of Commerce. Entrepreneur Year of the Year, California State Trade Association, 1987. Technical Achievement of the Year, IEEE, 1988 . . ."

Senator Deere read on about Pierre the Magnificent and the house that dGraph built. If this was an election for Sainthood, Pierre would be a shoo-in. But considering the beating that Rickfield had inflicted on a couple of earlier speakers, it looked like Nancy was trying to bolster Pierre for the upcoming onslaught.

". . .and he has just been appointed to the President's Council on Competitive Excellence." She closed her folder. "With that number of awards and credentials, I dare say I expect to be inundated with insights. Thank you Mr. Chairman."

"And, we thank you," Rickfield barbed, "for that introduction. Now, if there are no further interruptions," he glared at Nancy, "Mr. Trew-blow, would you care to read your prepared statement.

"No, Senator." Pierre came back. A hush descended over the entire room. He paused long enough to increase the tension in the room to the breaking point. "I never use prepared notes. I prefer to speak casually and honestly. Do you mind?" Pierre exaggerated his French accent for effect. After years of public appearances, he knew how to work and win a crowd. The cameras again flashed as Pierre had just won the first round of verbal gymnastics.

"It is a bit unusual, not to have an advanced copy of your statements, and then . . ." Rickfield stopped himself in mid sentence. "Never mind, I'm sorry. Please, Mr. Trew-blow, proceed."

"Thank you, Mr. Chairman." Pierre scanned the room to see how much of it he commanded. How many people were actually listening to what he was going to say, or were they there for the experience and another line item on a resume? This was his milieu. A live audience, and a TV audience as an extra added bonus. But he had planned it that way.

He never told anyone that he was the one who called the TV stations to tell them that there would be a significant news development at the Rickfield hearings. If he concentrated, Pierre could speak like a native American with a Midwest twang. He gave CNN, NBC, CBS and ABC down home pitches on some of the dirt that might come out. Only CNN showed up. They sent a junior producer. So what, everyone has to start somewhere. And this might be his big break.

"Mr. Chairman, committee members," his eyes scanned the dais as he spoke. "Honored guests," he looked around the hall to insure as many people present felt as important as possible, "and interested observers, I thank you for the opportunity to address you here today." In seconds he owned the room. Pierre was a captivating orator. "I must plead guilty to the overly kind remarks by Senator Deere, thank you very much. But, I am not feigning humility when I must lavish similar praises upon the many dedicated friends at dGraph, whom have made our successes possible."

Mutual admiration society, thought Scott. What a pile of D.C. horseshit, but this Pierre was playing the game better than the congressional denizens. As Pierre spoke, the corners of his mouth twitched, ever so slightly, but just enough for the observer to note that he took little of these formalities seriously. The lone TV camera rolled.

"My statement will be brief, Mr. Chairman, and I am sure, that after it is complete you will have many questions," Pierre said. His tone was kind, the words ominous.

"I am not a technical person, instead, I am a dreamer. I leave the bits and bytes to the wizards who can translate dreams into a reality. Software designers are the alchemists who can in fact turn silicon into gold. They skillfully navigate the development of thoughts from the amorphous to the tangible. Veritable artists, who like the painter, work from tabula rasa, a clean slate, and have a picture in mind. It is the efforts of tens of thousands of dedicated software pioneers who have pushed the frontiers of technology to such a degree that an entire generation has grown up in a society where software and digital interaction are assimilated from birth.

"We have come to think, perhaps incorrectly, in a discreet quantized, digital if you will, framework. To a certain extent we have lost the ability to make a *good guess*." Pierre paused. "Think about a watch, with a second hand. The analog type. When asked for the time, a response might be 'about three-thirty', or 'it's a quarter after . . .', or 'it's almost ten.' We approximate the time.

"With a digital watch, one's response will be more accurate; 'one-twenty-three," or '4 minutes before twelve,' or 'it's nine thirty-three.' We don't have to guess anymore. And that's a shame. When we lose the ability to make an educated guess, take a stab at, shoot from the hip, we cease using a valuable creative tool. Imagination!

"By depending upon them so completely, we fall hostage to the machines of our creation; we maintain a constant reliance upon their accuracy and infallibility. I am aware of the admitted parallel to many science fiction stories where the scientists' machines take over the world. Those tales are, thankfully, the products of vivid imaginations. The technology does not yet exist to worry about a renegade computer. HAL-9000 series computers are still far in the future. As long as we, as humans, tell the computer to open the pod bay doors, the pod bay doors will open." Pierre elicited a respectful giggle from the standing room only crowd, many of who came solely to hear him speak. Rickfield doodled.

"Yet, there is another viewpoint. It is few people, indeed, who can honestly claim to doubt the answer displayed on their calculator. They have been with us for over 20 years and we instinctively trust in their reliability. We assume the computing machine to be flawless. In many ways, theoretically it is perfect. But when man gets involved he fouls it up. Our fingers are too big for the digital key pad on our wristwatch-calculator-timer-TV. Since we can't approximate the answer, we have lost that skill, we can't guess, it becomes nearly impossible to know if we're getting the right answer.

"We trust our computers. We believe it when our spreadsheet tells us that we will experience 50% annual growth for five years. We believe the automatic bank teller that tells us we are overdrawn. We don't question it. We trust the computer at the supermarket. As far as I know, only my mother adds up her groceries by hand while still at the check-out counter."

While the image sank in for his audience, Pierre picked up the glass of ice water in front of him and sipped enough to wet his whistle. The crowd ate him up. He was weaving a web, drawing a picture, and only the artist knew what the climax would be.

"Excuse me." Pierre cleared his throat. "We as a people believe a computer print out is the closet thing to God on earth. Divinely accurate, piously error-free. Computerized bank statements, credit card reports, phone bills. . . our life is stored away in computer memories, and we trust that the information residing there is accurate. We want, we need to believe, that the machines that switch the street lights, the ones that run the elevator, the one that tells us we have to go to traffic court, we want to believe that they are right.

"Then on yet another hand, we all experience the frustration of the omnipresent complaint, *'I'm sorry the computer is down. Can you call back?'*" Again the audience emotionally related to what Pierre was saying. They nodded at each other and in Pierre's direction to indicate concurrence.

"I, as many of us have I am sure, arrived at a hotel, or an airport, or a car rental agency and been told that we don't have a reservation. For me there is an initial embarrassment of having my hand slapped by the computer terminal via the clerk. Then, I react strongly. I will raise my voice and say that I made a reservation, two days ago. I did it myself. Then the clerk will say something like, 'It's not in the computer'. How do you react to that statement?

"Suddenly your integrity is being questioned by an agglomeration of wire and silicon. Your veracity comes into immediate doubt. The clerk might think that you never even made a reservation. You become a liar because the computer disagrees with you. And to argue about it is an exercise in futility. The computer cannot reason. The computer has no ability to make a judgment about you, or me. It is a case of being totally black or white. And for the human of the species, that value system is unfathomable, paradoxical. Nothing is black and white. Yes, the computer is black and white. Herein again, the mind prefers the analog, the continuous, rather than the digitally discreet.

"In these cases, the role is reversed, we blame the computer for making errors. We tend to be verbally graphic in the comments we make about computers when they don't appear to work the way we expect them to. We distrust them." Pierre gestured with his arms to emphasize his point. The crescendo had begun.

"The sociological implications are incredible. As a people we have an inherent distrust of computers; they become an easy scapegoat for modern irritations. However, the balancing side of the scale is an implicit trust in their abilities. The inherent trust we maintain in computers is a deeply emotional one, much as a helpless infant trusts the warmth of contact with his parents. Such is the trust that we have in our computers, because, like the baby, without that trust, we could not survive."

He let the words sink in. A low rumbling began throughout the gallery and hall. Pierre couldn't hear any of the comments, but he was sure he was starting a stink.

"It is our faith in computers that lets us continue. The religious parallels are obvious, the evangelical computer is also the subject of fiction, but trust and faith are inextricably meshed into flavors and degrees. A brief sampling of common everyday items and events that are dependent on computers might prove enlightening.

"Without computers, many of lives' simple pleasures and conveniences would disappear. Cable television. Computer run. Movies like Star Wars. Special effects by computer. Magic Money Cards. Imagine life without them." A nervous giggle met Pierre's social slam. "Call holding. Remember dial phones? No computers needed. CD's? The staple diet of teenage America is the bread and butter of the music industry. Mail. Let's not forget the Post Office and other shippers. Without computers Federal Express would be no better than the Honest-We'll-Be-Here-Tomorrow Cargo Company."

"Oh, and yes," Pierre said dramatically. "Let's get rid of the microwave ovens, the VCR's and video cameras. I think I've made my point."

"I wish you would, Mr. Trew-blow," Senator Rickfield caustically interjected. "What is the point?" Rickfield was making no points taking on Pierre Troubleaux. He was too popular.

"Thank you, Senator, I am glad you asked. I was just getting there." Pierre's sugary treatment was an appropriate slap in Rickfield's face.

"Please continue." The Senator had difficulty saying the word 'please'.

"Yes sir. So, the prognostications made over a decade ago by the likes of Steve Jobs, that computers would alter the way we play, work and think have been completely fulfilled. Now, if we look at those years, we see a multi-billion dollar industry that has made extraordinary promises to the world of business. Computerize they say! Modernize! Get with the times! Make your operation efficient! Stay ahead of the competition! And we listened and we bought.

"With a projected life cycle of between only three and five years, technology progresses that fast, once computerized, forever computerized. To keep up with the competitive Jones', maintaining technical advantages requires upgrading to subsequent generations of computers. The computer salespeople told us to run our businesses on computers, send out Social Security checks by computer, replace typewriters with word processors and bank at home. Yet, somewhere in the heady days of phenomenal growth during the early 1980's, someone forgot. Someone, or more than likely most of Silicon Valley forgot, that people were putting their trust in these machines and we gave them no reason to. I include myself and my firm among the guilty.

"Very simply, we have built a culture, an economic base, the largest GNP in the world on a system of inter-connected computers. We have placed the wealths of our nations, the backbone of the fabric of our way of life, we have placed our trust in computers that do not warrant that trust. It is incredible to me that major financial institutions do not protect their computer assets as well as they protect their cash on hand.

"I find it unbelievable that the computers responsible in part for the defense of this country appear to have more open doors than a thousand churches on Sunday. It is incomprehensible to me that privacy, one of the founding principles of this nation, has been ignored during the information revolution. The massive data bases that contain vast amounts of personal data on us all have been amply shown to be not worthy of trust. All it takes is a home computer and elbow grease and you, or I, or he," Pierre pointed at various people seated around the room, "can have a field day and change anybody's life history. What happens if the computer disagrees with you then?

"It staggers the imagination that we have not attempted any coherent strategy to protect the lifeblood of our society. That, ladies and gentlemen is a crime. We spend $3 trillion on weapons in one decade, yet we do not have the foresight to protect our computers? It is a crime of indifference by business leaders. A crime against common sense by Congress who passes laws and then refuses to fund their enactment. Staggeringly idiotic. Pardon me." Pierre drained the water from his glass as the tension in the hearing room thickened.

"We live the paradox of simultaneously distrusting computers and being required to trust them and live with them. We are all criminals in this disgrace. Maybe dGraph more than most. Permit me to explain my involvement." The electricity in the room crackled and the novice CNN producer instructed the cameraman to get it right.

"Troubleaux!" A man's gruff accented voice elongated the syllables as he shouted from the balcony in the rear. A thousands eyes jerked to the source of the sound up above. Troubleaux himself turned in his seat to see a middle aged dark man, wearing a turban, pointing a handgun in his direction. Scott saw the weapon and wondered which politician was the target. Who was too pro-Israel this week? He immediately thought of Rickfield. No, he didn't have a commitment either way. He only rode the wave of popular sentiment.

Pierre too, wondered who was the target of a madman's suicide attack. It had to be suicide, there was no escape.

Scott's mind raced through a thousand thoughts during that first tenth of a second, not the endless minutes he later remembered. In the next split second, Scott realized, more accurately he knew, that Pierre was the target. The would-be victim.

As the first report from the handgun echoed through the cavernous chamber Scott was mid-leap at Pierre. Hell of a way to grab an exclusive, he thought. He fell into Pierre as the second shot exploded. Scott painfully caught the edge of the chair with his shoulder while pushing Pierre over sideways. They crumpled into a heap on the floor when the third shot fired.

Scott glanced up at the turbanned man vehemently mouthing words to an invisible entity skyward. The din from the panic in the room made it impossible to hear. Still brandishing the pistol, the assailant began to take aim again, at Scott and Pierre. Scott attempted to wiggle free from the tangle of Pierre's limbs and the chairs around them. He struggled to extricate himself but found it impossible.

A fourth shot discharged. Scott cringed, awaiting the worst but instead heard the bullet ricochet off a metal object above him. Scott's adrenal relief was punctuated by a loud and heavy sigh. He noticed that the assailant's shooting arm had been knocked upwards by a quick moving Capital policeman who violently threw himself at the turbanned man so hard that they both careened forward to the edge of the balcony. The policeman grabbed onto a bench which kept him from plummeting twenty feet below. His target was hurtled over the edge and landed prone on two wooden chairs which collapsed under the force. The shooting stopped.

Scott groaned from discomfort and a pain as he calmly began to pull away from Pierre. Then he noticed the blood. A lot of blood. He looked down at himself to see that his white pullover shirt, the one with Mickey Mouse instead of an alligator over the breast pocket, was wet with red. As was his jacket. His left hand had been on the floor, in a pool of blood that was oozing out of the back of Pierre's head. Scott tried to consciously control his physical revulsion to the body beneath him and the overwhelming urge to regurgitate.

Then Pierre's body moved. His chest heaved heavily and Scott pulled himself away completely. Pierre had been hit with at least two bullets, one exiting from the front of his chest and one stripping away a piece of skull exposing the brain. Gruesome.

"He's alive! Get a doctor!" Scott shouted. He lifted himself up to see over the tables. The mad shuffle to the exits continued. No one seemed to pay attention.

"Hey! Is there a doctor in the house?"

Scott looked down at Pierre and touched the veins in his neck. They were pulsing, but not with all of life's vigor. "Hey," Scott said quietly. "You're gonna be all right. We got a doctor coming. Don't worry. Just hang in there." Scott lied, but 40 years of movies and television had preprogrammed the sentiments.

"Drtppheeough . . ." Scott heard Pierre gurgle.

"What? What did you say?" Scott leaned his ear down closer to Pierre's mouth.

"DGOEROUGH."

"Take it easy," Scott said to comfort the badly injured Pierre Troubleaux.

"Nooo . . ." Pierre's limp body made a futile attempt at movement. Scott held him back.

"Hey, Pierre . . .you don't mind if I call you Pierre?" Scott adapted a mock French accent.

"Noo, DNGRAAAAPHJG . . ."

"Good. Why don't you just lay back and wait. The doctor'll be here in a second . . ."

"Sick . . ." Pierre managed to get out one word.

"Sick? Sick? Yeah, yeah, you're sick." Scott agreed sympathetically.

"DGRAF, sick." The effort caused Pierre to pant quickly.

"Dgraf, sick? What does that mean?" Scott asked.

"Sick. DGraph sick." Pierre's voice began to fade. "Sick. Don't use it. Don't use . . ."

"What do you mean don't use it? DGraph? Hey," Scott lightly shook Pierre. "You still with us? C'mon, what'd you say? Tell me again? Sick?"

Pierre's body was still.

* * * * *

The bullshit put out by the Government was beyond belief, thought Miles. How could they sit there and claim that all was well? It was common knowledge that computer security was dismal at best throughout both the civilian and military agencies. With the years he spent at NSA he knew that security was a political compromise and not a fiscal or technical reality. And these guys lied through their teeth. Oh, well, he thought, that would all change soon.

The report issued by the National Research Council in November of 1990 concurred with Miles' assessment. Security in the government was a disaster, a laughable travesty if it weren't for the danger to national security. The report castigated the results of decades of political in-fighting between agencies competing for survival and power.

He and Perky spent the day watching the hearings at Miles' high rise apartment. They had become an item in certain circles that Miles traveled and now they spent a great deal of time together. After several on-again off-again attempts at a relationship consisting of more than just sex, they decided not to see each other for over a year. That was fine by Miles; he had missed the freedom of no commitments.

At an embassy Christmas party months later, they ran into each other and the old animal attraction between them was re-released. They spent the weekend in bed letting their hormones loose to run rampant on each other. The two had been inseparable since. She was the first girl, woman, who was able to tolerate Miles' inflated ego and his constant need for emotional gratification.

Perky had little idea, by design, of the work that Miles was doing for Homosoto. She knew he was a computer and communications wizard, but that was all. Prying was not her concern. During his angry outbursts venting his frustration with Homosoto's pettiness, Perky supported him fully, unaware of his ultimate goal.

Perky found the testimony by Dr. Sternman to be educational; she actually began to understand some of the complicated issues surrounding security and privacy. In many ways it was scary, she told Miles. He agreed, saying if were up to him, things would get a lot worse before they get any better. She responded to his ominous comment with silence until Pierre Troubleaux began his testimony.

As well known as Bill Gates, as charismatic as Steve Jobs, Pierre Troubleaux was regarded as a sexy, rich and eligible bachelor ready for the taking. Stephanie Perkins was more stirred by his appearance and bearing than his words, so she joined Miles in rapt attention to watch his orations on live television.

When the first shot rang out their stunned confusion echoed the camera's erratic framing. As the second shot came across the TV, Perky sprang up and shouted, "No!" Tears dripped from the corners of her eyes.

"Miles! What's happening? They're shooting him . . ."

"I don't know . . ." A third shot and then the image of Scott and Pierre crumbling. "Holy shit, it's an assassination . . ."

"Miles, what's going on here?" Stephanie cried.

"This is fucking nuts . . .he's killing him . . ." Miles stared at the screen and spoke in a dull monotone. "I can't believe this is happening, it's not part of the plan . . ."

"Miles, Miles!" She screamed, desperately trying to get his attention. "Who? Miles! Who's killing him? What plan?"

"Fucking Homosoto, that yellow skinned prick . . ."

"Homosoto?" She stopped her bawling upon hearing the name.

Miles leapt up from the couch and raced over to the corner of the room with his computers. He pounced on the keyboard of the Nip-Com computer and told it to dial Homosoto's number in Japan. That son of a bitch better be there. Answer, damn it.

<<<AUTOCRYPT CONVERSATION>>>

Homosoto!!!!!

The delay seemed interminable as Miles waited for Homo to get on line. Perky followed him over to the computer and watched as he made contact. She knew that Miles and Homosoto spoke often over the computer, too often for Miles' taste. Homosoto whined to Miles almost every day, about one thing or another, and Miles complained to her about how irritating his childish interference was. But throughout it all, Perky had never been privy to their conversations. She had stayed her distance, until this time.

Miles had been in rages before; she had become unwillingly accustomed to his furious outbursts. Generally they were unfocused eruptions; a sophomoric way of releasing pent up energy and frustration. But this time, Miles' face clearly showed fear. Stephanie saw the dread. "Miles! What does Homosoto have to do with this? Miles, please!" She pleaded with him to include her. The screen finally responded.

MR. FOSTER. AN UNEXPECTED PLEASURE

You imperial mother fucker.

EXPLAINATION, PLEASE.

You're a fucking murderer

I TAKE EXCEPTION TO THAT

Take exception to this, Jack! What the hell did you kill him for?

I ASSUME YOU HAVE BEEN WATCHING TELEVISION

Aren't we the Einstein of Sushi land.

YOUR MANNERS

You killed him! Why?

Stephanie read the monitor and wept quietly as the conversation scrolled before her. She placed her hands on Miles' shoulders in an effort to feel less alone.

IT WAS A NECESSARY EVIL. HE COULD NOT BE PER-
MITTED TO SPEAK. NOT YET.

So you killed him?

ONE OF MY PEOPLE GOT A LITTLE OVER ZEALOUS. IT IS
REGRETTABLE, BUT NECESSARY

It is not necessary to kill anyone. Nowhere in the plan does it call for murder! That was part of our deal.

THE WINDS BLOW. CONDITIONS CHANGE.

The wind blows up your ass!

THAT DOES NOT CHANGE THE FACT THAT HE WAS GOING
TO TELL WHAT HE KNEW.

What the hell does he know?

DGRAPH. THAT'S THE PROGRAM WE INFECTED

DGraph? That's impossible. That's the most popular program in the world. How did you infect it?

I BOUGHT IT.

You own dGraph? I thought that Cross Tech owned them.

OSO OWNS DATA TECH. YOU DID NOT LISTEN TO YOUR
OWN ADVICE. I BOUGHT IT AFTER YOU VISITED ME FOR
THE SECOND TIME. IT SEEMED PRUDENT. WE ALSO

BOUGHT A HALF DOZEN OTHER SMALL, PROMISING
SOFTWARE COMPANIES, JUST AS YOU SUGGESTED.
VERY GOOD PLAN.

And Troubleaux knows?

OF COURSE. HE HAD INCENTIVE.

So you try to kill him?

HE LOST HIS INCENTIVE. IT WAS NECESSARY. HE WAS
GOING TO TELL AND, AS YOU SAID, SECRECY IS
PARAMOUNT. YOUR WORDS.

Yes, secrecy, but not murder. I can't be part of that.

BUT YOU ARE MR. FOSTER. I HOPE THAT THIS IS AN ISO-
LATED INCIDENT THAT WILL NOT BE REPEATED.

It had damn well better be.

DO NOT FORGET MR. FOSTER THAT YOU HAVE A SIZABLE
PAYMENT COMING. I WOULD HATE TO SEE YOU LOSE
THAT WHEN THINGS ARE SO CLOSE.

<<<CONNECTION TERMINATED>>>

"Son of a bitch," Miles said out loud. "Son of a bitch."

"What's going on? Miles?" Perky followed him back to the couch
in front of the TV and sat close with her arm around him. She was
still crying softly.

"It's gonna start. That's amazing." He blankly stared forward.

"What's gonna start? Miles, did you kill someone?"

"Oh, no!" He turned to her in sincerity. "That bastard Homosoto
did. Jesus, I can't believe it."

"What are you involved in? I thought you were a consultant."

"I was. Tomorrow I will be a very rich retired consultant." He
pulled her hands into his and spoke warmly. "Listen, it's better that
your don't know what's going on, much better. But I promise you, I
promise you, that Homosoto is behind it, not me. I couldn't ever kill
anyone. You need to believe that."

"Miles, I do, but you seem to know more than . . ."

"I do, and I can't say anything. Trust me," he said as he brought
her close to him. "This will all work out for the best. I promise you.
Look at me," he said and pulled up her chin so she gazed directly into
his eyes. "I have a lot invested in you, and this project. More than
you could ever know, and now that it is nearly over, I can put more
time into you. After all, you bear some of the responsibility." Miles'
loving attitude was a contradiction from his usual self centered pre-
occupation.

"Me?" She asked.

"Who got me involved with Homosoto in the first place?" he said glaring at her.

"I guess I did, but . . ."

"I know, I'm kidding," he said squeezing her closer. "I'm not blaming you for anything. I didn't know he could resort to murder, and if I did, I never would have gotten involved in the first place."

"Miles, I love you." That was the first time in their years of on-again off-again contact that she told him how she felt. Now she had to decide if she would tell him that he was just another assignment, and that in all likelihood she had just lost her job, too. "I really do love you."

* * * * *

"The last goddamned time this happened was in the 1950's when Puerto Rican revolutionaries started a shoot-em-up in the old gallery," the President shouted.

Phil Musgrave and Quinton Chambers listened to the angry President. His tirade began minutes after he summoned them both to his office. They were as frustrated and upset as he was, but it was their job to listen until the President had blown off enough steam.

"I am well aware a democracy, a true democracy is subject to extremist activists, but," the President sighed, "this is getting entirely out of hand. What is it about this computer stuff that stirs up so much bad blood?" He waited for an answer.

"I'm not sure that computers are to blame, sir," said Phil. "First of all, the assailant used a ceramic pistol. No way for our security to detect it without a physical search and that wouldn't go over well with anyone." The brilliant Musgrave was making a case for calm rationality in the light of the live assassination attempt. "Second, at this point there is no connection between Troubleaux and his attacker. We're not even 100% sure that Troubleaux was the target."

"That's a crock Phil," asserted the President. "It doesn't take a genius to figure out that there is an obvious connection between this computer crap and the Rickfield incident. I want to know what it is, and I want to know fast."

"Sir," Chambers said quietly. "We have the FBI and the CIA investigating, but until the perpetrator regains consciousness, which may be doubtful because his spine was snapped in the fall, we won't know too much."

The President frowned. "Does it seem odd to you that Mason, the Times reporter was there with Troubleaux at the exact time he got shot?"

388

"No sir, just a coincidence. It seems that computer crime has been his hot button for a while," Musgrave said. "I don't think he's involved at all . . ."

"I'm not suggesting that," the President interrupted. "But he does seem to be where the action is. I think it would be prudent if we knew a bit more of his activities. Do I need to say more?"

"No sir. Consider it done."

* * * * *

Chapter 22

Friday, January 8
Washington, D.C.

It seemed that everyone in the world wanted to speak to Scott at once. The FBI spent an hour asking him inane questions. "Why did you help him?" "Do you know Troubleaux?" "Why were you at the hearings?" "Why didn't you sit with the rest of the press?" "Where's your camera?" "Can we read your notes?"

Scott was cooperative, but he had his limits. "You're the one who's been writing those computer stories, aren't you?" "What's in this for you?"

Scott excused himself, not so politely. *If you want me for anything else, please contact the paper,* he told the FBI agents who had learned nothing from anyone else either.

He escaped from other reporters who wanted his reporter's insight. For the first time, he experienced what it was like to be hounded relentlessly by the press. Damned pain in the ass, he thought, and damn stupid questions. "How did you feel . . .?" "Were you scared . . .?" "Why did you . . .?"

The exhausted Scott found the only available solace in a third floor men's room stall where he wrote a piece for the paper on his GRiD laptop computer. Nearly falling asleep on the toilet seat, he temporarily refreshed himself with ice cold water from the tap and changed from his bloodsoaked clothes into fresh jeans and a pullover from his hanging bag that still burdoned him. One reporter from the Washington Post thought himself lucky to have found Scott in the men's room, but when Scott finished bombasting him with his own verbal assault, the shell shocked reporter left well enough alone.

After the Capital police were through questioning Scott, he wanted to make a swift exit to the airport and get home. They didn't detain him very long, realizing Scott would always be available. Especially since this was news. His pocket shuttle schedule showed there was a 6:30 flight to Westchester Airport; he could then grab a limo home and be in bed by ten. He was exhausted.

Three days in Europe on next to no sleep. Rush back to public Senate hearings that no one has ever heard about. Television cameras appear, no one admits to calling the press, and then, Pierre. He needed time to think, alone. Away from the conflicting influences that were tearing at him.

On one hand his paper expected him to report and investigate the news. On another, Tyrone wanted help on his investigation because official Washington had turned their backs on him. And Spook. Spook. Why is that so familiar? Then he had to be honest with his own feelings. What about this story had so captivated him that he had let many of his other assignments go by the wayside?

Doug was pleased with Scott's progress, and after today, well, what editor wouldn't be pleased to have a potential star writer on the National news. But Scott was drowning in the story. There were too many pieces, from every conceivable direction, with none too many of them fitting neatly together. He remembered Hurcule Poirot, Agatha Christie's detective, recalling that the answers to a puzzle came infinitely easier to the fictional sleuth than to him.

Scott called into Doug.

"Are you all right?" Doug asked with concern but didn't wait for an answer. "I got your message. Next time call me at home. I thought you were going to be in Europe till Wednesday."

"Hold you horses," Scott said with agitation. Doug shut up and listened to the distraught Scott. "I have the story all written for you. Both of them are going into surgery and the Arab is in pretty bad shape. The committee made itself scarce real fast and there's no one else to talk to. I've had to make a career out of avoiding reporters. Seems like I'm the only one left with nothing to say." Doug heard the exhaustion in Scott's voice.

"Listen," Doug said with a supportive tone. "You've been doing a bang up job, but I'm sending Ben down there to cover the assassination attempt. I want you to go to bed for 24 hours and that's an order. I don't want to hear from you till Monday."

Scott gratefully acknowledged Doug's edict, and might have suggested it himself if it weren't for his dedication to the story he had spent months on already. "O.K.," Scott agreed. "I guess not much will happen . . ."

"That's right. I want you fresh anyway," Doug said with vigor. "If anything major comes up, I'll see that we call you. Fair enough?"

Scott checked his watch as his cab got caught up in the slow late afternoon rush hour traffic on the George Washington Parkway. If he missed this flight, he thought, there was another one in an hour. The pandemonium of Friday afternoon National Airport had become legendary. Despite extensive new construction, express services and modernized terminals, the airport designers in their infinite wisdom had neglected in any way to improve the flow of automobile traffic in and out of the airport.

As they approached, Scott could see the American terminal several hundred yards away from his cab. They were stuck behind an interminable line of other taxis, limousines, cars and mini-busses that had been stacking for ten minutes. Scott decided to hike the last few yards and he paid the driver who tried to talk him into remaining till the ride was over. Scott weaved through the standstill traffic jam until he saw the problem. So typical. A stretch Mercedes 560, was blocking the only two lanes that were passable. Worse yet, there was no one in the car. No driver, no passengers. Several airport police were discussing their options when a tall, slender black man, dressed in an impeccably tailored brown suit came rushing from the terminal doors.

"Diplomatic immunity!" He called out with a thick, overbearing Cambridge accent.

The startled policemen saw the man push several people to the side, almost knocking one elderly woman to the ground. Scott reached the Mercedes and stayed to watch the upcoming encounter

"I said, Diplomatic immunity," he said authoritatively. "Put your tickets away."

"Sir, are you aware that your car has been blocking other cars from . . ."

"Take it up with the Embassy," the man said as he roughly opened the driver's door. "This car belongs to the Ambassador and he is immune from your laws." He shut the door, revved the engine and pulled out squealing his tires. Several pedestrians had to be fleet of foot to miss being sideswiped.

"Fucking camel jockeys," said one younger policeman.

"He's from equatorial Africa, Einstein," said another.

"It's all the same to me. Foreigners telling us how to live our lives," the third policeman said angrily.

"You know, I can get 10 days for spitting on the ground, but these assholes can commit murder and be sent home a hero. It's a fucking crime," the younger one agreed.

"O.K., guys, leave the politics to the thieves on Capital Hill. Let's get this traffic moving," the senior policeman said as they started the process of untangling airport gridlock.

Another day in the nation's capital, Scott thought. A melting pot that echoed the days of Ellis Island. Scott carried his briefcase, laptop computer and garment bag through the crowded terminal and made a left to the men's room next to the new blue neon bar. Drinks were poured especially fast in the National Airport Bar. Fliers were traveling on such tight schedules that they had to run to the bar, grab two quick ones and dash to the gate. The new security regulations placed additional premiums on drinking time. The bar accommodated their hurried needs well. Scott put down his baggage next to the luggage pile and stole a bar seat from a patron rushing off to catch his flight. One helluva chaotic day. He ordered a beer, and sucked down half of it at once. The thirst quenching was a superior experience. Brain dulling would take a little longer.

The clamorous rumble of the crowd and the television blaring from behind the bar further anesthetized Scott's racing mind. He finally found himself engrossed in the television, blissfully ignorant of all going on around him. Scott became so absorbed in the local news that he didn't notice the striking blonde sit next to him. She ordered a white wine and made herself comfortable on the oversized stool.

Scott turned to the bartender and asked for another beer during the commercial. It was then he noticed the gorgeous woman next to him and her golden shoulder length hair. Lightly tanned skin with delicate crow's feet at the edges of her penetrating blue eyes gave no indication of her age. An old twenty to a remarkable forty five. Stunning, he thought. Absolutely stunning. He shook the thought off and returned his attention to the television.

He heard the announcer from Channel 4, the local NBC affiliate. "Topping tonight's stories, Shooting at Senate Hearing." The picture changed from the anchorman to a live feed from outside the New Senate Office Building, where Scott had just been. "Bringing it to us live is Shauna Miller. Shauna?"

"Thank you Bill," she said looking straight into the camera holding the microphone close to her chin. Behind her was a bevy of police and emergency vehicles and their personnel in a flurry of activity.

"As we first reported an hour ago, Pierre Troubleaux, President of dGraph, one of the nation's leading software companies, was critically injured while giving testimony to the Privacy and Technology Containment subcommittee. At 3:15 Eastern Time, an unidentified assailant, using a 9mm Barretta, shot Mr. Troubleaux four times, from the visitor's balcony which overlooks the hearing room. Mr. Troubleaux was answering questions about . . . "

Scott's mind wandered back to the events of a few hours ago. He still had no idea why he did it. The television replayed the portion of the video tape where Pierre was testifying. While he spoke, the shots rang out and the camera image suddenly blurred in search of the source of the sound. Briefly the gunman is seen and then the picture swings back to Pierre being pushed out of his chair by a man in a blue sports jacket and white shirt. As two more gun shots ring out the figure covers Pierre. Two more shots and the camera finally settles on

393

Pierre Troubleaux bleeding profusely from the head, his eyes open and glazed.

Scott shuddered at the broadcast. It captured the essence of the moment, and the terror that he and the hundreds of others at the hearing had experienced. Shauna Miller reappeared.

"And we have here the man who dove to Mr. Troubleaux's rescue when the shooting began." The camera angle pulled back and showed Scott standing next to the newswoman.

"This is Scott Mason, a reporter from the New York City Times who is attending the hearings on behalf of his paper. Scott," she turned away from the camera to speak directly to Scott. "How does it feel being the news instead of reporting it?" She stuck the microphone into his face.

"Uh," Scott stammered. What a stupid fucking question, he thought. "It does give me a different perspective," he said, his voice hollow.

"Yes, I would think so," Shauna added. "Can you tell us what happened?"

Idiot can't come up with anything better than that? "Sure, be happy to." Scott smiled at the camera. "One of the country's finest software executives just had part of his head blown off so his brains could leak on my coat and the scumbag that shot him took a sayonara swan dive that broke every bone in his body. How's that?" He said devilishly.

"Uh," Shauna hesitated. "Very graphic." This isn't Geraldo she thought, just the local news. "Do you have anything to add?"

"Yeah? I got to get some sleep."

The camera zoomed into a closeup of Shauna Miller. "Thank you, Mr. Mason." She brightened up. "Mr. Troubleaux and the alleged gunman have been taken to Walter Reede Medical Center where they are undergoing surgery. Both are listed in critical condition and Mr. Troubleaux is still in a coma." Shauna droned on for another 30 seconds with filler nonsense. How did she ever get on the air, Scott thought. And, why does she remain?

"That was you."

Scott started at the female voice. He turned to the left and only saw salesmen and male lobbyists drinking heartily. He pivoted in the other direction and came face to face with Sonja Lindstrom. "Sorry?"

"That was you," she said widening her smile to expose perfectly formed brilliant white Crest teeth.

An electric tingle ran up Scott's legs and through his torso. The pit of his stomach felt suddenly empty. He gulped silently and his face reddened. "What was me?"

She pointed at the television. "That was you at the hearing today, where Troubleaux got shot."

"Yeah, 'fraid so," he said.

"The camera treats you well. I was at the hearing, too, but I just figured out who you were." Her earnest compliment came as a surprise to Scott. He raised his eyebrows in bewilderment.

"Who I am?" He questioned.

"Oh, sorry," she extended her hand to Scott. "I'm Sonja Lindstrom. I gather you're Scott Mason." He gently took her hand and a rush of electricity rippled up his arm till the hairs on the back of his neck stood on end.

"Guilty as charged," he responded. He pointed his thumb at the television. "Great interview, huh?"

"She epitomizes the stereotype of the dumb blond." Sonja turned her head slightly. "I hope you're not prejudiced?"

"Prejudiced?

She picked up her wine glass and sipped gingerly. "Against blondes."

"No, no. I was married to one," he admitted. "But, I won't hold that against you." Scott wasn't aggressive with women and his remark surprised even him. Sonja laughed appreciatively.

"It must have been rough," Sonja said empathetically. "I mean the blood and all."

"Not exactly my cup of tea. I don't do the morgue shift." Scott shuddered. "I'll stick to computers, not nearly so adventurous."

"And hacker bashing." she said firmly. She took another sip of wine.

"How would you know that?" Scott asked.

She turned and smiled at Scott. "You're famous. You're known as the Hacker Smacker by quite a few in the computer field. Not everyone appreciates what you have to say." Sonja, ever so politely, challenged Scott.

"Frankly my dear, I don't give a damn," he smirked.

"That's the spirit," she encouraged. "Not that I agree with everything you have to say."

"I assume you have read my dribble upon occasion."

"Upon occasion, yes," she said with a coy sweetness.

"So, since you know so much about me, I stand at a clear disadvantage. I only know you as Sonja."

"You're right. That's not fair at all." She straightened herself on the bar stool. "Sonja Lindstrom, dual citizenship U.S. and Denmark. Born May 11, 1964, Copenhagen. Moved here when I was two. Studied political science at George Washington, minored in sociology. Currently a public relations consultant to computer jocks. I live in D.C. but I'm rarely here."

"Lucky for me," Scott ventured.

Sonja didn't answer him as she slowly drained the bottom of her wine glass. She glanced slyly at him, or was that his imagination?

"Can a girl buy a guy a drink?"

The clock said there was fifteen minutes before Scott's flight took off. No contest.

"I'd be honored," Scott said as he nodded his head in gratitude.

Sonja Lindstrom bought the next two rounds and they talked. No serious talk, just carefree, sometimes meaningless banter that made them laugh and relish the moment. Scott didn't know he had missed his second flight until it was time for the 8:15 plane to LaGuardia. It had been entirely too long. longer than he cared to remember since he had relaxed, disarmed himself near a woman. There was an inherent distrust, fear of betrayal, that Scott had not released, until now.

"So, about your wife," she asked after a lull in their conversation.

"My wife?" Scott shrank back.

"Humor me," she said.

"Nothing against her, it just didn't work out."

"What happened?" Sonja pursued.

"She was an artist, a sculptor. And if I say so myself, an awful one. A three year old could do as well with stale Play-Dough."

"You're a critic, too?" Sonja bemused.

"Only of her art. She got into the social scene in New York, gallery openings, the she-she sect. You know what I mean?" Sonja nodded. "So, when I decided to make a career shift, well, she wasn't in complete agreement with me. Even though in 8 years she had never sold one single piece of art, she was convinced, by her socialite pals, that her work was extraordinarily original and would become, without any doubt, the next Pet Rock of the elite."

"So?"

"So, she gets the bug to go to the Coast and make her mark. I think some of her Park Avenue pals went to Beverly Hills and wanted her to come out to be their entertainment. She expected me to follow her hallucinations, but I just couldn't play that part. She's a little left of the Milky Way for me."

"How long has it been?" Sonja asked with warmth.

"Three years now."

"So, what have these years been like?"

"Oh, fine," he said. Sonja gave him a disbelieving dirty look. "O.K., kinda lonely. I'm not complaining, mind you, but when she was there, no matter how inane our conversations were, not matter how far out in the stratosphere her mind was, at least she was someone to talk to, someone to come home to. She's a sweet girl, I loved her, but she had needs that . . .well. It wasn't all bad, we had a great few years. I just couldn't let her madness, harmless though it was, run my life. We're still friends, we talk fairly often. I hope she becomes the next Dali."

"That's very gracious of you," Sonja said sincerely.

"Not really. I really feel that way. It's her life, and, she never wanted or tried to hurt me. She was just following her star."

"Has she sold any of her art?" Sonja asked.

"It's on perpetual display, she says," Scott said.

"Why don't you buy one? To make her feel good?"

"Ha! She feels fine. Beverly Hills is not the worst place in the world to be accepted." He lost himself in thought for a moment. "I think it has worked out for both of us."

"Except, you're lonely," she came back.

"I got into my work. A career shift at my age, you know, I had a lot to learn. So, I've really put myself into the job, and I've been getting a lot out of it." He stared at the gorgeous woman to whom he had been telling his personal feelings. "But, yes, I do miss the companionship," he hinted.

The clock over the bar announced it was quarter to ten. "Hey." Scott turned to face Sonja squarely. "I gotta go, you don't know how much I don't want to, but I gotta." He spoke with a pained sincerity.

"No you don't," she said exuberantly.

"Huh?"

Sonja's entire face glowed with effervescence. "Have you ever done anything crazy?"

"Sure, of course," Scott nonchalantly said.

"No, I mean really crazy. Totally off the wall. Spontaneous." She grabbed Scott's shoulders. "Haven't you ever wanted to go off the deep end and not care what anybody thinks?" Scott got caught up in Sonja's contagious enthusiasm. This absolutely stunning blonde bombshell exuded enough sexual enthusiasm for the entire NFL, and he was playing it cool. He wondered why.

"I was a real hell raiser as a kid . . ."

"Listen, Scott." Her demeanor turned serious. "Are you willing to do something nuts right now? And go through with it?"

Here was one of the most beautiful women he had ever seen asking him to make a borderline insane promise. Her painted lips broke into a thin smile. Ten minutes to the last flight.

"I'm game. What is it?" Scott played along. He could always say no. Right?

"Wait here a minute." Sonja grabbed her purse and dashed out of the bar. Scott's eyes followed her in amazement.

Scott finished his beer and the clock indicated that the last flight to New York had left. He wondered what was keeping Sonja so long, and then she suddenly whisked back into the bar.

"C'mon, we have to hurry." Sonja shuffled papers in and out of her purse. She threw enough money on the bar to cover their drinks.

Scott scooted off of his bar stool laughing. "Hurry? Where're we going?"

"Shhhh, get your bags," Sonja said urgently. "You do have a passport don't you?" She asked with concern.

"I just came from Europe, yeah." His bewilderment was clear while he retrieved his luggage.

"Good. Follow me."

Sonja dashed through the terminal to the security check with Scott struggling to keep up. The view of her exquisite figure was followed by more than just Scott. Her molded red dress left little to the imagination. She put her purse on the conveyor belt and Scott did the same with his two bags. She darted from the security station leaving Mason to reorganize himself. His ability to run was encumbered by his luggage so he watched carefully to see into which gate she was headed.

Gate, gate? Where am I going? And why? He would have laughed if he wasn't out of breath from wind sprinting through the airport. He followed Sonja into Gate 3.

She handed a couple of tickets to the attendant. "We're the last ones, hurry up, Scott," Sonja giggled.

"Where are we going . . .where did the tickets . . .how are you?" Scott stumbled through his thoughts.

"Get on, Scott. We'll talk." She held out her hand, beckoning him seductively.

The attractive flight attendant stared at Scott. His hesitancy was holding up the flight. He looked at Sonja. "This is nuts," he said quietly.

"Told you so."

"Where is it going?"

"Jamaica," she beamed.

"Oh, Sonja, come on, this isn't real." Why the hell was he trying to talk himself out of a fantasy in the making.

"I'm getting on. I need a weekend to cool out, and I bet that it wouldn't hurt you any. After what happened." Sonja took the separated boarding pass and looked back once before she left. Scott stood still. He stared as Sonja disappeared down the tunnel to the plane.

The flight attendant appeared quite annoyed. "Well, are you or aren't you?"

Scott reasoned that if he reasoned out the pros and the cons the plane would be gone regardless of his decision. "Fuck it," he said and he walked briskly down the ramp.

He entered the Airbus behind the cockpit and turned right to find Sonja. It didn't take long. She was the only person sitting in first class. "Fancy running into you here," she said waving from the plush leather seat.

"Quite," he said in his well practiced West London accent. "Dare I guess how long it's been?" He placed his bags in the empty first class storage compartment.

"Too long. Much too long. You had me worried," Sonja said melodramatically.

"I still have me worried."

"I thought you might chicken out," she said.

"I still might."

The three hour flight was replete with champagne, brie and similar delicacies. They gorged on the delicacies to their heart's content. One flight attendant, two passengers. Light talk, innocuous flirtations, not so innocuous flirtations, more chatting - time passed, hours disguised as seconds.

Half Moon Bay is a one hour cab ride from the airport and, true to Jamaican hospitality, the hotel staff expected them. They were led to two adjoining rooms after being served the obligatory white rum punch with a yellow umbrella. It was nearly 3 AM. Scott was working on 80 hours without sleep.

"Scott?" Sonja asked as they prepared to go into their respective rooms.

"Yes," he said.

"Thank you."

"For what?"

"For tomorrow night."

After four hours sleep, Sonja knocked on Scott's door. "Rise and shine! Beach time!"

Scott swore to himself, looked at the clock on the night stand, and then swore again. Ugh! Scott forced himself out of bed and opened the door. The vision of Sonja Lindstrom in a bathing suit that used no more than 4 square inches of material was instantly arousing. Despite 39 plus years of morning aversions, Scott readied himself at breakneck speed, thinking that reality and fantasy were often inseparable. The question was, what was this? Was he really in the Caribbean? *No!*, he thought. *This is real! Holy shit, this is real. I wasn't as drunk as I thought.* Intoxication takes many forms, and this appears to be a delicious wine. During breakfast she managed to talk him into going to the nude beach, about a half mile down Half Moon Bay.

"God, you're uptight," she said as she shed her g-string. on the isolated pristine coastline. She was a natural blond with a dancer's body where the legs and buttocks merge into one.

"I am not!" He defended.

"I bet you can't take them off. For personal reasons," she laughed out loud pointing at the baggy swim suit he borrowed from the resort. She lay down on her back, perfectly formed breasts pointing at the sky. Scott noticed only the faintest of tan lines several inches below her belly button. She patted the huge towel, inviting Scott to join her. There was room enough for three,

"Well," he agreed. "It might prove embarrassing. I thought my intentions were honorable."

"Bull. Neither are mine." She arched her back and patted the towel again.

"Fuck it," he said laughingly as he dropped his bathing suit and dropped quickly, facedown next to Sonja. "Ouch!" He yelled louder than the hurt was worth. "I hate it when that happens," he said checking to make sure that the pieces were still intact.

They spent the next two days exploring Half Moon Bay, the lush green hills behind the resort and each other. Scott forgot about work, forgot about the hackers, forgot about Tyrone. He never thought about Kirk, Spook, or any of the blackmail schemes he was so caught up in investigating. And, he forgot, at least temporarily about the incident with Pierre. The world consisted of only two people, mutually radiating a glow flush with passion; retreating into each other so totally that no imaginable distraction could disturb their urgings.

They slept no more than an hour all Saturday night, "I told you I wanted to thank you for tomorrow night!" she said. They made it to the water's edge early Sunday morning. Scott's body was redder in some places than it had ever been, and Sonja's tan line all but disappeared. They both knew that the fantasy was going to be over in the morning, a 7:00 AM flight back to reality, but neither spoke of it. The *Here and Now* was the only reality that they wanted to face.

"I'm impressed," Sonja said turning to face Scott on the beach towel. No matter in which direction she turned, her body stood tall and firm.

"Impressed, with what?" Scott giggled.

"I had two days to loosen you up before you went back to that big bad city. I'm ahead of schedule."

"What schedule?"

"Scott, we need to talk." Sonja reached over and touched Scott's shoulder. He couldn't take his eyes off of her magnificent nude figure. "Did you ever work on something, for a very long time; really get yourself involved, dedicated, and then find out in was all for the wrong reasons? That's how I feel now."

* * * * *

Saturday, January 10
Langley, Virginia

It is not uncommon for the day employees at the CIA in Langley to arrive at their desks before 6:00 AM. Even on a Saturday. Today, Martin Templer arrived early to prepare for an update meeting with the director. Nothing special, just the weekly report. He found that he could get more done early in the morning. He enjoyed the time alone in his quiet office so he could complete the report without constant interruption. Not fifteen minutes into his report, his phone rang. Damn, he thought, it's starting already.

"Yeah?" Templer said gruffly into the mouthpiece.

"Martin?"

"Yeah, who's this?"

"Alex."

Templer had almost forgotten about their meeting. "Will small wonders never cease. Where have you been?"

"Still in Europe. I've been looking for some answers as we discussed."

"Great! What have you got?" Templer grabbed a legal pad.

"Nothing," Alex said with finality. "Nothing. Nobody knows of any such operation, not even a hint." Alex had mastered the art of lying twenty years ago. "But I'll tell you," he added. "I think that you may be on to something."

"If there's nothing how can there be something?" asked Martin Templer.

This was Alex's opportunity to throw the CIA further off the track. Since he and Martin were friends, as much friends as is possible in this line of work, Alex counted on being believed, at least for a while. "Everybody denies any activity and that in itself is unusual. Even if nothing is happening, enough of the snitches on the street will claim to be involved to bolster their own credibility. However, my friend, I doubt a handful even know about your radiation, but it has gotten a lot of people thinking. I get the feeling that if they didn't know about your problems, they will soon enough. I wish I could be of further help, but it was all dead ends."

"I understand. It happens; besides it was a long shot," Martin sighed. "Do me a favor, and keep your eyes and ears open."

"I will, and this one is on the house," said Alex.

After he hung up something struck Martin as terribly wrong. In twenty years Alex had never, ever, done anything for free. Being a true mercenary, it wasn't in his character to offer assistance to anyone without sufficient motivation, and that meant money. Martin noted the event, and reminded himself to include this in his report to the Director.

$$* * * * *$$

The television coverage of the Senate hearings left Taki Homosoto with radically different emotions. He had to deal with them both immediately.

DIALING . . .

<<<AUTOCRYPT CONVERSATION>>>

I AM NOT PLEASED

Ahmed Shah heard his communications computer beep at him. He pushed the joystick control on his wheelchair and steered over to read Homosoto's message.

Greetings

THAT WAS A MOST SLOPPY JOB.

Some things cannot be helped.

WHY IS HE NOT DEAD?

It was a difficult hit

IS THAT WHAT YOU TELL ARAFAT WHEN YOU MISS?

I do not work for Arafat

YOUR MAN IS ALIVE TOO.

Yes, fortunately.

NO, THAT IS UNFORTUNATE. KILL HIM. AND MAKE SURE THAT TROUBLEAUX IS TAKEN CARE OF. HE CANNOT SPEAK TO ANYONE

He is in a coma

PEOPLE WAKE UP. I DO NOT WANT HIM TO WAKE UP.

It will be done. I promise you.

I DO NOT WANT PROMISES. I WANT THEM BOTH DEAD. TROUBLEAUX MUST NOT BE PERMITTED TO SPEAK TO ANYONE. IS THAT CLEAR?

Yes, it will be done.

FOR YOUR SAKE I HOPE SO. I DO NOT TOLERATE SLOP-PINESS.

<<<CONNECTION TERMINATED>>>

Homosoto dialed his computer again, to a number inside Germany. The encryption and privacy keys were automatically set before Alex Spiradon's computer answered. To Homosoto's surprise, Alex was there.

MR ALEX.

Yes

CONGRATULATIONS. RICKFIELD IS BEING MOST COOPERATIVE.

He has many reasons to.

MILLIONS OF REASONS

We merely gave him the incentive to cooperate. I do not expect that he will maintain his position for very long.

YOUR HANDLING OF HIM HAS BEEN EXCELLENT. I HAVE NOT SEEN A U.S. NEWSPAPER. HOW DO THEY REACT TO HIS COMMITTEE?

He took a small beating from a couple of papers, but nothing damaging. It's the way Washington works.

WHO IS SENATOR DEERE? SHE COULD PRESENT A PROB-LEM.

I don't think so. Between her and Rickfield, the sum total will be a big zero. There will be confusion and dissension. I think it works in our favor.

I WILL FOLLOW THE PROGRESS WITH INTEREST. WHEN ARE THE HEARINGS TO CONTINUE?

Next week. One other thing. You asked that I get to Scott. Consider it done. You found a most attractive weakness and he succumbed instantly. But, I should say, I don't think it was necessary. He is doing fine on his own.

I THINK IT IS NECESSARY. IT IS DONE?

We have a conduit.

KEEP THE PIPELINE FULL.

<<<CONNECTION TERMINATED>>>

* * * * *

Sunday, January 10
New York City Times

What's wrong with Ford?

by Scott Mason

Ford is facing the worst public relations disaster for an automobile manufacturer since the Audi acceleration problem made international news.

Last month in Los Angeles alone, over 1200 Ford Taurus and Mercury Sable cars experienced a total breakdown of the electrical system. Radios as well as anti-skid braking controls and all other computer controlled functions in the automobiles cease working.

To date, no deaths have been attributed to the car's epidemic failures.

Due to the notoriety and questions regarding the safety of the cars, sales of Taurus's have plummeted by almost 80%. Unlike the similar Audi situation where the alleged problem was found in a only a few isolated cases, the Taurus failures have been widespread and catastrophically sudden.

According to Ford, "There has never been a problem with the Taurus electronics' system. We are examining all possibilities in determining the real cause of the apparant failures."
What else can Ford say?

* * * * *

Chrysler Struck by Ford Failures
by Scott Mason

Chrysler cars and mini-vans have been experiencing sudden electrical malfunctions . . .

* * * * *

Mercedes Electrical Systems Follow Ford
by Scott Mason

Mercedes owners have already organized a legal entity to force the manufacturer to find answers as to why so many Mercedes are having sudden electrical failures. Following in the footsteps of Ford and Chrysler, this is the first time that Mercedes has not issued an immediate 'Fix' to its dealer. Three deaths were reported when . . .

* * * * *

Sunday January 10
National Security Agency

"What do you make of this Mason piece?"

"I'd like to know where the hell he gets his information," said the aide. "That's what I make of it."

"Someone's obviously leaking it to him," Marvin Jacobs, Director of the National Security Agency, said to his senior aid. "Someone with access to a great deal of sensitive data." The disdain in his voice was unmistakable

Even though it was Sunday, it was not unusual for him to be at his office. His more private endeavors could be more discreetly pursued.

A three decade career at the Agency had culminated in his appointment to the Directorship, a position he had eyed for years.

"We have specialists who use HERF technology," the aide said. "It's more or less a highly focused computer-gun. An RF field on the order of 200 volts per meter is sufficient to destroy most electrical circuits. Literally blow them up from the inside out."

"Spare me the details . . ."

"Sir, we can stop a car from a thousand yards by pointing electricity at it."

"I don't really care about the details."

"You should, sir. There's a point to this . . ."

"Well, get on with it." Jacobs was clearly annoyed.

"Unlike the EMP-T technology which is very expensive and on the absolute edge of our capabilities . . ."

"And someone elses . . ."

"Granted," the aide said, sounding irritated with the constant interruptions. "But HERF can be generated cheaply by anyone with an elementary knowledge of electronics. The government even sells surplus radio equipment that will do the job quite nicely."

Jacobs smiled briefly.

"You look pleased," the aide said with surprise.

Jacobs hid his pleasure behind a more serious countenance. "Oh, no, it's just the irony of. We've been warning them for years and now it's happening."

"Who, sir?"

"Never mind," Jacobs said, dismissing the thought momentarily. "Go on."

Jacobs arrogantly leaned back in his executive chair, closed his eyes and folded his hands over his barrel chest. This was his way of telling subordinates to talk, spill their guts.

"The real worry about cheap HERF is what it can do in the wrong hands." The aide obliged the ritual. "One transmitter and antenna in a small truck can wipe out every computer on main street during a leisurely drive. Cash registers, electric typewriters, alarms, phones, traffic lights . . .anything electronic a HERF is pointed at, Poof! Good as dead. What if someone used a HERF gun at an airport, pointing up? Or at the tower? From up to a distance of over a kilometer, too. Ten kilometers with better equipment."

"So it works," muttered Jacobs so softly under his breath his aide didn't hear.

"It's reminiscent of drive-by shootings by organized crime. In this case, though, the target is slightly different."

"I see." Jacobs kept his eyes closed as the aide patiently waited for his boss to say something or allow him to return to his family. "I gather we use similar tools ourselves?"

"Yessir. Very popular technique. Better kept quiet."

"Not any more. Not any more."

* * * * *

Chapter 23

Monday, January 11
Washington, D.C.

I don't think you're gonna be pleased," Phil Musgrave said at their early morning conclave, before the President's busy day began.

"What else is new?" asked the President acerbically. "Why should I have an easy today any more than any other day?" His dry wit often escaped much of the White House staff, but Musgrave had been exposed to it for over 20 years and took it in stride. Pre-coffee grumps. The President poured himself more hot de-caf from the silver service. "What is it?"

"Computers."

The President groaned. "Don't you ever long for the old days when a calculator consisted of two pieces of sliding wood or a hundred beads on rods?"

Musgrave ignored his boss's frustration. "Over the weekend, sir, we experienced a number of incidents that could be considered non-random in nature," Musgrave said cautiously.

"In English, Phil," insisted the President.

"MILNET has been compromised. The Optimus Data Base at Pentagon has been erased as has been Anniston, Air Force Systems Command and a dozen other computers tied through ARPANET."

The President sighed. "Damage report?"

"About a month. We didn't lose anything too sensitive, but that's not the embarrassing part."

"If that's not, then what is?"

"The IRS computers tied to Treasury over the Consolidated Data Network?" The President indicated to continue. "The Central Collection Services computer for the Dallas District has had over 100,000 records erased. Gone."

"And?" The President said wearily.

"The IRS has had poor backup procedures. The OMB and GAO reports of 1989 and 1990 detailed their operational shortcomings." The President waited for Phil to say something he could relate to. "It appears that we'll lose between $500 million and $2 Billion in revenues."

"Christ! That's it!" The President shouted. "Enough is enough. The two weeks is up as of this moment." He shook his head with his eyes closed in disbelief. "How the hell can this happen . . .?" he asked rhetorically.

"Sir, I think that our priority is to keep this out of the press. We need plausible deniability . . ."

"Stop with the Pentagon-speak bullshit and just clamp down. No leaks. I want this contained. The last damn thing we need is for the public to think that we can't protect our own computers and the privacy of our citizens. If there is one single leak, I will personally behead the offender," the President said with intensity enough to let Phil know that his old friend and comrade meant what he said.

"Issue an internal directive, lay down the rules. Who knows about this?"

"Too many people, sir. I am not convinced that we can keep this completely out of the public eye . . ."

"Isolate them."

"Sir?"

"You heard me. Isolate them. National Security. Tell them it'll only be few days. Christ. Make up any damn story you want, but have it taken care of. Without my knowledge."

"Yessir."

"Then, find somebody who knows what the hell is going on."

* * * * *

Monday, January 11
Approaching New York City

Scott called Tyrone from the plane to discover that the hearings were being delayed a few days, so he flew back to New York after dropping Sonja off in Washington. They tore themselves apart from each other, she tearfully, at National Airport where they had met. He would be back in a few days, once the hearings were rescheduled. In the meantime, Scott wanted to go home and crash. While being in Jamaica with Sonja was as exhilarating as a man could want, relaxing and stimulating at once, he still was going on next to no rest.

While the plane was still on the tarmac in Washington, Scott had fallen fast asleep. On the descent into New York, he half awakened, to a hypnagogic state. Scott had learned over the years how to take advantage of such semi-conscious conditions. The mind seemingly floated in a place between reality and conjecture - where all possibilities are tangible, unencumbered by earthly concerns. The drone of the jet engines, even their occasional revving, enhanced the mental pleasure Scott experienced. Thoughts weightlessly drifted into and out of his head, some of them common and benign and others surprisingly original, if not out and out weird.

In such a state, the conscious mind becomes the observer of the activities of the unconscious mind. The ego of Scott Mason restrained itself from interfering with the sublime mental processes that bordered on the realm of pure creativity. The germ of a thought, the inchoate idea, had the luxury of exploring itself in an infinity of possibilities and the conscious mind stood on the sidelines. The blissful experience was in constant jeopardy of being relegated to a weak memory, for any sudden disturbance could instantly cause the subconscious to retreat back into a merger with the conscious mind. So, Scott highly valued these spontaneous meditations.

Bits and pieces of the last few days wove themselves into complex patterns that reflected the confusion he felt. He continued to gaze on and observe as the series of mental events that had no obvious relationships assumed coherency and meaning. When one does not hold fixed preconceived notions, when one has the ability to change perspective, then, in these moments, the possibilities multiply. Scott watched himself with the hackers in Amsterdam, with Kirk and Tyrone at home; he watched himself both live and die with Pierre in Washington. Then the weekend, did it just end? The unbelievable weekend with Sonja. It was when he relived the sexual intensity on the Half Moon Bay beach, in what was becoming an increasingly erotic state, that his mind entered an extraordinary bliss.

The rear tires of the plane hitting the runway was enough to snap Scott back to the sober reality of where he was. But he had the thought and he remembered it.

Scott hired a stretch limousine at LaGuardia and slept all the way to Scarsdale, but lacking the good sense God gave him, he checked the messages on his phone machine. Doug called to find out if Scott still worked for the paper and Ty called requesting, almost pleading, that Scott call as soon as he got back. He had to see him, post haste.

The call to Doug was simple. Yes, I'm back. The hackers are real. They are a threat. Pierre is still alive, I have more material than we can use. I did take notes, and my butt is sunburned. If there's nothing else, I'm dead on my feet and I will see you in the morning. Click.

Now he wanted to talk to Tyrone as much as it sounded like Ty wanted to speak to him. Where was he? Probably at the office. He dialed and Sure enough, Tyrone answered.

"Are you back?" Ty asked excitedly.

"Yeah, just got in. I need to talk to you . . ."

"Not as much as we do, buddy. Where are you now?"

"Home. Why?"

"I'll see you in an hour. Wait there." The FBI man was in control. Where the hell else was I going to go, Scott thought.

410

Scott piddled around, making piles for his maid, unpacking and puttering around the kitchen. Everything in the fridge needed cooking, and there was not enough energy for that, so he decided to take a shower. That might give him a few more hours before he collapsed.

Exactly one hour later, as promised, Tyrone Duncan rang Scott's doorbell. They exchanged a few pleasantries and then dove into the meat of their excitement. They grabbed a couple of beers and sat opposite each other in overstuffed chairs by Scott's wide fireplace.

"Boy have I learned a lot . . ." said Scott.

"I think you may be right," said Tyrone.

"Of course I am. I did learn a lot," Scott said with a confused look on his face.

"No I mean about what you said."

"I haven't said anything yet. I think there's a conspiracy." Scott winced to himself as he said the one word that was the bane of many a reporter.

"I said I think you were right. And are right."

"What the devil are you talking about?" Scott was more confused then ever.

"Remember a few months back, on the train we were talking."

"Of course we were talking." Scott recognized the humor in the conversation.

"No! I mean we were . . .shit. Shut up and listen or I'll arrest you!"

"On what charge?"

"CRS."

"CRS?"

"Yeah, Can't Remember Shit. Shut up!"

Scott leaned back in his chair sipping away. He had gotten to Ty. Hooked him, reeled him in and watched him flop on the deck. It pissed Ty off to no end to allow himself to be suckered into Scott's occasional inanity.

"When this whole blackmail thing started up there was no apparent motivation," Tyrone began. "One day you said that the motivation might be a disruption of normal police and FBI operations. I think you might be right. It's looking more and more that the blackmail stuff was a diversion."

"What makes you think so now?" Scott asked.

"We had a ton of cases in the last few weeks, same victims as before, who were being called again, but this time with demands. They were being asked to cough up a lot of cash in a short time, and stash it in a very public place. We had dozens of stakeouts, watching the drop points for a pick up. It read like the little bastards were finally getting greedy. You know what I mean?" Scott nodded in agreement, thinking, where is this going?

411

"So we had a couple hundred agents tied up waiting for the bad guys to show up. And you know what? No one showed. No one, goddamnit. There must have been fifty million in cash sitting in bus terminals, train stations, health clubs, you name it, and no one comes to get any of it? There's something wrong with that picture."

"And you think it's a cover? Right?" Scott grinned wide. "For what?"

Ty shrank back in mild sublimation. "Well," he began, "That is one small piece of the puzzle I haven't filled in yet. But, I thought you might be able to help with that." Tyrone Duncan's eyes met Scott's and said, I am asking as a friend as well as an agent. Come on, we both win on this one.

"Stop begging, Ty. It doesn't befit a member of the President's police force," Scott teased. "Of course I was going to tell you. You're gonna read about it soon enough, and I know," he said half-seriously, "you won't fuck me again."

Ouch, thought Tyrone. Why not pour in the salt while you're at it. "I wouldn't worry. No one thinks there's a problem. I keep shouting and being ignored. It's infinitely more prudent in the government to fuck-up by non-action than by taking a position and acting upon it. I'm on a solo."

"Good enough," Scott assured Ty. "'Nother beer?" It felt good. They were back - friends again.

"Yeah, It's six o'clock somewhere," Tyrone sighed. "So what's your news?"

"You know I went over to this Hacker's Conference . . ."

"In Amsterdam . . ." added Tyrone.

"Right, and I saw some toys that you can't believe," Scott said intently. "The term Hacker should be replaced with Dr. Hacker. These guys are incredible. To them there is no such thing as a locked door. They can get into and screw around with any computer they want."

"Nothing new there," said Ty.

"Bullshit. They're organized. These characters make up an entire underground society, that admittedly has few rules, but it's the most coherent bunch of anarchists I ever saw."

"What of it?"

"Remember that van, the one that blew up and . . ."

"How can I forget."

"And then my Tempest article . . ."

"Yeah. I know, I'm sorry," Tyrone said sincerely.

"Fuck it. It's over. Wasn't your fault. Anyway, I saw the equipment in actual use. I saw them read computers with antennas. It was absolutely incredible. It's not bullshit. It really works." Scott spoke excitedly.

"You say it's Tempest?"

"No, anti-Tempest. These guys have got it down. Regardless, the shit works."

"So what? It works."

"So, let's say, if the hackers use these computer monitors to find out all sorts of dirt on companies," Scott slowly explained as he organized his thoughts. "Then they issue demands and cause all sorts of havoc and paranoia. They ask for money. Then they don't come to collect it. So what have they achieved?" Scott asked rhetorically.

"They tied up one shit load of a lot of police time, I'll tell you that."

"Exactly. Why?"

"Diversion. That's where we started," Ty said.

"But who is the diversion for?"

The light bulb went off in Tyrone's head. "The hackers!"

"Right," agreed Scott. "They're the ones who are going to do whatever it is that the diversion is covering. Did that make sense?"

"No," laughed Ty, "but I got it. Why would the hackers have to be covering for themselves. Couldn't they be working for someone else?"

"I doubt it. This is one independent bunch of characters," Scott affirmed. "Besides, there's more. What happened in D.C. . . . ."

"Troubleaux," interrupted Ty.

"Bingo. And there's something else, too."

"What?"

"I've been hearing about a computer system called the Freedom League. Nothing specific, just that everything about it sounds too good to be true."

"It usually is."

"And one other thing. If there is some sort of hacker plot, I think I know someone who's involved."

"Did he admit anything?"

"No, nothing. But, well, we'll see." Scott hesitated and stuttered. "Troubleaux, he said something to me . . ."

"Excuse me?" Ty said with disbelief. "I thought his brains were leaking out . . ."

"Thanks for reminding me; I had to buy a new wardrobe."

"And a tan? Where've you been?"

"With, well," Scott blushed, "that's another story . . ."

"O.K., Romeo, how did he talk? What did he say?" Ty asked doubtfully.

"He told me that dGraph was sick."

"Who's dGraph?"

"dGraph," laughed Scott, "is how your secretary keeps your life organized. It's the most popular piece of software in the world. Troubleaux founded the company. And I think I know what he meant."

"He's a nerdy whiz kid, huh?" joked Tyrone

"Just the opposite. Mongo sex appeal to the ladies. No, his partner was the . . . " Scott stopped mid sentence. "Hey, I just remembered something. Troubleaux had a partner, he founded the company with him. A couple of days before they went public, his partner died. Shook up the industry. Shortly thereafter Data Tech bought them."

"And you think there's a connection?"

"Maybe . . .I can't remember exactly," Scott said. "Hey, you can find out."

"How?"

"Your computers."

"They're at the office . . ."

Scott pointed to his computer and Tyrone shook his head violently. "I don't know how to . . . "

"Ty," Scott said calmly. "Call your secretary. Ask her for the number and your passwords." Scott persuaded Ty to be humble and dial his office. He was actually able to guide Ty through the process of accessing one of the largest collections of information in the world.

"How did you know we could do that?" Ty asked after they logged into the FBI computer from Scott's study.

"Good guess. I figured you guys couldn't function without remote access. Lucky."

Tyrone scowled kiddingly at Scott. "You going over to the other side boy? You seem to know an awful lot."

"That's how easy this stuff is. Anyone can do it. In fact I heard a story about octogenarian hackers who work from their nursing homes. I guess it replaces sex."

"Bullshit," Tyrone said pointing at his chest. "This is one dude who's knows the real thing. No placebos for me!"

They both laughed. "You know how to take it from here?" asked Scott once a main menu appeared.

"Yeah, let me at it. What the hell did you want to know anyway?"

"I imagine you have a file on dGraph, somewhere inside the over 400,000,000 active files maintained at the FBI."

"I'm beginning to worry about you. That's classified . . ."

"It's all in the company you keep," Scott chided. "Just ask it for dGraph." Tyrone selected an Inquiry Data Base and asked the computer for what it knew about dGraph. In a few seconds, a sub- menu appeared entitled "dGraph, Inc.". Under the heading appeared several options:

1. **Company History**
2. **Financial Records**
3. **Products and Services**
4. **Management**
5. **Stock Holders**
6. **Activities**
7. **Legal**
8. **Comments**

"Not bad!" chided Scott. "Got that on everyone?"

Tyrone glared at Scott. "You shouldn't even know this exists. Hey, do me a favor, will ya? When I have to lie later, at least I want to be able to say you weren't staring over my shoulders. Dig?"

"No problem," Scott said as he pounced on the couch in front of the desk. He knocked a few days of mail onto the floor to make room. "O.K., who founded the company?"

"Founded 1984, Pierre Troubleaux and Max Jones . . ."

"That's it!" exclaimed Scott. "Max Jones. Where?"

"Cupertino, California."

"What date did they go public?" Scott asked quickly.

"Ah, August 6, 1987. Anything else massa?" Tyrone gibed.

"Can you tie into the California Highway Patrol computers?"

"What if I could?"

"Well, if you could, I thought it would be interesting to take a look at the police reports. Because, as I remember, there was something funny about Max Jones." Scott said, and then added mockingly, "But that's only if you have access to the same information that anyone can get for $2. It's all public information anyway."

"You know I'm not supposed to be doing this . . ." Tyrone said as he pecked at the keyboard.

"Bullshit. You do it all the time . . ."

"Not as a public service." The screen darkened and then announced that Tyrone had been given access to the CHiP computers. "So suppose I could do that, I suppose you'd want a copy of it."

"Only if the switch on the right side of the printer is turned ON and if the paper is straight. Otherwise, I just wouldn't bother." Scott stared at the ceiling while the dot matrix printer sang a high pitched song as the head traveled back and forth.

Tyrone scanned the print out coming from the computers in California. "You have one fuckuva memory. Sheee-it." Scott sat up quickly.

"What, what does it say?" Scott pressured.

"It appears that your friend Max Jones was killed in an automobile accident on Highway 275 at 12:30 AM." Ty stopped for a moment to read more. "He was found, dead, at the bottom of a ravine where his car landed after crashing through the barriers. Pretty high speed. And, the brake lines were cut."

"Holy shit," Scott said rising from his chair. "Does two a pattern make?"

"You mean Troubleaux and Max?" asked Tyrone.

"Yeah, they'll do."

"In my mind it would warrant further investigation." He made a mental note.

"Anything else there?" Scott asked.

"This is the kicker," Ty added. "The investigation lasted two days. Upstairs told the department to make it a quick and clean, open and shut case of accident."

"I assume no one from dGraph had any reason to doubt what the police told them. It sounds perfectly rational."

"Why should they if nobody kicked up a stink?" Ty said to himself. "Hey," he said to Scott. "You think he was murdered, don't you?"

"You bet your ass I do," Scott affirmed. "Think about it. The two founders of a company the size of dGraph, they're huge, one dead from a suspicious accident, and the other the target of an assassination and in deep shit in the hospital."

"And it was the hackers, right?" laughed Tyrone.

"Maybe," Scott said seriously. "Why not? It's all tying together."

"There's no proof," Tyrone said.

"No, and I don't need it yet. But I sense the connection. That's why I said there's a conspiracy." He used that word again.

"And who is behind it and why? Pray tell?" Tyrone needled Scott. "Nothing's even happened, and you're already spouting conspiracy."

"I need to do something. Two things." Scott spoke firmly but vacantly. "I need to talk to Kirk. I think there's something wrong with dGraph, and he can help."

"And two?"

"I'd like to know who I saw in Amsterdam."

"Why?" Ty asked.

"Because . . .because, he's got something to do with . . .whatever it is. He as much as admitted it."

"I think I can help with that one," offered Ty.

"Huh?" Scott looked surprised.

"How about we go into my office and see who this guy is?" Tyrone enjoyed the moment. One upping Scott. "Tomorrow."

Scott decided that the fastest way to reach Kirk, he really needed Kirk, was to write a clue in an article. Scott dialed the paper's computer from his house and opened a file. He hadn't planned on writing today - God, how long have I been awake? This was the easiest way to contact Kirk now, but that was going to change. Tyrone left early enough for Scott to write a quick piece that would be sure to make an inside page, page 12 or 14.

* * * * *

Tuesday, January 12

The Computer As Weapon?

by Scott Mason

Since the dawn of civilization, Man has had the perverse ability to turn Good into Bad, White into Black, Hot into Cold, Life into Death. History bears out that technology is falling into the same trap. The bow and arrow, the gun; they were created to help man survive the elements and feed himself. Today millions of guns are bought with no purpose other than to hurt another human being. The space program was going to send man to the stars; instead we have Star Wars. The great advantages that technology has brought modern man have been continuously subverted for malevolent uses.

What if the same is true for computers?

Only yesterday, in order to spy on my neighbor, or my opponent, I would hire a private eye to perform the surveillance. And there was a constant danger of his being caught. Today? I'd hire me the best computer hacker I could get my hands on and sic him on the targets of my interest. Through their computers.

For argument's sake, let's say I want advance information on companies so I can play the stock market. I have my hacker get inside the SEC computers, (he can get in from literally thousands of locations nationwide) and read up on the latest figures before they're reported to the public. Think of betting the whole wad on a race with only one horse.

I would imagine, and I am no lawyer, that if I broke into the SEC offices and read through their file cabinets, I would be in a mighty poke of trouble. But catching me in their computer is an

417

extraordinary exercise in resource frustration, and usually futile. For unlike the burglar, the computer criminal is never at the scene of the crime. He is ten or a hundred or a thousand miles away. Besides, the better computer criminals know the systems they attack so well, that they can cover their tracks completely; no one will ever know they were an uninvited guest.

Isn't then the computer a tool, a weapon, of the computer criminal? I can use my computer as a tool to pry open your computer, and then once inside I use it to perhaps destroy pieces of your computer or your information.

I wonder then about other computer crimes, and I will include viruses in that category. Is the computer or the virus the weapon? Is the virus a special kind of computer bullet? The intent and the result is the same.

I recall hearing an articulate man recently make the case that computers should be licensed, and that not everyone should be able to own one. He maintained that the use of a computer carried with it an inherent social responsibility. What if the technology that gives us the world's highest standard of living, convenience and luxury was used instead as a means of disruption; a technological civil disobedience if you will? What if political strength came from the corruption of an opponent's computer systems? Are we not dealing with a weapon as much as a gun is a weapon?, my friend pleaded.

Clearly the computer is Friend. And the computer, by itself is not bad, but recent events have clearly demonstrated that it can be used for sinister and illegal purposes. It is the use to which one puts the tool that determines its effectiveness for either good or bad. Any licensing of computers, information systems, would be morally abhorrent - a veritable decimation of the Bill of Rights. But I must recognize that the history of industrialized society does not support my case.

Automobiles were once not licensed. Do we want it any other way? I am sure many of you wish that drivers licenses were harder to come by. Radio transmitters have been licensed for most of this century and many a civil libertarian will make the case that because they are licensed, it is a restriction on my freedom of speech to require approval by the Government before broadcast. On the practical side, does it make sense for ten radio stations all trying to use the same frequency?

Cellular phones are officially licensed as are CB's. Guns require licenses in an increasing number of states. So it might appear logical to say that computers be licensed, to prevent whatever overcrowding calamity may unsuspectingly befall us.

The company phone effectively licenses lines to you, with the added distinction of being able to record everything you do.

Computers represent an obvious boon and a potential bane. When computers are turned against themselves, under the control of humans of course, or against the contents of the computer under attack, the results can ripple far and wide. I believe we are indeed fortunate that computers have not yet been turned against their creators by faction groups vying for power and attention. Thus far isolated events, caused by ego or accident have been the rule and large scale coordinated, well executed computer assaults non-existent.

That, though, is certainly no guarantee that we will not have to face the Computer Terrorists tomorrow.

This is Scott Mason Searching the Galaxy at Warp 9.

* * * * *

Tuesday, January 12
Federal Square, New York

Tyrone was required to come to the lobby of the FBI headquarters, sign Scott in and escort him through the building. Scott didn't arrive until almost eleven; he let himself sleep in, in the hopes of making up for lost sleep. He knew it didn't work that way, but twelve hours of dead rest had to do something.

Tyrone explained as they took an elevator two levels beneath the street that they were going to work with a reconstructionist. A man with a very powerful computer will build up the face that Scott saw, piece by piece. They opened a door that was identified by only a number and entered an almost sterile work place. A pair of Sun workstations with large high resolution monitors sat on a large white tables by one wall, with a row of racks of floor to ceiling disk drives and tape units opposite.

"Remember," Tyrone cautioned, "no names."

"Right," said Scott. "No names."

Tyrone introduced Scott to Vinnie who would be running the computer. Vinnie's first job was to familiarize Scott with the procedure. Tyrone told Vinnie to call him in his office when they had something; he had other matters to attend to in the meantime. Of obvious Italian descent, with a thick Brooklyn accent, Vinnie Misselli epitomized the local boy making good. His lantern jaw and classic Roman good looks were out of place among the blue suits and white shirts that typified the FBI.

419

"All I need," Vinnie said, "is a brief description to get things started. Then, we'll fix it piece by piece."

Scott loosely described the Spook. Dark hair, good looking, no noticeable marks and of course, the dimples. The face that Vinnie built was generic. No unique features, just a nose and the other parts that anatomically make up a face. Scott shook his head, no that's not even close. Vinnie seemed undaunted.

"O.K., now, I am going to stretch the head, the overall shape and you tell me where to stop. All right?" Vinnie asked, beginning his manipulation before Scott answered.

"Sure," said Scott. Vinnie rolled a large track ball built into the keyboard and the head on the screen slowly stretched in height and width. The changes didn't help Scott much he but asked Vinnie to stop at one point anyway.

"Don't worry, we can change it later again. How about the eyes?"

"Two," said Scott seriously.

Vinnie gave Scott an ersatz dirty look. "Everyone does it," said Vinnie. "Once." He grinned at Scott.

"The eye brows, they were bushier," said Scott.

"Good. Tell me when." The eyebrows on the face twisted and turned as Vinnie moved the trackball with his right hand and clicked at the keyboard with his left.

"That's close," Scott said. "Yeah, hold it." Vinnie froze the image where Scott indicated and they went on to the hair. "Longer, wavier, less of a part . . ."

They worked for an hour, Vinnie at the computer controls and Scott changing every imaginable feature on the face as it evolved into one with character. Vinnie sat back in his chair and stretched. "How's that," he asked Scott.

Scott hesitated. He felt that he was making too many changes. Maybe this was as close as it got. "It's good," he said without conviction. There was a slight resemblance.

"That's what they all say," Vinnie said. "It's not even close yet." He laughed as Scott looked shocked. "All we've done so far is get the general outline. Now, we work on the details."

For another two hours Scott commented on the subtle changes Vinnie made to the face. Nuances that one never thinks of; the curve of the cheek, the half dozen angles of the chin, the hundreds of ear lobes, eyes of a thousand shapes - they went through them all and the face took form. Scott saw the face take on the appearance of the Spook; more and more it became the familiar face he had spent hours with a few days ago.

As he got caught up in the building and discovery process, Scott issued commands to Vinnie; thicken the upper lip, just a little.

Higher forehead. He blurted out change after change and Vinnie executed every one. Actually, Vinnie preferred it this way, being given the orders. After all, he hadn't seen the face.

"There! That's the Spook!" exclaimed Scott suddenly.

"You sure?" asked Vinnie sitting back in the plush computer chair.

"Yup," Scott said with assurance. "That's him."

"O.K., let's see what we can do . . ." Vinnie rapidly typed at the keyboard and the picture of the face disappeared. The screen went blank for a few seconds until it was replaced with a 3 dimensional color model of a head. The back of the head turned and the visage of the Spook stared at them both. It was an eerie feeling and Scott shuddered as the disembodied head stopped spinning.

"Take a look at this," Vinnie said as he continued typing. Scott watched the head, Spook's head, come alive. The lips were moving, as though it, he, was trying to speak. "I can give it a voice if you'd like."

"Will that help?" Scott asked.

"Nah, not in this case," Vinnie said. "But it is fun. Let's make sure that we got the right guy here. We'll take a look at him from every angle." The head moved to the side for a left profile. "I'll make a couple of gross adjustments, and you tell me if it gets any better."

They went through another hour of fine tuning the 3-D head, modifying skin tones, texture, hair style and a score of other subtleties. When they were done Scott remarked that the image looked more like the Spook than the Spook himself. Incredible. Scott was truly impressed. This is where taxpayer's money went. Vinnie called Tyrone and by the time he arrived, the color photographs and digital maps of the images were ready.

Scott followed Tyrone down one corridor, then another, through a common area, and down a couple more hallways. They entered Room 322B. The innocuous appearance of the door did not prepare Scott for what he saw; a huge computer room, at least a football field in length. Blue and tan and beige and a few black metal cabinets that housed hundreds of disparate yet co-existing computers. Consoles with great arrays of switches, row upon row of video and graphic displays as far as the eye could see. Thousands of white two by two foot square panel floors hid miles of wires and cables that interconnected the maze of computers in the underground control center. There appeared to be a number of discreet areas, where large computer consoles were centered amidst racks of tape or disk drives which served as the only separation between workers.

"This is Big Floyd," Tyrone said proudly. "Or at least one part of him."

"Who or what is Big Floyd?"

"Big Floyd is a huge national computer system, tied together over the Secure Automated Message Network. This is the most powerful computer facility outside of the NSA."

Quiet conversations punctuated the hum of the disk drives and the clicks of solenoids switching and the printers pushing reams of paper. The muted voices could not be understood but they rang with purpose. The room had an almost reverent character to it; where speaking too loud would surely be considered blasphemous. Scott and Tyrone walked through banks and banks of equipment, more computer equipment than Scott had ever seen in one location. In fact the Federal Square computer center is on the pioneering edge of forensic technology. The NSA computers might have more oomph!, but the FBI computers have more purpose.

Tyrone stopped at one control console and asked if they could do a match, stat. Of course, anything for Mr. Duncan. "RHIP," Tyrone said. Scott recognized the acronym, Rank Has Its Privilege. Tyrone gave the computer operator the pictures and asked him to explain the process to Scott.

"I take these pictures and put them in the computer with a scanner. The digitized images are stored here," he said pointing at a a a rack of equipment. "Then, we enter the subject's general description. Height, physique and so on." He copied the information into the computer.

"Now we ask the computer to find possible matches."

"You mean the computer has photos of everyone in there?" Scott asked incredulously.

"No, Scott. Just the bad guys, and people with security clearances, and public officials? Your Aunt Tillie is safe from Big Brother's prying eyes." The reason for Ty's sarcasm was clear to Scott. Tyrone was not exactly acting in an official capacity on this part of the investigation.

"How many do you have? Pictures that is?" Scott asked more diplomatically.

"That's classified," Tyrone said quickly.

"The hackers say you have files on over a hundred million people. Is that true?" Scott asked. Tyrone glared at him, as if to say, shut the fuck up. Scott took the non-verbal hint and they watched in silence as the computer whirred searching for similar photo files in its massive memory. Within a couple of minutes the computer said that there were 4 possible matches. At the end of the 10 minute search, it was up to 16 candidates.

"We'll do a visual instead of a second search," said the man behind the keyboard. "We'll start with the 90% matches. There are two of them." A large monitor flashed with a picture of a man, that while not unlike the Spook in features, was definitely not him. The picture was a high quality color photograph.

"No, not him," Scott said without pause. The computer operator hit a couple of keys, a second picture flashed on the monitor and Scott's face lit up. "That's him! That's the Spook!"

Tyrone had wondered if they would find any matches. While the FBI data base was probably the largest in the world, it was unlikely that there was a comprehensive library of teen age hackers. "Are you sure?" Tyrone emphasized the word, 'sure'.

"Positive, yes. That's him."

"Let's have a quick look at the others before we do a full retrieve," said the computer operator. Tyrone agreed and fourteen other pictures of men with similar facial characteristics to the Spook appeared on the screen, all receiving a quick 'no' from Scott. Spook's picture as brought up again and again Scott said, "that's him."

"All right, Mike," Tyrone said to the man running the computer, "do a retrieve on OBR-III." Mike nodded and stretched over to a large printer on the side of the console. He pushed a key and in a few seconds, the printer spewed out page after page of information. OBR-III is a super-secret computer system designed to fight terrorism in the United States. OBR-III and Big Floyd regularly spoke to similar, but smaller, systems in England, France and Germany. With only small bits of data it can extrapolate potential terrorist targets, and who is the likely person behind the attacks. OBR-III is an expert system that learns continuously, as the human mind does. Within seconds is can provide information on anyone within its memory.

Tyrone pulled the first page from the printer before it was finished and read to himself. He scanned it quickly until one item grabbed his attention. His eyes widened. "Boy, when you pick 'em, you pick 'em." Tyrone whistled.

"What, what?" Scott strained to see the printout, but Tyrone held it away.

"It's no wonder he calls himself Spook," Tyrone said to no one in particular. "He's ex-NSA." He ripped off the final page of the printout and called Scott to follow him, cursorily thanking the computer operators for their assistance.

Scott followed Tyrone to an elevator and they descended to the fifth and bottom level, where Tyrone headed straight to his office with Scott in tow. He shut the door behind him and showed Scott a chair.

"There's no way I should be telling you this, but I owe you, I guess, and, anyway, maybe you can help." Tyrone rationalized showing the information to Scott - both a civilian and a reporter. He may have questioned the wisdom, but not the intent. Besides, as had been true for several weeks, everything Scott learned from Tyrone Duncan was off the record. Way off. For now.

The Spook's real name was Miles Foster. Scott scanned the file. A lot of it was government speak and security clearance interviews for his job at NSA. An entire life was condensed into a a few files, covering the time from when he was born to the time he resigned from the NSA. Scott found much of his life boring and he really didn't care that Miles' third grade teacher remembered him as being a "good boy". Or that his high school counselor though he could go a long way.

"This doesn't sound like the Spook I know," Scott said after glancing at the clean regimented life and times of Miles Foster.

"Did you expect it to?" asked Ty.

"I guess I never thought about it. I just figured it would be a regular guy, not a real spook for the government."

"Shit happens."

"So I see. Where do we go from here?" Scott asked in awe of the technical capabilities of the FBI.

"How 'bout a sanity check?" Tyrone asked. "When were you in Amsterdam?"

"Last week, why?"

Tyrone sat behind his computer and Scott noticed that his fingers seemed almost too fat to be of much good. "If I can get this thing to work, let's see where's the Control Key?" Scott gazed on as Tyrone talked to himself while working the keyboard and reading the screen. "Foster, Airline, Foreign, ah, the dates," he looked up at a large wall calendar. "Al right . . .shit . . .Delete . . . OK, that's it."

"What are you doing?" asked Scott.

"Just want to see if your boy really was in Europe with you."

"You don't believe me!" shouted Scott.

"No, I believe you. But I need some proof, dig?" Tyrone said. "If he's up to something we need to find out what, step by step. You should know that."

"Yeah, I do," Scott resigned. "It's just that I'm not normally the one being questioned. Know what I mean?"

"Our training is more . . .well, it's a moot point now. Your Mr. Foster flew to Amsterdam and then back to Washington the next day. I believe I have some legwork ahead of me. I would like to learn a little more about Mr. Miles Foster."

Scott talked Tyrone into giving him a copy of one of the images of Miles *aka* Spook. He was hoping that Kirk would call him tonight. In any case, Scott needed to buy an image scanner if Kirk was going to be of help. When he got home, he made room on his personal nightmare, his desk, for the flatbed scanner, then played with it for several hours, learning how to scan an image at the right sensitivity, the correct brightness and reflectivity for the proper resolution. He learnd to bring a picture into the computer and edit or redraw the picture. Scott scanned the picture of the Spook into the computer and enjoyed adding moustaches, subtracting teeth and stretching the ears.

At midnight, on the button, Scott's computer beeped. It was Kirk.

WTFO

You got my message.

SUBTLETY IS NOT YOUR STRONG POINT

I didn't want to miss.

GOTCHA. YOU RANG

First of all, I want a better way to contact you, since I assume you won't tell me who you are.

RIGHT! AND I'VE TAKEN CARE OF THAT. CALL 212-555-3908. WHEN YOU HEAR THE BEEP, ENTER YOUR NUMBER. I'LL CALL YOU AS SOON AS I CAN.

So you're in New York?

MAYBE. MAYBE NOT.

Ah, Call forwarding. I could get the address of the phone and trace you down.

I DON'T THINK YOU WOULD DO THAT

And why not may I ask?

CAUSE WE HAVE A DEAL.

Right. You're absolutely right.

NOW THAT I'M RIGHT, WHAT'S UP

I met with the Spook

YOU DID????????

The conference was great, but I need to know more. I've just been sniffing around the edges and I can't smell what's in the oven.

WHAT ABOUT THE SPOOK? TELL ME ABOUT IT.

I have picture of him for you. I scanned it.

VERY GOOD, CLAP, CLAP.

I'll send you SPOOK.PIX. Let me know what you think.

OK. SEND AWAY

Scott chose the file and issued the command to send it to Kirk. While it was being sent they couldn't speak, and Scott learned how long it really takes to transmit a digital picture at 2400 baud. He got absorbed in a magazine and almost missed the message on the computer.

THAT'S NOT THE SPOOK!!!!

Yes it is. I met him.

NO, IT'S NOT THE REAL SPOOK. I'VE MET HIM. HE'S PARTIALLY BALD AND HAS A LONG NOSE AND GLASSES. THIS GUY'S A GQ MODEL

C'mon, you've got to be putting me on. I travel 3000 miles for an impostor?

I GUESS SO. THIS AIN'T THE SPOOK I KNOW

Then who is it?

HOW THE HELL SHOULD I KNOW?

Just thought I'd ask . . .

WHAT'S GOING ON REPO?

Deep shit, and I need your help.

GOT THE MAN LOOKING OVER YOUR DONKEY?

No, he's not here, honest. I have an idea, and you're gonna think it's nuts, I know. But I have to ask you for a couple of favors.

WHAT MAY THEY BE?

The Freedom League. I need to know as much about it as I can, without anyone knowing that I want the information. Is that possible?

OF COURSE. THEY'RE BBS'ERS. I CAN GET IN EASY. WHY?

Well that brings up the second favor. dGraph. Do you own it?

SURE, EVERYONE DOES. LEGAL OR NOT.

Can't you guys take apart a program to see what makes it tick?

REVERSE ENGINEERING, YEAH

Then I would like to ask if you would look at the dGraph program and see if it has a virus in it?

* * * * *

426

Chapter 24

Wednesday, January 13
New York City

No Privacy for Mere Citizens

by Scott Mason.

I learned the other day, that I can find out just about anything I want to know about you, or her, or him, or anyone, for a few dollars, a few phone calls and some free time.

Starting with just an automobile license plate number, the Department of Motor Vehicles will be happy to supply me with a name and address that go with the plate. Or I can start with a name, or an address or just a phone number and use a backwards phone book. It's all in the computer.

I can find more about you by getting a copy of the your auto registration and title from the public records. Marriage licenses and divorces are public as well. You can find out the damnedest things about people from their first or second or third marriage records. Including the financial settlements. Good way to determine how much money or lack thereof is floating around a healthy divorce.

Of course I can easily find all traffic offenses, their disposition, and any follow up litigation or settlements. It's all in the computer. As there are public records of all arrests, court cases, sentences and paroles. If you've ever been to trial, the transcripts are public.

Your finances can be scrupulously determined by looking up the real estate records for purchase price, terms, cash, notes and taxes on your properties. Or, if you've ever had a bankruptcy, the sordid details are clearly spelled out for anyone's inspection. It's all in the computer.

I can rapidly build an excellent profile of you, or whomever. And, it's legal. All legal, using the public records available to anyone who asks and has the $2.

That tells me, loud and clear, that I no longer have any privacy! None!

Forget the hackers; it's bad enough they can get into our bank accounts and our IRS records and the Census forms that have our names tied to the data. What about Dick and Jane Doe, Everyman USA, who can run from agency to agency and office

427

to office put together enough information about me or you to be dangerous.

I do not think I like that.

It's bad enough the Government can create us or destroy us as individuals by altering the contents of our computer files deep inside the National Data Bases. At least they have a modicum of accountability. However, their inattentive disregard for the privacy of the citizens of this country is criminal.

As a reporter I am constantly amazed at how easy it is to find out just about anything about anybody, and in many ways that openness has made my job simpler. However, at the same time, I believe that the Government has an inherent responsibility to protect us from invasion of privacy, and they are derelict in fulfilling that promise.

If the DMV needs to know my address, I understand. The IRS needs to know my income. Each computer unto itself is a necessary repository to facilitate business transactions. However, when someone begins to investigate me, crossing the boundaries of multiple data bases, without question, they are invading my privacy. Each piece of information found about me may be insignificant in itself, but when combined, it becomes highly dangerous in the wrong hands. We all have secrets we want to remain secrets. Under the present system, we have sacrificed our privacy for the expediency of the machines.

I have a lawyer friend who believes that the fourth amendment is at stake. Is it, Mr. President?

This is Scott Mason, feeling Peered Upon.

* * * * *

Wednesday, January 13
Atlanta, Georgia

First Federal Bank in Atlanta, Georgia enjoyed a reputation of treating its customers like royalty. Southern Hospitality was the bank's middle name and the staff was trained to provide extraordinary service. This morning though, First Federal's customers were not happy campers. The calls started coming in before 8:00 AM.

"My account is off $10," "It doesn't add up," "My checkbook won't balance." A few calls of this type are normal on any given day, but the phones were jammed with customer complaints. Hundreds of calls streamed in constantly and hundreds more never got through the busy signals. Dozens of customers came into the local branches to complain about the errors on their statement.

An emergency meeting was held in the Peachtree Street headquarters of First Federal. The president of the bank chaired the meeting. The basic question was, What Was Going On? It was a free for all. Any ideas, shoot 'em out.

How many calls? About 4500 and still coming in. What are the dates of the statements? So far within a couple of days, but who knows what we'll find. What are you asking people to do? Double check against their actual checks instead of the register. Do you really think that 5000 people wake up one morning and all make the same mistakes? Do you have any other ideas? Then what? If they don't reconcile, bring 'em in and we'll pull the fiche.

What do the computer people say? They think there may be an error. That's bright. If the numbers are adding up wrong, how do we balance? Have no idea. Do they add up in our favor? Not always. Maybe 50/50 so far. Can we fix it? Yes. When? I don't know yet. Get some answers. Fast. Yessir.

The bank's concerns mounted when their larger customers found discrepancies in the thousands and tens of thousands of dollars. As the number of complaints numbered well over 10,000 by noon, First Federal was facing a crisis. The bank's figures in no way jived with their customer's records and the finger pointing began.

The officers contacted the Federal Reserve Board and notified them. The Board suggested, strongly, that the bank close for the remainder of the day and sort it out before it got worse. First Federal did close, under the guise of installing a new computer system, a lie that might also cover whatever screwed up the statements. Keep that option open. They kept answering the phones, piling up the complaints and discovering that thus far there was no pattern to the errors.

By mid-afternoon, they at least knew what to look for. On every statement a few checks were listed with the incorrect amounts and therefore the balance was wrong. For all intent and purpose, the bank had absolutely no idea whose money was whose.

Working into the night the bank found that all ledgers balanced, but still the amounts in the accounts were wrong. What are the odds of a computer making thousands of errors and having them all balance out to a net zero difference? Statistically it was impossible, and that meant someone altered the amounts on purpose. By midnight they found that the source of the error was probably in the control code of the bank's central computing center.

First Federal Bank did not open for business Thursday. Or Friday.

First Federal Bank was not the only bank to experience profound difficulties with it's customers. Similar complaints closed down Farmer's Bank in Des Moines, Iowa, Lake City Bank in Chicago, First Trade in New York City, Sopporo Bank in San Francisco, Pilgrim's Trust in Boston and, as the Federal Reserve Bank would discover, another hundred or so banks in almost every state.

The Department of the Treasury reacted quickly, spurred into action by the chairman of Riggs National Bank in Washington, D.C. Being one of the oldest banks in the country, and the only one that could claim having a personal relationship with Alexander Hamilton, the first Secretary of the Treasury, it still carried political weight with its upper echelon.

The evening network and local news stations covered the situation critically. Questions proliferated but answers were hard to come by. The largest of the banks and the government announced that a major computer glitch had affected the Electronic Funds Transfers which had inadvertently caused the minor inconsistencies in some customer records.

The press was extremely hard on the banks and the Fed Reserve and the Treasury. They smelled a coverup, a lie; that they and the public were not being told the truth, or at least all of it. Only Scott Mason and a couple of other reporters speculated that a computer virus or time bomb was responsible. Without any evidence though, the government and the banks vigorously denied any such possibilities. Rather, they developed a convoluted story of how one money transaction affects another and then another. The domino theory of banking was explained to the public in graphs and charts, but an open skepticism prevailed.

Small businesses and individual banking customers were totally shut off from access to their funds. Tens of thousands of automatic tellers were turned off by their banks in the futile hope of minimizing the damage. Estimates were that by evening, almost 5 million people had been estranged from their money.

Rumors of bank collapse and a catastrophic failure of the banking system persisted. The Stock Market, finally operating at full capacity after November's disaster, reacted to the news with a precipitous drop of almost 125 points before trading was suspended, cutting off thousands more from their money.

The International Monetary Fund convened an emergency meeting as the London and Tokyo stock markets reacted negatively to the news. Wire transfers and funds disbursements were ceased across all state and national borders.

Panic ensued, and despite the best public relations efforts, the Treasury imposed financial sanctions on all savings and checking accounts. If the banks opened on Friday, severe limits would be placed on access to available funds. Checks would be returned or held until the emergency was past.

Nightline addressed the banking crisis in depth. The experts debated the efficiency of the system and that possibly an unforeseen overload had occurred, triggering the events of the day. No one suggested that the bank's computers had been compromised.

* * * * *

New York City Times

"Yes, it is urgent."

"What is this about?

"That is for the Senator's ears only."

"Can you hold for . . ."

"Yes, yes. I've been holding for an hour. Go on." Muzak interpretations of Led Zeppelin greeted Scott Mason as he was put on hold. Again. Good God! They have more pass interference in the front office and on the phones than the entire NFL. He waited.

At long last, someone picked up the other end of the phone. "I am sorry to keep you waiting, Mr. Mason, it has been rather hectic as you can imagine. How are you faring?" Senator Nancy Deere true to form, always projected genuine sincerity.

"Fine, fine, thank you, Senator. The reason for my call is rather, ah . . .sensitive."

"Yes?" She asked politely.

"Well, the fact is, Senator, we cannot discuss it, that is, I don't feel that we can talk about this on the phone."

"That makes it rather difficult, doesn't it." She laughed weakly.

"Simply put, Senator . . . "

"Please call me Nancy. Both my friends and enemies do."

"All right, Nancy," Scott said awkwardly. "I need 15 minutes of your time about a matter of national security and it directly concerns your work on the Rickfield Committee." She winced at the nick name that the hearing had been given. "I can assure you, Senator, ah, Nancy, that I would not be bothering you unless I was convinced of what I'm going to tell you. And show you. If you think I'm nuts, then fine, you can throw me out . . . "

"Mr. Mason, that's enough," Nancy said kindly. "Based upon your performance at the hearing the other day, that alone is enough to make me want to shake your hand. As for what you have to say? I pride myself on being a good listener. When would be convenient for you?"

"The sooner the better," Scott said with obvious relief that he hadn't had to sell her.

"How's . . .ah, four tomorrow? My office?"

"That's fine, perfect. We'll see you tomorrow then."

"We?" Nancy picked up the plural reference.

"Yes, I am working with someone else. It helps if I'm not crazy alone."

* * * * *

FBI, New York

"I'll be in Washington tomorrow, we can talk about it then," Tyrone Duncan said emphatically into his desk telephone.

"Ty, I've been on your side and defended you since I came on board, you know that." Bob Burnsen was pleading with Ty. "But on this one, I have no control. You've been poking into areas that don't concern you, and I'm catching heat."

"I'm working on one damn case, Bob. One. Computer crime, but it keeps on touching this fucking blackmail fiasco and it's getting on everyone's nerves. There's a lot more to this than ransoms and hackers and I've been having some luck. I'll show you what I have tomorrow. Sixish. Ebbets."

"I'll be there. Ty," Burnsen said kindly. "I don't know the specifics, but you've been shaking the tree. I hope it's worth it."

"It is, Bob. I'd bet my ass on in."

"You are."

* * * * *

Thursday, January 14
Walter Reed Medical Center

"How is he doing?" Scott asked.

"He's not out of the woods yet," said Dr. Sean Kelly, one of Walter Reede's hundreds of Marcus Welby look-alike staff physicians. "In cases like this, we operate in the dark. The chest wound is nasty, but that's not the danger; it's the head wound. The brain is a real funny area."

Tyrone's FBI identification was required to get him and Scott in to see Dr. Kelly. As far as anybody knew, Pierre Troubleaux had been killed over the weekend in an explosion in his hospital room. The explosion was faked at the suggestion of the management of dGraph, Inc. after Pierre's most recent assailant was murdered,

432

despite the police assigned to guard his room. Two of Ahmed's elite army had disguised themselves as orderlies, so well that they weren't suspected when one went in the room and the other occupied the guard. The media was having a field day.

All would have gone as planned but for the fact that one of the D.C. policeman on guard was of Lebanese decent. One ersatz orderly emerged from the room and spoke to his confederate in Arabic. "It's done. Let's get out of here."

The guard understood enough Farsi and instantly drew his gun on the pair. One of Ahmed's men tried to pull his gun but was shot and wounded before he could draw. The other orderly started to run down the hallway pushing nurses and patients out of his way. He slid as he turned left down another corridor that ended with a huge picture window overlooking the lush hospital grounds. He never slowed, shouting "Allah, I am yours!" as he dove through the plate glass window plummeting five floors to the concrete walk below.

The wounded and armed orderly refused to speak. At all. Nothing. He made his one call and remained silent thereafter.

The dGraph management was acutely concerned that there might be another attempt on Pierre's life, so the secrecy surrounding his faked death would be maintained until he was strong enough to deal with the situation on his own. The investigation into both the shooting and the meant-to-convince bombing was handled by the District Police, and officially the FBI had nothing to do with it.

Dr. Kelly continued, trying to speak in non-Medical terms. "Basically, we don't know enough to accurately predict the effects of trauma to the brain. We may be able to generally say that motor skills, or memory might be affected, but to what extent is unknown. Then there are head injuries that we can't fully explain, and Pierre's is one of them."

Scott and Ty looked curiously at Dr. Kelly. "Pierre had a severe trauma to the cranium, and some of the outer layers of brain tissue were damaged when the skull was perforated." Scott shuddered at the distinct memory of the gore. "Since he was in a coma, we elected to do minimal repair work until he gained consciousness and he could give us first hand reports on his memory and other possible effects. That's how we do it in the brain business."

"So, how is he?" Scott wanted a bottom line.

"He came out of a coma yesterday, and thus far, we can't find any problems that stem from the head injury."

"That's amazing," said Scott. "I saw the . . ."

"It is amazing," agreed Dr. Kelly. "But not all that rare. There are many references in the literature where severe brain damage was sustained without corresponding symptoms. I once saw a half inch re-bar go through this poor guy's forehead. He was still awake! We operated, removed the bar, and when he woke up he was hungry. He had a slight a headache. It was like nothing ever happened. So, who knows? Maybe we'll be lucky."

"Can we see him?" Scott asked the Irish doctor assigned to repair Pierre Troubleaux.

"He's awake, but we have been keeping him sedated, more to let the chest wound heal than his head," Dr. Kelly laughed at his words. "Like they say on TV, keep it short and don't upset the patient."

Pierre was recuperating in a virtual prison, a private room deep within the bowels of the Medical Center. There were 2 guards outside the room and another that sat near the hospital bed. Absolute identification was required every time someone entered the room and it took two phone calls to verify the identities of Scott and Tyrone despite the verbal affidavit from Kelly. The groggy Pierre was awake when the three approached the bed. Dr. Kelly introduced them and Pierre immediately tried to move to thank Scott for saving his life.

Dr. Kelly laid down the rules; even though Pierre was in remarkably good shape, still, no bouncing on the bed and don't drink the IV fluid. Pierre spoke quietly, but found at least a half dozen ways to thank Scott for his ad hoc heroics. He also retained much of his famed humor.

"I want to thank you," Pierre said in jest, "for putting the value of my life in proper perspective."

Scott's cheeks pushed up his glasses from the deep smile that Pierre's words caused. He hadn't realized that Pierre had been conscious. Tyrone looked confused.

"I begged him not to die," laughed Scott. "Because it wouldn't look good on my resume."

"And I have had the common courtesy to honor your request."

After suffering enough embarrassment by compliments, Scott asked Pierre for a favor, to which he readily agreed. No long term karmic debt here, thought Scott.

"I need to understand something," said Scott. Pierre nodded, what?

"You told me, in the midst of battle, that dGraph was sick. I took that to mean that it contained a virus of some kind, but, well, I guess that's the question. What did you mean?"

"You're right. Yes," Pierre said softly but firmly. "That's what I was going to say at the hearings. I was going to confess."

"Confess?" Tyrone asked. "To what?"

"To the viruses. About why I did it, or, really, why I let it happen."

"So you did infect your own software. Why?" Scott demanded.

Pierre shook his head back and forth. "No, I didn't do it. I had no control."

"Then who did?"

"Homosoto and his people."

"Homosoto? Chairman of OSO?" Scott shrieked. "You're out of your mind, no offense."

"I wish I were. Homosoto took over my company and killed Max."

* * * * *

The New Senate Office Building
Washington, D.C.

"The Senator will see you now," said one of Senator Deere's aides. Scott and Tyrone entered her office which was decorated more in line with a woman's taste than the heavy furniture men prefer. She stood to greet them.

"Gentlemen," Nancy Deere said shaking their hands. "I know that you're with the New York City Times, Mr. Mason. I took the liberty of reading some of your work. Interesting, controversial. I like it." She offered them chairs at an informal seating area on one end of the large office.

"And you are?" she said to Ty. He told her. "I take it this is official?"

"At this point ma'am, we just need to talk, and get your reactions," Ty said.

"He's having labor management troubles." Scott thought that was the perfect diplomatic description.

"I see," Nancy said. "So right now this meeting isn't happening."

"Kind of like that," Ty said.

"And him?" She said cocking her head at Scott.

"It's his story, I'm just his faithful sidekick with a few of the pieces."

"Well then," Nancy said amused with the situation. "Please, I am all ears." She and Tyrone looked at Scott, waiting.

How the hell was he going to tell a U.S. Senator that an organized group of anarchistic hackers and fanatic Moslem Arabs were working with a respected Japanese industrialist and building computer viruses. He couldn't figure out any eloquent way to say it, so he just said it, straight, realizing that the summation sounded one step beyond absurd. All things considered, Scott thought, she took it very well.

"I assume you have more than a headline?" Senator Deere said after a brief, polite pause.

Scott proceeded to describe everything that he had learned, the hackers, Kirk, Spook, the CMR equipment, his articles being pulled, the First State and Sidneys situation. He told her about the anonymous documents he had thus far been unable to use. Except for one which he would use today. Scott also said that computer viruses would fully explain the banking crisis.

Tyrone outlined the blackmail cases he suspected were diversionary tactics for another as yet unknown crime, and that despite more than $40 millions in payoffs had been arranged, no one had showed to collect.

"Ma'am," Tyrone said to Senator Deere. "I fought to get into the Bureau, and I made it through the good and the bad. And, I always knew where I stood. Akin, I guess to the political winds that change every four years." She nodded. "But now, there's something wrong." Nancy tilted her head waiting for Ty to continue.

He spoke carefully and slowly. "I have never been the paranoid type; I'm not conspiracy minded. But I do find it strange that I get so much invisible pressure to lay off a case that appears to be both global in its reach and dangerous in its effects. It's almost like I'm not supposed to find out what's happening. I get no cooperation from my upstairs, CI, the CIA. NSA has been predictably obnoxious when I started asking questions."

"So why come to me?" Nancy asked. "You're the police."

"Are you aware that Pierre Troubleaux is alive?" Scott asked Nancy, accidentally cutting off Tyrone.

"Alive? How's that possible?" She too, had heard the news. They told her they had spoken to Pierre and that his death had been a ruse to protect him. The reports on Pierre's prognosis brightened Nancy attitude.

"But, it's not all good news. It appears, that every single copy of dGraph, that's a . . ."

"I know dGraph," she said quickly. "It's part of the job. Couldn't live without it."

"Well, ma'am, it's infected with computer viruses. Hundreds of them. According to Pierre, the head of OSO Industries, Taki Homosoto, had Max Jones, co-founder of dGraph killed and has effectively held Pierre hostage since."

The impact of such an overwhelming accusation defied response. Nancy Deere's jaw fell limp. "That is the most unbelievable, incredible . . .I don't know what to say."

"I have no reason not to believe what Pierre is saying, not yet," said Tyrone.

"There are a few friends of mine working to see if dGraph really is infected." Scott whistled to indicate the seriousness of the implications.

"What, Mr. Mason, what if it is?" She thirsted for more hard information.

"I'm no computer engineer, Senator, er, Nancy, but I'm not stupid either. Pierre said that at least 500 different viruses have been installed in dGraph since Homosoto took over. A rough guess is that there are over four million copies of dGraph. Legal ones that is. Maybe double that for pirated copies." Nancy maintained rapt attention as Scott continued. . "Therefore, I would venture that at least eight to ten million computers are infected."

Scott paused as Nancy's eyes widened.

"Knowing that viruses propagate from one program to another according to specific rules, it would not be unreasonable to assume that almost every micro-computer in the United States is getting ready to self destruct." Scott sounded certain and final.

"I can't comprehend this, this is too incredible." Senator Deere shook her head in disbelief. "What will happen?"

"Pierre doesn't know what the viruses do, he's not a programmer. He's just a figurehead." Scott explained. "Now, if I had to guess, I would, well, I would do everything possible to keep those viruses from exploding."

"One man's word is an indictment, not a conviction." Nancy said soberly.

"There's more," Tyrone said, taking some of the onus off Scott. "We've learned quite a bit in the last few days, Senator, and it begins to pull some of the pieces together, but not enough to make sense of it all." He slid forward in his chair. "We know that Scott's hacker's name is Miles Foster and he's tied up with the Amsterdam group, but we don't how yet. We also know that he is ex-NSA and was a communications and security expert out at the Fort." Nancy understood the implication.

"When I asked for information on Foster from NSA I was stonewalled. I assume that I somehow pushed a button and that now they're retaliating. But, for the life of me, I don't know why." Tyrone shook his head in frustration. "It doesn't make any sense."

"At any rate," Tyrone said waving off the lack of cooperation, "I checked into his background since he left the Agency in '87. He went freelance, became a consultant, a Beltway Bandit." Nancy Deere nodded that she understood but she listened with a poker face. "We have him traveling to Japan shortly after his resignation, and then several times over the next few months. He has been to Japan a total of 17 times. Since his credit cards show no major purchases in Japan,

I assume that he was somebody's guest. The tickets purchased in his name were bought from a Tokyo travel agency, but we can't determine who paid for them."

"Seventeen times?" asked the Senator.

"Yes ma'am. Curious."

"How do you know what he used his credit cards for, Mr. Duncan?" she asked dubiously.

"We have our means. I can't get into that now." Tyrone held the party line which meant not confirming or denying that the FBI could access any consumer and credit data base in the world. In fact though, the National Crime Information Center is linked to hundreds of computers world wide over the Computer Applications Communications Network. They can generate a complete profile on any citizen within minutes of the request. Including all travel, credit card and checking activities. Scott found this power, entrusted to a few non-elected and non-accountable civil servants unconscionable.

"I have no doubt," she said caustically.

"There's more." Tyrone spoke without the benefit of notes which impressed Nancy. "The case concerning Max Jones' death is being reopened. It seems that the former Sheriff in San Mateo county was voted out and the new one is more than willing to assist in making his predecessor look bad." Tyrone spoke without the emotion that drove Scott.

"So what does this prove?" she asked.

"It turns out that Homosoto was in Sunnyvale the day that Jones died."

Nancy Deere sat in silence and stared out of the window which only provided a view of another office building across the street. Despondence veiled her normally affable countenance as she grappled internally with the implications of the revelations.

"Senator," Scott said as he handed her a file labeled General Young: GOVT-108. "I was wondering if this might have any bearing on the tone of the hearings? It's pretty obvious that you and Rickfield don't see eye to eye."

Nancy took the file cautiously, meeting Scott's eyes, looking for ulterior motives. She found none and scanned the first page that described the illicit relationship between General Young and Senator Merrill Rickfield. Her brow furrowed the more she read.

"Is this confirmed?" she asked quietly.

"No ma'am," Scott said. "I read it this weekend and added up two and two and, well, it does raise some questions."

"I should say it does. Ones that I'm sure he will not be anxious to answer."

* * * * *

6 PM, Washington, D.C.

"Who the hell are you pissing off and why?" Bob Burnsen met Tyrone and Scott at the Old Ebbett's Grill across the street from Treasury at 6:00 PM.

Burnsen insisted that their conversation be off the record, and reluctantly accepted that for Scott's assistance in Tyrone's investigation he would get an exclusive.

For a full half hour, Tyrone and Scott explained what they knew, just as they had to Senator Deere. Tyrone had other problems. "I've been running into all sorts of bullshit here, CI, and don't forget our midnight rendezvous."

Burnsen was a reasonable man, and had every reason, more than two decades of reasons to believe the tale that Tyrone was telling him. Yet, at the same time, the story carried a wisp of the implausible. Hackers and Arabs? But, then, why was he getting heat that Ty was peeking under the wrong logs?

"What are you planning?" Bob asked them both.

"Scott's going after Homosoto," said Tyrone. "See if he can get a few answers."

"And," Scott added, "the Max Jones angle. I'll be on that, too."

"Right. As for me?" Tyrone asked. "I sure would like to have a chat with Mr. Foster. I can't imagine that he's squeaky clean. There's no core, no substance, but a lot of activity, and I think it's about time to turn a few screws."

"Ty," Bob consoled. "Whoever's button you're pushing has pushed the Director's, whose aides have been all over my ass like stink on shit. And that's exactly what this smells of. From a political angle, it reeks, and by all rights I should make you back off." Burnsen gestured at Scott. "Then we'd have him doing the work while our asses stay clean." He referred to Scott. "A perfect case of CYA."

"But?" Tyrone suggested.

"But," Bob said, "just because you're paranoid doesn't mean someone's not out to get you. It smells like pure 100% Grade A Government approved horse shit here, but I'll be fucked if know why CI is such a problem. They normally love the espionage stuff."

"They think it's a crock. Said we should stick to tabloid crimes," Tyrone said defiantly.

"Unless," Scott thought out loud. Ty and Bob stopped to listen. "Unless, the NSA has something to hide about Miles Foster. Could they exert that kind of pressure?" He asked Bob.

"The NSA can do almost anything it wants, and it has tremendous political strength. It's possible," Bob resigned. "Listen, I'll cover you as long as I can, but, after that, it may get too thick for my blood. I hope you understand."

"Yeah, I know. I'll call you anyway. And, Bob? Thanks."

* * * * *

Friday, January 15
New York City

Skyway-I helicopter flew down the East River at 5:30 AM making the first of dozens of traffic reports that would continue until 10:00 AM. Jim Lucas flew during the AM and PM rush hours for 8 local stations and was regarded as the commuters's Dear Abby for driver's psychosis. His first live-report did not bode well; the FDR Drive was tied up very early; might be a rough commute.

He crossed 42nd. St. heading west to the Hudson River and noticed that there were already two accidents; one at 5th. Avenue and one at Broadway. He listened in on the police band for details to pass on to his audience.

At 5:50 AM, Skyway-I reported traffic piling up at the 72nd. Street and Riverside Drive exit of the decrepit and ancient West Side Highway. And another accident on West End Avenue and 68th. Street. Jim flew east across Manhattan to 125th. Street where the Triborough Bridge dumps tens of thousands of cars every morning onto southbound 2nd. Avenue. Two more accidents. He listened to the police calls and heard them say the accidents were caused because all of the traffic lights were green.

Every traffic light in Manhattan was green according to the police. Jim reported the apparent problem on the air and as many accidents as he could; there were too many accidents to name. He passed on the recommendations of the police: Best Stay Home.

By 6:30 two additional helicopters were ordered to monitor the impending crisis as the city approached real gridlock. Police helicopters darted about while the media listened in on the conversations from their police band radios.

At 7:00 AM The Traffic Commissioner was called at home, and told that he shouldn't bother trying to come to work. The streets were at a standstill. Thousands of extra police units dispersed throughout the city in a dubious attempt to begin the process of managing the snarl that engulfed the city.

Scott Mason exited from the 43rd. Street and Vanderbilt side of Grand Central Station and was met with a common sight - a massive traffic jam. He walked the one block to Fifth Avenue and it gradually dawned on him that traffic wasn't moving at all. At 8:15 AM it shouldn't be that bad. The intersection at Fifth was crowded with cars aiming in every direction and pedestrians nervously slipped in and around the chaos.

Scott walked the three blocks to the Times digesting the effects of the city's worst nightmare; the paralysis of the traffic system. At that thought his stomach felt like he had been thrown from an airplane. The traffic computers.

* * * * *

Washington, D.C.

Sonja Lindstrom watched the New York based Today show from the kitchen counter in her upscale Reston, Virginia townhouse. What a mess, she thought. She knew how bad traffic could be in New York even when the lights worked. A news flash pre-empted an interview with Joan Embry from the San Diego Zoo. Sonja watched intently. New York was entering panic mode, and the repercussions would be world wide. Especially with the banks closed.

The New York radio stations linked up with the Emergency Broadcast System so they could communicate with the half million drivers who had nowhere to go. Bridges and tunnels into Manhattan were closed and cars and busses on major arteries were being forced to exit onto side streets. Schools, shops and non-essential government services were shut down for the day.

The Governor of New York declared a state of emergency and the National Guard was called to assist the local police. Sonja compared New Yorkers' reactions to this crisis to the way they deal with a heavy snowfall when the city stops. Pretty much like any other day. No big deal, go to a bar, good excuse for a party. She giggled to herself as the phone rang.

"Hello?"

"Good morning, Sonja?"

"Oh, hi, Stephanie. Yeah. Kind of early for you, isn't it?" Sonja sipped her coffee.

"It is, I know, but I had to call you," Stephanie said quickly.

"Something wrong?" Sonja asked.

"I think so, maybe. Wrong enough that I had to tell you." Stephanie sighed audibly. "You don't have to play up to Scott Mason any more. I'm getting out."

"Out of what?" Sonja said with confusion.

"I've learned a few things that I don't like, and I've kinda got hung up on Miles, and, well, I feel funny about taking the money anymore. Especially since Miles doesn't know about the arrangements. You know what I mean?"

"Yes. With Scott it bothered me a little. So I made believe I was on the Dating Game. All expense paid date." Sonja knew exactly what Stephanie meant. Deep inside she had known that at one point or another she would have to meet the conflict between her profession and her feeling straight on and deal with it. She had not suspected that it would be for passion, nor because of one of her 'dates'.

"Besides," Sonja added, "I didn't need to push him into anything. He's so hung on this story that it's almost an obsession with him."

"That's good to know, I guess," Stephanie said vacantly until her thoughts took form. "Hey, I have an idea. Why don't the four of us get together sometime. I'm sure the boys have a lot in common."

"Scott should be down tonight."

"That should be fine. We were going to dinner anyway. Maybe we can put this behind us."

* * * * *

New York City

The traffic engineers frantically searched for the reason that the signals had all turned green. They reinitialized the switches and momentarily thousands of green lights flashed red and yellow, but there was no relief from the gridlock. Computer technicians rapidly determined that the processor control code was 'glitching', as they so eloquently described the current disaster. A global error, they admitted, but correctable, in time. The engineers isolated the switching zones and began manually loading the software that controlled each region's switches in the hope of piecing together the grid.

At noon the engineers and technicians had tied together the dozens of local switches into the network and watched as they synchronized with each other. The computers compare the date, the time, anticipated traffic flow, weather conditions and adjust the light patterns and sequences accordingly. Twenty minutes later, just as system wide synchronization was achieved, every light turned green again. It was then that the engineers knew that it was only the primary sync-control program which was corrupted.

The Mayor publicly commended the Traffic Commissioner for getting the entire traffic light system back in operation by 2:00 P.M.. The official explanation was a massive computer failure, which was partially true. Privately, though, Gracie Mansion instructed the police to find out who was responsible for the dangerous software and they in turn called the Secret Service. The media congratulated the NYPD, and the population of the City in coping with the crisis. To everyone's relief there were no deaths from the endless stream of traffic accidents, but almost a hundred were injured seriously enough to be taken to the hospital. Whoever was responsible would be charged with attempted murder among other assorted crimes. All they had to do was find him.

* * * * *

New York City

Telephoning to another day is about as close to time travel as we will see for a century, but that's how Scott felt when he called OSO Industries in Tokyo. Was he calling 17 hours into the next day, or was he 7 hours and one day behind? All he knew was that he needed an international clock to figure out when to call Japan during their business hours. Once he was connected to OSO switchboard, he had to pass scrutiny by three different operators, one of them male, and suffer their terrible indignities to the English language. He told Homosoto's secretary, whose English was acceptable, that he was doing a story on dGraph and needed a few quotes. It must have been slow in Tokyo as he was patched through almost immediately.

"Yes?"

"Mr. Homosoto?"

"Yes."

"This is Scott Mason, from the New York City Times. I am calling from New York. How are you today?"

"Fine, Mr. Mason. How may I help you?" Homosoto was obviously the gratuitous sort when it came to the press.

"We are preparing to run a story in which Pierre Troubleaux accuses you of murdering his partner Max Jones. He also says that dGraph software is infected with destructive programs. Would you like to comment, sir?" Scott asked as innocently as possible under the circumstances.

No answer.

"Sir? Mr. Homosoto?"

"Yes?"

"We are also interested in your relationship with Miles Foster. Mr. Homosoto?"

"I have nothing to say."

"Are you financing hackers and Arabs to distribute computer viruses?"

No answer.

"Sir, do you know anything about a blackmail operation in the United States?"

"I should have killed him."

"What?" Scott strained his ear.

"Mr. Troubleaux is alive?"

"I can't answer that. Do you have any comment, sir? On anything?"

"I have nothing to say. Good day." The phone went dead.

Guilty as sin. A non-denial denial.

* * * * *

Chapter 25

Saturday, January 16
Tokyo, Japan

Dressed as business-like on the weekend as during the week, Taki Homosoto sat at his regal techno-throne overlooking the Tokyo skyline from his 66th floor vista. It was time. Years of preparation and millions of dollars later, it was time. Perhaps a little earlier than he would have liked, but the result would be the same anyway.

The first call Homosoto made was to Ahmed Shah, in his Columbia University office. Ahmed responded with his PRG code as the computer requested.

<<<CONNECTION>>>
GOOD YOU ARE THERE.

I can't get too far without my man-servant.
I WANT TO THANK YOU FOR YOUR INVALUABLE ASSISTANCE. HE IS DEAD?

Yes. It took two martyrs, one is being tortured by the FBI, but he has Allah to guide him.
GOOD. CAN YOU DO MORE?

I am at your disposal. This is not the war I expected, but I serve Allah's will, and he is using you as his instrument of revenge.
THE BANK CARDS. THEY ARE FOR YOU AND YOUR PEOPLE TO FUND YOUR EFFORTS.

You speak strangely. Is something wrong?
NO, EVERYTHING IS ACCORDING TO PLAN. I EXPECT YOU WILL FULFILL MY WISHES.

Of course, that is the arrangement. But what has changed?
NOTHING. I AM FULFILLING MY DESTINY.

As am I.
THEN YOU WILL UNDERSTAND.

* * * * *

Alexander Spiradon relaxed in his Alpine aerie home overlooking the hilly suburbs of Zurich while watching a satellite feed of the Simpson's on his TV. He found that he learned American colloquialisms best from American television. They brutalized the language under the guise of entertainment. During a commercial for *'The Quicker Picker Upper'*, his computer announced a call.

He put the VCR on Quick-Record and sat at his Compaq Deskpro computer watching the screen display the incoming identification.

<<<AUTOCRYPT CONVERSATION>>>
<PRG RESPONSE?>

Alex entered the code displayed on his personal identification card.

G4-YU7-%T64-666.009
<ACCEPTED>

Alex figured it was Homosoto since this was a very private computer. His other computer, an AST 386SX with 330 MB of storage was the one his recruits called with reports. The 25 Sir George's of his army called twice a day. Once to get their assignments and once to send him the results of their efforts.

They didn't have to call long distance, though, and never knew that Alex ran his part of Homosoto's operation from Europe. Sir George and his hidden compatriots used their untraceable cellular phones and merely called a local phone number within their area code. Alex's communications group had set up a widely diverse network of call forwarding telephones to make tracing the calls impossible. They exploited all of the common services that helped make his and Homosoto's armies invisible.

MR ALEX.

Yes, sir.

THE TIME HAS COME.

So soon?

YES. MONDAY IS GROUNDHOG DAY.

Monday? Are you sure? With no warning?

HAVE I EVER BEEN WRONG?

No

THEN DO AS I SAY. PLEASE.

Alex started at the word 'please'. He had never seen Homosoto ever use it before.

Of course. As you wish.

WHAT ARE THE FIRST TARGETS OF THE GROUNDHOGS?

It is complex

TELL ME!

The reservations systems of American, Delta, Pan Am and TWA. It will shut down air travel for weeks.

GOOD. AND?

The NBC, CBS and ABC communications computers. We have people working in each network. Plus, we have land based transmitters to garble and override network satellite transmissions. Quite a neat trick actually. I'm impressed with the technology.

I DON'T CARE ABOUT YOUR TECHNOLOGY. I WANT TO KNOW THAT THEY WILL WORK. WHO ELSE?

The list is long. Groundhogs are at the Home Shopping Network, American Express and other credit card companies. The Center for Disease Control, Hospitals, the IRS, Insurance Companies. Within a week, their computers will be empty and useless.

THAT IS WHAT I WANT TO HEAR. THIS ENDEAVOR HAS BEEN MOST PROFITABLE FOR YOU, HAS IT NOT?

Very much so. It is appreciated.

THEN YOU WILL NOT MIND IF I INCREASE YOUR PAYMENT

No. Why?

YOU MUST MAINTAIN THE SANCTITY OF OUR ARRANGE-MENTS. NO MATTER WHAT HAPPENS. DO YOU UNDER-STAND?

Yes. I assume I ask no questions?

YOU KNOW MORE THAN YOU SHOULD, BUT YOU ARE A MAN OF HONOR, AS LONG AS I PAY THE MOST. THAT IS TRUE.

At least you know where I stand.

WILL YOU CONTINUE?

Consider it done. How much more?

ENOUGH. MORE THAN ENOUGH.

<<<CONNECTION TERMINATED>>>

* * * * *

He couldn't believe it. Scott had just watched Nightline, and who was the guest? Madonna. How ridiculous. She badly needed English lessons not to mention a brain. He was relieved when the call came.

WTFO?

I'm here, Kirk. You're two minutes late.

PICKY PICKY.

I had to sit through a half hour of Madonna explaining why she masterbates on MTV.

LIFE'S A CESSPOOL. THEN YOU DIE.

You sound happy tonight.

I'M NOT EXACTLY PLEASED, IF THAT'S WHAT YOU MEAN.

What have you got?

WE'VE LEARNED A LOT. FIRST OF ALL, DGRAPH IS IN-FECTED.

No shit.

PROFANITY. BIG BROTHER AND FREEDOM ARE LISTEN-ING. REALLY. WE FOUND DOZENS OF DIFFERENT VIRUSES IN LOTS OF DIFFERENT COPIES OF DGRAPH. SOMEONE PUT A LOT OF WORK INTO THIS. I HAVE NEMO AND EVERY PHREAK I KNOW WORKING ON IT TO SEE WHAT OTHER VERSIONS THERE ARE. AND I'M SURE THAT HALF THE HACKERS IN THE COUNTRY ARE DOING THE SAME THING NOW. WORD GETS AROUND. BUT THAT'S NOT THE HALF OF IT.

Continue, oh messenger of doom.

THERE'S MORE ABOUT THE FREEDOM BOARDS. I THOUGHT YOU MIGHT BE INTERESTED IN WHAT WE FOUND.

I'm hanging on your every byte.

GOOD. FIRST OF ALL, I HAD NO IDEA HOW BIG THE FREEDOM LEAGUE WAS. OVER 1600 MEMBER BBS'S HERE AND IN CANADA.

Is that large?

THAT MAKES THEM A FULL FLEDGED NATIONAL NET-WORK. ALMOST A MILLION PEOPLE BELONG. BUT THE BEST PART? THE FREEDOM LEAGUE SOFTWARE IS FILLED WITH VIRUSES TOO.

You've got to be kidding. A million people in on it?

NO, NOT AT ALL. COULD BE JUST A FEW.

A few? How many are a few?

QUIET! THE FREEDOM LEAGUE RUNS A SORT OF FRANCHISE SERVICE FOR BBS'S. THEY GIVE YOU ALL OF THE TOOLS AND TOYS AND SOFTWARE TO HAVE YOUR OWN FREEDOM LEAGUE BBS. SO ANYONE WHO WANTS TO, CAN SET THEMSELVES UP FOR FREE. FREEDOM GIVES THEM EVERYTHING BUT A COMPUTER AND A MODEM.

And in exchange, they have to sell Freedom Software.

NOT EXACTLY SELL, SHAREWARE IS FREE TO DIS-
TRIBUTE, IN THEORY ONLY A FEW PEOPLE MAY EVEN
KNOW ABOUT THE INFECTIONS. WHOEVER IS DESIGN-
ING THE PROGRAMS HAS TO BE IN ON IT.

*And the franchisers, of course! They set up their own distribu-
tion of viruses.*

I WOULD GUESS THAT ABOUT 100 OF THE FREEDOM
BBS'S KNOW ABOUT THE INFECTIONS.

Why, how do you know that?

GOOD GUESS. WHEN FREEDOM STARTED UP BACK IN
'88, IT HAD 100 LOCATIONS.

So it was staged, set up?

MUSTA BEEN. NOT CHEAP. A GOOD BBS TAKES ABOUT
$10,000 TO GET GOING.

A million bucks. Chump change.

FOR WHO?

Just a friend. What else?

THEY'VE DISTRIBUTED MILLIONS OF PROGRAMS. MIL-
LIONS.

Is every one infected?

I GUESS SO. EVERY ONE WE'VE LOOKED AT IS.

Who else knows.

NEMO, PHREAK PHRIENDS. IN A COUPLE OF DAYS YOU
WON'T BE ABLE TO GIVE FREEDOM AWAY. IF IT'S IN-
FECTED, WHICH IT IS, IT'S ALL OVER FOR THEM. THEIR
REP IS SHOT.

*Aren't you worried about a repeat performance on your com-
puters?*

NO. I MOVED WHAT WAS LEFT OF MY EQUIPMENT AND
WE SWITCHED TO CELLULAR CALL FORWARDING. CAN'T
BE TRACED FOR MONTHS. BUT I APPRECIATE THE CON-
CERN.

I'll call you. My main man is going to want to talk to you.

* * * * *

Monday, January 18
New York City Times

dGRAPH INFECTED WITH VIRUS:
DGI OFFERS FREE UPGRADES.

by Scott Mason

In an unprecedented computer software announcement, DGI President and industry magnate Pierre Troubleaux admitted that every copy of dGraph sold since late 1987 contains and is infected with highly dangerous and contagious computer viruses.

He blamed Taki Homosoto, chairman of OSO Industries, and the parent company of DGI for the viruses that Troubleaux said were implanted on purpose.

Mr. Homosoto had no comment on the allegations.

Since there are so many different viruses present in the dozens of dGraph versions, (Mr. Troubleaux estimates there may be as many as 500) it is impossible to determine the exact detonation dates or anticipated damage. Therefore DGI is offering free uninfected copies of dGraph to every registered user.

Industry reaction was strong, but surprisingly non-critical of DGI's dilemma. In general the reaction was one of shock and disbelief. "If this is true," said one source, "the amount of damage done will be incalculable." He went on to say that since the virus problem has been largely ignored, very few businesses have any sort of defensive measures in place. Estimates are that large companies have the most to lose when the dGraph Virus explodes.

The major software manufacturers came to DGI's support saying, ". . .it was bound to happen sooner or later. We're just glad it didn't happen to us." Leading software firms including Microsoft, Lotus, Computer Associates and Ashton Tate have offered their disk duplication and shipping facilities to assist DGI in distributing over four million copies of the program.

Even with such support policies by DGI and the assistance of the software industry, there is a great fear that the infected dGraph programs have communicated viruses to other programs and computers. According to Ralph Potter of the International Virus Association, "This is a disaster of unfathomable proportions. It could not be much worse than if DOS had been carrying a virus for years. The designers knew what they were doing, *waiting so long before the viruses were triggered to go off. The ultimate Trojan Horse."*

The National Computer Systems Laboratory at the National Institute of Standards and Technology issued a terse statement saying that they would soon publish recommended procedures to minimize the effects of the current virus crisis. They predicted at least 2 millions personal computers would be stricken with the dGraph Viruses.

One dGraph User Group in Milwaukee, Wisconsin has begun a class action suit against DGI and OSO on behalf of all users who have damage done to their computers and or data. They claim at least 10,000 co-plaintiffs on the initial filing with District Court in Milwaukee and are asking for $10 Billion in damages.

Scott's story went on to describe that the FBI and Secret Service were taking the threat as a national security risk and would make a public statement in a day or so. Leading software industry prophets were quoted, all taking credit for warning the computer industry that such massive assaults were predictable and preventable. They blamed the government and computer manufacturers for laxidazical handling of a serious problem that could have been prevented. Scott had to make a large chart to keep track of the competitive finger pointing from the experts.

DGI's stock fell 75% after the announcement until the SEC suspended its trading.

* * * * *

The Associated Press wire announcement was followed in seconds by the one from UPI. Doug tore it off the printer and raced it over to Scott.

"I believe this will be of interest to you . . ." Doug chuckled as Scott read the wire.

Tokyo, Japan: Taki Homosoto, the billionaire founder and chairman of OSO Industries, was found dead this afternoon in his opulent Tokyo office. According to police and company spokespersons, Mr. Homosoto died by his own hands in traditional Japanese warrior fashion; hari-kari. His body was found curled up in a pool of blood with the ritualistic sword penetrating his abdomen protruding from his lower back.

Police say they discovered a note on his person that explained the apparent suicide. The letter is believed to have been hand written by

451

Mr. Homosoto. The contents of that letter, as released by the Tokyo police follow:

Honorable Friends,

I now resign as Chairman of OSO Industries. My time is over.

For almost 50 years I have waited to see the United States and its people suffer as my people did during those terrible days in August. The United States gave our people no warning, and tens of thousands of innocent women and children died without purpose. This criminal sin is one which the United States and its people will have to live with for all eternity.

Yet, out of compassion for the millions of innocent bystanders who are helplessly trapped by their government's indifference to human life, I will give the American people a warning: Without your computers your future is dim, and your present becomes the past.

When I was told about the attack plans on the United States, I admit that I was a willing but skeptical buyer. I found it hard to believe, indeed incredible, that the greatest military power on Earth was so foolish. I learned that there were no defenses for the computers that run your country. How unfortunate for you.

It was shown me how to execute the plans which invade the very bastions of Western Imperialism; and I have succeeded admirably. You will not recover for years, as we did not after your hideous attack upon our land.

By the time you read this, I will be dead and happy. My creations will have taken hold, and unshakeable from their roots, will spread chaos and distrust. This is the world's first computer war and I have waged it and I will win it.

Retaliate! Retaliate, if you wish, if you can; but you will not, you cannot. Who do you attack? My country? They had nothing to do with it. My company? I will be dead and there is no double jeopardy in death.

You have nothing to say, and nothing to do in response. As we did not after your fire-bombs landed. We could say nothing.

Helplessness is a terrible feeling. It is one of loneliness, solitude in a personal hell which your people shall suffer as they learn to live without the luxuries of technology. You will pay for your ancestor's mistakes.

To the memory and honor of my family.

Taki Homosoto

* * * * *

Scott Mason called Tyrone Duncan immediately.

"I know," said Tyrone, sounding out of breath. "We're on it. Pierre's getting additional protection. It turns out that Mr. Homosoto isn't as pure as the driven snow like he pretends to be."

"How do you mean?" Scott asked.

"Off the record."

"Background." The negotiation on press terms was complete.

"All right, but be careful. It seems that since the 1940's Mr. Homosoto has been performing some very lucrative services for our friends at the Pentagon. He has some influential friends in Congress and uses an assortment of lobbying firms to promote his interests."

"What's so unusual about that?" Asked Scott.

"Nothing, until you see that certain Congressmen got very wealthy when OSO Industries built plants in their districts. Heavy PAC contributions, blind distribution of small contributing funds. It also appears that he regularly entertained high Pentagon officials in the finest fashion. Paris, Tokyo, Rio, Macao. Influence pedaling and bribery. We have traced a path from Tokyo to the Pentagon that has resulted in OSO subsidiaries receiving large non-classified government contracts. Take dGraph for example. That's a de facto standard for all agencies."

"I never though about that. Everyone in the government uses it."

"Just like the private sector. I'm on my way to have a little talk with your Mr. Foster. I don't believe in coincidences."

"Good, where?" Asked Scott excitedly.

"Whoah! Wait a minute. This is official now, and I can't have a civilian . . ."

"Bullshit!" Scott yelled into the phone. "Don't you get GI on me. I gave him to you. Remember? Besides, I know him. And I might have something else."

"What's that?"

"What if I told you that the Freedom League is part of it? And that it's being run by foreign nationals."

"So what?" asked Tyrone.

"How far did you check into the van driver's background? Wasn't he Arab?" Scott offered tidbits that he thought relevant.

"Yeah . . ."

"When are you meeting Foster?"

Tyrone thought carefully about Scott's words. "Listen, I have to get a warrant anyway. It'll probably take till tomorrow." Tyrone paused for the subtle offer to sink in to Scott. "He's listed. Gotta go."

One hell of a guy, thought Scott. If it ever got out that Tyrone worked with the media like this, he would be immediately retired, if not possibly prosecuted. But nobody else was doing anything, and Scott had given them Foster on a silver platter. He would save the Freedom League story for the moment.

* * * * *

The Motorola STU-III secure phone rang on the credenza behind Marvin Jacobs desk. He had been Director of the National Security Agency, DIRNSA, since 1984, installed in that position because he gave the distinct impression that he didn't care about anything except satisfying his mentor; in this case Vice President Bush.

The STU-III phone added funny electronic effects to the voices that spoke over it; all in the interest of national security.

"Hello?" Jacobs asked.

"Homosoto is dead."

"I heard," Jacobs said. "It sounded clean."

"Very pro. Won't be a problem."

* * * * *

Scott saw the galley for the afternoon paper. The headline, in 3 inch letters shocked him:

RICKFIELD RESIGNS

He immediately called Senator Nancy Deere.

"I was going to call you," she said. "I guess you've heard."

"Yes, what happened?" He shouted excitedly over the rumble of the high speed train.

"I guess I should take the blame," Nancy said. "When I confronted the Senator this morning, he just stared at me. Never said a word. I begged him for an explanation, but he sat there, expressionless. He finally got up and left."

"That's it? What happens now?"

"I see the President," she said.

"May I ask why?"

"Off the record," she insisted.

"Sure." Scott agreed. What's one more source I can't name.

"I heard about the resignation from the White House. Phil Musgrave. He said the President was very concerned and wanted a briefing from my perspective. He's beginning to feel some heat on the computer crimes and doesn't have a clue. I figure they need to get up to speed real fast."

"It's about time," Scott said out loud. "They've been ignoring this forever."

"And," Senator Deere added, "they want you there, too. Tomorrow, 9AM."

The hair on Scott's neck stood on end. A command performance from the White House?

"Why, why me?"

"You seem to know more than they do. They think you're wired into the hackers and Homosoto."

"I'll be there," Scott managed to get out. "What do I do . . .?"

"Call Musgrave's office at the White House."

"I bet the paper's going nuts. I didn't tell them I had left or where I was going," Scott laughed.

Scott called Doug who had half of the paper looking high and low for him. "You made the big time, huh kid?" Doug said feigning snobbery. "What world shattering events precipitated this magnanimous call?" In fact he was proud. Very proud of Scott.

Scott explained to Doug that he would call after the White House meeting, and he wasn't quite sure why he was going, and that Nancy was taking over the hearings and he would stay in DC for a few days. And no, he wouldn't tell more than was in print, not without calling Doug or Higgins - at any hour.

Doug sounded relieved when Scott volunteered that there would be no hotel bills. Phew. Forever the cheap skate. The story of the year and he's counting pennies. God, Doug was a good editor.

Scott's stories on computer crime and specifically the dGraph situation aroused national attention. Time, Newsweek and dozens of periodicals began following the story, but Scott, at Doug's suggestion, had wisely held back enough information that would guarantee the privacy and quality of his sources.

He was right in the middle of it, perhaps making news as much as reporting it, but with Doug's and the Times' guidance, Scott and the paper were receiving accolades on their fair yet direct treatment of the issues.

Doug thought that Scott was perhaps working on the story of the year, or maybe the decade, but he never told him so. However, Scott was warned that as the story became major national news, the exclusivity that he and the Times had enjoyed would be in jeopardy. Get it while the getting is hot.

No problem.

It just so happened Scott knew Miles Foster personally.

* * * * *

"Sonja? I'm coming down. Tonight. Can you recommend a good hotel?" He jibed at her while packing away his laptop computer for the trip to Washington. He called her and was going to leave a message, but instead he was rewarded with her answering the phone.

"Chez Lindstrom is nice, but the rates are kind of high."

"King or twin beds? Room with a view? Room service?"

"E, all of the above," she laughed. "Want me to pick you up at National?"

"Naw, I'll take the train from work. I may need to buy a few things when I get there, like a suitcase and a wardrobe. It's kind of last minute."

"I gather I wasn't the prime reason for your sudden trip." Sonja said in fun.

"No, it was, I wanted to come, but I had to do some . . .and then I found out about . . .well I have to be there tomorrow, but I am leaving a day early." He pleaded for understanding, not realizing she was kidding him. He couldn't tell her why he was being so circumspect. Nothing about the meeting.

"Well," she said dejectedly. "I guess it's O.K. If."

"If what?" Scott brightened.

"If we can have a couple of friends over for dinner. There's someone I'd like you to meet."

* * * * *

"Holy shit," Scott said as Sonja opened her apartment door and admitted Miles and the stunning Stephanie.

Miles stopped in his tracks and stared at Scott. Then at Stephanie. "What's the deal?" he said accusingly.

"This is Sonja Lindstrom and her friend Scott Mason," Stephanie said. "What's wrong, hon?" She still had her arm wrapped around Miles' arm.

"It's just that, well, we've met, and I was just kind of surprised, that's all." He extended a hand at Scott. "Good to see you again." Scott warmly reciprocated. This was going to be an interesting evening.

"Yeah, ditto," Scott said, confused. "What happened to you? I thought you were coming back?" He was speaking of Amsterdam.

"Well, I was a little occupied, if you recall," Miles said referring to the triplets in Amsterdam. "And business forced me back on the road."

"Where? To Japan?" Scott awaited a reaction by Miles, but was disappointed when there was none.

Stephanie and Sonja wondered how the two had already met; it was their job to report such things to Alex, but it really didn't matter any more. They were quitting.

The first round of drinks was downed quickly and the tension in the room abated slightly. The four spoke casually, albeit somewhat guardedly. The harmless small talk was only a prelude to Scott's question when the girls stepped into the kitchen. Perhaps they left the room on purpose.

"Listen," Scott whispered urgently to Miles. "I know who you are, and that you're tied up with Homosoto and the computer nutsiness that's going on everywhere. You have a lot of people looking for you and we only have a few seconds," Scott said glancing up at the kitchen door. "I see the situation as follows. You get to tell your side of the story to the authorities in private, or you can tell me first and I put it in tomorrow's paper. This may be your only chance to get your side of the story out. All of sudden, you're big news. What'll it be?" Scott spoke confidently and waited for Miles' answer.

Miles intently scanned every inch of Scott's face in minute detail. "That fucking gook. You're damn right I'll talk. First of all, it's a lie," Miles hissed. "If they're coming after me, I have to protect myself. Can't trust a fucking slant eye, can you?"

The girls returned with fresh drinks and sat down on the white leather couch. Miles and Scott continued their discussion.

"What happened?" Scott asked. Miles looked over at the stunning Sonja, stripping her naked with his stare and then at Stephanie who had caught his stare.

"It's very simple," Miles said after a while. His dimples deepened while he forced a smile. "Homosoto's fucked us all." He nodded his head as he looked at his three companions. "Me. Royally. How the hell can I defend myself against accusations from the grave." He shrugged his shoulders. "And you," he pointed at Scott. "You've kept the fear going. Haven't you. You picked up the scent and you've been writing about it for months. Setting his stage for him. Like a puppet. And then? After you sensitize the public, he commits suicide. He used you."

"And then, you two," Miles said to Stephanie and Sonja. "You could be out in the cold in days. Bet you didn't know you were in on it. Am I right?"

"In on what?" Scott asked Miles and Sonja.

457

"Tell him," Miles said to Sonja. "I've never met you, but I can guess what you do for a living."

"She's a PR person," interjected Scott.

"Go on, tell him, or I will," Miles said again.

Sonja's eyes pleaded with Miles to stop it. Please, stop. I'll do it in my own way, in time. Please, stop. Scott glowered at Miles' words and awaited a response from Sonja. How could he distrust her? But what did Miles mean?

The front door bell rang and broke the intense silence. It rang again as Sonja went to answer.

"Yes, he's here," she whispered.

The door opened and Tyrone Duncan came into the room while another man stood at the door. Tyrone walked up to Miles. Scott was in absolute awe. How the hell? Ty had said tomorrow.

"Mr. Foster? Miles Foster?" Tyrone asked without pleasantries.

"Yeah," Miles said haughtily.

"FBI," Ty said flashing his badge. "You're under arrest for trafficking in stolen computer access cards and theft of service." Tyrone took a breath and waved a piece of paper in the air. "We searched your apartment and found telephone company access codes that . . . "

"I want to call my lawyer," Miles interrupted calmly. "Now," he commanded.

" . . . have been used to bypass billing procedures."

"I said I want to call my lawyer," Miles again said emphatically.

"I'll be out in an hour," he said aside to Stephanie and kissed her on the cheek. His arrogance was unnerving; this wasn't the same Miles that Scott had known in Amsterdam. There, he was just another misguided but well-intentioned techno-anarchist who was more danger to himself than anyone else. But now, as Tyrone read a list of charges against him, mostly arcane FBI domain inter-state offenses, Miles took on a new character. A worldly criminal whom the FBI was arresting for potential terrorist activities.

"And those are for starters, Mister," Tyrone said after reading off a list of penal violations by code number. As if following a script, Tyrone added, "you have the right to remain silent . . ." He wanted to make sure that this was clean arrest, and with this many witnesses, he was going to follow procedure to the letter. Mirandizing was one of the steps.

Scott Mason's adrenaline flowed with intensity. Did he ever have a story to tell now! An absolute scoop. He was present, coincidentally, during the arrest of Miles Foster.

Front page.

"I want to call my lawyer," Miles repeated.

"Make it quick," said Tyrone. Miles rapidly dialed a number from memory.

Miles turned his back on Tyrone and the others and spoke calmly into the phone.

"It's me."

Pause.

"It's me. I need assistance."

Arrogance. Pause.

"A laundry list of charges."

Disinterest. Pause.

"Had to happen, sooner or later, yeah," Miles said happily. Pause.

"I gotta dinner party. I don't want to miss it." He smiled at Stephanie and blew a kiss. "Great. Make it quick." Miles hung up.

Miles turned to Tyrone and held his wrists out together in front of him. "Let's go," Miles said still smiling cooly.

Tyrone gently snapped the cuffs on Miles and ushered him toward the door.

"Back in an hour or so," Miles defiantly said to Scott, Sonja and Stephanie over his shoulder as the front door closed behind Miles and his escorts.

Scott watched in disbelief. Miles, the Spook, ever so calm, cool and collected. Not a fluster. Not a blush.

Who had he called? That was the question that bothered Scott throughout the rest of the evening.

* * * * *

The White House, Washington, D.C.

The President looked grim. The normally affable Republican had won his second term by a landslide and had maintained unprecedented popularity. The Democrats had again been unable to conjure up a viable candidate after another string of scandals rocked the primaries and the very election foundation of the party itself Their entire platform focused on increasing the Peace Dividend beyond the aggressively reduced $180 Billion Defense budget. It was not much of an attack on a President whose popularity never fell below an astounding 65% approval, and the only ebb was due to a minor White House incident involving a junior aide, the junior aide's boyfriend and the Lincoln Bedroom.

The recession that was started by the Iraqi situation in Kuwait during the summer of 1990 was not as bad as it could have been. The world wide militaristic fever, proper Fed Reserve response and the

459

Japanese all took credit for easing the problem through their specific efforts. In fact, the recession was eased due in part to all of their efforts as well the new Europe. The President was rewarded, ultimately, with the credit for renewing the economy almost glitch-free.

But the President was still grim. America was again at war, and only a handful of people in the upper echelons of the Government even knew about it. It would be in the paper in the morning.

* * * * *

Chapter 26

Midnight, Tuesday, January 19
Scarsdale, New York

Scott Mason awaited Kirk's midnight call.

Now that they had a deal, a win-win situation, Kirk and his phriends had become gung-ho. Kirk agreed to help Scott in the dGraph and Freedom situations if Scott would make sure that his articles clearly spelled out the difference between the white-hat and black-hat hackers.

Journalistic responsibility demanded fair treatment of all sides and their respective opinions, and Scott attempted to bring objectivity to his analyses. He did this well, quite well, and still was able to include his own views and biases, as long as they were properly qualified and disclaimed.

Additionally, Kirk wanted assurances of total anonymity and that Scott would not attempt to identify his location or name. Scott also had to agree to keep his Federal friends at a distance and announce if they were privy to the conversations.

In exchange for fair portrayals in the press, privacy and no government intervention, Kirk promised Scott that the resources of Nemo would be focussed on finding defenses to the virus attacks in dGraph and Freedom software. If Kirk and Homosoto were right, millions of computers would experience the electronic equivalent of sudden cardiac arrest in less than 2 weeks.

The Times, Higgins and Doug agreed to the relationship but added their own working caveats. In order to treat Kirk as a protected source, they treated him as if he were a personal contact. Instead of reporter's notes, Scott maintained an open file which recorded the entirety of their computer conversations. There were no precedents for real-time electronic note taking, but Higgins felt confident that the records would protect the paper in any event. Besides, Supreme Court rulings now permit the recording of conversations by hidden devices, as long as the person taping is actually present. Again, Higgins felt he had solid position, but he did ask Scott to ask Kirk's permission to save the conversations on disk. Kirk always agreed.

At midnight, Scott's computer beeped the anticipated beep.

WTFO

I heard a good one.

JOKE?

Yeah, do they work over computer?

461

TRY ME.

Snow White and the Seven Dwarfs were in Europe and got to meet the Pope. Dopey really wanted to asked the Pope a few questions. "Mr. Pope, Mr. Pope. Do you have pretty nuns?" "Of course we do, Dopey." "Mr. Pope, do you have fat ugly nuns?" "Why, yes, Dopey, we do." "And I bet, Mr. Pope, that you have some tall skinny nuns, too." "Yes, Dopey we do." "Mr. Pope? Do you have nuns in Chicago?" "Yes, Dopey, we have nuns in Chicago?" "And in San Francisco and New York?" "Yes, Dopey." "And do you have nuns in Africa and Australia and in France?" "Yes, Dopey. We have nuns everywhere." Dopey took a second to think and finally asked, "Mr. Pope? Do you have nuns in Antarctica?" "No, Dopey, I'm sorry, we don't have any nuns in Antarctica." The other six dwarfs immediately broke out into a laughing song: "Dopey fucked a penguin. Dopey fucked a penguin."

HA HA HA HA HA!!! LOVE IT. REAL ICE BREAKER. HA HA

Facetious?

NO, THAT'S GREAT. IS YOUR RECORDER ON?

You bet. No plagiarism. What have you got?

MORE THAN I WISH I DID. DGRAPH FIRST. WE HAVE IDENTIFIED 54 SEPARATE DGRAPH VIRUSES. I HAVE A FILE FOR YOU. IT LISTS THE VIRUS BY DETONATION DATE AND TYPE, SYMPTOMS AND THE SIGNATURES NEEDED FOR REMOVAL. ARE YOU REALLY GOING TO PRINT IT ALL?

Daily. Our science section has been expanded to every day from just Tuesday. I have all the room I need.

YOU MIGHT MAKE ME RECONSIDER MY OPINION OF THE MEDIA.

Just the facts, ma'am. Just the facts.

HA HA. WE'VE JUST TOUCHED THE SURFACE ON FREEDOM, BUT THE WORD'S OUT. FREEDOM WILL BE AS GOOD AS DEAD IN DAYS. THE NUMBER OF VIRUSES MUST NUMBER IN THE HUNDREDS. IT'S INCREDIBLE. I'VE SEEN A LOT OF VIRUSES, BUT NONE LIKE THIS. IT'S ALMOST AS THOUGH THEY WERE BUILT ON AN ASSEMBLY LINE. SOME ARE REAL CLOSE TO EACH OTHER, EVEN DO THE SAME THINGS, BUT THEIR SIGNATURES ARE DIFFERENT MAKING IT EXTRA HARD TO DETECT THEM. EACH ONE WILL HAVE TO BE DONE INDIVIDUALLY.

I suggest we start with the dGraph viruses. You said 54, right?

YEAH

Send me the file and I still may have time to get it into tomorrow's paper. They usually leave a little room.

I'LL SEND DGVIRUS.RPT. IT'S IN ASCII FORMAT, EASY TO READ INTO ANY FILE YOU'RE WORKING WITH.

I think I can handle it.

* * * * *

DGRAPH VIRUS LIST

by Scott Mason

The dGraph Virus Crisis has set the computer industry into a virtual tailspin with far reaching effects including stock prices, delayed purchasing, contract cancellation and a bevy of reported lawsuits in the making.

All the same, the effects of the Crisis must be mitigated, and the New York City Times will be providing daily information to assist our readers in fighting the viruses. DGraph is now known to contain at least 54 different viruses, each designed to execute different forms of damage to your computer.

According to computer security experts there are two ways to deal with the present virus crisis. The best way to make sure that an active security system is in place in your computer. Recommendations vary, but it is generally agreed by most experts that security, especially in the highly susceptible desktop and laptop personal computers, should be hardware based. Security in software is viewed to be ineffective against well designed viruses or other offensive software mechanisms.

The second way to combat the effects of the dGraph Virus, but certainly not as effective, is to build a library of virus signatures and search all of your computers for matches that would indicate a viral infection. This technique is minimally effective for many reasons: Mutating viruses cause the signature to change every time it invades another program, rendering the virus unidentifiable. There is no way to be sure that all strains have been identified. Plus, there is no defense against subsequent viral attacks, requiring defensive measures to be reinstituted every time.

Preliminary predictions by computer software experts are that between 1 and 5 million IBM compatible computers will be *severely effected by the dGraph Viruses. Computers tied to local area and wide area networks are likely to be hit hardest.*

Beginning today, we will publish the known dGraph Virus characteristics daily to help disseminate the defensive information as rapidly as possible.

dGraph Version 3.0

Virus #1

Detonation Date: 2/2/XX
Symptoms: Monitor blinks on an off, dims and gets bright.
Size: 2413
Signature: 0F 34 E4 DD 81 A1 C3 34 34 34

Virus #2, #3, #4, #5

Same as above but different dates:
2/3/XX, 2/4/XX, 2/5/XX, 2/6/XX

Virus #6

Detonation Date: 2/2/XX
Symptoms: Erases hard disk
Size: 1908
Signature: E4 EE 56 01 01 C1 C1 00 01 02

Virus #7

Detonation Date: 1/22/XX
Symptoms: Reformats hard drive
Size: 2324
Signature: 00 F1 8E E3 AA 01 F5 6B 0B 0D

Virus #8

Detonation Date: 1/23/XX
Symptoms: Over exercises hard disk heads causing failure. Requires hard disk to be replaced.
Size: 2876
Signature: FF 45 7A 20 96 E6 22 1F 07 0F 2E

Scott's article detailed all 54 dGraph Viruses. Every wire service and news service in the country picked up the story and reprinted it in their papers and magazines. Within 24 hours, everyone who owned or used a computer had some weapons with which to fight available to him. If they chose to believe in the danger.

* * * * *

Wednesday, January 20
The White House

"So what about this Mason character?" Secretary of State Quinton Chambers asked challengingly. The President's inner circle was again meeting to discuss the government's reaction to the impending chaos that Mr. Homosoto posthumously promised. The pre-dawn hours were viewed as an ideal time to have upper level meetings without the front door scrutiny of the press.

Phil Musgrave pulled a folder from the stack in his lap and opened it. "Born 1953, he had an Archie Bunker for a father but he came out a brain -IQ of 170. Against Nam, who wasn't, protested some, but not a leader. No real trouble with the law; couple of demonstration arrests. City College, fared all right, and then set up his own company, worked in the defense industry writing manuals until he hit it big and sold out. Divorced, no kids. Wife is kinda wacky. The news business is new to him, but he's getting noticed fast."

"Is he a risk?"

"The FBI hasn't completed their investigation," said Phil. "If he is a risk, it's buried deep. Surface wise, he's clean. Only one problem."

"What's that?"

"He's an independent thinker."

"How's he done so far?"

"So far so good."

"So we let him continue?"

"Last night he said he was willing to help, but I have a sneaky suspicion he'll do better on his own without our interference. Besides, he prints every damn thing he does."

"What about their identity?"

"No way. He will maintain source protection, and I don't think it matters right now. Maybe later."

"What about the FBI friend?"

"The FBI is aware of it, and views it favorably. Duncan's relationship has been exclusively personal until recently. It seems to serve both sides well."

"So you're saying he's working for us and not knowing it?"

"He probably knows it, and probably, like most of the media, doesn't care. His job is to report the news. It just so happens that we read the same newspapers. Let's leave him alone."

The President held up his hand to signal an end to the debate between State policy and the White House Chief of Staff. "Unless anyone can give me a good goddamned reason to fix something that seems to be working," he said, "let Mason do his job and let us do ours." He looked around the Oval Office for comments or dissent. It was a minor point and nobody thought it significant enough to pursue. Yet. "Next?" The President commanded.

Refills of coffee were distributed and the pile of Danishes was shrinking as the men casually dined during their 6:00 AM meeting.

"OSO Industries appears, by all first impressions, to have nothing to do with the threats." Henry Kennedy was expected to know more than anyone else at this point. "Investigations are continuing, but we have no reason to suspect a smoking gun."

"One man did all of this?" asked the President skeptically.

"We have no doubt that he accomplished at least the dGraph Viruses with accomplices and a great deal of money." Henry knew his material. With the combined help of the NSA, CIA, FBI and international contacts, the National Security Advisor was privy to an incredible range of information. He was never told directly that U.S. agents regularly penetrated target computers as part of any investigation, or that they listened in on computers and communications to gather information. But Henry Kennedy preferred it this way; not to officially know where he got his data. Professional deniability.

"We also have every reason to believe that he used technical talent outside of OSO," Kennedy continued. "Perhaps as many as thirty or forty people involved."

The inner circle whistled. "Thirty or forty? That's a conspiracy," commented Quinton.

"I agree with Quinton. What I think we need to do here," said Phil Musgrave to the others in the room and the President, "is expand our previous definition of terrorism. Doesn't a threat to international stability and the economic well being of this country constitute terrorism?" He gazed into each of the listener's eyes then said, "In my mind it clearly does." He referred to the work at the Department of State which, since the Iraqi War, had clearly expanded the operational definition of terrorism.

"There's more," Henry said soberly. "Four months ago the FBI was inundated with reports of blackmail. None materialized but still take up a great deal of manpower and resources. Classified defense technology is used to shut down the Stock Exchange and other major businesses. Two months ago an Irani foreign national was killed in New York. He was driving a vehicle which contained sophisticated computer monitoring equipment."

"Has anything developed on that front?" the President asked. "I remember reading about that. It was a tragedy."

"It was," agreed Phil Musgrave.

"We had the FBI, the CI division take apart what was left of the van and we began a cross trace," Henry pulled out yet another file from his stack. "It seems that during a 2 month period in 1988, a disproportionate number of identical Ford Econoline vans were paid for in cash. As far as the dealer is concerned, the customer disappeared. Unless they're using stolen plates, they're part of the DMV system. The New York van was registered to a non-existent address. Roadblocked."

"And don't forget the First State incident, INTERNET, the FAA radar systems," Quinton Chambers said to the President. He listed a long series of computer malfunctions from the last 60 days. "It appears at this point that we have been experiencing a prelude, the foreplay if you will, of something worse. The Homosoto letter makes him as good a candidate as anyone right now."

Even Andrew Coletree felt in concert with the others on this point. "If what has happened to computers, the traffic systems, airplanes, to the IRS, the Stock Exchange, Fed Ex, and God knows what else is all from one man, Homosoto, then yes, it's a army, an attack."

"What if we declare war?" Secretary of State Quinton Chambers said, fully expecting immediate agreement with his idea.

"On who? The Computers?" jibed Defense Secretary Coletree. "The goddamned Computer Liberation Organization will be the next endangered minority."

"Declaring war is a joke, excuse me Mr. President," said Phil Musgrave. "It's a joke and the American people won't buy it. They're getting hit where it hurts them the most. In their pockets. We have major business shut downs, and they want an answer. A fix, not a bunch of hype. We've had the war on crime, the war on drugs, the war on poverty and they've all been disasters. Things are worse now than before. They've had it with bullshit and they're scared right now."

The President bowed and rotated his head to work out a kink. "The position of think," Musgrave would say. Then the refreshing snap in the President's neck would bring a smile of relief to corners of Chief Executive's mouth.

"What if we did it and meant it?" asked the President with a devilish grin. No one responded. "What if we declared war, with the approval of Congress, and actually did something about it."

"A unique concept," quipped Musgrave. "Government accomplishing something." Penetrating glares from Coletree and Kennedy only furthered the President's amusement. He enjoyed the banter.

"No, let me run this by you, and see what you think," the President thought out loud. "We are facing a crisis of epic proportions, we all agree on that. Potential economic chaos. Why don't we deal with it that way. Why don't we really go out and fix it?" Still no reactions. "What is wrong with you guys? Don't you get it? Mediocrity is passé. It can't be sold to the this country again. For the first time in almost two centuries, the American people may have to defend themselves, in their homes and businesses on their home land. If that's the case, then I think that leadership should come from the White House."

The President rose and leaned on the back of his chair. There was quiet muttering among his top aides. "Aren't you stretching the point a little, sir?" asked the Chambers, the silver haired statesman. "After all, it was just one man . . ."

"That's the point!" shouted the President. "That's the whole damned point." He strode around to the old white fireplace with a photo of George Washington above it. If permitted, this spot would be labeled 'Photo Opportunity' by the White House tours.

"Look what one man can do. I never claimed to know anything about computers, but what if this was a warning?"

"Don't get maudlin on us . . ."

"I am not getting anything except angry," the President said raising his voice. "I remember what they said about Bush. They said if he was Moses, he would have brought down the ten suggestions. That will not happen to me."

The inner circle stole questioning glances from each other.

"This country has not had a common cause since Kennedy pointed us at the moon. We had the chance in the '70's to build a national energy policy, and we screwed it up royally when oil prices were stable. So what do we do?" His rhetorical question was best left unanswered. "We now import more than 50% of our oil. That's so stupid . . .don't let me get started." There was an obvious sigh of relief from Chambers and Musgrave and the others. When the President got like this, real pissed off, he needed a sounding board, and it was generally one or more of them. Such was the price of admission to the inner circle.

The President abruptly shifted his manner from the political altruist still inside him to the management realist that had made him a popular leader. He spoke with determination.

"Gentlemen, exactly what is the current policy and game plan." The President's gaze was not returned. "Henry? Andrew?" Musgrave and Chambers and Secretary of the Treasury Martin Royce wished they could disappear into the wallpaper. They had seen it before, and they were seeing it again. Senior aides eaten alive by the President.

"Henry? What's the procedure?" The President's voice showed increasing irritation.

"Sir, CERT, the Computer Emergency Response Team was activated a few months ago to investigate Network Penetrations," Henry Kennedy said. "ECCO, another computer team is working with the FBI on related events. Until yesterday we didn't even know what we were up against, and we still barely understand it."

"That doesn't change the question, Henry. What are the channel contingencies? Do I have to spell it out?" The President mellowed some. "I was hoping to spare myself the embarrassment of bringing attention to the fact that the President of the United States is unaware of the protocol for going to war with a computer." The lilt in his voice cut the edge in the room, momentarily. "Now that that is out in the open, please enlighten us all." The jaws were preparing to close tightly.

Henry Kennedy glanced nervously over at Andrew Coletree who replied by rubbing the back of his neck. "Sir," Henry said. "Basically there is no defined, coordinated, that is established procedures for something like this." The President's neck reddened around the collar as Henry stuttered. "If you will permit me to explain . . ."

The President was furious. In over 30 years of professional politics, not even his closest aides had ever seen him so totally out of character. The placid Texan confidence he normally exuded, part well designed media image, part real, was completely shattered.

"Are you telling me that we spent almost $4 trillion dollars, four goddamn trillion dollars on defense, and we're not prepared to defend our computers? You don't have a game plan? What the hell have we been doing for the last 12 years?" The President bellowed as loudly as anyone could remember. No one in the room answered. The President glared right through each of his senior aides.

"Damage Assessment Potential?" The President said abruptly as he forced a fork full of scrambled eggs into his mouth.

"The Federal Reserve and most Banking transactions come to a virtual standstill. Airlines grounded save for emergency operations. Telephone communications running at 30% or less of capacity. No Federal payments for weeks. Do you want me to continue?"

"No, I get the picture."

The President wished to God he wouldn't be remembered as the President who allowed the United States of America to slip backward 50 years. He waited for the steam in his collar to subside before saying anything he might regret.

"Marv?" For the first time the President acknowledged the presence of Marvin Jacobs, Director of the National Security Agency. Jacobs had thus far been a silent observer. He responded to the President.

"Yessir?"

"I will be signing a National Security Decision Directorate and a Presidential Order later today, authorizing the National Security Agency to lead the investigation of computer crimes, and related events that may have an effect on the national security." The President's words stunned Jacobs and Coletree and the others except for Musgrave.

"Sir?"

"Do you or do you not have the largest computers in the world?" Jacobs nodded in agreement. "And do you not listen in to everything going on in the world in the name of National Security?"

Jacobs winced and noticed that besides the President, others were interested in his answer. He meekly acknowledged the assumption by a slight tilt of his head.

"I recall, Marv," the President said, "that in 1990 you yourself asked for the National Computer Security Center to be disbanded and be folded into the main operations of the Agency. I issued a Presidential Order rescinding Reagan's NSDD-145. Do you recall?"

"Yes, of course I do," said Marvin defensively. "It made sense then, and given it's charter, it still makes sense. But you must understand that the Agency is only responsible for military security. NIST handles civilian."

"Do you think that the civilian agencies and the commercial computers face any less danger than the military computers?" The President quickly qualified his statement. "Based upon what we know now?"

"No, not at all," Jacobs felt himself being boxed into a corner. "But we're not tooled up for . . ."

"You will receive all the help you need," the President said with assurance. "I guarantee it." His words dared anyone to defy his command.

"Yessir," Jacobs said humbly. "What about NIST?"

"Do you need them?"

"No question."

"Consider it done. I expect you all here at the same time tomorrow with preliminary game plans." He knew that would get their attention. Heads snapped up in disbelief.

"One day?" complained Andrew Coletree. "There's no way that we can begin to mobilize and organize the research . . ."

"That's the kind of talk I do not want to hear, gentlemen," the President said. Coletree turned red.

"Mr. President," said Chambers. "If we were going to war . . ."

"Sir," the President said standing straight. "We are already at war. You're just not acting like it. According to you, the vital interests of this country have been attacked. It is our job to defend the country. I call that war. If we are going to sell a Computer War to America, we better start acting like we take it seriously. Tomorrow, gentlemen. Pull out the stops."

* * * * *

1:15 PM, New York City

Upon returning from lunch, Scott checked his E-Mail at the Times. Most of the messages he received were from co-workers or news associates in other cities. He also heard from Kirk on the paper's supposedly secure network. Neither he nor the technical network gurus ever figured out how he got in the system.

The network administrators installed extra safeguards after Scott tipped them that he had been receiving messages from outside the paper. They added what they called 'audit trails'. Audit trails are supposed to record and remember every activity on the network. The hope was that they could observe Kirk remotely entering the computer and then identifying the security breach. Despite their attempts, Kirk continued to enter the Times' computers at will, but without any apparent disruption of the system.

It took Scott some time to convince the network managers that Kirk posed no threat, but they felt that any breach was potentially a serious threat to journalistic privilege.

Reporters kept their notes on the computer. Sources, addresses, phone numbers, high level anonymous contacts and identities, all stored within a computer that is presumably protected and secure. In reality, the New York City Times computer, like most computers. is as open as a sieve.

Scott could live with it. He merely didn't keep any notes on the computer. He stuck with the old tried and true method of hand written notes.

His E-Mail this time contained a surprise.

IF YOU WANT TO FIND OUT HOW I DID IT, CALL ME TONIGHT. 9PM. 416-555-3165. THE SPOOK.

A pit suddenly developed in Scott's stomach. The last time he remembered having that feeling was when he watched Bernard Shaw broadcast the bombing of Baghdad. The sense of sudden helplessness, the foreboding of the unknown. Or perhaps the shock of metamorphosis when one's thoughts enter the realm of the unreal.

Then came the doubt.

"Ty," Scott asked after calling him at his office. "What happened to Foster?" He spoke seriously.

"True to his word," Tyrone laughed with frustration, "he was out in an hour. He said he was coming back to your party . . ."

"Never showed up." Scott paused to think. "How did he get out so fast?"

"He called the right guy. Charges have been reduced to a couple of misdemeanors; local stuff."

"So, isn't he your guy?"

"We're off, right?" Tyrone though to double check.

"Completely. I just need to know for myself."

"Bullshit," Tyrone retorted. "But for argument's sake, I know he had something to do with it, and so do a lot of other people."

"So what's the problem?"

"A technicality called proof," sighed Tyrone. "We have enough on him for a circumstantial case. We know his every move since he left the NSA. How much he spent and on whom. We know he was with Homosoto, but that's all we know. And yes, he is a computer genius."

"And he goes free?"

"For now. We'll get him."

"Who pulled the strings?"

"The Prosecutor's office put up a brick wall. Told us we had to get better evidence. I though we were all on the same side." Tyrone's discouragement was evident, even across the phone wires.

"Still planning on making a move?"

"I'll talk to you later." The phone went dead on Scott's ears. He had clearly said a no-no on the phone.

* * * * *

Cambridge, Massachusetts

Lotus Development Corporation headquarters has been the stage for demonstrations by free-software advocates. Lotus' lawsuits against Mosaic Software, Paperback Software and Borland created a sub-culture backlash against the giant software company. Lotus sued its competitors on the basis of a look-and-feel copyright of the hit program 1,2,3. That is, Lotus sued to keep similar products from emulating their screens and key sequences.

Like Hewlett Packard, Apple and Microsoft who were also in the midst of legal battles regarding intellectual-property copyrights, Lotus received a great deal of media attention. By and large their position was highly unpopular, and the dense university culture which represented free exchange of programs and information provided ample photo opportunity to demonstrate against the policies of Lotus.

Eileen Isselbacher had worked at Lotus as a Spreadsheet Customer Service Manager for almost two years. She was well respected and ran a tight ship. Her first concern, one that her management didn't necessarily always share, was to the customer. If someone shelled out $500 for a program, they were entitled to impeccable service and assistance. Despite her best efforts, though, Lotus had come to earn a reputation of arrogance and indifference to customer complaints. It was a constant public relations battle; for the salespeople, for customer service, and for the financial people who attempted to insure a good Wall Street image.

The service lines are shut down at 6 PM EST and then Eileen enters the Service Data Base. The SDB is a record of all service calls. The service reps logged the call, the serial #, the type of problem and the resolution. Eileen's last task of the day was to compile the data accumulated during the day and issue a daily summation report.

She commanded the data base to "Merge All Records". Her computer terminal, on the Service Department's Novell 386 network began crunching.

12,346 Calls between 7:31 AM and 5:26 PM.

That was a normal number of calls.

Serial Numbers Verified.

The Data Base had to double check that the serial number was a real one, issued to a legitimate owner.

712 Bad Disks

Her department sent out replacement disks to verified owners who had a damaged disk. A little higher than the average of 509, but not significant enough unless the trend continues.

FLAG!!

4,576 Computational Errors

Eileen's attention immediately focussed in on the FLAG!! message. The Computational Error figures were normally '0' or '1' a week. Now, 5,000 in one day?

She had the computer sort the 4,576 CE's into the serial number distribution. The Service Department was able to act as a quality control monitor for engineering and production. If something was wrong, once a few hundred thousand copies hit the field, the error would show up by the number of calls. But CE's were normally operator error. Not the computer's.

There was no correlation to serial numbers. Old Version 1.0's through Version 3.0 and 3.1 were affected as were the current versions. By all reports, Lotus 123 could no longer add, subtract, divide, multiply or computer accurately. Mass computational errors. The bell curve across serial numbers was flat enough to obviate the need for a statistical analysis. This was clearly not an engineering design error. Nor was it a production error, or a run of bad disks. Something had changed.

* * * * *

Scarsdale, New York

On the 6:12 to Scarsdale, Tyrone and Scott joined for a beer. The conversation was not to be repeated.

"ECCO, CERT, the whole shooting match," Tyrone whispered loud enough to be heard over the rumble of the train, "are moving to NSA control. NIST is out. They all work for the Fort now. Department of Defense."

"Are you shitting me?" Scott tried to maintain control.

"It'll be official tomorrow," Tyrone said. "Write your story tonight, call around tomorrow. The goddamned NSA has won again."

"What do you mean, again?"

"Ah," Tyrone said trying to dismiss his frustrated insight into agency rivalry. "It seems that whatever they want, they get. Their budget is secret, their purpose is secret, and now they have every computer security concern at their beck and call. Orders of the President."

"Aren't they the best suited for the job, though . . ."

"Technically, maybe. Politically, no way!" Tyrone said adamantly. "I think the Bureau could match their power, but they have another unfair advantage."

Scott looked curiously at Tyrone.

"They wrote the rules."

* * * * *

Scarsdale, New York

Speedo's Pizza was late, so Scott got the two $9 medium pepperoni pizzas for free, tipping the embarrassed delivery boy $10 for his efforts. Not his fault that his company makes absurd promises and contributes to the accident rate.

As 9:00 PM approached, Scott's stomach knotted up. He wasn't quite sure what he would find when he dialed the Canadian number. It was a cellular phone exchange meaning that while he dialed the Toronto 416 area code, the call was probably rerouted by call forwarding to another location, also connected by cellular phone. Untraceable. Damn sneaky. And legal. Technology For The People.

<<<DIALING 4165553165 . . . . .>

Scott listened to the small speaker on his internal modem card as it dialed the tones in rapid sequence. A click, a buzz and then in the background, Scott heard the faintest of tones. Was that crosstalk from another line, or was another secret number being dialed?

<<<CONNECTION 4800 BAUD>>>

The screen hesitated for few seconds then prompted . . .

IDENTIFY YOURSELF:

Scott wondered what to enter. His real name? Or the handle Kirk's hackers gave him.

Scott Mason aka Repo Man

Again the computer display paused, seemingly pondering Scott's response.

I SUPPOSE ASKING FOR FURTHER IDENTIFICATION WOULD OFFEND YOU.

I'm getting used to it. Paranoia runs rampant in your line of work.

LET'S SAVE THE EDITORIALIZING FOR NOW. GIVE ME THE WARM AND FUZZIES. PROVE YOU'RE SCOTT MASON.

You can't keep your eyes off of Sonja's chest as I recall.

GOOD START. NICE TITS.

So you're Miles Foster.

THERE ARE GROUNDRULES. FIRST. MY NAME IS THE SPOOK. MR. SPOOK. DR. SPOOK. PROFESSOR SPOOK. KING SPOOK. I DON'T CARE WHAT, BUT I AM THE SPOOK AND ONLY THE SPOOK. MY IDENTITY, IF I HAVE ONE, IS TO REMAIN MY LITTLE SECRET. UNLESS YOU ACCEPT THAT, WE WILL GET NOWHERE FAST.

Like I said, you're Miles Foster.

NO. AND IF I WAS, IT WOULDN'T MATTER. I AM THE SPOOK. I AM YOUR PERSONAL DEEP THROAT. YOUR BEST FRIEND.

Let me see if I understand this right. You will tell all, the whole story on the record, as long as you stay the Spook? Use your name, Spook, in everything?

THAT'S IT.

The paper has given me procedures. I have to record everything. Save it to disk, and give a copy to the lawyers.

ARE YOU SAVING THIS YET?

No. Not until we agree. Then we outline the terms and go.

I'M IMPRESSED. YOU ARE THE FIRST REPORTER I'VE HEARD OF TO USE COMPUTERS AS A SOURCE. WHO DEVELOPED THE RULES?

The lawyers, who else?

FIGURES.

So. Do we have a deal?

LET ME SEE THE CONTRACT.

Scott and the Spook exchanged notes over their modems and computers until they arrived at terms they both could live with. After Kirk, the rules Higgins had established were clear, easy to follow and fair. Scott set his computer to Save the conversation.

This is Scott Mason, speaking to a person who identifies himself only as the Spook. I do not know the sex of this person, nor his appearance as all conversations are occurring over computer modem and telephone lines. The Spook contacted me today, through my office computer. This is his amazing story.

Spook. Why did you call me?

I DESIGNED THE COMPUTER INVASION OF THE UNITED STATES FOR TAKI HOMOSOTO. WOULD YOU LIKE TO KNOW HOW I DID IT?

* * * * *

Wednesday, January 20
National Security Agency

Marvin Jacobs had a busy day and evening. And night, preparing for his meeting with the President. He would have a chance to make his point, and win it, with an audience in attendance. The high level bureaucrat craved to aspire within the echelons of the government hierarchy, but competence prevented his goals from being realized.

During Korea Lt. Marvin Jacobs served his country as 90 day wonder straight out of ROTC. A business major with a minor in civic administration did not prepare him for the tasks the Army had in store for him. Army Intelligence was in desperate need of quality analysts, people with minds more than marshmallows for brain. The Army Intelligence Division, G-2 personnel staff poured through new recruit files in hopes of recruiting them into the voluntary program. But the catch phrase, 'Military Intelligence, a contradiction in terms' made their job doubly difficult. So they resorted to other tactics to recruit qualified people for an unpopular and often despised branch of the military: they made deals, and they made Lt. Marvin Jacobs a deal he couldn't refuse.

Young Captain Jacobs returned to the United States at the end of the conflict as a highly skilled and experienced communications manager for the evolving communications technology; as antiquated as it appears today. His abilities were widely needed by emerging factions of the government as McCarthyism and the fear of the Red Menace were substituted for Hot War.

The super secret NSA, whose existence was unknown to a vast majority of Congress at that time, made him the best offer from all the Federal Agencies. The payscales were the same, but the working conditions promised were far superior at the Agency. Marvin Jacobs had studied to serve as a civil servant, but he imagined himself in Tecumseh, Michigan politics, not confronting the Communist Threat.

He was rewarded for his efforts, handsomely. In the sports world, they call it a signing bonus. In the deep dark untraceable world of the National Security Agency they call it All Paid Reconnaissance. APR, for short. Travel when and where you like, ostensibly on behalf of your government. If worse comes to worst, attend a half day seminar and make yourself seen.

By the time he was 35, Marvin Jacobs, now a well respected management fixture at the NSA, had seen the world twice over. Occasionally he traveled on business. For the first ten years with the Agency he traveled with his wife, college sweetheart Sarah Bell, and then less so as their three children matured. Still, although he now travels alone more often than not, he was on a plane going somewhere at least twice a month, if only for a weekend.

The Directorship of the NSA landed in his lap unexpectedly in 1985, when the schism between the Pentagon and the Fort became an unsurvivable political nightmare for his predecessor. Marvin Jacobs, on the other hand, found the job the deserved cherry on a career dedicated to his country. It was largely a political job, and managing the competing factions of his huge secret empire occupied most of his time.

The prestige, the power, the control and the responsibility alone wasn't enough for Marvin Jacobs. He wanted more. He wanted to make a difference. A very dangerous combination.

* * * * *

"It is so good to hear your voice, Ahmed Shah," Beni Rafjani said in Farsi over an open clear overseas line.

"And you. I am but Allah's servant," replied Ahmed, bowing his head slightly as he spoke.

"As we all are. But today I call to say you can come home."

"Home? Iran?" The excitement in Ahmed's voice was more due to the call than the news. "Why?"

"I thought you would be pleased, now that the Red Sun has set." The cryptic reference to the death of Homosoto wouldn't fool anybody listening, but inuendo was non-admissible.

"Yes, my work is going well, and I have learned much, as have hundreds of students that attend my classes. However, with all due respect, I think we may accomplish more by continuing the work that our esteemed leader began. Why should we stop now? It goes very well, in our favor."

"I understand," Rafjani said with respect. "You are honored for your sacrifice, living among the infidels."

"It must be done. I mean no disrespect."

"You do not speak disrepectfully, Ahmed Shah. Your work is important to your people. If that is your wish, continue, for you do it well."

"Thank you, thank you. Even though one grain of sand has blown away, the rest of the desert retains great power."

"Ahmed Shah, may Allah be with you."

* * * * *

Chapter 27

Thursday, January 21
The White House, Washington, D.C.

He wanted to make them wait.

The President decided to walk into the breakfast room for their early morning meeting a few minutes late. Even with intimates, his inner circle, the awe of the Presidency was still intact. His tardiness added to the tension that they all felt as a result of the recent revelations. Perhaps the tension would further hone their attention and dialogue.

He had not slept well the night before; he was prepared for anything he understood, but computers were not on his roster of acquired fluencies. A President has to make decisions, tough decisions, life and death decisions, but decisions of the type that have a history to study and a lesson to learn. And like most of those before him, he was well equipped to make tough decisions, right or wrong. Presidents have to have the self confidence and internal resolve to commit themselves, and their nation, to a course of action. This President's political life trained him well; lawyer, local politics, state politics and then Washington.

But not computers. He was not trained in computers. He had learned to type, a little, and found that sending E-Mail messages was great fun. To him it was a game. Since the first days when microcomputers had invaded the offices of governmental Washington, he had been able to insulate himself from their day to day use. All the same, every desk he occupied was adjoined by a powerful microcomputer fitted with the finest graphics, the best printer and an elite assortment of software. He used the memory resident calculator and sent and received electronic mail. That was it.

The President, as most men of his generation, accepted the fact that computers now ran the show. The whole shooting match. Especially the military. The communications and computer sophistication used by the Allies enthralled the world during the Iraqi War: bombs smart enough to pick which window they would enter before detonating, missiles smart enough to fly at 2000 mph and destroy an incoming missile moving at 3000 mph. It turned out that hitting a bullet with a bullet was possible after all. Intuitively, the President knew that the crisis developing before his eyes meant massive computer damage, and the repercussions would be felt through the economy and the country.

However, the President did not have enough computer basics to begin to understand the problem, much less the answers. This was the first time during his administration that major tactical and policy decisions would be made primarily by others. His was a duty of rubber stamping. That worry frustrated his attempts at sleeping and nagged at him before the meeting. And then, of course, there was the press.

"Gentlemen," the President said sauntering towards his chair at the head of the large formal breakfast table. He opened the door with enough vigor to startle his guests. He maintained his usual heads-up smile and spry gait as he noticed that there were new faces present.

In addition to the inner circle, Marvin Jacobs asked two key NSA security analysts to be observers at the meeting. Only if the President asked a question was it then all right to speak. Accompanying Phil Musgrave, under admitted duress to repay a previous favor, was Paul Trump, Director of NIST, the eternal rival of the NSA in matters of computers. The President was introduced to the guests and smiled to himself. He recognized that the political maneuvering was beginning already. Maybe the competition would help, he thought.

"Marv," the President said leaning away from the waiter pouring his coffee. This was the same waiter who had spilled near boiling liquid in his lap last month. "I guess it's your show, so I'll just sit back and keep my mouth shut." He leaned even further away as the waiter's clumsiness did not inspire confidence.

Group chuckle notwithstanding, everyone in the inner circle knew what the President really meant. The President was hungry and Marv Jacobs would not be eating breakfast. He would be answering questions.

"Thank you, sir," Marv said as he courteously acknowledged the presence of the others in the inner circle. He handed out a file folder to everyone in the room. Each was held together with a red strap labeled TOP SECRET that sealed the package. Not until the President began to open his package did the others follow suit.

"We've only had a day to prepare . . ." Marvin Jacobs began.

"I know," the President said wiping the corner of his mouth with a white linen napkin. "That should have been plenty of time." Marvin, wisely avoided responding to the President's barb. He took the caustic hit as the other breakfast guests quietly thanked the powers on high that it was someone elses turn to be in the hot seat. All in all, though, the President was a much calmer person this morning than during his verbal tirade the day before. But, if needed, the acerbity of his biting words would silence the boldest of his advisors or enemies. The President was still royally pissed off.

"We have developed a number of scenarios that will be refined over the next weeks as we learn more about the nature of the assault by Homosoto." He turned into his report and indicated that everyone should turn to page 4. "This is sketchy, but based upon what we have seen already, we can estimate the nature of what we're up against."

Page 4 contained three Phrases.

1. Malevolent Self Propagating Software Programs (Viruses)

2. Unauthorized Electromagnetic Pulses and Explosions

3. Anti-TEMPEST Coherent Monitor and Pixel Radiation.

Marvin Jacobs described the observed behavior of each category, but nonetheless the President was unhappy. A rehash from the newspapers.

"That's it?" the President asked in disbelief. "You call that an estimate? I can find out more than that from CNN."

"At this point, that's about it."

"I still can't believe this," the President said, shaking his head. "What the hell am I going to say when I have to face the press? 'Sorry folks, our computers and the country are going down the toilet, and we really don't know what to do about it. Seems as if no one took the problem seriously'" The President gazed at Marvin and Henry Kennedy, half expecting them to break into tears. "Bullshit!"

"Sir, may I be blunt?" Marvin asked.

"Of course, please. That's what we're here for," the President said, wondering how blunt was blunt.

"Sir, this is certainly no time to place blame on anyone, but I do think that at a minimum some understanding is in order." All eyes turned to Jacobs as he spoke. "Sir, the NSA has been in the business of safeguarding military computer systems for years."

"That's arguable," said the President critically.

Marvin continued unaffected. "Cryptography and listening and deciphering are our obvious strong points. But neither Defense nor Treasury," he said alluding to each representative from their respective agencies, "can spend money without Congress's approval. Frankly sir, that is one of the major stumbling blocks we have encountered in establishing a coherent security policy."

"That's a pile of bull, Marv," said NIST's feisty Paul Trump. Paul and Marv had known each other for years, became friends and then as the NIST-NSA rift escalated in 89 and 90, they saw less of each other on a social basis. "Sir," Paul spoke to the President. "I'm sorry for interrupting . . ."

"Say what you have to say."

"Yessir." Trump had no trouble being direct either. Nearing mandatory retirement age had made Trump more daring. Willing to take more risks in the best interest of NIST and therefore the nation.

Spry and agile, Paul Trump looked twenty years younger with no signs of slowing down.

"Sir, the reason that we don't have any security in the government is due to Congress. We, Marv and I, agree on that one point. Martin, do you concur?"

Treasury Secretary Martin Royce vigorously nodded in agreement. "We've been mandated to have security for years, but no one says where the money's coming from. The hill made the laws but didn't finish the job."

The President enjoyed the banter among his elite troops. He thrived on open dissent and debate, making it easier for him to weigh information and opinions. That freedom reminded him of how difficult it must have been for the Soviets to openly disagree and consider unpopular positions.

It seems that after Khrushchev took over, in one Politburo meeting, he received a handwritten note which said: 'If you're so liberal, how come you never stood up to Stalin.' Khrushchev scoured the room for a clue as to who made the insulting comment. After a tense few seconds he said, 'would the comrade who wrote this stand up so I may answer him face to face?' No one stood. 'Now, you know the answer.'

The President's point was, around here anything goes, but I'm the boss. The difference is the democratic process, he would say, the voters elect me by a majority to institute a benevolent oligarchy. And I, he pointed at himself, am the oligarch.

Paul Trump continued. "In reality sir, NIST has tried to cooperate with NSA in a number of programs to raise the security of many sectors of the government, but, in all fairness, NSA has put up constant roadblocks in the name of national security. The CMR problem for the commercial sector has been completely ignored under the cloak of classified specifications."

"TEMPEST is a classified program . . ." Marvin objected strenuously.

"Because you want it to be," Trump retorted instantly. "It doesn't have to be, and you know it. Sir," he turned to the President. "TEMPEST is . . ." The President nodded that he knew. "The specification for TEMPEST may have been considered a legitimate secret when the program started in the '70's. But now, the private sector is publishing their own results of studies duplicating what we did 20 years ago. The Germans, the Dutch, the French, just about everybody but the English and us has admitted that CMR is a problem for everyone, not just the military. Jesus, you can buy anti-Tempest plans in Popular Science. Because of NSA's protectiveness of a secret that is no longer a secret, the entire private sector is vulnerable to CMR and anti-TEMPEST assaults. As a country, we have no electronic privacy."

Marvin nodded in agreement. "You're damn right we keep it a secret. Why the hell should we tell the world how to protect against it? By doing that, we not only define the exact degree of our own exposure, but teach our enemies how to protect themselves. It should be classified."

"And everyone else be damned?" Trump challenged Jacobs.

"I wouldn't put it that way, but NSA is a DoD oriented agency after all. Ask Congress," Marvin said resolutely.

"That's the most alienating, arrogant isolationist attitude I've ever heard," Paul Trump said. "Regardless of what you may think, the NSA is not the end-all be-all, and as you so conveniently dismiss, the NSA is not trusted by many outside the U.S.. We do not have a technology monopoly on TEMPEST any more than we do on the air we breathe." Trump threw up his hands in disgust. "Patently absurd paranoia . . ."

"Paul, you don't have all the facts . . ." objected Marv to no avail. Trump was a master at debate.

"Sir," Trump again turned from the argumentative Jacobs to the President. "I don't think this is proper forum for rehashing history, but it should be noted that NIST is responsible for non-defense computer security, and we have a staff and budget less than 1% of theirs. The job just isn't getting done. Personally, I consider the state of security within the government to be in total chaos. The private sector is in even worse shape, and it's our own fault."

"Phil?" the President said. "Emergency funding. Congress." Phil nodded as the debate continued. "None of this is saying a damn thing about what we should do. How do we best defend?" He bit off the end of crispy slice of bacon waiting for the answer he knew would be unsatisfactory.

"We improvise."

"Improvise! That's the best you can do?" The President threw down his napkin and it slipped off the table to the floor as he shoved his chair back.

"This country is run by goddamned computers," the President muttered loudly as he paced the breakfast room. Those who had been eating ceased long ago. "Goddamned computers and morons."

* * * * *

Thursday, January 21

SPREADSHEETS STOP CRUNCHING
LOTUS AND MICROSOFT STRUCK

by Scott Mason

Last weekend's threats made by the late OSO Industries Chairman, Taki Homosoto appear to be a trustworthy mirror of the future.

Lotus Development Corporation and Microsoft, two of the software industry's shining stars are the latest victims of Homosoto's vengeful attack upon the computer systems of the United States.

With cases of 20-20 hindsight proliferating, security experts claim that we should have seen it coming.

The last several months has been filled with a long series of colossal computer failures, massive virus attacks and the magnetic bombing of major computer installations. These apparently unrelated computer crimes, occurring with unprecedented frequency have the distinct flavor of a prelude to the promises Homosoto made in the self penned note that accompanied his seeming suicide.

The latest virus debacle comes immediately on the heels of the announcement of the dGraph infections.

Yesterday, Lotus and Microsoft and their dealers were inundated with technical support calls. According to reports, the industry standard 123 and the popular Excel spreadsheets have been experiencing cataclysmic failures in the field. Typical complaints claim the powerful spreadsheet programs are performing basic mathematical functions incorrectly; a veritable disaster for anyone who relies upon the accuracy of their numbers.

The leading theory held by both companies as well as software and security experts, is that a highly targeted computer virus was designed to only affect Lotus and Microsoft spreadsheet files. While some viruses are designed to erase files, or entire hard disks, the Lotus Virus as it has been informally named, is a highly sophisticated virus designed only to make subtle changes in the results of mathematical calculations.

Viruses of this type are known as Slight Viruses. They only infect small portions of the computer or program, and then only in ways that will hopefully not be detected for some time - thus compounding the damage.

Fortune 100 companies that use either 123 or Excel nearly unanimously announced that they will put a moratorium on the use of both programs until further notice. Gibraltar Insurance issued a terse statement: "Due to the potential damage caused by the offending software, we will immediately begin installation of compatible spreadsheet programs and verify the accuracy of all data. Our attorneys are studying the matter at this time."

Lotus and Microsoft stock plummeted 36% and 27% respectively.

* * * * *

GOOD ARTICLE. DO YOU WANT TO GET IT RIGHT NOW?

I see humility reigns right up there with responsibility.

THE FIRST LOTUS VIRUSES WERE WRITTEN IN LATE 1988. CUTE, HUH? THE LONGEST VIRUS INCUBATION PERIOD EVER!

Not many people share your sense of achievement.

I DON'T EXPECT SO.

We should get something straight right off.

ARE YOU SAVING?

I am now. I do not approve, in fact I despise what you say you've done.

I AM NOT LOOKING FOR APPROVAL. MAYBE UNDERSTANDING.

Not from me.

YOU'RE BETTER THAN THAT. IF WE DO THIS, YOU NEED TO PRESENT BOTH SIDES. IT'S TO YOUR BENEFIT. YOU'RE GOING FOR A PULITZER.

Don't tell me how to do my job.

LET'S GET TO IT.

Fine. Where did I go wrong in the article?

NOT WRONG, INCOMPLETE. THERE ARE REALLY 6 VERSIONS OF THE LOTUS VIRUS. ONLY THE FIRST ONE HAS BEEN DETECTED. THE OTHERS AREN'T SET TO GO OFF UNTIL LOTUS HAS TIME TO CLEAN UP THE FIRST MESS.

You mean you built several viruses all aimed at Lotus programs?

AND MICROSOFT, ASHTON TATE, BORLAND, CA, NOVELL, LAN MANAGER, WORDPERFECT, AND A WHOLE BUNCH MORE. THE LIST WAS OVER 100 TO BEGIN WITH.

100? How many viruses? When?

SLIGHT VIRUSES! I LOVE IT. WHAT A NAME. LIKE I SAID,
YOU'RE GOOD. I GUESS 500. MAYBE MORE. THEY'RE
SET TO GO OFF FOR THE NEXT TWO YEARS. TIME
RELEASED. TIME RELEASE SLIGHT VIRUSES. WHEW!

Why? Why tell me, now?

SLOW DOWN. NOT ALL AT ONCE. FIRST OF ALL, WE
HAVE TO BUILD YOU A LITTLE CREDIBILITY. CONVINCE
YOUR PUBLIC THAT I AM WHO I SAY I AM AND THAT I CAN-
NOT BE TOUCHED. SO HERE'S THE FIRST LOTUS VIRUS
SIGNATURE - THE CURRENT ONE: 05 55 EF E0 F4 D8 6C
41 44 40 4D. IN COMPUTERS THAT ARE INFECTED, BUT
HAVEN'T YET STRUCK THE PROGRAM, THE VIRUS IS TWO
HIDDEN FILES: ONE SHORT ONE NAMED 7610012.EXE.
IT'S ONLY 312 BYTES LONG AND HIDES ITSELF IN THE
ROOT DIRECTORY BY LOOKING LIKE A BAD CLUSTER TO
THE SYSTEM. IT'S NEVER EVEN NOTICED. WHEN THE
TIME COMES, IT AWAKENS THE SECOND PART OF THE
VIRUS, 7610013.EXE WHICH IS SAVED IN A HIDDEN DIREC-
TORY AND LOOKS LIKE BAD SECTORS. ONLY A FEW K.
THAT'S THE FILE THAT SCREWS AROUND WITH 123 MATH
FUNCTIONS. AFTER 123 IS INFECTED, THE FILE LENGTH
STILL SAYS IT HASN'T BEEN CHANGED AND THE VIRUS
ERASES ITSELF AND RETURNS THE SECTORS TO THE
DISK. IN THE MEANTIME, LOTUS IS SHOT AND IT IS IN-
FECTING OTHER PROGRAMS. BRILLIANT IF I SAY SO
MYSELF.

And you want me to print this? Why?

IT WILL GIVE YOU AND ME CREDIBILITY. YOU'LL BE
BELIEVED AND THAT IS ABSOLUTELY NECESSARY. WE
HAVE TO STOP IT FROM HAPPENING.

What from happening?

THE FULL ATTACK. IT CAN'T BE TOTALLY STOPPED, BUT I
CAN HELP.

How much of an attack?

YOU HAVE NO IDEA. NO IDEA AT ALL. THERE WERE
THOUSANDS OF PEOPLE INVOLVED AND NOW IT'S ON
AUTOPILOT. THERE'S NO WAY TO TURN IT OFF.

*That's incredible . . .more than incredible. Why? For what pur-
pose?*

MAYBE LATER. THAT DOESN'T MATTER NOW. I WILL SAY,
THOUGH, THAT I NEVER THOUGHT HOMOSOTO COULD
PULL IT OFF.

So you worked for him?

I WAS HIRED BY OSO INDUSTRIES TO WORK ON A SECRET CONTRACT TO DESIGN METHODS TO COMBAT COMPUTER VIRUSES AND STUDY MILITARY APPLICATIONS. AS THE PROJECT CONTINUED, IT TOOK ON A NEW SCOPE AND WE WERE ASKED TO INCLUDE ADDITIONAL ELEMENTS AND CONSIDERATIONS IN OUR EQUATIONS.

Equations?

COMPUTER DESIGN IS MATHEMATICAL MODELING, SO THERE'S A LOT OF PENCIL AND PAPER BEFORE ANYTHING IS EVER BUILT. WE FIGURED THE EFFECTS OF MULTIPLE SEQUENCED VIRUSES ON LIMITED TARGET DEFINITIONS, COMPUTER SOFTWARE DISTRIBUTION DYNAMICS, DATA PROPAGATION PROBABILITIES. OUR CALCULATIONS INCLUDED MULTI-DIMENSIONAL INTERACTIONS OF INFECTION SIMULTANEITY. EVERY POSSIBILITY AND HOW TO CAUSE THE MOST DAMAGE.

It's a good thing I kind of understand the technical gobbledygook.

OH, IN ENGLISH? WE STUDIED WHAT HAPPENS IF YOU ENDLESSLY THROW THOUSANDS OF COMPUTER VIRUSES AT THE UNITED STATES.

I got that. So what does happen?

YOU'RE FUCKED FOR LIFE. ONE VIRUS IS A PAIN IN THE ASS. 1000 IS FATAL.

You have a way with words.

GOD GIVEN GIFT. I GUESS YOU COULD CALL US A THINK TANK FOR COMPUTER WARFARE.

So what happens next? Mr. Spook.

PATRONIZING, NOW, NOW, NOW. LET'S SEE HERE (FLIP, FLIP) SATURDAY, JANUARY 23, NO, THAT WAS THE STOCK EXCHANGE, NO DECEMBER 11, THE PHONE COMPANY AND FEDERAL EXPRESS . . .

Cocky son of a bitch aren't you?

AH YES! HERE IT IS. MONDAY, JANUARY 25. SCOTT, YOU'RE MY FRIEND, SO LET ME GIVE YOU A TIP. DON'T TRY TAKING AN AIRPLANE FOR THE NEXT FEW WEEKS.

Why not?

THE NATIONAL RESERVATION SERVICE COMPUTERS ARE GOING TO BE VERY, VERY SICK.

"Yeah," the deep sleepy voice growled in Scott's ear.

"Ty, wake up."

"Wha?"

"Tyrone, get up!" Scott's excited voice caught Tryone's notice.

"Scott," he yawned. "What's the matter?"

"Are you awake?"

"Don't worry, I had to get up to answer the phone." Then in a more muffled voice, Scott heard Tyrone say, "No, it's all right dear. Go back to sleep, I'll take it in the den." Tyrone got back on the phone and barked, "Hold on."

Scott paced across his junked up home office, sidestepping some items, stepping on others, until Tyrone came back on the line.

"Shit, man," were Tyrone's first words. "You have any idea what time it is?"

"Hey, I'm sorry," Scott said mocking Tyrone's complaint. "I'll write you a letter tomorrow and lick a stamp and let the Post Office take it from there . . ."

"You made your point. What is it?"

"The airlines are going to be hit next. Homosoto's next target."

"How the hell would you know that?"

"I've been talking to Foster. He told me."

"Foster told you what?"

"It's a huge attack, an incredibly large computer attack. He worked for Homosoto. But the point is, the airlines. They're next. Worse than the radar computer problems."

"Can I get right back to you?"

Waiting for Ty's call, Scott wrote an article for the following morning's paper and submitted it from home to the office computer.

* * * * *

COMPUTER TERRORISM

An Exclusive Interview With The Man Who Invaded America

By Scott Mason

The man who claims to be the technical genius behind the recent wave of Computer Crimes has agreed to tell his story exclusively to the New York City Times.

Only known as the Spook, a hacker's handle which represents both an alter-ego and anonymity, he says that he was hired by Taki Homosoto, late chairman of OSO Industries to design and prepare a massive assault against the computer systems of the United States.

The incredible claims made by the Spook appear to be grounded in fact and his first statements alone were astounding. Please note, these are exact quotes from a computer conversation with the Spook. The only editing was done for typos.

"There will be thousands of viruses. Thousands of them. I have to imagine by now that every program in America is infected with ten different viruses. There is only one way to stop them all. Never turn on your computers.

"You see, most virus programmers are searching for immediate gratification. They write one and want it to spread real quick and then see it blow up. So most amateur virus builders are disappointed in the results because they don't have patience. But we, I had patience.

"To maximize the effects of viruses, you have to give them time. Time to spread, to infect. Many of the viruses that you will experience are years old. The older viruses are much cruder than those made recently. We learned over time to build better viruses. Our old ones have been dormant for so long, their contagion is complete and they will be just as effective.

"We have built and installed the greatest viruses of all time. Every PC will probably be dead in months if not weeks, unless you take my advice. There are also VAX viruses, VMS viruses, SUN viruses, we even built some for Cray supercomputers, but we don't expect much damage from them."

The Spook's next comments were just as startling.

"The blackmail operation was a sham, but a terrific success. It wasn't for the money. No one ever collected any money, did they? It was pure psychological warfare. Making people distrust their computers, distrust one another because the computer makes them look like liars. That was the goal. The money was a diversionary tactic.

"Part of any attack is the need to soften the enemy and terrorism is the best way to get quick results. By the time the first viruses came along, whoa! I bet half the MIS directors in the country don't know whether they're coming or going.

According to the Spook, he designed the attack with several armies to be used for different purposes.

One for Propaganda, one for Infiltration and Infection, one for Engineering, one for Communications, and another for Dis-

tribution and another for Manufacturing. At the pinnacle was Homosoto acting as Command and Control.

"I didn't actually infect any computers myself. We had teams of Groundhogs all too happy to do that for us."

According to security experts, Homosoto apparently employed a complex set of military stratagem in the execution of his attack.

It has yet to be determined if the Spook will be of any help in minimizing the effects of the First Computer War.

Scott finally went to bed. Tyrone never called him back.

* * * * *

Thursday, January 21
New York City

The cavernous streets of New York on a cloud covered moonless night harbor an eerie aura, reminiscent of the fog laden alleys near the London docks on the Thames in the days of Jack the Ripper. A constant misty rain gave the city an even more depressing pallor than winter normally brought to the Big Apple. In other words, the weather was perfect.

On the corner of 52nd. and 3rd., in the shadow of the Citibank tower, Dennis Melbourne stuck a magnetic strip ID card into a Cirrus 24 Hour Bank Teller Machine. As the machine sucked in the card, the small screen asked for the personal identification number, the PIN, associated with that particular card. Dennis entered the requested four digit PIN, 1501. The teller whirred and asked Dennis which transaction he would like.

He selected:

Checking Balance.

A few seconds later $4,356.20 appeared. Good, Dennis thought.

He then selected:

Withdrawal - Checking

Dennis entered, $2,000.00 and the machine display told him that his request exceeded the daily withdrawal limit. Normal, he thought, as he entered an 8 digit sequence: 00330101. The supervisor control override.

The teller hummed and thought for a moment, and then $20 bills began tumbling out of the "Take Cash" drawer. One hundred of them.

The teller asked, "Another Transaction?" and Dennis chose 'No'. He retrieved the magnetic card from the machine and the receipt of this transaction before grabbing a cab to a subway entrance on 59th. and Lexington Ave. The ID card he used was only designed to be used once, so Dennis saw to it that the card was cut and disposed of in a subterranean men's room toilet.

Dennis Melbourne traveled throughout New York all night long, emptying Cirrus cash machines of their available funds. And the next night, and the next. He netted $246,300 in 3 days. All told, Cirrus customers in 36 states were robbed by Dennis Melbourne and his scores of accomplices of nearly $10 Million before the banks discovered how it was being done.

The Cirrus network and it's thousands of Automatic Tellers were immediately closed. For the first time in years, America had no access to instant cash.

Bank lines grew to obscene lengths and the waiting for simple transactions was interminable. Almost one half of personal banking had been done by ATM computer, and now human tellers had to deal with throngs of customers who had little idea of how to bank with a live person.

Retail sales figures for the week after the ATM machines were closed showed a significant decline of 3.2%. The Commerce Department was demanding action by Treasury who pressured the FBI and everybody looked to the White House for leadership. The economic impact of immediate cash restriction had been virtually instantaneous; after all the U.S. is a culture of spontaneity demanding instant gratification. Cash machines addressed that cultural personality perfectly. Now it was gone.

Dennis Melbourne knew that it was time to begin on the MOST network. Then the American Express network. And he would get rich in the process. Ahmed Shah paid him very well. 25% of the take.

* * * * *

Friday, January 22
New York City

"We had to take the part out about the airlines," Higgins said in response to Scott's question about the heavy editing. To Higgins' and Doug's surprise, Scott understood; he didn't put up a stink.

"I wondered about that," Scott said reflecting back on the last evening. "Telling too much can be worse than not telling enough. Whatever you say, John."

"We decided to let the airlines and the FAA and the NTSB make the call." Higgins and Scott had come to know and respect each other

491

quite well in the last few weeks. They didn't agree on everything, but as the incredible story evolved, Higgins felt more comfortable with less conservative rulings and Scott relinquished his non-negotiable pristine attitude. At least they disagreed less often and less loudly. Although neither one would admit it, each made an excellent sounding board for the other - a valuable asset on a story this important.

Higgins continued, "The airlines are treating it as a bomb scare. Seriously, but quietly. They have people going through the systems, looking for whatever it is you people look for." Higgins' knowledge of computers was still dismal.

"Scott, let me ask you something." Doug broke into the conversation that like all the others, took place in Higgins' lawyer-like office. They occurred so often that Scott had half seriously convinced Higgins' secretary that he wouldn't attend unless there were fresh donuts and juice on the coffee table. When Higgins found out, he was mildly annoyed, but nonetheless, in the spirit of camaraderie, he let the tradition continue. "Children will be children," he said.

"How much damage could be done if the Spook's telling the truth?" Doug asked.

"Oh, he's telling the truth," Scott said somberly. "Don't forget, I know this guy. He said that the effects would take weeks and maybe months to straighten out. And the airline assault would start Monday."

"Why is he being so helpful?" Higgins asked.

"He wants to establish credibility. He says he wants to help now, but first he wants to be taken seriously."

"Seriously? Seriously? He's a goddamned terrorist!" shouted Higgins. "No damn different than someone who throws a bomb into a crowded subway. You don't negotiate with terrorists!" He calmed himself, not liking to show that degree of emotion. "But we want the story . . ." he sighed in resignation. Doug and Scott agreed in unison.

"Personally, it sounds like a macho ego thing," commented Doug.

"So what?" asked Higgins. "Motivation is independent of premeditation."

"Legally speaking . . ." Doug added. He wanted to make sure than John was aware that there were other than purely legal issues on the table.

"As I was saying," Scott continued. "The reservation computers are the single most important item in running the nation's airlines. They all interact and talk to each other, and create billing, and schedule planes; they interface on line to the OAG . . .they're the brains. They all use Fault Tolerant equipment, that's spares of everything, off site backup of all records - I've checked into it. Whatever he's planned, it'll be a doosey."

"Well, it doesn't matter now," Higgins added with indifference. "Legally it's unsubstantiated hearsay. But with the computer transcripts of all your conversations, if anything happens, I'd say you'd have quite a scoop."

"That's what he wants! And we can't warn anybody?"

"That's up to the airlines, the FAA, not us." The phone on Higgins disk emitted two short warbles. He spoke into the phone. "Yeah? Who? Whooo?" He held the phone out to Scott and curled his lips. "It's for you. The White House." Scott glanced over at Doug who raised his bushy white eyebrows.

Scott picked up the phone on the end table by the leather couch; the one that Scott seemed to have made a second home. "Hello?" he asked hesitantly. "Yes? Well, I could be in Washington . . ." Scott looked over to Doug for advice. "The President?" Doug shook his head, yes. Whatever it is, go. "I'd be happy to," he said reading his watch. "A few hours." He waited a few seconds. "Yes, I know the number. Off the record? Fine. Thank you."

"Well?" asked Higgins.

"The President himself wants to have a little chat with me."

* * * * *

Friday, January 22
The White House

Only the President, Musgrave and Henry Kennedy were there to meet Scott. They did not want to overwhelm him, merely garner his cooperation. Scott rushed by cab to the White House from National Airport, and used the Press Gate even though he had an appointment with The Man. He could have used the Visitor's Entrance. Scott was whisked by White House aides through a *"Private"* door in the press room to the surprise of the regular pool reporters who wondered who dared to so underdress. Definitely not from Washington.

Scott was running on short notice, so he was only wearing his work clothes: torn blue jeans, a sweatshirt from the nude beach he and Sonja had visited and Reeboks that needed a wash. January was unusually warm, so he got away with wearing his denim jacket filled with a decade of patches reflecting Scott's evolving political and social attitudes. He was going to have to bring a change of clothes to the office from now on.

Before he had a chance to apologize for his appearance, at least he was able to shave the three day old stubble on the train, the President apologized for the suddenness and hoped it wasn't too much of an inconvenience. Kennedy and Musgrave kept their smirks to themselves, knowing full well from the very complete dossier on Scott Mason, that he was having a significant intimate relationship with one Sonja Lindstrom, here in Washington. Very convenient was more like it, they thought.

The President sat Scott down on the Queen Anne and complimented him on his series of articles on computer crime. He said that Scott was doing a fine job awakening the public to the problem, and that more people should care, and how brave he was to jump in front of flying bullets, and on and on and on. Due to Henry and Phil's political savvy and professional discipline, neither of their faces showed that they both wanted to throw up on the spot. This was worse than kissing babies to get elected. But the President of the United States wanted a secret favor from a journalist, so some softening, some schmoozing was in order.

"Well, let me get right to the point," the President said a half hour later after two cups of coffee and endless small talk with Scott. He, too, had wondered what the President wanted so much that the extended foreplay was necessary. "I understand Scott, that you have developed quite a rapport with this Spook fellow." He held up a copy of the New York paper headlines blaring:

Computer Terrorism - Exclusive.

Aha! So that's what they want! They want me to turn him in. "I consider myself to be very lucky, right place, right time and all. Yessir." Scott downplayed his position with convincing humility. "It seems as if he has selected me as his mouthpiece."

"All we want, in fact, all we can ask," Musgrave said, "is for you to give us information before it's printed." Scott's eyes shot up in defense, protest at the ready. "No, no," Mugrave added quickly. "Nothing confidential. We know that Miles Foster is the Spook, but we can't prove it without giving away away too many of our secrets." Scott knew they were referring to their own electronic eavesdropping habits that would be imprudent in a court. "Single handedly he is capable of bringing down half of the government's computers. We need to know as much as we can as fast as we can. So, whatever you print, we'd like an early copy of it. That's all."

Scott's mind immediately traveled back to the first and only time an article of his was pulled. At the AG's request. Of course it finally got printed, but why the niceties now? They can take what they want, but instead they ask? Maybe they don't want to get caught fiddling around with the Press too much. Such activities snagged Nixon, not saying that the President was Nixon-esque, but politics is politics. What do I get in return? He could hear it now, the *'you'll be helping*

494

your country,' speech. Bargaining with the President would be gauche at the least.

So he proposed to Musgrave instead. "I want an exclusive interview with the President when this thing is over."

"Done!" said Musgrave too quickly. Scott immediately castigated himself for not asking for more. He could shoot himself. A true Washington denizen would have asked for a seat in the Cabinet. But that was between Scott and his conscience. Doug would hear a dramatized account.

"And no other media finds out that you know anything until . . ." Scott added another minor demand.

"Until the morning papers appear at the back door with the milk," joked Musgrave. "Scott, this is for internal use only. Every hour will help."

Scott was given a secret White House phone number where someone would either receive via FAX or E-Mail message. Any hour, any day. He was also given a White House souvenir pen.

"It went fine," Kennedy said to Marvin Jacobs from his secure office in the White House basement. He spoke to Marvin Jacobs up at Fort Meade on the STU-III phones.

"Didn't matter," Marvin said munching on what sounded to Kennedy like an apple. A juicy one.

"What do you mean, it didn't matter?"

"We're listening to his computers, his phones and his fax lines anyway," Marvin said with neutrality.

"I don't know if I want to know about this . . ."

"It was just a back up plan," Jacobs said with a little laugh. He wanted to defuse Kennedy's panic button. For a National Security Advisor, Kennedy didn't know very much about how intelligence is gathered. "Just in case."

"Well, we don't need it anymore," Kennedy said. "Mason is cooperating fully."

"I like to have alternatives. I expect you'll be telling the President about this."

"Not a chance. Not a chance." Kennedy sounded spooked.

Jacobs loudly munched the last bite through the apple skin. "I'll have something else for you on Mason tomorrow. Let's keep him honest."

* * * * *

Friday, January 22
Reston, Virginia

"No, mom, I'm not going to become a spy," Scott calmly said into the phone while smiling widely at Sonja. "No, I can't tell you what he wanted, but he did give me a present for you." Scott mouthed the words, 'she's in heaven' to Sonja who enjoyed seeing the pleasure the woman received from her son's travels. "Yes, I'll be home in a couple of days," he paused as his mother interrupted again. "Yes, I'll be happy to reprogram your VCR. I'm sorry it doesn't work . . ." He sat back to listen for a few seconds and watch Sonja undress in front of a full length mirror. Their guests were expected in less than 15 minutes and she rushed to make herself beautiful, despite Scott's claims that she was always beautiful. "Yes, mom, I'm paying attention. No ma'am, I won't. Yes, ma'am, I'll try. O.K., goodnight, I love you." He struggled to pull the phone from his ear, but his mother kept talking. "Don't worry, mom. You'll meet her soon." Finally he was able hang up and start worrying about one of their dinner guests. Miles Foster.

Scott had told Sonja nothing about Miles. Or the Spook. As far as the world was concerned, they were two different people with different goals, different motivations and different lives. The unresolved irreconcilliation between the two faces of Miles Foster put Scott on edge, though. Does he treat Miles like Miles or like the Spook? Or is the Spook coming to dinner instead of Miles. Does he then treat the Spook like the Spook or like Miles?

In kind, Sonja had not told Scott that she had been hired to meet him, nor that she had quit after meeting him. The night Miles was arrested, she had successfully evaded his queries about her professional PR functions. Scott accepted at face value that Sonja was *between jobs*.

She had made a lot of money from Alex and his references, but that was the past. She had no desire to be dishonest with Scott, on the contrary. It was not an easy topic to broach, however, and if things between them got beyond the frenzied sexual savagery stage, she would have to test the relationship. But not yet.

The doorbell of Sonja's lakefront Whisper Way townhouse in Reston rang before either she or Scott were ready, so Scott volunteered for first shift host and bartender duty. He took a deep breath, ready for another unpredictable evening, and opened the door.

"Scott," Stephanie Perkins said putting her arms around his neck. "Welcome back. It's good to see you." The three of them, Stephanie, Sonja and Scott had gotten along very well. "Maybe Miles can see his way clear to spend the entire evening with us tonight," she said teasing Miles.

Miles ignored Perky's shot at him and brushed the incident aside without explanation. Apparently he had provided Stephanie with an acceptable excuse for getting arrested by the FBI. So be it far from Scott to bring up a subject that might ruffle the romantic feathers which in turn were likely to ruffle the feathers of his source.

Miles dressed in summer khaki pants, a yachtsman's windbreaker and topsiders without socks; the most casual Scott had seen either the Spook or Miles. Scott prepared the drinks and Stephanie went upstairs with her glass of wine to see Sonja, and let the boys finish their shop talk. Miles opened the sliding glass doors to the deck overlooking the fairly large man-made lake.

"I won't ask," Scott said as soon as Stephanie's feet disappeared from view on the elegant spiral staircase to the second floor.

"Thanks. And, by the way, Perky probably doesn't need to hear too much about Amsterdam," Miles said with a mild sinister touch

"We used to call it the rules of the road," Scott remembered.

"I call it survival. Christ, sometimes I get so fucking horny, I swear the crack of dawn is in trouble."

Scott's mind played with the varied imagery of Miles' creative phraseology. The name was different, he thought, but the character was the same.

"You know," Scott said as the two stood on the deck, drinks in hand, soaking up the brisk lake air. "I really don't understand you."

"What's to understand?" Miles' gaze remained constant over the moonlit water.

"I see that you weren't overly detained the other evening."

"No reason to be. It was a terrible mistake. They must have me confused with someone else." Miles played dead pan.

"You know what I'm talking about," urged Scott. "The Spook and all that . . ."

"Fuck you!" Miles turned and yelled with hostility. He placed the glass of Glenfiddich on the railing and pointed his forefinger in Scott's face. "You're getting what you want, so back the fuck off. Got it?"

Scott's blood pressure joined his fight or flight response in panic. Was this the Mr. Hyde of Miles Foster? Or the real Spook? Had he blown it?

Just then, the sliding glass door from the living room opened and Sonja and Stephanie shivered at the first cool gust of wind. Miles instantly swept Stephanie in his arms and gave her an obscene sounding kiss. His face emerged from the lip melee with no trace of anger, no trace of displeasure. The sinister Miles was magically transformed into Miles the lover.

He had had no chance to respond to Miles' outburst, so Scott was caught with his jaw hung open.

"You boys finish shop yet?" Stephanie said nuzzling at Miles' ear.

"We were just discussing the biographical inconsistencies in the annotated history of Alfred E. Neumann's early years," Miles said convincingly. He glanced over at Scott with a wise cracking dimple filled smile. "We disagree on the exact date of his second bris."

Incredible, thought Scott. The ultimate chameleon.

Gullibility was one of Stephanie's long suits, so Sonja helped out. "That's right up there with the bathing habits of the Jamaican bob-sledding team."

"C'mon," Stephanie said tugging at Miles. "It's chilly out here."

Dumbfounded, Scott shrugged at Miles when the girls weren't looking. Whatever you want. It's your game. Miles mouthed back at Scott, *'you're fucking right it is.'*

The remainder of the evening comprised a little of everything. Except computers. And computer crime. And any political talk that might lead to either of the first two no-nos. They dined elegantly, drank expensive French wine and overindulged in Martel. It was the perfect social evening between four friends.

* * * * *

Chapter 28

Sunday, January 24
New York City Times

HARDWARE VIRUSES: A NEW TWIST

By Scott Mason

In conversations with the Spook, the man who claims to be the technical genius behind the Homosoto Invasion, I have learned that there are even more menacing types of computer viruses than those commonly associated with infected software programs. They are hardware viruses; viruses built right into the electronics. The underground computer culture calls the elite designers of hardware viruses Chippers. It should come as no surprise then that Chipping was a practice exploited by Homosoto and his band under the wizardry of the Spook.

Chippers are a very specialized group of what I would have once called hackers, but whom now many refer to as terrorists. They design and build integrated circuits, chips, the brains of toys and computers, to purposefully malfunction. The chips are designed to either simply stop working, cause intentional random or persistent errors and even cause physical damage to other electronic circuits.

You ask, is all of this really possible? Yes, it is possible, it is occurring right now, and there is good reason to suspect that huge numbers of electronic VCR's, cameras, microwaves, clock radios and military systems are a disaster waiting to happen.

It takes a great many resources to build a chip - millions of dollars in sophisticated test equipment, lasers, clean rooms, electron beam microscopes and dozens of PhD's in dozens of disciplines to run it all.

According to the Spook, OSO Industries built millions upon millions of integrated circuits that are programmed to fail. He said, "I personally headed up that portion of the engineering design team. The techniques for building and disguising a Trojan Chip were all mine. I originally suggested the idea in jest, saying that if someone really wanted to cause damage, that's what they would do. Homosoto didn't even blink at the cost. Twelve million dollars."

When asked if he knew when the chips would start failing he responded, "I don't know the exact dates because anyone could easily add or change a date or event trigger. But I would guess that based upon timing of the other parts of the plan, seemingly isolated electronic systems will begin to fail in the next few months. But, that's only a guess."

The most damaging types of Trojan Chips are those that already have a lot of room for memory. The Spook described how mostly static RAM, (Random Access Memory) chips and various ROM chips, (Read Only Memory) such as UV-EPROM and EEPROM were used to house the destructive instructions for later release in computer systems.

"It's really simple. There are always thousands of unused gates in every IC. Banks and banks of memory for the taking. Homosoto was no slouch, and he recognized that hardware viruses are the ultimate in underground computer warfare. Even better than the original Trojan Horse. No messy software to worry about, and extensive collateral damage to nearby electronic components. Makes repairs terrifically expensive."

Which chips are to be considered suspect? The Spook was clear.

"Any RAM or ROM chips with the OSO logo and a date code after 1/89 are potentially dangerous. They should be swapped out immediately for new, uninfected components. Also, OSO sold their chips, in die form, to other manufacturers to put their own names on them. I wish I knew to whom, but Homosoto's firm handled all of that."

The Spook also said to beware of any electronic device using OSO labeled or OSO made LS logic chips. Hundreds of millions of the LS logic chips, the so called Glue of electronics, are sold every year. In the electronics world they are considered 'dime-store' parts, selling for a few pennies each. However, in most electronic systems, an inexpensive component failure is just as bad as an expensive component failure. In either case, it stops working.

The Spook continues: *"The idea was to build a small timebomb into VCR's, televisions and radios. Not only computers, but alarm systems, cash registers, video games, blowing up all at once. At times it got very funny. Imagine dishwashers spitting up gallons of suds in kitchens everywhere. The ovens will be cooking pork tartar and toast a la burnt. What happens when Betty-Jean doesn't trust her appliances any more? The return line at Sears will be a week long."*

I asked the Spook how this was possible? How could he inflict such damage without anyone noticing? His answer is as indicting as is his guilt. *"No one checks. If the chip passes a few simple tests, it's put into a calculator or a clock or a telephone or an airplane. No one expects the chip to be hiding something destructive, so no one looks for it. Not even the military check. They just expect their chips to work in the frozen depths of space and survive a nuclear blast. They don't expect a virus to be lurking."*

No matter what one thinks of the nameless, faceless person who hides behind the anonymity of these computerized confessions, one has to agree that the man known as the Spook has awakened this world to many of the dangers that unbridled technical proficiency brings. Have we taken too much liberty without the concomitant responsibility? I know that I find I wish I could run parts of my life in fast forward. Sitting in a movie theater, I feel myself tense as I realize I cannot speed up the slow parts. Has the infinite flexibility we have given ourselves outpaced social conscience?

Ironically, conversations with the Spook tended to be impersonal; not machine-like, but devoid of concern for people. That many people would suffer. I asked him if he cared.

"That was not the idea, as far as I know. In a way this was electronic warfare, in the true sense of the word. Collateral damage is unavoidable."

Hardware viruses in addition to software viruses. Is nothing sacred?

* * * * *

Sunday, January 24
Washington, D.C.

"Does he know what he's saying?" Henry Kennedy said doubtfully.

"I think so, and I also think it's a brilliant way to put a huge dent in the Japanese monopoly on integrated circuits." Marvin Jacobs had an office installed not two doors from Kennedy's in the subterranean mazes beneath the White House lawn.

"He can't blame the Japanese for everything . . ."

"Don't you see? He's not? All he's saying is that OSO did it, and he's letting the Japanese national guilt by association take its course." Jacobs seemed pleased. "Mason's chippers will cast a shadow of doubt on everything electronic made in Japan. If it has OSO's name on it, it'll be taboo. Toshiba, Mitsubishi, Matsushita . . .all the big Nippon names will be tarnished for years."

"And you actually want this to happen?" asked Henry.

501

"I didn't say that," Marvin said slithering away from a policy opinion. "Hey, what are you complaining about? Mason gave us the article like you wanted, didn't he?"

"I told you there were other ways," Kennedy shot back.

"Well, for your information, there's a little more that he didn't tell us about," said Jacobs haughtily.

"And how did you find out? Pray tell?"

Marvin grinned devilishly before answering. "CMR. Van Eck. Whatever. We have Mason covered."

"You're using the same . . ."

"Which is exactly how we're going to fight these bastards."

"At the expense of privacy?"

"There is no clear cut legal status of electromagnetic emanations from computers," Marv said defensively. "Are they private? Are they free to anyone with a receiver, like a radio or TV? No one has tested the theory yet. And that's not to say we've tried to publicize it. The FCC ruled in 1990 that eavesdropping on cellular telephone calls was legal. By anyone, even the government." Marvin was giving a most questionable technical practice an aura of respectability hidden behind the legal guise of freedom. Kennedy was uncomfortable with the situation, but in this case, Marv had the President's ear.

"And screw privacy, right? All in the name of national security." Henry did not approve of Marvin's tactics.

"It's been done before and it'll be done again," Marvin said fairly unconcerned with Kennedy's opinions and whining. "Citing National Security is a great antidote to political inconvenience."

"I don't agree with you, not one iota!" blasted Kennedy. "This is a democracy, and with that comes the good and the bad, and one premise of a democracy is the right to privacy. That's what shredded Nixon. Phone taps, all the time, phone taps."

"Henry, Henry," begged Marv to his old time, but more liberal minded friend. "This is legal." Marvin's almost wicked smile was not contagious. "It's not illegal either."

Kennedy frown deeply. "I think you take the NSA's charter as national listening post to an extreme," he said somberly.

"Henry, Are you going to fight me on this?" Marv asked finally.

"No," sighed Henry Kennedy. "The President gave you the task, I heard him, and I'm here to support his efforts. I don't have to agree . . .but it would help."

* * * * *

"Don't worry. The speech will make him sound like an expert, like he actually knows what he talking about. Not a man who thinks Nintendo is Japanese slang for nincompoop." Phil Musgrave called Henry Kennedy's office in the basement.

Phil joked with Henry about the President's legendary technical ineptness. One time while giving a speech to the VFW, the sound went out. Trying to be helpful, the President succeeded in plugging an 'in' into an 'out' which resulted in a minor amount of smoke, an embarrassing false security alert, and the subsequent loss of any sound reinforcement at all.

"You know how I feel about him, Phil," said Henry with concern. "I support him 110%. But this is a new area for all of us. We don't have the contingency plans. Defense hasn't spent years studying the problem and working out the options or the various scenarios. Phil, until recently viruses and hackers were considered a non-problem in the big picture."

"I know, Henry, I know, but the politicians had to rely on the experts, and they argued and argued and procrastinated . . ."

"And Congress, as usual, didn't do shit." Kennedy completed the statement. "That doesn't change the fact that he's winging it. Christ, we don't even know the questions much less the answers and, well, we know he calls 911 to change a lightbulb." His affection for the President was clear through the barb. "And you know what really pisses me off?"

"What's that?"

"Jacobs. He seems pleased with the turn of events."

"He should," agreed Phil nonchalantly. "He just won a major battle. He's got security back under his thumb. A nice political coup."

"No, not that," Henry said cautiously. "It's just that I think he's acting too much the part of the renegade. Do you know what I mean?"

"No, not at all," laughed Phil. "He's just playing it his way, not anyone elses. C'mon, now, you know that."

"I guess . . ."

"Besides, Henry," he said glancing at his watch. "It's getting to be that time." They agreed to watch the speech from the sidelines, so they could see how the President's comments were greeted by the press.

"Ladies and Gentlemen, the President of the United States." An assistant White House press agent made the announcement to the attendant Washington press pool. The video was picked up by the CNN cameras as it was their turn to provide a feed to the other networks. Sunday evening was an odd time to call a press conference, but everyone had a pretty good idea that the subject was going to be computers. Thus far, government comments on the crisis had come from everywhere but the White House.

The President rapidly ambled up to the podium and placed his notes before him. He put on his glasses and stared at the camera somberly. It was speeches that began this way, without a preannounced subject matter, that caused most Americans who grew up during the Cold War to experience a sinking feeling in their stomachs. They still thought about the unthinkable. As usual the press corps was rapt with attention.

"Good evening," the President of the United States began slowly. "I am speaking to you tonight on a matter of great concern to us all. A subject of the utmost urgency to which we must address ourselves immediately.

"That subject is, information. The value of information.

"As I am sure most of you are aware, one man, Taki Homosoto, threatened the United States this last week. It is about that very subject that I wish to speak to the country, and the world." The President paused. He had just told the country what he was going to say. Now he had to say it.

"For all practical purposes, the United States is undergoing an electronic Pearl Harbor, and the target is one of the most crucial segments of our way of life: Information.

"Information. What is information? Information is news. Information is a book, or a movie or a television show. Information is a picture, it's a word and it's a gesture. Information is also a thought. A pure idea.

"Information is the single commodity, a common denominator upon which all industrial societies must rely. Data, facts, opinions, pictures, histories, records, charts, numbers. Whether that data is raw in nature, such as names addresses and phone numbers, or it consists of secret governmental strategies and policies or proprietary business details, information is the key building block upon which modern society functions.

"Information is the lifeblood of the United States and the world.

"As first steam, and then coal and then gas and oil, now information has become an integral driving force of the economy. Without information, our systems begin to collapse. How can modern society function without information and the computers that make America what it is? Effectively there are no longer any nationalistic boundaries that governments create. Information has become a global commodity. What would our respective cultures look like if information was no longer available?

"We would not be able to predict the weather. Credit cards would be worthless pieces of plastic. We would save less lives without enough information and the means to analyze it. We need massive amounts of information to make informed decisions in government policies and actions.

"What if banks could no longer transfer money because the computers were empty? How could the airlines fly if there were no passenger records? What good is an insurance company if its clients names are nowhere on file? If there was no phone book, who could you call? If hospitals had no files on your medical history, what treatment is required? With a little effort, one can imagine how difficult it would be to run this planet without information.

"Information, in short, is both a global and a national strategic asset that is currently under attack."

"Information and the information processing industry has come to represent a highly significant piece of our gross national product; indeed, the way we live as Americans, enjoying the highest standard of living in the world, is due in large part to the extraordinary ability of having information at our fingertips in a second's notice. Anything we want in the form of information can literally be brought into our homes; cable television, direct satellite connections from the back yard. The Library of Congress, and a thousand and one other sources of information are at our fingertips from our living room chair.

"Without information, without the machinery that allows the information to remain available, a national electronic library, the United States steps back 30 years.

"Information is as much a strategic weapon in today's world as is the gun or other conventional armaments. Corporate successes are often based upon well organized data banks and analytic techniques. Government functions, and assuredly the Cold War was fought, on the premise that one side has more accurate information than its adversary. Certainly academia requires the availability of information across all disciplines. Too, the public in general relies upon widespread dissemination of information for even the simplest day to day activities.

"It is almost inconceivable that society could function as we know it without the data processing systems upon which we rely.

"It is with these thoughts that those more expert than I can speak at length, but we must realize and accept the responsibility for protecting that information. Unfortunately, we as trusting Americans, have allowed a complacency to overshadow prudent pragmatism.

"Over the last weeks we have begun to see the results of our complacency. The veins of the nation, the free flow of information, is being poisoned.

"Both the government and the private sector are to blame for our state of disarray and lack of preparedness in dealing with the current crisis. We must be willing, individually and collectively, to admit that we are all at fault, then we must fix the problem, make the sacrifice and then put it behind us.

"It is impossible for the Government to deny that we have failed miserably in our information security and privacy implementation. Likewise, the value of the accumulation of information by the private sector was overlooked by everybody. Fifteen years ago, who could have possibly imagined that the number of businesses relying on computers would have jumped more than a hundred thousand fold.

"Today, the backbone of America, the small businessman, 20,000,000 strong, the one man shop, provides more jobs than the Fortune 1000. And, the small businessman has come to rely on his computer as Big Business has for decades. His survival, his success is as critical to the stability of the United States' economy as is a General Motors or an IBM. We must defend the small business as surely as we must defend our international competitiveness of industrial leaders.

"The wealth of this country was once in steel mills, in auto plants, in manufacturing. The products built by the United States were second to none. Made in the U.S.A. was a proud label, one that carried a premium worldwide. Our technological leadership has never been in question and has been the envy of the world for over 200 years. Franklin, Fulton and Edison. The Wright Brothers, Westinghouse, Ford. As a nation the Manhattan Project reaffirmed our leadership. Then Yaeger and the speed of sound. The transistor. DNA decoded. The microchip. The Moon. The computer.

"Yet there was a subtle shift occurring that escaped all but the most vigilant. We were making less things, our concentration on manufacturing was slowly shifting to an emphasis on technology. Communications, computers. Information processing. No longer are cities built around smokestacks spewing forth the byproducts of the manufacturing process. Instead, industrial parks sprout in garden-like settings that encourage mental creativity. Fifteen percent of the American workforce no longer drive to the office. They commute via their computers at home.

"The excitement of the breakneck pace of technology masked the danger in which we were placing ourselves. Without realizing it, a bulk of this nation's tangible wealth was being moved to the contents of a computer's memory. We took those first steps toward computerization hesitantly; we didn't trust the computer. It was unfamiliar, foreign, alien. But when we embraced the computer, we unquestioningly entrusted it with out most precious secrets.

"Unlike the factory though, with the fence, the gates, the dogs, the alarms and the night guards, we left our computers unprotected. Growing bigger and faster computers took precedence over protecting their contents.

"We were warned, many times. But, as I said earlier, neither your government nor its constituency heeded the warnings with enough diligence. Protection of government information became a back-burner issue, a political hot cake, that in budget crunches, was easy to overlook. Overclassification of information became the case of the *The Spy Who Cried Wolf.*' The classification system has been abused and clearly does not serve us well. At my direction it will receive a thorough overhaul.

"Personal privacy has been ignored. Your government is in possession of huge amounts of data and yet there is no effort at protecting the non-classified privacy of individuals in our computers.

"The private sector faces another dilemma. The unresponsiveness of the Federal Government to the protection of its own information did not set a good example for industry, and their computers, too, remained vulnerable.

The President paused from reading his speech to pour a glass of ice water.

"Nothing can stop the fact that the United States is under attack. Nothing can change the fact that the attack cannot be turned away. And nothing can change the fact that America will suffer significant disruptions and inconvenience for some time. But we can minimize the damage. We can prepare for the inevitable obstacles we will face.

"The poison that Mr. Homosoto put into the American information society is the equivalent of electronic biological warfare. He has senselessly and vengefully struck out against the United States in a manner that I describe as an act of war.

"In order to deal with this real threat to the security of the United States of America, I have taken several steps that are designed to assist in weathering the storm.

"First, I am assigning the Director of the National Security Agency to coordinate all efforts at defending against and minimizing the effects of the current crisis. The NSA has the experience and resources, and the support of this President ᴗ manage an operation of this complexity and importance. In addition, representatives from GCHQ in the United Kingdom and other ITSEC members from Germany, France and Holland will coordinate European defensive strategies.

"Second, I am activating the following four groups to assist the NSA in their efforts. ECCO, the Emergency Computer Crisis Organization, has acted as an advisor to law enforcement agencies across the country and has been instrumental in providing the technical support to the FBI and the Secret Service in their computer crime investigations.

"CERT, the Computer Emergency Response Team was created by the Defense Advanced Research Projects Agency as an outgrowth of the 1988 INTERNET Worm incident. Carnegie Mellon University where CERT is headquartered has donated the complete facilities and staff of their Software Engineering Institute to deal with the invasion of our computers.

"The Defense Data Network Security Coordination Center was based at the Stanford Research Institute by the Defense Communications Agency to coordinate attacks against non-classified computer systems.

"Lastly, CIAC, the Computer Incident Advisory Capability manages computer crises for the Department of Energy at Lawrence Livermore Laboratories.

"These are the organizations and the people who will guide us through the coming adversities. It is they who are responsible to insure that America never again finds itself so vulnerable. So open to attack. So helpless in our technological Achilles Heel.

"The organizations I mentioned, and the government itself have not yet been tested in a crisis of significant magnitude. This is their maiden voyage, so to speak, and it is incumbent on us, the American people, to make their job as easy as we can by offering our complete cooperation.

"And, tonight, that is what I am asking of you. Your assistance. Your government cannot do it alone. Nor can small localized individual efforts expect to be successful against an army of invaders so large. We must team together, act as one, for the good of the entire country. From the big business with 100,000 computers to the millions of men, women and children with a home computer; from the small businessman to the schools, we need to come together against the common enemy: the invasion of our privacy and way of life.

"Americans come together in a crisis, and my fellow Americans, we face a crisis. Let me tell you what my advisors tell me. They tell me without taking immediate drastic steps to prevent further destruction of America's information infrastructure, we face a depression as great as the one of the 1930's.

"They tell me that every computer in the country, most in Canada, a significant number in England and other countries, can expect to be attacked in some manner within two years. That represents over 70 million casualties!

"The international financial and monetary system will come to a halt and collapse. Financial trading as we know it will cease and wild speculative fluctuations will dominate the world currency markets.

America is already feeling the change since the ATM networks were removed from service.

"As we have seen, the transportation facilities of this country, and indeed the world, are totally dependent on computers and therefore vulnerable. That is why today we take so seriously the threats against the airlines. There is no choice but success. Together, the American people must stand up to this threat and not succumb to its effects.

"While your government has the resources to develop solutions to the problems, it has not been within our power to mandate their use in the private sector.

"We will need unity as never before, for the battleground is in our homes, our schools, our streets and our businesses. The children of this great country will have as much opportunity to contribute as their parents will, and as the leaders of business will. As we all will and all must.

"In conclusion, ladies and gentlemen, the very structure of our country is in imminent danger of collapse, and it is up to us, indeed it is within our power, to survive. The sacrifices we will be called upon to make may be great, but the alternative is unacceptable.

"Indeed, this is a time where the American spirit is called upon to shine, and shine bright. Thank you, and God Bless the United States of America."

* * * * *

Sunday, January 24
Scarsdale, New York

"One fuckuva speech," Tyrone Duncan said to Scott Mason who was downing the last of a Coors Light. "You should be proud of yourself." They had watched the President's speech on Scott's large screen TV.

"Ahhhh," grunted Scott. "It's almost anti-climatic."

"How the hell can you say that?" Tyrone objected. "Isn't this what you've been trying to do? Get people to focus on the problem? Christ, you can't do much more than a Presidential speech."

"Oh, yeah," agreed Scott cynically. "Everyone knows, but not a damn thing's gonna be done about it. Nothing. I don't care what the President says, nothing's going to change."

"You have become one cynical bastard. Even Congress is behind the President on this one. His post-speech popularity is over 70%. according to CNN's Rapid Sample Poll."

"CNN. Bah, Humbug. Sensationalist news. And you think the proposed computer crime bills will pass?" Scott asked doubtfully.

Tyrone hesitated. "Sure, I think so. And you don't?"

"No, I don't. At least not in any meaningful way. C'mon, you're the constitutionalist not me. Sure, the original authors of the bill will write something with punch, maybe even effective. But by the time it gets committee'd to death, it'll be another piece of meaningless watered down piece of shit legislation. And that's before the states decide that computer crime is a state problem and not an inter-state issue. They'll say Uncle Sam is treading on their turf and put up one helluva stink." Scott shook his head discouragingly. "I see nothing but headaches."

"I think you just feel left out, like your job's done and you have nothing to do anymore. Post partum depression." Ty rose from the comfortable leather reading chair to get a couple more beers. "I kind of know how you feel."

Scott looked up at Tyrone in bewilderment. "You do? How?"

"I'm definitely leaving. We've made up my mind." Tyrone craned his neck from the kitchen. "Arlene and I, that is." Tyrone came back and threw a silver bullet at Scott. "This part of my life is over and it's time I move on to something else."

"Computers and the Law I suppose?" Scott said drearily.

"Don't make it sound like the plague," Tyrone laughed. "I'm doing it because I want to, and it's needed. In fact I would expect a good amount of the work to be pioneering. Pro bono. There's no case history; it'll be precedent setting law. I figure someone's got to be there to keep it honest. And who better than . . ." Tyrone spread his arms around the back of the chair.

"You, I know. The great byte hope." Scott laughed at his own joke which triggered a similar response from Tyrone. "Hey, man. I wish you all the best, if that's what you really want."

From Scott's office a sudden beeping began. "What's that?" asked Tyrone.

"A computer begging for attention. Let me see who it is." Tyrone followed Scott into his office, still astonished that anyone could work in such a pig pen. And the rest of the house was so neat.

<<<CONNECTION>>>

The computer screen held the image of the single word while whoever was calling caused Scott's computer to beep incessantly.

"What the hell?" Scott said out loud as he pecked at the keyboard standing rather than sitting at his desk.

wtfo

YOU'RE THERE. GOOD.

kirk?

YUP. WANNA GO TO A DEBATE?

Excuse me?

YOU WATCH THE PRESIDENT?

Of course. I have a mild interest in the subject.

SO DID I AND EVERY OTHER PHREAK IN THE COUNTRY,
AND THEY'RE NOT HAPPY.

Why?

SEE FOR YOURSELF. THE CONVERSATION PIT AT NEMO
IS BRIMMING. I GOT YOU AN INVITE.

I have a guest.

FRIEND OR FOE

friend. definitely.

REMEMBER HOW TO USE MIRAGE?

I can fake it.

To Tyrone's amazement, Scott seemed to know what he was doing
at the computer. Scott sat down, put his electronic conversation with
Kirk on hold, and called up another program as the colorful screen
split into two.

I got you on the bottom window.

YOU'LL SEE THE PIT ON THE TOP. JOIN IN WHEN YOU
WANT.

Maybe I'll just listen.

WHATEVER. I'M LOGGING ON.

The top window on Scott's computer screen blinked off momentarily and then was filled with a the words from the dissident phreaks.

CONVERSATION PIT: KIRK, RAMBO, PHASER, FON MAN,
POLTERGEIST,

AND WHAT ARE WE GOING TO DO ABOUT IT? <FON MAN>

THE FASCIST GOVERNMENT IS JUST TRYING TO TAKE
OVER. THE BILL OF RIGHTS IS GOING RIGHT DOWN THE
SHITTER <POLTERGEIST>

I AGREE. THEY LOOK FOR ANY EXCUSE TO TAKE AWAY
ANY FREEDOM WE MAY HAVE LEFT AND THEY TOOK THIS
HOMOSOTO THING AND BLEW IT RIGHT OUT OF PROPOR-
TION. JUST LIKE VIETNAM. <PHASER>

YOU DON'T BELIEVE THAT, DO YOU? <RAMBO>

YOU BET YOUR SWEET ASS I DO. SINCE WHEN HAS THE
GOVERNMENT GIVEN A SHIT ABOUT US? ONLY SINCE
THEY REALIZED WE HAVE POWER WITHOUT THEM.
THEY'RE NO LONGER IN CONTROL AND THEY'LL DO ANY-
THING THEY HAVE TO TO GET IT BACK. <POLTERGEIST>

I DON'T THINK THAT IT'LL BE THAT BAD <KIRK>

YOU BEEN HANGING OUT WITH THAT MASON GUY TOO MUCH <PHASER>

CAREFUL WHAT YOU SAY. HE'S LISTENING <KIRK>

ALL THE BETTER. HE'S AS BAD AS THE FEDS. <PHASER>

May I say something?

WHY DID YOU WAIT SO LONG?

I must beg to differ with Phaser with a question.

IT'S YOUR DIME <PHASER>

Believe me, I understand that you guys have a point, about hacking and the free flow of information. But who's in control now? From my viewpoint, it's not you and it's not the government. It's Homosoto.

SO? <PHASER>

So, if freedom is the issue as you say, I assume that you want to keep your electronic freedom at all costs.

RIGHT! <PHASER>

THAT'S THE POINT ‾ <POLTERGEIST>

Therefore, regardless of your opinions, you must realize that the government will do everything it thinks it needs to do to protect the country.

MAKE YOUR POINT <PHASER>

It seems to me that the best way for you to keep the electronic freedom you crave, might be to help fight Homosoto and the viruses and all. Minimize the damage, help defend the Global Network.

HE MAKES A POINT. I'VE HELPED. *<KIRK>*

THEN WE FALL INTO THEIR TRAP. SAVE IT ALL AND THEN THEY CLOSE DOWN THE NETWORK. I CAN'T PLAY INTO THEIR DECEIT AND TREACHERY. (POLTERGEIST>

DO YOU THINK THE FREEDOM LEAGUE IS DOING GOOD? <KIRK>

OF COURSE NOT. <PHASER>

That's Homosoto. Thousands of viruses. NEMO already helped.

ONLY THOSE THAT AGREE. WE ARE NOT A DEMOCRACY. <POLTERGEIST>

SO YOU DON'T WANT TO FIGHT THE VIRUSES? <RAMBO>

NOT YOU, TOO? <PHASER>

IT'S A MATTER OF RIGHT AND WRONG. ELECTRONIC FREEDOM, ANARCHY IS ONE THING. BUT WE DO NOT ABUSE. WE LIVE BY THE CODE AND WANT TO KEEP THE NETWORK OPEN. HOMOSOTO WANTS TO CLOSE THE NETWORK DOWN. BY SCARE TACTICS. <RAMBO>

THAT DOESN'T CHANGE THE FACT THAT THE FASCIST GOVERNMENT WILL TAKE EVERYTHING AWAY. <PHASER>

Only if they have to. Wouldn't you rather help? and keep that from happening?

IF I TRUSTED THE GOVERNMENT. <PHASER>

Can I introduce you to someone? His handle is FBI.

KIRK, WHAT ARE YOU DOING, GIVING US AWAY? <POLTER-GEIST>

THEY'RE TIED IN ON MIRAGE. THEY CAN PLAY BUT THERE'S NO REDIAL. <KIRK>

Gentlemen, this is FBI. Let me tell you something. I don't agree with hacking, theft of service and the like. But I also am pragmatic. I recognize the difference between the lesser of two evils. And as of today, based upon what I know, you guys are a pain the ass, but not a threat to national security. That is why Washington has taken little interest in your activities. But at the same time, you are part of an underground that has access to the electronic jungle in which we find ourselves. We would like your help.

OFFICIALLY? <PHASER>

No, unofficially. I am law enforcement, associated with ECCO, if you've ever heard of them.

ECCO. YOU GUYS FIGHT THE REAL COMPUTER JERKS, DON'T YOU? LIKE ROBERT MORRIS AND PUNJAB. DID YOU EVER CATCH THE GUY WHO STOPPED THE SHUTTLE FLIGHT? <POLTERGEIST>

Sadly, no. I am talking to you as a friend of Scott's. And I will tell you, that anything I learn I will use to fight Homosoto's attack. But frankly, you are little fish. I don't know who you are, nor do I really care. In all honesty, neither does Washington, the NSA or anyone else. You're merely an underground protest group. If anything, you help keep us honest. But even protesters should have their limits.

MINE HAS BEEN REACHED *<KIRK>*

AND MINE <RAMBO>

There is a big difference between freedom of speech and insurrection and invasion.

WHAT ABOUT PRIVACY? <PHASER>

THERE IS NONE, AND YOU KNOW IT. <KIRK>

THAT'S THE POINT. WE HAVE TO STOP THE MILITARISTIC WAR MONGERS FROM PRYING INTO OUR LIVES. THEY KNOW EVERYTHING ABOUT US, AND MORE. I WANT TO SEE THAT STOPPED. NOW. <PHASER>

This is Mason. At the expense of true freedom? Freedom of choice? By your logic, you may end up with no Compuserve. No electronic mail boxes. No networks. Or, they'll be so restricted that you'll never get on them.

IT'LL HAPPEN ANYWAY. <PHASER>

And you'll just speed up the process. What do you have to lose by helping out?

I WANT TO CONTINUE HELPING. MY FREEDOM TO HACK RESPONSIBLY IS IN DANGER BY ONE MAN, AND I AIM ON KEEPING MY FREEDOM. <KIRK>

It may be the only way to keep the digital highways open. I'm sorry to say.

IS THAT A THREAT? <PHASER>

Merely an observation.

I NEED TO THINK. <PHASER>

WHAT DO YOU NEED TO KNOW <RAMBO>

A lot. We need a complete list of phone numbers for every Freedom BBS. They provide wide distribution of infected software.

WE KNOW. BFD. <PHASER>

This is FBI. We want to shut them down.

HOW? <KIRK>

We have our means.

SEE WHAT I MEAN! THEY'RE ALL PIGS. THEY TAKE, TAKE, TAKE. BUT IF YOU ASK SOMETHING THEY CLAM UP. <KIRK>

All right. If it works you'll find out anyway. There are a number of underused laws, and we want to keep this on a Federal level. USC 1029, 1030, they're a bunch of them including racketeering. Then there are a number of Federal laws against doing anything injurious to the United States.

WHICH GIVES YOU THE RIGHT TO PROSECUTE ANYONE YOU DAMN WELL PLEASE WHENEVER YOU DAMN WELL WANT. <POLTERGEIST>

As a lawyer, I could make that case.

I AM A LAWYER, TOO. I PHREAK FOR PHREEDOM. <POL-TERGEIST>

Then you also know, that you have to really be on someone's shit list to get the FBI after you. Right now, Homosoto and his gang are on our shit list big time.

THEN WHEN YOU'RE THROUGH WITH THEM, IT'S US NEXT. THEN WHO'S LEFT? <PHASER>

RIGHT. <POLTERGEIST>

We can argue forever. All I'm saying is we could use whatever help you can give us. And I honestly don't care who you are. Unless of course you're on my shit list.

FBI HUMOR <KIRK>

WHAT ELSE DO YOU NEED? <RAMBO>

As many signatures as possible. We figure that there are thousands of you out there, and you can probably do a better job than any government security group punching in at nine and out at five. You have more people, no bureaucracy and a bigger sample of the software population.

SIGNATURES? NO QUESTIONS ASKED? <PHASER>

None. Also, rumors.

WHAT KIND OF RUMORS? <KIRK>

Like who might want to disrupt the Air Reservations System.

YOU'RE KIDDING? <POLTERGEIST>

I wish I was. You see, we are up against the wall.

THAT COULD REALLY FUCK THINGS UP <POLTERGEIST>

REALLY <KIRK>

IS IT REALLY THAT BAD? <POLTERGEIST>

Worse.

MAYBE I'LL THINK ABOUT IT. <POLTERGEIST>

ME TOO. <PHASER>

MASON. I'M GOING TO CUT YOU OFF. <KIRK>

It won't be the first time.

<<<CONNECTION TERMINATED>>>

Tyrone stretched his limbs searching for a bare place to sit down. Leaning over Scott's shoulders for the slow paced computer conversation stiffened his muscles. Scott motioned to slide whatever was in the way, out of the way, to which Tyrone complied.

"Dedicated mother fuckers. Misguided, but dedicated." Ty sat back in thought. "What do you think they'll do?"

"I don't think, I know," said Scott confidently. "Most of them will help, but they won't admit it. They openly distrust you, Washington and me. But, they value their freedom, and instinctively they will protect that. Kirk will be the conduit. I'm not worried."

"And what will they do?"

"Once they get around to it, they'll commandeer every hacker in the country and at least stop the viruses. Or some of them. I think that we need to elicit their trust, and I can do that by giving them more than they give me."

"Can you do that?"

"Just watch. If they play their cards right, they can be heroes."

* * * * *

Chapter 29

Monday, January 25
The White House

We had a pretty good handle on parts of it," said Marvin Jacobs glibly. Phil Musgrave, Martin Royce, Henry Kennedy and Quinton Chambers joined Marvin in one of the private White House conference rooms at 5 AM. Jacobs had called all members of the inner circle, personally, early that morning. He had received word that last evening's computer conversations between Scott Mason and the Spook had been intercepted and the preliminary analysis was ready.

Scott Mason's computer screens had been read by the NSA's remote electromagnetic receivers while he prepared his article for the following day. The actual article had also been transmitted to the White House, prior to publication, as agreed.

"And Mason seems to be living up to his part of the bargain," Jacobs continued. "He only edits out the bullshit, pardon my French. Gives the public their money's worth."

"You said we were close. How close?" Musgrave tended to run these meetings; it was one of the perks of being the President's Number One.

"His organization was a lot more comprehensive than we thought," Henry Kennedy said. "We underestimated his capabilities, but we caught the essence of his weapons by good guessing."

"If we could get our hands on this Spook character," sighed Martin Royce. He was thinking of the perennial problems associated with identifying the exact location of someone who doesn't want to be found.

"That's not the problem," said Chief of Staff Phil Musgrave. "We know who the Spook is, but we can't prove it. It's only hearsay, even with Mason's testimony, and it's a pretty damn safe bet he won't be inclined to testify. But Marv has given us a ton on him. After all, he is Marv's fault."

"You guys sort that out on your own time," yawned Phil. "For now, though we need to know what we're up against."

"If the President hadn't gone on television last night, we might have been able to keep this quiet and give the press some answers in a few days . . ." Marv said.

"Dream on," Phil said emphatically. "Mason broke the story and we were caught with our pants down. The President did not, and I repeat, did not, want to be associated with any cover up . . ."

"I didn't say cover up . . ."

"He wants to take his lumps and fix it. He will not lie to the American people."

"If we shut Mason up . . ." Marv suggested.

"We need him right where he is," Henry Kennedy said about Scott to stem the escalating argument.

"The subject is closed." Phil's comment silenced the room. After all was said and done, Musgrave was the closet thing to the President in the room. As with the President, the discussion was over, the policy set, now let's get on with it. "So, Marv? What are we up against."

The seasoned professional in Marvin Jacobs took over, conflicting opinions in the past, and he handed out a series of TOP SECRET briefing folders.

"You've got to be kidding," laughed Martin Royce holding up his file. "This stuff will be in today's morning paper and you classify it?"

"There are guidelines for classification," Marvin insisted. "We follow them to the letter."

"And every letter gets classified . . ." muttered Royce under his breath. The pragmatist in him saw the lunacy of the classification process, but the civil servant in him recognized the impossibility of changing it. Marv ignored the comment and opened his folder.

"Thanks, Phil," began Marv. "Well, I'll give it to him, Foster that is. If what he says is accurate, we have our work cut out for us, and in many cases all we can do is board up our windows before the hurricane hits."

"For purposes of this discussion, assume, as we will, that the Spook, Foster, is telling the truth. Do we have any reason to disbelieve him?"

"Other than attacking his own country? No, no reason at all." Marvin showed total disdain for Foster. His vehemence quieted the room, so he picked up where he left off.

"The first thing he did was establish a communications network, courtesy of AT&T. If Foster is right, then his boys have more doors and windows in and out of the phone company computers than AT&T knows exist. For all intents and purposes, they can do anything with the phone system that they want.

"They assign their own numbers, tap into digital transmissions, reprogram the main switches, create drop-dead billings, keep unlimited access lines and Operator Control. If we do locate a conversation, they're using a very sophisticated encryption scheme to disguise their communications. They're using the same bag of tricks we tried to classify over 20 years ago, and if anyone had listened . . ."

"We get the point, Marv," Phil said just before Henry was about to say the same thing.

"We can triangulate the cell phone location, but it takes time. Perhaps the smartest thing Foster did was recognize the need for an efficient distribution system. In order for his plan to work, he had to insure that every computer in the country was infected."

"Thus the dGraph situation?" Quinton Chambers finally began to look awake.

"And the Lotus Viruses, and the Freedom software," Henry said. "What about FTS-2000?" He was asking about the new multi-billion dollar voice and data communications network. FTS stands for Federal Telecommunications System.

"I have no doubt that it's in the same boat," suggested Marv. "But we have no sure data yet. We should ask Scott to ask Foster."

"What could happen?"

"Worst case? The government shuts down for lack of interest and no dial tone."

"And these viruses?"

"According to Foster, they designed over 8,000 viruses and he assumes that all or most of them have been released over the last several years," Marv said to a room full of raised eyebrows.

"How bad is that?" asked Chambers.

"Let's put it this way," said Marv. "In the last 14 years, only 313 viruses have been confirmed. Of those, the longest gestation period, from release to detonation . . .was eight months. And that one was discovered a couple of weeks after they were released. What Foster counted on was the fact that if software behaved normally, it wouldn't be suspect. And if it became popular, it was automatically above suspicion. He was right."

"I've heard that every computer is infected?"

"At the minimum, yes." Jacobs turned the pages of his dossier. "To continue, one of Foster's most important tools was the construction of road maps."

"Road maps?" questioned Phil.

"Connections, how it all ties together. How MILNET ties to INTERNET to DARPANET to DockMaster, then to the Universities." Marv wove a complex picture of how millions of computers are all interconnected. "Foster knew what he was doing. He called this group Mappers. The maps included the private nets, CompuServe, The Source, Gemini, Prodigy . . .BBS's to Tymenet . . .the lists go on forever. The road maps, according to Foster, were very detailed. The kind of computer, the operating system, what kind of security if any. They apparently raked through the hacker bulletin boards and complied massive lists of passwords for computers . . ."

"Including ours?" asked Quinton Chambers.

"Quite definitely. They kept files on the back doors, the trap doors and the system holes so they could enter computers undetected, or infect the files or erase them . . .take a look at Social Security and the IRS. Martin?"

Treasury Secretary Royce nodded in strong agreement. "We got hit but good. We still have no idea how many hundreds of thousands of tax records are gone forever, if they were ever there. So far it's been kept under wraps, but I don't know how long that can continue. The CDN has been nothing but trouble. We're actually worse off with it than without it."

"How can one person do all of that?" Chambers had little knowledge of computers, but he was getting a pretty good feel for the potential political fallout.

"One person! Ha!" exclaimed Jacobs. "Look at Page 16." He pointed at his copy of the Secret documents. "According to Foster he told Homosoto he needed hundreds of full time mappers to draw an accurate and worthwhile picture of the communications and networks in the U.S.."

"That's a lot of money right there," added Royce.

"It's obvious that money wasn't a consideration." Phil spouted the current political party line as well as it was understood. "Retaliation against the United States was the motivation, and to hell with the cost."

"Homosoto obviously took Foster's advice when it came to Propaganda," Marv continued. "The FBI, I believe, saw the results of a concentrated effort at creating distrust in computers. We've got a team working on just finding the blackmailers. Their version of a disinformation campaign was to spread the truth, the secret undeniable truths of those who most want to keep their secrets a secret."

"That's also where the banks got hit so hard," offered Henry Kennedy. "Tens of thousands of credit card numbers were spirited away from bank computers everywhere. You can imagine the shock when tens of millions of dollars of purchases were contested by the legitimate credit card holders."

"It's bad," agreed Royce.

"And we haven't even seen the beginning yet, if we believe Foster. There were other groups. Some specialized in Tempest-Busting . . ."

"Excuse me?" asked Quinton Chambers.

"Reading the signals broadcast by computers," Marv said with some derision. The Secretary of State should know better, he thought. "It's a classified Defense program." He paused while Chambers made a note. "Others used stolen EMP-T bomb technology to blow up the Stock Exchange and they even had antennas to focus HERF . . ."

"HERF?" laughed Phil.

"HERF," said Marv defensively. "High Energy Radiated Fields. Pick a frequency, add an antenna, point and shoot. Poof! Your computer's history."

"You're kidding me . . ."

"No joke. We and the Soviets have been doing it for years; Cold War Games," said Kennedy. "Pretty hush-hush stuff. We have hand held electric guns that will stop a car cold at a thousand yards."

"Phasers?" asked Chambers.

"Sort of, Quinton," chimed in Phil.

"Foster's plan also called for moles to be placed within strategic organizations, civilian and government." Marv continued. "They were to design and release malicious software from inside the company. Powerful technique if you can find enough bodies for the dirty work . . ."

"Again, according to Foster, Homosoto said that there was never a manpower problem," Marv said. "He's confident that an Arab group is involved somewhere. The MacDonald's accident was caused by Arabs who . . ."

"And we still can't get shit out of the one who we're holding. The only one that's left. Troubleaux was shot by an Arab . . .the FBI is working hard on that angle. They've given themselves extraordinary covers." Phil was always on top of those things that might have a political cause and/or effect. "How extensive an operation was this?"

Marvin Jacobs ruffled through some notes in his files. "It's hard to be sure. If Homosoto followed all of Foster's plan, I would guess 3 - 5,000 people, with a cost of between $100 - $300 Million. But mind you, that's an uneducated guesstimate."

Quinton Chambers dropped his pen on the table. "Are you telling us that one man is bringing the United States virtually to its knees for a couple of hundred million?" Marv reluctantly nodded. "Gentlemen, this is incredible, more than incredible . . .does the President know?"

Even Phil Musgrave was antsy with the answer to that question. "Not in any detail, but he is very concerned. As for the cost, terrorism has never been considered expensive."

"Well thank you Ron Ziegler, for that piece of information," scowled Chambers. "So if we know all of this, why don't we pick 'em all up and get this over with and everything working again?"

"Foster claims he doesn't know who anyone other than Homosoto is. He was kept in the dark. That is certainly not inconsistent with the way Homosoto is known to do business - very compartmentalized. He didn't do the recruitment, he said, and all communications were done over the computer . . .no faces, no names. If it wasn't for Mason, we wouldn't even know that Foster is the Spook. I consider us very lucky on that point alone."

"What are we going to do? What can we do?" Royce and Chambers both sounded and looked more concerned than the others. Their agencies were on the front line and the most visible to the public.

"For the government we can take some mandatory precautions. For the private sector, probably nothing . . ."

"Unless." Phil said quietly.

"Unless what?" All heads turned to Phil Musgrave.

"Unless the President invokes martial law to protect the country and takes control of the computers until we can respond." Phil often thought out loud, even with his extremist possibilities.

"Good idea!" said Jacobs quickly.

"You think that public will buy that?" asked Chambers.

"No, but they may have no choice."

* * * * *

Tuesday, January 26

PRESIDENT DECLARES WAR ON COMPUTERS

By Scott Mason

Support for the President's Sunday night call to arms has been virtually unanimous by industry leaders.

According to James Worthington, Director of Computing Services at First National Life, "We take the threat to our computers very seriously. Without the reliable operation of our MIS systems, our customers cannot be serviced and the company will suffer tremendous losses. Rates will undoubtedly rise unless we protect ourselves."

Similar sentiments were echoed by most industry leaders. IBM announced it would be closing all of its computer centers for between two and four weeks to effect a complete cleansing of all systems and products. A spokesperson for IBM said, "If our computers are threatened, we will take all necessary steps to protect our investment and the confidence of our customers. IBM prefers a short term disruption in normal services to a long term failure."

Well placed persons within the government concur that the NSA, who is responsible for guiding the country through the current computer crisis, is ideally suited for managing the situation. Even agencies who have in the past been critical of the super-secret NSA are praising their preliminary efforts and recommendations to deal with the emergency.

In a several page document issued by the NSA, a series of safeguards is outlined to protect computers against many of the threats they now face. In addition, the NSA has asked all long distance carriers to, effective immediately, deny service to any digital communications until further notice. Despite high marks for the NSA in other areas, many of their defensive recommendations have not been so well received.

"We are actually receiving more help from the public BBS's and local hacker groups in finding and eradicating the viruses than from the NSA or ECCO," said the Arnold Fullerman, Vice President of Computer Services at Prudential.

AT&T is also critical of the government's efforts. "The Presidential Order gives the NSA virtual control over the use of our long distance services. Without the ability to transmit digital data packets, we can expect a severely negative impact on our first quarter earnings . . ." While neither AT&T nor the other long distance carriers indicated they would defy the executive decree, they did say that their attorneys were investigating the legality of the mandate.

The NSA, though, was quick to respond to criticism. "All the NSA and its policies are trying to achieve is a massive reduction in the rate of propagation of the Homosoto Viruses, eliminate further infection, so we can isolate and immunize as many computers as possible. This will be a short term situation only." Detractors vocally dispute that argument.

AT&T, Northern TelCom and most telephone manufacturers are taking additional steps in protecting one of Homosoto's key targets: Public and Private Branch Exchanges, PBX's, or phone switches. They have all developed additional security recommendations for customers to keep Phone Phreaks from utilizing the circuits without authorization. Telephone fraud reached an estimated $5 Billion last year, with the courts upholding that customers whose phones were misused are still liable for all bills. Large companies have responded by not paying the bills and with lawsuits.

The NSA is further recommending federal legislation to mitigate the effects of future computer attacks. They propose that computer security be required by law.

"We feel that it would be prudent to ask the private sector to comply with minimum security levels. The C2 level is easy to reach, and will deter all but the most dedicated assaults. It is our belief that as all cars are manufactured with safety items such as seat belts, all computer should be manufactured with security and information integrity mechanisms in place. C2 level will meet 99% of the public's needs." A spokesman for ECCO, one of the emergency computer organizations working with the NSA explained that such security levels available outside of the highest government levels range from D Level, the weakest, to A Level, the strongest.

It is estimated that compliance with such recommendations will add no more than $50 to the cost of each computer.

The types of organizations that the NSA recommend secure its computers by law is extensive, and is meeting with some vocal opposition:

Companies with more than 6 computers connected in a network or that use remote communications.

Companies which store information about other people or organizations.

All Credit Card merchants.

Companies that do business with local, state or federal agencies.

The entire Federal Government, regardless of data classification.

All publicly funded organizations including schools, universities, museums, libraries, research, trade bureaus etc.

Public Access Data Bases and Bulletin Boards.

"It is crazy to believe that 45 million computers could comply with a law like that in under 2 years," said Harry Everett, a Washington D.C. based security consultant. "In 1987 Congress passed a law saying that the government had to protect 'sensitive but unclassified data' to a minimum C2 level by 1992. Look where we are now! Not even close, and now they expect to secure 100 times that many in half the time? No way."

Another critic said, "C2? What a joke. Europe is going by ITSEC and they laugh at the Orange Book. If you're going to make security a law, at least do it right."

NSA also had words for those computers which do not fall under the umbrella of the proposed legislation. Everyone is strongly urged to practice safe computing.

* * * * *

Tuesday, January 26
St. Louis, Missouri

"I'm sorry sir, we can't find you in the computer" the harried young woman said from behind the counter.

"Here's my boarding pass," he said shoving the small cardboard pass into her face. "And here's a paid for ticket. I want to get on my flight."

"Sir, there seems to be a complication," she nervously said as she saw at least another hundred angry people behind the irate customer.

"What kind of complication?" he demanded.

"It seems that you're not the only one with a ticket for Seat 11- D on this flight."

"What's that supposed to mean?"

"Sir, it seems that the flight has been accidentally overbooked, by about 300 people . . ."

"Well, I have a ticket and a boarding pass . . ."

"So do they, sir."

Delta and American and Northwest and USAir were all experiencing problems at every gate their airlines serviced. So was every other airline that used the National Reservation Service or Saber. Some flights though, were not so busy.

"What kind of load we have tonight, Sally?" asked Captain David Clark. The American red-eye from LAX to Kennedy was often a party flight, with music and entertainment people swapping cities and visiting ex-wives and children on the opposite coast.

"Light," she replied over the galley intercom from the middle of the 400 seat DC-10.

"How light?"

"Crew of eleven. Two passengers."

By midnight, the entire air traffic system was in total chaos. Empty airplanes sat idly in major hubs awaiting passengers that never came. Pilots and flight crews waiting for instructions as take-offs from airports all but ceased. Overbooking was so rampant that police were called into dozens of airports to restore order. Fist fights broke out and despite pleas for calm from the police and the airlines, over 200 were arrested on charges of disorderly conduct, assault and resisting arrest. Tens of thousands of passengers had confirming tickets for flights that didn't exist or had left hours before.

Arriving passengers at the international airports, LAX, Kennedy, San Francisco, Miami were stranded with no flights, no hotels and luggage often destined for parts unknown. Welcome to the United States.

The FAA had no choice but to shut down the entire air transportation system at 2:22 AM.

* * * * *

Wednesday, January 27
National Security Agency
Fort Meade, Maryland

"Did you get the President to sign it?"

"No problem. Public opinion swung our way after yesterday."

"And now?"

"Essentially, every long and short distance phone company works for Federal Government.."

"Tell me how it works."

"We have lines installed from the 114 Signal Transfer Points in every phone district to a pair of Cray-YMP's at the Fort. Every single AT&T long distance phone call goes through these switches and is labeled by an IAM with where the call came from and where it's going. What we're looking for is the high usage digital lines. Including fax lines. So the phone company is kind enough to send us a list of every call. We get about seven million an hour."

"We can handle that?"

"We have enough to handle ten times that."

"I forget about the international monitors. That's millions more calls a day we listen to."

"Yessir. The computers go through every call and make a list of digital calls. Then we get a list of all billing records and start crunching. We compare the high usage digital lines with the phone numbers from the bills and look for patterns. We look to see if it's a private or business line, part of a private PBX, hours and days of usage, then who owns the line. Obviously we eliminate a great many from legitimate businesses. After intensive analysis and profile comparison, we got a a few thousand candidates. What we decided to look for was two things.

"First, we listen to the lines to make sure it's a computer. If it is, we get a look at the transmissions. If they are encrypted, they get a red flag and onto the Hit List."

"The President bought this?"

"We told him we'd only need the records for a short time, and then we would dispose of them. He agreed."

"What a sucker. Good work."

* * * * *

Friday, Fbruary 12
New York City Times

Computer License Law Possible?

by Scott Mason

Senator Mark Bowman's proposed legislation is causing one of the most stirring debates on Capital Hill since the divisive decision to free Kuwait militarily.

The so-called "Computer License Law" is expected to create as much division in the streets and homes of America as it is politically.

The bill calls for every computer in the country to be registered with the Data Registration Agency, a working component of the Commerce Dept. The proposed 'nominal fees' are intended to insure that the technology to protect computer systems keeps up with other computer technology.

*Critics, though, are extremely vocal in their opposition to a bill that they say sends a strong message to the American people: **We don't trust you.** The FYI, Freeflow of Your Information says that passage of the Computer License Law will give the federal government the unrestricted ability and right to invade our privacy. Dr. Sean Kirschner, the chief ACLU counsel, is considering a lawsuit against the United States if the bill passes. Kirschner maintains that " . . .if the License Law goes into effect, the streets will be full of Computers Cops handing out tickets if your computer doesn't have a license. The enforcement clauses of the bill essentially give the police the right to listen to your computer. That is a simple invasion of privacy, and we will not permit a precedent to be set. We lost too much freedom under Reagan."*

Proponents of the bill insist that the low fee, perhaps only $10 per year per computer, is intended to finance efforts at keeping security technology apace with computer technology. "We have learned our lesson the hard way, and we now need to address the problem head on before it bites us again." They cite the example of England, where televisions have been licensed for years, with the fees dedicated to supporting the arts and maintaining broadcasting facilities.

527

"Does not apply," says Dr. Kirschner. *"With a television, there isn't an issue of privacy. A computer is like an electronic diary, and that privacy must be respected at all costs."*

"And," he adds, *"that's England, not the U.S.. They don't have freedom of the press, either."*

Kirschner vowed a highly visible fight if Congress *" . . .dares to pass that vulgar law . . ."*

* * * * *

Monday, February 15
Scarsdale, New York

"ECCO reports are coming in."

"At this hour?" Scott said sleepily.

"You want or no?" Tyrone Duncan answered with irritation.

"Yeah, yeah, I want," Scott grumbled. "What time is it?"

"Four A.M. Why?"

"I won't make the morning . . ."

"I'm giving you six hours lead. Quit bitching."

"O.K., O.K., what is it?"

"Don't sound so grateful."

"Where the hell are you?" Scott asked sounding slightly more awake.

"At the office."

"At four?"

"You're pushing your luck . . ."

"I'm ready."

"It looks like your NEMO friends were right. There are bunches of viruses. You can use this. ECCO received reports of a quarter million computers going haywire yesterday. There's gotta be ten times that number that haven't been reported."

"Whose?"

"Everybody for Christ's sake. American Gen, Compton Industries, First Life, Banks, and, this is almost funny, the entire town of Fallsworth, Idaho."

"Excuse me?"

* * * * *

Thursday, February 25

TOWN DISAPPEARS

By Scott Mason

The town of Fallsworth, Idaho is facing a unique problem. It is out of business.

Fallsworth, Idaho, population 433, has a computer population of 611.

But no one in the entire incorporation of Fallsworth has ever bought or paid for a single piece of software or hardware.

Three years ago, the town counsel approved a plan to make this small potato farming community the most computerized township in the United States, and it seems that they succeeded. Apparently the city hall of Fallsworth was contacted by representatives of Apple Computer. Would they like to be part of an experiment?

Apple Computer provided every home and business in the Fallsworth area with a computer and the necessary equipment to tie all of the computers together into one town-wide network. The city was a pilot program for the Electronic City of the future. The residents of Fallsworth were trained to use the computers and Apple and associated companies provided the township beta copies of software to try out, play with and comment on.

Fallsworth, Idaho was truly the networked city.

Lily Williams and members of the other 172 households in Fallsworth typed out their grocery lists on their computer, matching them to known inventories and pricing from Malcolm Druckers' General Store. When the orders arrived at the Drucker computer, the goods just had to be loaded in the pick up truck. Druckers' business increased 124% after the network was installed.

Doctors Stephenson, Viola and Freemont, the three town doctors modem'ed prescriptions to Baker Pharmacy so the pills were ready by the time their patients arrived.

Mack's Messengers had cellular modems and portable computers installed in their delivery trucks. They were so efficient, they expanded their business into nearby Darbywell, Idaho, population, 5,010.

Today, Fallsworth, Idaho doesn't use its computers. They lie dormant. A town without life. They forgot how to live and work and play and function without their computers. Who are the slaves?

The viruses of Lotus, of dGraph. The viruses of Freedom struck, and no one in the entire town had registration cards. The software crisis has left Fallsworth and a hundred other small test sites for big software firms out in the digital void.

Apple Computer promised to look into the matter but said that customers who have paid for their products come first . . .

* * * * *

Friday, March 5
FBI Building, Federal Square

Tyrone Duncan was as busy as he had ever been, attempting to coordinate the FBI's efforts in tracking down any of the increasing number of computer criminals. And there were a lot of them at the moment. The first Copy-Cat computer assaults were coming to light, making it all that much more difficult to isolate the Foster Plan activities from those other non-coordinated incidents.

Tyrone, as did his counterparts in regional FBI offices nationwide, created teams of agents who concentrated on specific areas of Homosoto's assault as described by the Spook. Some specialized in tracing missing electronic funds, some in working with the phone company through the NSA. More than any other goal, the FBI wanted desperately to locate as many of the invisible agents that the Spook, Miles Foster, had told Homosoto to use. Tyrone doubted they would catch anywhere near the 3000 or more he was told that were out there, but at this point any success was welcome.

FBI agents toiled and interviewed and researched sixteen and eighteen hours a day, seven days a week. There hadn't been such a blanket approval of overtime since the Kennedy assassination. The FBI followed up the leads generated by the computers at the NSA. Who and where were the likely associates of Homosoto and Foster?

His phone ringing, the private line that bypasses his secretary, startled Tyrone from the deep thought in which he was immersed. On a Saturday. As the voice on the other end of the phone uttered its first sound, Tyrone knew that it was Bob Burnsen. Apparently he was in his office today as well.

"Afternoon, Bob," Tyrone said vacantly.

"Gotcha at a bad time?" Burnsen asked.

"No, no. Just going over something that may prove interesting."

"Go ahead, make my day," joked Burnsen.

"I know you don't want to know . . ."

"Then don't tell me . . ."

"But Mason's hackers are coming through for us."

"Jeez, Ty," whined Bob. "Do you have to . . ."

"Do you know anybody else that is capable of moving freely in those circles? It's not exactly our specialty," reprimanded Tyrone.

"In theory it's great," Bob reluctantly agreed, "but there are so damn many exposures. They can mislead us, they're not professionals, and worst of all, we don't even know who they are, to perform a background check."

"Bob, you went over to the other side . . .playing desk man on me?"

"Ty, I told you a while ago, I could only hang so far out before the branches started shaking . . ."

"Then you don't know anything." Tyrone said in negotiation. Keep Bob officially uninformed and unofficially informed. "You don't know that NEMO has helped to identify four of the blackmailers, and a handful of the Freedom Freaks. You don't know that we have gotten more reliable information from Mason's kids than from ECCO, CERT, NIST and NSA combined. They're up in the clouds with theory and conjecture and *what-iffing* themselves silly. NEMO is in the streets. A remote control informer if you like."

"What else don't I know?"

"You don't know that NEMO has been giving us security holes in some of our systems. You don't know that Mason's and other hackers have been working on the Freedom viruses . . .

"Some systems? Why not all?"

"They still want to keep a few trapdoors for themselves . . ."

"See what I mean!" exclaimed Burnsen. "They can't be trusted."

"They are not on our payroll. Besides, it's them or no one," Tyrone calmly said. "They really would like to keep the real-bad guys off of the playing field, as they put it."

"And keep the spoils for their own use."

"It's a trade-off I thought was worthwhile."

"I don't happen to agree, and neither does the Director's office."

"I thought you didn't know . . ."

"Word gets around. We have to cap this one, Ty. It's too hot. This is so far from policy I think we could be shot."

"You know nothing. Nothing."

But Burnsen and the FBI and the White House all knew they wanted Foster. Tyrone instinctively knew as did Scott, that Miles Foster was the Spook. Other than meager unsubstantiated circumstantial evidence, though, there was still no convincing legal connection between Miles Foster and the Spook. Not enough of one, anyway.

Miles Foster had done an extraordinary job of insulating himself and his identity from his army.

There had to be another way.

* * * * *

Monday, March 8
New York City Times

Lawsuit Cites Virus

by Scott Mason

Will stockholders of corporations soon require that all Corporate assets be appropriately protected? Including those contained in the computers? Many people see a strong possibility of a swell of Wall Street investor demands to secure the computers of publicly held companies. The SEC is planning on issuing a set of preliminary regulations for firms under its aegis.

Last week, a group of 10,000 Alytech, Inc. stockholders filed the first class action suit along this vein. They are suing the current board of directors for " . . .willful dereliction of fiduciary responsibility in the adequate security and protection of corporate information, data, communications and data processing and communications equipment." The suit continues to say that the company, under the Directors' leadership and guidance knew and understood the threat to their computers, yet did nothing to correct the situation.

Attorneys for the plaintiffs have said that they are in possession of a number of internal Alytech documents and memos which spelled out security recommendations to their board of directors, upon which no action was taken.

Alytech was one of the many companies hit particularly hard by the Computer War. The dGraph virus, the Lotus viruses and the Novell viruses were among those that infected over 34,000 of the company's computers around the world; bringing the company to a virtual halt for over two weeks. Immediately after getting their computers back up and running, they were struck by several Freedom viruses which were designed to destroy the hard disks on the computers.

As of this date, Alytech still has over 10,000 computers sitting idly waiting for the much delayed shipments of hard disks required to repair the machines.

Spokesman for Alytech, Inc. say that the lawsuit is frivolous and without merit.

A date of June 14 has been set for the courts to hear the first of many rounds of motions.

* * * * *

Sunday, March 21
Paris, France

Spring in Paris is more glorious than any reviewer can adequately portray.

The clear air bristles with fresh anticipation like lovers on a cool afternoon. Bicycles, free from a winter of hiding in garages, fill the streets and parks. All of Paris enjoys the first stroll of the year.

Coats and jackets are prematurely shed in favor of t-shirts and skimpy tank-tops and the cafes teem with alfresco activity. The lucky low-season American tourist experiences firsthand the French foreplay to summer.

Looking down to the streets from the 'deuziemme etage' of the Eiffel Tower, only a hundred feet up, the sheer number of strollers, of pedestrian cruisers, of tourists and of the idly lazy occupies the whole of one's vista.

Martin Templer leaned heavily on the wrought iron railing of the restaurant level, soaking up the tranquility of the perfect Sunday afternoon. He gazed across the budding tree-lined Seine toward the Champs Elysee and the Arc de Triumph; from Notre Dame to the skyscrapered Ile de la Cité. He mentally noted the incongruity between the aura of peace that Paris radiated with its often violent history. He hoped nothing today would break that spell.

A sudden slap on the back aroused Templer from his sun warmed daydream. He turned his head in seeming boredom. "You'd make a lousy pickpocket."

"That's why I avoided a life of crime." Alexander Spiradon was immaculately dressed, down to the properly folded silk handkerchief in his suit jacket. "How are you today my friend? Did I interrupt your reverie?"

Templer swung his London Fog over his shoulder. His casual slacks and stylish light weight sweater contrasted severely with Alex's comfortable air of formality. "I don't get here often. Paris is a very special place," Templer mused, turning from his view of the city to face his old comrade.

"It is indeed," agreed Alex. "Then why do you look so melancholy? Does Paris bring you memories of sadness?"

"I hope not," Templer said, eyes down.

"You didn't give me much notice," Alex said good naturedly. "I left the most beautiful woman in the world in a jacuzzi at St. Moritz."

"No, I'm sorry. I know I didn't, but it was urgent. Couldn't wait." A slight breeze caused Templer to shiver. He slowly put on his tan rain coat and looked right into Alex's eyes. "I'm going to ask you straight."

Alex confidently grinned. "Ask what?"

"Was Taki Homosoto a client of yours?" The biting words seemed to have little impact on Alex.

"My clients trust me to keep their identities confidential." The expression on Alex's face didn't change.

"The guy's dead. What the hell can it hurt?" Templer laughed. "What's he gonna do? Sue you for breach of contract?"

Alex didn't say a word. He saw Templer laugh the confident laugh of a chess player one move from checkmate and he realized how uncomfortable a position this was for him. How do you behave when you're on the losing end of the stick? Alex was thinking like he cared what Templer knew or thought. In reality, though, he didn't care any more about what anyone thought of him. He had enough money, more than enough money, to lead a lavish lifestyle without worry. So what did it matter. As friends nothing would change between him and Martin. But professionally, that was a different matter.

"I'd love to tell you, but, it's a matter of ethics," Alex said happily. "You understand."

"It really doesn't matter," laughed Templer. "Let's walk. The wind's picking up." They unconsciously joined in the spontaneous promenade of walkers who shuffle around the mid level of the Tower to share in the ambience that only Paris offers.

"You know, I'm officially retired," Alex said breathing in deeply.

"I'm not surprised. Must have been a very profitable endeavor."

"I saved a little and made prudent investments," Alex lied and Templer knew it. No need to push the point.

"How well did Sir George do? He wouldn't tell us."

Alex stopped in his tracks and glared at Martin with a blank emotionless expression for several seconds until his deep set brown eyes began to twinkle. A knowing smile and nod of recognition of accomplishment followed, telling Martin he had hit a home run. "You're good. Very good." They both began walking again, as if on cue. "For future edification, how did you find him?"

"Them. Sir George was the most helpful, though."

"I remember him. Real character, kind of helpless but with the gift of gab." Alex seemed unconcerned that any of his network had been discovered. "He talked?"

"Second rate criminal. Definitely deportable."

"And you made him an offer he couldn't refuse."

"Something like that," Templer said coyly. "Let's just say he prefers the vineyards of California to the prisons in England."

Alex nodded in understanding. "How'd you find him?"

"Telephone records."

"That's impossible," Alex said, shrugging off Martin's answer.

"Never underestimate the power of silicon," Martin said cryptically.

"Computers? No way," Alex said defiantly. "Every year there are almost 40 Billion calls made within the United States alone. There's no way to trace that many calls."

"Who needs to trace?" Templer enjoyed the joust. Thus far. "The phone company is kind enough to keep records of every call made. Both local and long distance. They're all rather complete. From what number, to what number, if it's forwarded, to what number and at what time and for how long. They also tell us if the calls were voice, fax, or other types of communications. It even identifies telephone connections that use encryption. Believe me, those are flagged right off."

"You monitor every conversation? I thought it was just the overseas calls. That's incredible. Incredibly illegal."

"But necessary. The threat of terrorism inside the United States has reached unacceptable levels, and we had the capability. It was just a matter of flipping the switch."

"Since when can you do that?" Alex asked, stunned that he had overlooked, or underestimated a piece of the equation.

"Since the phone company computers were connected to the Fort. And, I guarantee you, it's not something they want advertised," Martin said in a low voice. "Did you fuck up?" They had circled the Tower twice and stopped back where they started, overlooking the Seine.

Alex's professional composure returned as they leaned over the Tower's railing.

"I guess I wasn't as right as I usually am," he snickered. Templer followed suit. "How many did you get?"

"How many are there?"

"That would be telling," Alex said coyly.

"I assume, then, that you would be averse to helping us out of our current dilemma." Being friends with potential adversaries made this part of the job all the more difficult.

"Well," Alex said turning his head toward Martin. "I guess I could be talked into one more job, just one, if the price was right."

Templer shook his head. "That's not the right answer."

Alex was taken off guard by the sullenness in Martin's voice. "Right answer? There are no right and wrongs in our business. Only shades of gray. You know that. We ride a fence, and the winds blow back and forth. It's not personal."

Martin straightened up and put both hands deep into the pockets of his London Fog. "Among the professionals, yes. But Sir George and his cronies, and you by default, broke the rules. Civilians are off limits. We were hoping that you would want to help."

Alex ignored the second request. "I won't do it again. I promise," he said haughtily.

"Is there anything I can say that will make you reconsider? Anything at all?" Martin implored.

"No," Alex said. "Unless we can discuss an equitable arrangement."

Martin took his hands out of his pockets and said, "I don't think that will work. I'm sorry."

"Sorry?"

Martin quickly moved his right hand up to Alex's neck and touched it briefly. Alex reached up and slapped his neck as terror overtook his face. He grabbed Martin's arm and twisted it with his free hand to expose a small needle tipped dart projecting from a ring on one finger. Templer wrested his arm free from Alex's weakening clutch and tore off the ring, tossing it away from the Tower.

Alex weakened further as he leaned both hands on the railing to steady himself. His mouth gaped wide, intense fear and utter disbelief competing for control of his facial muscles. Martin ignored his collapsing adversary and walked deliberately to the open elevator which provided escape down to street level. Before the doors had closed, Templer saw a crowd converge over the crumpled body of Alexander Spiradon.

Martin Templer crossed the Seine and performed evasive maneuvers to make sure he was not being followed. The *cleansing* process took about three hours. He flagged down a taxi and the most uncooperative driver refused to acknowledge he understood that the destination was the American Embassy on Gabriel. Only when Templer flashed a 100 Franc note did the driver's English improve.

Templer showed his CIA credentials to the Marine Sergeant at the security desk, and told him he needed access to a secure communications channel to Washington.

After his identity was verified, Templer was permitted to send his message. It was electronically addressed to his superiors at CIA headquarters in Langley, Virginia.

PLATO COULDN'T COME OUT AND PLAY.
UNFORTUNATE STROKE INTERRUPTED THE INTER-VIEW.

* * * * *

536

Chapter 30

Monday, March 22
National Security Agency

He had two separate offices, each with a unique character. One ultra modern and sleek, the other befitting a country gentleman. The two were connected by a large anteroom that also provided immediate access and departure by a private elevator and escape stairs. He could hold two meetings at once as was occasionally required in his position as DIRNSA, Director, National Security Agency. Each office had its own secretary and private entrance, selected for use depending upon whom was expected.

The meeting in the nouveau office was winding down to a close and the conversation had been reduced to friendly banter. Marvin Jacobs had brought in three of his senior advisors who were coordinating the massive analytical computing power of the NSA with the extraordinary volume of raw data that the 114 AT&T 4ESS switches downloaded daily.

Since they had been assigned to assist the FBI, the NSA had been hunting down the locations of the potential conspirators with the assistance of the seven Baby Bells and Bell Laboratories in Princeton, New Jersey. The gargantuan task was delicately balancing a fine line between chaos and stagnancy; legality and amorality.

As they spoke, Jacobs heard a tone emit from his computer and he noticed that Office-2 had a Priority Visitor.

"Gentlemen," Marvin Jacobs said as he stood. "It seems that my presence is required for a small matter. Would you mind entertaining yourselves for a few minutes?" His solicitous nature and political clout demanded that his visitors agree without hesitation.

He walked over to a door by the floor to ceiling bookshelf and let himself in, through the gracious ante-room by the commode and into his heavy wood and leather office. He immediately saw the reason for the urgency.

"Miles, Miles Foster, my boy! How are you?" Marvin Jacobs walked straight to Miles, vigorously shook his hand and gave him a big friendly bear hug.

Miles smiled from ear to ear. "It's been cold out there. Glad to be home." He looked around the room and nodded appreciatively. "You've been decorating again."

"Twice. You haven't been in this office for, what is it, five years?" Jacobs held Miles by the shoulders. "My God it's good to see you. You don't look any the worse for wear."

"I had a great boss, treated me real nice," Miles said.

"Come here, sit down," Marvin said ushering Miles over to a thickly padded couch. "If you don't already know it, this country owes you a debt of thanks."

"I know," Miles said, even though he had been paid over three million dollars by Homosoto.

"A drink, son?" At fifty-five, the red faced paunch bellied Jacobs looked old enough to be Miles' father, even though they were only fifteen years apart.

"Glenfiddich on the rocks." Miles felt comfortable. Totally comfortable and in control of the situation.

"Done." DIRNSA Jacobs pressed a button which caused a hidden bar to be exposed from a mirror paneled wall. The James Bondish tricks amused Miles. "Excuse me," he said to Miles. "Let me get rid of my other appointments." Jacobs handed Miles the clear drink and leaned over his desk speaking into telephone. "Uh, Miss Greeley, cancel my dates for the rest of the day, would you please?"

"Of course, sir." The thin female voice came across the speaker phone clearly.

"And my regrets to the gentlemen in One."

"Yessir." The intercom audibly clicked off.

"So," Marvin asked. "How does it feel to be both the goat and the hero?"

"Hey, I fixed it, just like we planned, didn't I?" Miles said arrogantly, but his deep dimples said he was joking. "I remember everything you taught me," he bragged. "Lesson One: If you really want to fix something, first you gotta fuck it up so bad everyone takes notice. Well, how'd I do?" Miles still grinned, his dimples radiating a star pattern across his cheeks. Jacobs approved whole heartedly.

"You were a natural. From day one."

"Homosoto thought that fuck-it to fix-it was entirely too weird at first, so I quit calling it that." Miles fondly remembered those early conversations. "As you said, it takes a disaster to motivate Americans, and we gave them one."

"I'm glad you see it that way," Marvin said obligingly. "It occurred to me that you might have gotten soft on me."

"Not a chance." Miles countered. "How many men get to lead armies, first of all. And I may be the first, ever, to lead an invasion of my own country with my government's approval. This was a sanctioned global video game. I should thank you for the opportunity."

"That's a hell of a way to look at it, my boy. You show a lot of courage." Marvin drank to Miles' health. "It takes men of courage to run a country, and that's what we do; run the country." Miles had heard many of Marvin's considerable and conservative speeches

538

before, but this one was new. After over 5 years, that was to be expected.

"It doesn't make a damn bit of difference who the President is. The Government stays the same regardless of who's elected every 4 years." Marvin continued as Miles listened reverently.

"The American public thinks that politicians run the country; they think that they vote for the people who make the policies, who set the tone of the government, but they are so wrong. So wrong." Marvin shook his head side to side. "And it's probably just as well that they never find out for sure." He held Miles' attention. Marv walked around the room drink in hand, gesturing with his hands and arms.

"The hundreds of thousands of Government employees, the ones that are here year after year after year, we are the ones who make policy. It's the mid-grade manager, staff writer, the political analysts who create the images, the pictures that the White House and Capital Hill see.

"This town, the United States is run by lifers; people who have dedicated their lives to the American way of life. The military controls more than any American wants to know. State Department, Justice, HUD; each are their own monolithic bureaucracies that do not change direction overnight because of some election in Bumfuck, Iowa. It takes four years to find your way through the corridors, and by then, odds are you'll be packing back to Maine, or Georgia or California or wherever you came from." Marvin Jacob's vitriolic oration was grinding on Miles, but he had to listen to his boss.

"So when this country gets into trouble, someone has to do something about it. God knows the politicians won't. This country was in real trouble and someone had to fix it. In this case it was me. It's been a decade since the first warnings about how vulnerable our computers, our economy, shit, our National Security were. The reports came out, and Congress decided to ignore them. Sure, they built up the greatest armaments in the history of civilization, sold the future for a few trillion, but they neglected to protect their investment." Jacobs angrily poured himself another drink.

"I couldn't let that happen, so I decided that I needed to expose the weaknesses in our systems before somebody else did." Marvin spoke proudly. "And what better way than to fuck it up beyond all recognition. FUBAR. At least this way we were in charge, and we were able to pick the damage. Thanks to you. Lessons tend to be painful, and I guess we're paying for some of our past sins." He drank thirstily.

"Did those sins mean that I would have to be arrested by the FBI. I couldn't say a thing; not the truth. They'd never have believed me." Miles shuddered at the thought. "For a moment, I thought you might leave me in jail to rot."

"Hey," Marvin said happily. "Didn't our people get you out, just like I promised? Less than an hour." He sounded proud of his efforts. "Besides, most of them were bullshit charges. Not worth the effort to prosecute."

"I never underestimate the power of the acronym," Miles said about the NSA, CIA and assorted lettered agencies. "There was a lot of not so quiet whispering when it was released that the charges were dropped by the Federal Prosecutor. Think that was smart, so soon? Maybe we should have waited a couple of months . . ."

Jacobs looked up sharply at Miles' criticism of his actions but spoke with understanding. "We needed to get the cameras off of you and onto the real problem; it was the right thing to do. Your part is over. You started the war. Now it's up to me to stop it. It could not have gone any smoother. Yes," he reflected. "It's time for us to take over. You have performed magnificently. We couldn't ask for any more."

Miles sipped at his vodka accepting the reasoning and asked, "I've wondered about a few things, since the beginning."

"Now's as good a time as any," Marv said edging himself behind his desk. "I'd imagine you have a lot of holes to fill in."

"How did you get Homosoto to cooperate? He seemed to fall right into place."

"It was almost too easy," Jacobs commented casually. "We had a number of candidates. You'd be surprised how many people with money and power hold grudges against Uncle Sam," he snickered. "It's hard to believe, but true."

"Meaning, if it wasn't him, it would have been someone else?"

"Exactly. There's no shortage of help in the revenge business. There are still many hibakusha, survivors of Hiroshima and Nagasaki, who still want revenge on us for ending the war and saving so may lives. Ironic, isn't it? That someone like Homosoto is twisted enough to help us, just to fuel his own hatred." Marvin Jacobs asked rhetorically.

"But he didn't know he was helping, did he?" Miles asked.

"Of course not. Then he would have been running the show, and this was my production. No, it worked out just fine."

Jacobs paused for more liquor and continued. "Then we have a few European industrialists, ex-Nazis who are available . . .the KGB, GRU, Colombian cartel members. The list of assets is long. Where's there's money, there's help, and most of them prefer the Yankee dollar to any other form of payment. They forget that by hurting us, they also hurt the world's largest economy, as well as everybody else's and then the fiscal dominoes start falling uncontrollably."

"You mean you bought him?" Miles asked.

"Oh, no! You can't buy a billionaire, but you can influence his actions, if he thinks that it's his idea. It just so happens that he was the first one to bite. Health problems and all."

"What problems?"

"In all likelihood it's from the radiation, the Bomb; his doctors gave him a couple of years to live. Inoperable form of leukemia."

"I didn't know . . ."

"No one did. He insisted on complete secrecy. He had not picked a successor to run OSO, and in some ways he denied the reality."

"Excuse my tired old brain, but you're talking Spook-Speak. How did you know . . .?"

"Old habits . . ." Marvin agreed. "As you well know, from your employ here, we have assets in every major company in the world. Especially those companies that buy and sell elected officials in Washington. OSO and Homosoto are quite guilty of bribing their way into billions of dollars of contracts. Our assets, you see, can work in two directions. They let us know what's going on from the inside and give us a leg up on the G2. Then, we can plant real or false information when needed. The Cold Economic War."

"So you told Homosoto what to do?" Miles followed closely.

"Not in so many words." Marvin wasn't telling all, and Miles knew it. "We knew that through our assets we gave Homosoto and several others the idea that U.S. computers were extremely fragile. Back in 1983 the DoD and CIA prepared classified reports saying that computer terrorism was going to be the international crime of choice in the last decade of the century. Then the NRC, NSC and DIA issued follow-up reports that agreed with the original findings. We saw to it that enough detail reached Tokyo to show just how weak we were."

Jacobs continued to tell Miles how the NSA effected the unwitting recruitment of Homosoto. "That, a well timed resignation on your part, and advertising your dissatisfaction with the government made you the ideal person to launch the attack." Marvin smiled widely holding his drink in the air, toasting Miles.

Miles responded by raising his glass. "And then a suicide, how perfect." Jacobs did not return the salute, and Miles felt sudden iciness. "Right? Homosoto's suicide." Jacobs still said nothing. "Marv? It was a suicide, wasn't it?"

"Miss Perkins was of great help, too," Marvin said ignoring Miles questions.

"Perky? What's she got to do with this?" Miles demanded.

"Oh? You really don't know?" Marvin was genuinely shocked. "I guess she was better than we thought. I thought you knew." He looked down to avoid Miles's eyes. "Didn't you think it odd . . .?"

"That she introduced me to Homosoto?" Miles asked acrimoniously.

"She didn't."

"Of course she did," Miles contradicted.

"We have a tape of the conversation," Marv disagreed. "All she did was ask you if you would work for a foreigner and under what circumstances. Perkins' job was to prep you for Homosoto or whoever else we expected to contact you. An admirable job, huh Miles?" Marvin Jacobs seemed proud of her accomplishments, and given the stunned gaping expression on Miles' face, he beamed even more. Miles didn't say a word, but his glazed eyes said loud and clear that he felt defiled.

"I'm sorry Miles," Marvin said compassionately. "I really assumed you knew that she was a toy. You certainly treated her that way." No reaction. "If it helps any, she was on Homosoto's payroll. She was a double."

Miles jerked his head back and then let out a long laugh. "Well, fuck me dead. Goddamn, she was good! Had me going. Not a fucking clue." Miles stood from his chair and laughed and smiled at Marvin. "What a deal. I get blow jobs courtesy of the American taxpayer and you get paid to watch."

"Miles, we know how you felt for her . . ."

"Bullshit," Miles said quickly. "That's fucking bullshit." He pounded on the desk.

"She's already on another assignment," Marvin said calmly.

Miles couldn't completely hide the dejection, the feeling of loss, no matter how loudly he denied it. "Fuck her!" Miles exclaimed. He walked over to the high tech bar and made himself another Absolut on the rocks. Perfect drink to get dumped by. "Another?" he asked Marvin who handed Miles his glass for a refill.

"As I was saying," Marvin said. "This country owes you a thanks, beyond any medals or awards, and unfortunately, there is no way we can publicly express our appreciation." Marvin sat down with his drink and addressed Miles.

"Hey," Miles said holding his hands in front of him. "I knew that going into the deal. I did my job, for my country, and maybe I lose some face, but I didn't do this for fame. Retiring in style, maybe the Alps is a nice consolation prize." The pain, so evident seconds ago about Stephanie, was gone. Miles gloated in his achievement.

A low warble came from the phone on Marvin's desk. He read a message that appeared on the small message screen attached to the phone and struck a few keys in response. At that moment, the double doors from the Office-2 reception opened and in came Tyrone Duncan and two other FBI agents. Miles turned to see who was interrupting their meeting. It was the same man who had arrested him a few weeks before.

Miles gulped deeply and felt his heart skip a beat. *What the hell is going on*, he thought. He quickly glanced at Jacobs. His pulse and respiration increased to the point of skin sweat and near hyper-ventilation.

Tyrone spoke to the Director. "Mr. Jacobs, we are here to see Mr. Foster." Jacobs gestured to Miles in the deep chair across from the marble desk.

Miles' mind raced. What was Marv doing? And Duncan again?

"Mr. Foster," Tyrone Duncan said. Miles looked up. "You are under arrest for violation of the espionage and sedition laws of the United States of America. In addition, you are charged with violating the Official Secrets Act and ..." Tyrone read off 94 federal crimes including racketeering and 61 assorted counts of conspiracy.

As Tyrone read the extended list of charges, Miles shook to his core, turned to Marvin in abject terror. His face cried out, please, help me. Jacobs watched with indifference as Tyrone continued with the new charges.

"You have the right to remain silent ..." Tyrone read Miles his Miranda rights as he lifted him from the chair to put on the cuffs.

"Marv!" Miles shouted in panic. "This is a joke, and it's not funny .. .Marv .. .Jesus Fucking Christ!" The girls shriveled as Miles struggled like an animal. He thought he was free. "I'm the fucking fish food. Aren't I? Marv," he shouted even louder. "Aren't I?"

"It seems to me that you've dug your own grave, son. I can't tell you how disappointed I am in your actions." Jacobs played the role perfectly.

"You fucking liar! The President doesn't even know about what I did for you? Does he?" Miles was screaming as Tyrone and another agent restrained him by the arms. "Why not? You told me that this project had approval from the highest level."

"Are you mad?" Marvin sounded like a caring parent admonishing a misbehaving lad who knew no better. "Do you think that he would have approved of such a plan? Ruin his own country? Is that why you went to Homosoto? Because we said you were crazy?"

"You told me he approved it!" Miles screamed at Marvin. "You lied! About that, about Stephanie, what else have you lied to me about?"

Jacobs sat silently as Tyrone turned the handcuffed Miles toward the door.

"Why don't you just admit it? I'm the fucking fall guy for your scheme, aren't I?" Miles shouted. "Admit it goddamnit, admit it!"

Jacobs looked down at his desk and shook his head from side to side as if he were terribly disappointed.

"I'll get you, I will get you for this," Miles shrieked. "I trusted you, like a father and then you fuck me. Fucked me like every other dumb shit that works here." His vicousness intensified. "Suck my dick!" he shoutedwith finality.

Tyrone tugged at Miles to keep him from the Director's desk. "Is there anything else Director Jacobs?"

"Yes, Agent Duncan, here." Jacobs opened a drawer and pulled out a large envelope, marked with Miles' name. Miles stared at it, eyes bulging with fear. Tyrone looked questioningly at Marvin.

"I believe you will find enough in there to put Mr. Foster in Tokyo with Mr. Homosoto at the time he died." Tyrone took the package. "I think the Tokyo Police would be most interested in making a possible case for murder."

Miles screamed, "Scum bucket! You're fucking nuts." His vicious verbal assaults were aimed directly at Marvin who ignored them. "You know I had nothing to do . . .goddamn you! I spend five years of my life helping my country and you . . ."

"I think very few would agree that what you've done can be considered helpful."

"I will get even! Even, do you hear!" Miles' voice was getting hoarse from the outrageous tirade.

DIRNSA Marvin Jacobs raised his right hand to Tyrone indicating that Miles was dismissed. Miles continued bellowing at Marvin and Tyrone and the two other agents tried to keep him in tow. When they had left, and the door closed behind them, Jacobs pushed a button on his phone and spoke casually.

"Miss Greeley? Could you please get me a 2:00 PM tee off time?"

* * * * *

544

Epilogue

The Year After

The newspaper headlines during the first year of the attack revealed as much about the effects of the attacks on American society, its politics and economy as could any biased editorial. They ironically and to the dismay of many of those in the government, echo the pulse of the country, regardless of the political leaning of the Op-Ed pages.

Foster Indicted By Federal Grand Jury
Faces 1800 Years If Convicted

Washington Post

Economy Loses $300 Billion in First 6 Months
$1 Trillion Loss Possible

Tampa Tribune

Senator Urges Sanctions Against Japanese

Washington Post

NSA Admits Its Own Computers Sick

New York City Times

NASA Launch Stopped By Faulty Computers

Orlando Sentinal

MacMillan Indicted - Skips Country
Employee's Testimony Crucial

New York Post

Credit Card Usage Down 84%
Retailers In Slump

Chicago Sun-Times

OSO Denied Access to Government Contracts
Investigation Expected to Take Years

Los Angeles Times

Most Companies Go Unprotected
Do Nothing In Spite of Warnings

USA Today

Commercial Tempest Program Kicks Off
Safe Computers Begin Shipping

Houston Mirror

Secret Service Stops Freedom
BBS Software Company Built Viruses

Tampa Tribune

New York Welfare Recipients Suffer
No Payments For 3 Months: 3rd Night of Riots

Village Voice

Allied Corporation Loses 10,000 Computers
Viruses Smell of Homosoto

Dallas Herald

ACLU Sues Washington
Class Action Privacy Suit First of a Kind

Time Magazine

3rd. Quarter Leading Indicators Dismal
Deep Recession Predicted If 4th. Qtr. Is Worse

Wall Street Journal

Supreme Court Rules on Privacy
4th Amendment Protects E-Mail

San Diego Union

Waves of VCR Failures Plague Manufacturers
OSO Integrated Circuits Blamed

San Jose Register

Mail Order Ouch!
Thousands of Dead Computers Kill Sales

Kansas City Address

Chicago Traffic SNAFU
New York Tie Up Remembered

Chicago Sun Times

Homosoto Worked For Extraterrestrials
Full Scale Alien Invasion Imminent

National Enquirer

* * * * *

Power to the People

by Scott Mason

The last few months have taught me, and this country, a great deal about the technology that has been allowed to control our lives. Computers, mainframes, mini computers, or millions of personal computers - they do in fact control and monitor our every activity, for better or for worse. A marriage of convenience?

Now, though, it appears to be for worse.

I am reminded of the readings of Edgar Cayce and the stories that surround the myth of Atlantis. According to Cayce and legend, Atlantis was an ancient ante-deluvian civilization that developed a fabulous technology which achieved air flight, levitation, advanced medical techniques and harnessed the sun's energy.

However, the power to control the technology which had exclusively been controlled by the high priests of Atlantis was lost and access to the technology was handed to the many peoples of that ancient culture. Through a series of unintentional yet reckless events, the Atlanteans lost control of the technology, and despite the efforts of the Priests, their cities and cultures were destroyed, eventually causing Atlantis to sink to the bottom of the depths of the Atlantic Ocean.

Believing in the myth of Atlantis is not necessary to understand that the distribution of incredible computing power to 'everyman' augers a similar fate to our computerized society. We witnessed our traffic systems come a halt, bringing grid lock to small rural communities. Our banks had to reconstruct millions upon millions of transactions in the best possible attempt at reconciliation. The defensive readiness of our military was in question for some time before the Pentagon was satisfied that they had cleansed their computers.

The questions that arise are clearly ones to which there are no satisfying responses. Should 'everyman' have unrestrained access to tools that can obviously be used for offensive and threatening purposes? Is there a level of responsibility associated with computer usage? If so, how is it gauged? Should the businessman be subject to additional regulations to insure security and privacy? Are additional laws needed to protect the

547

privacy of the average citizen? What guarantees do people have that information about them is only used for its authorized purpose?

Should 'everyman' have the ability to pry into anyone's personal life, stored on hundreds of computers?

One prominent group calling themselves FYI, Freeflow of Your Information, represented by the ACLU, represents one distinct viewpoint that we are likely to hear much of in the coming months. They maintain that no matter what, if any, restrictive mandates are placed on computer users that, both an invasion of privacy and violation of free speech have occurred. "You can't regulate a pencil," has become their informal motto emblazoned across t-shirts on campuses everywhere.

While neither group has taken any overt legal action, FYI is formidably equipped to launch a prolonged court battle. According to spokesmen for FYI, "the courts are going to have to decide whether electronic free speech is covered by the First Amendment of the Constitution. If they find that it is not, there will be a popular uprising that will shake the foundation of this country. A constitutional crisis of the first order."

With threats of that sort, it is no wonder that most advocates of protective and security measures for computers are careful to avoid a direct confrontation with the FYI.

* * * * *

Foster Treason Trials Begin
Jury Selection to Take 3 Months

Associated Press

Unemployment Soars to 9.2%
Worst Increase Since 1930

Wall Street Journal

SONY's Threat
Soon Own New York

New York Post

Homosoto Hackers Prove Elusive
FBI says, "I doubt we'll catch many of them."

ISPN

Hard Disk Manufacturers Claim 1 Year Backlog
Extraordinary Demand To Replace Dead Disks

San Jose Citizen Register

Security Companies Reap Rewards
Fixing Problems Can Be Profitable

Entrepreneur

Auto Sales Down 34%

Automotive Week

92% Distrust Computers

Neilson Ratings Service

Compaq Introduces 'Tamper Free' Computers

Info World

IBM Announces 'Trusted' Computers

PC Week

Dow Jones Slides 1120 Points

Wall Street Journal

Senator Nancy Investigates Gov't Security Apathy

Washington Times

Hollywood Freeway Halts
Computer Causes 14 Hour Traffic Jam

Los Angeles Times

* * * * *

A Day In The Life:
Without Computers

by Scott Mason.

As bad as a reformed smoker, but without the well earned battle scars, I have been, upon occasion, known to lightly ridicule those who profess the necessity of computers to enjoy modern life. I have been known as well to spout statistics; statistics that show the average homemaker today spends more time homemaking than her ancestor 100 or 200 years ago. I have questioned the logic of laziness that causes us to pull out a calculator rather than figure 10% of any given number.

I have been proven wrong.

Last Saturday I really noticed the effects of the Foster Plan more than any time since it began. I must confess that even though I have written about hackers and computer crime, it is axiomatically true that you don't notice it till it's gone. Allow me to make my point.

Have you recently tried to send a fax? The digital phone lines have been scrupulously pruned, and therefore busy most of the time.

The check out lines at the supermarket have cob webs growing over the bar code price scanner. The system that I used when I was a kid, as a delivery boy for Murray and Mary Meyers Meat Market, seems to be back in vogue; enter the cost of the item in the cash register and check for mistakes when the receipt is produced.

I haven't found one store in my neighborhood that still takes credit cards. Have you noticed the near disdain you receive when you try to pay with a credit card? Its real and perceived value has been flushed right down the toilet.

Not that they don't trust my well known face and name, but my credit cards are as suspect as are everybody's. Even check cashing is scarce. Seems like the best currency is that old time stand-by, cash. If you can make it to the bank. The ATM at my corner has been rented out to a flower peddler.

All of this is happening in reasonably affluent Westchester County. And in impoverished East Los Angeles and in Detroit and Miami and Boston and Atlanta and Dallas as well as a thousand Oshkosh's. America is painfully learning what life is like without automation.

* * * * *

OSO Puts Up Foster Defense Costs
Effort At Saving Face

Miami Herald

Hackers Hacked Off
Accuse Government of Complicity

Atlanta Constitution

Microwaves Go Haywire
Timers Tick Too Long

Newsday

1 Million School Computers Sit Idle
Software Companies Slow to Respond

Newsweek

Federal Computer Tax Bill Up For Vote
John and Jane Doe Scream 'No'!

San Diego Union

Cable Shopping Network Off Air 6 Months

Clearwater Sun

Bankruptcies Soar 600%

Money Magazine

Banking At Home Programs On Hold
Unreliable Communications Blamed

Computers In Banking

Slow Vacation Travel Closes Resorts
But Disneyland Still Happiest Place on Earth

San Diego Tribune

* * * * *

Hacker Heroes

By Scott Mason

 I have occasionally wreaked verbal havoc upon the hacker community as a whole, lumping together the good and the bad. The performance of hackers in recent months has contributed as much to the defense of the computers of this country as has the government itself.
 An estimated one million computer users categorize themselves or are categorized as hackers. After the Homosoto bomb was dropped on America, a spontaneous underground ad hoc hacker effort began to help protect the very systems that many of them has been violating only the day before. The thousands of bulletin boards that normally display new methods of attacking com-

puters, invading government networks, stealing telephone service, phreaking computers and causing electronic disruptions, are now competing for recognition.

Newspapers interested in providing the most up to date information on fighting Homosoto's estimated 8000 viruses, and methods of making existing computers more secure have been using hacker BBS's as sources.

* * * * *

Foster Defense Coming to An End
Foster won't take stand

New York City Times

AIDS Patients Sue CDC For Releasing Names
Actors, Politicians and Leaders on Lists

Time Magazine

FBI Arrests 15 Fosterites
Largest Single Net Yet

Miami Herald

Congress Passes Strongest Computer Bill Yet
Washington Post

American Express Declares Bankruptcy
United Press International

No New Passports For Travelers
3 Month Department Hiatus Till System Repaired

Boston Globe

138 Foreign Nationals Deported
Homosoto Complicity Cited

San Francisco Chronicle

National Identification Cards Debated
George Washington Law Review

* * * * *

Ex Foster Girl Friend Key
Prosecution Witness

by Scott Mason

A long time girl friend of Homosoto associate Miles Foster, testified against her former lover in the Federal Prosecutor's treason case against him today. Stephanie Perkins, an admitted high class call girl, testified that she had been hired to provide services to Mr. Foster on an 'as-needed' basis.

Over a period of four years, Ms. Perkins says she was paid over $1 Million by a '. . .man named Alex . . .' and that she was paid in cash at a drop in Chevy Chase, Maryland.

She stated that her arranged ralationship with Mr. Foster 'was not entirely unpleasant,' but she would have picked someone 'less egotistical and less consumed with himself.'

"I was supposed to report his activities to Alex, and I saw a lot of the conversations on the computer."

"Did Foster work for Homosoto?"

"Yes."

"What did he do?"

"Built viruses, tried to hurt computers."

"Did you get paid to have sex with Mr. Foster?"

"Yes."

"How many times?"

"A few hundred, I guess."

"So you liked him?"

"He was all right, I guess. He thought I liked him."

"Why is that?"

"It was my job to make him think so."

"Why?"

"So I could watch him."

"What do you do for a living now?"

"I'm retired."

* * * * *

Prosecution Witnesses Nail Foster
Defense Listens to Plea Bargain Offer

Newsday

50% Of Americans Blame Japan - Want Revenge
Rocky Mountain News

La Rouche Calls For War On Japan
Extremist Views Speak Loud

Los Angeles Time

12% GNP Reduction Estimated
Rich and Poor Both Suffer

USA Today

Soviets Ask For Help
Want To Avoid Similar Fate

London Telegraph

International Monetary Fund Ponders Next Move
Christian Science Monitor

* * * * *

Security: The New Marketing Tool

by Scott Mason

American business always seems to turn a problem into a profit, and the current computer confidence crisis is no different.

In spontaneous cases of simultaneous marketing genius, banks are attempting to garner new customers as well as retain their existing customers. As many banks continue to have unending difficulties in protecting their computers, the Madison Avenue set has found a theme that may set the tone of banking for years to come.

Bank With Us: Your Money Is Safer.
Third Federal Savings and Loan
Your Money Is Protected - Completely,
Mid South Alliance Bank

Banks have taken to advertising the sanctity of their vaults and the protective measures many organizations have hastily installed since the Foster Plan was made public. In an attempt to win customers banks have installed extra security measures to

554

insure that the electronic repositories that store billions of dollars are adequately protected; something that banks and the ABA openly admit has been overlooked until recently.

The new marketing techniques of promoting security are not the exclusive domain of the financial community. Insurance companies, private lending institutions, police departments, hospitals and most major corporations are announcing their intentions to secure their computers against future assaults.

* * * * *

Foster GUILTY! Plea Deal Falls Apart
Sentencing Hearing Date Set

New York Post

Universities Protest "Closed Computing"
Insist Freedom on Information Critical For Progress

US News and World Report

More New Viruses Appear Daily
Complacency Still Biggest Threats

Tampa Tribune

NSA/ITSEC Agreement Near
International Security Standards Readied

Federal Computer Week

Justice Department Leads Fight Against Organized Computer Crime

Baltimore Sun

Novell Networks Now Secure

Government Computer News

OSO Offers Reparations: Directors Resign
Wall Street Journal

American and Delta Propose Merger
Nashville Tennessean

Citizen Groups Promote Safe Computing
St. Paul Register

April 15 IRS Deadline Extended 90 Days
Washington Post

49 States Propose Interstate Computer Laws
Harvard Law Review

Courts Work Overtime on Computer Cases
Christian Science Monitor

AT&T Plans New Encryption For Voice
Communications

Microsoft Announces Secure DOS
Admits Earlier Versions "Wide Open"
PC Week

3500 Foster Viruses Identified: 5000 To Go
Info World

National Computer Security Plan Cost: $500 Billion
Wall Street Journal

An End Is In Sight Says NSA
Public Skeptical
New York City Times

Foster Receives Harsh Penalty: 145 Years
Appeal Process Begins, Foster Remains in Custody
Washington Post

* * * * *

The press is often criticized for 'grand standing' and 'sensationalizing' otherwise insignificant events into front page news, but in this case the government said little about the media's handling of the situation. In fact, privately, the White House was pleased that the media, albeit loudly and crassly, was a key element in getting the message to the American public:

Secure Your Computers Or Else.

Everyone agreed with that.

* * * * *

December 17
Overlooking Charlotte Amalie,
St. Thomas, U.S. Virgin Islands

"You must feel pretty good. Pulitzer Prize. Half of the writing awards for last year, nomination for Man of the Year."

"The steaks are burning." The hype had been too much. Scott alone had to carry forward the standard. He had become expected to lead a movement of protest and dissent. Despite his pleas, his neutrality as a reporter was in constant danger of compromise.

"It's kind of strange talking to a living legend . . ."

Scott's deeply tanned body and lighter hair was quite a contrast to the sickly paleness of New Yorkers in winter. "Get the spritzer, water the coals and then fuck yourself."

"Isn't this what you wanted?" Tyrone scanned the exquisite view from the estate sized homestead overlooking Charlotte Amalie Harbor on St. Thomas, U.S. Virgin Islands. The safe enclosed harbor housed three cruise ships, but the hundreds of sailboats in the clear Caribbean dominated the seascape.

After the last year, Scott had decided to finally take time off for a proper honeymoon. He and Sonja elected to spend an extended holiday on St. Thomas, in a rented house with a cook and a maid and a diving pool and a satellite dish and all of the luxuries of stateside living without the residual headaches.

Their head over heels romance surprised no one but themselves and they both preferred to let the past stay a part of the past. Scott decided quickly to take Sonja at her word. Her past was her past, and he had to not let it bother him or they would have no future. Even if he was one of her jobs for a short while.

Scott's name was in constant demand as a result of his exposé of Homosoto and the hackers. Fame was something Scott had not wanted specifically. He had imagined himself the great translator, making the cacophony of incomprehensible technical polysyllabics intelligible to 'everyman'. He had not planned for fame; merely another demand on his time, his freedom and his creativity.

"What I wanted was a break." Scott poked at the steaks. In the pool Arlene Duncan and Sonja kicked their feet and chattered aimlessly. The perfect respite. The Times made Scott the most generous tenure offers in a generation of writers, and Scott recognized the fairness of the offers. It was not now, nor had it ever been a question of money, though.

"What's next?"

"The book, I suppose. The Trial of Miles Foster."

"And then back to the Times?"

"Maybe, maybe. I haven't given it much thought," Scott said watering down the coals to reduce the intensity of the barbecue inferno he had created. "I promised to help out once in a while. Officially they call it a sabbatical."

"How long do you think you can hold out on this rock before going nuts?"

"We've managed pretty well, so far." Scott said admiring his bride whose phenomenal physical beauty was tightly wrapped in the high French cut one piece bathing suit that Scott insisted she wear in honor of their more conservative guests. Tyrone, he was sure, would not have minded Sonja's nudity, but Arlene would have been on the next flight to Boston and her parents.

"Three months so far, and nine months to go. I think I can take it," he said staring at Sonja and motioning to the view.

Tyrone silently conveyed understanding for Scott's choice of an island retreat to get away from it all. But Tyrone's choices demanded his presence within driving distance of civilization.

"So the bureau wasn't too upset about your leaving?" Scott changed the subject.

"I guess not," Tyrone said laughing. "I was approaching mandatory anyway and I'd become too big a pain in their asses. Using your hackers didn't endear me to too many of the Director's staff."

"What about your friend . . ."

"You mean Bob Burnsen?"

"Yeah, the guy we met at Ebbett's . . ."

"He got his promotion right after I left. I guess I was holding him back," Tyrone said with tongue in cheek. "On the other hand, I could have stayed and really made his life miserable. We're both at peace. Best of all? Still friends."

"I have to say, though, I never thought you'd go through with it," said Scott turning the steaks. "You and the Bureau, a thirty year affair."

"Not quite thirty . . ."

"Whatever. You've certainly built up a practice and a half in six months."

"Yeah," chuckled Tyrone. "Like you, I never planned on becoming a big player . . .Christ. Who ever thought that Computer Law would be the next Cabbage Patch Doll of the courts?" Tyrone saw the smirk in Scott's face. "O.K., you did. Yes, you predicted a mess in the courts. Yes, you did Mr. Wisenheimer. I just saw it as a neat little extension of constitutional law and then whammo! All of sudden, computer litigation is the hip place to be. Every type of lawsuit you predicted is somewhere in the legal system - SEC suits, copyright suits, privacy suits, theft of data, theft of service."

"Sounds like everyone who was scared to admit they had a problem in the past is going balls to the wall . . ."

"The Japanese lawyers are living their worst nightmare: OSO Industries is up to top of its colon with lawsuits, including one asking for OSO to be denied any access to the American market for 100 years."

Scott whistled long and loud, then laughed. "And that's fun?"

"You're goddamned right, it's fun," Ty asserted, popping another beer from the poolside cooler. "It's a shit load more interesting that rotting here," he spread his arms to embrace the lush beauty from their 1500 foot high aerie. "How much sun and peace and quiet and sex and water and beach can one man take?" He spoke loudly, like a Southern Spiritual Minister. "Too much scuba diving and swimming and sailing and sunsets and black starry nights can be bad for the health. This is a goddamned Hedonist's Heaven." He brought his hands to his side and gave a resigned sigh. "I guess if you can stomach this kind of life."

"Jealous?" Scott asked gently. He knew about Arlene's reticence to try anything new, out of the ordinary. She was very pleased with her life in Westchester. She felt that knowing someone who lived in Paradise whom she could visit once a year was new-ness enough.

"No, man," Tyrone said genuinely, speaking as himself again. "I got exactly what I wanted." He cocked his head at the pool, where Arlene seemed more relaxed than she had in years. "Can't you see? She's miserable, but she's mine. Scott, you've lived your fantasy, made a difference. Now, it's my turn."

Scott looked over at Arlene. "Hey, shit for brains," he said to Tyrone. "She's no slouch. It's what the hell she's doing with you I never understood." Scott lunged at Tyrone's attention- getting sized abdomen with the steak fork.

"Nice and juicy," retorted Tyrone and patting his prominent stomach.

"You're not my type. I like mine lean. I cut off the fat," Scott barbed. Before Tyrone could get in his jibe Scott called out, "Steaks' on. Outside black, inside mooing."

The girls smacked their lips in anticipation and sat in the elegant all weather PVC furniture. A red sailor's delight sun was mere inches above the horizon, setting to the west over Hassel and Water Islands which provide umbrage to Blue Beard's harbor of choice.

The men were providing all services this evening and the ladies were luxuriating in this rare opportunity. Little did they know, or little did they let on, that they knew the men enjoyed the opportunity to demonstrate their culinary skills without female interference. Beside, thought Scott, it was the maid's day off.

"Seriously, though," Tyrone said quietly as Scott piled the plates with steaks and potatoes. "I know you better than that. I don't see how you can do nothing. You don't know how to sit your ass still for ten minutes. It's not your personality. Don't you agree Arlene?"

"Yes dear," she said, still talking to Sonja.

"And that room you call your office, Jesus. You have more equipment in there than . . ."

"It looks like more than it is . . ." Scott downplayed the point. "Mainly communications. The local phone company is a joke, so I installed an uplink. No big deal."

"C'mon, man, I just can't see you sitting on the sidelines." Tyrone stressed the word 'you'. "Not with what's happening now? There must be a thousand stories out there . . ."

"And a thousand and one reporters. Too much noise, too busy for my liking. After the Homosoto story, if there's one luxury I've learned to live with, it's that I can pick and choose what I do." Scott spoke much too reserved for the Scott Mason Tyrone knew.

"Aha! So you are up to something. I knew it. I gave you one, maybe two months, but I never figured you'd last three."

They carried the four plates laden with steaks and potatoes over to the table where their spouses waited. Fresh beers awaited their much appreciated efforts.

"I do get a little itchy and I read a lot." Tyrone glared at Scott with disbelief. "No really, just a little research," laughed Scott in mock defense. "O.K., I received a call, and it sounded kind of interesting, so I've been looking into it."

"Poking around, here and there and everywhere?"

"Kinda, just following up a few leads."

"Just a few?"

"Well, maybe more than a few," Scott admitted.

"When did this little project begin?" Tyrone asked accusingly. He suspected Scott was hiding a detail or two.

"It's not really a project . . ."

"Don't skirt the issue. When?"

Scott lowered his head. "Two weeks after we got here."

Tyrone stifled what might otherwise have become a volcanic roar of laughter. "Two weeks? Ha!" Tyrone needled. "You only lasted two weeks? How did Sonja feel about that?" He looked over Scott's better half listen in.

"Ah, well, she sort of insisted . . ."

"You drove her nuts? In two weeks?" Sonja shook her head vigorously in agreement but kept speaking to Arlene Duncan..

"Kind of; semi-sorta-kinda-maybe." Scott grinned impishly. "But, yeah, I have been working on something." He couldn't keep it to himself.

"Dare I ask?"

"Off the record?" Scott sounded insistent.

"This is a twist. How about attorney-client privilege?" Tyrone asked. Scott didn'd disagree. "Good," said Tyrone. "Give me a dollar. That's my yearly fee."

Scott complied, finding a soaking wet dollar bill in his swimming trunks. He laid it next to Tyrone's plate.

"Well?" Tyrone asked with great interest.

"Well, I discovered we never developed the A-Bomb to end World War II."

"Excuse me?"

"Someone gave it to us."

* * * * *

What You Can Do

Safeguarding the information infrastructure of the United States and protecting our electronic privacy are responsibilities we all share. Take a stand and let your elected representatives know how you feel. To make your voice heard, write your congressman, senator and the President of the United States. These fine organizations can provide additional topical information.

ISPN/MIS

498 Concord Street
Framingham, MA 01701
(508) 879-7999
The best information security magazine around.

CSI - Computer Security Institute

360 Church St.
Northborough, MA 01532
(617) 393-2600
Well established, professional organization.

Data Pro Research

600 Delran Parkway
Delran, NJ 08075
(609) 764-0100
Solid, solid research.

Computers and Security

Elsevier Publications
655 Ave. of the Americas
New York, NY 10010
Scholarly and Authoritative

ISSA

PO Box 9457
Newport Beach, CA 92658
Management Oriented

Crisis Magazine

94 North High Street
Dublin, OH 43017
614-793-9909
Worst Case Analyis